PARIS
AND ENVIRONS

THE BLUE GUIDES

PARIS

AND ENVIRONS

TC

Edited by

IAN ROBERTSON

Street Atlas and 12 Maps & Plans

LONDON
ERNEST BENN LIMITED

RAND McNALLY & COMPANY
CHICAGO, NEW YORK, SAN FRANCISCO

PARIS

FIRST *(post-war)* EDITION 1951
SECOND EDITION 1960
THIRD EDITION 1968

PARIS AND ENVIRONS
FIRST EDITION *(in this form)* 1977

Published by Ernest Benn Limited
25 New Street Square, London EC4A 3JA
& Sovereign Way, Tonbridge, Kent TN9 1RW

Rand McNally & Company
Chicago, New York, San Francisco

© Ernest Benn Limited 1977

Printed in Great Britain

ISBN *Library* 0 510-01000-8   528-84650-7 (USA)
ISBN *Paperback* 0 510-01003-2   528-84659-0 (USA)

PREFACE

This fourth post-war edition of the BLUE GUIDE TO PARIS, although in the same format as the edition of 1968, has not only been substantially revised textually, but also typographically. The typeface has been changed, the plans redrawn, and an entirely new Atlas section has been provided to bring it into line with recent editions of the other *Blue Guides* devoted to such capital cities as *London* and *Rome*. The summary historical introduction to Paris in relation to French history in general, will, it is hoped, provide the chronological framework necessary to an understanding of her monuments and institutions. The section giving practical information of a general nature about the city's amenities has been expanded. The itineraries have been to a certain extent rearranged to provide a more natural coverage of the city, district by district, taking into account the changing character of many *arrondissements,* and to assist those visiting Paris briefly or for the first time, advice is given (see p. 14) on a progression of routes to be followed which will take them to many of the more important and interesting monuments, etc., while at the same time offering them a general view of the capital. The contents of museums (with the exception of the *Louvre,* which is given a separate chapter) have been detailed immediately after the building itself has been described, rather than relegated to a separate section.

A number of additional routes have been written, radiating approximately 100 km. from the centre, for while most visitors to Paris will as a matter of course make the expedition to *Versailles,* and many will also endeavour to include the longer excursions to *Fontainebleau* and *Chantilly* (which had already been described in previous editions), and which inevitably overshadow other sites in the area, there are also a number of other important towns, châteaux, and monuments in the environs and in the *Île de France* which well deserve the attention of the discriminating traveller or resident with time to spare, and which, historically, are so much a part of Paris.

Included in this edition are the towns of *Soissons, Provins, Sens, Chartres, Évreux, Beauvais,* and *Compiègne,* which define the perimeter of the area covered.

In many cases two routes may be combined with ease by those wishing to return to Paris by a different road. Paris itself is divided into twenty urban routes, most of which can be accomplished in essence on foot by the energetic traveller in a day. The *Musée du Louvre* itself deserves and physically demands several visits. Indeed, visitors to Paris are warned that, because of the sheer scale of many of her monuments, and the extensive sweep of many of her vistas, it is only too easy to underestimate distances, and one should not attempt too much sight-seeing in a day.

Travellers returning to Paris after a period of years will find many changes, not all for the good. Certainly the cleaning of façades (even if *only* the façades in many cases) has done much to beautify the city, and indeed, in spite of traffic flowing along the Quais of the Seine (unobtrusively underground at some stretches), much of the centre still retains its immense charm. One awaits with interest the result of the projected plan for the Georges Pompidou Centre, replacing the old Halles—still, when recently visited, an immense hole. Meanwhile, many familiar horizons have been broken by the erection of vast blocks of buildings, perhaps the most injudiciously placed being the new *Tour Montparnasse,* which, dominating the surrounding area, has also irreparably affected the townscape. Nevertheless, much of the modern architecture of Paris is of a high standard, and while certain squalid outlying districts are being completely and essentially transformed, others of considerable architectural interest, such as the Marais, continue to be tastefully restored. Unfortunately the view of many monuments is spoiled by shoals of coaches blatantly parked in their immediate vicinity, but not every site is surrounded by such swarms of tourists. There is still much to see not far off the track beaten by the majority.

It is of course only too easy to be critical; it would be better perhaps to repeat Montaigne's words with regard to this great and vital city: 'I am never so exasperated against France that I cease to have a kindly feeling for Paris; she has had my heart since boyhood. And, as in the case of all excellent things, the more I have since seen of other fine cities, the more does the beauty of this one impress me and gain on my affection. I love her for herself, and more in her own being than overladen with foreign pomp. I love her tenderly, even her warts and blemishes. I am a Frenchman only through this great city, great in its people, great in the happiness of its site, but above all great and incomparable in variety and diversity of amenities, the glory of France and one of the noblest ornaments of the world'.[1]

Only a small number of restaurants have been mentioned in the practical information section, and omission does not imply any derogatory judgement; a complete list of hotels and inexpensive restaurants is readily obtainable free of charge from French tourist offices. See also pp. 33-5.

The text, although based upon the authoritative descriptions published in earlier editions, both of *Paris* and the corresponding sections of the Blue Guides to *North-Western* and *North-Eastern France,* has been thoroughly revised and augmented, although in certain places the hand of previous editors will still be discerned. Many museums continue to be rearranged, and while endeavouring to keep abreast of all the most recent changes, inevitably the very latest information is not always forthcoming.

The continuing practice of 'starring' the highlights always comes in for some criticism, but although the system is subjective and inconsistent, such asterisks do help the hurried traveller to pick out those things which the general consensus of opinion (modified occasionally by the Editor's personal prejudice, admittedly) considers he should not miss. In certain cases a museum has been starred, rather than individual objects among those described, when the standard of its contents is remarkably high.

Selection is the touchstone by which guide-books are judged, and it is hoped that this edition will provide a comprehensive and balanced account of most aspects of a great city and its environs without intentionally neglecting any that might appeal to the intelligent resident or visitor, and without being so exhaustive as to leave him no

[1] *Essays,* Book III, ch. 9, Trechmann's translation, Oxford University Press.

opportunity of discovering additional pleasures for himself. The present Editor does not pretend to have visited in person every château or early Gothic church in this astonishingly rich area; time and cost inevitably impose certain limitations, and not every facet has been brought to the standard he would like. The Editor alone is responsible for all inexactitudes, inconsistencies, and shortcomings. No one is better aware of the difficulty of avoiding errors both of omission and commission, and any constructive suggestions and corrections for the improvement of future editions of the Guide will be most gratefully welcomed.

The cartography has been entrusted to the capable hands of *Mr John Flower*. In the preparation of this edition, the Editor must acknowledge the assistance he has received from *Mlle Brigitte Godfroy* at the Office de Tourisme de Paris; and the facilities granted to him by *M. Jacques Dupont* (Inspecteur-Général des Monuments Historiques); *Mlles Sylvie Alvarez* and *Geneviève Ravaux* (Direction des Musées de France); *Mlles Germaine Pelegrin, Geneviève Monnier,* and *Claudie Ressort* (Musée du Louvre); *Mlle Clare Constant* (le Château de Versailles); *M. Olivier Lepine* and *Mlle Fabienne de Sèze* (Musée des Arts-Décoratifs); *M. Bernard de Montgolfier* (Musée Carnavalet); *M. Georges Poisson* (Musée de l'Île de France, Sceaux); the Conservateurs des Musées de Marine and Malmaison; *Mme Françoise Dumas* (Cabinet des Médailles, Bibliothèque Nationale); *M. René Baillargeat* and *M. Jean Humbert* (Musée de l'Armée); *Mlle M.-M. Deneck* (Musée Guimet). The Editor must also acknowledge his indebtedness to *Stuart Rossiter,* Editor of the Blue Guides from 1963 to 1973, and author of several exemplary editions; to *Paul Langridge,* General Editor since 1975, for his patience and invaluable criticism; to *Henry Hankey,* for his encouragement at an early stage in the revision of this Guide; and to *John Collis,* for tendering material assistance and advice during the latter stages of its preparation.

Thanks are due also to M. and Mme André Caspueñas, M. and Mme Jean-Jacques Châtelard-Zamora, and to my wife, herself a Parisienne, who have helped me in a variety of practical ways, while suggestions and advice have been offered also by many friends both in Paris itself and elsewhere in France, in Spain, and in London.

CONTENTS

I THE CITÉ AND THE ÎLE-ST-LOUIS

II THE SOUTH OR LEFT BANK: LA RIVE GAUCHE

III   THE NORTH OR RIGHT BANK: LA RIVE DROITE

IV   THE ENVIRONS OF PARIS

MAPS AND PLANS

TOPOGRAPHICAL INTRODUCTION

Paris, the capital of France, lies on both banks of the *Seine,* and near the centre of the so-called Paris Basin. Its height above sea-level varies from 85 to 419 ft, and its distance from the sea is 92 miles (or over 200 by the windings of the river). The SEINE, the third in length of the four great rivers of France, enters the capital some 300 miles from its source in Burgundy, and describes a curved course through the town, also forming two islands, the *Île St-Louis* and the larger *Île de la Cité.* Much of the attraction of Paris stems from the way the river, with its numerous bridges, has been used to unite rather than divide the northern or Right Bank (*Rive Droite*) and the southern or Left Bank (*Rive Gauche*); indeed, the two are much more nearly of equal importance than the N. and S. banks of the Thames. Unlike London, Paris was always (until comparatively recently) bounded by a definite line of ramparts, which although they have long been demolished and their sites built upon, served to contain its population, denser than in any other European city. The line of the last defensive walls (19C) can be imagined by following the exterior BLVD. PÉRIPHÉRIQUE, and certain forts still remain some distance beyond, although engulfed by suburbs (*banlieues*).

The total municipal population of *Paris,* according to the census of 1975, is 2,290,000; the combined population of the surrounding *urban* departments (Hauts-de-Seine, Seine-Saint-Denis, and Val-de-Marne) totals almost 3,963,000, making a figure of 6,253,000 for Greater Paris.

A recent demographic survey has confirmed that some 20 per cent (almost 500,000) of the population of Paris itself is made up of foreigners, including 67,000 Algerians, 33,000 Tunisians, 20,000 Moroccans, and 15,000 from Black Africa. From the poorer nations of S. Europe 69,000 Spaniards (including exiles, presumably), 44,000 Portuguese, 28,000 Italians, and 19,000 from Yugoslavia, now live and work in Paris.

The populations of the circumjacent departments are as follows: Seine-et-Marne, 752,000; Yvelines, 1,076,000; Essonne, 915,000; and Val-d'Oise, 830,000.

The total for the Région Parisienne, together with that of Greater Paris, is now 9,826,000, or approx. 18.7 per cent of the present population of France (52,568,000).

The topography of Paris can perhaps be best understood by taking the PL. DE LA CONCORDE (Pl. 13; 3) as a focal point, although historically the *Pl. du Parvis-Notre-Dame* (from which kilometric distances are measured) might be more appropriate. Hence (and elsewhere) we can appreciate the artistic town-planning of the past, which deliberately allowed vistas from one bank of the river to extend to the far bank in further impressive perspectives. Indeed it is these great perspectives that are particularly memorable about Paris.

Turning to the N.W., we can discern the *Arc de Triomphe* (and *La Défense* beyond), at the far end of the *Av. des Champs-Élysées:* in the opposite direction, the immense bulk of the *Louvre* beyond the gardens of the *Tuileries.* This is flanked, to the N., by the *Rue de Rivoli,* which with its continuation, the *Rue St-Antoine,* leads to the *Pl. de la Bastille;* and further E., by the *Rue du Faubourg St-Antoine,* to the *Pl. de la*

Nation, and *Vincennes* beyond. It is perhaps this diagonal road axis, which, more than the river, cuts Paris into two almost equal parts.

The **Arrondissements.** These municipal districts, of which there are twenty in central Paris, each with its Maire and *Mairie,* or town hall, are important administrative and topographical entities, and their names and numbers convey far more than that of a municipal borough or mere postal district in London, and the visitor should make himself familiar with the situation of some of them: see plan on pp. 2-3 of Atlas.

As in London, certain areas are known more familiarly by their unofficial titles. Those arrondissements which the visitor will most likely enter are printed in the larger type. The numeration (which is often given in Roman figures) follows a spiral working out from the centre.

1er; Louvre; the W. half of the CITÉ, the *Louvre,* PL. VENDÔME, and *Palais-Royal.*

2e; Bourse: containing also the *Bibliothèque Nationale.*

3e; Temple: comprising the N. half of the MARAIS, the TEMPLE, and *Archives.*

4e; Hôtel de Ville: includes the E. half of the CITÉ, with *Notre-Dame,* the ÎLE ST-LOUIS, the *Hôtel de Ville,* and the S. part of the MARAIS, with the PL. DES VOSGES, and the PL. DE LA BASTILLE to the E.

5e; Panthéon: the 'Quartier Latin', with the *Sorbonne, Panthéon, Val-de-Grâce,* and *Jardin des Plantes.*

6e; Luxembourg: with *St-Germain-des-Prés, St-Sulpice,* and the *Palais du Luxembourg.*

7e; Palais-Bourbon: comprising the Faubourg St-Germain. *Les Invalides,* the *École Militaire,* and the *Eiffel Tower* at its W. end.

8e; Élysée: with the PL DE LA CONCORDE, the *Madeleine,* the CHAMPS-ÉLYSÉES, and Faubourg St-Honoré, and including the PARC MONCEAU to the N., and containing the Av. George-V to the W.

9e; Opéra: reaching up to the BLVD. DE CLICHY and PL. PIGALLE.

10e; Enclos St-Laurent: with the *Gares du Nord,* and *de l'Est,* and *Hôpital St-Louis.*

11e; Popincourt: the area N.E. of the PL. DE LA BASTILLE, and reaching to PL. DE LA NATION.

12e; Reuilly: the area S.E. of the PL. DE LA BASTILLE, including the *Gare de Lyon* and Bercy.

13e; Gobelins: the area S. of the *Gare d'Austerlitz,* including the *Gobelins,* and PL. D'ITALIE.

14e; Observatoire: including the *Cimetière de Montparnasse,* PARC DE MONTSOURIS, and *Cité Universitaire.*

15e; Vaugirard: the area S.W. of the *Gare Montparnasse* and *École Militaire.*

16e; Passy: between the *Seine* and BOIS DE BOULOGNE, its N. half crossed by the Avenues Foch, Victor-Hugo, and Kléber, radiating from the *Étoile,* and containing the districts of Chaillot, Passy, and Auteuil.

17e; Batignolles Monceau: the area N.W. of the *Étoile.*

18e; Butte Montmartre: the area N.E. of the PL. DE CLICHY, and reaching as far E. as the Rue d'Aubervilliers.

19e; Buttes-Chaumont: and including the district of La Villette.

20e; Ménilmontant: including *Père Lachaise.*

It must be admitted that few of the *banlieues* of Paris merit the attention of the visitor, unless he is interested in the cult of 'Urbanisme', but whatever one may feel about the usual vast schemes of 'aménagement' and 'rénovation' which are taking place in all areas, proceeding on a scale resulting too often in huge windswept spaces between ugly horizontal and/or vertical boxes, the efforts of the road engineers have been conspicuously successful.

Further out, work is in progress with the construction of five New Towns: *Cergy-Pontoise* (84,000; c. 32 km. N.W. of Paris); *St Quentin-en-Yvelines* (88,000; c. 12 km. S.W. of Versailles); *Évry* (18,500; c. 34 km. S. of Paris, and not far beyond Orly); *Melun-Senart* (95,000; c. 50 km. S.E. of Paris); and *Marne-La-Vallée* (47,300; c. 23 km. E. of the city, adjacent to the *Château de Champs*).

France is now divided into 95 **Départements** (including *Corsica*), and each has its number, the majority of these being formed arbitrarily, for administrative purposes, in 1790, out of the old provinces or military governments, and with certain exceptions are named after some natural feature, often a river.

Each department is administered by a *préfet*, appointed by the President, and assisted by a *conseil général*, and its main town is the seat of the *préfecture*. Departments are subdivided into *arrondissements*, each with its *sous-préfet*, and its *sous-préfecture*. The *canton*, a subdivision of the arrondissement, is the judicial unit, under a *juge de paix*. The canton includes a number of *communes* or parishes, each presided over by a *maire*, and the commune is the administrative unit of local government.

With the growth of Paris (the chief magistrate of which is the *Préfet de la Seine*), by a decree which took effect in 1968, the old department of the *Seine* was subdivided into four new departments: VILLE-DE-PARIS (75); HAUTS-DE-SEINE (92), préfecture *Nanterre;* SEINE-SAINT-DENIS (93), préfecture *Bobigny;* and VAL-DE-MARNE (94), préfecture *Créteil.* The old department of *Seine-et-Oise* was similarly subdivided into three: VAL-D'OISE (95), préfecture *Pontoise;* YVELINES (78), préfecture *Versailles;* and ESSONNE (91), préfecture *Évry.* At the same time the department of SEINE-ET-MARNE (77), préfecture *Melun,* was incorporated to make up the DISTRICT DE LA RÉGION PARISIENNE.

This *Blue Guide to Paris and Environs,* however, takes in a somewhat wider area, to include parts of the departments of OISE (60; préfecture *Beauvais*) to the N.W.; AISNE (02) to the N.E.; YONNE (89) to the S.E.; EURE-ET-LOIR (28; préfecture *Chartres*) and EURE (27; préfecture *Évreux*) to the S.W. and W. respectively.

EMPLOYMENT OF TIME

A good deal of Paris itself may be seen in a week by the energetic traveller, but this will allow only a superficial glance at some few treasures of its museums. With the information given on pp. 37-9, the visitor will be able to plan his campaign, and should have no difficulty, using the index and Atlas section, in choosing and following his own itinerary. The arrangement of routes has been designed to assist the less experienced traveller to explore the city systematically.

A list of convenient *Métro stations* is given at the beginning of most routes: see also Atlas, pp. 4-5.

For those with the time and curiosity, an interesting general view of parts of Paris may be had, for the price of a single ticket, by taking the Métro at the *Étoile* (for example, or indeed anywhere on Ligne 6), direction *Nation;* there changing onto Ligne 2, direction *Porte Dauphine* (two stops beyond *Étoile*). In this way, because much of the journey is made *over*ground rather than under, one can get a glimpse of certain areas which one would not otherwise have any particular reason for visiting. The journey can of course be made in the reverse direction.

For those with little time in Paris it is perhaps advisable to visit first the *Cité* (Rte 1), before crossing to the Left Bank, where one might concentrate on the Latin Quarter and the Faubourg St-Germain (Rtes 2 and 5). The *Invalides* should not be overlooked (Rte 7).

Crossing to the Right Bank, one may follow Rte 8 to the *Louvre*, the contents of its departments being described in Rte 9. One may combine Rte 10 with a view of the *Madeleine* and the *Opéra*. A visit to the *Pl. des Vosges* and the *Musée Carnavalet* should be attempted, in addition. It must be emphasized, however, that this recommended itinerary will only provide an imperfect view of the capital, and each visitor will have his own priorities and preferences.

As far as the environs are concerned, perhaps the most important routes are those concentrating on *Versailles* itself (Rte 21); *Chantilly* (Rte 24), which may be combined with a visit to *Senlis* (Rte 25); *Fontainebleau* (Rte 31), which may include an excursion to *Provins* (Rte 29); *Chartres* (Rte 33C); and *Beauvais* (Rte 38). In most cases they may be approached directly and rapidly by motorways.

HISTORICAL INTRODUCTION

Confined on an island in the Seine, the fortified capital of the *Parisii*, an insignificant Gallic tribe, is first mentioned under the name of *Lutetia* by *Julius Caesar* in 53 B.C., the year before his decisive defeat of *Vercingetorix* at *Alésia*. He appointed it as the meeting-place of deputies from conquered Gaul. The speech, culture, and the roads of Rome soon spread over *Gallia Narbonensis*, and Romanization proceeded apace, in spite of local revolts.

By c. A.D. 250 *St Dionysius* (Denis), its first bishop, had introduced Christianity, and in 292 it became a residence of the emperor *Constantius Chlorus*, but it was not until 360 that the name Paris was applied to the town.

On the advice of *St Geneviève*, Paris opened its gates to the invading Franks in 497, after the conversion of *Clovis*, their king, and grandson of *Merovius*, who had defeated the degenerate Gallo-Romans at *Soissons* in 486. He made Paris his official capital in 508, but after his death three years later, having divided his kingdom, internecine warfare further weakened the **Merovingian** dynasty. Paris remained the political centre of conflicting Frankish interests, and during the next 200 years the population, grown too large for the island, overflowed to form suburbs around the monasteries situated on both banks of the river. Much political influence passed into the hands of the Mayors of the Palace, one of whom, *Charles Martel*, was to check at *Poitiers*, in 732, the invading Moors who had already overrun Spain during the previous two decades. His son, *Pepin le Bref* (the short), deposed the last of the Merovingians in 752.

Carolingian Period. Although Pepin lived occasionally at Paris, his son *Charlemagne* (768-814), in close alliance with the Pope, extended his dominion over France, Germany, and Italy, and, created Emperor of the

West, moved the seat of government to Aix-la-Chapelle. The system of dividing territories on the death of kings was to cause the eventual disintegration of Charlemagne's empire, but by the Treaty of Verdun (843), those areas which were eventually to form modern France, were transferred to his grandson *Charles le Chauve* (the bald), who reigned until 877. Meanwhile, raiding Norman pirates had by 885 reached Paris itself, which was besieged from their encampment on the present site of the Louvre, but the Cité was successfully defended by *Bp Gozlin* and *Count Eudes*. Although the country had become little more than a collection of feudal states, out of which the Normans had by 912 carved out a duchy for themselves, what remained of the Carolingian monarchy (the Île de France) was taken over by Eudes's nephew, *Hugues Capet, Duke of France*, who in 987 was elected king.

The House of Capet. Paris grew steadily in size and importance particularly on the North Bank, and during the reign of *Louis VI* (d. 1137), or even earlier, a second town wall was erected. The Hanse Parisienne, or merchants' league, was established, marking the foundation of the municipality, whose arms, a freighted vessel on a sea argent, with the device 'Fluctuat nec mergitur' (tossed, but not engulfed), probably dates from this period. The continual struggle between the central power and the subordinate feudal lordships was further complicated by the marriage in 1152 of the future *Henry II of England* to *Eleanor of Aquitaine* (the divorced wife of Louis VII), who brought him about one-third of France as her dowry, which precipitated a long struggle between the two countries. In 1163 the foundation-stone of Notre-Dame was laid, while some years later *Philippe Auguste* (1180-1223) built the fortress of the Louvre. During his reign the schools of Paris were united to form one University, which was granted its first statutes by Pope Innocent III in 1208, and established itself on the Left Bank of the Seine. While a growing student population settled there, the northern Right Bank became the centre of commerce, industry, and administration. Some streets were paved, the two ancient wooden bridges were replaced by stone, and the town was enclosed by an extensive line of fortifications. In the political field, Philippe Auguste won back a large part of the lost provinces, having inflicted a heavy defeat on the allies of *John of England* at *Bouvines* in 1214.

During the long reign of *Louis IX* (St Louis; 1226-70), the Hospice des Quinze-Vingts and theological college of the Sorbonne were founded (1253), which was to become a dominant influence in the University. The Palais de la Cité was rebuilt (parts of which, notably the Ste Chapelle, still exist), and the office of Provost was reformed; statutes were drawn up for the many guilds, which were to remain in force until the Revolution.

House of Valois. With the death of *Charles IV* in 1328, the direct branch of the Capetians became extinct, and the claim of *Philippe de Valois* (1328-50) to the throne of France was disputed by *Edward III of England*, who routed the French army at *Crécy* (1346), and inflicted a further defeat on *Jean II* at *Poitiers* in 1356. The ravages and depredations of both French and English soldiery roused both the peasants (the Jacquerie) and the burgesses to revolt. In Paris, *Étienne Marcel*, 'Maire du Palais' and 'prévôt des marchands', took advantage of the situation to increase the strength of the municipality, but he offended public opinion by seeking to hand over the city to *Charles the Bad* (Carlos II, el Malo) *of Navarre*, and was assassinated in 1358. Two years later, by the Treaty of Brétigny, England abandoned her claims, but before long desultory warfare between the two countries was to break out again.

Charles V (1364-80) raised the fortress of the Bastille, and was able to bring back some order to his kingdom, but anarchy returned during the following reign, when his son, *Charles VI,* weak-minded and incapacitated by madness, provoked the citizens of Paris by excessive taxation. The resulting revolt of the 'Maillotins' (maillet = mallet or mace) was bloodily suppressed (1380), but the king became the pawn of rival regents, and for the next 40 years France suffered from dissensions between the aristocratic party, the Armagnacs, and the Burgundians, the popular party (*Jean II* had made his fourth son *Duke of Burgundy*). Seizing the opportunity, *Henry V of England* invaded France, and supported by the Burgundians defeated a French force at *Agincourt* (1415). By the Treaty of Troyes (1420), he received the hand of *Catherine,* the daughter of Charles VI, together with the right of succession to the French throne. Indeed, from 1420, when Henry entered Paris, until 1436, the English controlled the city, *John, Duke of Bedford* having repelled an assault led by *Joan of Arc* in 1429. By 1453, however, all that remained of the once extensive English possessions in France, was Calais.

With the reign of *Louis XI* (1461-83), the change from a medieval social system to the modern state was accelerated. An unscrupulous politician (and relieved from the menace of England), he proceeded to crush the great feudal lordships which encroached on his territory, the most threatening being that of *Charles the Bold,* 'le Téméraire', of Burgundy; and eventually brought Artois, the Franche-Comté, Provence, Anjou, and Maine into direct alliance. In 1469 the first French printing-press was set up in the Sorbonne.

The following three reigns were occupied largely with indecisive campaigns in Italy, the only tangible result of which—particularly during the reign of *François I* (1515-47)—was the establishment in France of the literary and artistic concepts of the Italian Renaissance. In 1532 Brittany was formally united to France, and there was a further expansion towards the Rhine. At the instigation of his domineering mother, *Catherine de Médicis, Charles IX* signed the order for the massacre of Protestant Huguenots on the Eve of St Bartholomew (23 Aug. 1572), and until the promulgation of the Edict of Nantes in 1598, the country was ravaged by the Religious Wars of the League (*La Ligue*). The ultra-Catholic *Henri, Duc de Guise* was assassinated in 1588 by *Henri III,* against whom he was an overt rebel, who was himself assassinated at *St-Cloud* the following year. *Henri IV* (of Navarre), a Protestant, eventually defeated the Catholics at *Ivry* (near Évreux) in 1590, but was unable to enter besieged and famished Paris until 1594, when, as a condition, he abandoned his faith with (it is said) the cynical remark that "Paris vaut bien une messe".

House of Bourbon. Peace established, Henri IV (1589-1610, when he also was assassinated, in the Rue de la Ferronnerie) enlarged the *Louvre* and the *Tuileries,* planned several squares, including the *Place Royale,* completed the *Pont Neuf,* and, with his minister *Sully,* instituted a number of valuable reforms and economies, but these were brought to naught by the extravagant favourites of his successor, *Louis XIII*, at least until *Card. Richelieu* came to power in 1624. In 1623 the archbishopric of Paris was created, and in 1635 and 1640 respectively, the Académie Française and Imprimerie Royale were founded. A fifth wall was erected, and several new quarters arose, e.g. in the Pré-aux-Clercs (Faubourg St-Germain), the Île St-Louis, and the Marais, which became the favourite residence of the nobility. *Marie de Médicis*, the king's mother, built the Luxembourg; *Anne of Austria*, his wife, founded the church of Val-de-Grâce; and Richelieu built for himself the Palais-Cardinal, later the Palais-Royal. The great minister's main aims were the establishment of absolute royal power, the suppression of Protestant influence in politics, and French supremacy in Europe.

In 1643 *Louis XIV* succeeded as a minor, while *Card. Mazarin*, Richelieu's successor—for he had died the previous year—carried on his predecessor's policy. But on Mazarin's death in 1661, Louis decided to govern alone, duped by the conviction that "L'État c'est moi". The nobility were reduced to ineffectual courtiers, the king selecting his ministers from the 'hauts bourgeois', some, such as *Colbert*, being very able. The king's indulgence in costly wars, the least successful being those of the Grand Alliance (1686-97) and of the Spanish Succession (1702-13), in which French forces suffered repeatedly at the hands of *Marlborough* and *Prince Eugene*, was to bring Louis's long reign to a disastrous and bankrupt close.

Meanwhile, in 1672, boulevards were laid down on the lines of Étienne Marcel's wall, and the University quarters were incorporated into the city, now containing about 560,000 inhabitants and 25,000 houses. But although Paris had become one of the cultural centres of Europe—*Corneille, Racine, Molière, La Fontaine*, and *Pascal* making their home there—in 1672 the king chose to transfer his court to *Versailles*, another extravagant project, which further beggared the country. The life of the court there during the latter part of the reign and subsequent regency is brilliantly described in the 'Memoires' of the *Duc de Saint-Simon*.

The following reign (of *Louis XV*) was likewise blighted by ruinous warfare—the campaigns of the Polish Succession, the Austrian Succession, and particularly the Seven Years War were disastrous to French arms, and saw the loss of her flourishing colonies in India, North America, and the West Indies. But grandiose buildings continued to be erected, such as the *Panthéon, Les Invalides*, and the *Palais-Bourbon;* and a sixth wall, thrown up as a simple customs-barrier at the instigation of the farmers-general of taxes, only caused further discontent ("Le mur murant Paris rend Paris murmurant"). *Louis XV* was too weak to cope with the interminable financial crises, and although they inspired reforms, they inspired those which, if accepted, would have adversely affected the privileged estates, the clergy and the nobility, who therefore rejected them.

As a result, the Estates-General were summoned to meet at *Versailles* in 1789, for the first time since 1614. Their first political act was the creation of the *National Assembly* (17 June), when the Third Estate (the representatives of the majority of the nation) swore not to disband until a constitution had been given to the country which would limit royal autocracy, and would guarantee liberty, equality, and fraternity.

This **'Revolution'** was naturally resisted by the privileged classes, which in turn provoked the Parisians to a more open rebellion, culminating in the storming of the *Bastille* on 14 July. Many of the nobility—a class shortly to be abolished—sought asylum abroad, but *Louis XVI* was virtually a prisoner in the Tuileries whence he attempted to flee the country and was arrested (at Varennes) and brought back to Paris. On 1 Oct. 1791 a new Legislative Assembly was formed, which was at first swayed by the moderate *Girondists*, but the following year the extreme *Jacobins* seized power under *Danton, Robespierre*, and *Marat*, and, as the *National Convention*, established the *Republic*. On 21 Jan. 1793 the king was executed in the Pl. de la Révolution, and this act was soon followed by the setting-up in March of the dictatorial *Committee of Public Safety*, which, suspicious of the moderate party, ruthlessly suppressed all royalist sympathizers, and the guillotine was in constant action. In July Marat was assassinated, and even the Dantonists found themselves to be a moderating force opposed to the sanguinary *Hébertists*, even more extreme in their rigorous reign of terror. But Robespierre's personal ambition brooked no rivals, and early in 1794 both *Hébert* and Danton were guillotined. However, after some months of ferocious intimidation of the people, the reaction came, and on 27 July (9 Thermidor, see Republican Calendar, p. 23), his own head fell.

By the following year the Girondists were again in control, although the Royalists continued to make determined efforts to change the course of events, which on 5 Oct. 1795 *Napoleon Bonaparte*, with his 'whiff of grape-shot', to a large extent quelled. On the 28th of that month a *Directory* of five members assumed power. During the next four years French republican armies were particularly successful abroad under their young commander, Bonaparte. But he, on returning to Paris after the less effectual attempt to destroy the British fleet at the battle of the *Nile*, finding the tyrannical Directory generally detested, with the help of the army, and with the support of *Siéyès*, established the *Consulate* by a coup d'état on 9-10 Nov. 1799. Bonaparte himself became First Consul, assisted by Siéyès and *Roger Ducos*. A new constitution awarded him the consulate for life, but such was his personal ambition, that four years later he caused himself to be declared Emperor of the French, and on 18 May 1804 was crowned in Notre-Dame by Pope *Pius VII*.

A Civil Code, largely retaining the liberal laws of the Revolution, was laid down. Paris itself was suitably embellished with monuments and bridges, as befitted the capital of an empire, and further enriched with the spoils of conquest.

First Empire. Brought face to face with a new coalition of England, Austria, and Russia, Napoleon I crushed the last two at *Austerlitz* in 1805, and imposed on them the humiliating Peace of Pressburg. But his fleet had been destroyed at *Trafalgar* only six weeks earlier. In the following year Prussian armies were cowed at *Jena* and *Auerstadt*, and a further campaign against Russia was ended by the Treaty of Tilsit, which brought temporary peace to the Tsar. Austria attempted to renew the struggle, but suffered disastrous defeats at *Essling* and *Wagram*. The subsequent Peace of Vienna (1809) marked perhaps the apogee of the emperor's power. Meanwhile, his brother *Joseph* had been imposed on the Spaniards, whose guerrilla methods of carrying on the war were to cause a continual drain in Napoleon's reserves of manpower. England sent two expeditionary forces to assist the Spaniards, and under *Wellington*, they inflicted a series of defeats on the French, culminating in the battles of *Vitoria* (1813), and—on French territory itself—*Toulouse*. Napoleon himself had just returned from the suicidal invasion of Russia, where great armies were virtually annihilated at the crossing of the *Beresina* by 'Generals January and February'. The Prussians, having recovered from their previous defeats, were able to retaliate at *Leipzig*, and also entered France. Paris itself surrendered to the Allies (31 Mar. 1814) after skirmishing on the heights of Montmartre; the emperor abdicated at Fontainebleau, and retired to the island of Elba.

The Bourbons were restored, but the Treaty of Paris (30 May 1814) humiliated *Louis XVIII* by setting at naught almost all the conquests of the Republic and Empire. The king himself had to escape from Paris during 'the Hundred Days' (26 Mar.-24 June 1815), while Napoleon made his desperate attempt to regain absolute power. His defeat at *Waterloo* (18 June), and subsequent banishment to St Helena, where he died in 1821, enabled the king to resume his precarious throne. The reign of his successor, *Charles X*, under whom were passed the reactionary ordinances of St-Cloud, suppressing the liberty of the press, and reducing the electorate to the landed classes, only proved that the Bourbons could 'learn nothing and forget nothing', and led to the 'July Revolution' of 1830.

House of Orléans. *Louis-Philippe*, son of '*Philippe-Égalité*' d'Orléans of the Revolution, was chosen as head of the 'July Monarchy', and the upper-middle class, who had striven for power since 1789, now achieved it. The king devoted himself, with perhaps more energy than taste, to the further embellishment of Paris, and many somewhat pretentious buildings date from this period. In 1840, the body of Napoleon I (1769-1821) was transferred with much pomp and ceremony to its last resting-place at the Hôtel des Invalides. The city was surrounded by fortifications during the years 1841-45, but this could not defend the king against the mass of his people, among whom socialist ideas were spreading, nor did the conservative policy of *Guizot* suit their temper, and by the 'February Revolution' of 1848, Louis-Philippe was overthrown.

A *Second Republic* was set up by the provisional government, and Louis Napoleon (nephew of the great emperor, who as pretender had already made two abortive attempts to regain the throne) was elected president, but such was the sentimental prevalence of the idea of Empire, that in December 1851 a coup d'état placed him in a position to be almost unanimously accepted by a plebiscite as the emperor *Napoleon III* some months later. Having adopted the clever but misleading slogan of 'L'Empire c'est la paix', he embroiled the country in a succession of wars, notably in the Crimea and in Italy. Meanwhile, he continued the expedient policy of his predecessor, by clearing the mass of congested, evil-smelling, and tortuous lanes of old Paris, which had so favoured the erection of barricades in 1830 and 1848, and in their place *Baron Haussmann* laid out a number of broad boulevards which are still a characteristic of much of the centre, and the Bois de Boulogne and the

Bois de Vincennes were transformed into public parks. But these peaceful occupations were halted abruptly by the outbreak, in 1870, of the Franco-Prussian War. Napoleon III was himself taken prisoner at *Sedan* (and died at Chislehurst, near London, in 1873).

The *Third Republic* had been proclaimed while German troops advanced on Paris, which, invested on 19 Sept., capitulated four months later, on 28 Jan. 1871, after much suffering and famine. The Louvre had been turned into an armament workshop, the Gare d'Orléans into a balloon factory, and the Gare de Lyon into a cannon-foundry. Order was not re-established until after the Communard Insurrection, which then broke out (18 Mar.-29 May 1871), had been overthrown at the cost of pitched battles in the streets, and the destruction of parts of the Tuileries and other public buildings, including the Hôtel de Ville. Retaliatory measures included the massacre of some 20,000 Parisians. *Thiers* was declared president. By Sept. 1873 the last German occupation troops had gone, but France was left to pay a heavy war indemnity, and lost the provinces of Alsace and Lorraine. Various political crises, embittered by the reprehensible 'Dreyfus affair', coloured much of the period up to the outbreak, on 3 Aug. 1914, of the **First World War.** During these decades building continued apace, even if much of it was of a meretricious nature, of which the basilica of Sacré-Coeur is perhaps the most obvious example of the taste of an age so well described by *Proust.*

At the battle of the *Marne,* at the commencement of the war, French forces were dramatically reinforced by 11,000 men rushed to the front in taxis from Paris, whose citizens had the satisfaction of hearing the din of battle gradually recede, and little damage was done to the capital by air raids or long-range bombardment. On 11 Nov. 1918 an armistice was declared, and in the following July the Treaty of Versailles was signed. The loss in manpower had been staggering, but slowly the country recruited her strength, even if, politically, she showed little initiative. The Thiers fortifications were demolished in 1919-24, affording an opportunity to lay out a new ring of boulevards round Paris, but at the same time a costly and supposedly impregnable system of defence was constructed along the German frontier—the Maginot Line—which was immediately side-stepped by invading armoured divisions at the commencement of the **Second World War.** French forces, in no state to resist, ostensibly capitulated to the triumphant Reich, while a high proportion of the British army was able to recross the Channel from Dunkerque in a fleet of small boats sent to its rescue. For the rest of the war, the underground Resistance Movement did what it could to thwart the collaborating policy of the Vichy government presided over by the octogenarian *Marshal Pétain,* hero of Verdun. Meanwhile, a provisional French government had been set up in London by *Gen. Charles de Gaulle,* and Free French forces helped in the liberation of France. Allied troops disembarking in Normandy and in the South of France (on 6 June and 15 Aug. 1944, respectively) converged on Paris, which was liberated by late August, and the occupying Germans were eventually driven from French soil.

In Oct. 1946 the *Fourth Republic* was proclaimed. Women now had the vote, and proportional representation was adopted. Slowly, despite many changes in government, the country was restored to prosperity after the devastation of war. In 1958 de Gaulle prepared a new constitution, which was approved by a referendum, and the general was elected the first president of the *Fifth Republic* by universal direct suffrage for a period of seven years. The powers of the president were considerably increased; he nominates the prime minister, who in turn recommends the members of the government; he can make laws and refer decisions of major importance to popular vote by referendum; in extreme cases he has the power to dismiss the National Assembly. In 1965 de Gaulle was returned to power with enthusiasm, but with a reduced majority.

In May 1968 took place a serious 'Student Revolution' in Paris, which precipitated overdue educational reforms.

In 1969 de Gaulle was succeeded by *Georges Pompidou,* followed in turn, on the latter's death in office, by *Valéry Giscard d'Estaing.*

RULERS OF FRANCE

Merovingians, among which were

481-511	CLOVIS, king of the Franks
561-84	CHILPERIC I, king of Neustria
622-38	DAGOBERT, king of Austrasia, and from 628, of France

Carolingians

751-68	PEPIN (le Bref)
768-814	CHARLEMAGNE
814-40	LOUIS (le Débonnaire)
840-77	CHARLES (le Chauve)
877-79	LOUIS II (le Bègue)
879-82	LOUIS III, and CARLOMAN
882-84	CARLOMAN
884-87	CHARLES (le Gros)
887-98	COUNT EUDES
898-922	CHARLES (le Simple)
936-54	LOUIS IV d'Outremer
954-86	LOTHAIRE
986-87	LOUIS V (le Fainéant)

Capetians

987-96	HUGUES CAPET

996-1031	ROBERT (le Pieux)
1031-60	HENRI I
1060-1108	PHILIPPE I
1108-37	LOUIS VI (le Gros)
1137-80	LOUIS VII (le Jeune)
1180-1223	PHILIPPE AUGUSTE
1223-26	LOUIS VIII (le Lion)
1226-70	LOUIS IX (St Louis)
1270-85	PHILIPPE III (le Hardi)
1285-1314	PHILIPPE IV (le Bel)
1314-16	LOUIS X (le Hutin)
1316	JEAN I (proclaimed king at birth, but died 4 days old)
1316-22	PHILIPPE V (le Long)
1322-28	CHARLES IV (le Bel)

House of Valois

1328-50	PHILIPPE VI
1350-64	JEAN II (le Bon)

1364-80	CHARLES V (le Sage)
1380-1422	CHARLES VI (le Bien-Aimé)
1422-61	CHARLES VII (le Victorieux)
1461-83	LOUIS XI
1483-98	CHARLES VIII (l'Affable)
1498-1515	LOUIS XII (le père du peuple)
1515-47	FRANÇOIS I
1547-59	HENRI II
1559-60	FRANÇOIS II
1560-74	CHARLES IX
1574-89	HENRI III

House of Bourbon

1589-1610	HENRI IV (le Grand)
1610-43	LOUIS XIII (le Juste)
1643-1715	LOUIS XIV (le Grand), 'le Roi Soleil'
1715-74	LOUIS XV (le Bien-Aimé)
1774-92	LOUIS XVI
	LOUIS XVII never reigned

Revolution and First Empire

| 1792-1804 | *First Republic* |
| 1804-14 | NAPOLEON I |

House of Bourbon (restored)

| 1814-24 | LOUIS XVIII |
| 1815 | ('the hundred days') |

| | NAPOLEON I |
| 1824-30 | CHARLES X |

House of Orléans

| 1830-48 | LOUIS-PHILIPPE |

Second Republic

| 1848-52 | |

Second Empire

| 1852-70 | NAPOLEON III |

Third Republic

Presidents

1871-73	ADOLPHE THIERS
1873-79	MARSHAL MAC-MAHON
1879-87	JULES GRÉVY
1887-94	SADI CARNOT
1894-95	JEAN CASIMIR-PÉRIER
1895-99	FÉLIX FAURE
1899-1906	ÉMILE LOUBET
1906-13	ARMAND FALLIÈRES
1913-20	RAYMOND POINCARÉ
1920	PAUL DESCHANEL
1920-24	ALEXANDRE MILLERAND
1924-31	GASTON DOUMERGUE
1931-32	PAUL DOUMER
1932-40	ALBERT LEBRUN
1941-44	MARSHAL PÉTAIN (Vichy government)

Fourth Republic

| 1947-54 | VINCENT AURIOL |
| 1954-58 | RENÉ COTY |

Fifth Republic

1958-69	CHARLES DE GAULLE
1969-74	GEORGES POMPIDOU
1974-	VALÉRY GISCARD D'ESTAING

A **Republican Calendar** was instituted on 24 Nov. 1793, and remained in force until 1 Jan. 1806, when it was officially replaced by the Gregorian. Year I was considered to have begun at the autumnal equinox (22 Sept.) of 1792, the day of the proclamation of the Republic.

The year was divided into 12 months of 30 days each; each month being divided into 3 periods of 10 days or *décades;* and 5 days ('Sans-culottides') were added at the end of each year (6 in leap years).

Poetic names, devised by Fabre d'Églantine, were given to the months: VENDÉMIAIRE (the month of the vintage, *vendange*); BRUMAIRE (*brume,* fog); and FRIMAIRE (*frimas,* hoar-frost) being the autumn months; NIVÔSE (*neige,* Lat. *nix, nivis,* snow); PLUVIÔSE (*pluie,* rain); and VENTÔSE (*vent,* wind) being the winter months; GERMINAL (*germination,* seed-time); PRAIRIAL (*prairie,* meadow); and FLORÉAL (*fleur,* flower) typifying spring; and MESSIDOR (*moisson,* Lat. *messem,* harvest); THERMIDOR (Greek *therme,* heat); and FRUCTIDOR (Lat. *fructus,* fruit) typifying summer.

BIBLIOGRAPHY

This brief list does not attempt to do more than suggest a few books which may be found useful for reference, or of interest in providing background, for the visitor to Paris. Many of them contain comprehensive bibliographies for further or more specialized reading.

TOPOGRAPHICAL AND GENERAL: *Pierre Couperie,* Paris au fil du temps (atlas historique d'urbanisme et d'architecture); *Jacques Hillairet,* Dictionnaire historique des rues de Paris; *Thomas Okey,* The Story of Paris (1906); *Hilaire Belloc,* Paris (1900); *E. V. Lucas,* A Wanderer in Paris (1909); *Henri Bidou,* Paris; *John Russell,* Paris; Larousse, Dictionnaire de Paris.

HISTORICAL: *Saint-Simon,* Historical Memoirs (trans. and edited by Lucy Norton, 3 vols); *A. Cobban,* A History of Modern France, 1715-1962 (3 vols); *Nancy Mitford,* The Sun King; and Madame de Pompadour; *D. W. Brogan,* The Development of Modern France (1870-1939); *T. Zeldin,* France, 1848-1945; *A. Horne,* The Terrible Year: the Paris Commune, 1871; *J. Ardagh,* The New France; *Joan Evans,* Life in Medieval France; *J. Huizinga,* The Waning of the Middle Ages; *J. H. M. Salmon,* Society in Crisis: France in the Sixteenth Century.

LITERARY: *Sir Paul Harvey* and *J. E. Heseltine,* The Oxford Companion to French Literature; A Literary History of France (in 6 vols; published by Ernest Benn); *George Orwell,* Down and Out in Paris and London; *Sylvia Beach,* Shakespeare and Company; *Henry James,* The Ambassadors (1903); *George Painter,* Marcel Proust.

ART AND ARCHITECTURE: *Anthony Blunt,* Art and Architecture in France, 1500-1700; *Kalnein* and *Levey,* Art and Architecture of the 18C in France; *Joan Evans,* Monastic Architecture in France, 1500-1700; Art in Medieval France; *V. Rowe,* Royal Châteaux of Paris; *Ian Dunlop,* Versailles.

MISCELLANEOUS: *P. Morton Shand,* A Book of French Wines; *A. Lichine,* Wines of France; *P. Andrieu,* Fine Bouche: a history of the Restaurant in France; *Elizabeth David,* French Provincial Cooking.

See p. 29 for **Maps.**

PRACTICAL INFORMATION

APPROACHES TO PARIS AND TRANSPORT IN PARIS

Paris may be reached directly from Great Britain by a variety of ways, and although a car taken across the Channel (or hired in Paris) will render the tourist independent of other forms of transport in the Île de France, it is not essential if only Paris and its immediate surroundings are to be visited.

There are a number of rapid *rail* services from London to Paris, while the quickest (but least interesting) means of transit is by *air*.

Travel Agents. General information may be obtained gratis from the *French Government Tourist Office,* 178 Piccadilly, London, W1, and any accredited member of the *Association of British Travel Agents* will sell tickets and book accommodation.

Among these are *Thomas Cook & Son,* 45 Berkeley Street, W1, with many branches in central London, and *American Express,* 6 Haymarket, SW1, 89 Mount St, W1, and 82 Brompton Road, SW3, etc. Travellers are warned that these, and some other agents, have chosen to impose an additional charge when booking open-dated return air tickets not originally issued by themselves, and it is often preferable to visit the individual airline's offices in such cases.

There are *French Government Tourist Offices* in the United States at 610 Fifth Av., New York; 111 N. Wabash Av., Chicago; 9401 Wilshire Blvd., Beverly Hills; 323 Geary Street, San Francisco: and in Canada, at 1840 West, Rue Sherbrooke, Montreal; and 372 Bay Street, Toronto.

Numerous and frequent Passenger and Car Ferry Services are operated by British and French Railways, Townsend Thoresen, and Southern Ferries Ltd, from British to northern French ports. For the latest information about services available, inquiries should be made to the *Continental Car Ferry Centre,* 53 Grosvenor Gardens, London SW1. Those wishing to make use of the various *Hovercraft* services should be warned that the quality of service can be erratic, and not only in adverse weather.

The *British Railway Travel Centre,* Rex House, Lower Regent St, London SW1, provides travel tickets, sleeping-berth tickets, seat reservations, etc., on Continental (as well as British) transport services; the offices of *French Railways* (S.N.C.F. or Société des Chemins de Fer Française), adjacent to the French Tourist Office in Piccadilly, are equally helpful, and perhaps more informative in certain cases.

Motorists driving to Paris will save much trouble by joining the *Automobile Association* (Fanum House, Basingstoke, Hants, RG21 2EA), the *Royal Automobile Club* (83 Pall Mall, SW1), the *Royal Scottish Automobile Club,* 17 Rutland Square, Edinburgh, or the *American Automobile Association.* These organizations will provide any necessary documents, as well as information about rules of the road abroad, restrictions regarding caravans and trailers, arrangements for spare-parts, insurance, etc. Motorists who are not the owners of their vehicle should possess the owner's permit for its use abroad. The use of safety-belts is now compulsory in France. Both the A.A. and R.A.C. have offices in Paris, at 2 Pl. Madeleine and 8 Pl. Vendôme respectively.

The *Automobile Club de France,* 6 Pl. de la Concorde, and the *Touring Club de France,* 65 Av. de la Grande-Armée, 16e, may also be found useful.

The latest edition of the *Michelin* map of France (No. 989) is recommended for those disembarking at the Channel ports; it is also preferable to buy other maps of Paris and environs before leaving home if it is intended to tour en route. See section on *Maps,* below.

The simplest approach to Paris from *Calais* and *Dunkerque* is viâ the Autoroute A1. From *Dunkerque* it is possible to travel on the A25 to *Lille* and join A1 there. From *Calais* the Autoroute should be joined at *Arras.* From *Boulogne* follow N1 viâ *Abbeville* and *Beauvais.* From *Dieppe* N15 and N31 to *Beauvais,* thence N1.

Parking is restricted in central Paris, and in the *Zone Bleu* is regulated by the 'disc' system or by meters. Beware the female traffic-wardens in their plum-coloured uniforms (familiarly known as 'aubergines'). Use should be made of the increasing number of underground parks being constructed, a list of which is available at Tourist Offices; see also under Map section, p. 29.

Regular **Air Services** between England and Paris are maintained by *Air France,* working in conjunction with *British Airways.* Full information about flights may be obtained from British Airways, Dorland House, Lower Regent St, SW1, and from Air France, 158 New Bond St, W1. There are also daily flights from Gatwick with British Caledonian, 65 Regent St, W1.

There are also regular international flights from most European capitals and larger cities to Paris, and direct services from New York and Montreal to Paris, and from many other non-European countries, apart from those provided by Charter companies.
Apart from flights from London (Heathrow and Gatwick), Bristol, Cardiff, Manchester, Edinburgh, Birmingham, and Glasgow, have direct air connections with Paris.

British Airways have Paris offices at 91 Av. des Champs-Élysées and 38 Av. de l'Opéra; Air France offices are at 119 Av. des Champs-Élysées.

Internal or domestic services are maintained by *Air Inter,* 232 Rue de Rivoli, Paris 1er and branches.

Paris is served by three airports: *Le Bourget* and *Charles de Gaulle* (near the village of Roissy-en-France), 15 and 23 km. N.E. of Paris respectively; and at *Orly* (*South* and *West*), 14 km. S. of the city. All three are linked with each other by regular Air France buses, and to the two town terminals at *Porte Maillot* and *Les Invalides.* Taxis will also meet planes, and many car-hire firms have offices at the airports. Both at Charles de Gaulle and Orly, and at Porte Maillot, are expensive hotels and restaurants, shopping and exchange facilities, and information bureaux, etc.

Railway Stations. The main termini, all on Métro lines, have most of the facilities required by the traveller, including left-luggage offices (*consigne*), lockers, trolleys, etc. They also provide exchange facilities, Post Offices, restaurants (not cheap), and the *Gares de l'Est, de Lyon,* and *du Nord* also have information bureaux (see p. 31).

The main stations of the S.N.C.F. are:
Gare d'Austerlitz, serving the Région Sud-Ouest (Tours, Bordeaux, Toulouse, Bayonne, Madrid, etc.).

Gare de l'Est, for the Région Est (Reims, Metz, Strasbourg, Frankfurt, Bâle, Zurich, etc.).

Gare de Lyon, for the Région Sud-Est (Lyon, Dijon, Provence, Nice, Barcelona, etc.).

Gare Montparnasse, terminus for the Région Ouest (Brittany, La Rochelle, etc.).

Gare du Nord, for the Région Nord (Lille, Brussels, Amsterdam, Cologne, Hamburg, etc.; also for boat-trains to Boulogne, Calais, Dunkerque).

Gare St-Lazare, another terminus of the Région Ouest (Normandy lines, and for boat-trains to Dieppe, Le Havre, Cherbourg, etc.).

Public Transport in Paris. All the buses (*autobus*) and the underground railway (*Métro*) in Paris are controlled by the R.A.T.P. (Régie Autonome des Transports Parisiens), with offices at 53bis Quai des Grands-Augustins (just S. of the *Pont Neuf*), and in the Pl. de la Madeleine (on the E. side of the church). They issue a useful map of the Métro and bus system (*Plans Métro-Autobus*), also available in a larger format for the Autobus (*Plan du Réseau*), etc., and also a leaflet giving details of numerous Summer Excursions.

They also sell a 4-or 7-day *billet de tourisme* (also available at thirty of the main Métro stations and from the Tourist Office at 127 Av. des Champs-Élysées; also from French Railways in London) allowing unlimited travel on the R.A.T.P. system for the period concerned, which can be useful and comparatively cheap if used constantly. Normally, the most convenient way is to buy a '*carnet*' of 10 tickets at the booking offices of the Métro. First and Second class tickets are available, but the latter compartments are usually perfectly satisfactory although occasionally more crowded. Tickets, which operate a turnstile, should be retained until the end of the journey, as at some stations they may be required to make an exit or change, and they may also be inspected.

The **Métro** (*Métropolitain*) provides a rapid means of transit in Paris, and its modernization continues. Many trains now glide silently on rubber wheels through impressively clean stations, approximately 500 metres apart—the platform of the *Louvre* station is lavishly decorated with castes from the collections of the museum—and the service, from 5.30 in the morning until approx. 12.30 at night, is normally frequent and regular. The fare is the same for any distance on the main network, including all necessary changes, making long journeys reasonably inexpensive in comparison with shorter distances covered.

The various lines of the Métro (the first of which was opened in 1900, and certain stations, notably the Bois de Boulogne entrance of *Porte Dauphine,* retain their 'art nouveau' decoration) are called by the names of their terminal stations: e.g. Ligne 1, *Vincennes-Neuilly.* The direction of the trains, which keep to the right, is indicated by a sign naming the terminal station. Entry to some platforms is still controlled by automatic barriers closing as the train arrives. The platforms themselves are reached by stairs, including some escalators. At interchange stations, the passages leading to the line concerned are clearly indicated by an orange-lighted sign marked 'Correspondance', followed by the name of the terminal stations of the connecting line. See Pl. 4-5.

The fast exterior lines of the **R.E.R.** (*Réseau Express Régional*), at present running W. from *Auber* (nr the Opéra) viâ *Étoile* to *Saint-*

Germain-en-Laye; E. from *Nation* to *Boissy St-Léger;* and S. from *Luxembourg* to *Sceaux* and *Robinson,* and to *St-Rémy-lès-Chevreuse* (the latter connecting with the Métro at *Denfert-Rochereau*), are *not* covered by the inclusive price, and a separate ticket must be bought at the interchange station, many of which have elaborate automatic ticket machines.

The lines of the R.E.R. will eventually cross the centre of Paris, running E. from *Auber* to *Les Halles, Gare de Lyon,* and *Nation;* while a transverse line will join *Luxembourg* to *Les Halles,* and to the *Gare du Nord.* A newly opened line now runs from the latter station to the *Charles de Gaulle airport.* A bus shuttle-service from *Orly,* which will be superseded eventually by a direct line to *Luxembourg,* connects with a line to the *Gare d'Austerlitz* and the *Gare d'Orsay,* which is in course of extension to *Les Invalides,* and will also be connected to the Métro at *Champs-Élysées Clemenceau* on the line to *Porte Maillot.*

Those making the excursion to *Versailles* will find the line running along the Seine S.W. from *Les Invalides* a useful means of transport.

Buses. Bus-stops, which are now all 'request stops' (*arrêt facultatif*), are indicated by small placards showing the numbers of the routes and their destinations. Depending on the length of the journey, either one or two tickets of the *carnet* will be required, the tickets for buses and the Métro being interchangeable. Buses therefore are generally more expensive than the Métro; ask the driver-conductor if in doubt as to the fare. It will be noticed that buses, owing to the large number of one-way streets, do not necessarily return along the same route that they follow to their destination, and this can lead to confusion until the visitor finds the position of the stops concerned.

Smoking is forbidden on both buses and the Métro. Where possible, care should be taken to avoid the use of public transport during 8.00-9.00, and during 17.30-19.30, when the Paris 'rush-hour' is at its height. In some areas traffic is also heavy between 12.00 and 14.00.

Excursions. Apart from those excursions organized by the R.A.T.P., many tourist agencies run daily coach tours to sites outside Paris, and, during the summer, to view the floodlighting in Paris. Tourist Offices will be able to advise on the termini of the various regular coach routes into the outer environs of Paris, and into the provinces.

River Trips. *'Les Bateaux-Mouches'* (*Pont de l'Alma;* Right Bank), and *'Vedettes'* (*Pont d'Iéna* or *Pont Neuf;* Left and Right Banks respectively) run trips along the Seine at frequent intervals during the summer months, and less frequently in winter. Although these river excursions offer many attractive low-level vistas as the launch emerges from beneath the numerous bridges spanning the Seine, perhaps a better idea of the importance of the river in the growth and planning of Paris is made more apparent by taking a leisurely walk, between the *Pont d'Iéna* and the *Pont de Sully,* along the embankment or the Quais. Unfortunately these are less attractive than they once were since traffic has been diverted along the water's edge.

Taxis. There are over 14,000 taxis in Paris, and many will be found cruising or waiting at a rank, marked 'Tête de Station', and with a telephone. Visitors making regular use of a taxi from their place of residence should make a note of the telephone number of the nearest rank. Taxi-drivers still optimistically expect a tip of 10-15% in addition to the charge on the meter. Rates are displayed inside the vehicle; note that the night tariff (after 23.00) is considerably higher than the day.

There are extra charges for luggage placed in the boot, etc.

No one need be intimidated by the fact that Parisian taxi-drivers have gained for themselves an unenviable reputation over the years for truculence and rapacity. Usually their bark is worse than their bite, even if the many female taxi-drivers are escorted by their protective Alsatians, etc.; but in case of real trouble, make for the nearest *gendarme*.

Maps, etc. For Paris itself, and its immediate environs, the following are recommended: *Michelin, Plan de Paris* (No. 10; 1:10,000), also available in atlas form as *Paris, index et plan* (more convenient when walking); No. 11, which is sold with the loose inset (No. 9) entitled *Paris transports* (with maps of the Métro and bus systems, and also including a plan showing the position of underground car-parks and 24-hour petrol-stations). The atlas, with 60 pp. of maps, contains a useful list of names, addresses, and telephone numbers of organizations likely to interest visitors, and a vital street index, forming an invaluable complement to this *Blue Guide*. The *Michelin; Sorties de Paris* (No. 100; 1:50,000) will be found helpful when negotiating the interchanges of the Blvd. Périphérique, and extends as far W. as Versailles and St-Germain-en-Laye.

Michelin Map 96, *Environs de Paris* (1:100,000), extends to Chartres, Senlis, and Fontainebleau, covering the same area as the I.G.N. (Institut Géographique National) *Carte Touristique* of the *Environs de Paris,* at the same scale. The latter may be supplemented by their Cartes Touristiques (Série Verte; 1:100,000) Nos. 8, 9, 20, and 21, covering slightly more than the area described in this guide. *Michelin* Map 97, at 1:200,000, covers the same area in one sheet. The I.G.N. Map 3 (Série Rouge) may also be of interest.

The *I.G.N. Carte Routière* for France, and *Michelin*'s *France-Grandes Routes* (Map 989), both at 1:1,000,000, may help in planning one's route to Paris.

It is always advisable to have the *latest* edition of all such maps (stocked by Stanfords, 12-14 Long Acre, London WC2, and Sifton Praed, 54 Beauchamp Pl., Knightsbridge, SW3). While most of the above-mentioned will be found without great difficulty in general bookshops in Paris and environs, a visit to the salerooms of the *Institut Géographique National* at 107 Rue La Boétie (Champs-Élysées end) may be found rewarding. They have an extensive range of impressions of old maps on sale also.

FORMALITIES, CURRENCY, POST OFFICE, ETC.

Passports are necessary for all British and American travellers entering France, and must bear the photograph of the holder. An *Identity Card* is also accepted. British passports (£5.00) valid for ten years are issued at the Passport Office, Clive House, Petty France, London SW1 (9.30-16.30; Sat. 9.30-12.30), or may be obtained for an additional fee through any tourist agency. No visa is required for British or American visitors, but should any foreigner intend to remain in France for more than three months, he should apply in advance to the nearest French Consulate, or, if already in France, to the Préfecture de Police in the department in which he is residing, or to the Préfecture de Police (Service des Étrangers) in Paris.

British subjects seeking employment in France should write to the *Consular Section* of the Embassy, now at 109 Rue du Faubourg-St-Honoré, 8e (4th floor), but it should be emphasized that they are *not* an employment agency, nor can they help to find accommodation. They will advise on the procedure to be followed, according to the status of the person concerned under the E.E.C. regulations.

Custom House. Except for travellers by air, who have to pass customs at the airport of arrival, or those travelling on international expresses, where their luggage is examined in the train, luggage is scrutinized at the frontier, or ports of departure and disembarkation. Provided that dutiable articles are declared, bona-fide travellers will find the French customs authorities (*douaniers*) courteous and reasonable.

Currency Regulations. The allowance permitted per person by the British government for pleasure travel is (in 1975) £300 each trip, up to a maximum of £2,000 in one year, all of which may be held in foreign notes. In sterling notes, not more than £25 may be taken out of Great Britain by British or American travellers. Application should be made to the Bank of England for the export of larger amounts of currency, and for business travelling allowances.

The complicated regulations, which lay down even what you may spend your money on in countries not subject to British law, are set out in the leaflet 'Notice to Travellers', which may be obtained from most banks.

Money. The monetary unit is the *franc,* subdivided into *centimes.* Banknotes for 10, 50, 100, and 500 francs are in circulation, and there are also coins of 5, 10, 20, and 50 centimes (½fr.), 1 franc, and 5 francs.

Branches of all French **Banks** are open from 9.00 to 16.30 from Mon. to Fri.; most banks close on Sat. morning, but many central branches of the principal banks (including the British and American banks, see below) have a 'bureau de change' open from 9.00 to 12.00. At the main-line stations, the 'bureaux de change' are open daily from 6.00 or 7.30 to 22.00 or 23.00. Those at the airports of Charles de Gaulle, Orly, and Le Bourget operate a 24-hour service; the air terminals at Les Invalides and Porte Maillot, and the Office de Tourisme at 127 Av. des Champs-Élysées, also provide this service from 9.00 to 22.00 or 24.00.
Larger hotels will also accept travellers' cheques, which may be convenient, but they will give a lower rate of exchange. It is advisable to obtain a small supply of French change for incidental expenses before leaving home, particularly if arriving in France during the week-end.
BRITISH BANKS: *Barclays,* 33 Rue du Quatre-Septembre, 2e; *Lloyds,* 43 Blvd. des Capucines, 2e; *Westminster,* 18 Pl. Vendôme, 1er.
AMERICAN: *Bank of America,* 28 Pl. Vendôme, 1er, *Chase Manhattan,* 41 Rue Cambon, 1er; *First Nat. City Bank,* 60 Av. Champs-Élysées, 8e; *Morgan Guaranty,* 14 Pl. Vendôme, 1er.
CANADIAN: *Canadian National,* 47 Av. George-V, 8e; *Royal Bank of Canada,* 3 Rue Scribe, 9e.
Chambers of Commerce: *British,* 6 Rue Halévy, 9e; *American,* 21 Av. George-V, 8e; *Canadian,* 9 Av. Franklin-Roosevelt, 8e.

Postal and other Services. The main *Post Office* in Paris is at the Hôtel des Postes, 52 Rue du Louvre, 1er, which provides a 24-hour service, as do those at 8 Pl. de la Bourse, 2e; 103 Rue de Grenelle, 7e; and 71 Av. des Champs-Élysées, 8e (8.00-23.00). Most other post offices, indicated by the sign **P.T.T.,** are open from 8.00 to 19.00 on weekdays, and until noon on Sat.

English-speaking hostesses can help with postal queries at the Champs-Élysées and Rue du Louvre Post Offices, the latter being the destination of all letters, etc., marked merely 'Poste Restante, Paris', without an arrondissement number being given. When this has been added, the head post office in the appropriate arrondissement should be visited. Correspondence marked 'poste restante' may be addressed to any post office, and is handed to the addressee on proof of identity (passport preferable). Letters may be sent registered ('recommandé') for a small fee, and are likewise not delivered without proof of identity.

Telegrams in English may be *telephoned* to 233 21 11. There is a public *Telex* office at 7 Rue Feydeau, just N. of the Bourse.

Letter-boxes are now painted blue. Postage-stamps (*timbres*) are on sale at all post offices and most tobacconists.

Among other services, that of the *pneumatiques* (peculiar to Paris) may be mentioned as a much cheaper way of sending messages within Paris and suburbs, which is almost as rapid as a telegram. Both letters and '*cartes télégrammes*' may be transmitted by these pneumatic tubes, and should be posted in special letter-boxes so marked.

Telephones. The telephone service is not all that it might be, but public call-boxes may be found at most post offices, Métro stations, cafés, restaurants, and recently at some bus stops (taxiphones). Unfortunately, too often, they seem to be out of order, but with patience, and sufficient small change, one should eventually make the correct connection. Paris now has S.T.D. telephonic communication with the British Isles and most of Europe, etc. Reversed-charge calls ('P.V.C.') are accepted. Some call-box instruments are constructed to take 'jetons' only, which have to be bought at the counter near which they are installed.

Information Bureaux. The *Office de Tourisme de Paris,* with its head office at 127 Av. des Champs-Élysées, open daily from 9.00 to midnight, has an exceptionally patient and helpful English-speaking staff. These long-suffering blue-uniformed 'hostesses' endeavour to answer most general queries concerning Paris and Environs (apart from giving information on the rest of France). For a small charge they will book hotel accommodation in Paris, and from this head office, by telex, in the provinces. They will supply visitors with leaflets giving information about temporary exhibitions, entertainment, inexpensive restaurants, etc. A useful map of Paris and environs may be supplied on request. They are *not* set up to give detailed information concerning train timetables, etc., but at the head office there is also a Travel Agency, and exchange facilities.

Otherwise known as *Le Bureau Central d'Accueil* ('Welcome' reception office; tel. 720 04 96 and 720 16 78), it has subsidiary branches at the Gare de l'Est, Gare du Nord, Gare de Lyon, Aérogare des Invalides, Aérogare de Porte Maillot, and at 9bis Rue Norvins, Montmartre.

There is a *municipal* Tourist Information Office in the N. vestibule of the *Hôtel de Ville,* 29 Rue de Rivoli, 4e.

Students and young people generally may find the following organizations of assistance: *Service d'Accueil aux Étudiants Étrangers.* 13 Rue de Vaugirard, 6e; the *Centre d'Information et de Documentation Jeunesse,* 101 Quai Branly, 15e; the *Office du Tourisme Universitaire et Scolaire,* 137 Blvd. St-Michel, 5e; and the *Bureau Information Logements,* 12 Rue des Barres, 4e.

Lost Property Office. Articles lost on the Métro or in buses (in which case they are held for claiming for the first 48 hrs at the terminus of the route concerned), in the street, theatres or cinemas, etc., should be enquired for at the *Bureau des Objets Trouvés,* 36 Rue des Morillons, 15e (open Mon.-Fri., 8.30-17.00); the nearest Métro is Convention.

USEFUL ADDRESSES

Directories. Any required address may be turned up in 'Le Bottin' (the *Annuaire-Almanach du Commerce et de l'Industrie Didot-Bottin*, to give its full title), which may be consulted at post offices, hotels, restaurants, shops, etc., where a notice may be displayed: 'Ici on consulte le Bottin'. Residential and official addresses may be found also in the 'Bottin Mondain'. *Le Bottin* was initiated in 1819 by Sébastien Bottin (1764-1853), who took over an earlier *Almanach du Commerce* founded in 1798. At Bottin's death it merged with the *Annuaire général du commerce* published by Didot. Although a somewhat ponderous example of Gallic methodology, it can be found useful on occasions.

Embassies and Consulates. *British Embassy*, 35 Rue du Faubourg St-Honoré, 8e; Consulate at 109, some 5 minutes walk to the W. *American Embassy*, 2 Av. Gabriel, 8e (just N. of the Pl. de la Concorde); other services at 2 Rue St-Florentine, ler. *Canadian Embassy*, 35 Av. Montaigne, 8e. *South African Embassy*, 38 Rue Bassano, 8e. *Australian Embassy*, 64 Av. d'Iéna, 16e. *New Zealand Embassy*, 9 Rue Léonard-de-Vinci, 16e. *Irish Embassy*, 4 Rue Rude, 16e.

Hospitals with English-speaking staff. The *British Hospital* (*Hertford*), 48 Rue de Villiers, N.W. of the *Porte de Champerret* (737 94 10); *American Hospital*, 63 Blvd. Victor-Hugo, Neuilly (637 72 00). In an emergency, dial 17 for the *Police*, or 887 27 50 for the *Public Assistance Ambulance Service*. The *British* (and American) *Pharmacy* is at 1 Rue Auber, 9e (073 49 40).

Churches. The *British Embassy Church*, 5 Rue d'Aguesseau, is at present closed: other English churches include *St George's*, 7 Rue Aug.-Vacquerie (off the N. end of the Av. d'Iéna), and *St Joseph's* (R.C.), 50 Av. Hoche (nr the Étoile); *Methodist chapel*, 4 Rue Roquépine, 8e; *Church of Scotland*, 17 Rue Bayard, 8e; *Society of Friends*, 114 Rue de Vaugirard, 6e. The *American Church* is at 65 Quai d'Orsay, 7e; *Holy Trinity* at 23 Av. George-V, 8e. The *Great Synagogue* is at 44 Rue de la Victoire, 9e.

Sports. General information about a variety of sports may be obtained from the *Comité National des Sports*, 25 Rue d'Anjou, 8e; *Service Académique de la Jeunesse et Sports*, 11 Rue Auber, 9e; the Préfecture de Paris (*Service de la Jeunesse et des Sports*), 17 Blvd. de Morland, 4e; or from the *Standard Athletic Club*, Meudon.

Among the innumerable French sporting federations, the following may be found useful: Féd. Française de *Golf*, 4 Rue Bassano, 16e; Féd. Française des *Sports Equestres*, 164 Rue du Faubourg-St-Honoré, 8e, and Féd, Nationale des Sociétés de Courses de France, 11 Rue du Cirque, 8e; the main racecourses in the vicinity of Paris are at Longchamp and Chantilly (flat-races), and at Auteuil (steeplechases); Union Nationale des Centres sportifs de plein air (U.C.P.A.), 62 Rue de la Glacière, 13e (for *mountaineering*); Féd. Française de *Ski*, 34 Rue Eugène-Flachat, 17e; Féd. de la *Pêche*, 10 Rue Péclet, 15e; Conseil supérieur de la *Chasse*, 85 Av. de Wagram, 17e; Union des *Polos* de France, Polo de Paris, Bois de Boulogne, 16e; Soc. des *Steeple Chases* de France, 137 Rue du Faubourg-St-Honoré, 8e; Féd. Française de *Lawn Tennis*, 15 Rue de Téhéran, 8e (also information from 74 Rue de Rome, 8e); Féd. Française de *Montagne* (et Club Alpin Français), 7 Rue La Boétie, 8e.

HOTELS AND RESTAURANTS

Hotels of every class, size, and price abound in Paris, but it is prudent to book rooms in advance either directly or through a travel agency, for they are often full during the tourist season, particularly at Easter and during the course of Exhibitions, Trade Fairs, etc. Branches of the *Office de Tourisme de Paris* (see p. 31) will, for a small charge, endeavour to make on-the-spot bookings, which are automatically cancelled if not taken up within 1½ hours. They can also provide an up-to-date *Guide des Hôtels* for Paris and region. Another useful list is that published annually by *Michelin*, entitled *Paris et sa banlieue: Hôtels et Restaurants*, which lists the better-known and well-equipped hotels by arrondissements, and may be recommended. This edition of the *Blue Guide*, by the inclusion of the word *'Hotels'* after certain towns, indicates the existence of reasonable accommodation elsewhere in the Île de France.

Most of the luxury and correspondingly expensive hotels are situated in the 1st, 2nd, 6-10th, and 16-17th arrondissements. In his own interest, a traveller should have a precise understanding as to the charge before taking possession of his room. Valuables should be deposited with the manager in exchange for a receipt.

All hotels are officially classified by the Secrétariat au Tourisme, and their grading is shown by stars, depending on their amenities and the type of hotel, from 4-stars 'L' (Luxury) to the 1-star (plain but comfortable). A surprisingly large number of hotels in the 1-, 2-, and even 3-star category still have only a proportion of rooms with a private W.C. en suite. Similarly, a high percentage of hotels, including some with 4 stars, have no restaurant. In most hotels 15% is added to the bill for 'service'—whether provided or not—and certainly when the bill is marked 'service et taxes compris' (s.t.c.), no additional gratuity need be given.

Hostel for the Disabled. The French are to be highly commended for their consideration for the disabled, and those who have difficulties in coping with hotels might find the solution to their problem at a hostel run by the Association des Paralysés de France, 17-21 Blvd. Auguste-Blanqui, 13e. The disabled person can have a single room or, sharing with an able-bodied helper, a studio equipped with cooking facilities, refrigerator, shower, and wash-basin. The warden and his wife are available at all times (and will even supply meals if due notice is given); and there is an underground lock-up garage. Lifts and special lavatories are provided for those in wheelchairs.

Disabled people will find 'Access in Paris' useful. It is available from 'The Paris Survey Project', 68b Castlebar Road, Ealing, London W5. Helpful advice can also be given by the Central Council for the Disabled, 34 Eccleston Sq., SW1.

Restaurants of every kind and category are plentiful in Paris, and although prices tend to be comparatively high, very often (but by no means always) one will obtain better value for money than in some other countries who do not take the ritual and etiquette of eating so seriously, and who are prepared to accept low standards. At most restaurants the day's set menu, 'à prix fixe', is available, and at a much lower price than 'à la carte', even if somewhat unimaginative in the more modest establishments; and this is displayed, with prices, at the entrance. Sometimes there are more than one selected menu to choose from, apart from the recommended 'plat du jour'.

The **wine**, either *rouge, blanc,* or *rosé,* in carafes or 'pichets' (jugs) is usually very fair at most restaurants, while many can also provide a liberal choice of superior wines at relatively high prices. When dining *à la carte,* the traveller should not allow the suggestions of the waiter, however plausible, to add more dishes to the menu than he really wants, for the slightest additions can easily swell the bill by a disproportionate amount. The bill ('l'addition'), which should be carefully scrutinized, should be in writing; the 'normal' 15% gratuity is usually added, but any misunderstanding can be avoided by asking 'Le service est-il compris?'. If no gratuity has been included, the waiter may be rewarded with 10-12% of the bill, according to the quality of service; somewhat less where a considerable proportion of the total is for a single bottle. See also *Tipping,* p. 40.

A useful list of *inexpensive* restaurants, classified by districts, and offering a good-quality meal, is available from Tourist Offices. Information about restaurants may also be obtained by telephoning 359 12 12. There are, of course, a number of French gastronomic guides listing a great range of eating-places, but it must be admitted that the traveller will often have better value for his money at the less pretentious establishments. Unfortunately there is a tendency, particularly in the areas frequented by tourists rather than by a regular clientele, to serve stereotyped meals of a mediocre quality for the price charged. It will be noted that many restaurants are closed on Sundays, and during August. It is advisable to book a table in advance whenever possible.

Among the better-known 'de-luxe' restaurants, where French cookery *should* reach its perfection, are the following (listed according to arrondissement):

1er: *Grand Véfour,* 17 Rue Beaujolais; 2e: *Drouant,* Pl. Gaillon; 5e: *Tour d'Argent,* 15 Quai Tournelle; 7e: *Archestrate,* 84 Rue Varennes; 8e: *Lasserre,* 17 Av. Franklin D. Roosevelt; *Ledoyen,* Carré Champs-Élysées; *Maxim's,* 3 Rue Royale; *Taillavent,* 15 Rue Lamennais; *Lucas-Carton,* 9 Pl. Madeleine; *La Marée,* 1 Rue Daru; 10e: *Chez Michel,* 10 Rue Belzunce; 14e: *Chez Albert,* 122 Av. Maine; 16e: *Vivarois,* 192 Av. V.-Hugo; 17e: *La Coquille,* 6 Rue Tocqueville; 19e: *Cochon d'Or,* 192 Av. Jean-Jaurès.

The thousand **Cafés** of Paris—there were said to be 300 as early as 1715—are more numerous in the larger streets, and in many cases tables and chairs are set out on the pavement in front (the 'terrasse')—or behind a glazed conservatory/observatory—where the customer may spend an entertaining hour watching the passers-by. The *café* or *café crème* is usually very good, but tea-making is still a perfunctory performance. A 'Continental breakfast' or 'petit déjeuner' may be obtained in the mornings, with rolls, *croissants,* or *brioche,* and butter, with coffee or chocolate.

The usual order for a small beer is a *demi;* draught beer is *à la pression.* It is cheaper to stand at the bar, but prices are automatically raised if one subsequently takes a seat. The waiter should not be paid after each drink, but just prior to the time one wishes to leave. Travellers are warned that the prices charged at some pretentious cafés or patisseries for a mere coffee, beer, *vin ordinaire,* or other beverage, are quite exorbitant, and it is always as well to check before ordering, to avoid an unpleasant shock.

The standard of toilet facilities in restaurants, brasseries, bistros, bars, and cafés, is slowly improving; they are not all the Stygian bogs they once were, but towels (paper or otherwise) are often hard to come by.

ENTERTAINMENT

Topical information about theatres, cinemas, cabarets, night clubs, etc., may be found in any of the guides to What's On, among them 'Une Semaine de Paris', 'L'Officiel des Spectacles', 'Allo Paris', 'Paris selection', etc., available from most tourist agencies and kiosks.

Theatres. The National, or State-subsidized, theatres are the *Comédie-Française*, Pl. du Théâtre-Français, 1er; the *Théâtre de France* (de l'Odéon), Pl. Paul-Claudel, 6e; *Théâtre National Populaire* (T.N.P.), Palais de Chaillot; *Théâtre de l'Est Parisien* (T.E.P.), 17 Rue Malte-Brun, 20e; and the *Théâtre de la Ville*, Pl. du Châtelet, 4e. In addition, there is the 'Théâtre Lyrique', the world-famous *Opéra*, Pl. de l'Opéra, 9e (see p. 151); the *Opéra-Comique* is now used mainly as an experimental theatre.

In addition to the productions to be seen in these and the many other theatres of Paris, there are also any number of *Music Halls, Chansonniers*, etc., most of them—with certain exceptions—devoted to revues of no very refined nature. Some specialize in political satire, but these can only be appreciated by those with a thorough knowledge of the language.

While few **Cabarets** leave much to the imagination, although some present more or less 'artistic performances', they attempt to provide something to suit all tastes in these entertainments, from the exotic (or simply érotique) to the grossly vulgar, but visitors are warned that the announcement of 'free admission' (*entrée libre*) to any of these *boîtes* or night-clubs simply means that the price of admission is added to the already high charge for 'consommations' which he is expected to order.

Cinemas of all types are numerous in all parts of Paris, many of the larger converted to show various films in the same building. Most run continuously from 14.00. Programmes normally change on Wednesdays.

Note that theatre tickets bought through any agency will cost more than at the box-office of the theatre concerned, usually open between 11.00 and 18.30 or 19.00. Most theatres close for some weeks in the summer, and on one evening a week (usually Mon. or Tues.). Smoking is forbidden. Ushers expect a tip.

Concert Halls. The main halls are the *Théâtre des Champs-Élysées*, 15 Av. Montaigne; *Théâtre du Châtelet*, Pl. du Châtelet; *Salle Gaveau*, 45 Rue La Boétie; *Salle Pleyel*, 252 Rue du Faubourg-St-Honoré; *Salle Cortot*, 78 Rue Cardinet; the *Palais de Chaillot*, Pl. du Trocadéro; the *Maison de l'O.R.T.F.*, 116 Av. du Président-Kennedy; and at the *Palais des Congrès*, Porte Maillot.

Good **Church Music,** or *Organ Recitals,* can be heard at a number of churches, particularly at Notre-Dame, St-Eustache, St-Séverin, St-Sulpice, St-Roch, St-Clotilde, St-Étienne-du-Mont, and the Madeleine.

Art Exhibitions. Although smaller exhibitions devoted to individual artists can be seen at any of the innumerable galleries and art-dealers' shops, many of them in the 6e arrondissement, the main national exhibitions are held at the *Grand Palais, Musée d'Art Moderne,* the *Petit-Palais, Musée des Arts Décoratifs,* etc., while the new *Beaubourg Centre* will also be an important focus of exhibitions of modern art.

Shopping. Many of the smartest, and most expensive, shops are to be found in the 1er, 6e, 8e, and 16e arrondissements, particularly in the area of the Rue du Faubourg-St-Honoré, but in fact good shops can be found in most districts of central Paris, and their prices are usually less extravagant. The best of the many department stores are perhaps 'Les Galeries Lafayette', and 'Au Printemps', at 40 and 69 Blvd. Haussmann, respectively (just N. of the Opéra). Many of the Antique shops and *brocanteurs* (second-hand dealers) are to be found in the 6e, while the so-called *Village Suisse* (shut Tues.-Wed.; W. of the École Militaire), and the extensive *Marché aux Puces* (open Sat.-Mon.; a few minutes walk N. of the Porte de Clignancourt Métro), attract crowds in search of the rare bargain among the bric-à-brac.

Auctions are held regularly at the *Salle Drouot,* 6 Rue Rossini, 9e. Nearby, in the Rue Drouot and further S. in the arcades of the Palais-Royal, are the haunts of philatelists; while an open-air *Stamp* Market is held at weekends and Thurs. mornings at the junction of the Av. de Marigny and Av. Gabriel. Other colourful markets are devoted to *flowers:* in the Pl. Louis-Lépine (not far E. of the Conciergerie), on the E. side of the Madeleine, and at the Pl. des Ternes, and Pl. de la République. On Sundays the flowers of the Pl. Louis-Lépine give way to a *Bird* Market, while opposite, on the Quai de la Mégisserie, is a *Pet* Market (not Sun.).

On the N. side of the Pl. de la Madeleine some superbly displayed Food Shops may be seen, although less sumptuous establishments will tempt the eye and palate throughout Paris; indeed, one of the great pleasures of wandering about the city is the quality of the merchandise seen in many of the smaller shops selling cheese, *patisserie,* or *charcuterie.* Although *Les Halles* have been transferred to *Rungis* (near Orly airport), other Food Markets not too far from the centre may be visited (not Sun. or Mon.) in the Rue de Montorgueil (leading N. from Les Halles Métro); the Rue Mouffetard, 5e; the Rue Buci (just N. of the Odéon Métro); and there are of course many others. Food shopping on a Sunday morning at one of the street markets of Paris is almost always an agreeable occupation.

Bookshops, Libraries, and Cultural Centres. The former continue to proliferate throughout central Paris, but differ widely in the range of books stocked, and in the quality of their service. English newspapers and magazines can be found at many kiosks near the centre. For books in English both *Librairie Brentano*'s, 37 Av. de l'Opéra, and *Librairie Galignani,* 224 Rue de Rivoli (nr the Tuileries Métro), provide a better selection than others, and *W. H. Smith*'s, at 248 Rue de Rivoli, has a propitiatory teashop.

A *British Cultural Centre* (incorporating the British Institute and Council Offices, Library, etc.), has recently been opened at 9-11 Rue du Constantine, W. of the Esplanade des Invalides. There is a good *American Library* at 10 Rue du Gén. Camou, 7e, and a Student Centre at 261 Blvd. Raspail, 14e.

MUSEUMS, COLLECTIONS, AND MONUMENTS

A table giving hours of admission, etc., is given below, but it should be noted that opening times vary and often change without warning. Lecture tours are organized by several bodies; those promoted by the *Caisse Nationale des Monuments Historiques* are listed in a bi-monthly leaflet entitled 'Informations permanentes et visites conférences des Musées Nationaux', obtainable from the Hôtel de Sully, 62 Rue St-Antoine, 3e, Tourist Offices, *Bureau d'Action Culturelle de la Direction des Musées de France,* Palais du Louvre, etc. A list of such visits will also be found in some newspapers. No advance application is normally necessary: the visitor merely goes to the place indicated at the time stated, and pays a small fee. The group is conducted by competent official French-speaking guide-lecturers. Guided tours by English-speaking lecturers may be arranged.

It may be remarked that visitors coming from countries where they are used to entering museums free of charge may sometimes baulk at paying the fee imposed. In fact, in many cases, the charge is in no way disproportionate to the size and quality of the collections to be seen, an increasing number of which are being reformed and displayed with considerable taste. Unfortunately this is not always so, and the same charge can apply to museums and monuments whose conservateurs appear to remain unconcerned as to whether they are giving value for money, and who are insensitive to the comparative excellence of other collections.

It may also be mentioned that although considerable work seems to have gone into the preparation and production of lavishly illustrated catalogues, selling at high prices, of temporary exhibitions, few of the important museums—perhaps because they are still undergoing change—publish good catalogues of use to the discriminating visitor for whom the few 'Publications scientifiques' available are both too detailed and highly priced, and who find the slighter booklets too superficial; a situation which it is hoped will be improved before too long.

Hours of admission to the main Museums, Collections, and Monuments in Paris and environs

With the exception of those marked with a dagger, all the following collections, etc., are closed on **Tuesdays.** Certain museums are also closed on public holidays. In many, the admission fee is reduced on Sundays, when in a few cases entry may be free (but the museum may be crowded). The more important are indicated by bolder type.

NAME	OPEN	ALSO CLOSED	DESCRIBED ON PAGE
Arc de Triomphe Pl. Charles-de-Gaulle, 8e	10.00–17.00 or 18.00		162
Art Moderne, Musée Municipal d' 11 Av. Prés.-Wilson	10.00–17.45	Mon.	168
Art Moderne, Musée National d' 13 Av. Prés.-Wilson, 16e	9.45–17.15		168
Arts Africains 293 Av. Daumesnil, 12e	9.45–12.00; 13.30–17.00		183
Arts Décoratifs 107 Rue de Rivoli, 1er	10.00–12.30; 13.30–17.00		94
Arts et Traditions Populaires 6 Route du Mahatma-Gandhi (Bois de Boulogne)	10.00–12.30; 14.00–17.00		176

†*Bibliothèque Nat. Cabinet des Médailles* 58 Rue de Richelieu, 2e	9.00 or 10.00—17.00 or 18.00	Sun. and for two weeks after Easter	128
Carnavalet 23 Rue de Sévigné, 3e	10.00—17.50		140
Cernuschi 7 Av. Vélasquez, 8e	10.00—17.50	Mon.	166
Chasse 60 Rue des Archives, 3e	10.00—17.00		145
Cinéma Palais de Chaillot, 16e	10.00—17.00		172
Cluny 6 Pl. Paul-Painlevé, 5e	9.45—12.45; 14.00—17.15		58
Cognacq-Jay 23 Blvd. des Capucines, 2e	10.00—17.50	Mon.	150
Guimet 6 Pl. d'Iéna, 16e	9.45—12.00; 13.30—17.15		169
Hôtel de Soubise 60 Rue des Francs-Bourgeois, 3e	14.00—17.00		144
Homme, Musée de l' Palais de Chaillot, 16e	10.00—17.00 or 18.00		173
†**Invalides, Les (Musée de l'Armée)** Esplanade des Invalides, 7e	10.00—17.00 every day		83
Jacquemart-André 158 Blvd. Haussmann, 8e	13.30—17.30	Mon.	164
Jeu de Paume *(Impressionnisme)* Pl. de la Concorde, 1er	9.45—17.00		89
Louvre, Musée du Palais du Louvre, 1er	9.45—17.15 Parts of certain departments are closed in rotation during the week and between 11.30 and 14.00		97
Marmottan 2 Rue Louis-Boilly, 16e	10.00—18.00	Mon.	174
Monuments Français Palais de Chaillot, 16e	9.45—12.30; 14.00—17.15		171
Nissim de Camondo 63 Rue de Monceau, 8e	10.00—12.00; 14.00—17.00	Wed.	165
Panthéon Pl. du Panthéon, 5e	10.00—12.00; 14.00—17.00 or 18.00		55
Petit-Palais Av. Churchill, 8e	10.00—17.50		160
Rodin, Musée 77 Rue de Varenne, 7e	10.00—12.15; 14.00—17.00		79
Sainte-Chapelle Blvd. du Palais, 4e	10.00—12.00; 14.00—17.00 or 18.00		46
†*Techniques* (Science Museum) 292 Rue St-Martin, 3e	13.30—17.30 10.00—17.00 on Sun.	Mon.	147
Vincennes, Château de	10.00—12.00; 14.00—17.00 or 18.00		181

Environs of Paris

Chantilly (Musée Condé)	10.30—17.00	208
Compiègne, Château de	10.00—12.00; 13.30—17.30	217
Écouen, Château d' (Musée de la Renaissance)	Due to open 1977—79. For information, apply locally	207
Fontainebleau, Château de	**10.00—12.30; 14.00—16.15 or 17.15**	235

	Certain guided tours start at 12.00, 16.15 or 17.15	
Malmaison and Bois-Préau, Châteaux de	10.00—12.00;13.30—17.00	**200**
St-Denis, Basilique de	10.00—12.00; 14.00—17.00 or 18.00	**204**
St-Germain-en-Laye (Musée des Antiquités Nat.)	9.45—12.00; 13.30—17.15	**203**
Sceaux, Château de (Musée de l' Île de France)	10.00—12.00; 14.00—19.00 on Sat. and Sun.; open to 17.00 on Wed. and Thur.; and from 14.00 to 17.00 only on Mon. and Fri.	**243**
†**Versailles, Château de**	10.00—17.00 or 9.30—17.30	**187**
Grand Trianon	10.00—12.00; 14.00—17.30	**198**
Petit Trianon	(closed for restoration)	**199**
Musée des Voitures	14.00—17.00 or 17.30	
Vaux-le-Vicomte, Château de	10.00—12.00; 14.00—18.00 from April to Oct.	**232**

Although this table includes many of the principal attractions of Paris and its environs, it by no means exhausts the list of things to see. The traveller is reminded of the following additional points of interest, to mention a few only which deserve a visit, details of which will be found in the text. In **Paris:** the *Arènes de Lutèce;* the *Palais-Royal; Palais Luxembourg; Palais de Justice;* the *Hôpital St-Louis,* and *Hôpital de la Salpêtrière; École Militaire;* and the churches of *La Madeleine, Val-de-Grâce, St-Eustache, St-Étienne-du-Mont, St-Germain-l'Auxerrois, St-Germain-des-Près, St-Roch, St-Médard, St-Séverin, St-Sulpice, Ste-Ursule de la Sorbonne;* the cemeteries of *Père Lachaise, Montmartre, Montparnasse,* and *Picpus;* the *Pl. Vendôme* and *Pl. des Vosges,* without listing individually the numerous hôtels of the Marais and the Faubourg St-Germain.

The cemeteries are normally open from 7.30 to 18.00 in summer, and from 8.00 to 16.30 in winter; that of *Picpus* is open during the afternoon only.

Among the outstanding buildings of interest in the **environs** of Paris which should be visited, one may mention: the churches of *Morienval, St-Leu-d'Esserent,* or *St-Loup-de-Noud;* the châteaux at *Dampierre, Maintenon,* or *Rosny-sur-Seine;* but throughout the whole region of the Île de France those that merit a detour are legion. An up-to-date brochure giving times of admission to some châteaux and gardens open to the public may be obtained from *La Demeure Historique,* 55 Quai de la Tournelle, 5e (329 02 86)

Examples of medieval architecture range from the Merovingian crypt at *Jouarre* to the cathedrals of *Sens* and *Évreux,* and to the even greater churches at *Chartres* and *Beauvais;* the impressive ruins of *Royaumont, Longpont,* or *St-Jean-des-Vignes* (Soissons); the imperious ramparts of *Gisors,* or *Château-Gaillard;* the agreeable towns of *Senlis, Montfort-l'Amaury,* or *Provins,* are among the more obvious: the area is rich indeed, and the historical associations are endless.

Unfortunately, as in every country, certain sites are spoiled by the sheer density of tourists congregating in their vicinity, but once beyond the suburbs of Paris and the other towns in its neighbourhood, the attractions of the landscape of the Île de France offer a welcome relief, and forest tracts, verdant valleys, and fertile agricultural land extend in every direction.

GENERAL HINTS

Season. The main characteristic of the weather in Paris is changeability, particularly in the winter and spring, although long periods of fine weather occur each year. Perhaps because of its long wide boulevards, which sometimes act as wind tunnels, the wind is more noticeable than in London, and bitterly cold blasts can be experienced in some quarters during certain seasons, and it can remain cold until well after Easter. At other times it can be oppressively hot. In spring and autumn, although the days are shorter, the weather is better adapted for the active sightseer, for in summer (June-Aug.) Paris is packed with tourists, although in Aug. the city is almost deserted by its regular residents, and many of the theatres, libraries, etc., and even restaurants, are closed.

Language. The visitor who knows no language but English can usually get along without too much trouble in Paris, although he will probably pay in cash for his ignorance. Some attempt to speak some French is always appreciated.

Manners. Forms of politeness in France are still less casual than in some other countries, and there is more handshaking at meeting and parting. It is also polite to continue to use 'Monsieur', 'Madame', or 'Mademoiselle' as a form of address (without the surname) even after some acquaintance, but such standing on ceremony is becoming progressively relaxed in many circles.

Tipping. However anachronistic may be this stultifying system of rewarding waiters, taxi-drivers, cloakroom attendants, et al., who now invariably expect more than they deserve for the quality of service often grudgingly given, it still persists. However, many restaurants and hotels have replaced it by adding 15% (no less) to the bill, leaving little room for discussion, even when the 'service' has been indifferent or merely perfunctory.

Working Hours, etc. It will be found that in France, work starts earlier than in the U.K., and generally meals are also begun at an earlier hour. Although there is a movement towards the 'English' week-end, most food shops are open on Sunday mornings, and remain open later on weekday evenings; but they are likely to be shut on Mondays. *Note also that the majority of Museums, etc.* (see pp. 37-9) *are shut on Tuesdays,* although open on Sundays. Many, however, are closed between 12.00 and 14.00 on weekdays.

Public Holidays. The main public holidays are 1 Jan.; Easter Monday; Whit Monday; Ascension Day; 1 May; 14 July (Fête Nationale); 15 Aug. (Assumption); 1 Nov. (All Saints); 11 Nov. (Armistice Day); and Christmas Day. Banks are likely to be shut at noon on days preceding public holidays.

CALENDAR OF EVENTS

The dates, some only approximately fixed, of some of the more important annual events (other than 'sporting' events) or 'manifestations' taking place in Paris, are listed below. Numerous other activities, fairs, exhibitions, etc., are advertised in the Press, and in magazines devoted to 'What's on'.

1 JAN.	*Jour de l'An;* gifts exchanged (étrennes).
6 JAN.	*Journée des Rois* (Epiphany); special cakes (galettes) baked for family parties.
EASTER WEEK.	Foire aux Pains d'Épice (Gingerbread Fair) in the Pl. de la Nation.
MARCH/ APRIL.	Opening of the Salon des Indépendants, Grand Palais.
MAY.	'Labour Day'; Lily of the Valley sold in the streets.
1 MAY.	(usually fortnight ending Whit Monday). Foire de Paris at the Porte de Versailles.
JUNE.	Salon opens.
1 JUNE.	Air Show at Le Bourget.
14 JULY.	Fête Nationale; reviews at the Champs-Élysées; fireworks, dancing, and general festivity.
26 AUG.	Celebration of Liberation (1944).
OCT.	Salon de l'Automobile in the Palais de la Défense.
9 OCT.	Feast of St Denis.
OCT./NOV.	Salon d'Automne at the Grand Palais.
1-2 NOV.	*Toussaint* and *Jour des Morts;* principal cemeteries visited and graves decorated.
11 NOV.	Armistice Day; military parades at the Arc de Triomphe.
DEC.	Salon d'Hiver opens at the Musée d'Art Moderne.
24 DEC.	Midnight masses.
25 DEC.	*Noël.*

EXPLANATIONS

TYPE. The main routes are described in large type. Smaller type is used for branch-routes, excursions, or deviations, and for historical and preliminary paragraphs, and (generally speaking) for descriptions of greater detail or minor importance.

ASTERISKS indicate points of special interest or excellence.

DISTANCES in Rtes 21-38 are given cumulatively from the starting-point of the route (i.e., from *Notre-Dame*), or from the commencement of the sub-route. Road distances are measured and signposted in kilometres, and it was felt that motorists would prefer the distances recorded in the *Guide* to conform, since Britain is to change to metric measurement. It should be noted, however, that the constant realignment of roads makes it certain that these distances will vary slightly from those measured by motorists on their milometers.

STREET NUMBERING. In Paris, in streets parallel to the river the houses are numbered from E. to W.; in those at right-angles to the Seine, from the end nearest the river.

ANGLICIZATION. For the sake of consistency, most place-names and the names of kings, etc., have retained their French form.

Abbreviations. In addition to generally accepted and self-explanatory abbreviations, the following occur in the *Guide:*

Av. = Avenue
C = Century
Blvd. = Boulevard
l. = left
N.-D. = Notre-Dame
Pl. = Place or Plan
R = Room
r. = right
Rte = Route
S. = Salle
St- or Ste- = Saint
S.I. = Syndicat d'Initiative or Tourist Office

GLOSSARY OF ARCHITECTURAL AND ALLIED TERMS

ACAJOU = mahogany

ARC-BOUTANT = flying buttress

AUTEL = altar

CARREFOUR = crossroads

CASERNE = barracks

CHEVET = apse (also ABSIDE)

COLONNETTE = little column; a term used in France for a vaulting shaft

CONTREFORTS = buttresses

DESSUS DE PORTE = a painting above a doorway

EBÉNISTE = cabinet-maker

ÉGLISE = church

ÉMAIL = enamel

FLÈCHE = spire

HÔTEL = mansion

HÔTEL-DIEU = principal hospital in many towns

MANSARD ROOF = roof of which each face has two slopes, the lower steeper than the upper

MAIRIE = town-hall or municipal building; also Hôtel de Ville

NACRE = mother or pearl

NEF = nave

OEIL-DE-BOEUF = small circular window (bull's eye)

REZ DE CHAUSSÉE = ground floor

TIERCERON = curved rib in Gothic vaults springing from the same point as the intersecting diagonal rib, and rising to the end of the ridge-rib

VERMEIL = silver-gilt

VITRAIL = stained-glass window

VOUSSOIR = wedge-shaped stones used in constructing vaults

I THE CITÉ AND THE ÎLE-ST-LOUIS

1 THE ÎLE DE LA CITÉ AND THE ÎLE-ST-LOUIS

MÉTROS: *Cité, St-Michel, Pont-Neuf, Châtelet, Pont-Marie, Sully-Morland.*

The **Île de la Cité** (Pl. 14; 4-6), the earliest inhabited part of Paris, lies in the river like a ship, the 'Pointe' as its prow and *Notre-Dame* as its poop, moored to the banks by numerous bridges; and the ship which has always figured in the arms of Paris is indeed appropriate. The Cité was the site of the original Gallic settlement of Lutèce or Lutetia Parisiorum, and after the destruction of the later Roman city on the Left Bank, became the site of Frankish Paris.

It remained the royal, legal, and ecclesiastical centre long after the town had extended onto both river-banks, and for the visitor with but little time even a brief tour of the Cité will give a good idea of its importance in the historical development of Paris.

The Cité derives its importance from its situation at the crossroads of two natural routes across France. The Capetian kings were the great builders of the Cité, and it remained little changed from 1300 to the Second Empire, when Haussmann, after massive demolition, left it with its present appearance.

From the QUAI DU LOUVRE, the picturesque **Pont-Neuf** crosses the W. extremity of the island. It is, in spite of its name, the oldest existing bridge in Paris, begun by *Baptiste du Cerceau*, completed in 1607, and several times repaired since then. It was also the first bridge to be built without houses lining each side, and with pavements. This 'Pointe de la Cité' is occupied by the SQUARE DU VERT-GALANT, so-called in allusion to the amorous adventures of Henri IV, a statue of whom, by *Lemot*, stands close to the bridge.

The Statue was set up in 1818 in place of another, by Giambologna and Tacca, which stood here from 1635 to 1792. The foundryman, an ardent Bonapartist, placed a statuette of Napoleon within the right arm, because he was constrained to use metal from the melted-down statue of his hero which had surmounted the Vendôme column.

East of the Pont-Neuf, entered by the Rue Henri-Robert, is the ***Pl. Dauphine**, retaining two rows of houses dating from the reign of Louis XIII, although many have been altered since. Unfortunately the E. wing of the triangle was demolished to provide a view of *Louis Duc*'s W. façade of the *Palais de Justice* (1857-68; see below).

During the 17th and 18C the PL. DU PONT-NEUF and the bridge swarmed with pedlars and mountebanks. Tabarin set up his 'théâtre' in the Pl. Dauphine. Here, too, was the original site of the *Samaritaine*, one of the earliest hydraulic pumps, constructed by a Fleming for Henri IV to supply water for the royal palaces of the Louvre and Tuileries. It derived its name from a figure of the Good Samaritan on the fountain.

Other bridges connecting the Cité to the Right Bank of the Seine are the *Pont au Change* (1858-59), replacing a stone bridge dating from 1639 lined with moneylenders' shops; the *Pont Notre-Dame*, rebuilt in 1913 on the site of the main Roman Bridge; and beyond is the *Pont d'Arcole*, built under the restoration, and named after a young man killed in 1830 leading insurgents against the Hôtel de Ville.

To the S., the Cité is connected to the Left Bank by the *Pont St-Michel*, rebuilt several times since the 14C (last in 1857), affording a fine view of the façade of *Notre-Dame*. Beyond is the *Petit Pont* (1853), on the site of another Roman bridge. Until 1782 it was defended at the S.

end by the *Petit Châtelet*, the successor of the Tour de Bois, which in 886 held Norman marauders at bay. From the W. front of *Notre-Dame*, the *Pont-au-Double* (1881) replaced a 17C bridge, for crossing which the toll of a 'double' ($\frac{1}{12}$d) was charged; while from the E. extremity of the Cité after skirting the cathedral, on the site of the archbishop's palace (pulled down in 1831), is the *Pont de l'Archevêché* (1827), providing a good view of the apse, with its profusion of flying buttresses.

Following the QUAI DE L'HORLOGE (N. of the *Palais de Justice*), and entered just beyond twin towers (see below), is the ***Conciergerie**, one of the world's famous prisons, occupying part of the lower floor of the Palais, and originally the residence of the 'Concierge', chief executive of the Parlement. Adm. daily 10.00-12.00, 13.30-16.00 or 18.00; closed Tues.

Its historical associations are numerous. In 1418 the Comte d'Armagnac was massacred here with many of his partisans by the hired assassins of the Duke of Burgundy. The Marquise de Brinvilliers, the poisoner, was held here. During the Revolution, first Marie-Antoinette, then Bailly, Malesherbes, Mme Élisabeth, Mme Roland, Mme du Barry, Camille Desmoulins, Charlotte Corday, Danton, André Chénier, and Robespierre passed their last days in the Conciergerie. 288 prisoners perished here in the massacres of Sept. 1792. Later prisoners were Georges Cadoudal (d. 1804), the Chouan leader, Marshal Ney, and the Duc d'Orléans (1890).

The SALLE DES GARDES, a handsome vaulted room of the 14C (restored 1877), where visitors await the guide, contains two small stairs (no. adm.) ascending (r.) to the *Tour de César*, where Ravaillac, the murderer of Henri IV, was imprisoned (1610); the other leads to the *Tour d'Argent,* which served as a prison for Damiens, who attempted to kill Louis XV (1757). The little spiral staircase in the r.-hand corner as we leave the room was climbed by Marie-Antoinette and over 2,200 other prisoners on their way from their cells to the Tribunal.

The impressive four-aisled Gothic *SALLE DES GENS-D'ARMES (restored in 1868-80) rivals those of Mont St-Michel and the Palace of the Popes at Avignon. This was the original 'Salle des Pas-Perdus', said to be so called because the victims of the Revolution walked through it on their way to the Cour du Mai and execution; the name has since been transferred to the hall above (and to the waiting-rooms of other public buildings).

Near the far end, to the l. a curious open spiral stair leads to the so-called *CUISINES DE ST-LOUIS (14C), also vaulted, and with four huge fireplaces. Returning to the first bay, we turn l, past a grille flanking the Rue de Paris, reserved for the 'pailleux' (prisoners who slept on straw, being unable to bribe their gaolers). We next enter the diminutive GALERIE DES PRISONNIERS, the windows of which look out onto the COUR DES FEMMES, where the female prisoners were allowed to take exercise, and also the scene of the massacres of Sept. 1792. A railing which still exists divided off a section for men. To the l. in the Gal. des Prisonniers was the cell where condemned prisoners had their hair shorn and awaited the departure of the tumbril for the guillotine, and at the end is the iron wicket which was the only entrance to the prison in Revolutionary times.

At the opposite end of this gallery is the original door (but in a different position) of Marie-Antoinette's cell, where the queen remained

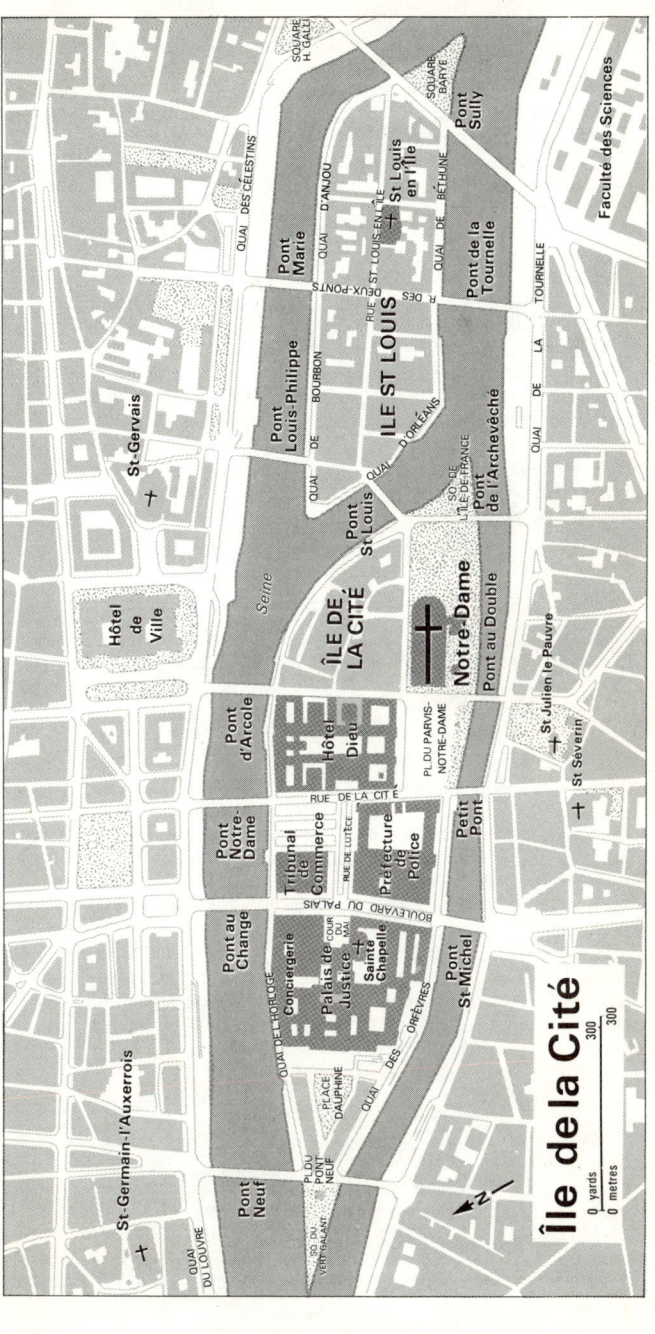

Île de la Cité

Faculté des Sciences

Pont Sully

SQUARE BARYE

SQUARE H. GALLI

QUAI DES CÉLESTINS

QUAI D'ANJOU

St-Louis en l'Île

Pont Marie

QUAI DE BÉTHUNE

QUAI DE BOURBON

R. DES DEUX-PONTS

RUE ST-LOUIS-EN-L'ÎLE

St Louis en l'Île

Pont Louis-Philippe

ÎLE ST LOUIS

QUAI D'ORLÉANS

Pont de la Tournelle

QUAI DE LA TOURNELLE

St-Gervais

Pont St-Louis

QUAI DE BÉTHUNE

QUAI DE LA TOURNELLE

Seine

QUAI DE L'ÎLE-DE-FRANCE

SQ. DE L'ÎLE-DE-FRANCE

Pont de l'Archevêché

QUAI DE L'ARCHEVÊCHÉ

Hôtel de Ville

ÎLE DE LA CITÉ

Notre-Dame

Pont au Double

St Julien le Pauvre

Pont d'Arcole

Hôtel Dieu

PL. DU PARVIS-NOTRE-DAME

St Séverin

RUE DE LA CITÉ

Pont Notre-Dame

Tribunal de Commerce

Préfecture de Police

Petit Pont

RUE DE LUTÈCE

Pont au Change

QUAI DE L'HORLOGE

Conciergerie

Palais de Justice

Sainte Chapelle

BOULEVARD DU PALAIS

COUR DU MAI

Pont St-Michel

St-Germain-l'Auxerrois

QUAI DU LOUVRE

SQ. DU VERT-GALANT

PL. DU PONT-NEUF

PLACE DAUPHINE

QUAI DES ORFÈVRES

Pont Neuf

| 0 yards | 300 |
| 0 metres | 300 |

from 2 Aug. to 16 Oct. 1793. Adjacent, and now communicating with it, is Robespierre's cell. Next comes the CHAPEL (with a gallery for the prisoners) where the Girondins were incarcerated. It now displays a small collection of souvenirs, including a blade of the guillotine, a crucifix found in Marie-Antoinette's cell, orders for arrest, etc.

On making our exit, we turn r. into the Blvd. du Palais, passing the COUR DU MAI, on the E. side of the Palais de Justice, named after the maypole set up here annually by the 'Basoche' or society of law-clerks.

The **Palais de Justice,** a huge block of buildings occupying the whole width of the island, also includes within its precincts the *Sainte Chapelle* (see below), which, with the four towers on the N. side, is the oldest surviving portion. The main buildings, of the 18C, were greatly enlarged in 1857-68 and 1911-14. The 14C *Tour de l'Horloge*, at the N.E. corner, with an enormous clock copied from the original dial designed c. 1585 by *Germain Pilon*, was almost rebuilt in 1852. The upper part of the N. façade was also rebuilt in the style of the original work of the 14C, by *Enguerrand de Marigny*. The domed *Galerie Marchande*, dominating the *Cour du Mai*, is adorned with sculptures by *Pajou*.

Adm. 9.00-6.00 daily, except Sun.; the Sainte Chapelle is open the same hours as the Conciergerie.

History. The site of the *Palais de Justice* was occupied as early as the Roman period by a palace, which was a favourite residence of Julian the Apostate, proclaimed Emperor here in 360. The Merovingian kings divided their time between the Thermes and this Palais de la Cité, which was inside the walls, when not in the country. Louis VI died in the palace in 1137; Louis VII in 1180; and in 1200 or 1201 Philippe Auguste was married here to Ingeborg of Denmark. St Louis altered the palace and built the *Sainte Chapelle*. From 1431 it was occupied entirely by the Parlement, who had previously only shared it with the king, but it was not until the Revolution that it acquired its present function.

The most interesting part of these law courts may be entered directly from the Boulevard just N. of the Cour du Mai, by stairs ascending to the ***Salle des Pas-Perdus.** This magnificent hall, which replaced the great hall of the medieval palace (where in 1431 the coronation banquet of Henry VI of England was celebrated), was rebuilt in 1622 by *Salomon de Brosse,* and restored in 1878 after being burned by the Communards. At the far end of the room, divided in two by a row of arches, and to the r., is the entrance to the PREMIÈRE CHAMBRE CIVILE, formerly the *Grand' Chambre* or *Chambre Dorée* (restored in the style of Louis XII), perhaps originally the bedroom of St Louis. Later it was used by the *Parlement*, in contempt of which Louis XIV here coined his famous epigram "L'État, c'est moi". The Revolutionary Tribunal, with Fouquier-Tinville as public prosecutor, sat here in 1793 and condemned many people to death (see *Conciergerie*, above).

A vaulted gateway leads from the *Cour du Mai* to the *Cour de la Sainte-Chapelle.*

The ***Sainte Chapelle** was built in 1243-48 by St Louis as a shrine for the Crown of Thorns and a fragment of the True Cross. Its design is ascribed to *Pierre de Montreuil* (comp. St-Denis, and St-Germain-en-Laye), and is remarkable for the impression of lightness it conveys. It was often the scene of royal marriages, and Richard II of England was betrothed here in 1396 to Isabel of France. It was 'restored' in 1837-57 by *Duban, Lassus* (who added a leaden flèche in the 15C style), and the ubiquitous *Viollet-le-Duc*.

118 ft long, 56 ft wide, and 138 ft high, the building gives an impression of great height in proportion to its length and breadth. It consists in fact of two superimposed chapels, the lower for servants and retainers, the upper reserved for the royal family and court. The lofty windows of the upper chapel, an innovation, are surmounted by delicately sculptured gables and a graceful balustrade. The leaden roof is modern. The portal consists of two porches, one above the other; the statues are 19C restorations.

The interior of the CHAPELLE BASSE, already low (21 ft), with carved oak bosses, and forty columns sustaining the upper chapel, is further darkened by the repellent decoration of *Émile Boeswillwald* (1815-96). There are a number of 14-15C tombstones in the pavement.

A spiral staircase leads to the CHAPELLE HAUTE (67 ft high), certainly one of the outstanding achievements of the Middle Ages; but sadly in need of cleaning. With the walls stripped of its 19C painting and gilding, the simple lines of its architecture would be seen to better advantage; its *Stained-Glass (restored 1845) would glow more luminously.

The eighty-six panels from the Apocalypse in the large rose-window were a gift of Charles VIII. The 1st window on the r. represents the Legend of the Cross and the removal of the relics. The other windows in the nave and apse depict scenes from the Old and New Testaments. Beneath the windows on either side runs a blind arcade; of the apostles against the pillars, the 4th, 5th, and 6th on the l., and the 3rd, 4th, and 5th on the r., are original. The two deep recesses under the windows of the 3rd bay were the seats reserved for the royal family. In the centre of the restored arcade across the apse is a wooden canopy beneath which the relics used to be exhibited on Good Friday. Any remaining relics, not destroyed during the Revolution, are in Notre-Dame. We make our exit by a second spiral stair.

To the S., in the QUAI DES ORFÈVRES (No. 36), is a *Museum of Police History* (open Thurs. 14.00-17.00), with a room devoted to the part they played in the Resistance, and Liberation of Paris.

Opposite the Cour du Mai, the Rue de Lutèce leads between (r.) the *Préfecture de Police* and (l.) the domed *Tribunal de Commerce* (by *Bailly;* 1860-65), behind which the *Marché aux Fleurs* offers a colourful contrast. A Bird Market is held here on Sundays.

Crossing the Rue de la Cité, we turn r. and then l. into the PL. DU PARVIS NOTRE-DAME, the area of which Haussmann increased sixfold by his demolitions. To the l. is the *Hôtel-Dieu*, rebuilt here in 1868-78 to the N. of its original site. The first hospital was founded here by St Landry, Bp. of Paris, c. 660.

On the *Parvis* the archbishops of Paris tried heretics, and here the condemned knelt before execution to acknowledge their sin and beg absolution. In 1314 Jacques de Molay, grand master of the Templars, summoned to repeat his confession publicly and accept sentence of imprisonment, unexpectedly protested the innocence of his Order, and was hustled off to the stake. Excavations in the Parvis have uncovered relics of all ages back to the 2C, including late 3C walls.

To the E. rises the **Cathedral of Notre-Dame** (Pl. 14; 6), the exterior of which has been cleaned. Although archaeologically one of the most interesting of the Gothic cathedrals of France, in beauty it ranks after Chartres, Reims, Amiens, and Bourges. Taken in hand at the time when

Gothic art was beginning to throw off the traditions of the Romanesque style, Notre-Dame was completed in the 13C, so that it is possible to follow the gradual progress of the new style until its decadence in the 14C.

Road distances in France are calculated from the W. door of the cathedral.

History. The idea of replacing by a single building, on a much larger scale, the cathedral of St-Étienne (founded by Childebert in the 6C) and that of Notre-Dame, further E., was due to Maurice de Sully, Bp. of Paris (d. 1196). The old Notre-Dame replaced a Roman temple of Jupiter more or less on the site of the present cathedral, the foundation stone of which was laid by Pope Alexander III in 1163. The choir was finished by 1182, except for the roof; the nave was added in 1208; and the W. front and its towers c. 1225-50. A girdle of chapels was added: in the nave (1235-50) and apse (by *Pierre de Chelles* and *Jean Ravy;* 1296-1330). The side porches were begun in 1258; the crossings of the transept were built by *Jean de Chelles* and *Pierre de Montreuil* (1250-67).

Henry VI of England was crowned king of France in the cathedral choir in 1430, at the age of ten; and here were celebrated the marriages of François II to Mary Stuart (1558), Henry of Navarre to Marguerite de Valois (1572), and Charles I of England (by proxy) to Henrietta Maria (1625).

Until the end of the 17C Notre-Dame had preserved intact its appearance of the 14C, but the reigns of Louis XIV and Louis XV brought deplorable alterations, particularly in the destruction of tombs and stained glass. The baptistery of St-Jean-le-Rond, adjoining the N. tower, was demolished in 1748. Many sculptures and treasures were destroyed during the Revolution, when an opera-singer, Mlle Maillard, was enthroned here as the Goddess of Reason. In 1804, Napoleon I and Joséphine were crowned here by Pius VII; Napoleon III and Eugénie de Montijo were married here in 1853. In 1845 a thorough 'restoration' was begun under the direction of Lassus and Viollet-le-Duc.

On 26 Aug. 1944 the thanksgiving service, following Gen. de Gaulle's entry into Paris, was interrupted by sniping from the galleries, both inside and outside the cathedral. It continues to be the scene of many ceremonial functions, state funerals, etc.

Exterior. The *W. front, in three distinct storeys, forms one harmonious whole. The central *Porte du Jugement* (23 ft high), ruined by *Soufflot* in 1771, has a 19C Christ on the pier, and in the tympanum, the Last Judgment, restored by Viollet-le-Duc; only the upper tier of sculptures is ancient.

The *Porte de la Vierge* (l.) contains a restored Virgin on the pier; three kings and three prophets, and the Resurrection of the Virgin, in the lower part of the tympanum; above is the Coronation of the Virgin.

The sculptures of the *Porte de Ste-Anne* (r.) are mostly of 1165-75, designed for a narrower portal, with additions of c. 1240. On the pier is St Marcellus (19C); above, scenes from the life of St Anne and the Virgin, and the Virgin in Majesty, with Louis VII (r.) and Maurice de Sully (l.). The two side doors retain their medieval wrought-iron hinges.

Above the portals is the GALLERY OF THE KINGS OF JUDAH (reconstructed by Viollet-le-Duc), destroyed in 1793 because the Parisians took them to represent kings of France. The magnificent rose-window, 31 ft in diameter, is flanked by double windows within arches. Higher still is an open arcade.

The TOWERS, 223 ft high, originally intended to be crowned with spires, may be ascended (except Tues.) for the view; entrance in the N. tower. In the S. tower hangs the great bell, recast in 1686 and weighing 13 tons; Hugo's bell-ringer, Quasimodo, may be remembered. The Chimières (gargoyles), grotesque figures of devils, birds, and beasts, were designed by *Viollet-le-Duc.*

The side façades and apse likewise consist of three distinct and receding storeys; the bold flying buttresses of the latter, by *Jean Ravy*, are also admired for their

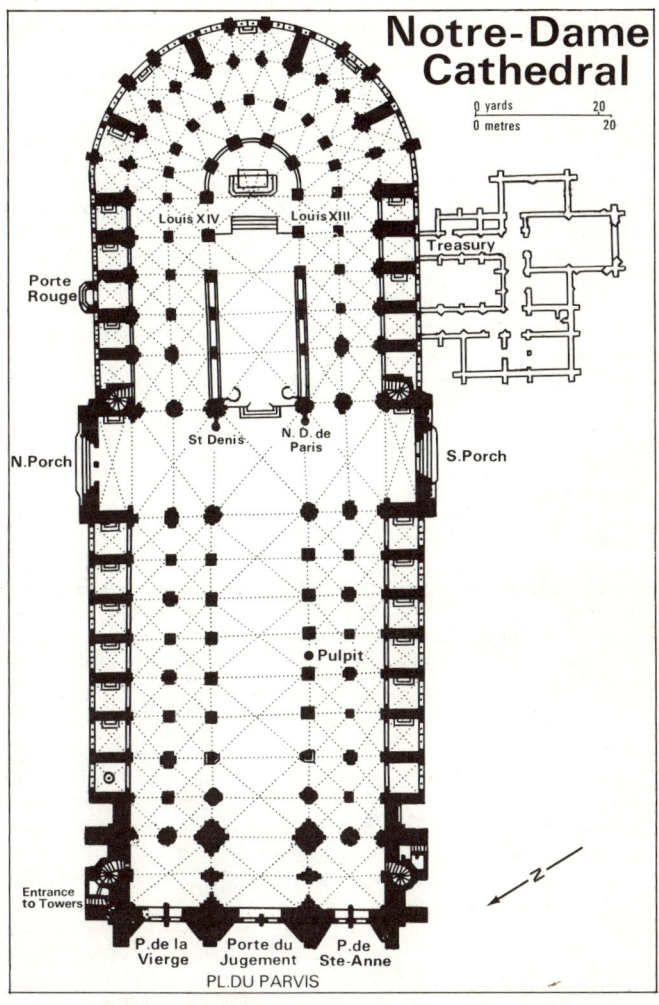

Notre-Dame Cathedral

0 yards 20
0 metres 20

Louis XIV Louis XIII

Treasury

Porte
Rouge

St Denis N. D. de
Paris

N.Porch S.Porch

Pulpit

Entrance
to Towers

P.de la Porte du P.de
Vierge Jugement Ste-Anne

PL.DU PARVIS

elegance. The S. porch, according to a Latin inscription at the base, was begun in 1257 (1258 n.s.) under the direction of *Jean de Chelles.* The story of St Stephen, as depicted in the tympanum, and the medallions of student life, are original. The N. porch, of the same period, retains an original statue of the Virgin, and in the tympanum, the story of Theophilius. Just to the E. of this porch is the graceful *Porte Rouge,* probably by *Pierre de Montreuil.* To the l., below the windows of the choir chapels, are seven 14C bas-reliefs. The *Flèche* (312ft above the ground), a lead-covered oak structure, was rebuilt by Viollet-le-Duc in 1859-60, the original having been destroyed in the 18C.

The best view of the **Interior** is obtained from beneath the organ

(1733, later rebuilt, and enlarged 1960), at the W. end. The cathedral (427 ft long, 157 ft wide, and 115 ft high) consists of a nave of ten bays of great purity of design, flanked by double aisles continued round the choir (of five bays). 37 chapels surround the whole. A vaulted gallery overlooks the nave; the windows above were altered in the 13C. The vaulting is supported by 75 piers, surmounted by bold yet graceful capitals. New glass, with an abstract design, was placed in the nave in 1963-64. Of the three *Rose-windows, retaining their original 13C glass, the N. is the best preserved and finest. At the crossing, 'Notre-Dame de Paris', a 14C figure, stands against the S.E. pillar; against the N.E. pillar is St Denis, by *N. Coustou.* On the S.W. pillar a tablet commemorates the million subjects of the British Empire who died in the *First* World War, the greater part of whom rest in French soil. Seven paintings (by *Ch. Le Brun, Seb. Bourdon,* and others), presented by the Goldsmiths' Guild of Paris in 1634-51, hang in the side-chapels of the nave.

The CHOIR, modified in 1708-25 by Louis XIV in fulfilment of his father's vow of 1638, attracted Viollet-le-Duc's 'restoring' hand. 78 of the original 114 *Stalls remain, adorned with bas-reliefs from the designs of *Jules Degoullons* (1711-15). Canopied archiepiscopal stalls stand at either end. The bronze angels (1712-13) against the apse-pillars escaped the Revolutionary melting-pot.

In front of the high-altar Geoffrey Plantagenet, son of Henry II of England, was buried in 1186. Behind Viollet-le-Duc's altar is a Pietà by *N. Coustou* with a base sculptured by *Girardon,* part of the 'Voeu de Louis XIII'. The statue of Louis XIII (S.) is also by *Coustou;* that of Louis XIV (N.) is by *Coysevox.* In the first four bays of the choir may be seen the remains of the screen which, until the 18C, extended round the whole apse; the expressive bas-reliefs on the exterior, finished in 1351, were unfortunately restored and repainted by Viollet-le-Duc. In the blind arches below are listed some of the eminent people buried in the church.

The AMBULATORY contains the tombs of 18-19C prelates. Behind the high altar is the tomb-statue of Bp. Matiffas de Bucy (d. 1304). In the 2nd chap. S. of the central chapel is the theatrical tomb, by *Pigalle,* of the Comte d'Harcourt (d. 1769); here are also the restored tomb-statues of Jean Jouvenel des Ursins and his wife (d. 1431, 1451).

The entrance to the *Sacristy,* which contains the *Treasury,* is on the S. side of the ambulatory.

Part of the nave of the *Chapelle St-Aignan* (1115-18) is preserved at No. 19 Rue des Ursins, N. of the cathedral. Mass was said in secret here in 1789-91; enquire at 3 Rue de la Colombe, adjacent. Nicolas Boileau (1636-1711) died nearby.

In the SQUARE DE L'ÎLE-DE-FRANCE, at the extreme E. end of the Cité, is a *Memorial* (by *H. Pingusson*) to some 200,000 Frenchmen deported to German concentration camps.

Hence the *Pont St-Louis,* damaged by a lighter in 1936 and replaced in 1969, crosses to the **Île St-Louis** (Pl. 15; 5), still a comparatively quiet backwater, but in danger of over-exploitation. Formerly two islets, it was not built over until the 17C, when as an annexe of the Marais to the N., it became the site of a number of fine mansions. It is connected to the

N. bank by the *Pont Louis-Philippe*, rebuilt in 1862; beyond stands the *Pont Marie* (1614-28), named after its builder, crossing to the QUAI DES CÉLESTINS. Further E., the island is crossed obliquely by the *Pont Sully* (1874-76), at the N. end of which, beyond the SQUARE H.-GALLI, stands the striking *Hôtel Fieubet* (see p. 137). On the S. side, from the Rue des Deux-Ponts, the old *Pont de la Tournelle*, originally (1369) built of wood, rebuilt in 1634, again under Louis-Philippe, and finally in 1925-28, crosses to the QUAI DE LA TOURNELLE. To the S.E. is the new *Science Faculty Building* replacing the old 'Halles aux Vins'. The island has many associations with Restif de la Bretonne, who once lodged in the Rue des Deux-Ponts.

In the transverse Rue St-Louis-en-l'Île is the *Hôtel Chenizot* (No. 51, with a balcony), of 1730. No. 21, the richly decorated church of **St-Louis-en-l'Île**, was begun by *Le Vau* in 1664 and finished in 1726 by *Jacques Doucet*. The tower and curious openwork spire were added in 1765. The ornamental stone-carving in the interior was executed under the direction of *J.-B. de Champaigne* (d. 1681; buried in the church). It contains six Nottingham alabasters from the same series of those in *St-Leu-St-Gilles*. There is a plaque in the N. aisle, presented in 1926, to the memory of St Louis after whom the city of Saint Louis, Missouri, is named. At No. 12 in this street Philippe Lebon first introduced the principle of lighting by gas in France (1799). Between Nos. 7 and 9 is an arch of the *Hôtel de Bretonvilliers*, finished by *Jean I du Cerceau* in 1640. Fénelon (1651-1715) lived at No. 3. No. 2 is the *Hôtel Lambert* by *Le Vau* (c. 1650), once the residence of Voltaire and Mme du Châtelet, and later the home of the Czartoryski family and a centre of Polish life in Paris.

On the N. side of the island, in the QUAI D'ANJOU, No. 3 belonged to Le Vau; No. 9 was the home of Honoré Daumier (1808-79) from 1846. The **Hôtel de Lauzun** or *de Pimodan* (No. 17; 1657), by *Le Vau*, was the residence in 1682-84 of the Duc de Lauzun, commander of the French troops at the Battle of the Boyne, who lived here with 'la Grande Mademoiselle'. In 1845 Baudelaire lived on the third floor, and Gautier had apartments here in 1848, where meetings of the Club des Haschichins took place. It became the property of the city in 1928.

For admission, apply to the Centre d'accueil, Hôtel de Ville. The artists responsible for its splendid decoration were *Lebrun, Le Sueur, Patel,* and *Sébastien Bourdon.*

Further W., Nos. 13 and 15 QUAI DE BOURBON were the *Hôtel Le Charron* (17C), with a delightful courtyard; while No. 11 was owned by Philippe de Champaigne. No. 1 was the *Franc-Pinot*, an inn kept during the Revolution by the father of Cécile Renault, who tried to murder Robespierre.

Turning S., in the QUAI D'ORLÉANS, No. 6 is the *Musée Adam Mickiewicz*, with an important Polish library, and souvenirs of the poet, and also of Chopin (with his death-mask, by *Clésinger*). Further E., in the QUAI DE BÉTHUNE, is the mansion of Armand, Duc de Richelieu, grand-nephew of the cardinal (No. 18); the poet Francis Carco (1886-1958) died here. No. 20 was built by *Le Vau*. At the eastern extremity of the island is the triangular SQUARE BARYE.

II THE SOUTH OR LEFT BANK: LA RIVE GAUCHE

2 THE LATIN QUARTER

MÉTROS: *St-Michel, Maubert-Mutualité, Card. Lemoine, Luxembourg.*

The **'Quartier Latin'**, deriving its present name (conferred by Rabelais) from the language spoken by the early students, is a district S. of the *Île de la Cité*, which grew up with Abélard's removal in c. 1200 to the Montagne Ste-Geneviève from the school attached to Notre-Dame. Originally known as the *Université*, it has remained to a large extent the learned quarter of Paris, and still contains the main educational and scientific institutions. Not the least interest of the district is that it occupies the site of Roman *Lutetia*. With the growth of the University, the student population overflowed, and occupied a much more extensive area than the originally confined and swarming alleys on either side of the Rue St-Jacques. In the mid-19C the BLVD. ST-GERMAIN was driven E. through the old streets, and many ancient buildings were swept away. In 1968 its paving-blocks were found to be useful missiles during the 'student revolution'. Cafés and bookshops abound, and the students appear to spend more time in the former than in the various faculty buildings. In 1922 a 'Cité Universitaire' was founded in the 14th Arrondissement, to the S. (see p. 64).

From the PL. ST-MICHEL (Pl. 14; 6), linked to the Cité by the *Pont St-Michel*, and with the *Fontaine St-Michel* at its S. end, erected by *Davioud* in 1860, and incorporating a memorial of the Resistance of 1944, the busy BLVD. ST-MICHEL (popularly known as the 'Boul Mich') leads S. to the *Carrefour de l'Observatoire.*

It was laid out by Haussmann as a direct continuation of the *Blvd. de Strasbourg* and the *Blvd. de Sébastopol,* and shortly crosses the *Blvd. St-Germain*, running roughly parallel to the Seine. Almost the only interest of these main thoroughfares lies in their animation; the architectural and historical character of the Quartier is found in the side-streets.

Immediately to the E. of the Pl. St-Michel, in a still decrepit corner of Old Paris, diverges the Rue de la Huchette (the 'Narrow Street' of Elliot Paul), off which run the Rue Xavier-Privas and Rue du Chat-qui-Pêche, an alley named after an old shop-sign. Théophile de Viau composed his 'Parnasse Satirique' at No. 1 Rue de la Huchette, and at No. 8 (or 10) Napoleon lodged in 1795; the *Théâtre de la Huchette* is the smallest in Paris.

Diverging r. along the Rue de la Harpe, and taking the first turning l., brings us to *St-Séverin (under restoration), rebuilt in the 13-16C on the site of an oratory of the time of Childebert I, where in the 12C Foulque of Neuilly-sur-Marne preached the Fourth Crusade. The lower part of the W. front and the W. bays of the nave date from the early 13C; the outer S. aisle was added c. 1350, the outer N. aisle and the E. part of the church were in construction in 1450-96, the chapels in 1500-20. The main W. portal, of the early 13C, was brought piecemeal from St-Pierre-aux-Boeufs in the Cité in 1837. The upper two storeys date from the 15C. On the l. is a tower of the 13C, completed in 1487, with a door which was once the main entrance; the tympanum dates from 1853, but in the frame is a 15C inscription: "Bonnes gens qui par cy passés, Priez Dieu pour les trespassés". To the l. of the tower, a niche holds a statue of St Séverin.

The INTERIOR impresses by the breadth of its double ambulatory. The most striking details are the ribs of the vaulting and the choir triforium, which approach English Perpendicular in style. The apse was partially classicized in the 17C at the expense of Mlle de Montpensier. In the nave, the first three bays contain late-14C glass from St-Germain-des-Prés, but much restored; from the fourth bay on the glass is mid-15C. The ambulatory is disfigured by modern glass. One of the subjects on the S. side of the nave is the murder of Thomas Becket, while the W. rose-window contains a Tree of Jesse (c. 1500) obscured by an organ of 1745.

To the S. of the choir are the 15C galleries of the graveyard, beneath which the first operation for the stone was successfully carried out in 1474.

On the far side of the Rue St-Jacques, diverges the Rue Galande, one of the oldest existing streets in Paris (14C), with, on No. 42, a carved representation of the life of St Julian. The church of **St-Julien-le-Pauvre,** rebuilt c. 1170-1230 and used in the 13-16C as a university church and in 1655-1877 by the old Hôtel-Dieu for various secular purposes, has since 1889 been occupied by the Melchites, Greek Catholics subject to papal authority. The present W. front was built in 1651. Note the foliated capitals within; an iconostasis obscures the E. end. A good *View of the *Cathedral of Notre-Dame* may be had from the SQUARE RENÉ-VIVIANI, just to the N.

From the N.E. side of this square the Rue de la Bûcherie runs through an area under restoration, where No. 13 was occupied by the École de Médecine from 1483 to 1775, with a rotunda built in 1745 by the Danish doctor Jacques-Bénigne Winslow. Restif de la Bretonne (1734-1806) died at No. 16 (prev. No. 27). S. of the Square René-Viviani is the Rue du Fouarre (named after the 'straw' on which the students sat), the centre of four 14C schools of the University, and referred to by Dante, who is supposed to have attended lectures here. The Rue Lagrange leads S.E. to meet the Blvd. St-Germain at the PL. MAUBERT ('la Maub'), where Étienne Dolet (1509-46) was burnt as a heretic. Crébillon fils (1707-77) was born in a house here.

The ancient Rue de Bièvre runs N.E., off the Pl. Maubert, in which Dante is said to have written part of the 'Divina Commedia'. To the W. is the Rue des Anglais, inhabited by English students in medieval times.

A short distance along the Rue Monge, leading S.E., is (l.) **St-Nicolas-du-Chardonnet** ('of the thistle-field'), a Renaissance church built mostly in 1656-1709, but the clumsy tower (1625) is a relic of an earlier edifice. Some of the statues and stucco work are by *Nicolas Legendre.*

In the dark interior, in the 1st chapel on the r., is *Corot*'s study for the Baptism of Christ; the 2nd chapel on the r. of the choir, beyond the transept, contains a monument by *Girardon* of Bignon, the jurist (d. 1656). In the 8th chapel (round the apse) is the tomb of Le Brun's mother, by *Tuby* and *Collignon*, designed by *Le Brun* in the theatrical style of Bernini; against the window is a monument of Le Brun (d. 1690) and his widow, by *Coysevox*. Note the fine 18C organ-case; a Crucifixion by *Brueghel the Younger* is preserved in the Sacristy.

Diverging l. along the Rue St-Victor, we pass (l.) the Rue de Poissy, where at No. 24 are the remains of the 14C refectory of the ancient *Collège des Bernardins*; a museum is projected. At the far end of this street, where it meets the QUAI DE LA TOURNELLE, stands the 17C *Hôtel de Nesmond* (No. 55). At No. 47 in the quai is a small *Museum* devoted to Hospitals of Paris, accommodated in what was once the convent of the 'Miramiones' or Filles Ste-Geneviève, founded by Mme de Miramion (d. 1696). No. 15 is *La Tour d'Argent*, a famous restaurant which gained its gastronomic reputation in the Second Empire, although built on the site of an earlier tavern dating from 1582.

At No. 32 in the Rue du Card.-Lemoine, running S. parallel to the Rue de Poissy, stood the *Collège des Bons-Enfants*, where St Vincent de Paul founded his congregation of mission-priests. Further S., No. 49 is the 17C *Hôtel Le Brun*, built by *Boffrand* for the artist, and later occupied by Watteau and Buffon.

Ascending S.W. at the junction of the Rue du Card.-Lemoine with the Rue Monge, we approach the Rue Clovis, where a section of Philippe Auguste's perimeter *Wall* may be seen. No. 65 Rue du Card.-Lemoine, the *Institution Ste-Geneviève*, was the old **Scots College** (*Collège des Écossais*; apply to the concierge), founded in 1665 by Robert Barclay.

The *Chapel*, on the first floor, contains the tomb of Frances Jennings, Duchess of Tyrconnel (d. 1731), the spirited elder sister of Sarah, Duchess of Marlborough; a memorial erected to James II (who bequeathed his brain to the college) by James Drummond, Duke of Perth, with a long Latin epigraph; the tomb of Sir Patrick Menteith, who died in 1675 in the service of Louis XIV, etc.

Blaise Pascal (1623-62) died on the site of No. 67.

No. 5 Rue Descartes, to the r. of the Rue Clovis, is the entrance to the influential *École Polytechnique*, founded by Monge in 1794 for the training of artillery and engineer officers, and transferred in 1805 to the buildings of the *Collège de Navarre*, which were considerably enlarged in 1929-35.

Founded in 1304 by Jeanne de Navarre, queen of Philippe le Bel, the Collège de Navarre numbered among its pupils Gerson, Ramus, Henri III, Henri IV, Henri de Guise, Richelieu, Bossuet, Condorcet, and André Chénier. The *Collège de Boncourt* (No. 21), taken over by the Collège de Navarre in the 17C. had earlier contained perhaps the first theatre in Paris. In 1792 G. B. Piranesi's sons established their engraving works in the college.

At No. 34 Rue Montagne-Ste-Geneviève, further down the hill, are remains of the *Collège des Trente-Trois*, founded in 1633 by Claude Bernard, friend and follower of St Vincent de Paul, and named after its 33 scholarships (one for each year of Christ's life).

At No. 23 Rue Clovis is the entrance to the *Lycée Henri-IV*, the **Tower** of which (restored) has a Romanesque base and two Gothic upper storeys (14-15C) and is a relic of the church (demolished 1802) of the *Abbaye Ste-Geneviève*. Practically the whole of the conventual buildings were rebuilt in the 18C, but the former refectory (now the chapel), is an over-restored 13C building; the kitchens are likewise medieval. The fact that the abbey came under papal jurisdiction, not that of the Bp. of Paris, influenced Abélard's choice of this area (comp. above). Bernardin de Saint-Pierre lived at No. 4 Rue Rollin from 1781 to 1786, where he wrote 'Paul et Virginie'. Mérimée (1803-70) was born at No. 7 Carré de Ste-Geneviève, which was adjacent.

On the r. is the interesting church of **St-Étienne-du-Mont* (Pl. 14; 8), showing the transition from the Gothic to the Renaissance style. It was almost continuously in construction from 1492 to 1586. Marguerite de Valois laid the foundation stone of the portal in 1610 and even this preserves certain Gothic motives. The tower, begun in 1492, was completed in 1628. The N. side, with its picturesque porch, dates from 1630-32.

The church replaced an earlier parish church dependent upon and entered through the abbey church of *Ste-Geneviève* (comp. above). During the Revolution, it became the 'Temple of Filial Piety'.

The INTERIOR has lofty columns, a wide ambulatory, and ribbed vaulting with pendent keystones. Its originality lies in the balustrade which runs along the supporting pillars of the nave and choir. The beautiful fretted * *Rood Screen*, built in 1525-35, is a masterpiece of design and carving; the date 1605 on the side refers only to the door admitting to the spiral staircases by which it is ascended. The organ-case by *Jean Buron* dates from 1631-32; the pulpit of 1651 is the work of *Germain Pilon*, with sculptures designed by *Laurent de la Hire*. The *Stained-glass ranges in date from c. 1550 to c. 1600; the oldest windows are those in the apse.

Between the 6th and 7th chapels in the S. aisle a tablet commemorates the Jacobins, an order of preaching friars established in the Rue St-Jacques in 1218. Above the 1st chapel in the choir is an ex-voto to St Geneviève, with the provost and merchants of Paris, by *F. de Troy* (1726), while higher, to the r., is a similar painting by *Largillière*, of 1696. On either side of the chapel are the epitaphs of Pascal and Racine (by Boileau), whose graves are at the entrance to the LADY CHAPEL. Also buried in the church are Rollin, and the painter Le Sueur. The next chapel S. of the choir contains the copper-gilt shrine of St Geneviève (1853). Within is a fragment of her tomb; her bones were burned by the mob in the Pl. de Grève in 1801.

From the next bay runs a corridor, at the end of which (r.) is the Presbytery, built in 1742 for Louis d'Orléans (son of the Regent), who died here in 1752. On the l. is the *Charnier*, or gallery of the graveyard, with twelve superb *Windows of 1605-09; note one depicting the Mystic Wine-press. Most of them are after the designs of *Léonard Gautier*.

To the W. of the PL. STE-GENEVIÈVE (Pl. 14; 8) rises the grandiose bulk of the **Panthéon**, situated on the 'Mont de Paris', the highest point on the Left Bank (200 ft) and the original burial-place of St Geneviève, the patron saint of Paris (422-509/12).

In 1744, lying ill at Metz, Louis XV vowed that if he recovered, he would replace the former church, and the present building was begun some twenty years later, although not completed until 1789. The architect *Soufflot* died, of anxiety it is said, owing to criticism that subsidence of the walls (noticeable near the choir) would occur because the foundations had been laid on clay pits dug by Roman potters. In 1791, after the death of Mirabeau, the Constituent Assembly decided that the church should be used as a Panthéon or burial-place for distinguished citizens, and the pediment was inscribed with the words "Aux Grands Hommes la Patrie reconnaissante". From the Restoration to 1831 and from 1851 to 1885 it was again used as a church, but on the occasion of Victor Hugo's interment it reverted to the name and purpose decreed in 1791.

Exteriorly imposing, the *Panthéon* is built in the shape of a Greek cross, 360 ft long, 275 ft wide, and 270 ft high to the top of the majestic *Dome. The pediment above the portico of 22 Corinthian columns is a masterpiece of *David d'Angers*, representing France between Liberty and History, distributing laurels to famous men. Forty-two windows were walled in during the Revolution.

The INTERIOR may be visited daily, except Tuesday, but is of little interest. Coldly Baroque, it is adorned with paintings, among which are some pallid works by *Puvis de Chavannes*, while in the S. transept is a monument to unknown heroes by *Landowski*, and opposite is his monument to unknown artists. The colossal group of the Convention, at the E. end, is by *Sicard*.

The *Dome*, supported by four piers united by arches, contains three distinct cupolas, of which the first is open in the centre to reveal the second, with a fresco by *Gros*. By the first pillar (r.) is a monument to Rousseau by *Bartholomé*: on the l. a monument to Diderot and the Encyclopædists by *Terroir*. Other tablets commemorate Saint-Exupéry and Bergson. Within the dome, in 1852, Léon Foucault, the physicist, gave the first public demonstration of his pendulum experiment proving the rotation of the Earth.

Conducted tours of the **Crypt** (entrance in the N. E. corner) may be made, first passing a shrine containing the heart of *Gambetta* (d. 1882). Among the tombs are those of *Rousseau* (d. 1778; and transferred here in 1794); *Voltaire* (d. 1778; trans. 1791), with a statue attr. to *Houdon*; and *Jacques-Germain Soufflot* (1714-80), the architect. Of men whose remains have been reinterred in the vaults, the most famous are *Victor Hugo* (d. 1885); *Émile Zola* (d. 1902); *Marcelin Berthelot* (1827-1907), the chemist; *Jean Jaurès* (1859-assassinated 1914), the socialist politician; *Louis Braille* (1809-52), benefactor of the blind; and the explorer *Bougainville* (1729-1814; from Montmartre, see p. 159). *Mirabeau* and *Marat* were interred here with great state, but their remains were soon cast out with ignominy: the former now rests in the cemetery of Ste-Catherine, the latter in the graveyard of St-Étienne-du-Mont.

In the N.W. corner of the PL. DU PANTHÉON was the *École de Droit*, begun by Soufflot in 1771 and subsequently enlarged and now known as Universities I and II, see p. 57. Opposite is the *Mairie of the 5th Arrondissement* (1844-50), built in the same style. The **Bibliothèque Ste-Geneviève**, on the N. side of the Place, originated in the library of the famous Abbey of Ste-Geneviève. The present building, also of 1844-50, by *Labrouste*, is on the site of the *Collège de Montaigu*, founded in 1314, where Loyola, Erasmus, and Calvin were students. It was also known as the *Hôtel des Haricots*, as it was presumed that beans were the staple fare of its inmates. It was in later years a prison.

The library contains c. 700,000 vols (nearly 4,000 MSS.) and over 30,000 prints and engravings (including 10,000 portraits). Rooms are devoted to Scandinavian literature (c. 90,000 vols) and the *Bibliothèque Jacques Doucet* comprising c. 8,000 vols of late 19th and 20C French authors, including MSS. of Rimbaud, Verlaine, Baudelaire, Gide, and Valéry. Among the illuminated MSS., which are occasionally exhibited, are an English Bible, copied by Manerius in the 12C; the Chronicles of St-Denis (late 13C); several MSS. of the Carolingian period; the 'De Proprietatibus Rerum' of Barthélemy l'Anglais (Catalan translation of the 15C); and 'La Cité de Dieu' of St Augustine (late 15C). The building also contains a number of busts by *Coysevox, J.-J. Caffieri, Lemoyne,* and *Houdon*.

On the r. of the Library, in the Rue Valette, are the interesting remains of the *Collège Fortet* (No. 21), dating from 1397, where Calvin was a student in 1531. Further downhill to the r., in the Rue des Carmes, is *St-Ephrem*, a Syrian Catholic church, formerly the chapel (1760) of a community of Irish priests, who established themselves in the 17C buildings of the *Collège des Lombards*.

To the l. of the Library, on the r. in the Rue Cujas, is the *Collège Ste-Barbe*, founded in 1460, the oldest existing public educational establishment in France, at which St Francis Xavier was a scholar. The *Law Faculty Library* has been built on part of the grounds.

Leading W. from the Panthéon towards the *Luxembourg Gardens* is the Rue Soufflot, where (r.) at No. 14 a tablet commemorates the site of the Dominican or Jacobin convent (1217-1790) where Albertus Magnus and Thomas Aquinas taught.

The Rue St-Jacques, which we first cross, an important thoroughfare in medieval times, following the course of the Roman road from Lutetia to Orléans, formed part of the pilgrim route to St James of Compostella (Santiago; whence its name), and so attracted many convents. The S. section is described on p. 62.

Turning N. along the Rue St-Jacques, we pass (r.) the *Lycée Louis-le-Grand*, formerly the Jesuit *Collège de Clermont*, founded in 1560 and rebuilt in 1887-96. Molière, Voltaire, Robespierre, Desmoulins, Delacroix, and Hugo studied here.

We next pass the **Collège de France**, with its entrance in the PL. MARCELIN-BERTHELOT (Pl. 14; 6-8). It was founded by François I in 1530 under Budé's influence to spread humanism and counteract the narrow scholasticism of the Sorbonne. It was independent of the University and its teaching was free and public. The present building was begun in 1610, finished by *Chalgrin* c. 1778, and since enlarged. During work in 1894 traces were found of Gallo-Roman baths. In the courtyard, with its graceful portico, is a statue of Guillaume Budé (Budæus; 1468-1540), and also tablets recording the names of all its professors since the foundation.

In a garden on the N.E. side of the college is a monument to the Pléïade, the 16C poetical coterie (notably du Bellay and Ronsard) which originated in a vanished college near this site (tablet on No. 11 Impasse Chartière).

To the W. of the *Collège de France* stands the **Sorbonne**, founded as a modest theological college in 1253 by Robert de Sorbon, chaplain to St Louis. It was rebuilt at Richelieu's expense by *Jacques Lemercier* in 1629, but, with the exception of the church, the present buildings date from 1885-1901.

The *University of Paris*, which disputes with Bologna the title of the oldest university in Europe, arose in the first decade of the 12C out of the schools of dialectic attached to *Notre-Dame*. Transferred by Abélard to the Montagne Ste-Geneviève, it obtained its first statutes in 1208, and these served as the model for Oxford and Cambridge and other universities of northern Europe. By the 16C it comprised no fewer than forty separate colleges.

Before the end of the 13C the *Sorbonne* had become synonymous with the faculty of theology, overshadowing the rest of the University and possessing the power of conferring degrees, and was distinguished for its religious rancour, supporting the condemnation of Joan of Arc (Pierre Cauchon came from the Sorbonne), justifying the massacre of St Bartholomew, and refusing its recognition of Henri IV. Nevertheless, in 1469, by allowing Ulrich Gering and his companions to set up their presses within its precincts, it introduced printing into France. In the 18C it attacked the 'philosophes', and in 1792 was itself suppressed. It was refounded by Napoleon, and in 1821 became the official headquarters of the University of Paris. The student 'revolution' of May 1968 eventually had the effect of instigating overdue reforms in the university system, and in 1970 the University of Paris was replaced by the formation of thirteen autonomous universities in the region. The Sorbonne accommodates Universities III and IV.

The ponderous buildings, which still accommodate the University Library of 700,000 volumes, the *Académie de Paris*, and minor learned institutions, include the *Grand Amphithéâtre* (the main lecture hall, containing *Puvis de Chavannes'* mural, 'Le Bois sacré'), which may be visited on application at the main entrance in the Rue des Écoles. Apply here also to visit the Church of *Ste-Ursule de la Sorbonne**, facing the PL. DE LA SORBONNE, founded in the 13C and rebuilt by *Lemercier* in 1635-59 at the expense of Richelieu. The dramatic *Tomb of the great cardinal (1585-1642) was designed by *Le Brun* and sculptured by *Girardon* (1694). The *Dome was the first example of a true dome in Paris.

Opposite the entrance to the Sorbonne is the SQUARE PAUL-PAINLEVÉ (Pl. 14; 6; with a statue of Montaigne by *Landowski),* to the N. of which is the *Hôtel de Cluny**, built at the end of the 15C on the site of Roman ruins and one of the finest extant examples of medieval French domestic architecture. It now houses the **Musée de Cluny**, devoted to the arts and crafts of the Middle Ages, the entrance to which is in the r.-hand corner of the courtyard, beyond an archway surmounted by the Amboise arms.

The property was bought in 1340 by Pierre de Chalus, Abbot of Cluny in Burgundy, and the mansion was built c. 1490 by Abbot Jacques d'Amboise as the town house of the abbots, although rarely occupied by them. In 1515 it became the residence of Mary Tudor (1496-1533), daughter of Henry VII and later widow of Louis XII. She was known as 'La Reine Blanche' from the white mourning worn by her as queen-dowager of France. In 1537 James V of Scotland was lodged here before his wedding with Madeleine, daughter of François I. Later occupants were the Card. de Lorraine, Claude de Guise, Mazarin, and the papal nuncios (1600-81). In the 18C the tower was used as an observatory by the astronomer Messier. At the Revolution the mansion became national property, but in 1833 it was bought by *Alexandre Du Sommerard* (1779-1842) and filled with the treasures which he spent his lifetime in collecting. These were bought by the State and supplemented by many new acquisitions, but only part of the collection is on view.

A complete reorganization of the Museum is imminent, and as any detailed description will be superseded, only certain outstanding objects are listed below.

At the far end of the GROUND FLOOR, steps descend to the *Palais des Thermes**, or briefly the *Thermes*, which adjoins the building to the W. This consists of the ruined baths of a Roman building (almost certainly not a 'palace'), probably built during the reign of Caracalla (212-17). The main room (65 ft long and 38 ft wide), preserving its vault, unique in France, was probably the *Frigidarium*, with the *Bath*, or *Piscina*, on the N. side. Fragments of Gallo-Roman sculpture are displayed here.

In the N. wing of the FIRST FLOOR is the *Chapel**, with a central pillar and a star vault, a masterpiece of sculptural decoration, with God the Father blessing His dying Son, and angels with the instruments of the Passion in the vault of the oriel window.

Among the tapestries in the collection are the series of six exquisite early-16C French works known as **La Dame à la Licorne' (or Unicorn); those depicting the Life of St Stephen in 23 scenes, woven for Jean Baillet, Bp. of Auxerre (c. 1490), and 'La Vie Seigneuriale', illustrating the activities of a nobleman's household, of c. 1500.

Other sections are devoted to the *Accessories of Medieval Costume* (pins, buckles, clasps, girdles, shoes—one 'à la poulaine', with a pointed toe—etc.); *Textiles and Embroidery,* including ecclesiastical vestments; *Sculpture and Painted Woodwork of the Late Middle Ages,* including *Four mutilated statues of the Apostles from the Sainte Chapelle (c. 1245); *Jewellery, Enamels, and Goldsmiths' and Silversmiths' work; Ceramics; Metal Work* in brass, bronze, copper, wrought iron, pewter, and lead, etc.; examples of medieval furniture, arms and armour, utensils, locks and keys, medallions, pilgrims' badges (and their moulds), Ivories, etc., and numerous other treasures.

3   JARDIN DES PLANTES; GOBELINS; ST-MÉDARD

MÉTROS: *Monge, Gare d'Austerlitz, St-Marcel, Gobelins, Censier-Daubenton.*

At the E. end of the Rue des Écoles (conveniently approached from Métros. Maubert Mutualité or Cardinal Lemoine) rises the extensive new utilitarian block of buildings housing the departments of the *Faculty of Science* (Universities V and VI; see p. 57), to the N. of which the Rue des Fossés-Saint-Bernard descends towards the Seine at the *Pont Sully* (see p. 51). Here, until their transfer to Bercy, stood the huge bonded warehouses of the Halles aux Vins, itself on the site of the Abbaye de St-Victor. This had been dispersed in 1790: here Thomas Becket and Abélard resided, and in its important library, Rabelais studied.

Bearing S. we ascend the Rue Linné, off which the Rue des Arènes climbs r. to the ruins of the **Arènes de Lutèce** (2-3C), the amphitheatre of Roman Paris, only discovered in 1870 and fully excavated since 1883. It is 62 yds long and 51 yds wide, and is now surrounded by the gardens of the SQUARE CAPITAN.

At the junction of the Rue Linné with the Rue Geoffroy-St-Hilaire stands the *Fontaine Cuvier* (1840), and the N.W. entrance to the **Jardin des Plantes** (previously known, until 1793, as the *Jardin du Roi*), officially the *Muséum National d'Histoire Naturelle* (Pl. 15; 7), 60 acres in area, and combining the attractions of a menagerie, botanical gardens, and natural history galleries. Its collections of wild and herbaceous plants are unrivalled, and in May and June the peonies make a magnificent show. The *Library* contains a remarkable collection of botanical MSS., including the *Vélins du Roi,* illustrated by *Nicolas Robert* and others (from 1630); also works by *Redouté,* etc.

Adm. The *Gardens* are open daily from 9.00 to 17.30 or 19.00; likewise the *Menagerie, Aquarium,* and *Vivarium.* The *Jardin d'Hiver* is open from 14.00 to 17.00 except Tues.; the *Jardin Alpin* is closed from Nov. to April; and the *Zoological Galleries* are open from 13.30 to 17.00 daily, except Tues.
   There are other entrances in the Rue Geoffroy-St-Hilaire, and in the semicircular PL. VALHUBERT to the E. opposite the *Gare d'Austerlitz.* The nearest *Métro* stations are *Jussieu, Monge, Censier Daubenton,* and *Austerlitz.*
   Founded in 1626 under Louis XIII as a 'physic garden' for medicinal herbs by the royal physician Guy de la Brosse, the garden was first opened to the public in 1650. Its present importance is mainly due to the great naturalist *Buffon* (1707-88), who was superintendent from 1739, and greatly enlarged the grounds. In 1793 it was reorganized by the Convention under its present official title, and provided with twelve professorships. The animals from the royal collection at Versailles were brought to form the nucleus of a menagerie. In 1792, Richard Twiss was told by the director that the names of some plants had been changed: "We will not have any aristocratic plants"! Many distinguished French naturalists have taught and studied here, and are commemorated by monuments in the garden or nearby. A statue of Lamarck (1744-1829) faces the E. entrance.

Entering from the N.W. we pass near (l.) *Chevreul's House* and *Cuvier's House,* where Georges Cuvier (1769-1832), zoologist and paleontologist, gave Saturday evening receptions during the 1820s and 30s, attended by Mérimée, Stendhal, and Delacroix, among others. Here also are the *Administrative Building,* in a mansion of 1785, and the *Amphithéâtre* or lecture hall, of 1788 (restored). The *Menagerie* occupies most of the N. side of the gardens. It is said that many of its earlier occupants were killed in 1870-71 to feed besieged Parisians during the Franco-Prussian War.

On the r. as we enter is the *Butte,* a hillock with a maze, the first cedar of Lebanon (from Kew Gardens) to be planted in France (by Jussieu, in 1734), and on the summit, a *belvedere.* The sundial here bears the inscription 'Horas non numero nisi serenas': I only count the sunny hours. In the centre are the *Jardin d'Hiver* and *Jardin Alpin,* while along the S. side of the gardens are ranged the *Zoological Galleries,* in the N. vestibule of which is the tomb of Guy de la Brosse (d. 1641); the *Mineralogical Galleries,* with the *Library* (c. 500,000 vols and 2500 MSS.) and *Buffon's House,* occupied by him from 1773 to his death; the *Botanical Gallery;* and *Paleontological Gallery.* To the S., on the far side of the Rue Buffon, is an Annexe to the museum.

To the W. of the Rue Geoffroy-St-Hilaire stands the *Institut franco-musulman,* with a green-tiled *Mosque,* complete with minaret, opened in 1925. Slightly further W. (in the Rue Puits-de-l'Ermite) stood the *Prison de Ste-Pélagie,* where Joséphine, the future empress, and Mme du Barry, were confined under the Revolution, and where Mme Roland wrote her memoirs.

Not far to the S., we reach the BLVD. ST-MARCEL, near which point was the *Cimitière Ste-Catherine,* where the bodies of Mirabeau and other revolutionaries were reburied after being ejected from the *Panthéon.* This thoroughfare leads N.E. to meet the BLVD. DE L'HÔPITAL. To the r. of this junction stands the huge **Hôpital de la Salpêtrière* (Pl. 19; 5), founded in 1656 as a home for aged or insane women, on the site of a gunpowder factory.

In 1684 a criminal wing was added, in which Manon Lescaut and Mme de la Motte were gaoled, and which was notorious for its filth and vice. Aged couples were later admitted, and in 1790 there were said to be 8,000 people living there. Part of the building, named 'La Force', contained political prisoners during the Revolution, and here took place some of the worst massacres of Sept. 1792.

The main building, by *Le Vau* and *Le Muet,* dates from 1657-63; the domed *Church of St-Louis,* built in 1670-77, is by *Libéral Bruant.* Statues by *Étex* were added after 1832. As a whole, it is a notable example of the austere magnificence of the architecture of the period, and may be compared in many ways to the Invalides.

Dr Charcot (1825-93), the hypnotist, is commemorated by a monument to the l. of the gateway; his consulting-room, laboratory, and library have been preserved intact.

Adjacent to the S. is the *Hôpital de la Pitié,* transferred in 1911 from the Rue Lacépède, where it had been founded by Marie de Médicis in 1612.

To the N.E. is the **Gare d'Austerlitz,** the main railway terminus for Bordeaux, Bayonne, Toulouse, etc.; see Pl. 19; 3.

The Blvd. St-Marcel leads S.W. to meet the Av. des Gobelins, beyond which it divides to be continued by the BLVD. ARAGO (leading due W. to the *Pl. Denfert-Rochereau*), and the BLVD. DE PORT-ROYAL (eventually meeting the *Blvd. du Montparnasse*).

A short distance S. of the former junction stands (r.) the **Gobelins** (Pl. 18; 8; adm. Wed., Thurs., Fri. 14.00-16.00; guided tour), the famous tapestry factory which has been a state institution for over three hundred years, and still retains some of its 17C buildings.

The original manufactory at Fontainebleau was moved to Paris by Henri II. Suspended during the 16C Religious Wars, the industry was revived by Henri IV and installed in 1601 in the buildings of the Gobelins, named after *Jean Gobelin*(d. 1476), head of a family of dyers, who made their reputation with the discovery of a scarlet dye, and who had set up their dye-works here on the banks of the Bièvre. In 1662, under Colbert, the royal carpet factory of the *Savonnerie*, started in 1604 in the galleries of the Louvre, and subsequently moved to a 'savonnerie' (soap-factory) at Chaillot, was placed under the same management (it transferred its workshops to the Gobelins' factory in 1826). In 1667 Louis XIV added the royal furniture factory, and Charles Le Brun and then Pierre Mignard were appointed as directors. The workshops of the Beauvais tapestry, destroyed in 1940, have likewise been transferred here (comp. pp. 269-70).

On the l. are two workshops, separated by a staircase. The tapestry is woven on high-warp looms, several of which date from the time of Louis XIV. The weaver works on the reverse side of the tapestry, having the painting which he is copying behind him and reflected in mirrors. The average amount of tapestry that a weaver can produce in a day is $2\frac{1}{5}$ sq. inches. We are conducted to the former *chapel*, where hang two tapestries made for it, and cross the Rue Berbier-du-Mets, behind the factory, which now covers the non-calcareous waters of the Bièvre, which used to flow between the dye-works and workshops. A new building has been erected here, containing workshops for the weaving of carpets, where the original methods are still followed.

Adjacent are the buildings of the *Mobilier National*, and beyond them, where stood the allotments of tapestry workers, is the SQUARE RENÉ-LE-GALL (with the hunting lodge of M. de Julienne, the patron of Watteau).
The Av. des Gobelins ends to the S. at the PL. D'ITALIE, the hub of seven important thoroughfares, on the N. side of which is the *Mairie of the 13th Arrondissement*.

Turning N. down the Av. des Gobelins, we shortly reach the picturesque church of **St-Médard** (Pl. 18; 6), dedicated to the 'St Swithin' of France. The nave and W. front are of the late 15C; the choir, in construction from 1550 to 1632, was 'classicized' in 1784, when the *Lady Chapel* was added. Sacked by the Huguenots in 1561, not much of the 16C glass survives. The churchyard, now a garden, was notorious for the orgies of the Jansenist fanatics or 'convulsionnaires' at the tomb of the Abbé Pâris (d. 1727).

The shabby and populous Rue Mouffetard (closed to traffic at its lower end) climbs N. from the front of the church through a squalid district (but with a good street market) past (l.) the Rue de l'Arbalète, where at No. 3 Auguste Rodin was born in 1840. Eventually we pass (r.) the PL. DE LA CONTRESCARPE, where No. 1 has a tablet commemorating the 'Cabaret de la Pomme-de-Pin', immortalized by Rabelais and the 'Pléiade'. There was another cabaret of the same name in the Rue de la Cité. The historian Charles Rollin died in 1741 at No. 8 in the nearby Rue Rollin, where at No. 14, Descartes once lived. We shortly enter the Rue Descartes, at No. 39 in which Paul Verlaine (1844-96) died, before reaching the Rue Clovis, see p. 54.

Also in this district, but slightly to the W., and best approached by the Rue d'Ulm (leading S. from the *Panthéon*), is the Maronite church of *N.-D. du Liban* (No. 17). The *Collège des Irlandais*, founded in 1578 and established here as a seminary in 1769, stands at the corner of the adjacent Rue des Irlandais. At No. 29 Rue Lhomond, leading S.E., with an 18C façade seen from the Rue Amyot, Mme du Barry and Juliette Drouet were educated in the *Couvent de Ste-Aure*. A short distance beyond, at the *Ecole de Physique et de Chimie industrielles*, in the Rue Pierre-Brossolette, Pierre and Marie Curie did their experimental work in 1883-1905.

At No. 45 Rue d'Ulm is the *École Normale Supérieure,* established in 1794 for the training of teachers, and sited here since 1843. Pasteur worked in laboratories here between 1864 and 1888. Among its pupils were Taine, Bergson, Péguy, Romain Rolland, Giraudoux, Jules Romains, Jean Jaurès, and Éd. Herriot.

4   VAL-DE-GRÂCE; OBSERVATOIRE; MONTPARNASSE

MÉTROS: *Luxembourg, Port-Royal, Denfert-Rochereau, Cité-Universitaire, Vavin, Montparnasse-Bienvenue.*

Turning S. from the Rue Soufflot along the RUE ST-JACQUES (Pl. 18; 3; see p. 57) we pass No. 218, which occupies the site of the house of Jean de Meung, part-author of the 'Roman de la Rose' (c. 1300). On the r. is *St-Jacques-du-Haut-Pas,* a plain classical building (1630-88), the favourite church of the Jansenists, completed with the help of the Duchesse de Longueville. No. 254, at the corner of the Rue de l'Abbé-de-l'Épée, is the *Institut National des Sourds-Muets,* a Deaf and Dumb Asylum founded by the Abbé de l'Épée about 1770 and taken over by the State in 1790; the building, once the Oratorian seminary of St-Magloire, was reconstructed in 1823. In the courtyard is a statue of the Abbé by *Félix Martin,* a deaf and dumb sculptor (1789).

Further on, at No. 269 (l.) is the **Schola Cantorum** (visitors admitted), a free conservatoire of singing and music established in 1894 by three pupils of César Franck, including Vincent d'Indy. The buildings (1674) are those of the English Benedictine monastery of St Edmund, founded in France in 1615, and established on this site from 1640 to 1818. The salon and staircase are good examples of the Louis-XIV style; the lower part of the chapel is now a concert hall; the 'chapelle ardente', where James II's body lay in state, may also be seen.

James II (d. 1701), his daughter Louisa Maria-Theresa (1692-1712), and the Duke of Berwick (1670-1734), his son by Arabella Churchill, were buried here; their bodies, hidden at the Revolution, are probably in the catacombs, which were once accessible from the house. The last burial here was that of Berwick's second son Charles (d. 1787). Dr Johnson (1775) and Benjamin Franklin were guests of the English monks here.

At No. 284 (l.), the door between columns at the end of the courtyard was once the entrance to the distinguished Carmelite convent to which Louise de la Vallière, mistress of Louis XIV, retired in 1674. Another relic of the convent is a crypt beneath No. 25 Rue Henri-Barbusse, to the W.

The street widens (at Nos. 277-279) opposite the impressive front of the ***Val-de-Grâce** (Pl. 18; 5), since 1790 a military hospital, and from 1624 the house of the Benedictine nuns of Val-Profond, whose patroness was N.-D. du Val-de-Grâce. The present much more extensive buildings were erected by Anne of Austria in thanksgiving for the birth of Louis XIV in 1638 (she had been married 23 years without issue), and the first stone of the new works was laid by the young king in 1645. In the courtyard is a bronze statue of Napoleon's surgeon, Baron Larrey (1766-1842), by *David d'Angers.*

François Mansart was succeeded as architect before 1649 by *Jacques Lemercier,* and after 1654 the buildings were finished by *Le Muet* and *Le Duc,* the church being completed in 1667. The remains (often only their hearts) of royal personages interred here, including Anne of Austria and

Henrietta Maria, were dispersed at the Revolution. The Army Medical School was added in 1850.

The façade of the church (by *Mansart*) is a fine example of the Jesuit style, and the *DOME (by *Le Duc*) is one of the best in France. The sculptures within are by *François* and *Michel Anguier, Pierre Sarazin,* and others. The high-altar, with its six huge twisted marble columns, is inspired by Bernini's in St Peter's at Rome; but the sculptured Nativity on it is a copy of Anguier's original (now at *St-Roch*). The painting in the dome is by *Pierre Mignard;* in the chapel on the r. of the choir is a portrait of Anne of Austria borne by an angel; and in the CHAPEL OF THE SACRAMENT (shown by the sacristan), is the Communion of the Angels, by *J.-B. de Champaigne.* The imposing CLOISTERS may be visited, and also, in the former refectory, a museum of military hygiene.

The *Val-de-Grâce* was only one of the many religious houses which, until the Revolution, were established in this district. To the N. are the Rue des Ursulines and Rue des Feuillantines, whose names recall vanished convents; almost opposite were the Carmelites (see above); to the S. stood *Port-Royal* (see below), beyond which, in the BLVD. ARAGO, stood a 13C Franciscan nunnery. Victor Hugo spent part of his youth (1808-13) in the Rue des Feuillantines.

To the r. on the far side of the BLVD. DE PORT-ROYAL, a maternity hospital has, since 1814, occupied the buildings of *Port-Royal de Paris,* a branch of the Jansenist abbey of *Port-Royal-des-Champs,* destroyed at the instigation of the Jesuits and its site ploughed over in 1709 (see p. 252). In the chapel, built by *Le Pautre* in 1647, is the tomb of Angélique Arnauld (1591-1661), the famous reforming abbess.

The extensive buildings of the *Hôpital Cochin* lie to the l. of the Rue Faubourg-St-Jacques, where No. 38 (r.), the *Hôtel de Massa* (1784), is now occupied by the Société des Gens de Lettres. The building was transferred here from the Champs-Élysées in 1927.

We turn up the Rue Cassini, where at No. 2 lived Alain-Fournier in 1910-14, and wrote 'Le Grand Meaulnes'; Balzac lived in 1829-34 at a house on the site of No. 1, where he wrote 'La Peau de Chagrin'.

We pass (l.) the entrance of the **Observatoire** (Pl. 18; 5), founded by Louis XIV in 1667 and completed by *Claude Perrault* in 1672.

The four sides of the building face the cardinal points of the compass, and the latitude of the S. side is the recognized latitude of Paris (48° 50′ 11″ N.). A line bisecting the building from N. to S. is the meridian of Paris (2° 20′ 14″ E. of Greenwich), which until 1912 was the basis for the calculation of longitude on French maps. The Observatoire is also the headquarters of the *Bureau International de l'Heure,* and a 'speaking' clock (tel. 033 84 00) is installed in its cellars.

Application to attend a guided tour (on the 1st Sat. of each month, at 14.30) should be made in advance to the Secrétariat at 61 Av. de l'Observatoire.
On the first floor of the main building is a *Museum of Instruments,* and the contents of the Rotunda in the W. tower illustrate the history of astronomy. The room on the second floor, on the pavement of which is traced the Paris meridian, contains older instruments. A shaft descending from the roof of the main building into the catacombs has been used for the study of falling bodies. In the E. cupola is an equatorial telescope of 14 inches aperture.

Turning N. from the *Observatoire,* we shortly cross the Av. Denfert-

Rochereau to reach the CARREFOUR DE L'OBSERVATOIRE, to the N.W. of which is *Rude*'s statue of Ney (1769-1815), who was shot close by for traitorously espousing Napoleon's cause on his return from Elba. Behind it is the *Closerie des Lilas,* long a literary resort, and frequented by Baudelaire, Verlaine, Gide, Jarry, Apollinaire, etc. To the N. is the *Fontaine de l'Observatoire* (1875) by *Davioud, Frémiet,* and *Carpeaux.*

The Av. Denfert-Rochereau leads S.W. to the PL. DENFERT-ROCHEREAU, passing (r.) the *Hôpital St-Vincent-de-Paul,* with a chapel of 1650-55. Chateaubriand lived in 1826-38 in the grounds of the Infirmerie Marie-Thérèse, which occupied an adjacent site, and which was directed by his wife.

This focus of traffic was known as the '*Pl. d'Enfer'* until 1879, when it received its present name in honour of the defender of Belfort during the Franco-Prussian War. In the centre is a reduced copy of Bartholdi's sculpture of the 'Lion of Belfort'.

On the S.W. side of the Place, in one of the octroi pavilions of the old Barrière d'Enfer (1784), is the main entrance to the **Catacombs,** a labyrinthine series of underground quarries dating from the time of the Romans and extending from the *Jardin des Plantes* to the *Porte de Versailles* and into the suburbs of Montrouge, Montsouris, and Gentilly. In the 18C they were converted into a charnel-house for bones removed from disused graveyards, and most of the victims of the massacres of the Terror were later transferred here. In 1944 they became a headquarters of the Resistance Movement.

Escorted tours are arranged on the 1st and 3rd Saturdays of each month at 14.00; every Sat. in summer. It is advisable to take a torch. The perambulation lasts over an hour, through a macabre series of galleries lined with bones and skulls, to a huge ossuary containing the remains of c. 3 million skeletons, but tends to be monotonous.

Leading S. from the Pl. Denfert-Rochereau, the Av. René-Coty approaches the **Parc de Montsouris,** some 40 acres in area and laid out in 1875-78. Near its N.E. corner is a lake (which suddenly dried up on the day of inauguration, and the engineer responsible committed suicide); near the centre of the S. side is a reproduction of the *Bey's Palace* at Tunis (erected for the Exhibition of 1867), now used as a meteorological observatory.

Among artists who lived in this quarter was Braque (1882-1963), with a studio in the Rue du Douanier (Rousseau), to the W. Lenin lived at No. 4 Rue Marie-Rose, some minutes walk further N.W., in 1909-12.

Facing the S. side of the park, flanked by the BLVD. JOURDAN, is the **Cité Universitaire,** founded in 1922, accommodating c. 7,000 students in some 37 halls of residence, the individual style of each reflecting the characteristic architecture of their own country. The U.S. foundation dates from 1928; the British hostel from 1937; and the huge *Maison Internationale* (with a swimming-pool, theatre, etc.) from 1936. Few of these heterogeneous buildings are of any great interest, although *Le Corbusier* (the designer of the Swiss and Brazilian halls) will have his admirers.

The church of *Sacré-Coeur,* reached by a footbridge over the BLVD. PÉRIPHÉRIQUE to the S., is a landmark to traffic approaching Paris by the A6 autoroute and Orly.

Montparnasse

From the CARREFOUR DE L'OBSERVATOIRE, the long BLVD. DU MONTPARNASSE leads N.W. across the BLVD. RASPAIL, where to the N. stands *Rodin*'s statue of Balzac. This junction may be regarded as the centre of a quarter which replaced Montmartre as the principal artistic and bohemian rendezvous, when they no longer found inspiration on the N. heights of Paris. Gauguin had a studio at No. 8 Rue de la Grande-Chaumière, leading N.E. Then, inexorably, the smaller intimate cafés were replaced by *Le Dôme, La Coupole, La Rotonde,* etc., and the district was invaded by a horde of hangers-on and parasitic pseudo-bohemians; the 'boîtes' in the Rue de la Gaité and elsewhere still attract this polyglot crowd.

Nevertheless, the neighbouring streets are full of (fast fading) associations with late-19C and early 20C artists and intellectuals. Trotsky and his fellow-revolutionaries frequented the *Rotonde* prior to 1917. Rilke and Modigliani lived in the Rue Campagne-Première, to the S.E., as did Whistler, who, with Rodin, had studios at 132 Blvd. du Montparnasse (demolished). In earlier decades, Sainte-Beuve, the critic (1804-69), lived at No. 19 Rue N.-D.-des Champs, to the N.E., and died at No. 11 Rue du Montparnasse. Romain Rolland lived at No. 162 Blvd. du Montparnasse in 1901-14. Both Henry Miller and Hemingway have described the café life, disreputable and otherwise, of the district in its heyday, which was largely blighted by the mid-1930s, and which may disappear for ever with the present transformation and development of the area, already dominated by the hideously obtrusive **Tour Montparnasse** (completed in 1973, and 656ft high), which has little to recommend it except for the impressive panoramic views (fee) from the 56th floor (Adm. 9.30 or 10.00-22.00 or 23.30). An open-air terrace forms its 58th floor.

To the S.W. and parallel to the Blvd. de Montparnasse, is the BLVD. EDGAR-QUINET, with the main entrance of the **Cimetière Montparnasse** (Pl. 17; 5), a 45-acre site laid out in 1824. Maupassant, Louÿs, Baudelaire, J.-K. Huysmans, and Sainte-Beuve, among writers; César Franck, D'Indy, Saint-Saëns, and Clara Haskil, among composers and musicians; Fantin-Latour, Gérard, Houdon, and Rude, among artists and sculptors; Proudhon, the socialist reformer, and Alfred Dreyfus, were all buried here; as was Pierre Laval, prime minister in the wartime Vichy régime.

Adjacent to the *Tour,* and forming part of the glass and concrete complex, is the **Gare Montparnasse** (Pl. 17; 5), 18 storeys high, surrounding, on three sides, the station platforms, over which hanging gardens are promised.

The BLVD. DE VAUGIRARD flanking the Station to the N.W., with a *Postal Museum* at No. 34, leads shortly to the BLVD. PASTEUR, off which runs the Rue du Docteur-Roux, with (l.) the *Institut Pasteur,* founded by Louis Pasteur in 1887-89 and built by private subscription. Pasteur (1822-95) is buried in the crypt; the tomb of Dr Émile Roux (1853-1933), inventor of the treatment of diphtheria by serum-injection, lies in the garden.
In the Rue Antoine-Bourdelle, N. of and parallel to the Blvd. de Vaugirard, is a *Museum* devoted to the sculptor *Bourdelle* (1861-1929).

The Métro at Montparnasse-Bienvenue is well-connected with lines returning to the centre.

5   THE FAUBOURG ST-GERMAIN: EASTERN SECTOR

MÉTROS: *Pont-Neuf, Odéon, Luxembourg, St-Sulpice, St-Germain-des-Prés, Mabillon.*

The district still known as the Faubourg St-Germain stretches S. from the Seine opposite the *Louvre,* from the *Pont des Arts* on the E. to the *Pont de la Concorde* to the W. Until the end of the 16C, much of this area, the property of the *Abbaye St-Germain-des-Prés,* was open country. In the following century, with the religious revival, several convents were built here, and in 1670, the *Hôtel des Invalides* was constructed on the outskirts to the W. By 1685 the new *Pont Royal* provided easy access to the *Château des Tuileries,* which became the home of the court during the Regency, and this, together with the creation of the *École Militaire,* were the main reasons for the building of this new aristocratic quarter, which gradually took the place of the *Marais.* About half the houses were built between 1690 and 1725, a quarter between 1725 and 1750, and most of the rest between 1750 and 1790. In style they are very similar; often the most handsome façade faces the garden, and the gateway from the street leads to the 'Cour d'Honneur'.

Today, the main thoroughfares are the Blvd. St-Germain and the Blvd. Raspail, which have done much to alter the character of the quarter. The most characteristic streets of the once 'noble faubourg' are the Rue de Lille, Rue de l'Université, Rue St-Dominique, and Rue de Grenelle. About a hundred old mansions remain, many of them converted to house embassies or government offices, but the whole area still retains numerous characteristic streets, and the 6th and E. half of the 7th Arrondissements remain two of the most delightful districts of Paris in which to linger.

It is convenient to divide the large area into two sections: *Route 5* describing the Luxembourg and St-Germain-des-Prés (from the Blvd. St-Michel to the Rue des Saints-Pères and Blvd. Raspail): *Route 6* describing the rest of the 7th Arrondissement.

At the S. end of the *Pont des Arts,* facing the *Louvre,* is the PL. DE L'INSTITUT, flanked by the curved wings of the *Institut de France (Pl. 14; 3), surmounted by a dome, which, since its recent cleaning and restoration, is one of the outstanding features of this reach of the quays.

The building may be visited on Sat. afternoons by arrangement with the Secrétariat, 23 Quai de Conti.

The E. wing of the *Institut* and the adjacent *Hôtel des Monnaies* (see below) cover the site of the *Hôtel de Nesle* (13C), in which was incorporated the 12C *Tour de Nesle* or *Tour Hamelin,* the river bastion of Philippe Auguste's (which ran S.E. parallel to the Rue Mazarine). The tower was notorious in legend as the scene of the amours of Marguerite (c. 1290-1315) and Jeanne of Burgundy, wives of Louis X and Philippe V, who are said to have had their lovers thrown into the river. Later occupants were Isabeau de Bavière, Charles the Bold, and Henry V of England. The W. part, known as the *Petit-Nesle,* was the workshop of Benvenuto Cellini in 1540-45, and was demolished in 1663. The E. part, or *Grand-Nesle,* rebuilt in 1648 by *Fr. Mansart,* became the *Hôtel de Conti,* and in 1770, the *Mint.*

The present building was erected in accordance with the will of Card. Mazarin, who bequeathed 2 million fr. in silver and 45,000 fr. a year for the establishment of a college for sixty gentlemen of the four provinces acquired by the Treaties of Münster and the Pyrenees; viz. Flanders, Alsace, Roussillon, and Piedmont (Pinerolo). The building, designed by *Louis Le Vau,* was erected in 1662-74. The official name of the new college was the *Collège Mazarin,* but its popular name was the *Collège des Quatre-Nations.* The Institut, founded in 1795, and installed first in the Louvre, acquired the former Collège Mazarin in 1806.

The INSTITUT DE FRANCE comprises five academies: the *Académie Française,* founded by Richelieu in 1635 and restricted to forty members, whose particular task was the editing of the dictionary of the French language; the *Académie des Beaux-Arts* (1816), founded by Mazarin in 1648 as the *Académie Royale de*

Peinture et de Sculpture; the *Académie des Inscriptions et Belles-Lettres,* founded by Colbert in 1663; the *Académie des Sciences,* founded by Colbert in 1666; and the *Académie des Sciences Morales et Politiques,* founded in 1795 and reconstituted in 1832.

The *Académie Française* holds special receptions for newly elected members, tickets of admission to which are much sought after (apply to the general secretary). An annual general meeting of all five academies is held on 25 Oct. (adm. by ticket only).

Members are known, satirically, as 'Les Immortels', but it may be remarked that among the considerable list of great figures of French literature who were *not* members were Pascal, Descartes, Molière, La Rochefoucauld, Diderot, Rousseau, Beaumarchais, Balzac, Flaubert, Maupassant, Zola, and Proust.

Passing into the first octagonal courtyard (beyond which are two others, the third being the *Kitchen Court* of the old Collège Mazarin), the door on the l. leads to the *Bibliothèque Mazarine,* containing c. 350,000 vols, 5,800 MSS., and 1,900 incunabula. This was the cardinal's personal library, which, opened to scholars in 1643, became the first public library in France.

The *Institute Library* is also in this wing, together with a number of rooms decorated with academic statues and busts of distinguished academicians. Among many of little merit, *Pigalle*'s Voltaire is striking.

In the W. wing is the *Salle des Séances Solennelles,* in the former chapel. Recent restoration has undone the damage caused by Vaudoyer, and Mazarin's tomb by *Coysevox* has been returned from the Louvre. His niece, the Duchesse de Mazarin (d. 1699), the famous beauty of the court of Charles II, was also buried here. The room contains about 400 seats (green for members of the Académie Française; red for the others), and here take place receptions and general meetings.

At No. 13 QUAI DE CONTI (the riverside embankment here, as elsewhere in this central reach of the Seine, lined with the bookstalls of the *bouquinistes)* is the *Hôtel Guénégaud* or *de Sillery-Genlis,* by *Fr. Mansart* (1659), often visited by Napoleon when on leave from the École Militaire. Larrey lived here from 1805 to 1832.

No. 11, the ***Hôtel des Monnaies,** the *Mint,* is a simple dignified building by *J.-D. Antoine* (1771-75). The handsome doorway is ornamented with Louis XVI's monogram and elegant bronze knockers; above is the fleur-de-lys escutcheon with Mercury and Ceres as supporters. From the vestibule, a notable example of 18C architecture, a double staircase on the r. ascends to the second landing, from which we enter the *Musée de la Monnaie* (open Mon. to Fri., 11.00-17.00), containing an impressive collection of stamping presses, punches, medals, and coins. Medals are for sale in the far wing.

The SALLE GUILLAUME DUPRÉ, in the centre of the building, is (apart from the modern ceiling) representative of the best period of the Louis-XVI style; showcases display medals from the Renaissance to the present. The SALLE SAGE contains new acquisitions; the SALLE JEAN WARIN, portraits of the Walloon medallist Warin (1604-72) and directors of the Mint; the SALLE DENON is devoted to medals of the Consulate and Empire period and the SALLE DUVIVIER displays examples of coins illustrating the evolution of French currency from Merovingian times.

On the r. of the second courtyard is the entrance to the *Ateliers* or workshops, where, under escort (no gratuity) one may see processes in the production of coins and medals (adm. only Tues. and Thurs. 14.00-15.30; closed during summer vacation).

At No. 5, on the corner of the Rue Guénégaud, Col. de Marguerittes, of the Resistance, set up his headquarters while conducting operations for the liberation of Paris 19-28 Aug. 1944. At the end of the adjacent Rue de Nevers (entered below an arch), one may see part of Philippe Auguste's *Wall.*

From the S. end of the *Pont Neuf,* the Rue Dauphine leads S., passing (l.), at No. 9 Rue Mazet, the site of *chez Magny,* a famous restaurant and literary rendezvous in the 1860s, to the CARREFOUR DE BUCI, with its street market. The parallel Rue des Grands-Augustins (with the restaurant *Lapérouse* on the corner), contains the *Hôtel d'Hercule,* dating from the 17C (Nos. 3-7); No. 21 was the birthplace of the lexicographer Émile Littré (1801-81), and Heine lived at No. 25 in 1841, as had La Bruyère in 1676-91.

At No. 35 QUAI DES GRANDS-AUGUSTINS is another pleasant 17C mansion at the corner of the Rue Séguier, lined with old houses, which likewise leads S. to meet the Rue St-André-des-Arts, also containing several notable 17-18C buildings (Nos. 47 and 52).

From the PL. ST-ANDRÉ, to the E., where at No. 11 Gounod was born in 1818, the Rue Hautefeuille leads S., with (No. 5) the *Hôtel des Abbés de Fécamp,* with a pretty turret. Among its occupiers was Godin de Sainte-Croix, an accomplice of the Marquise de Brinvilliers. Baudelaire (1821-67) was born at No. 15 (demolished). J.-K. Huysmans (1848-1907) was born at No. 9 Rue Suger, leading W. from the Pl. St-André.

Leading S. from the Rue St-André-des-Arts, the Rue de l'Éperon shortly meets (r.) the Rue du Jardinet, in which Saint-Saëns (1835-1921) was born. Continuing along the latter alley, we enter the *Cour de Rohan* (16-17C), originally part of the palace of the Abp. of Rouen. Turning l. on passing through an archway, No. 4 in the ancient *Cour de Commerce-St-André* is the basement of one of Philippe Auguste's towers. At No. 8, Marat's journal 'L'Ami du Peuple' was printed; while at No. 9, opposite, popular myth has it that Dr Joseph-Ignace Guillotin perfected his 'philanthropic beheading machine'.

The Rue de l'Ancienne Comédie (the next street to the W.) takes its name from the Comédie Française of 1689-1770, which occupied No. 14, while opposite, the *Café Procope,* which originated before 1700, was a favourite haunt of Voltaire and the Encyclopaedists, Musset, George Sand, Balzac, Gautier, Verlaine, Huysmans, and Wilde, among others.

To the N. the Rue Mazarine leads back to the *Institut,* passing the *sites* (at No. 42) of the *Théâtre de Guénégaud* (occupied by the Opéra in 1671-72, by Molière's company in 1673-80, and by the Comédie-Française in 1680-89); and at No. 12, the former tennis-court where the *Illustre Théâtre* was opened in Dec. 1643 by Molière's company.

In the mid-19C the BLVD. ST-GERMAIN was cut through this picturesque area of narrow lanes leading S. from the river. Opposite the Rue de l'Ancienne Comédie is the CARREFOUR DE L'ODÉON (Pl. 17; 4), beyond the PL. H.-MONDOR, both busy crossroads, where the *Benjamin Franklin Library* has replaced the Café Voltaire (No. 1), where a banquet was held in honour of Gauguin before he left for Tahiti in 1891. At No. 2 Camille Desmoulins was arrested in 1794; the statue of Danton (1759-94) marks the site of his house, where he was likewise apprehended.

To the E. is a building of the **Faculty of Medicine** (University V) erected by *Gondouin* in 1769-76 on the site of the *Collège de Bourgogne* and *Collège des Prémontrés,* and since enlarged. The older part, facing the Rue de l'École-de-Médecine, is considered one of the most classical works of the 18C. The façade facing the Blvd. St-Germain was added in 1878.

In the courtyard is a statue of the anatomist Bichat (1771-1802) by *David d'Angers.*
The *Library* contains c. 600,000 vols, and commentaries of the heads of the faculty from 1395 onwards. Also of interest are the *Lecture Hall,* the *Musée d'Histoire de la Médecine,* and the *Salle du Conseil,* hung with four Gobelins tapestries of the Louis-XIV period, *after Le Brun.*

Opposite is the entrance to the former *Refectory* of the *Couvent des Cordeliers,* a 15C Franciscan convent, which during the Revolution was a meeting-place of the extremist Club des Cordeliers, the leaders of which were Marat (a doctor by profession, and partly educated at Edinburgh), Camille Desmoulins, and Danton. The former was stabbed in his bath by Charlotte Corday in 1793 at No. 20 (demolished). At No. 5, the *Institut des Langues Modernes* occupies the old *Amphithéâtre de St-Côme* (1691-94), with a beautiful portal. This was originally the lecture-hall of the College of Surgery. A plaque here commemorates the birth of the actress Sarah Bernhardt in 1845.

Further E. (l.) at the corner of the S. section of the Rue de Hautefeuille (No. 32), Gustave Courbet (1819-77) had his studio in the former chapel of the *Collège des Prémontrés.*

The Rue de l'École-de-Médecine narrows before meeting the BLVD. ST-MICHEL.

From its W. end, we may ascend steps before turning l. along the Rue Monsieur-le-Prince (de Condé). At No. 10, Auguste Comte (1798-1857), the positivist philosopher, lived from 1841. Saint-Saëns lived at No. 14 in 1877-89, and Longfellow had lodgings at No. 49 in 1826 (and in a subsequent winter, at No. 5 in the adjacent Rue Racine). At No. 54 (altered) Pascal lived in 1654-62 and wrote his 'Pensées'. To the l., on meeting the Rue de Vaugirard, is the *Lycée St-Louis,* built by *Bailly* on the site of the *Collège d'Harcourt,* the greatest of the University colleges (1280), its entrance facing the Pl. de la Sorbonne. Racine and Boileau studied here.

Adjacent to the S. end of the Rue Monsieur-le-Prince is the PL. EDMOND-ROSTAND, with a good view of the *Panthéon* (see p. 55). George Sand's last Paris home, in the 1870s, was at No. 5 Rue Gay-Lussac, to the S.E. To the S., on the r. of the BLVD. ST-MICHEL, the *École Supérieure des Mines* occupies the *Hôtel de Vendôme,* an 18C building enlarged after 1840, and having its principal façade towards the Luxembourg Gardens. It contains a *Museum of Mineralogy and Geology.* At No. 95 in the Boulevard died César Franck (1890). Leconte de Lisle lived at No. 64 in 1872-94.

One of many entrances to the **Jardin du Luxembourg* (Pl. 14; 7) is a few yards S. of the Pl. Edmond-Rostand. These extensive gardens (c. 57 acres), embellished by numerous statues, form one of the pleasanter and more colourful open spaces in central Paris. Laid out in the 17C, they were deplorably mutilated in 1782 and 1867, and perhaps little remains of the original garden as known by Marie de Médicis (see Palais de Luxembourg, below).

Steps descend from the E. Terrace to lawns surrounding an octagonal pond with its fountain. Beyond the formal W. Terrace is the Jardin Anglais; while to the S., beyond the PL. ANDRÉ-HONNORAT, gardens are continued between the two branches of the Av. de l'Observatoire, which were laid out under the First Empire on the site of a Carthusian monastery demolished at the Revolution.

Turning N. from the central pond, we pass on our r., at the end of an oblong pool, the **Fontaine Médicis,** attr. to *Salomon de Brosse* (c. 1627), moved here in 1861. In the central niche is Polyphemus about to crush Acis and Galatea; on either side are Pan and Diana, and at the back a bas-relief, the Fontaine de Léda, brought from the Rue du Regard in 1855.

At No. 19 Rue de Médicis, flanking the gardens to the N.E., was born André Gide (1869-1951).

The ***Palais du Luxembourg,** once a royal residence, with its heavily rusticated masonry, is more visually attractive externally than internally, although the S. façade, facing the gardens, is a 19C copy, by *Gisors.* The N. façade is the original, where the main entrance is surmounted by an eight-sided dome. The two wings, terminating in steep-roofed pavilions, with three orders of columns superimposed, are connected by a single-storeyed gallery.

The Luxembourg was built by *Salomon de Brosse* in 1615-27 for Marie de Médicis, widow of Henri IV, who, it is said, wished to have a palace which reminded her of the Pitti Palace in Florence, her birthplace. She also acquired the adjacent mansion of the Duc de Tingry-Luxembourg (the *Petit-Luxembourg;* 1570-1612), hence its name. The building was altered in 1808 and enlarged in 1831-44.

After Louis XIII's death, the palace passed to her second son Gaston, Duc d'Orléans, and the 'Palais Médicis' became known as the 'Palais d'Orléans'. Subsequently, it belonged in succession to Mlle de Montpensier, the Duchesse de Guise (1672), Louis XIV (1694), and the Orléans family. Among prisoners confined here during the Revolution were Marshal de Noailles (executed at the age of 79 with his wife, daughter, and granddaughter); Hébert, Danton, Desmoulins, Fabre d'Églantine, the painter David, and Tom Paine (imprisoned here in 1793 for voting in the Assembly against the king's execution, and who escaped the guillotine only by an accident). In 1794 the Directory transferred the seat of government from the Tuileries to the Luxembourg, and here Gen. Bonaparte presented the Treaty of Campo Formio. In 1800 the 'Palais Directorial' became the 'Palais du Consulat'; under the Empire it was the 'Palais du Sénat', and later, the 'Palais de la Pairie'. Marshal Ney was confined and tried here in 1815. The ministers of Charles X were tried here under Louis-Philippe in 1830, and Louis-Napoléon Bonaparte after landing at Boulogne in 1840. From 1852 to 1940 the Palais was the meeting-place of the Senate, the upper chamber of the French Republic, except in 1871-79, when it was the seat of the Préfecture de la Seine.

In 1940-44 it was occupied by Field Marshal Sperrle, commander-in-chief of the Luftwaffe on the Western Front. In 1946 it was the seat of the Conseil de la République, but in 1958 it reverted to the Senate.

Adm. 9.30-12.00, 16.00-19.00 on Sun. only, when small groups are conducted round parts of the building.

The INTERIOR, drastically remodelled by *Chalgrin* under Napoleon I, is decorated in the sumptuous but decadent 19C manner, replete with statues, and paintings, historical and allegorical, few of which are of any merit. The series of paintings devoted to the Life of Marie de Médicis, by *Rubens,* which once hung in the palace, are now in the Louvre; see p. 103. By far the most interesting room is the luxuriously gilt **Cabinet Doré,** Marie de Médicis's audience chamber. Other rooms (on the First Floor) through which parties are conducted are the SALLES DES CONFÉRENCES; the hemicycle of the SALLE DE SÉANCES; the LIBRARY, overlooking the gardens, and containing some mediocre paintings by *Delacroix*, that in the cupola being the Limbo of Dante's Inferno.

The adjoining **Petit-Luxembourg** (now the residence of the President of the Senate; no adm.) was presented to Richelieu by Marie de Médicis in 1626. It includes the cloisters and chapel of the Filles du Calvaire, for whom the queen built a convent; the chapel is a charming example of the Renaissance style, the cloister forms a winter-garden. To the W. is the *Orangery*, once occupied by a museum.

A few yards to the N.E. of the Palais stands the ***Théâtre de France** (or *de l'Odéon*), built in the form of a classical temple by *Wailly* and *Peyre* in the garden of the *Hôtel de Condé*, which was demolished by Louis XV to this end.

The vanished Hôtel, the site of which was Nos. 5-9 in the adjacent Rue de Condé, was the town house of the family from 1612 to 1764.

The theatre was opened in 1782 with the title of *Théâtre-Français,* but was rebuilt by *Chalgrin* after a fire in 1807. Its auditorium, with an interesting ceiling, is one of the finest in Paris.

From its N. entrance, the Rue de l'Odéon, bordered by 18C houses, slopes downhill towards the Carrefour de l'Odéon. At No. 22 in the parallel Rue de Condé, to the W., lived Lucile Duplessis before her marriage to Desmoulins; No. 26 was the home of Beaumarchais in 1763-76, the period of 'Le Barbier de Séville'. The Marquis de Sade (1740-1814) was born at No. 20.

From the main entrance of the *Palais de Luxembourg,* in the Rue de Vaugirard (the longest street in Paris, stretching from the Blvd. St-Michel to the Porte de Versailles) the wide and stately Rue de Tournon leads gently down to the Blvd. St-Germain.

To the N. it is extended by the Rue de Seine, also containing a number of attractive houses, to the *Institut.*

Balzac lived at No. 2 in the Rue de Tournon in 1827-30; Marie Lenormand, the fortune-teller consulted by so many Revolutionary celebrities, lived at No. 5 for over fifty years and died there in 1843; Hébert (Père Duchesne; 1755-94), the journalist, lived here in 1793, and Charles Cros, one of the pioneers of the phonograph, died here in 1888. No. 6, the *Hôtel de Brancas,* was reconstructed during the Regency by *Bullet;* Gambetta lived on the top storey of No. 7, the *Hôtel du Sénat,* where Alphonse Daudet also resided when he first came to Paris. No. 10 (now barracks of the Garde Républicaine) was the *Hôtel de Concini.* Paul Jones died at No. 19 in 1792; the actor Gérard Philipe (1922-59) died at No. 17.

Parallel to the Rue de Tournon, to the W., is the Rue Garancière, with the *Hôtel de Sourdéac* (No. 8; 1640).

At No. 20 Rue de Vaugirard stood the Café Tabourey, a famous literary rendezvous; while at No. 48 the composer Massenet (1842-1912) long resided, and died. In the picturesque Rue Férou, diverging r., died Mme de La Fayette (1634-93), fifteen years after writing 'La Princesse de Clèves'; No. 50, at the corner, her birthplace, later became the *Hôtel de la Trémoille.* Fantin-Latour lived at No. 15.

Turning r. down the next street, the Rue Bonaparte (which narrows as it approaches the Seine), containing numerous antique shops and galleries, one of the most pleasant and characteristic in the commercial part of the Faubourg, we shortly enter the PL. ST-SULPICE (Pl. 14; 5) dominated to the E. by the church. In the centre is the *Fontaine des Quatre-Évêques,* by *Visconti,* with statues of four famous preaching bishops: Bossuet, Fénelon, Massillon, and Fléchier.

In 1843-44 Renan was a scholar at the seminary which stood on the S. side; opposite, No. 6 is a dignified mansion by *Servandoni* (1754), the first of a range which never materialized. Too many of the neighbouring shops display cloying modern ecclesiastical art and furniture.

St-Sulpice, the wealthiest church on the Left Bank, and noted for its music (frequent organ recitals; enquire at the church for details), is a somewhat ponderous classical building, imposing mainly for its size, although described by Gibbon as "one of the noblest structures in Paris". The W. front consists of an Ionic colonnade over a Doric. The N. tower, 240 ft high, has seated figures of the Evangelists; the S. tower is 16 ft lower. Hugo compared them to clarionets.

It was begun in 1646 by *Gamard* on the site of an older church, and continued on a larger scale by *Le Vau* in 1655 and *Gittard* in 1670. After an interval from 1675 to 1719 the work was resumed by *Oppenordt.* The building of the W. front was entrusted to *Servandoni,* who, however, failed to give satisfaction, and was replaced in 1745 by *Maclaurin.* His successor, *Chalgrin,* rebuilt the N. tower in 1777, since Maclaurin's design had also failed to please, but the S. tower was left incomplete.

Camille Desmoulins was married here to Lucile Duplessis in 1790. Under the Convention St-Sulpice became the 'Temple de la Victoire', and in 1799 a public banquet was given here by Gen. Bonaparte. Saint-Simon, writing earlier, was contemptuous of its clergy, with their 'barbes sales'.

The stately INTERIOR, a representative example of the 'Jesuit' style, is 360 ft long, 184 ft wide, and 108 ft high. The famous Organ, one of the largest in existence (6,588 pipes), was built in 1781 and remodelled in 1860-62; the case was designed by *Chalgrin,* and is adorned by statues by *Clodion* and decoration by *Duret.* At the beginning of the nave are two huge tridacna gigas shells serving as holy-water stoups, presented to François I by the Venetian Republic; the marble 'rocks' on which they rest were sculpted by *Pigalle.* The late-18C pulpit, by *Wailly,* bears gilded figures of Faith and Hope by *Guesdon,* and Charity by *Dumont.*

In the paving of the S. transept is a bronze tablet connected by a meridian line with a marble obelisk in the N. transept; at noon the sun's rays, passing through an aperture in a blind window in the S. transept, strike the meridian at different points according to the time of year.

The CHAPELS encircling the church are decorated with frescoes. In the first (r.) are some late works by *Delacroix* (1853-63). In the 5th chapel, the tomb, by *Slodtz,* of the curé Languet de Gergy (1674-1750), founder of the *Enfants Malades,* and responsible for the completion of the church. In the *Choir,* works by *Bouchardon.* The *Lady Chapel* was designed by *Servandoni.* In a niche behind the altar is a marble Virgin by *Pigalle,* with angels by *Mouchy.* The wall-paintings are by *Carle Van Loo;* those in the dome, by *Lemoyne.*

Remains of the 16C church may be seen in the crypt.

After crossing the Rue du Four, we shortly reach the busy intersection of the PL. ST-GERMAIN-DES-PRÉS (Pl. 14; 5). Diagonally opposite, at Nos.

170 and 172 respectively, are the *Café des Deux Magots* (grotesque Chinese figures), and the *Café de Flore;* while at No. 151 is the *Brasserie Lipp.* All were once known for the artistic and literary set which frequented them; perhaps poseurs are now predominant.

To the N.E. the square is dominated by the church of *St-Germain-des-Prés, the oldest in Paris, and also the only one retaining any considerable remains of Romanesque work.

The church, a relic of the great Benedictine abbey founded in 558 by Childebert I, who was buried there, as was St Germanus, Bp. of Paris (d. 576), was rebuilt at the beginning of the 11C (body of the W. tower), in the late 11C (nave), and in the mid-12C (choir), and was consecrated by Pope Alexander III in 1163. It was the chief house of the reformed Congregation de Saint-Maur in the 17C, and numbered the scholar Jean Mabillon (1632-1707) and Bernard de Montfaucon (1655-1741) among its distinguished members. The massive flying buttresses of the choir are among the earliest in France. The W. porch dates from 1607, but preserves the jambs of a 12C door and a battered lintel depicting the Last Supper. The transepts were remodelled c. 1644. The bell-chamber of the tower was added in the 17C. Flanking the choir are the bases of two towers pulled down in 1822, when the church was drastically restored, after its use as a saltpetre factory in 1794-95.

The INTERIOR (213 ft by 69 ft, and 62 ft high) would be more imposing if stripped of its 19C decoration; but is nevertheless interesting architecturally for the combination of the Romanesque style in the nave with the first attempts at the Gothic style in the choir. The vault of the nave and aisles dates from 1644-46. The pillars are flanked by four columns, the sculptured capitals of which in 1848-53 were either re-cut or removed to the Musée de Cluny and replaced by copies, with the exception of one remaining in the N.W. corner. Both nave and choir are daubed with murals by *Hippolyte Flandrin* (1842-64), among others.

S. AISLE. To the r. is a marble statue of N.-D. de Consolation, presented to the Abbey of St Denis by Queen Jeanne d'Évreux in 1340. In the S. transept is the tomb of Olivier and Louis de Castellan, killed in the king's service in 1644 and 1669, by *Girardon.* In the *first ambulatory-chapel* is the tomb of Lord James Douglas (d. 1645; son of the first Marquess of Douglas), a Scottish gentleman in the service of Louis XIII. *2nd chapel:* tombstones of Descartes (1596-1650), removed from Ste-Geneviève (1819), and of Mabillon (see above). *4th chapel:* fragments of stained glass of 1245-55.

CHOIR. The small marble columns in the triforium are re-used material from the 6C abbey of St Vincent; their bases and capitals are of the 12C. The *Lady Chapel* was rebuilt at the beginning of the 19C.

N. AISLE (as we return). *3rd chapel:* tombstones of Nicolas Boileau (1636-1711) removed from the Sainte Chapelle. *4th:* the tomb of William Douglas, 10th Earl of Angus (d. 1611), who died in the service of Henri IV. In the N. transept are a statue of St Francis Xavier, by *G. Coustou;* and the theatrical tomb, by *G.* and *B. Marsy,* of John Casimir, King of Poland, who became abbot of St-Germain in 1669 and died in 1672.

In the garden to the N. of the church are fragments of sculptures from the great lady-chapel built in 1212-55 by Pierre de Montreuil within the precincts of the abbey. In the Rue de l'Abbaye, but further E., are the buildings of the old *Abbot's Palace,* erected c. 1586 by Card. de Bourbon, behind which was the *Prison de l'Abbaye* (its site crossed by the present boulevard), where Brissot wrote his memoirs, and Charlotte Corday spent her last days.

In 1857, six years before he died at 6 Rue de Furstenberg, Delacroix built a studio in the adjoining PLACE, still one of the quietest backwaters of central Paris. This was later shared by Monet and Bazille, and now contains a small *Delacroix Museum* (open 10.00-17.00 except Tues.).

No. 1 Rue Bourbon-le-Château, a few yards E., was Whistler's first home in Paris (1855-56), while the *Pré-aux-Clercs,* which lay to the N. (now crossed by the Rue Jacob), was a favourite promenade, and the scene of medieval student brawls.

For streets radiating S.W. and W. of the Pl. St-Germain-des-Prés, see below.

The Rue Bonaparte continues N., crossing the Rue Jacob. At No. 18 in the former street the Czech government was formed in 1916; No. 14 is the main entrance to the *École des Beaux-Arts* (see below), while the *Hôtel du Marquis de Persan* (Nos. 7-9) was the home of Monge in 1803, and the birthplace of Manet (1832-83).

Both the Rue Jacob, and two streets diverging r. off the Rue Bonaparte, have interesting associations. Laurence Sterne put up in the Rue Jacob on his arrival in Paris in 1762 (at the 'Hôtel de Modène'), and was later a guest of Mme de Rambouillet at No. 46. Wagner lodged at No. 14 in 1841-42, working on 'The Flying Dutchman'; the social reformer Pierre-Joseph Proudhon later resided at the same address. In 1848 Mérimée lived at No. 18 (rebuilt); No. 32 belonged to du Cerceau, architect of the Pont Neuf; Stendhal stayed at both Nos. 28 and 52 in 1808-10. At No. 56 was signed a provisional treaty recognizing the independence of the United States (3 Sept. 1783); since 1810 it has been the offices of the printer Didot. Gen. Sikorski, head of the free Polish government, lived at No. 58 in 1939-40.

To the N. in the parallel Rue Visconti (then the Rue des Marais) Racine (1639-99) lived from 1693 until his death (house demolished); at No. 16 Adrienne Lecouvreur (1692-1730) died in the arms of Marshal Saxe; at No. 17 Balzac had a printing business, liquidated in 1828, and on the 2nd floor is a studio once occupied by Delaroche (1827-34) and Delacroix (1838-43).

In the next street to the r., the Rue des Beaux-Arts, Mérimée (1842-46) and Corot (1849-55) lived at No. 10; Fantin-Latour lived at No. 8. At No. 13 Oscar Wilde died destitute in 1900; his drama *Salomé* had been produced in Paris in 1896, while he was in Reading Gaol; he was buried in *Père Lachaise.*

The **École des Beaux-Arts** (Pl. 14; 3), begun in 1820 by *Debret* and finished in 1862 by *Duban,* replaced the convent of the Petits-Augustins, founded in 1608, of which certain relics remain. It was here that Alexandre Lenoir collected together so many pieces of sculpture, saving them from destruction during the Revolutionary period (comp. St-Denis). The buildings were further enlarged in 1885 on the acquisition of the *Hôtel de Chimay* (see below).

Regrettably, the buildings are no longer open to the general public, but scholars and artists should make application to the director, who may give permission to use the *Library,* containing c. 80,000 vols and approx. one million engravings, drawings, etc.

The main points of interest are the former convent *Chapel* (c. 1600), against the S. wall of which is the central part of the façade of the Château d'Anet, by *Philibert*

Delorme; in the adjoining *Chapel of Marguerite de Valois,* the small domed hexagon has claims to be the first dome built in Paris. Part of a Renaissance façade from the Château de Gaillon (1500-10) in Normandy separates the first courtyard from the second. An arcade from the *Hôtel de Torpane* (c. 1570) and the façade from the *Hôtel de Chimay* are also preserved. Both in the courtyards and inside the buildings are many sculptured fragments, antique marbles, etc., while the Salle de Melpomène is used for the display of students' work when competing for the Grands Prix de Rome.

Leading S.W. from the PL. ST-GERMAIN-DES-PRÉS is the Rue de Rennes, at the far end of which obtrudes the *Tour Montparnasse* (see p. 65). To the l. diverges the Rue Madame, at No. 25 in which in 1832 was the home of Mlle George, once Napoleon's mistress. Turning r. at the junction with the Rue de Vaugirard, we pass the domed church of *St-Joseph-des-Carmes,* once the chapel of a Carmelite convent dating from 1613-20 and containing a number of interesting 17C canvases, etc. The crypt contains the bones of some 120 priests massacred in the convent garden in Sept. 1792. Prisoners held here and later released included Gen. Hoche, Joséphine de Beauharnais, and Mme Tallien. Adjacent are the buildings of the *Institut Catholique,* where, in 1890, radio waves were discovered by Branly.

The de Musset family lived during 1818-32 in the nearby Rue Cassette (No. 27); Alfred Jarry (1873-1907) died at No. 20. Rainer Maria Rilke lived at No. 29 in 1906. Gertrude Stein lived at No. 27 Rue de Fleurus, not far S.

Some distance S. in the next crossroad, the Rue d'Assas, is No. 62, where Strindberg lived in 1895-96; Auguste Bartholdi (1834-1904), sculptor of the Statue of Liberty (New York), died at No. 82.

Turning r. into the Rue d'Assas, and recrossing the Rue de Rennes, we shortly reach the Rue du Cherche-Midi (deriving its name from an 18C sign on No. 19 representing an astronomer tracing a sundial), containing a number of attractive 17-18C houses. For its W. section, beyond the *Blvd. Raspail,* see p. 80. From the animated CARREFOUR DE LA CROIX-ROUGE (Pl. 14; 5) the Rue de Sèvres leads S.W. At No. 11 lived J.-K. Huysmans from 1872 to 1898. Off the N. side of the street, the Rue Récamier recalls the *Abbaye aux Bois,* the home of Mme Récamier in 1819-49, where the most frequent visitor to her famous salon was Chateaubriand. For the W. section of the Rue de Sèvres, see p. 80; likewise for the Rue de Grenelle, which also commences at the *Carrefour de la Croix-Rouge.* Crossing this junction, we enter the Rue du Dragon, the possible site of the pottery workshop of Bernard Palissy (1510-89). Hugo lived at No. 30 in 1821; No. 3 is an American Cultural Centre.

At No. 71 in the parallel Rue des Saints-Pères, to the W., died Rémy de Gourmont (1858-1915).

At the junction of the Rue des Saints-Pères and the Blvd. St-Germain stood the *Hôtel de Selvois,* where the Duc de Saint-Simon (1675-1755) was born and lived until 1714. At No. 184 in the Boulevard is the *Hôtel de la Société de Géographie,* founded in 1821.

The E. side of the Rue des Saints-Pères, after crossing the Boulevard, is the *Chapelle St-Pierre,* rebuilt in 1611, the sole relic of the Hôpital de la Charité, which stood on this site from 1605 to 1937. It is now the church of the Ukrainian Catholic community in Paris (St-Vladimir-le-Grand). Adjacent are buildings of the *Faculty of Medicine* (1936-53), while opposite, in the 18C *Hôtel de Fleury,* by *Antoine,* is the *École des Ponts et Chaussées,* a civil engineering school founded in 1747.

At the corner of the Rue de Lille is the *École des Langues Orientales,* founded by the Convention in 1795. Manet died at No. 5; and the organist Widor (1844-1937) lived at No. 7, the *Hôtel de Falconet* (c. 1650). From the *Hôtel Tessé,* on the corner of the Quai Voltaire, the Marquis de Becqueville attempted to glide with wings across the Seine in 1742.

In the QUAI MALAQUAIS, leading E. to the *Institut,* are some charming 17-18C mansions. Anatole France (1844-1924) was born at No. 19 (the home of George Sand in 1832-36), but until 1853 he lived at No. 15. At No. 17, part of the *Hôtel de Chimay,* built by *Fr. Mansart* c. 1640, and altered in the 18C for the Duchesse de Bouillon (d. 1714), the friend of La Fontaine, lived Henrietta Maria of France (the widow of Charles I of England; 1662). No. 9, at the corner of the Rue Bonaparte, the *Hôtel de Transylvanie,* is a good example of Louis-XIII architecture (1622-28). No. 5 was occupied by Marshal Saxe from 1744 until his death in 1750; and No. 3 was the residence of the naturalist Alexander Humboldt during the Restoration.

6   THE FAUBOURG ST-GERMAIN: WESTERN SECTOR

MÉTROS: *Solferino, Chambre des députés, Invalides, Varenne, Sèvres-Babylone, Rue du Bac.*

From the *Louvre,* the *Pont du Carrousel* crosses the Seine to the QUAI VOLTAIRE (Pl. 13; 6), which continues the *Quai Malaquais* to the W., and was formerly the *Quai des Théatins.* Voltaire died in 1778 at the house of the Marquis de Villette (No. 27); *St-Sulpice* refused to accept his corpse, which was rushed to an abbey near Troyes to save it from a common grave. Louise de Kéroualle, Duchess of Portsmouth, occupied Nos. 3-5 in 1695-1701. Ingres died at No. 11 in 1867. At No. 13 was installed the 'Moniteur Universel', an influential newspaper during the Revolution. Here as a tenant in 1829-36, Delacroix was preceded by Horace Vernet and followed by Corot. At No. 19 Baudelaire lived in 1856-58, working on 'Les Fleurs du Mal', while Wagner completed the libretto of 'Die Meistersinger' there in 1861-62; both Jean Sibelius and Oscar Wilde were later tenants. De Musset lived at No. 25 in 1841-49.

To the W., the QUAI ANATOLE-FRANCE and the QUAI D'ORSAY are the focus of foreign affairs. The *Gare d'Orsay,* built in 1898-1900 on the site of the old Cour des Comptes, is being rebuilt internally to house the *Musée du XIXe Siècle* (to be opened 1981; Pl. 13; 6), devoted to paintings, sculpture, and objets d'art from the period 1850-1905, including the work of the Impressionists at present housed in the *Jeu de Paume.* The main Paris auction rooms are also being moved here. We now reach the *Palais de la Légion d'Honneur, the entrance to which, in the parallel Rue de Lille, is flanked by a colonnade with bas-reliefs by *Roland* on the attic storey. The Corinthian portico in the courtyard is adorned with a frieze of arabesques with the device 'Honneur et Patrie'. Facing the quay is a rotunda with Corinthian columns and symbolic busts, etc.

Built by *Rousseau* in 1782-86 for the Prince de Salm-Kyrbourg, at the Revolution it was raffled and won by a former wig-maker's apprentice who had made a fortune. He was later imprisoned for forgery, and the house became the

Swedish Embassy in 1797. Mme de Staël, the ambassador's wife, gave her famous receptions here under the Directory, but in 1804 it was bought by the government for the grand chancellery of the Legion of Honour. The entrance to the *Musée National de la Légion d'Honneur et des Ordres de Chevalerie* (to give it its full title), exhibiting medals, decorations, etc., relating to the history of the Order, together with foreign heraldic trappings, is to be found at No. 2 Rue de Bellechasse, adjoining (adm. weekdays 14.00-17.00; guided tours on Sat. at 15.00).

At No. 80 Rue de Lille (to the S.) is the *Hôtel de Seignelay* by *Boffrand*, architect also of the adjacent *Hôtel de Beauharnais* (1714), once the home of Queen Hortense, and later the German Embassy (now the ambassador's residence).

A few minutes walk to the W. brings one to the **Palais-Bourbon**, seat of the *Assemblée Nationale*, facing the *Pont de la Concorde* (see p. 87; Pl. 13; 5).

In 1722 a mansion was erected on this site for the Dowager Duchess of Bourbon (legitimized daughter of Louis XIV and the Marquise de Montespan), of which only the inner courtyard and main entrance (at 128 Rue de l'Université) have survived. The Prince de Condé, forced to leave his home because of the construction of the *Théâtre de l'Odéon* (see p. 71), bought the palace from Louis XV and enlarged it from 1764 until the Revolution. He incorporated the *Hôtel de Lassay*, in which he lived after the Revolution. The Palais became national property under the name of Maison de la Révolution, the meeting-place of the Council of Five Hundred, and was later occupied by the Archives (1799-1808). Since 1815 it has been used by the French equivalent to the House of Commons, although in 1946 its name was changed from the Chambre des Députés.

In 1940-44 the *Palais-Bourbon* was the headquarters of the German military administration of the Paris region, and at the time of the Liberation considerable fighting took place in the neighbourhood, causing some damage to the building, and the destruction of over 30,000 vols in the Library.

Adm. Those wishing to visit the interior, or to attend a session of the Assembly, must first apply in writing to the Questor's Office. The main entrance is in the Pl. du Palais-Bourbon.

The N. façade, a neo-Hellenistic piece of imperial bombast designed principally to balance the *Madeleine* when seen from the *Pl. de la Concorde*, is entirely decorative, and consists of a portico, by *Poyet* (1804-07), of twelve Corinthian columns, with statues of statesmen, allegorical bas-reliefs, etc.

The decoration of the interior is likewise of little artistic merit; certain rooms contain historical paintings by *Horace Vernet* and *Ary Scheffer*; and by *Delacroix* (in the SALON DU ROI and LIBRARY); theSALLE DES SÉANCES retains bas-reliefs by *Lemot* (1798).

The GALERIE DES FÊTES (1848) connects the building to the *Hôtel de Lassay* (1724), the official residence of the President of the Assembly.

Further along the QUAI D'ORSAY (with which it is synonymous) stands the *Ministère des Affaires Étrangères* (Foreign Office), built by *Lacornée* in 1845.

Adjacent, on the ESPLANADE DES INVALIDES, is the *Gare des Invalides* and *Aérogare* (or Air Terminus).

For the *Hôtel des Invalides* and *Musée de l'Armée*, see Rte 7.

Turning E. along the Rue de l'Université, we shortly reach the PL. DU PALAIS-BOURBON, an elegant ensemble of Louis-XVI mansions all built to the same pattern after 1776.

At No. 108 Rue de l'Université (but with its entrance at No. 121 in the

Rue de Lille, parallel to the N.) is the *Institut Néerlandais*, with a good collection of Dutch and German paintings. Jacques Turgot (1727-81), the economist, died here; La Fayette lived at No. 123, adjacent, in 1799.

Further E. (on the far side of the Blvd. St-Germain), at No. 51 Rue de l'Université, is a fine 18C mansion by *Lassurance*; No. 24 has a notable façade by *Servandoni* in the courtyard (1700). Franklin's first lodging on his arrival in Paris in 1776 was at the Hôtel de Hambourg in this street. Alphonse Daudet (1840-97) died at No. 41; and from 1885 he had lived in the neighbouring Rue de Bellechasse, which leads S. to regain the BLVD. ST-GERMAIN, flanked to the W., at this point, by the extensive buildings of the *Ministère de la Défense Nationale* (by *Bouchot;* 1867-77), with a clock-tower at the corner of the Rue de Solferino.

Nos. 1, 3, and 5 Rue St-Dominique, running W. from the BLVD. ST-GERMAIN, date from c. 1710; No. 5 was the home of Gustave Doré (1832-83) from 1849 until his death. Nos. 10-12 (now part of the *Ministère de la Défense Nationale*) occupy the former *Couvent des Filles de St-Joseph* (1641), established for orphaned girls, and generously supported by Mme de Montespan, who retired here in 1687 after her fall from royal favour. Mme du Deffand in 1755 likewise supported it, and here in retirement held her literary salons. Nos. 14-16, in the same block of buildings, the *Hôtel de Brienne* (1714 and 1730), was once the home of Lucien Bonaparte, and later of Laetitia Bonaparte. No. 28 was once the *Hôtel Rochefoucauld-d'Estissac* (1710), while further W., the *Hôtel de Sagan* (No. 57) was built by *Brongniart* in 1784 for the Princess of Monaco.

S. of the Rue St-Dominique rises the uninspired Gothic-revival church of *Ste-Clotilde*, built in 1846-56, where for over thirty years César Franck was organist; a commemorative monument, by *Lenoir*, stands opposite.

The Rue de Grenelle, flanked by a number of Embassies and Ministries, may be conveniently approached by following the Rue de Bellechasse S., in which, at No. 41, the *Conseil de la Résistance* and the *Comité Parisien de la Libération* organized operations for the rising of 19 Aug. 1944. Turning l. at their junction, we pass, at No. 106, the *Temple de Panthemont* (by *Constant d'Ivry;* 1747-56), once the chapel of a convent where Joséphine de Beauharnais lived for several years. Its main buildings (now Nos. 37-39 in the Rue de Bellechasse) housed an aristocratic school for girls, where Jefferson's daughter was a pupil during her father's embassy.

No. 102, the *Hôtel de Maillebois*, built early in the 18C by *Deslisle-Mansart*, was the home of the Duc de Saint-Simon from 1738, when he was working on his 'Mémoires', until his death in 1755. Robert Browning and his wife were later tenants. No. 87 is the *Hôtel de Bauffremont* (1721-36), with a curved façade; No. 85, the *Hôtel d'Avaray* (1718; by *Leroux*), where Horace Walpole lived, is now the *Netherlands Embassy*. No. 79, the *Hôtel d'Estrées*, the *Russian Embassy*, was built by *Robert de Cotte* in 1713.

Retracing our steps towards the W., we pass No. 110, the *Hôtel de Courteilles* (1778; now the *Min. de l'Éducation Nationale*); No. 116, the old *Hôtel de Brissac*, rebuilt for Marshal de Villars by *Boffrand* and *Leroux* (1731), and now the *Mairie of the 7th Arrondissement*. No. 101, the former *Hôtel Rothelin* (or *de Charolais*), built by *Lassurance* in 1700, is now the *Min. du Développement Industriel et Scientifique*. Nos.

138 and 140 were built by *Jean Courtonne* in 1724 and decorated by *Lassurance* in 1734 for Mlle de Sens. Marshal Foch died in the former; the latter is occupied by the *Institut Géographique National* (whose maps are available from 107 Rue La Boétie). No. 127, the *Min. du Travail*, was the *Hôtel du Châtelet*, one of the finest examples of the Louis-XV style; it was at one time used as the Archbishop's Palace. The *Hôtel de Chanac*, at No. 142, opposite (by *Delamair;*1750) is now the *Swiss Embassy.*

We turn l. along the BLVD. DES INVALIDES, and back into the Rue de Varenne. At No. 77, at the corner, the *Hôtel Biron* (Pl. 13; 5-7), is installed the *Musée Rodin* (MÉTRO: *Varenne*), open daily except Tues.; 10.00-12.15 and 14.00-17.00. It contains an important and impressive collection of sculpture by *Auguste Rodin* (1840-1917), which he left to the State, many being the originals of works executed in marble or bronze, and a fine selection of drawings.

The *Hôtel Biron*, built in 1728-30 by *Aubert* and *Gabriel*, was occupied by the Duc de Biron in 1753, and in 1820 by the aristocratic convent of the Sacré-Coeur. The State bought the mansion and its extensive gardens in 1901. In 1910 two ground-floor rooms were used as a studio by Rodin, who lived here from 1907 until his death. Much of the painted and gilt panelling, which had been removed by the Philistine superior of the convent as being mere ostentation, has been recovered, and is in the process of being replaced.

Of the many outstanding examples of Rodin's work displayed here, a few only are listed. GRAND SALON: St John the Baptist; 'L'Homme qui marche'; the Kiss; the Hand of God; Iris; and two studies of hands.—In a room to the l.: 'L'Age d'Airain'; busts of Carrier-Belleuse, Mahler, and Puvis de Chavannes. In rooms to the r. of the Grand Salon: the Thinker; Orpheus; Eve; bust of Lady Sackville-West; of Eve Fairfax, the suffragette; Rodin's father, etc.—On the STAIRCASE: Three Shades (from the Gate of Hell).

FIRST FLOOR. Case of models for the Gate of Hell; two busts of Hugo; four nude studies of Balzac; Man with a broken nose; the Good Genius; Eternal Spring; Triton and Nereid on a dolphin; Water-fairy; Young Mother. Also shown are dance studies by *Renoir*, and paintings by *Renoir, Monet,* and *Van Gogh*, including the latter's Le Père Tanguy.

The GARDENS contain numerous bronzes and marbles, including: the Thinker; Hugo at Guernsey, formerly in the gardens of the Palais-Royal; Balzac; and the Gate of Hell; also, near the entrance, and seen from the street, the Burghers of Calais.

An Annexe to the Museum is at *Meudon*, see p. 184.

———

No. 72 in the Rue de Varenne is the *Hôtel de Castries*, sacked by the mob in 1790 after the duel between the reactionary Duc de Castries and the radical Comte Charles de Lameth. No. 69, the *Hôtel de Clermont* by *Leblond* (1708), is now the *Haut Commissariat à l' Energie atomique.*— At 1bis in the Rue Vaneau (r.) André Gide (1869-1951) died.—Just beyond is the *Hôtel de Matignon* (No. 57), built by *Courtonne* about 1721 and altered in the 19C; having served as the Austro-Hungarian Embassy (1888-1914), since 1935 it has been the residence of the *Présidence du Conseil.* One of the most beautiful mansions in the Faubourg, it has an unusually large garden. Talleyrand lived here in 1808-11. No. 50, the handsome *Hôtel de Gallifet*, with an Ionic peristyle built by *Legrand* in 1775-96, is now the *Italian Institute;* their *Embassy* is at No. 47.

We shortly reach the Rue du Bac. See below for the continuation of the route N.

To the S., No. 98, with gilt angels above the door, and good iron balconies, was the *Café des Deux-Anges*, the secret rendezvous of the Chouans (c. 1800), and here Cadoudal hatched the conspiracy of 1804. At No. 108bis died Laplace (1749-1827), the astronomer and mathematician. At No. 110 Whistler (from 1892) was visited by Beardsley and Mallarmé, and got into trouble with his landlord for letting his child-models run naked in the garden. Nos. 118-120, with doors designed by *Toro*, are the *Hôtel de Clermont-Tonnerre*, where Chateaubriand (1768-1848) lived from 1838 until his death. On the third and fourth floors Mrs Mary Anne Clarke and her daughter Mary (later Mme Mohl; 1793-1883) had their salon, and were visited by Dean Stanley, Mrs Gaskell, and Florence Nightingale. No. 128 is the *Séminaire des Missions Étrangères*, founded in 1663, with mementoes and relics of martyred missionaries. Nos. 136-140 are the *Hôtel de la Vallière*, with handsome portals, occupied by the Sœurs de Charité.

To the l. is the *Grands Magasins du Bon Marché*, built on the site of an earlier asylum, the Petites Maisons, to the E. of which is the SQUARE BOUCICAUT (Pl. 13; 8; named after the foundress of the *Bon Marché*).

Slightly to the W. in the Rue de Sèvres (No. 42) is the *Hôpital Laënnec*, formerly a home for incurable women, founded by Card. de la Rochefoucauld c. 1635, which retains its original courtyard and chapel. At No. 95 is the *Église des Lazaristes*, with a silver shrine preserving the body of St Vincent de Paul. Barbey d'Aurevilly (1808-89) lived for thirty years and died at No. 25 in the adjacent Rue Rousselet.

At No. 31 Rue St-Placide, the S. extension of the Rue du Bac, J.-K. Huysmans (1848-1907) died; David d'Angers and Michelet lived in the same street, while Parmentier resided in the parallel Rue de l'Abbé-Grégoire.

No. 40 in the Rue du Cherche-Midi, near the BLVD. RASPAIL, belonged to Rochambeau (1725-1807), who fought for the Americans in the War of Independence, notably at Yorktown. At No. 38, the *Maison des Sciences de l'Homme* has been built on the site of the *Prison Militaire du Cherche-Midi*, where many French patriots were imprisoned between 1940 and 1944.

The Rue du Bac leads N. from the Rue de Varenne, shortly crossing the Rue de Grenelle, where to the r. (Nos. 57 and 59) is the ***Fontaine des Quatre-Saisons**, designed by *Bouchardon* in 1739, with sculptures of the City of Paris with the Seine and Marne at her feet, and with bas-reliefs of the Seasons. Alfred de Musset lived at No. 59 from 1824 to 1840.

Half-l. across the BLVD. ST-GERMAIN, government offices occupy Nos. 244-248, two early-18C houses. No. 246, the *Hôtel de Roquelaure* (1722), by *Lassurance* and *Leroux*, has a fine courtyard. Cambacérès, Second Consul in 1799, lived here in 1808.

Guillaume Apollinaire (1880-1918) lived and died at No. 202 BLVD. ST-GERMAIN; off which, to the r., leads the Rue St-Guillaume, where the 16C *Hôtel de Mesmes* (No. 27), enlarged in 1933, is the Institut National des

Sciences Politiques; No. 16, the *Hôtel de Créqui*, built in 1660-64, and extended in 1772, was for a time the home of Lamartine, and later of Renan.

Crossing the Boulevard, the Rue du Bac leads N. to the Seine, and is named after the ferry operating there before the construction of the Pont Royal.

No. 46 Rue du Bac, the former *Hôtel de Boulogne*, has a fine courtyard; built in 1744 by *Boffrand* for Jacques Bernard, who died after a scandalous bankruptcy in 1753; it was the lodging of Chateaubriand in 1815-18. To the E. is **St-Thomas-d'Aquin**, begun in 1682 by *Pierre Bullet* in the Jesuit style, and completed, with the construction of the façade, in 1787. The ceiling-painting in the Lady Chapel is a characteristic 18C work by *Lemoyne.*

7   THE INVALIDES AND MUSÉE DE L'ARMÉE; ÉCOLE MILITAIRE; EIFFEL TOWER

MÉTROS: *Invalides, Varenne, La Tour-Maubourg, St-François-Xavier, École-Militaire, Cambronne, Bir Hakeim-Grenelle.*

The districts to the W. of the Faubourg St-Germain are overshadowed by the *Dôme* of the *Invalides*, the *Tour Eiffel* to the W., and now by the *Tour Montparnasse* to the S. (see p. 65).

From the Right Bank, the best approach is by the *Pont Alexandre-III*, which affords an impressive vista of the *Invalides* at the end of its esplanade. This walk can be conveniently combined with a return viâ the Palais de Chaillot.

The ESPLANADE DES INVALIDES, 490 by 270 yds, was laid out in 1704-20 by *Robert de Cotte*, and planted with trees along the sides. At its N.E. corner is the *Aérogare* (see p. 31).

To the W., the QUAI D'ORSAY extends as far as the *Pont de l'Alma.* At No. 63 on the Quai is the *American Church*, built in the Gothic style in 1927-31; the playwright Jean Giraudoux (1882-1944) died at No. 89. At No. 7 Rue Edmond-Valentin, a short distance S.W., off the Av. Bosquet, lived James Joyce from 1935 to 1939.

From the PL. DES INVALIDES, S. of the Esplanade, the Av. de la Motte-Picquet leads S.W. past the front of the *École Militaire* (see below); the Blvd. des Invalides skirts the E. side of the *Hôtel des Invalides,* the formal façade of which contrasts with the domestic architecture opposite. To the l. diverges the Rue de Grenelle and the Rue de Varenne (see Rte 6), and near the corner of the latter is the *Musée Rodin* (p. 79).

The ****Hôtel des Invalides** (Pl. 12; 6-8; headquarters of the military governor of Paris) was founded by Louis XIV in 1671 as a home for disabled soldiers, the first enduring institution of its kind; at one time it housed 4,000 pensioners. At present about 70 wounded live there. The buildings, which form a majestic ensemble, were erected from the designs of *Libéral Bruant* (d. 1697), and *J. Hardouin-Mansart* continued the work. It was restored under Napoleon I, who was later buried beneath its Dôme. Part of the building now houses the *Musée de l'Armée* (see below), one of outstanding interest and importance.

Tickets, which cover both the museum and entry to Napoleon's Tomb, may be used on two *consecutive* days. The courtyards of the Invalides, and the Dôme, with Napoleon's Tomb (main entrance in the Pl. Vauban) are open daily, *including* Tuesdays, 7.00-19.00.

Facing the Esplanade is a row of eighteen pieces of captured artillery, of which the eight on gun-carriages form the *Batterie Triomphale* (removed by the Germans in 1940). On either side of each half-battery are twenty unmounted pieces.

From the entrance gate we approach the dignified façade, 230 yds long. The dormer windows take the form of trophies, each different. Flanking the main entrance are recent copies of the original statues of Mars and Minerva, by *Guillaume Coustou* (1735). The equestrian bas-reliefs above the central door, of Louis XIV accompanied by Justice and Prudence, by *Pierre Cartellier,* replaced (in 1815) an earlier design by Coustou.

Opposite the entrance to the *COUR D'HONNEUR (111 by 68 yds) is the door of the church of St-Louis, above which are *Seurre*'s original bronze statue of Napoleon, formerly surmounting the *Vendôme Column* (see p. 123), and an astronomical clock (1781). On the E. side of the courtyard is the main entrance to the *Musée de l'Armée.* At the foot of the staircase to the r. of the entrance to the church, is one of the Renault cars (the Marne taxis), which, commandeered by Gen. Gallieni, carried troops to the Front in Sept. 1914.

The ***Church of St-Louis** (the chapel of the *Invalides*) was built by *Bruant* and *Mansart.* The plain but imposing interior, decorated with captured ensigns, has a gallery built at the same level as that of the dormitories of the disabled. In 1837 it resounded to the first performance of Berlioz's 'Grande Messe des Morts', the orchestra being reinforced by a battery of artillery on the esplanade. Concerts still take place here. Behind the high-altar a sheet of plain glass separates the chapel from the *Dôme des Invalides.*

In vaults below (no adm.) are the graves of many French marshals (and generals), among them Jourdan, Bertrand, Grouchy, and Oudinot, and, more recently, Leclerc (de Hautecloque; d. 1947).

On leaving the chapel, we turn l. along the Corridor de Nîmes to reach the entrance of the *Dôme.* Visitors approaching from the Pl. Vauban, to the S., will find the ticket-office just W. of its main entrance (Pl. 14;8).

The ***Dôme des Invalides,** begun by *J. Hardouin-Mansart* in 1675, and finished in 1706, was added to the church of St-Louis as a chapel royal. In the niches on either side of the entrance are statues of Charlemagne and St Louis by *Coysevox* and *Nic. Coustou.* The ribbed dome is roofed with lead, adorned with gilded trophies, and crowned with a flèche 345 ft above the ground.

The admirably proportioned interior, 184 ft square, is in the form of a Greek cross.

But the focus of attention is the **Tomb of Napoleon,** 13 by 6½ ft, and 15 ft high, of dark red porphyry from Finland, resting on a pedestal of green Vosges granite.

It is surrounded by a gallery with ten bas-reliefs *after Simart* representing the benefits conferred on France by the emperor, and facing the sarcophagus are twelve figures by *Pradier* symbolizing his great victories, between which are six trophies of 54 flags taken at Austerlitz. The statue of Napoleon in his coronation robes is also by *Simart.*

The error of placing the tomb in an inappropriately inferior position as seen from the circular gallery, is now generally recognized. An imposing view is gained by descending to the CRYPT, the inscription on the impost of the entrance to which may be translated: "I desire that my ashes rest on the banks of the Seine, in the midst of the French people whom I have loved so dearly".

On re-ascending, we may visit the surrounding chapels. In that at the S.E. corner (ST-AUGUSTIN) is the tomb of Joseph Bonaparte (d. 1844). Walking in an anti-clockwise direction, we pass that of Vauban (d. 1707). In the CHAP. ST-AMBROISE is the bronze tomb of Marshal Foch (d. 1929), by *Landowski;* in that of ST-GRÉGOIRE, that of Marshal Lyautey (d. 1934), by *Albert Laprade* (1963), and also the heart of La Tour d'Auvergne (d. 1800; 'the first grenadier of the Republic'). We next pass the tomb of Turenne (d. 1675): the CHAP. ST-JÉRÔME stands anticipatively empty. In an adjacent chapel is the sarcophagus of the Roi de Rome (1811-32), Bonaparte's only son, who died prematurely of phthisis. Originally buried in Vienna, his remains were brought here by the Germans in 1940, on the hundredth anniversary of the burial of his father in the crypt.

The **Musée de l'Armée** comprises one of the world's most interesting, extensive, and well-displayed collections of arms and armour, weapons, uniforms, military souvenirs, etc., and without an excessive display of chauvinism. The building also houses a library, and a small cinema.

Unlike most other museums, it is open every day, including Tues., except 1 Jan., 1 May, 1 Nov., and 25 Dec.; 1 Oct.-31 March, 10.00-17.00; 1 April-30 Sept., 10.00-18.00.

From the main entrance (E. side of the *Cour d'Honneur*), the SALLE VAUBAN (l.) with cavalry uniforms and equipment, and the SALLE TURENNE (r.), with colours of French regiments from the First Republic to the present, may be visited. The original frescoes are by *van der Meulen.* The maquette of the Invalides (made prior to 1757) is also of interest, while an English colour taken at Bergen-op-Zoom in 1795 may also be seen among the captured trophies.

From the Vestibule, stairs ascend to the SECOND FLOOR. To the r. is the entrance to a series of rooms (opened in 1972) devoted to the military exploits of the Ancienne Monarchie (1618-1792), set out in chronological order. It should be emphasized that most figures are displayed in such a way that the visitor may see them 'in the round': this applies likewise to the suits of armour to be seen in the W. wings. Among the numerous plans, engravings, prints, and portraits, those individual objects which may be pointed out are the cannon-ball that killed Turenne (1694), and the perforated back plate of his cuirass, his marshal's baton, and his portrait attr. to *Le Brun.* Note also the colours of the Irish Clancarty regiment (1642).

Another room contains souvenirs of Gen. La Fayette (1757-1834). We next enter recently opened compartments concentrating on the Revolutionary, Directory, and Consulate periods, with many Napoleonic souvenirs, including one of Bonaparte's grey coats; his tent and furniture; and the stuffed skin of his white horse, 'Vizier', which outlived the emperor by eight years. Among portraits of his marshals, that of Ney, by *Gérard,* is notable. A further series of cabinets devoted to Napoleon at St Helena, and the period 1830-52, bring us back to the stairs.

On the floor above are attic rooms in which is housed the autonomous **Musée des Plans-Reliefs,** an important collection (founded by Louvois) of models, maquettes, maps, and plans which, regrettably, are not displayed as well as they deserve. Among those illustrating the construction of fortresses since the time of Vauban, which are of considerable historical and topographical interest, are such strongholds as *Strasbourg, Neuf-Brisach* (nr. Mulhouse), *Grenoble, Briançon, Bayonne, Perpignan, Mont Saint-Michel, Saint-Martin* (l'Île de Ré), *Antibes,* and (even) *St-Tropez:* all to the scale 1:600.

On the W. side of the *Cour d'Honneur* are the ****Collections of Arms and Armour,** extraordinarily rich in weapons of all periods, many exhibits being of great artistic interest, and masterpieces of damascening and chasing. To the r., the SALLE FRANÇOIS I, retaining the original frescoes (restored) of the dining-rooms and a painting of the Founding of the Invalides by *Pierre Dulin,* contains suits of armour (including parade armour) and the horse armour of François I, his sword, and plaques from his tomb. Note the heavy armour of the Elector Palatine Otto Henry.

To the l. of the entrance to this wing is the SALLE HENRI IV, with frescoes by 'Martin des Batailles', concentrating on jousting armour. Note the diminutive 'sample' suits made by the armourer to obtain orders for complete suits.—From the Vestibule we may enter, straight ahead, galleries containing the important **Collection Pauilhac.** Among the numerous medieval and Renaissance pieces are suits belonging to Louis XIII, Henri III, Henri IV, and Louis XIV. The extensive ***Collection of Firearms,** showing the evolution of such weapons, is outstanding.

A small room near the entrance, containing arms *before the 9C,* may also be visited on request.

On the SECOND FLOOR are a series of rooms devoted to the 1914-18 War, with uniforms, and other souvenirs of the armed forces of France *and* her Allies. Two 'animated' maps describe graphically the movements of troops, with an accompanying verbal explanation (in French).—To the r., other rooms describe aspects of the 1939-45 War. The two main sections concern *Occupied France* and *France Liberated:* others cover the sad history of deportations; and the *Normandy Landings.*

Other rooms are in the course of rearrangement, and the completion of this considerable work will be eagerly awaited. An important descriptive volume, profusely illustrated, 'Les Invalides: trois siècles d'histoire', available at the entrance, will interest not only the military historian.

From the PL. VAUBAN (Pl. 12; 8), to the S. of the *Hôtel des Invalides,* the Av. de Tourville leads W. towards the *École Militaire,* and the Av. de Villars leads S.E., shortly meeting the S. section of the BLVD. DES INVALIDES (by the church of *St-François-Xavier;* 1875), which continues as far as the Rue de Sèvres, beyond which it is extended by the BLVD. DE MONTPARNASSE. At this junction are the buildings of the *Institut National des Jeunes Aveugles,* founded in 1793 by Valentin Haüy. Vincent d'Indy (1851-1931) lived for 70 years and died at No. 7 Av. de Villars.

S. of the Rue de Sèvres are the *Hôpital des Enfants-Malades* (founded 1724) and *Hôpital Necker,* once a Benedictine nunnery, founded in 1779 by Louis XVI, directed at one time by Mme Necker, and rebuilt in 1840.

Also radiating from the PL. VAUBAN are the wide tree-lined Av. de Breteuil, its S. end providing a good view of the *Invalides;* and to the S.W., the Av. de Ségur passing (r.) the *Min. des Postes et Télécommunications,* and behind the controversial buildings of the UNESCO headquarters, perhaps best approached by the Av. de Lowendal.

The **UNESCO Buildings** (by *Breuer, Zehrfuss,* and *Nervi;* 1958), flanking the semicircular Pl. de Fontenoy, consist in fact of three buildings: one for the permanent delegation; a *Conference Building,* with its accordion-pleated concrete roof covered in copper, and containing murals by *Picasso* and *Rufino Tamayo;* and the dominating Y-shaped *Secretariat* of seven floors supported by 72 pylons. In the *Piazza* are 'decorative works' by *Henry Moore, Alexander Calder, Jean Arp,* and *Miro,* et al., and a Japanese Garden has been designed by *Noguchi.*

To the N. lies the **École Militaire* (Pl. 12; 7-8), a handsome structure covering 29 acres of the former 'ferme' and 'château' of Grenelle, built by *J.-A. Gabriel,* and enlarged in 1856.

The school was founded in 1751 by Louis XV, influenced by Mme de Pompadour, for the training of noblemen as army officers. It was opened in 1756 and completed in 1770. In 1777 its rigid rules for entry were modified so that it could take in the élite of provincial military academies; thus in 1784 Bonaparte (who was confirmed in the chapel during his training) was chosen from the Collège de Brienne. It was closed in 1787 and used as a depot and barracks. It is now occupied by the *École Supérieure de Guerre,* or staff college.

18C railings separate the *Cour d'Honneur* from the PL. DE FONTENOY, which has lost its 18C character. On the entablature of the entrance façade, the figure representing Victory is in fact Louis XV, and is probably the only likeness that escaped the Revolution.

On written application to the Commandant, 1 Pl. Joffre, a guided tour of the interior can be arranged. The most impressive room is the SALON DES MARÉCHAUX, with its fine woodwork. The CHAPEL is open to the public daily.

Between the *École Militaire* and the Seine lies the **Champ-de-Mars,** c. 1000 yds in length, laid out in 1765-67 as a parade ground on the old Plaine de Grenelle, with its market-gardens; it was used as a racecourse after the Restoration, and made into a park after 1913.

The ground was the scene of several early aeronautical experiments by the Montgolfiers, by Charles and Robert, and by Blanchard (1783-84). Numerous revolutionary festivals were held here, the most famous of which was the Fête de la Fédération on 14 July 1790, when the king, the Assembly, and the delegates from the provinces, and the army, took the oath at the Autel de la Patrie to observe the new Constitution; the 'Champ de Mai', held by Napoleon on his return from Elba; and many international exhibitions.
Bailly, president of the Constituent Assembly, was brutally executed here in 1793; and Capt. Alfred Dreyfus was publicly degraded here in Dec. 1894.

The **Eiffel Tower** (Pl. 12; 5), with its base at the river end of the Champ-de-Mars, still one of the tallest 'buildings' in the world (984 ft high, and just over 1,040 ft including the television installation), continues to dominate this quarter of Paris, although the equally obtrusive *Tour Montparnasse* threatens to divide one's attention. Built in 1889, the *Tour Eiffel* was originally granted only 20 years of life, but its use in radio-telegraphy in 1904 saved it from the demolition it deserved.

Constructed by the engineer *Gustave Eiffel* (1832-1923), it weighs over 7,000 tons, and is composed of 12,000 pieces of metal, fastened by 2,500,000 rivets, while its four feet are supported by masonry piers sunk 30-45 ft in the ground. The first and second platforms contain restaurants, the third (at 902 ft) sports a bar, all reached by the lift.

The ascent is not recommended in misty, windy, or cold weather, but

on a clear day, particularly about one hour before sunset, the extensive
*Views are remarkable.

Hence the *Pont d'Iéna* (see p. 171) crosses the Seine to the *Palais de Chaillot,* see
p. 171.

———————

The Champ-de-Mars is bounded on the S.W. by the Av. de Suffren.
Further S.W. is the BLVD. DE GRENELLE, leading from the *Pont de Bir-
Hakeim* to the PL. CAMBRONNE. (It was Gen. Cambronne who made the
famous and defiant expletive "Merde!" when the Imperial Guard was
summoned to surrender at Waterloo.) Hence the Rue Frémicourt and its
extension the Av. Émile-Zola lead due W. to the *Pont Mirabeau* (1895-
97), crossing the Seine to Auteuil. To the r. new blocks of buildings flank
the river. To the S. (in the Rue de la Convention) in this not very
interesting 15th Arrondissement, are the buildings of the *Imprimerie
Nationale,* founded in 1640, and moved here in 1925 from the *Hôtel de
Rohan.*

Beyond, to the S.W. is a Citroën factory, and on the far side of the BLVD.
PÉRIPHÉRIQUE (*Porte de Sèvres*) is the *Héliport de Paris,* while adjacent, to the
E., are various buildings of the *Armée de l'Air* and other Service departments.

III THE NORTH OR RIGHT BANK:
LA RIVE DROITE

8 FROM THE PL. DE LA CONCORDE TO
THE PL. DU LOUVRE

MÉTROS: *Concorde, Tuileries, Palais-Royal, Louvre.*

The *Pl. de la Concorde* (Pl. 13; 3), occupying a central position by the Seine, and midway between the *Étoile* and the *Île de la Cité*, is one of the world's most impressive squares. Although its perspectives were evidently a design of the First Empire, the present appearance of the square dates from 1852, when the surrounding ditch was filled in.

The site, then a vacant space to the W. of the main built-up area of the city (but within the enceinte of the Fermiers-Généraux raised some thirty years later), was chosen in 1757 to receive a bronze statue of Louis XV commissioned by the 'échevins' (or magistrates, see p. 134), and unveiled in 1763. The surrounding square was named after the king, but already in 1770 panic during a firework display celebrating the marriage of the dauphin Louis and Marie-Antoinette had provided its first holocaust (133 dead).

In 1792 the statue was replaced by a huge figure of Liberty (the object of Mme Roland's famous apostrophe: "O liberté, que de crimes on commet en ton nom!"), and the square was called Pl. de la Révolution. In the same year a guillotine was erected here for the appropriate execution of the robbers of the crown jewels (comp. below).

Louis XVI was guillotined on 21 Jan. 1793, on the site now occupied by the fountain nearest the river, and between May 1793 and May 1795 the knife claimed among its numerous victims Charlotte Corday (17 July 1793), Marie-Antoinette (16 Oct.), the Girondins (31 Oct.), Philippe-Égalité (6 Nov.), Mme Roland (10 Nov.), Hébert (24 Mar. 1794), Danton (5 Apr.), Mme Élisabeth (9 May), and Robespierre (28 July). The square first received its present name in 1795 at the end of the Reign of Terror.

On the N. side of the square are two handsome mansions designed by *Gabriel* in 1763-72 (with pediment sculptures by *M.-A. Slodtz* and *G. Coustou* the younger) and originally intended as official residences. That to the r., from which the crown jewels were stolen in 1792, has been since 1789 the *Ministère de la Marine;* that to the l. is shared between the *Automobile Club* and the *Hôtel Crillon.* Between these buildings passes the Rue Royale, at the end of which appears the *Madeleine* (see p. 149), while in the opposite direction the southern perspective is designedly completed by the assertive classical façade of the *Palais-Bourbon,* see p. 77.

To the W. of the *Pl. de la Concorde,* the *Av. des Champs-Élysées* (see Rte 16A) rises gently towards the *Arc de Triomphe,* the vista framed by the *Marly Horses,* two groups by *G. Coustou*—"ces marbres hennissants" as Hugo called them—which were brought from the Château de Marly in 1794 and now form pendants to the winged horses at the W. entrances of the *Tuileries.*

In the opposite direction the view extends to the Louvre. On the S. side of the Place, the *Pont de la Concorde,* offering fine perspectives, was built by *Perronet* in 1788-90. Stone from the Bastille was used in the construction of the upper part; one reason for this is said to be that the Parisians would be able to tread under foot the symbol of royal despotism. It was widened in 1931-32.

In the centre of the Place rises the **Obelisk of Luxor,** a monolith of pink syenite, 75 ft high and 250 tons in weight. It originally stood before a temple at Thebes in Upper Egypt, and commemorates in its hieroglyphics the deeds of Rameses II (13C B.C.).

The obelisk was presented to Louis-Philippe in 1831 by Mohammed Ali (the donor of Cleopatra's Needle in London). The pedestal, of Breton granite, bears representations of the apparatus used in its erection (see also p. 172). The two fountains, by *Hittorf,* copies of those in the piazza of St Peter's at Rome, are embellished with figures emblematic of Inland (N.) and Marine Navigation.

The eight stone pavilions round the Square, built by *Gabriel* in the 18C, support statues personifying the great provincial capitals. Strasbourg (as capital of Alsace, lost to France in 1871) was hung with crape and wreaths until 1918. *Pradier*'s model for Strasbourg was Juliette Drouet.

Near the statue of Lille is the entrance to the **Sewers** (*Égouts*) of Paris, a formidable system laid out by the engineer *Belgrand,* which may be visited at 14.00, 15.00, 16.00, and 17.00 every Thurs., July-mid-Oct.; 2nd and 4th Thurs. in May-June; and last Sat. in the months May-Sept.; closed when raining. The tour is not so hazardous as that experienced by Jean Valjean in 'Les Misérables'. The total combined length of the sewers of Paris has been estimated at 2,100 km.

The **Jardin des Tuileries,** a formal garden of 63 acres adorned with a wealth of statues, extends eastwards to the *Pl. du Carrousel,* and is crossed by the Av. du Gén.-Lemonnier. The W. section was the private garden of the Tuileries, and has been little altered since it was laid out anew by *'Le Nôtre* in 1664. The earlier gardens, in the Italian style, had been designed by his grandfather. It became the favourite promenade of the fashionable nobility until superseded by the Palais-Royal just before the Revolution.

The gateway opening from the *Pl. de la Concorde* has pillars crowned by equestrian statues of Fame and Mercury, by *Coysevox* (brought from Marly in 1719). A tablet on the r. commemorates the ascent of the first gas-balloon from Paris in Dec. 1783. The large octagonal pond is surrounded by statuary of the 17-18C by *N.* and *G. Coustou* and *Van Cleve;* on the steps to the S. is 'Hommage à Cézanne' by *Maillol;* to the N., a copy of Coysevox's bust of Le Nôtre (original in *St-Roch*).

Terraces extend along both sides of the gardens. On the S., overlooking the QUAI DES TUILERIES (from which the *Pont Solferino* crosses to the *Quai Anatole-France*), is the *Terrasse du Bord-de-l'Eau.* Beneath this, a passage led from the palace cellars to the *Pl. de la Concorde,* providing Louis-Philippe with an escape route in 1848. At the W. end of the terrace is the *Orangerie* (1853), see below.

On the N. side, the *Terrasse des Feuillants,* skirting the Rue de Rivoli, is named after a Benedictine monastery which in 1791 was the meeting-place of the 'Club des Feuillants' (moderate republicans, among whom were Lavoisier and André Chénier).

Below the E. side of the terrace are fragments of the *Palais des Tuileries, not* in situ. Further E., nearly opposite the Rue de Castiglione, was the site of the *Manège,* the riding-school of the palace, where the National Assembly met from 1789 to 1793, and where Louis XVI was condemned to death.

Here, the ****Musée du Jeu-de-Paume,** or '*de l'Impressionnisme*' (Pl. 13;3; MÉTRO: *Concorde*), is accommodated in a real tennis-court built in 1861. On the terrace on its S. side is a monument to Charles Perrault

(1628-1703), the writer of fairy tales, at whose suggestion the gardens were thrown open to the public by Colbert.

The Museum, which it is planned to move to the new *Musée du XIXe Siècle* (see p. 76), entered at the W. end of the building, contains the admirably arranged national collection of paintings by the Impressionist School, and several rooms are named after the donators of bequests to the collection, a well-illustrated but expensive Catalogue of which is available from the bookstall. From the Vestibule, displaying panels by *Toulouse-Lautrec*, we enter **R 1** (to the r., but unnumbered; SALLE DEGAS), containing: *Degas* (1834-1917), Self-portrait and other early portraits including H.-R. de Gas, his grandfather (painted on his visit to Italy in 1857), and of the Bellelli family; 'Danseuse sur la Scène'; Orchestra (with portraits of the musicians); A young woman; The absinthe drinker; The pedicure; Horse-racing scenes (and bronzes of horses).

R 2 (SALLE CAMONDO). *Degas,* studies of dancers, including 'Répétition', and bronzes; 'Les repasseuses'; 'Le tub'; and other bath scenes.

R 3 (SALLE FANTIN-LATOUR). Four large portrait groups, of historical interest, by *Fantin-Latour* (1836-1904), including Hommage to Delacroix (with portraits of Baudelaire, Manet, and Whistler), The corner of the table, and Studio in the Batignolles; Portrait of Renoir by *F. Bazille* (1841-70), and Portrait of Monet, by *Renoir* (1841-1919). Near the stairs, illustrations of Impressionist techniques, etc.

R 4 (SALLE EDUARDO MOLLARD). Landscapes by *Camille Pissarro* (1830-1903), *Boudin* (1824-98), *Corot* (1796-1875), *Jongkind* (1819-91), *Lépine* (1836-92), and *Sisley* (1839-99).—There are more landscapes in **R 5** (SALLE BAZILLE), including *Sisley's* Snow at Louveciennes; Portrait of Bazille, by *Renoir;* La Charrette (a snow scene), and Women in a garden, by *Monet* (1840-1926); and Family Reunion, and The pink dress, by *Bazille.*

R 6 (SALLE MANET). Works by *Manet* (1832-83), including 'Déjeuner sur l'herbe', which caused much scandal in 1863, as did 'Olympia', which met with the usual shower of abuse at the Salon of 1865. Portraits of Zola and Mallarmé; The balcony (portrait of Berthe Morisot); The fifeplayer; Mme Manet on a blue couch; 'Angelina'; 'Lola de Valence'; 'La serveuse de bocks'. Also The cradle, *Berthe Morisot* (1841-95); Box at the theatre, *Eva Gonzalès* (1849-83).

R 7 (SALLE MOREAU-NÉLATON). *Manet,* Lady with a fan (Berthe Morisot); Still-lifes, and flower paintings; 'La Blonde aux seins nus'; and 'Déjeuner sur l'herbe' by *Monet.*

R 8 (SECOND SALLE MOREAU-NÉLATON). Mainly landscapes by *Pissarro* and *Sisley,* including the latter's The Saint-Martin canal; and 'Les coquelicots' (poppies) and 'Le repos sous les lilas', by *Monet.*

R 9 (SALLE ARGENTEUIL: M. ET R. KAGANOVITCH). *Monet,* The church at Vetheuil; The hospital of St-Paul at St-Rémy, *van Gogh* (1853-90); Breton peasants, *Gauguin* (1848-1903); Auvers, *Cézanne;* landscapes by *Sisley, Seurat,* and *Pissarro.*

At the foot of the stairs: *G. Caillebotte* (1848-94), The floor. Ascending, we pass a Judgement of Paris (original plaster), by *Renoir.*

Turning r., we enter **R 10** (SALLE MONET), with five studies of Rouen Cathedral; The Gare St-Lazare; and landscapes by *Monet;* also further examples of the art of *Sisley* and *Pissarro* (Red roofs).

R 11 (SALLE CAILLEBOTTE). *Monet,* Two studies of water-lilies; The Houses of Parliament; Turkeys; 'Le déjeuner'; *Renoir,* various voluptuous nudes, and portraits of Mme Georges Charpentier, Mme Alphonse Daudet, and Richard Wagner, among others; also 'Le moulin de la Galette'; The swing; and The path through long grass. Some studies by *Toulouse-Lautrec* (1864-1901) are provisionally displayed in the centre of the room.

R 12 (SALLE PERSONNAZ). *Degas,* 'La repasseuse'; *Toulouse-Lautrec,* 'Le lit'; Woman dressing her hair; *Mary Cassatt* (1845-1927), Woman sewing; *Monet,* The bridge at Argenteuil; landscapes by *Pissarro* (The vegetable garden), and *Guillaumin* (1841-1927).

We return to **R 13** (at the head of the stair), displaying *Cézanne* (1839-1906), Still-lifes; Self-portrait (c. 1880); 'La douleur'; Card-players; 'L'Estaque'; Poplars; Dr Gachet's house at Auvers; 'La femme à la cafétière'; Dahlias in a Delft vase (and the original vase).

R 14 (SALLE GACHET). *Pissarro,* Route de Louveciennes; *Sisley,* Canal Saint-Martin; *Guillaumin,* Self-portrait; *van Gogh,* Cottages at Cordeville, Portrait of Dr Gachet, Auvers church, and Self-portrait.

R 15 (SALLE GAUGUIN). *Gauguin,* The Seine, 'La belle Angèle', 'Les Alyscamps', The white horse, Vaîrumati, Breton scenes, Haystacks, Arearea, Tahitian women, and others. Carvings by Gauguin and other souvenirs from Tahiti are displayed in the centre case. Also *van Gogh,* Restaurant de la Sirène, His bedroom at Arles, 'La Guinguette', 'L'Arlésienne'; *Odilon Redon* (1840-1916), Portrait of his wife; *Rousseau, 'le douanier'* (1844-1910), Snake-charmer, War, and Portrait of a woman; *Seurat* (1859-91), Nude studies; and *Signac* (1863-1935), The river bank.

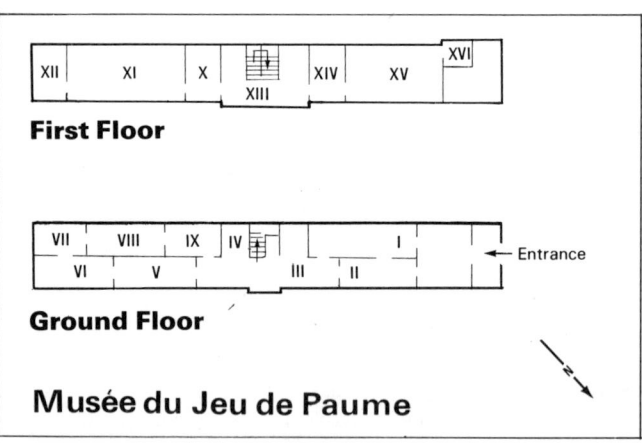

First Floor

Ground Floor

Musée du Jeu de Paume

In the **Orangerie,** 3 min. walk to the S. across the Tuileries gardens, are displayed *Monet's* series of mural paintings, 'Les Nymphéas' (see also *Musée Marmottan,* p. 174). Temporary exhibitions are frequently held in the remaining rooms of this building.

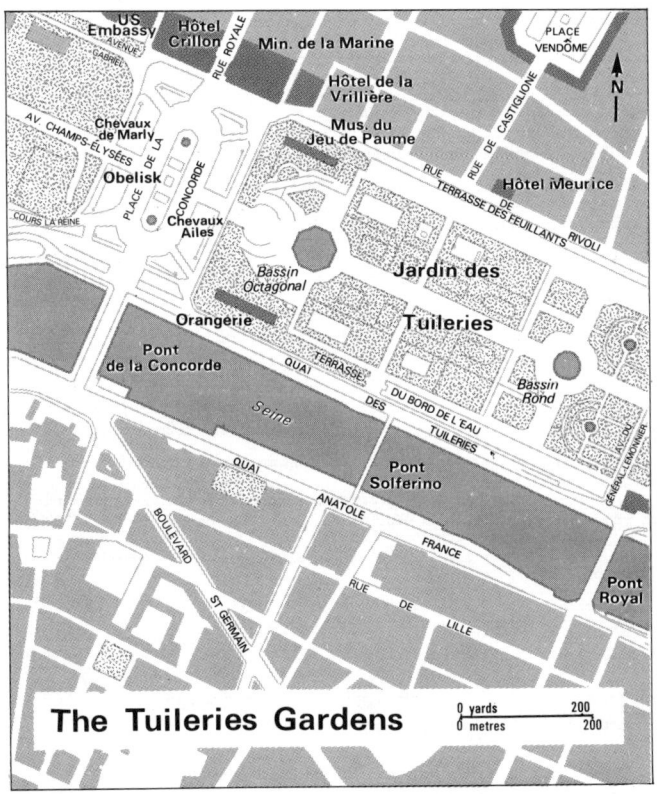

The Tuileries Gardens

The central avenue of the **Jardin des Tuileries,** of chestnuts and plane trees, leads to the Round Pond, between which and the Av. du Gén.-Lemonnier survive the railings put up by Louis-Philippe to isolate the 'private garden'. *Galignani*'s 'New Paris Guide' (1841 ed.) stated that "Great care is taken in keeping the garden clean; persons in working habits or carrying any parcels, except books, are not allowed to enter it"! Among the flower-beds are groups of sculpture, notably by *G.* and *N. Coustou, Coysevox,* and *Le Pautre.*

The main W. wing of the famous *Palais des Tuileries,* which used to flank the E. side of the Av. du Gén.-Lemonnier, no longer exists, except for the *Pavillons de Flore* and *de Marsan* (to the S. and N. respectively), both of which have been restored or rebuilt, and which now form the W. extremities of the wings of the Louvre. The *Pavillon de Marsan* accommodates the *Musée des Arts Décoratifs* (see below).

The palace was begun in 1564 by *Philibert Delorme* (c. 1515-70) for Catherine de Médicis, who left the *Hôtel des Tournelles* after Henri II's lingering death. The site beyond the city walls was known as the 'Sablonnière' and occupied by tile-kilns (tuileries). Delorme was succeeded by *Jean Bullant* and then, in 1595, by *Jacques du Cerceau*, who built the *Pavillon de Flore*. The *Pavillon de Marsan* was built in 1660-65 by *Louis Le Vau* and his son-in-law *François d'Orbay*. Louis XVI was confined here after being brought from Versailles (except during his ineffectual attempt to escape in 1791) until the riot of 10 Aug. 1792, when his Swiss Guards were massacred. In 1793-96 it was the headquarters of the Convention. Pius VII was lodged in the *Pavillon de Flore* for four months in 1804-05. The Tuileries became the permanent residence of Napoleon I, Louis XVIII (who died here), Charles X, Louis-Philippe, and Napoleon III. In May 1871, the Communards set fire to the building, which, like the Hôtel de Ville, was completely gutted. Its charred remains stood until 1884, and the site was converted into a garden in 1889, which is now embellished by nineteen heavy female statues in bronze, by *Aristide Maillol* (1861-1944).

The **Arc de Triomphe du Carrousel,** a reduced copy of the Arch of Septimius Severus at Rome (48 ft high instead of 75 ft), was begun in 1806 from the designs of *Fontaine* and *Percier* to commemorate the victories of Napoleon I in 1805. It constituted then the main entrance to the courtyard of the Tuileries from the Cour du Carrousel.

On the top are figures of Soldiers of the Empire and a bronze chariot-group by *Bosio* (1828) representing the Restoration of the Bourbons. The original group incorporated the antique horses looted from St Mark's, Venice, and replaced there in 1815. The four sides are decorated with marble bas-reliefs: the Battle of Austerlitz; the Capitulation of Ulm; the Meeting between Napoleon and Alexander at Tilsit; the Entry into Munich; the Entry into Vienna; and the Peace of Pressburg.

The PL. DU CARROUSEL, lying to the E. of the Arch, was until the middle of the 19C a small square amidst a labyrinth of narrow streets, which for centuries had remained almost encircled by the royal palaces. It derives its name from an equestrian fête given here in 1662 by Louis XIV. The archways to the N. lead to the Rue de Rivoli and beyond to the S. end of the Av. de l'Opéra; those on the S. give onto the QUAI DES TUILERIES opposite the *Pont du Carrousel* (see below).

To the E. lies the *Square du Carrousel;* westwards the Square commands an impressive view towards the *Arc de Triomphe* (see Rte 16 A).

The ****Palais du Louvre** (Pl. 14; 3), surrounding three sides of the square, and occupying 40 acres between the Rue de Rivoli and the Seine, is the most important public building in Paris, and one of the most magnificent of the world's great palaces. The history of its construction, which extended over three centuries, is of considerable interest. The **interior** is described with its contents; see Rte 9.

History. The name is derived either from an early wolf-hunter's rendezvous known as 'Lupara' or 'Louverie', or from a 'Louver', a blockhouse. It first appears in history as one of Philippe Auguste's fortresses (1190-1202), fragments of which survive in the basement store-rooms (perhaps from the time of Dagobert I, 628-38). Charles V made it an official residence, and surrounded it by a moat. The W. and S. sides were rebuilt under François I (1515-47) and extended by his successor Henri II. Catherine de Médicis, Henri II's widow, began the LONG GALLERY

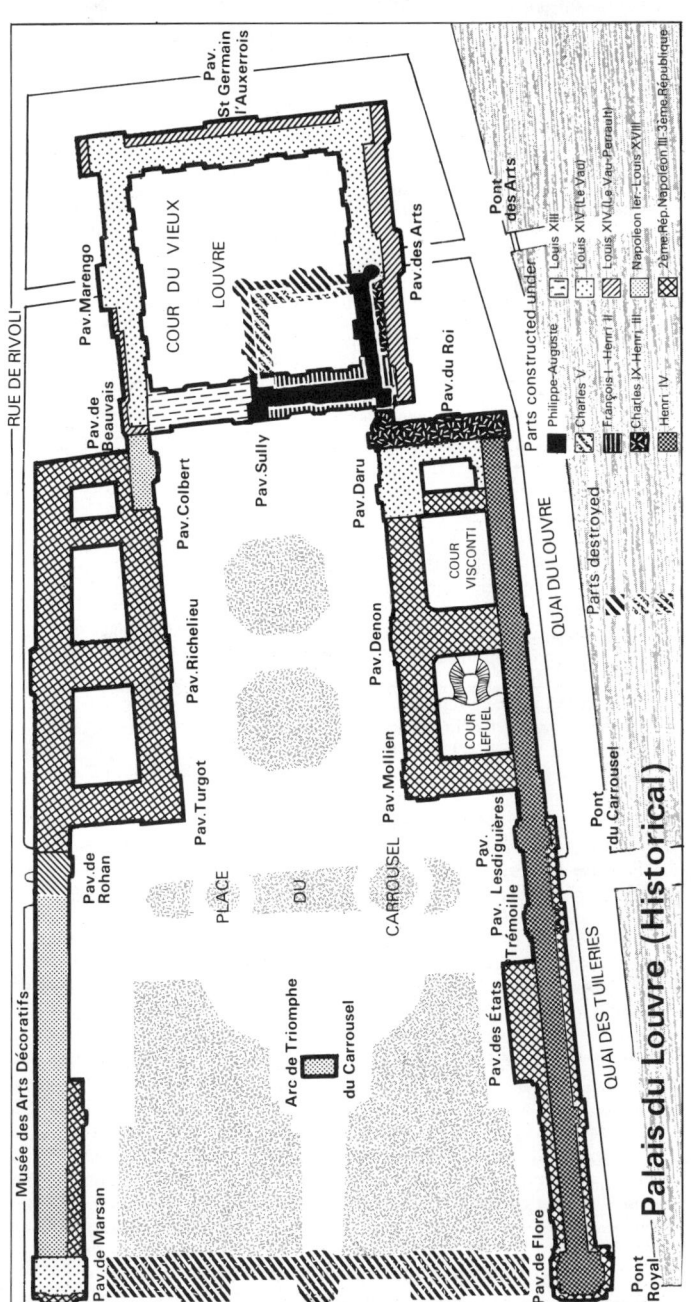

Palais du Louvre (Historical)

RUE DE RIVOLI

Musée des Arts Décoratifs

Pav. de Marsan
Pav. de Rohan
Pav. Turgot
Pav. Richelieu
Pav. Colbert
Pav. de Beauvais
Pav. Marengo

St Germain l'Auxerrois
Pav. St Germain l'Auxerrois

COUR DU VIEUX LOUVRE

Pav. Sully
Pav. des Arts

Pont des Arts

PLACE DU CARROUSEL

Arc de Triomphe du Carrousel

Pav. Denon
Pav. Mollien
Pav. Daru
Pav. du Roi

COUR VISCONTI
COUR LEFUEL

Pav. Lesdiguières
Pav. Trémoille
Pav. des États
Pav. de Flore

QUAI DU LOUVRE

Pont du Carrousel

QUAI DES TUILERIES

Pont Royal

Parts constructed under:
- Philippe-Auguste
- Charles V
- François I–Henri II
- Charles IX–Henri III
- Henri IV
- Louis XIII
- Louis XIV (Le Vau)
- Louis XIV (Le Vau–Perrault)
- Napoléon Ier–Louis XVIII
- 2ème Rép. Napoléon III–3ème République

Parts destroyed

flanking the river, to connect the Louvre with her new palace at the *Tuileries*. The building was further extended during the reigns of Henri IV and Louis XIII, and the quadrangle was completed, on Colbert's orders, during the minority of Louis XIV. The king soon lost interest in the new buildings, and they were left in a state of disrepair, and were occupied by squatters until 1754, when Louis XV commissioned *Gabriel* to renovate and restore the palace. Under Napoleon I the W. part of the northern gallery was erected, and under Napoleon III the main wings which enclose the Square du Carrousel on the N. and S. were completed.

Catherine de Médicis lived in the palace after the death of her husband. Here she extorted from Charles IX (whose sister Marguerite de Valois had married Henry of Navarre—later Henri IV—five days earlier) the order for the Massacre of St Bartholomew (24 Aug. 1572). In 1591, during the Wars of the League, the Duc de Mayenne hanged three members of the 'Council of Sixteen' in the *Salle des Gardes* (now the *Salle des Cariatides*). Henrietta Maria, the widowed queen of Charles I of England, found refuge in the Louvre. In 1658 Corneille's 'Nicomède' was performed in the Salle des Gardes. In 1793 the *Musée de la République* was opened in the Louvre, which has remained the national art gallery and museum ever since. During 1830, the Louvre was stormed by the revolutionaries; and it was set on fire by the Communards, but serious damage was limited to the library.

The Louvre consists of two main divisions: the OLD LOUVRE, comprising the buildings surrounding the *Cour du Louvre* (or Cour Carrée); and the NEW LOUVRE, the 19C buildings N. and S. of the *Square du Carrousel*, together with their extensions to the W.

On the W. side of the *Cour du Louvre*, to the S. of the *Pavillon Sully*, is the oldest visible part of the early 16C Palace, by *Lescot*, with sculptural decorations by *Jean Goujon* and *Paul Ponce*. The N. half of the W. façade, and part of the N. façade, were designed by *Lemercier* in imitation of Lescot; the caryatids on the *Pavillon Sully* are after *Sarazin*. The remainder of the court was built by *Le Vau* after 1660. The top storeys on the N., E., and S. sides, out of keeping with *Lescot's* attic, were added in the 17-18C, to bring them up to the height of the great colonnade of 52 Corinthian columns and pilasters that now forms the exterior E. façade. The work of *Claude Perrault* (1667-70), it was designed without due regard to dimensions, and a new outer façade was added to the S. side of the OLD LOUVRE to meet the projecting S. end. To give this E. façade its correct proportions, as intended by Perrault, a moat was excavated and terreplein added (1966-67), during which works the base was discovered of an earlier façade begun by *Le Vau* and abandoned when Colbert became superintendent of the building.

The *Galerie du Bord de l'Eau*, the long S. façade flanking the Seine, was the work of *Pierre Chambiges*, architect to Catherine de Médicis, and *Thibaut Métezeau*, as far as the *Pavillon de Lesdiguières*. *Jacques du Cerceau* was responsible for the prolongation of this wing, largely rebuilt in 1863-68. The building of the NEW LOUVRE (N. and S. of the *Square du Carrousel*) was undertaken by *Visconti* in 1852 and completed in 1871 by *Lefuel;* the N. side has since been occupied by the *Ministère des Finances*, who, it is hoped, will be moved elsewhere before long.

The N.W. wing of the *Palais du Louvre*, the *Pavillon de Marsan*, is occupied by the **Musée des Arts Décoratifs** (MÉTRO *Tuileries* or *Palais-Royal*), with its entrance at 107 Rue de Rivoli. It contains an outstanding collection of French decorative and ornamental art from medieval times, and is one of the most interesting and rewarding museums to visit in Paris. Much has already been done in the way of rearranging its extensive collections, which the quality of the objects displayed deserves, and the completion of this considerable work is eagerly awaited. Until then, some rooms may be temporarily closed. The contents of each room are fully described in conveniently placed lists.

The following itinerary will take the visitor round all the galleries, which are somewhat erratically and unsystematically numbered.

The GROUND FLOOR is reserved for temporary exhibitions, while on the MEZZANINE FLOOR a *Design and Textile Centre* is being set up.

From the Vestibule, with bookstalls, we ascend a staircase (r.) to the SECOND FLOOR, to enter **R 23**, which with **R 22** adjoining displays a collection of French sculpture and tapestries of the 13-16C.—**R 24** is sparsely but tastefully furnished as a medieval chamber.—**R 21**: dominated by the tapestry known as 'The woodcutters' (Tournai; 15C), among other hangings and furniture of the period, further representative examples of which, together with metalwork, are seen in **R 20**.—Passing (l.) the CABINET DES DESSINS, we cross to the S. side of the wing.

R 55 with a richly carved and painted retable (Brussels; early 16C); 'floral' tapestries; portrait of a young girl (Bruges; c. 1550).—**R 54** portrait of Madeleine de France, Queen of Scotland, by the '*Maître de Marie Tudor*'.—**R 53**: Limoges enamels (16-17C).—**R 52**: Renaissance bronzes and furniture.—**R 51**: medieval German work.—**R 49** displays furniture in the Chinese taste, together with Chinoiserie objects (18C).—**R 48**: marquetry commode and secretaire, etc.; Sceaux faïences.—**R 47**: collections of watches, rings, ivory boxes, snuff grinders, shuttles, walking-sticks, 'necessaires', cutlery, etc.—**R 46**: panelled in oak (c. 1735). In the passage, dress swords.—**R 45**: faïences 'en trompe-l'oeil', and 'fine blanche'; provincial silverware.—**R 44** with a ceiling painted in the style of Watteau (c. 1715) from the *Hôtel de la Comtesse de Verrie* in the Rue du Cherche-Midi; silverware.—**R 43**: carved wood picture-frames; curious terracotta of a girl playing with her pet dog, by *Clodion* (1738-1814).—**R 42** with a painted ceiling (c. 1710) by *Claude Audran* (1658-1734) from the *Hôtel Bertier de Flesselles*, Rue de Sévigné; panelling (c. 1707) from 7 Pl. Vendôme; faïences de Strasbourg.—**R 41**: carved wood brackets, panels, etc.—**R 40**: clocks; bronze ornaments, etc.; marquetry armoire by *Charles Cressent* (c. 1725).

We now approach (l.) **R 39**. Note the wax portrait moulds at the entrance, some by *G. B. Nini* (c. 1717-80). The collection of 17-18C chairs is arranged to show the evolution in style; also displayed here are collections of pewter, St-Cloud porcelain, door furniture, and bronze appliqués, etc.— **R 35**: in cases near the window: mathematical instruments, etc. Other cases display faïences 'de grand feu' from Moustiers, Strasbourg, Rouen, Sinceny, and Marseilles, etc.; and bookbindings. Note the portrait of Chancellor d'Aguesseau by *R. Tournières*.—**R 34**: more Rouen ware, showing strong Chinese influence: Chinese works of art entered France at nearby Dieppe. Marquetry armoire (c. 1680-90) attr. to *Boulle;* a pastel of Molière; and painted panels by *N. Coypel*.—**R 33**: marquetry cabinet (c. 1670); bindings and decorative embossed leather cases, etc.

On the adjacent landing, embroidered purses, etc.—In **R 31,** beyond, are further examples of the art of book-binding; the walls are covered with Spanish stamped leather panels, or *guadameciles*. Note the bizarre collection of ivory skulls.

The suite of rooms along the N. side of this wing accommodates the *Jean Dubuffet* Donation.

The stairs ascend to the THIRD FLOOR, with a series of gallery rooms decorated and furnished to show typical interiors from the period of the First Empire to the beginnings of the Second Empire. Wall coverings and borders have been copied from the originals. Note also the designs for interior decoration on the passage walls, and the displays of porcelain and miniatures, etc., in the wall-cases.

RR 73-75 (First Empire). Classical influence is seen in the furniture; paintings by *Boilly*, including Houdon's studio.—The decoration of the second room reproduces that of the palace at Compiègne; chairs by the *Jacob* brothers; an early painting by *Ingres*, the 'Casino de Raphael à Rome'.—**R 75**: silverware and bronze 'coiffeuse' used by Joséphine at the Tuileries.—**R 76**: 'Restoration' furniture.— **R 77** with 'Inca' wall-papers, by *Dufour* and *Leroy* (1826); boat-shaped bed by *F. Baudry* (1827).—**RR 78-79** furnished in the Louis-Philippe taste; collections of pipes, statuettes, glass ornaments, paperweights, etc.—**RR 80-81**: Second Empire furniture (Napoleon III).

Beyond the landing are a '*Centre de Documentation*' for designers and students, and an extensive collection of painted wallpapers. After returning along the gallery, cross to **R 69**, with examples of decorative woodwork; plaster plaques, etc. **R 68** contains charming water-colours by *Lafrensen (Lavreince), Huet,*

Debucourt, and *Mallet*.—**R 67** with decorative panels by *Hubert Robert*.—**R 65** with five garden scenes by *J. Pillement*.—**R 64** with painted panels in the Etruscan style (c. 1780).—**RR 63-60** contain collections of porcelain: biscuit figures (**R63**); Vincennes and Sèvres ware (**R 62**); Mennecy ware (**R 61**); and Chantilly ware (**R 60**).

Beyond, stairs ascend to the FOURTH FLOOR, parts of it not yet rearranged. Turning r. on entering the main gallery (adorned with huge paintings representing the Months, by *Charles Lebrun*), we pass an important collection of Chinese cloisonné.—**RR 91-96** contain a collection of (mostly *anon.*) Italian paintings and furniture.—**R 93** is handsomely carved, painted, and mirrored; **R 95** with three attractive flower studies (1614-15) by *G. Pini*.—**RR 97-99** are devoted to the arts of Spain, including (**R 97**) Catalan paintings by *Jaume* and *Pere Serra*, and the retable of St John the Baptist (c. 1415-20) by *Luis Borrassa*. In **R 98**, stalls from Rueda (Valladolid; early 16C).

The remaining collections of porcelain (Delft and Meissen) are displayed in the main gallery, along the N. side of which are rooms (**129-122**) devoted to the period 1880-1925.—From the far (W.) end of the gallery, we may enter **RR 113, 115, 119-120**, accommodating the *ISLAMIC COLLECTIONS: carpets and fabrics; tiles, glassware, and Turkish porcelains; Iranian bronzes; Persian miniatures, etc.

Two bridges cross the Seine from the Louvre to the *Quai Voltaire*. To the W. is the *Pont Royal*, a five-arched bridge by *Père F. Romain* and *Gabriel* (1685-89); the last pillar on either bank has a hydrographic scale indicating the low-water mark (zero; only 80 ft above sea-level), besides various flood-marks.

The *Pont du Carrousel* (1834, but rebuilt in 1935-39) retains four seated figures by *Petitot* and *Pradier*, from the original structure. The *Pont des Arts* (pedestrians only; under restoration), built in 1802-04, and crossing to the *Quai Malaquais*, with some fine 17-18C mansions, derives its name from the 'Palais des Arts', as the Louvre was then called.

Immediately E. of the Louvre is the PL. DU LOUVRE, which claims to be the area where Caesar's legions encamped in 52 B.C. Opposite stands the *Mairie of the 1st Arrondissement* (1859), which, according to Viollet-le-Duc, seems to have been intended as a caricature of the adjoining church, to which the conspicuous N. tower was added in the following year.

St-Germain-l'Auxerrois (Pl. 14; 4), a Gothic church of the 13-16C, was itself drastically restored in the 18-19C. The most striking exterior feature is the porch, by *Jean Gaussel* (1435-39), with a rose-window, and a balustrade above, which encircles the whole church. The transeptal doorways (15C) and Renaissance doorway (1570), N. of the choir, are noteworthy. Nothing remains of the cloister.

In 885, the Norman invaders turned the church dedicated to the 5C St Germanus, Bp. of Auxerre, into a fortress. A second church was built on the site in the 11C, which, in the following century, being the parish church of the adjacent palace, was found to be too small, and was replaced by the present building in the 13C. In 1572 it was involved unwittingly in the massacre of St Bartholomew (24 Aug.), for the ringing of its bells for matins that day was to be the signal for the slaughter of Huguenots to commence.

Molière was married and his first son baptized here, and Danton was also married here. During the Revolution, having first served as a granary and then as a printing-works, it became the 'Temple of Gratitude'. It was sacked in 1831, and poorly restored after 1838.

Among those buried in St-Germain are the poet Malherbe; the architects Lemercier, de Cotte, Gabriel, and Le Vau; the painters Coypel, Boucher, and Chardin; the sculptors Coysevox, N. and G. Coustou; and the engraver Israël Silvestre.

The INTERIOR (256 by 128 ft) is double-aisled. The 'restoration' of

1745, mingling the classicism of the 18C with 14-15C architecture, mangled the choir-arches, converted the piers into fluted columns, and heightened their capitals. Fragments of the destroyed rood-screen are preserved in the Louvre. The pulpit and royal pew are fine examples of late 17C woodwork by *Fr. Mercier* (designed by *Le Brun*). Behind the latter is a sculptured triptych with painted wings (16C; Flemish), and in the aisle-chapel opposite is another altarpiece (1519; from Antwerp) in carved wood. The wrought-iron choir-railings date from 1767. On the l., at the choir entrance is a wooden statue of St Germanus, on the r. a stone figure of St Vincent (both 15C). The outer S. aisle is occupied by the *Chap. de la Vierge* (late 13C), containing a 14C Virgin of the Champagne School, a 15C St Mary of Egypt, a 13C St Germanus (of the Paris School), and a 13C wooden Crucifixion. The transepts alone have preserved their 15-16C stained-glass. Above a small door in the *Ambulatory* (S. side) is a late-15C polychrome Virgin. The first inner bay is the base of the 12C belfry. In the 4th chapel are marble statues of Étienne d'Aligre and his son, both Chancellors of France (d. 1635; 1677); 6th chapel, a Dead Christ, the only relic of a Pietà by *Jean Soulas* (1505); and in the 7th chapel, effigies from the tomb of the Rostaing family (1582 and 1645).

Gabrielle d'Estrées (1573-99) died at No. 21 Rue de l'Arbre-Sec, behind the church, a few days before she was to have married Henri IV. No. 17 Rue des Prêtres, to the S., was the site of the *Café Momus* from 1841 to 1861.

9 THE MUSÉE DU LOUVRE

The *Palais du Louvre* as a building is described on pp. 92-4; Pl.p. 93.

Convenient MÉTROS are *Tuileries, Palais-Royal, Louvre,* and *Pont-Neuf.*

ENTRANCES. The principal entrance to the ****Musée du Louvre** is in the *Pavillon Denon,* on the S. side of the Square du Carrousel. Other entrances are by the *Porte Barbet-de-Jouy,* on the Quai du Louvre some 200 yds W. of the Pont des Arts; by the *Porte La Trémoille,* opposite the Pont du Carrousel; by the *Porte Jaujard,* on the N. side of the Pavillon de Flore; by the *Porte Champollion,* in the Passage des Arts, on the S. side of the Cour Carrée and opposite the Pont des Arts.

Admission. The galleries of the Louvre, in common with most other museums in Paris, are closed on Tuesdays, but are otherwise normally open every day from 9.45 to 17.15. However, certain rooms are closed in rotation between 11.30 and 14.00: see notice-board at the entrance.
Tickets may be obtained at each entrance, and in the *Salle du Manège,* inside the Porte Denon.
Admission is free on Sundays. Hand cameras are admitted without charge, but a special ticket is required for those with tripods: the use of 'flash' is prohibited.
An *Information Bureau* may be found in the Salle du Manège (or Galerie de Vente), who can advise on lectures, etc. A guided tour (in English), lasting approx. 1½ hours, starts every weekday at 10.30 and 15.00.
A range of stalls selling catalogues, photographs, postcards, and books (not necessarily concerned with the collections of the Louvre), a selection of over 3,000 casts, and jewellery (often of very fine quality and priced accordingly), may also be found here.
Of particular interest, and often overlooked by the visitor, is the **Chalcographie du Musée du Louvre**, to be found on the floor above, to the S., where engravings from a range of some 14,000, many of them from the original plates, may be purchased. Selective lists of casts and prints are available gratis: one may buy the Catalogue of Engravings, which is somewhat out-of-date.

Umbrellas, parcels, capacious bags, etc., *must* be handed in at the Cloakrooms (no charge). Here also, and elsewhere, lavatories will be found. Refreshments are available in the GALERIE MOLLIEN (first floor). Lifts are at the disposal of the aged and infirm.

History of the Collections. The nucleus of the royal art collection was formed by François I (d. 1547). At his request Leonardo da Vinci spent the last few years of his life in France, dying there in 1519. Henri II and Catherine de Médicis carried on the tradition; Louis XIV made some notable additions to his collection of Old Masters, and Louis XVI acquired some important paintings of the Spanish and Dutch Schools. In 1793, the *Musée de la République* was opened to the public, and during the next few years a large number of the most famous paintings of Europe—spoils of conquest by the victorious Republican and Napoleonic armies—were exhibited here; although after 1815 the French government was obliged to restore some 5,000 of them to their former owners. Under Louis XVIII, the Vénus de Milo and over a hundred pictures were acquired. In 1848 the Museum became the property of the State, and an annual grant was made for the purchase of works of art, and these have been supplemented subsequently by private bequests. During the years 1939–45, the collections were dispersed throughout the country, for the sake of security, since when they have been restored more or less to their permanent place.

The Collections of the *Musée du Louvre* are divided into seven sections (although Paintings and Drawings are considered as one in this *Guide*); the colour representing them on the Plan (Atlas 24), and the pages on which each department is described, are noted below.

A Paintings (Pl. Solid Blue (SBl), pp. 99–107) and Drawings (Pl. Grey (Gr), p. 106). B Greek and Roman Antiquities (Pl. Solid Green (SG), pp. 107–10). C Egyptian Antiquities (Pl. Blue Tint (BlT), pp. 110–13). D Oriental Antiquities (Pl. Green Tint (GT), pp. 114–16). E Objets d'Art (Pl. Solid Brown (SB), pp. 116–20). F Sculpture: Medieval, Renaissance, and Modern (Pl. Brown Tint (BT), pp. 120–2).

This *Guide* can only list a certain number of the finest or most representative works in each department. Although considerable changes in the positioning of certain sections, or of individual items, will continue to take effect, it is hoped that the majority will be found in the places in which they are described (but see below).

N.B. It is very easy to underestimate the size of the *Louvre*, and while each Department is described in sequence, this is not in any way a suggestion that the perambulation of all their galleries should be attempted at one visit. It is recommended that the visitor plans his campaign carefully: many will have their priorities.

The picture galleries themselves are enough for one day, for, in the words of that experienced 19C connoisseur and traveller Richard Ford, 'picture-seeing is more fatiguing than people think, for one is standing all the while, and with the body the mind is also at exercise in judging, and is exhausted by admiration'.

The more important analogous or supplementary Collections *in Paris itself,* which may well interest the visitor to the Departments of the Louvre, are: for *Paintings:* Musée du Jeu-de-Paume (p. 88), Musée du Petit-Palais (p. 160).— *Greek and Roman Antiquities:* Cabinet des Médailles (p. 128), Musée du Petit-Palais (p. 160).—*Oriental Antiquities:* Musée Guimet (p. 169), Musée Cernuschi (p. 166), Musée des Arts Décoratifs (p. 94), and Musée d'Ennery (p. 175).—*Objets d'Art:* Musée des Arts Décoratifs (p. 94), Musée Carnavalet (p. 140), Musée Cognacq-Jay (p. 150), Musée Nissim de Camondo (p. 165), Musée Jacquemart-André (p. 164), Musée de Cluny (p. 58), and Cabinet des Médailles (p. 128).—

Sculpture: Musée de Cluny (p. 58), Musée des Arts Décoratifs (p. 94), Musée Rodin (p. 79).

The more important collections or museums in the *environs of Paris* are those at Versailles, St-Germain-en-Laye, Chantilly, Compiègne, and Fontainebleau.

A Paintings

Note. Certain groups of paintings are likely to be moved to other galleries in the Louvre during forthcoming months. The most drastic of these changes will be the transference of the *Dutch* and *Flemish* Schools to the N. galleries on the SECOND FLOOR OF THE COUR CARRÉE, together with paintings of the *German* and *English* Schools. This will allow the paintings of the *Italian* Schools (some of them at present in the Salle des Sept Cheminées and the Salle des États) to be shown in a sensible chronological order; the collections of each School may then be visited without the intrusion of the paintings of other Schools or periods, an enlightened policy on the part of the curators, which continues to be implemented.

The following brief description of some of the more important paintings (which, as with the other contents of the Louvre here described, are *not* asterisked), will take the visitor through every gallery at present open to the public. The present contents of each are indicated, although certain sections may well have been moved to a more permanent position before the next revision of this *Guide* is published.

The most convenient approach to the galleries of the Department of Paintings may be made by passing from the main entrance along the GAL. DENON (Pl. SBl), containing a collection of Roman sarcophagi. We then ascend the monumental ESCALIER DARU, itself dominated by the **Nike of Samothrace,** or *'Winged Victory'.*

This magnificent statue of Parian marble, the centrepiece of a fountain, was found in the Sanctuary of the Great Gods, on the island of Samothrace, in 1863. Further excavations in 1950 led to the discovery of the mutilated right hand (in a case to the r.), and established the probable date of the statue as c. 200 B.C.; the breast and left wing are of plaster.

Turning r., we enter the PERCIER AND FONTAINE GALLERIES, the former with a ceiling by *Charles Meynier* (1819). On the l. are frescoes by *Botticelli* from the Villa Lemmi, near Florence.

SALLE DUCHÂTEL, with 14C **French** paintings, notable amongst which is a portrait of Jean II of France (le Bon; 1319-64), ascribed to *Girard d'Orléans* or *Jean Coste.*

THE SALON CARRÉ, in which the wedding feast of Napoleon and Marie-Louise was celebrated in 1810, also with a richly decorated ceiling, is devoted primarily to the Schools of Fontainebleau. Among several outstanding works displayed here are *Henri de Vulcop,* The raising of Lazarus; *Jean Fouquet* (c. 1420-c. 1480), Portraits of Charles VII of France and of Guillaume Juvénal des Ursins; *Jean Hey,* the 'Master of Moulins' (fl. 1480-1500), two panels from a triptych (c. 1492) of Pierre II, sire de Bourbon and Anne de Beaujeu, and a small portrait of their daughter Suzanne de Bourbon, probably from the same panel; *Enguerrand Quarton,* The Pietà of Villeneuve-lès-Avignon; *School of Avignon,* Three prophets; an *anon.* Flemish panel of the Parlement of Paris (note background); *Master of the Annunciation of Aix,* Books in a niche; *Nicolas Froment* (fl. 1461-83), The Matheron Diptych, with portraits of King René of Anjou and his wife Jeanne de Laval; *Josse Lieferinxe,* Calvary, and an Adoration of the Child; *Jean Cousin the Elder* (c. 1490-c. 1561), Eva Prima Pandora; *Pseudo-Félix Chrétien,* Portrait of a Man à l'antique; *First School of Fontainebleau,* Diana the

huntress; *Jean Clouet* (c. 1480-1541), François I; *Toussaint Dubreuil,*
The toilette; *anon.,* Double portrait, possibly by *Daniel Dumoustier;*
anon, One-eyed flautist; *François Quesnel,* Henri III; *anon,* Gabrielle
d'Estreés and the duchesse de Villars, her sister.

GRANDE GALERIE: 17th and 18C French Schools. *Valentin de
Boullogne* (1591-1634), Tavern scene; *Nicolas Poussin* (1594-1665),
Echo and Narcissus, and The poet's inspiration. Among many other
Arcadian scenes by Poussin displayed in this gallery, Orpheus and
Eurydice, Diogenes throwing his bowl, and The Four Seasons are
notable; also a self-portrait; *Phillippe de Champaigne* (1602-74),
Portrait of Arnauld d'Andilly (?), The artist's daughter with Mère
Catherine-Agnès Arnauld, and The magistrates of Paris; *Georges de la
Tour* (1593-1652), The cardsharper, Adoration of the shepherds, Joseph
the carpenter, and Magdalen watching the candle; *Louis le Nain* (1593-
1648), The guard house, The peasants' meal, and Peasant family, among
others; *Lubin Baugin* (1612-63), Still-life; *Claude Gellée,* better known
as *Claude Lorrain* (1600-82), View of the Campo Vaccino, Rome,
Ulysses and Chryseis, and Three luminous port scenes; *Charles le Brun*
(1619-90), Chancellor Séguier; *Joseph Parrocel* (1646-1704), Louis
XIV's army crossing the Rhine; *François de Troy* (1645-1730), Mouton,
the musician; *Hyacinthe Rigaud* (1659-1743), The sculptor Martin
Desjardins, Portrait of the artist's mother; *Nicolas de Largillière* (1656-
1746), Self-portrait, with his wife and daughter, Portrait of Président De
Laage; *François Desportes* (1661-1743), Self-portrait 'en chasseur';
Jean-Baptiste-Siméon Chardin (1699-1779), The skate and 'Le
souffleur'; *Antoine Watteau* (1684-1721), Gilles, the clown; *Jean-
Honoré Fragonard* (1732-1806), Two figures; *Jean-Baptiste Oudry*
(1686-1755), Bittern and partridge watched by a white dog; *Louis
Tocqué* (1696-1772), The painter Louis Galloche; *Joseph Silfrein-
Duplessis* (1725-1802), Allegrain, the sculptor; *Pierre Subleyras* (1699-
1749), The Abbé Cesare Benvenuti; *Hubert Robert* (1733-1808), The
Pont du Gard; *Élisabeth Vigée-Lebrun* (1755-1842), Portrait of Hubert
Robert; and examples of the work of *François Boucher* (1703-70),
Nicolas Lancret (1690-1743), and *Jean-Baptiste Greuze* (1725-1805).

The SALLE DES ÉTATS, entered (r.) some distance along the Grande Galerie, will
eventually display paintings of the French School also (17-18C): at present it is
devoted to the Italian Schools (16C), which will be transferred to the Pavillon des
États (Pl. SBl); these are described below (p. 101).

To follow the development of the French Schools, turn r. at this point
to enter the *Mollien Wing.* The earlier paintings of the Italian Schools
are accommodated in the *western extension* of the *Grande Galerie* (Pl.
SBl), and are described below (p. 102).

MOLLIEN WING. *Fragonard,* Inspiration, and Study; *Jean-Baptiste
Perronneau* (1715-83), Mme de Sorquainville; *Chardin,* Boy with a
teetotum, and Man with a violin; Baron *Gros* (1771-1835), Bonaparte at
the bridge of Arcole (1796); *Jean-Auguste-Dominique Ingres* (1780-
1867), Portraits of the Rivière family, and of M. Bertin, senior; *François
Gérard* (1770-1837), Comtesse Regnauld de Saint-Jean-d'Angély;
Eugène Delacroix (1798-1863), Self-portrait, and Portrait of Chopin.

The SALLE MOLLIEN, to the r., is largely devoted to the vast canvases
popular during the Napoleonic period, but mostly of greater historical
than artistic significance, including *Jacques-Louis David* (1748-1825),

M. Sériziat, his wife and son, Mme Trudaine, The Marquise d'Orvilliers, Pope Pius VII, and Mme Récamier in a familiar pose. Opposite is his immense Coronation of Napoleon I (by Pius VII in Notre-Dame, 2 Dec. 1804); *Gérard,* Portrait of the artist J.-B. Isabey; *Prud'hon,* The Empress Joséphine at Malmaison; *Gros,* Christine Boyer, first wife of Lucien Bonaparte; *Ingres,* Portraits of the composer Cherubini, of M. Cordier, 'La grande odalisque', and 'La baigneuse'.

Passing through the SALLE DENON (note ceiling), we enter the Salle Daru.

SALLE DARU. *Gros,* Bonaparte visiting the plague-stricken at Jaffa, and Napoleon at Eylau (with portraits of Berthier, Murat, Soult, and Davoust); *Théodore Géricault* (1791-1824), Officer of the Chasseurs de la Garde, The raft of the 'Medusa'; *Delacroix,* Liberty guiding the people, or 'Les Barricades', Scenes of the massacre of Chios, Algerian women at home; *Alexandre Decamps* (1803-60), Defeat of the Cimbri; *Gustave Courbet* (1819-77), The artist's studio, The wave.

The remaining paintings of the French School in the collection are at present housed on the *Second Floor* of the COUR CARRÉE (see p. 106), but some of them will, in due course, be accommodated in the SALLE DES SEPT MÈTRES (Pl. SBl, to the r.). It is recommended that this latter gallery should be next visited, which at present displays works of the **Dutch** School: these will eventually be transferred to northern galleries of the Cour Carrée.

SALLE DES SEPT MÈTRES. *Frans Hals,* Portraits of Paulus van Berestyn, and of his third wife, Catherine Both van der Eem; The van Berestyn family, now attr. to *Pierre Soutman;* also by *Hals,* The charming gipsy girl; *Gérard Verspronck,* Portrait of Agathe van Schoonhoven; *Salomon van Ruysdael,* The landing-stage; *Jan van Goyen,* View of Dordrecht. The next section is devoted to *Rembrandt:* Self-portrait, bareheaded; another wearing a toque and with an architectural background; and a third with a toquè and gold chain. A fourth self-portrait is of the artist in his old age (1660) at his easel. Other works by Rembrandt include Christ at Emmaus, Portrait of Hendrikje Stoffels, Bathsheba bathing, St Matthew inspired by an angel, The meditating philosopher, and The carcase of an ox. Later sections contain *Albert Cuyp,* Cavaliers; *Allart van Everdingen,* Landscape with hunters and fishermen; *Paul Potter,* Horses at a cottage door; *Jacob van Ruysdael,* The bush; *Philips Wouwerman,* Landscape with a cart; *Salomon van Ruysdael,* Still life with a turkey; *Karel Dujardin,* Italian charlatans; *Jan van der Heyden,* The Town Hall, Amsterdam; *Bol,* The mathematician.

On turning r. along the *Grande Galerie,* we shortly reach (r.) the SALLE DES ÉTATS, now containing a number of 16C masterpieces of the **Italian** Schools. Among these, on the far wall, *Veronese*'s huge Marriage at Cana; others by Veronese are the so-called 'La belle Nani', a Calvary, and Supper at Emmaus; *Titian,* Lady at her toilet (called 'Alfonso da Ferrara and Laura de' Dianti'), St Jerome in the desert, Man with a glove, and another male portrait, Supper at Emmaus, The Entombment, Allegory representing the wife of Alfonso d'Avalos being entrusted to Chastity and Cupid, François I, painted from a medal of the king the artist never saw, Jupiter and Antiope, known as 'the Venus of the Pardo', and Pastoral concert (once attr. to Giorgione); *Tintoretto,* Susanna and the elders, and Self-portrait (1590); *Palma Vecchio,* Adoration of the shepherds; *Giulio Romano,* Portrait of Joanna d'Aragón (the face by Raphael); *Andrea del Sarto,* Charity; *Correggio,* The Mystic Marriage of St Catherine of Alexandria, Jupiter and Antiope; *Lotto,* The woman taken in adultery; *Raphael,* St George, and St Michael, Portrait of Baldassare Castiglione (author of 'The Courtier'), 'La belle Jardinière', Self-portrait with a friend; *Leonardo da Vinci,* Annunciation, Madonna and Child with St Anne, The Virgin of the Rocks (1482; probably earlier than the similar composition in London), St John the Baptist (apparently painted from a female model or worked on later by another hand); *School of Leonardo,* Bacchus, and the so-called 'La belle ferronnière' (from the chain round her forehead). A Portrait by *Leonardo da Vinci,* traditionally assumed to be of Monna Lisa Gherardini, third wife of Francesco di Zanobi del Giocondo, hence also 'La Gioconda', or in French, 'La Joconde'.

Leonardo worked intermittently on this portrait for four years from 1500. In spite of drastic restoration at different periods, this remains one of the outstanding achievements of the Italian Renaissance. In Aug. 1911 it was stolen from the Salon Carré by a thief disguised as a workman, but was recovered in Florence in Dec. 1913. It has also been claimed that the sitter was Costanza d'Avalos, mistress of Giuliano de' Medici, and that another somewhat similar portrait in a private collection represents Monna Lisa.

Re-entering the GRANDE GALERIE, and turning r., we shortly reach the first section of this wing devoted to the **Italian** primitives.

Cimabue, Madonna with angels; *Giotto,* St Francis receiving the stigmata; an *anon.* 14C Florentine Calvary; *Bernardo Daddi,* Annunciation; *Bartolo di Maestro Fredi,* Presentation in the Temple; *Barnaba da Modena,* Madonna and Child; *Lorenzo Veneziano,* Madonna enthroned; twelve *anon.* Venetian scenes from the Life of the Virgin; *Simone Martini,* Christ bearing the Cross; *Guido da Siena,* Nativity, and Presentation in the Temple; *Pisanello,* A princess of the House of Este; *Gentile da Fabriano,* Presentation; *Jacopo Bellini,* Madonna and Child with donor; *Benozzo Gozzoli,* The triumph of St Thomas Aquinas; *Alessio Baldovinetti,* Madonna adoring the Child; *Paolo Uccello,* Battle of San Romano, in 1432; *Fra Angelico,* Coronation of the Virgin, and The martyrdom of St Cosmas and St Damian; *Sano di Pietro,* Five episodes from the dream of St Jerome; *The Master of the Observance,* St Anthony; *Sassetta,* Madonna and Child with angels, St Anthony of Padua and St John the Evangelist, and The miraculous deliverance of the poor incarcerated in the prisons of Florence; *School of Fra Filippo Lippi,* Nativity; *Botticelli,* Madonna and Child surrounded by angels, Portrait of a young man, 'The Madonna of the Guidi of Faenza', Madonna and Child with St John the Baptist; *Mantegna,* St Sebastian, and Calvary; *Antonello da Messina,* The condottiere; *Giovanni Bellini,* Portrait of a man.

We now reach the ROTUNDA (note ceiling), with, in a showcase (l.), *Catena,* Portrait of Giulio Mellini; *Bernardo Parentino,* Adoration of the Magi. In a case to the r., *School of Fra Angelico,* Herod's banquet; *Pesellino,* St Francis of Assisi receiving the stigmata, and St Cosmas and St Damian nursing the sick; *Signorelli,* Birth of St John the Baptist.

In the next section of the gallery, *Bartolomeo di Giovanni,* Marriage of Thetis and Peleus, and Wedding procession; *Ghirlandaio,* The bottlenosed old man and his grandson, The Visitation; *Piero di Cosimo,* Madonna and Dove; *Perugino,* Madonna with saints and angels, and

Tondo showing the Madonna and Child with St Catherine and St John the Baptist; *Giovanni Bellini,* Crucifixion, Resurrection, and Blessing, Portrait of two men (once attr. to Cariani); *Carpaccio,* St Stephen preaching; *School of Gentile Bellini,* Reception in Cairo of the Venetian Ambassador Dom. Trevisano; *Cima da Conegliano,* Madonna and Child with St John the Baptist and the Magdalen; *Jacopo de Barbieri,* Madonna at the fountain; *Palmezzano,* Christ supported by two angels.

We now enter the first of the rooms of the PAVILLON DES ÉTATS, which will eventually accommodate the 16-17C Italian School (at present in the Salle des États and Salle des Sept Cheminées: see pp. 101 and 105 respectively). The present contents of these rooms (**Dutch, Flemish,** and **German** Schools) are described below, but in due course they will be transferred to the Cour Carrée.

SALLE VAN DYCK. Among the paintings by *van Dyck* are the following portraits: The Marchesa Spinola Doria; Francisco de Moncada, Conde de Osuna and Gov.-Gen. of the Spanish Netherlands; the Duke of Richmond; Charles Louis, Elector Palatine, and his brother Prince Rupert, later Duke of Cumberland; Charles I of England; A gentleman with his sword; A lady of quality with her daughter; and A gentleman with his daughter. *Rubens,* Kermesse (the village fair), Portraits of his wife Helen Fourment with two of her children, her sister Suzanne, Baron Henri de Vicq—a portrait of the ambassador who obtained for the artist the commission to paint the Medici canvases (see below)—and The Adoration of the Magi; *Jan Fyt,* Still life with game; *Victor Boucquet,* Standard-bearer; *Jordaens,* The king drinks; and *David Teniers the Younger,* Riverside tavern.

The MEDICI GALLERY (*Galerie Médicis*) contains twenty-one large allegorical paintings depicting the Life of Marie de Médicis, which were designed in 1622-25 by **Rubens** for the decoration of the Luxembourg Palace (see p. 70), in the execution of which he was largely aided by his pupils.

To follow the chronological sequence, begin with the paintings on the l. of the entrance. I. The Fates spin her destiny; II and III. Her Birth and Education; IV. Henri IV receives her portrait; V. Marriage at Florence in Oct. 1600; the Grand Duke Charles stands proxy for Henri IV; VI. Marie lands at Marseilles; VII. Marriage at Lyon with Marie as Juno and Henri as Jupiter; VIII. Birth of Louis XIII at Fontainebleau in 1601, with Fortuna and the Genius of Health; IX. Henri IV starts for the war in Germany, and entrusts the regency to the queen; X. Coronation of the queen at St-Denis (1610), with the king (already crowned) in the gallery at the back; XI. Apotheosis of Henri IV (assassinated in 1610), with Marie as regent; XII. The Government of Marie; XIII. The queen's journey to Ponts-de-Cé to quell rebellion; XIV. Exchange of the two princesses (1615), by treaty between France and Spain; Elizabeth of France is betrothed to Philip IV of Spain, and Anne of Austria to Louis XIII of France; XV. Prosperity of the Regency; the queen enthroned, with Minerva, Fortuna, and Abundance; XVI. Majority of Louis XIII, to whom the Regent mother entrusts the ship of state; XVII. Marie's nocturnal flight from the Château of Blois (Feb. 1619); XVIII. The queen receives overtures of peace from her son; XIX. Conclusion of Peace (April 1619); XX. Reconciliation of the queen and her son, with the dragon of rebellion overcome; XXI. to the l. as we leave, the Triumph of Truth.

Returning to the vestibule, we may enter the PETITS CABINETS flanking the gallery, descending steps to the r. (facing the Seine). *Joos van Cleve,* Triptych of the Descent from the Cross, Francis of Assisi receiving the stigmata, and The Last Supper; *Master of the St Bartholomew Altarpiece,* Descent from the Cross.

Cabinet 1: *Master of the View of St Gudule,* Pastoral instruction;

Thierry Bouts, Descent from the Cross, Virgin and Child; *Gérard de Saint-Jean,* Raising of Lazarus; *Jan van Eyck,* Chancellor Nicolas Rolin before the Virgin; *Rogier van der Weyden,* Salvator Mundi, triptych of the Braque family; *Petrus Christus,* Pietà.

Cabinet 2: *Memling,* The Mystic Marriage of St Catherine, with the donor praying under the protection of St John the Baptist, Portrait of an old lady, The martyrdom of St Sebastian, Resurrection of Christ, Ascension, The Virgin of Jacques Floreins; *Gerard David,* Triptych of Mary, Marriage at Cana.

Cabinet 3: *Cornelis van Dalem,* Farmyard in winter; *Brueghel the Elder,* Beggars; *the Brunswick Monogramist,* Sacrifice of Abraham; *Lucas van Leyden,* The card-dealer, Lot and his daughters; *Mabuse,* Diptych of Jean Carondelet (Chancellor of Flanders) and the Virgin; *Quinten Massys,* Moneylender and his wife, The dead Christ; *van Orley,* Portrait of an old man; *van Cleve,* Monk offering his heart to the Virgin and Child; *Patinir,* St Jerome in the desert; *Hieronymus Bosch,* The Ship of Fools.

Cabinet 4: *van Valckenborgh,* The Tower of Babel; *Brueghel the Elder,* contemporary copy of The blind men; *Antonio Moro* (Anthonis Mor van Dashorst), Card. de Granvella's dwarf, A nobleman in the Cardinal's entourage; *anon.,* Portrait of a lady of quality.

Cabinet 5: Portraits, mostly from the collection of Roger de Gaignières (1642-1715), which included 1,096 items, from the workshops of *Corneille de Lyon* (fl. 1540-74), *Pourbus the Younger* (1569/70-1622)—note his portrait of Henri IV—and *François Clouet* (c. 1505-72). Note the latter's portrait of Elisabeth of Austria, wife of Charles IX, painted in 1571.

Cabinet 6: German Schools. *Hans Baldung Grien,* A knight, a woman, and Death; *Master of the Legend of St Ursula,* Pagan ambassadors at the court of St Ursula; *anon. painter from Cologne,* Pietà of St-Germain-des-Prés; *Ludger Tom Ring, the Elder,* Sibyl; also a fine *anon.* (L.C.Z.) Flagellation.

Cabinet 7: *Hans Holbein the Younger,* Portraits of Sir Henry Wyatt, Anne of Cleves, Erasmus (painted for Sir Thomas More), Nicolas Kratzer (Henry VIII's astronomer), and William Warham, Abp. of Canterbury; *Dürer,* Self-portrait (1493); *Wolf Huber,* The grieving Christ; *Lucas Cranach the Elder,* Venus in a landscape, A young girl (?Magdalena Luther); *Hans Maler,* Matthias Schwartz (?).

Cabinet 9: Studies for the decoration of the Ducal Palace at Urbino, by *Justus of Ghent* and *Pedro Berruguete.*

Hence we should return through the Galerie Médicis, and turn l. to enter the PETITS CABINETS facing the gardens of the Tuileries.

Cabinet 1: *Nicolaes Berchem,* Landscape with animals; *Gerard Dou,* Woman with dropsy; *Gabriel Metsu,* The female toper, Soldier and young girl, and The grass-market at Amsterdam; *Nicolaes Maes* (?), Bathing scene; *Gerard Ter Borch,* The military gallant, Reading lesson; *Pieter de Hooch,* Card-players.

Cabinet 2: *Ter Borch,* The concert, Portrait of a man; *Jan van der Heyden,* The Herengracht in Amsterdam; *Adriaen Coorte,* Shells; *Vermeer,* The lacemaker; *van Ostade,* The schoolmaster; *Michiel Sweerts,* Young man and matchmaker (?).

Cabinet 3: Sketches by *Rubens.*

Cabinet **4**: *Frans Post*, Tropical landscapes painted in Brazil; *Cornelis van Poelenburgh*, Orpheus charming the beasts, and Ruins of Rome with the Castel Sant'Angelo, etc.; *Willem Claesz. Heda*, The dessert; *Willem Cornelisz. Duyster*, Robbers; *Pieter Codde*, Dancing-lesson; *Hendrik Pot*, Copy of Daniel Mytens's portrait of Charles I of England.

Cabinet **5**: *David Teniers*, The Seven Works of Mercy, 'Les joueurs de Hoquet', Winter scene, Tavern interior; *Frans Francken the Younger*, The Prodigal Son; *Adrien Brouwer*, The inn, Landscape at dusk; *Joos van Craesbeek*, The smoker (? self-portrait).

Cabinet **6**: *Denis van Alsloot*, Winter landscape; *Paul Bril*, Landscape with a pond, Fishing; *Gotthard de Wedig*, Still-life; *Roelant Savery*, Polish mercenaries in the forest.

Cabinet **7**: *Pietersz. van de Venne*, Celebrating the truce of 1609; *Jan Brueghel the Younger (Velours)*, The battle of Arbela, Virgin and Child with a garland of flowers, Air and Earth (part of a series of the four elements: Fire and Water are in the Ambrosiana Museum, Milan), and Landscapes.

Passing through Cabinet **8**, we turn r. towards the Pavillon de Flore, along a gallery displaying further paintings of the **Italian** Schools, notably *Caravaggio*, portrait of Alof de Vignacourt, and The fortune-teller; *Bart. Schedone*, Entombment; *Guido Reni*, St Sebastian, Ecce Homo; *Domenichino*, Herminia among the shepherds, St Cecilia; *Pietro da Cortona*, Venus as a huntress appearing to Aeneas; *Carlo Maratta*, Maria-Magdalena Rospigliosi, niece of Pope Clement IX; *Lionello Spada*, Return of the Prodigal Son; *Bernardo Strozzi*, Holy Family; *Salvator Rosa*, Landscape with hunters; *Paolo Porpora*, Still life; *Aniello Falcone*, Battle scene; *Giuseppe Angeli*, The little drummer; *G.-M. Crespi*, Woman with a flea; *Guardi*, 8 of 12 scenes depicting festivities organized for the coronation of the Doge Alvise IV Mocenigo; *Longhi*, The Presentation; *G.-P. Panini*, Concert in Rome (26 Nov. 1729) to celebrate the birth of the Dauphin Louis to Marie Leczinska and Louis XV, and Preparations for festivities in the Piazza Navona; *Michele Marieschi*, View of S. Maria della Salute, Venice; *Guardi*, View of the church of SS Giovanni e Paolo; *G.-B. Tiepolo*, The Last Supper; *Domenico Tiepolo*, Carnival scene, and The charlatan.

The only other Italian paintings not listed are those at present in the SALLE DES SEPT CHEMINÉES (Pl. 5Bl), which it is planned to move to the Pavillon des États. Among these large 17-18C canvases may be mentioned *A. Carracci*, The Virgin appearing to St Luke and St Catherine, Hunting, and Fishing; *Caravaggio*, Death of the Virgin; and *Guercino*, The raising of Lazarus.

The last section of this gallery contains the undispersed *Beistegui Collection* (donated to the Louvre in 1953), with an *anon. Franco-Flemish* Virgin and Child; *Master of Moulins*, Portrait of the Dauphin Charles Orlando (1494; son of Charles VIII and Anne of Brittany): among other portraits are *François-Hubert Drouais* (1727-75), Anne-Françoise Doré, his wife; *van Dyck*, A Genoese gentleman (*not* Livio Odescalchi); *Lawrence*, Mrs Cuthbert; *Zuloaga*, Carlos de Beistegui (donor of the Collection); *David*, Gen. Bonaparte, sketched near Rivoli (c. 1797), M. Mayer, envoy from the Batavian Republic; *Gérard*, Mme Lecerf, his cousin; *Ingres*, Mme Panckoucke; and *Goya*, The Condesa del Carpio, Marquesa de Solana.

PAVILLON DE FLORE: **Spanish** Schools. **R I,** to the l., *Jaime Huguet,* The Flagellation, and Entombment; *Barnat Martorell,* Four episodes from the life of St George; Man with a glass of wine (Portuguese School).— **R II:** *El Greco,* Crucifixion with two donors (signed in Greek characters), St Louis of France; *Ribera,* St Paul the hermit.—**R III:** *Ribera,* The Entombment, Adoration of the shepherds, and Club-footed boy; *Zurbarán,* St Bonaventura at the Council of Lyon, and The saint's corpse exposed; *Murillo,* Legend of S. Diego, known as 'the angels' kitchen' (one of a series of 16 painted for the Franciscan convent at Seville, another of which has been recently acquired by the Louvre); *Carreño,* Foundation of the Trinitarian Order.—**R IV:** *Zurbarán,* Sta Apollina; *Velázquez,* Mariana of Austria, her daughter The infanta Margarita, and The infanta María Teresa; *Collantes,* The Burning Bush; *Murillo,* The young beggar.—**R V:** *Meléndez,* Self-portrait, and Still-life; *Goya,* The unequal wedding, Woman with a fan, and Two portraits, of Ferdinand Guillemardet, and Don Evaristo Pérez de Castro.

While at this end of the Louvre, it is as well to visit the SECOND FLOOR OF THE PAVILLON DE FLORE, where many masterpieces of pastel portraiture are displayed, a very small part of the collection of the *Cabinet de Dessins* (Pl. Gr): also some miniatures.

The **Cabinet de Dessins** itself is not open to the general public, but researchers and connoisseurs (who on their first visit will require a letter of introduction) are courteously allowed to study its superb collections, which include some 1,200 miniatures, 30,000 engravings, and 75,000 drawings.

Approximately one hundred pastel portraits are exhibited in a suite of rooms. **R I:** *Leonardo da Vinci,* Isabella d'Este, Duchess of Mantua; and new acquisitions.—**R II:** *Charles Le Brun* (1619-90), Three portraits of Louis XIV; *Robert Nanteuil* (c. 1623-78), Jean Dorien, Dominique de Vigny, Bp. of Meaux, Henri de la Tour d'Auvergne, vicomte de Turenne (attrib. doubtful); *Joseph Vivien* (1657-1734), The sculptor François Girardon, and The architect Robert de Cotte, among others; *Rosalba Carriera* (1675-1757; who did much to popularize the technique in France), Young girl with a monkey (the model may have been the daughter of the financier John Law).—**R III:** *Maurice-Quentin de Latour* (1704-88), Hermann-Maurice, Comte de Saxe, Philibert Orry, Jacques Dimont, and The Marquise de Pompadour; *Jean-Baptiste Perronneau,* Abraham van Robais, The engraver Laurent Cars; *Chardin,* His second wife, Self-portraits, with spectacles, with a green eye-shade, and at his easel.

Other portraits by *Gustav Lundberg, Adélaïde Labille-Guiard, Joseph Boze,* and *John Russell* (1745-1806) follow, together with a representative selection of 19C pastels.

The remaining galleries of the Louvre at present containing paintings are to be found on the SECOND FLOOR of the S. side of the COUR CARRÉE, best approached by retracing one's steps to the *Nike of Samothrace,* there turning r. through the Salle des Sept Cheminées (see p. 105), to traverse the Egyptian Rooms, at the far end of which we ascend the small spiral *Escalier du Chien.*

Here are assembled, temporarily, further 19C **French** paintings, and the few examples of the English School in the collection.

The latter, together with those of the Dutch, Flemish, and German Schools, will eventually be displayed together on the far side of the Cour Carrée.

R I: *Joseph Berger*, Portrait of a man; *Mme Benoist*, A black woman; *Henri-François Riesener*, Maurice Quaï; *Gros*, Madeleine Pasteur; *David*, Alexandre Lenoir; *Martin Drolling*, Kitchen interior; *A.-L.-C. Pagnest*, M. de Nanteuil-Lanorville.—**R II:** *Ingres*, The Turkish bath; *Amaury Duval*, Mme de Loynes; *Gérard*, Portrait of his wife.—**R III:** *P.-H. Valenciennes* (1750-1819), 24 views of Rome and the Campagna; *Louis Boilly* (1761-1845), Genre scenes; works by *A.-E. Michallon;* and *Camille Corot* (1796-1875), Views, and Portraits.—**R IV:** *Géricault*, Equestrian portraits, including horses at Epsom, and also The Vendéen; *Delacroix*, Hamlet and Horatio, etc.—**R V:** *Corot*, Landscapes; and *Delacroix*, The orphan at the cemetery.—**R VI:** minor Romantic works, including *Eugène Isabey* (1803-86), The wooden bridge.—**R VII:** *Eugène Fromentin* (1820-76), Hawking in Algeria; *Théodore Rousseau* (1812-67), Oak-trees; *Charles Daubigny* (1817-78), The sluicegate.— **R VIII:** more landscapes by *Corot*, and *Jean-François Millet* (1814-75), Paintings of peasants.—**R IX:** *Millet*, The gleaners, and Mme Lecourtois, his sister-in-law; *Honoré Daumier* (1808-79), Crispin and Scapin, Don Quixote and the dead mule; *Courbet*, Portrait of Pierre-Joseph Proudhon.—**R X:** *Pierre Puvis de Chavannes* (1824-98), Poor fishermen, etc.; *Whistler*, The artist's mother.

Dutch 17C paintings from the *de Croy Bequest* are exhibited in the W. wing of the COUR CARRÉE, including *van Honthorst*, The dentist, and Portrait of Frederic-Henri of Nassau; *Samuel van Hoogstraten* (?), The slippers; *Jan Verspronck*, Young woman from Haarlem; *Joos van Craesbeek*, Spring; *Barent Avercamp* and *Jan van Goyen*, Skating scenes.

18C **French** paintings. Works by *Watteau, Lancret, Boucher*, and *Fragonard*, but dominated by *Chardin*, Still-lifes and Genre scenes; *Greuze*, The broken pitcher; and *Claude-Joseph Vernet* (1714-89), The Ponte Rotto.

The **English** School. *Ramsay*, Lord Elcho (?); *Gainsborough*, Conversation in the park, Lady Gertrude Alston; *Reynolds*, Master Hare; *Romney*, Sir John Stanley; *Wright of Derby*, The Lake of Nemi; *Lawrence*, Charles William Bell, John Julius Angerstein and his wife; *Raeburn*, Capt. Robert Hay of Spott; *Bonington*, The Adriatic; and examples of the work of *John Hamilton Mortimer, Fuseli, Constable, Turner, Angelica Kauffmann*, and *Burne-Jones*.

B   Greek and Roman Antiquities

This Department, in common with others, is undergoing a thorough re-formation, and not all the rooms are open to the public. Meanwhile, many representative objects are on display, temporarily, in the GALERIE MOLLIEN on the *Ground Floor* to the r. of the *Porte Denon* (main entrance).

To visit the collection, as it is at present exhibited, pass through the *Gal. Denon* (l.), and turn to the l. below the *Nike of Samothrace* (already described on p. 99). Continue through the Rotunda, and a short distance beyond, in the SALLE DE L'APOLLON DE PIOMBINO (**R I**), stands the unusually fine 5C bronze Apollo, with copper incrustations—lips and nipples—which was retrieved from the sea near Piombino: it is perhaps a replica of a work by *Kanaknos;* also a female torso similar in type to the

Esquiline Venus at Rome.—**R 2:** Frieze with Apollo and Hermes and nymphs and graces (early 5C), from Thasos, and the upper part of the stele 'Exaltation of the Flower' from Pharsalus.—**R 3:** dominated by the *Vénus de Milo,* one of the most beautiful and celebrated surviving antique sculptures, found by a peasant in 1820 on the island of Melos in the Greek archipelago. It is now regarded as a copy by an unknown master of the 2C after a 4C original. When discovered, it was in five fragments, and was restored in the Louvre.—From **R 4** turn r. into **R 5,** containing the so-called 'Dame d'Auxerre', possibly of Cretan origin.— **R 6:** the 'Rampin' head, with a plaster cast of the equestrian figure (in the Acropolis Museum at Athens) to which it belongs (6C); Hera of Samos, one of the oldest and best authenticated works of island sculpture (c. 520 B.C.), inscribed *Cheramues;* torso of Apollo (Miletus; 5C); and black-figure ceramic ware.—**R 7:** metopes from the temple of Zeus at Olympia, with Hercules overcoming the Cretan bull, and presenting to Athene one of the Stymphalian birds; statue of Persephone, *after Pheidias.*

R 8: SALLE DU PARTHENON, with fragments of the E. frieze of the Parthenon at Athens (5C B.C.; the greater part of the frieze, which represents the Panathenaic procession, is in the British Museum); a fine head of a goddess, the 'Laborde Head', from one of the pediments on the Parthenon; Centaur carrying off a Lapith woman; the so-called Barberini Supplicant, etc.—Turning r., we now cross to the SALLE DES CARIATIDES (**R 9;** Pl. SG).

This is the oldest surviving room in the palace, built by *Pierre Lescot* for Henri II, who commissioned *Jean Goujon* to execute the caryatids supporting the gallery at the far end. Other decorations and the chimneypiece at the near end are by *Percier* and *Fontaine* (c. 1806). Mary Stuart married François II in this room in 1558, and here Louis XIV washed the feet of thirteen poor men on Maundy Thursday.

Displayed here are the 'Borghese Warrior', signed on the tree-trunk by *Agasias,* an otherwise unknown sculptor of the late Hellenistic period (found at Anzio in the 17C); replicas of work by Praxiteles and his school, including the Venus of Arles, altered by Girardon; the huntress Artemis, known as the Diana of Versailles (c. A.D. 100), acquired from Rome by François I; Hermes fastening his sandal, and Eros stringing his bow, antique copies of originals by *Lysippus;* Silenus and Dionysus, Apollo Sauroktonos (killing a lizard); the Aphrodite of Cnidos, and the so-called Kaufman Head, all *after Praxiteles;* and Aphrodite and Eros, *after Scopas.*

Passing through the ROTONDE D'ANNE D'AUTRICHE (decorated by *Michel Anguier* (1635), and with a ceiling-painting by *Mauzaisse*) we return to the VESTIBULE DES PRISONNIERS BARBARES (**R 12;** Pl. SG), displaying decorative monumental vases and sculptures in porphyry, etc., of the late Roman period. Turning l., we enter the COUR DU SPHINX (**R 13**), with a façade by *Le Vau,* containing bas-reliefs from the architrave of the Temple of Assos (nr Troy, in Asia Minor), representing Hercules battling against the Triton, a banquet, a procession of animals and centaurs, etc.; frieze from the temple of Artemis at Magnesia on the Maeander, illustrating a battle between Greeks and Amazons (2C B.C.); the God of the Tiber, a colossal group found in the 16C; in the centre, a huge mosaic of the Seasons (4C) from near Antioch.

R 15: SALLE D'AUGUSTE, built for Henri IV, and originally the *Salle des*

Ambassadeurs: among the many powerfully sculpted heads, those of Augustus (earlier than the body); Octavius representing Mercury, of Parian marble, and found in Rome: it is signed 'Cleomenes of Athens, son of Cleomenes' on the tortoise at the foot; Agrippa; and Livia (in black basalt), are outstanding.—We may return to the foot of the *Escalier Daru* by turning r. through the SALLE DES FRESQUES (**R16**), with, among others, a fine mosaic of the Judgement of Paris on the l. wall.

Ascending to the *First Floor,* passing the *Nike of Samothrace,* we shortly enter the SALLE 'DES BIJOUX' (Pl. SG), with, on the N. wall, fragments of Graeco-Roman frescoes; in window-cases, Roman cameos, and two ivory plaques (Etruscan; 6-5C B.C.); in the central showcase, the 'Treasure of Boscoreale' (nr Pompeii), a collection of superbly decorated silver objects discovered in 1895 in a fine state of preservation on the site of a villa overwhelmed by an eruption of Vesuvius in A.D. 79. Also seen here are the two silver masks from the Gallo-Roman 'Treasure of N.-D. d'Allençon', and the silver Treasure of Graincourt-les-Havrincourt (the latter temporarily on display in the *Gal. Mollien*).

Passing through the *Salle des Sept Cheminées* (see p. 105), we reach the SALLE CLARAC, with exhibits of the pre-Hellenic civilizations: pithoi from Knossos (Crete; 1700-1600 B.C.), and from Thera and Rhodes (14C B.C.); marble idols from the Cyclades (2500-2000 B.C.); terracotta and bronze figurines and painted ceramics (Minoan) from Crete (14-12C B.C.), and funerary objects.

Turning r., we enter the GALERIE CAMPANA, a series of nine rooms devoted to a superlative collection of Antique Pottery from the 10C B.C. to the 4C B.C.—**R1** (Pl. SG): pottery of the Geometric style. Boeotian figurines, etc.; Attic vases found in the Dipylon cemetery (c. 800 B.C.); pottery from the Greek Islands, and vessels in the 'orientalized' style.—**R2:** pottery from Corinth; Tyrrhenian amphorae, kraters, and other vessels; and black-figure Attic ceramics.—**R3:** Oenochoai and vases in the Attic style, signed by *Nikosthenes* and *Andokides* respectively, including both black and red figures; coloured terracottas.—**R4:** Attic red-figure pottery (c. 500 B.C.), including works by *Euphronius* (a large krater with the combat of Hercules and Antaeus), *Douris* (a kylix with Eros and Memnon), and *Myson* (amphora with Croesus on a pyre).—**RR5-7:** further examples of the Attic style.—**R8:** terracotta figurines, and statuettes from Tanagra.—**R9:** figurines of the Hellenistic period; and antique glassware.

Retracing our steps through this gallery, we may cross the *Salle des Sept Cheminées* to enter the SALLE HENRI II (the *Etruscan Room;* Pl. SG), with a ceiling by *Braque.* Among the fine collection of pottery, mostly in the Greek style, is some black ('bucchero') ware; and five terracotta panels from Cerveteri (600 B.C.); but the room is dominated by the terracotta Sarcophagus (also discovered at Cerveteri, by Campana, in 1850), where as if on a funeral couch recline the lifelike figures of a man and his wife represented as if still alive and conversing. The woman wears a cap (tutulus) and a small gorget; the man, barefooted, is draped.

The adjoining SALLE LA CAZE (Pl. SG) contains an impressive collection of Greek, Etruscan, and Roman bronzes, jewellery, arms, utensils, etc. The exhibits are arranged chronologically (as listed below), and in geographical groups.

Case **1**: Archaic Greek Art. Note the Minotaur; statuette of Athene; a warrior; javelin-thrower; and Silenus dancing (all 6C B.C.).—Case **18**: Pan and his syrinx.—Case **21**: mirrors, including one in its box decorated with scenes in relief.—Case **2**: Classical Greek statuettes (5C B.C.). Group of Lycurgus and the Maenads; a stag; Ephebus (*School of Polykleitos*); Hercules fighting; and Zeus.—Case **26**: athlete's head (Greek; 5C B.C.), found at Benevento, Italy.—Case **3**: Hellenistic Art. Aphrodite fastening her sandal; a hermaphrodite figure; and 'Napoleon's cist' (a cylindrical box in which women kept jewels and toilet accessories).—Cases **4** and **17**: Etruscan Art. The latter case containing small bronzes.—Case **12**: Roman Gaul. Statuettes and busts: note eyes; bull; and boar; and near the entrance to the room (r.), a cock found at Lyon.—Case **8**: winged helmet encircled by a gold crown.— Case **7**: gladiator's armour.—**Central showcase,** containing a magnificent collection of jewellery and goldsmiths' work from all the periods and regions covered by the other exhibits.

C Egyptian Antiquities

This Department (in the S. half of the COUR CARRÉE) is conveniently approached from the main entrance by descending into the *Crypt* behind the *Vénus de Milo* (Pl. SG, p. 108), and ascending into R 1 (BIT). This may also be entered direct from the *Porte Champollion* (in the Passage des Arts), named after the great Egyptologist and first curator, J.-F. Champollion (1790-1832).

Crypt. On the staircase (l.), the stele of Antef, first herald in the service of King Thothmes III (1504-1450 B.C.), and other steles of the 12th Dynasty. In the crypt itself, l., stele dedicated by Queen Hatshepsut to her father Thothmes (1530-1520 B.C.). To the r., colossal sphinx in pink granite, from Tanis (Lower Egypt, 22nd Dyn.). On the staircase, six canopic jars that contained the entrails of Apis bulls (18th Dyn.).

R 1: colossal statue of Seti II (19th Dyn.) in red sandstone.

R 2 (r., S. 135): r., the cult chamber of the 'mastaba' or tomb of Akhouthotep, a high Egyptian dignitary (c. 2500 B.C., 5th Dyn.), found at Sakkara and built of limestone; inscribed in the architrave above the door are the occupant's name and titles. Within, the walls are covered with vivid scenes in bas-relief of contemporary life in the Old Kingdom, as well as those depicting the funeral of the deceased; some of them among the finest extant examples of the art. The offerings of food and drink were placed on the table of pink granite, now by the window.

R 3 (S. 133): diorite statues of an official and a woman of the 3rd Dyn. (c. 2750 B.C.); stele of King Zet, known as the Serpent King, his name being represented here as a serpent; the falcon above symbolizes Horus, the god of kingship. The sculpture was found near the king's tomb at Abydos (c. 3000 B.C.).

R 4 (S. 131): Old Kingdom (2650-2100 B.C.). Wall-case in the passage: stele of Nefertiabet, in painted stone (4th Dyn.); she is seated before a table of offerings, dressed in a leopard's skin. Three fine columns of pink granite with palm-leaf capitals; that on the l. being marked with the name of King Uni (5th Dyn.); the other two, which were taken by Rameses II, are of the same period. In the centre, a sarcophagus in the 'palace façade' style, found at Abu Roash (5th Dyn.). Note the charming low relief in limestone of a girl smelling a flower. Also a case displaying the more important models found in the pyramid of Didoufri, son of Cheops, including a red quartzite head of King Didoufri.

R 5 (S. 129): in the centre, a small limestone figure of a scribe seated cross-legged, known as the 'Scribe Accroupi', remarkable for its lifelike appearance, with eyes of white quartz, rock crystal, and ebony. In wall-cases, alabaster and hard-stone vessels dating from pre-dynastic times to the 6th Dyn. (c. 3400-2300 B.C.). In the passage, a limestone group of the official Raherka, and his wife Merseankh (5th Dyn.).

R 6: Middle Kingdom (2100-1750 B.C.). On the l. (W. wall), a fine limestone lintel of Sesostris III (1887-1850 B.C.); the king is shown making an offering of bread to the hawk-headed god Montou. In a recess (N. wall), a colossal royal statue in diorite; and, N. wall, sandstone statue of the scribe Mentuhotep.

R 7 (S. 128): on the r. in cases: statuette of Sesostris III in green schist, and part of the head of the same king in grey granite; statues in black granite of Sesostris III in his youth, and as an old man; wooden statue of the Chancellor Nakhti, from Assiut, one of the largest wooden funerary effigies known of this period (c. 2100 B.C.). In the l.-hand case of the third recess, a statue of stucco and painted wood known as the 'Porteuse d'Auge', a young girl, clothed in a tunic of netted pearls, carrying on her head a trough containing a joint of an ox, an essential of the funeral offering. Red sandstone group of two priests of Ptah, from Memphis (12th Dyn.). Wall-cases: on the r., statuette of a royal concubine, the thumbs of which have been intentionally cut off; on the l., five little wooden figures of girls carrying offerings. Huge statue of Sebekhotep IV (13th Dyn.).

R 8 (S. 127): on the l., the inner case of the coffin of Chancellor Nakhti; note the two mystical eyes painted on the outside. In a case (l.), silver and lapis-lazuli treasure discovered in four bronze caskets, marked Amenemhat II (1938-1904 B.C.), in the foundations of the temple of Tod. On the r., models of funerary boats for transporting the dead down the Nile. A portico with papyrus-like columns (13th Dyn.). To the l., limestone statue of the bull of Apis, of the 30th Dyn. (378-341 B.C.); statue of the scribe Sethi, kneeling, and holding a naos containing a figure of Osiris (19th Dyn.). N. wall, a huge basalt statue of Isis (Roman period).—The GAL. ÉPIGRAPHIQUE (S. 126) is temporarily closed.

The Escalier Percier, which we shortly ascend, leads to the Egyptian rooms on the First Floor.

R 11 (SALLE HENRI IV; S. 125): New Kingdom. Outstanding among the objects displayed here are (centre) a black granite statue of the god Amon protecting King Tutankhamen (18th Dyn.); the head (the r. half eroded by sand and wind) and feet of a huge pink granite statue of Amenophis III (18th Dyn.), with a list of the peoples he subdued inscribed on the base; the sarcophagus of Rameses III (20th Dyn.), the lid of which is in the Fitzwilliam Museum at Cambridge; painted bas-relief of Seti I and the goddess Hathor, from the tomb of the former (19th Dyn.); a red granite fragment from the base of the Obelisk of Luxor (see Rte 8), with four cynocephali (dog-faced baboons) adoring the rising sun, and cartouches of Rameses II; also several statues of Sekhmet, the lion-headed goddess; Hathor capital of pink granite, from Bubastis, where Sekhmet was especially worshipped; limestone statue of a dog; by the stairs to the crypt—at present closed—a statue of a Nubian woman from Korosko; and mummy-shaped sarcophagi, including that of Tenthapi.

The CRYPT contains a number of imposing funerary monuments of the late Saïte period, among them a wooden statue of Osiris. Cases display smaller funerary objects and statues—many zoomorphic—of the Ptolemaic and Roman periods. On the ceiling the zodiac of Dendera (see below) will be displayed.

We retrace our steps to **R 8** and turn r. into the first of three rooms devoted to **Coptic Antiquities** (S. 130), its r.-hand wall displaying painted cloths used as shrouds, showing masks of the deceased, outstanding amongst which is the Fayoum portrait, and the mummy of a woman showing the form of its wrapping, and how the mask was mounted. Near the window is a plaster mask of a child. On the l.-hand wall are colourful Coptic woven fabrics.

In the **2nd** room (S. 132), fragments of mural-paintings from one of the first monasteries, and a collection of bronze statuettes, crosses, lamps, and candlesticks, etc.—Round the **3rd** room (S. 134) is reconstructed part of the nave of the chapel of the monastery of Bawit (5-9C A.D.). Note the Coptic icon, painted on wood, of Christ protecting Apa Mena, Superior of the Monastery.

To continue the study of *Egyptian Antiquities,* we return to the foot of the ESCALIER PERCIER. Here are collected a number of objects discovered by Mariette in 1850-53 at the Serapeum at Memphis, including the limestone sphinxes which bordered its approach. The canopic jars held the entrails of two Apis bulls (18th Dyn.), supposedly the incarnation of Ptah, the great god of Memphis. The serapeum itself was the underground burial-chamber of the sacred bulls. On the half-landing is a large circular sandstone zodiac from the temple of Hathor at Dendera: on the upper landing, a sphinx (post-Ptolemaic period) from Medamoud; a limestone statue of the god Bes from the temple of Nectanebo; and a huge bust of Amenophis IV (who adopted the name of Akhnaton), from Karnak.

We turn l. into the first of a series of eight rooms devoted to smaller objects from the Egyptian collection.

R 'A' (S. 236): prehistoric and Thinite periods (4000-2800 B.C.).— *Cases 6-7:* schist palettes, for grinding and mixing paints, one decorated with a bull—symbolizing the king—pinning an enemy to the ground, and another depicting both imaginary and real animals (giraffes, etc.).— In the case facing the fireplace is the knife from Gebel-el-Arak (c. 3400 B.C.), and small ivory nudes, known as 'concubines of the dead'.

R 'B' (S. 238): Old Kingdom (2650-2100 B.C.).—*Case 4:* models of granaries.—*Case 5:* funerary furniture from the tomb of Chancellor Nakhti (c. 2159 B.C.).—*Case 8:* a remarkable carved wood couple (4th Dyn.), unfortunately damaged.—*Case 9:* ivory head-rest of Pepi II.— *Case 10:* painted limestone head (4th Dyn.; known as the 'Salt head').

R 'C' (S. 240): Middle Kingdom (2100-1750 B.C.), Intermediate Period (1700-1560 B.C.), and New Kingdom (1560-1320 B.C.). In the centre, Prince Ahmosis, a seated statue of painted limestone; to the r. of the entrance, cynocephalous statue (limestone), connected with sun-worship; over the chimneypiece, bas-relief in painted limestone of Amenmes and his wife Depet.—*Case 1:* realistic statuettes.—*Case 2:* alabaster and hard-stone vases; casket; and a blue-glaze pottery hippopotamus.—*Case 3:* further examples of blue-glaze ware.—*Case 9:* ivory wands, and 'heart' scarabs.—*Case 11:* wooden statuettes, including the priestess Toui (1200 B.C.), Queen Ahmes-Nefertari, and a naked girl with a fringe.—*Case 12:* jewellery of the New Kingdom, and a royal head in blue glass paste (18th Dyn.).—*Cases 13-14:* papyrus 'Books of the Dead'.

R 'D' (S. 242): Ramesside Period (1320-1086 B.C.).—*Case 1:* stone 'Ushabti' figures, placed in tombs to serve the dead.—*Case 8:* green enamelled schist statuette of the priestess Nacha; two statuettes of the scribe Nebmertuf writing to the dictation of the cynocephalic god Thot.—*Case 10:* bronze mirrors, the handle of one in the form of a girl.—*Case 11:* bronze 'kneeling prisoner', inlaid with silver.

R 'E' (S. 244): Amarna Period. In the centre, limestone bust (abnormal) of Akhnaton.—*Case 1:* well-preserved everyday objects: note the adjacent wooden head; between the columns is a display of scarabs.—*Case 7:* statue of the young King Akhnaton.—Near *Case 2,* a painted limestone head of a princess of El-Amarna.—*Cases 3-5:* writing and cosmetic articles, including spoons.—*Case 9:* bas-relief of Akhnaton and his queen Nefertiti; a fragment of a stele; the gold seal of Horemhep.—*Case 6:* musical instruments and games. Adjacent is a quartzite female torso.—*Case 10:* a chair of state; also a small case containing, on a wooden, silver-plated stand, a bronze statuette of King Taharqa kneeling before the falcon-god Hemen, of gold-plated schist.

R 'F' (S. 246): Pre-Saïte Period (1085-663 B.C.), and Saïte Period (663-525 B.C.).—*Case 2:* Pre-Saïte statuary.—*Case 3:* bronzes.—*Case 4:* models, possibly votive offerings.—*Case 8:* bronze sistrum; triad of Osorkon II, in gold and lapis-lazuli, with the divinities Osiris, Isis, and their son Horus; bronze tablet-cover, decorated in silver, gold, and electrum; necklace of Pinedjem I, of gold and lapis-lazuli.—*Case 11:* bronzes representing Bastet, the cat-faced goddess of Bubastis.—*Case 12:* bronze figures of kings and priests.—Displayed in the centre of the room, the damascened bronze statue of Queen Keramana, wife of Takelot II (847-823 B.C.).

R 'G' (S. 248): Saïte Period and Later Dynasties (663-333 B.C.). On either side of the entrance, statues of an ibis (sacred to Thot), and a goose (sacred to Amon).—*Case 1:* images of Bes, god of recreation, and (in *Cases 3-4,* and *8-9*) of other deities in the form of animals; and protective steles.—*Case 2:* basalt head of an old man.—*Case 10:* amulets.—*Case 11:* lion-shaped vases, from the time of the Persian domination.—Between **RR 'G'** and **'H'** is a black basalt 'healing statue' representing Horus on the crocodiles, covered with magic signs.

R 'H' (S. 250): Ptolemaic and Coptic Periods.—*Case 1:* architects' models. Note also the adjacent Duck.—*Case 2:* statues of Montou, the bull-headed god, and his wife.—*Case 6:* lower half of a sarcophagus from Chelidonia.—*Case 9:* jewellery, etc.—*Case 10:* highly decorated 'Mit Rahiné' pottery objects. In the centre, bronze statue of the falcon-god Horus, offering a libation.

D   Oriental Antiquities

This Department is most conveniently approached viâ the Salle des Cariatides (*Ground Floor*, Pl. SG), at the far end of which it is necessary to descend into the *Crypte Sully* (GT), which is situated beneath the *Pavillon de l'Horloge* (or *de Sully*).

CRYPTE SULLY. Antiquities from Palestine, including an ossuary in the form of a house, from Azor (4th millennium). In the centre of the 2nd Bay, one of the jars in which were preserved the Dead Sea Scrolls (2C B.C. and 1C A.D.), found by Bedouin in 1947. Moabite Stone, or stele of Mesha, king of Moab (842 B.C.), found in 1868 in a remote village E. of the Dead Sea.

The 34-line inscription, recording victories over the Israelites in the reigns of Omri, Ahab, and Ahaziah, is one of the most important, if not the earliest, examples of the alphabetic writing which has come down to us from the Phoenicians through Greek and Latin.—Cases contain jewellery, glass, and metalwork.

We ascend to **R1** (S. 103), with Sumerian antiquities from Lagash (Mesopotamia), and Semitic reliefs and sculptures of the Akkadian Dynasty (2340-2190 B.C.) from Susa.—*Case 5* (3rd millennium): bas-reliefs of a 'plumed figure' from Girsu (Sumer) and of Ur-Nanshe, prince of Lagash, carrying a basket of bricks on his head, with his sons; bronze bull's head, etc. Opposite, stele of the Vultures, commemorating the victory of Eannadu, king of Lagash, over a rival city, Umma. In the centre, silver vase of Entemena, with a frieze of incised animals and the Lagash 'crest', a lion-headed eagle. Stele of the victorious Naram-Sin, king of Akkad.

R2 (S. 104): neo-Sumerian antiquities of c. 2150 B.C., including eleven diorite statues of Gudea, ruler of Lagash.—*Case 4:* one large clay cylinder recording, in cuneiform, Gudea's achievements as a builder.— *Case 10:* 'turbaned' head (Gudea); goblet belonging to Gudea, decorated with serpents and winged dragons with scorpion tails.—*Small case:* alabaster statuette of Ur-Ningirsu, son of Gudea.—*Case 9:* woman with a scarf, from Girsu.—*Case 11:* the dog of Sumu-ilu.—*Case 12:* terracotta figurines (one strangling a bird).—*Case 6:* late cuneiform documents (3-2C B.C.).—2 cases containing seals and cylinders.

R3 (S. 105): Mari and Larsa. Objects from the temple of the goddess Ishtar (c. 2500 B.C.) at Mari, including an alabaster statue of the intendant of Mari, Ebih-Il (*Case 9*), and head of Ishtar (*Case 7*).—*Case 1* contains a mosaic panel showing a scene of war. On the wall, two murals from the 2nd millennium palace, depicting Ishtar investing King Zimrilim with regal powers, and a sacrificial scene.—*Small case:* two bronzes, one of Hammurabi on bended knee, his face and hands covered in gold leaf; the other of a group of three rampant ibex, with horns interlaced, from Larsa.—*Case 5:* ceremonial vase from Larsa, with Ishtar and figures of animals.—*Case 3:* relief of a goddess smelling a flower. Statuette of Idi Ilum, prince of Mari.—By the exit, a bronze lion from the temple of Dagon.

R4 (S. 106): Babylon. In the centre, the Codex of Hammurabi, a block of black basalt, covered with the closely written text of the 282 laws embracing practically every aspect of Babylonian life of c. 1800 B.C., at the top of which the god Shamash dictates the law to the king.—

'Kudurrus' or boundary-stones, with inscriptions. Along the E. wall, statues of the princes of Ashnunnak, a rival state, captured by Shutruk-Nakhuntè, an Elamite prince, who erased the original inscriptions and substituted his own (c. 1100 B.C.).—In cases, alabaster statuettes, including reclining female figures, some with jewelled eyes and navels; bronze horned dragon (6C B.C.), symbol of Marduk; terracottas (c. 2000-1700 B.C.).

RR 5-13 contain mainly the results of excavations made at Susa (Mesopotamia).

R 5 (S. 107): *Cases 1, and 4-9:* pottery and first attempts at metallurgy from Susa (4th millennium).—*Case 12:* northern Iran, 3rd-2nd millennia.—*Case 2:* Tepe Giyan and Tepe Sialk.—*Case 3:* silverware and jewellery (12-5C B.C.); note the ornamental vase-handle in the form of a winged ibex (6C B.C.).—On the walls, brick reliefs from Achemenian times, of lions, winged bulls, and griffins.

R 6 (S. 108): Susa, 3rd and 2nd millennia. Vase 'à la cachette', with treasure hidden inside it. In the centre, headless bronze statue of Queen Napir Asu, and ritual scene celebrating the sunrise, known as the Sit Shamshi.—*Cases 5-6:* vessels in bitumen and terracotta; votive offerings and toys.

R 7 (S. 109): monumental capital in grey marble from the palace of Darius I at Susa (521-486 B.C.). In the centre (*Case 1*), a lion in enamelled terracotta (700 B.C.); on the walls, reliefs in enamelled brick of a winged bull and a lion, and two warriors.—*Case 6:* two rhytons (silver and bronze); bronze fibula; alabaster vase; and bronze cup decorated with an ostrich hunt, etc.—*Case 2:* charter of Darius (521-486 B.C.), reporting how the king had the raw materials needed for building his palace brought from distant lands.

R 8 (S. 110): frieze of enamelled brick with royal archers in relief; also lions, griffins, and winged sphinxes, from the palace of Darius I (6-4C).—**RR 9-10** (S. 111-112): further enamelled brick reliefs. A man's head of stone; bronze lamp with a monkey on the lid, etc.—**R 11** (S. 113): another frieze of archers; Luristan bronzes.—**R 12** (S. 114): Parthian and Sassanid antiquities (3-9C A.D.). Cast of a mural niche from the palace of Shapur (3-4C A.D.).

Passing four large earthenware pots from Susa (3-2C B.C.), and funerary lions, we descend into the CRYPTE MARENGO, with lead Phoenician sarcophagi, and the black sarcophagi of Eshmunazar, king of Sidon (5C B.C.), which although Egyptian in style, has an inscription in Phoenician (cursing the eventual violator of the tomb); also statues from the sanctuary of the god Mithra.

R 14 (S. 115): busts and funerary reliefs from tombs found at Palmyra in Syria, and three divinities in military attire (2-3C A.D.). On the r. of the staircase are Phoenician sculptures, and in the following rooms, the collections from their great cities of Baalbek (Heliopolis), Sidon, Tyre, Byblos, and Rase-Shamra (Ugarit).

R 16 (S. 116): bust of the pharaoh Osorkon (924-895 B.C.); the 'Lady of Byblos' stele (5-4C), and an unusual three-sided stele in relief; woman's head in marble (3C B.C.). In cases: statuettes of Jupiter of Heliopolis, flanked by bulls (3-2C), votive hand, and other examples of the same cult; head of a sphinx (Roman; Baalbek); terracotta figurines; gold plaquettes; Syrian glass, etc.—In the adjoining room is a headless

Aphrodite from Dura-Europos, and a wall-painting of a wild-ass hunt (194 B.C.).

R 18 (S. 117): *Case 1:* gilded bronze figurines of the god Reshef, from Byblos.—*Case 2:* sphinx dedicated by princess Itar, daughter of pharaoh Amenemhat II (20C B.C.), found at Qatna.—Antiquities from excavations at Ras Shamra Ugarit: *Cases 12-17:* Cypriot, Mycenaean, and Canaanite pottery.—*Case 10:* ivory pyxis depicting a goddess of fertility in Minoan style; gold cup with hunting scene; bronze and gold figurines of the god Ba'al.—*Case 11:* alphabetic tablets describing Canaanite epics, etc.

The Hittite and Cappadocian antiquities previously shown here have been replaced temporarily by a small representative display of Islamic Antiquities (**R 20;** S. 120), including ceramics, metalware and arms, wood and ivory carvings, enamels, fabrics and rugs, Persian miniatures, etc.

R 19 (S. 118): Cyprus. In the centre, the 'Vase of Amathus', a huge monolithic cistern (5C B.C.). Among the statues, the 'King of Cyprus' (5C B.C.); also sculptured heads in the Greek style; a bronze charioteer with silver inlay; gold jewellery and repoussé work from Enkomi (*Case 7*); Bronze Age ceramics, Mycenaean kraters, terracotta and painted stone figurines, etc.

RR 21-23 (S. 121-123) are mainly devoted to reliefs (9-7C B.C.) from the great Assyrian palaces of Nimrud (Nos. 1-11), Khorsabad (Nos. 12-58), and Nineveh (Nos. 59-74). In the cases (l.) in **R 21** are carved ivories from Arslan-Tash.—In the four corners of **R 22,** winged bulls from Khorsabad (7C B.C.), each with an extra leg, for the sake of symmetry. Note the reliefs of King Assurnasirpal (No. 7), of King Tiglathpileser III (No. 9), and of King Sargon with his ministers (Nos. 28-30); also a fine bronze lion from Khorsabad.

The staircase leading down to the crypt—at present closed—containing Egyptian antiquities (see p. 110), is decorated with reliefs from the palace of Assurbanipal at Nineveh. The two bulls at the foot of the stairs come from the temple at Arslan-Tash (8C B.C.).

E   Objets d'Art

The collections of Objets d'Art are at present displayed in three sections of the *First Floor* of the Louvre: in the APOLLO GALLERY (Pl. SBl), the COLONNADE GALLERIES (along the E. side of the *Cour Carrée;* Pl. SB), and in rooms in the N. and N.W. wings of the *Cour Carrée* (Pl. SB).

The APOLLO GALLERY is entered from the *Rotonde d'Apollon,* behind the *Nike of Samothrace* (Pl. SG), through impressive wrought-iron gates of c. 1650, brought from the Château de Maisons, near Paris. The gallery, built originally during the reign of Henri IV, burned down in 1661, and rebuilt by *Le Brun,* is admirably decorated. The central ceiling painting is of Apollo's Victory over the Python, by *Delacroix.*

The various cabinets contain a magnificent collection of Medieval and Renaissance goldsmiths' work, gems, rock-crystal vessels, etc.

In front of the entrance is a large Florentine mosaic table (from the Château de Richelieu). In the centre, *cases 1, 3, and 5* contain what is left of the important collections belonging to the French royal house.—*Case 1:* semi-precious vessels of lapis-lazuli, jade, amethyst, amber, and red and green jasper.—*Case 2:* crown of St Louis (c. 1255); crown of Louis

XV (1722): after his coronation the gems were replaced by coloured stones, according to custom; crown of Napoleon I (after Charlemagne's), never placed on his head.—*Case 3:* rock-crystal vase with decorations illustrating Noah in his vineyard, and other vessels.— *Case 4* contains the *Crown Jewels* that were retained when the rest were sold in 1887, and include the Regent diamond (137 carats), discovered in India, and bought by the Regent in 1717; 'Côte de Bretagne', a ruby once owned by Marguerite de Foix, Anne of Brittany, Claude de France, and François I, and later cut into the shape of a dragon as a decoration of the Order of the Golden Fleece; the 'Hortensia' diamond, acquired in 1691; reliquary brooch of the Empress Eugénie (1855); plaque of the Order of the Saint-Esprit.

Case 5: vessels in agate, sardonyx, and basalt.—Beyond the case is a coloured marble table-top dating from the reign of Louis XIV; and at the far end of the room, one of the 13 Savonnerie carpets (1667; usually rolled) which originally covered the floor.—*Wall-case 6* (r.): ecclesiastical ornaments from the Abbey of St-Denis, presented by Abbot Suger: antique porphyry vase mounted in silver gilt as an eagle; rock-crystal vase given by Eleanor of Aquitaine to Louis VII, who gave it to Suger; antique sardonyx ewer, mounted c. 1150; crystal ewer of the 10C (Islamic); serpentine paten inlaid with gold dolphins (5-6C) set in an 8-9C border; lapis-lazuli plaque with figures of Christ and the Virgin (Byzantine; 11-12C); two Byzantine reliquary plaques from the Sainte Chapelle and the so-called 'Ring of St Louis' (14-15C) from St-Denis.— *Wall-case 7:* silver-gilt statuette of the Virgin (14C), presented in 1339 to St-Denis by Jeanne d'Évreux; gold sceptre of Charles V; coronation gold spurs, set with garnets and fleurs-de-lys (12C; restored); coronation sword 'of Charlemagne' (? 11C).—*Wall-case 8:* enamelled gold shield and morion of Charles IX; sword of Charles X; candlestick and rock-crystal mirror presented to Marie de Médicis on her marriage to Henri IV (1600); sword and dagger of the Grand Master of the Knights of Malta (Augsburg; 16C), given to Napoleon in 1797.—*Wall-cases 9 and 10:* reliquaries and church plate from the chapel of the Saint-Esprit, founded by Henri III in 1578.

On leaving the gallery, turn r. and traverse the Egyptian galleries to enter (l.) the SALLES DE LA COLONNADE (Pl. SB). accommodating the collections of Medieval and Renaissance Art. The Vestibule (**R 1**) is decorated with fine 17C woodwork from the Queen's Pavilion of the Château de Vincennes. In the cases are four ceremonial mantles of the Order of the Saint-Esprit.

R 2, the CHAMBRE À ALCÔVE, has panelling (restored by Louis XIV) from Henri II's apartments in the Louvre, on the site of the Salle des Sept Cheminées. On the walls, a tapestry of the Battle of Jarnac from the workshop of Claude de Lapierre; between the windows, a chest belonging to Marie de Médicis, with her monogram; in the alcove, a richly decorated late 17C altarpiece.

R 3, the CHAMBRE DE PARADE, contains good panelling, mostly of the period of Henri II; also a Mortlake tapestry (1630-35), and 17C wall-hangings in silver thread.

R 4: Early Middle Ages. Ivories, silver and goldsmiths' work, and enamels. Near the window the shrine of St Potentin in copper gilt, from Steinfeld near Treves (13C). The beautiful and extensive collection of ivories includes the Harbaville Triptych (Byzantine; 10C); triptych of the Nativity (Byzantine; 11C); caskets with scenes from the Life of Christ (Metz; 10C), and with mythological scenes (Byzantine; 10C); plaques, including Christ and St Peter (5-6C), Miracle of the Loaves (Ottoman; 10C), and the Rout of Silenus (Alexandria; 3C); two 6C pyxes; Virgin (English ?; 11C); liturgical comb with Samson and the lion (Metz; 10-11C); 12C chessmen, etc.—Enamels: reliquary of the arm of Charlemagne (Mosan; c. 1170) from Aix-la-Chapelle and—in centre—a bronze equestrian statuette of the emperor (9C); cross-reliquary given to the abbey of St-Vincent at Laon (1174-1205); champlevé work from Cologne and the Moselle (12-13C); chalice and paten (Spanish; c. 1200). The two porphyry columns are from the 4C basilica of St Peter at Rome. On the walls, three hangings illustrating the life of St Anatole de Salins (Bruges; early 16C), and a 15C Flemish tapestry of the Adoration of the Magi. To the l., by the exit, are Limoges and other enamels of the 12-13C, including a small shrine, a Crucifixion, and a Eucharistic dove.

R 5: by the window, a huge ivory altarpiece by the *Embriachi* (c. 1400), presented to the abbey of Poissy by Jean, duc de Berri. In the centre, 13-14C ivories from Paris workshops; also the casket of St Louis, a wooden box with enamel and metal decoration (Limoges; late 13C); enamelled ciborium (mid-13C), signed 'G. Alpais of Limoges'.—*Case 3:* Limoges enamels with repoussé work (13C).—*Case 4:* more ivories of the Paris School (c. 1320-40), with distinctive decoration.—*Case 5:* Limoges champlevé work (12-13C).—*Case 6:* reliquaries, including that of the arm of St-Louis of Toulouse (Italian; 1337), of St Martin (14C), and of Jaucourt (Byzantine 11-12C work with French 14C supporters); a ring containing a portrait of Jean sans Peur, and a ring of the Black Prince.— *Case 7:* Spanish and Italian ivories and enamel work, notably a 14C communion cup (Spanish).—In other cases, less important metalwork and 'dinanderie' (12-15C), etc. Also noteworthy, an embroidered cross from a chasuble (Bohemia; early 15C). On the walls, tapestries of St Luke painting the Virgin (Brussels; 16C), and the Virgin in Glory (Flanders; 1485). We pass fragments of 13C stained-glass from Reims, on our exit.

R 6, first of the two SALLES DE LA RENAISSANCE: By the windows, 15-16C Florentine bronzes, including a Flagellation attr. to *Donatello* (*Case 10*); Gnome with a snail (Paduan School, 15C); eight bronze reliefs from the tomb of Marcantonio della Torre, in San Fermo, Verona, by *Andrea Riccio* (1470-1532).—Cases by the third window contain 16C engraved Italian crystals, including work by *Valerio Belli;* twelve small busts of Caesars (16C), etc. Also a collection of French and Italian medals by *Pisanello, Matteo de' Pasti, G. Pilon,* and *G. Dupré.*— In the centre, the 'Spinario', a Renaissance cast of the antique original (c. 1541); 16C Florentine table, with a bronze fountain (Spanish). In the central cases, bronzes of the Florentine and Paduan Schools (15-16C), including works by *Donatello, Bellano,* and *Riccio.*

R 7. The cases in the centre contain a superb collection of Italian and Limoges enamels, mainly of the 15-16C: *Case 1:* medallion with a self-portrait by *Jean Fouquet.*—*Cases 3-5:* Limoges enamels from the workshops of *Poillevé, Jean* and *Pierre Pénicaud, Nouailher,* and others; and by *Léonard Limousin* and his School.—*Case 5:* Portrait of the Constable Anne de Montmorency, by *Léonard Limousin* (1556).—

Cases 6-7: enamels by Pierre Reymond and his School.—*Cases 8-10:* enamels by *Jean* and *Suzanne de Court, Pierre Courteys, J.* and *Martial Reymond, Jacques I* and *Jacques II Laudin, Jean Limousin, Jacques* and *Pierre Nouailher.*

The eight wall-cases and *Case 17* display a magnificent collection of Hispano-Moresque, French, and Italian ceramics of the 15-17C, with fine examples of the art of *Bernard Palissy* (c. 1510-89) in *Cases 18-19,* and from the St-Porchaire workshop (*Case 17*). Note also three intarsia panels attr. to *Fra Vicenzo da Verona* (c. 1500), and four ceramic medallions attr. to *Girolamo della Robbia,* from the Château of St-Germain-en-Laye (16C).

Around the walls (starting from the N.E. corner) is a series of twelve tapestries of the months, 'Les Chasses de Maximilien', *after B. van Orley* (Brussels, c. 1530).

We now turn l. along the N. galleries of the COUR CARRÉE, devoted to collections of **French Furniture** and **Objets d'Art.**

R8: tapestries by *Jean Cousin the Elder* of the Martyrdom of St Mammès, and another of an elephant hunt (mid-16C).—**R 9** (Pl. SB), with a walnut coffer from the château of Azay-le-Rideau, in the Italian manner. To the r. is a magnificent collection of silverware (16-18C) donated by the David-Weill family, including work by *Thomas Germain.*—**R 10,** with more silverware, jewellery, clocks and watches, and 15-16C ivories.—**R 11:** pre-Gobelins tapestries *after Simon Vouet,* including Moses in the bulrushes, and bronzes from the workshops of *Jean Bologne* and *F. Tacca,* some inspired by Michelangelo.—**R 12** (CHAMBRE DU MARÉCHAL D'EFFIAT), with a Gobelins tapestry of the Life of Scipio, from designs by *Jules Romain* (1689), a Delft tulipière (17C), and an inlaid desk belonging to Marie de Médicis.—**R 13:** devoted to the ornate furniture of André-Charles Boulle (1642-1732); to the r., in **R 14,** are further works of the period, including a pair of ebony cupboards once owned by William Beckford.—**R 16** (l.; SALLE CRESSENT), with French Regency furniture.

The rooms on the N. side of this wing (often closed) contain, among other objects, a superb collection of snuffboxes and watches of the 17-18C, with examples dating from 1746-59, by *Moynat, Noël Hardivilliers* (1752-79), *J.-J. Barrière* (1765-76), the *Drais* family (1769-82), and *P.-J. Menière* (1773-82), as well as representative works from other countries, notably Switzerland.

R 24 (l.): Louis-XV style, to the l. of which is a room devoted to Marie Leczinska, with her 'nécessaire' (1729), and a brass marquetry clock.—**R 26** continues with the display of furniture of this period.—**R 27,** with a fine Gobelins tapestry of sheepshearing (1735), and a screen woven in the Savonnerie after a design by *Desportes,* a bureau by *Mignon* and *Dubois,* and four armchairs by Heurtaut.—**R 28:** works by the ébéniste *J.-F. Oeben* (d. c. 1765).—**R 29:** Gobelins tapestries, bed-hangings from the Chambre Rose, woven for the Condé family at the workshop of *Neilson,* c. 1775; roll-top desk 'of the King of Sardinia' by *M. G. Cramer,* (c. 1770); and a portrait of the Baron de Breteuil by *Ménageot.*—**R 30:** 'Chinese' hangings *after Blain de Fontenay* and *Vernansal* (Beauvais, early 18C); a flat-topped bureau by *Hauré* and *G. Beneman* (1787) made for Louis XVI's library at Fontainebleau; roll-topped secrétaire in mottled mahogany by *J.-H. Riesener* (1784); a large commode by *Beneman,* from Compiègne.—**R 31** (SALLE LEBAUDY), with gilt and white panelling from the Hôtel de Luynes, and armchairs by *Sené.*—**R 32** (CABINET CHINOIS), with panels of Chinese papers of the late 18C, and lacquered corner-pieces and commodes by *Martin Carlin* (c. 1780-85); chairs by *Georges Jacob* and *Rode.*—**RR 33-35** contain Gobelins tapestry representing the story of Don Quixote *after Tessier* and *Ch. Coypel* (c. 1785). Note (in **R 35**) Marie-Antoinette's travelling-case made in Paris c. 1787.

R 36, with Napoleon's throne from Saint-Cloud (by *Jacob-Desmalter*), and a cradle for his son, the King of Rome, also by *Jacob-Desmalter* and *Thomire* after a design by *Proudhon* (1811); the 'Grand Écrin' jewellery-case by *Jacob-Desmalter* and *Thomire* after a design by *Percier* (1809); a commode decorated with Wedgwood plaques (1790); and a nécessaire by *M.-G. Biennais* and *Lorillon* offered by Napoleon to Tsar Alexander I in 1808.

R 37: silver-gilt tea-service by *Biennais* ordered by Napoleon for his marriage with Marie-Louise, and a Sèvres porcelain coffee-service decorated with views of Egypt, made for the wedding, and which the emperor later took with him to St Helena; bed belonging to Louis XVIII at the Tuileries, by *Jacob-Desmalter.*

R 38 (*Collection Adolphe de Rothschild*), with a 15C Flemish tapestry of the Miracle of the Loaves; bas-relief of the Madonna and Child by *Agostino di Duccio;* and remarkable late-13C polyptych-reliquary from the abbey of Floreffe, Flanders.

R 39 (*Collection Camondo;* see also p. 165): Four armchairs by *S. Brizard* (c. 1775), a chaise-longue by *Delanois* (c. 1765); marble clock, 'the Three Graces', attr. to *Falconet* (c. 1770); a bed signed *G. Jacob,* covered with Genoa velvet; six chairs by *Tilliard* (c. 1755; W. wall); and a collection of Meissen porcelain, etc.

R 41 (r.; *Collection Schlichting*): roll-top desk attr. to *David Roentgen* (c. 1780), once the property of the Tsarina Catherine II; a child's-armchair (? the Dauphin's) by *Gay* (1780); and a portrait of Louis-Élisabeth de Maillé by *Drouais.*

Returning through **R 39**, we see in **R 42** (*Collection Thiers;* Pl. SB) a number of Italian Renaissance bronzes, ivory carvings, etc., collected by the statesman, together with—in the adjoining room—examples of Sèvres and Vincennes porcelain (18C), among others.

F   Sculpture

The collections of Medieval, Renaissance, and 17-19C Sculpture in the Louvre are at present separated into two sections. The main entrance is the *Porte La Trémoille,* towards the PAVILLON DE FLORE; the other, the *Porte Jaujard,* is on the N. side of this pavilion.

R 1 (SALLE ROMANE; Pl. BT): sculpture of the 11-12C. To the r. of the entrance, fragments of the cloister of St-Genis-des-Fontaines; a Descent from the Cross (painted wood), probably Burgundian (early 12C); two capitals from Moutiers-St-Jean, one depicting the vintage, rare at this period; others of the Sacrifice of Abraham, and of David and Goliath, from Parthenay; a marble Merovingian capital recarved in the 11C of Daniel in the Lion's den, from the former abbey of Ste-Geneviève, Paris. To the l., a relief of St Michael and the Dragon, from Nevers. Passing through a doorway from the priory of Estagel (Gard), we enter

R2: Early French 'Gothic' Sculpture. On the r., fragments of a frieze from N.-D.-en-Vaux (Châlons-sur-Marne); column-statues of Solomon and the Queen of Sheba from N.-D. de Corbeil (c. 1180-90); l., two historiated spiral columns from the abbey of Coulombs (mid-12C); and a remarkable head of St Peter (1170-89), with eyes lined with lead, from Autun.

R3 (SECOND GOTHIC ROOM): in the centre, the Virgin 'de la Celle' (Île de France; 14C); tomb statues of Charles IV (le Bel) and Jeanne d'Évreux, from the abbey of Maubuisson (1372) by *Jean de Liège;* in a recess in the form of a vault is a marble figure of Guillaume de Chanac (d. 1348); painted wooden statue of a woman praying (early 14C).

From **R4** (THIRD GOTHIC ROOM) we descend into **R5** (SALLE PAUL VITRY), with the imposing tomb of Philippe Pot, Grand Seneschal of Burgundy (d. 1493), formerly in the abbey of Cîteaux.

R6 (far end): marble high relief of St George and the Dragon by *Michel Colombe* (c. 1508); r., marble tomb (1515-24) of Renée d'Orléans-Longueville, from the Célestins church, Paris; tomb of Louis de Poncher and his wife, from St-Germain-l'Auxerrois.

R7 (SALLE JEAN GOUJON): French 'Renaissance'. The Three Graces, *Germain Pilon* (c. 1535-90), a funeral monument for the heart of Henri II; Diana leaning on a stag, an early garden figure, from the Château of Anet; tomb-statue of Adm. Philippe Chabot in armour, attr. to Pierre Bontemps (1505-68); Deposition and the Evangelists (reliefs, c. 1545), *Jean Goujon;* effigies of the Constable Anne de Montmorency and his wife, *Barthélemy Prieur* (c. 1540-1611); and tomb of Valentine Balbiani, by *Pilon.*

We follow a passage to **R9** (HIGH GALLERY) and the adjacent room—German School—with the Virgin of the Annunciation, kneeling, *Tilman Riemenschneider* (1468-1531), of painted and gilded marble; a naked Magdalene, 'the beautiful German girl', by *Gregor Erhardt* (1470-1541), of painted wood.

Steps descend to **R11** (Pl. BT). Above the door, the Nymph of Fontainebleau, a bronze bas-relief by *Benvenuto Cellini* (1500-72); at the end of the room, the monumental portal of the Palazzo Stranga at Cremona, attr. to *Pietro da Rho;* on the landing, Mercury, *Jean Bologne* (1524-1608).

Stairs lead to the LOWER GALLERY, containing a collection of enamelled earthenware from the Florentine workshop of *Della Robbia,* and Italian sculpture of the 14-15C. Among the more notable works are: Madonna and Child surrounded by angels (marble bas-relief), *Agostino di Duccio;* Dietisalvi Nerobi (marble), *Mino da Fiesole* (1418-81); Madonna and Child, and a St John the Baptist as a youth, both by *Donatello* (1386-1468); in a case, a Bust of a Woman, in painted and gilded wood, attr. to the workshop of *Desiderio da Settignano.*

Adjacent rooms are at present closed. Retracing our steps through these galleries, it is possible, by ascending a small stair in **R8** and then turning W. through the picture galleries, to descend to the *Ground Floor* of the *Pavillon de Flore:* alternatively, walk round the N. side of the building to the PORTE JAUJARD.

Ascending steps ahead, we enter the VESTIBULE DE FLORE (R7; Pl. BT), with statues of La Fontaine, by *Pierre Julien* (1731-1804); Pascal,

Augustin Pajou (1730-1809), dated 1785; Corneille, *Jean-Jacques Caffieri* (1725-92), dated 1779; and Poussin, also by *Julien*.

RR 1-5 are not always on view but display representative works by *Antoine Coysevox* (1640-1720), *Sébastien Slodtz* (1655-1726), *Nicolas* and *Guillaume Coustou* (1658-1733 and 1677-1746 respectively), *J.-L.* and *J.-B. Lemoyne* (1665-1755 and 1704-78), *René Fremin* (1672-1744), *Edme Bouchardon* (1698-1762), *Allegrain* (1710-95), *J.-J. Caffieri, J.-B. Pigalle* (1714-85), and *E.-M. Falconet* (1716-91).

To the l. is **R 6**, devoted to the works of *Jean-Antoine Houdon* (1741-1828). Outstanding among these are the bronze Diana (1790), and busts of his contemporaries, including Voltaire, the singer Sophie Arnould, Rousseau, his smiling wife (original plaster), Diderot, Washington, Franklin, the Brongniart children, and Mme Adélaïde.

Also displayed here are busts of Mme du Barry, and Mme Vigée-Lebrun, both by *Pajou*, and his bronze bust of Lemoyne, his master; and a bust of Pajou by his pupil *Roland* (1746-1816). The 'Egyptian' by *Clodion* (1738-1814), and the clay models of *Joseph Chinard* (1756-1813) are also noteworthy.

Crossing the Vestibule, we enter **R 8**, containing Psyche revived by the kiss of Cupid, and Cupid and Psyche standing, both by *Antonio Canova* (1757-1822); Sappho, *Claude Ramey* (1754-1838); Cupid and Psyche, *F.-N. Delaistre* (1746-1832); Niobe wounded, *James Pradier* (1790-1852); bust of a young woman, *Chinard;* Gen. Marceau, *J.-E. Dumont* (1761-1844); La Tour d'Auvergne, *C.-L. Corbet* (1758-1808); Alexandre Lenoir, *Claude Michallon* (1751-99).

The following rooms (**9-12**) are devoted to *François Rude* (1784-1855), including his Mercury, and bust of the painter Louis David, showing the deformation of his mouth; to *A.-L. Barye* (1795-1875), *J.-B. Carpeaux* (1827-75), and other 19C French sculptors of varying merit. Note the bust of Mme Sabatier (1847), who inspired some of Baudelaire's poems, by *Auguste Clésinger* (1814-83); that of Mme Renoir; and several nudes and ballet studies by *Degas*.

A stair leads to a basement displaying the Two Slaves of *Michelangelo Buonarotti* (1475-1564), intended for the tomb of Pope Julius II, but given to Henri II in 1550 by Robert Strozzi. Also shown here is a bronze bust of Michelangelo by one of his pupils.

10   PL. VENDÔME; PALAIS-ROYAL; BIBLIOTHÈQUE NATIONALE AND CABINET DES MEDAILLES

MÉTROS: *Concorde, Tuileries, Pyramides, Palais-Royal, Bourse.*

The RUE DE RIVOLI, constructed in 1811-56, and named in honour of Bonaparte's victory over the Austrians in 1797, runs E. from the *Pl. de la Concorde* (Pl. 13; 3). The S. side of the street, flanking the *Tuileries Gardens* and the *Louvre*, is, in its W. half, uniform in design and is built above arcades, but except for the inveterate window-shopper, it makes a tiring promenade.

Right at the W. end, at the corner of the Rue St-Florentin, stands the 18C *Hôtel de la Vrillière*, built to designs by *Chalgrin*, where Talleyrand

(1754-1838) died, and where the Princesse de Lieven held her salon in 1846-57. The design of the *American Embassy* (see p. 160) was inspired by this building, and completes the symmetry of the N. side of the PL. DE LA CONCORDE. At No. 228 Rue de Rivoli, the *Hôtel Meurice,* von Choltitz, commander of the German forces in Paris, allowed himself to be captured (25 Aug. 1944), having refused orders to destroy the capital's principal buildings.

Turning l. into the Rue Cambon, where at No. 5 (prev. No. 3) Stendhal lived from 1810 to 1814 and at No. 22 Hubert Robert died in 1808, we cross the Rue du Mont-Thabor, where Alfred du Musset (1810-57) died at No. 6 and where Washington Irving lodged at No. 4 in 1821, to enter the Rue St-Honoré, leading E., parallel to the Rue de Rivoli. At its junction with the Rue Cambon stands the church of the *Assumption,* built in 1670 as the chapel of the convent of the Haudriettes and now used by the Polish community. At No. 398 (opposite) once stood the house where Robespierre lodged with the cabinet-maker Duplay from July 1791 to the day of his arrest. Turning E., we shortly cross the Rue de Castiglione, leading N. into the octagonal ****Pl. Vendôme** (Pl. 13; 4), a superb example of the Louis-XIV style, surrounded by houses with uniform façades, designed by *Hardouin-Mansart* (1645-1708). Many of the buildings here were erected after Mansart's death, but the façades of all conformed to the original design. Originally called *Pl. des Conquêtes,* it owes its present name to a mansion built here in 1603 by`César, Duc de Vendôme, son of Henri IV and Gabrielle d'Estrées.

A number are now hotels (the *Bristol* at No. 3; the *Ritz* at No. 15), or luxury shops, etc. Nos. 5, 22, and 28 were built for John Law (who also lived at No. 23 as controller-general of finance); Chopin died at No. 12 (1849); Nos. 11-13 are the *Ministère de la Justice* (since 1815); No. 16 was let to Dr Mesmer, the famous quack, in 1778; the composer Piccinni lived at No. 17 in 1787.

The centre of the Place is dominated by the **Vendôme Column,* constructed by *Denon, Gondouin,* and *Lepère* in 1806-10 in the style of Trajan's Column in Rome. It replaced an equestrian statue of Louis XIV by Girardon, which stood there previously.

Encircling the column (143 ft high and c. 12 ft in diameter) is a spiral band of bronze bas-reliefs, designed by *Bergeret* and made of the metal of Russian and Austrian cannon, in which the principal feats of arms in the campaigns of 1805-07 are glorified. The statue of Napoleon surmounting it is a copy (1863) of the original by *Chaudet* thrown down by the royalists in 1814 and replaced at the Restoration by a fleur-de-lys. In 1833 Louis-Philippe put up a statue of Napoleon, which is now at the Invalides. The present statue narrowly escaped destruction in 1871, when a group of Communards, led by the painter Courbet, brought the whole column crashing to the ground, an act that led to Courbet's exile in Switzerland and his ruin, since he had to pay for its re-erection in 1874.

The once fashionable Rue de la Paix (now lined with travel agencies and airline offices) leads N. to the *Pl. de l'Opéra* (see p. 151), crossing the Rue Danielle-Casanova (named after a Resistance heroine; previously Rue des Petits-Champs), with 17-18C houses, where at No. 22 Stendhal (1783-1842) died of apoplexy. We may regain the Rue St-Honoré by turning down the Rue du Marché-St-Honoré, passing the site of a Dominican convent where the Jacobin Club met in 1789-94. To the E., steps ascend to the Baroque church of **St-Roch** (Pl. 13; 4), begun by *J. Lemercier* in 1653. Work was abandoned in 1660, but a donation by

John Law on his conversion to Rome in 1719 enabled the nave to be completed; *Robert de Cotte* was responsible for the façade (1735).

The unkempt INTERIOR (413 ft long) contains monuments of interest. To the l. of the entrance is a medallion of Corneille (1606-84), who died in the neighbouring Rue d'Argenteuil (plaque on No. 6), and is buried in the church. In the 1st bay (r.) are a bust of François de Créquy (d. 1687) by *Coysevox,* and the tomb of the Comte d'Harcourt (d. 1666) by *Renard.* 2nd bay: statue of Card. Dubois (d. 1723) by *G. Coustou,* and a monument to the astronomer Maupertuis (d. 1759) by *Huez.* In the Lady Chapel, by *Hardouin-Mansart,* is a marble group of the Nativity by *Fr.* and *Michel Anguier,* from Val-de-Grâce.

W. AISLE. On the last pillar of the ambulatory (r.) is a bust of Le Nôtre (d. 1707) by *Coysevox.* The 3rd chapel (beyond the transept) contains a mourning figure, by *J.-B. Le Moyne the Elder,* of Catherine, comtesse de Feuquières (c. 1700) incorporated in a monument, the central feature of which is the bust of her father, Pierre Mignard (1610-95), by *Girardon.* Diderot, Holbach, Mme Geoffrin, and the Abbé de l'Épée (see p. 62) are also buried in St-Roch.

The adjoining Rue St-Roch, where Vauban (1633-1707) died (plaque on the corner), rejoins the Rue de Rivoli just W. of the PL. DES PYRAMIDES, with a bronze-gilt statue of Joan of Arc, by *Frémiet.*

Continuing E. along the Rue St-Honoré, the scene both here and in neighbouring streets of Bonaparte's suppression of the royalist rising of 5 Oct. 1795 (some marks of his 'whiff of grape-shot' may be detected on the front of *St-Roch*), we shortly enter the PL. DU THÉÂTRE-FRANÇAIS(Pl. 14;1), with a view N..W. towards the *Opéra.* The two fountains are by *Davioud.* To the r. the short Rue de Rohan leads to the Rue de Rivoli opposite the arch leading to the *Pl. du Carrousel.* On the E. stands the **Théâtre Français,** built in 1786-90 by *Victor Louis,* but largely remodelled after a fire in 1900, and again the object of restoration.

As an institution the *Théâtre-Français* (or *Comédie-Française*) dates from the amalgamation in 1680 of the Hôtel de Bourgogne actors with Molière's old company, which had already absorbed the Théâtre du Marais. In 1812 Napoleon signed a decree (at Moscow) reorganizing the Comédie-Française, which is still a private company although controlled by a director nominated by the government and enjoying a state subsidy.

The vestibule contains, among other statues of actors, Talma, by *David d'Angers;* the staircase and foyer display busts of eminent dramatists including Dumas fils by *Carpeaux* and Mirabeau by *Rodin,* a statue of George Sand, by *Clésinger* (her son-in-law), and a *Seated statue of Voltaire, by *Houdon.* The chair in which Molière was sitting when acting in 'Le Malade Imaginaire', when taken fatally ill, is also preserved. The Library may also be consulted.

An inscription at the corner of the Rue de Valois (on the E. side of the *Palais-Royal*) marks the site of the 'Salle de Spectacle du Palais-Cardinal', occupied by Molière's company from 1661 to 1673, and by the 'Académie Royale de Musique' from 1673 until a fire in 1763.

Abutting the *Théâtre Français,* the ****Palais-Royal** constitutes one of the most attractive and interesting areas of Paris. The name is now applied not only to the original palace, but also to the extensive range of buildings and galleries surrounding the gardens to the N. The latter, a pedestrian thoroughfare, entered from neighbouring streets by several passages, now a delightful backwater and haunt of the philatelist, played an important role in the Revolutionary period, and among the profligate society of the late 18th and early 19C, was the scene of licence and revelry.

History. The Palais-Royal proper was originally known as the 'Palais-Cardinal', having been built by *J. Lemercier* in 1634-39 for Richelieu, who, as chief minister, wished to be near the Louvre. He died there in 1642. Bequeathed to Louis XIII, it was first called 'Palais-Royal' during the residence of Anne of Austria (d. 1666), then regent, and her sons Louis XIV and Philippe d'Orléans. Richelieu's apartments were then occupied by Card. Mazarin. During the Fronde they all had to escape to St-Germain-en-Laye; Louis therefore disliked the palace and it was Philippe and his wife Henriette d'Angleterre who returned to live there, as did the latter's mother, Queen Henrietta Maria, in 1652.

Louis housed the Royal Academy of painting and sculpture in the W. wing, and also his mistress Louise de la Vallière. This was the period of Mansart's alterations. In 1692 the palace was given by Louis to his brother and his heirs. It acquired an equivocal reputation from the dissolute 'petits soupers' given by the Regent (1715-23). Changes were made for the latter's son by *Constant d'Ivry* and *Cartaud*. In 1763 a fire destroyed the E. wing and the theatre. The houses and galleries around the gardens were built as a speculation by Philippe-Égalité, the Regent's great-grandson, in 1781-86, under pressure of debt, and let out as shops and cafés, etc. He also built the *Théâtre-Français;* and the *Théâtre du Palais-Royal,* in the N.W. corner, dates from the same period.

The cafés became a meeting-place for malcontents, since the police were excluded from entry, and on 13 July 1789 Camille Desmoulins delivered in the gardens the fiery harangue which precipitated the fall of the Bastille the following day. Its name was changed to the 'Palais-Égalité', and it was used as government offices. In 1814 it was returned to the Orléans family, and reverted to its earlier name; and Louis-Philippe lived there until 1832. In 1848 it was plundered by the revolutionaries, and occupied for a time by the 'Rights of Man' club.

During the Second Empire it was the residence of Jérôme Bonaparte, and Taine, Flaubert, Sainte-Beuve, and the brothers Goncourt were often entertained there. The Palais was rebuilt by *Chabrol* in 1872-76 after damage during the Commune. It is now occupied by the *Conseil d'État* and the *Ministère des Affaires Culturelles.*

The *Hôtel de Rambouillet*, built on part of the site of the Palais-Royal, was, during c. 1618-50, a famous intellectual centre; Saint-Évremond, Malherbe, La Rochefoucauld, the Scudérys, Bossuet, and the Duchesse de Longueville being among its habitués.

The buildings in the *Cour de l'Horloge,* facing the PL. DU PALAIS-ROYAL, were erected by *Constant d'Ivry* (1763-70), with sculptures by *Pajou* (l. wing) and *Franceschi* (r.; 1875). The façade on the N. side, overlooking the *Cour d'Honneur,* was begun by *d'Ivry,* continued by *Louis,* and completed by *Fontaine,* who also restored the E. and W. wings. The so-called *'Galerie des Proues',* on the E. side of the court, is the only relic of *Lemercier's* 17C building. To the N., the *Cour d'Honneur* is separated from the gardens by the *Galerie d'Orléans,* a double Doric colonnade by *Fontaine* (1829-31), which was restored and cleared of its shops in 1935.

The **Gardens** of the *Palais-Royal* are surrounded on three sides by arcades and buildings (by *Louis;* 1781-86), still occupied by shops and dwellings; Colette (1873-1954) died at No. 9 Rue de Beaujolais, beyond the *Galerie Beaujolais* to the N. On the W. side is the *Galerie de Montpensier,* and opposite is the *Galerie de Valois,* altogether a charming and harmonious ensemble. Other residents in recent times were Jean Cocteau and Jean Marais, while at Nos. 79-82 Gal. de Beaujolais, the 'Grand Véfour' was the fashionable rendezvous of writers in the Second Empire. Earlier, in the same house, Mlle de

Montansier entertained the leaders of the Revolution in 1789. Charlotte Corday bought her knife at No. 177 Gal. de Valois; No. 17 Gal. de Montpensier was in 1785 a museum of waxworks, having been founded by Curtius, the uncle of Mme Tussaud.

Immediately E. of the *Palais-Royal* lies the Rue de Valois, with (Nos. 1-3) the *Pavillon du Palais-Royal* (1766, by *d'Ivry* and *Moreau*); at Nos. 6-8, once the *Hôtel Melusine,* took place the first meetings of the French Academy in 1638-43, and the ox sculptured above the door recalls its period as the restaurant 'Boeuf à la Mode' from 1792 to 1936.

Students of architecture will find the *Caisse Nationale des Monuments Historiques* (No. 1 Rue de Valois), with extensive photographic archives, of value.

In the parallel street to the E., the Rue Croix-des-Petits-Champs, is the entrance to the **Banque de France** (Pl. 14; 1), founded in 1800 and accommodated here in 1811. The buildings incorporate the former *Hôtel de la Vrillière,* built by *Mansart* in 1635-38 and restored by *Robert de Cotte* in 1719. Later known as the *Hôtel de Toulouse* from its occupancy by the Comte de Toulouse, son of Louis XIV and Mme de Montespan, it became the residence of the Princesse de Lamballe, murdered in the prison of *La Force* in 1792.

The *Hôtel Portalis* (by *Ledais;* 1750) is on the corner of the Rue de la Vrillière and the Rue Croix-des-Petits-Champs, No. 13 of which was occupied by Malherbe in 1606. St Vincent de Paul lived in the street in 1613-16, and Bossuet in 1699-1702, at No. 52. Another resident was Mme de Pompadour (1721-64), from 1725 to 1745, before her departure for Versailles; she was born (as Antoinette Poisson) in the Rue de Cléry, a short distance to the N.E. Richelieu is believed to have been born in the Rue du Bouloi, just to the E.

No. 33 in the Rue Radziwill, on the N. side of the *Banque de France,* has an unusual double staircase; while Mansart's projecting angle here, supported by a bracket, is admired as a masterpiece of stonework.

The profusely decorated *GALERIE DORÉE, within the Bank, may be visited by those providing suitable bona fides.

To the N.E. of the Bank lies the circular **Pl. des Victoires,** laid out by *J. Hardouin-Mansart* in 1685; the surrounding houses were designed by *Pradot.* The equestrian statue of Louis XIV by *Bosio* (1822) replaces the original, destroyed in 1792; the bas-reliefs on the pedestal depict the Passage of the Rhine, and Louis XIV distributing decorations.

Thackeray lived in the Rue Hérold, to the S.E., after his marriage in 1836.

Immediately N.W. is the PL. DES PETITS-PÈRES, with a surprisingly provincial aspect, off which the Rue du Mail leads N.E., where Colbert lived (at No. 5, richly decorated) and Mme Récamier (No. 12), while Liszt was a frequent visitor at No. 13.

On the N. side of the Place stands **N.-D.-des-Victoires,** or the church of the *Petits-Pères,* dedicated in 1629 by Louis XIII in memory of the capture of La Rochelle from the Huguenots, but not finished until 1740. Every interior wall is plastered with ex-voto tablets. In the 2nd chapel on the l. is the tomb of the composer Jean-Baptiste Lulli (1633-87) by *Michel Cotton,* with a bust by *Gaspard Collignon;* in the choir are elaborately carved stalls, and seven paintings by *C. Van Loo.*

The adjoining street leads N. to the **Bourse** or *Stock Exchange* (open daily, 12.00-16.00; closed for business at 15.00), built by *Brongniart* and *Labarre* in 1808-27, and resembling the Temple of Vespasian in Rome. The N. and S. wings were added in 1903.

The Rue Feydeau, to the N., built on Louis-XIII fortifications, and the Rue des Colonnes, to the W., retain some interesting houses in an old district through which the Rue du Quatre-Septembre was driven in 1864, before being renamed on the proclamation of the Third Republic.

The Rue Vivienne leads S. from the *Bourse* along the E. side (r.) of the *Bibliothèque Nationale* (see below), and retains several 17-18C houses; Simón Bolívar lived at No. 2bis in 1804.

Of more interest is the parallel Rue de Richelieu, to the W., laid out by the great cardinal, running S. to the Pl. du Théâtre-Français. Rossini and Meyerbeer lived in its N. half; Grétry resided at No. 52, further S., in 1780. No. 101, with decorative masks in the courtyard, was the home of the Abbé Barthélemy (1716-95), author of the 'Voyage du jeune Anacharsis' and antiquary, who had charge of the royal collection of medals, then housed in the *Hôtel de Nevers* (see below). Anthelme Brillat-Savarin (1755-1826), author of the 'Physiologie du goût', died at No. 66; Ninon de L'Enclos (1620-1705) had lived there in 1653-59. On the l., at the corner of the Rue Colbert, stands part of the *Hôtel de Nevers,* built by Mazarin in 1649 to house his library (see below). As the home of Mme de Lambert it was a famous literary salon in 1710-33, where Montesquieu and Marivaux met. Further on is a fountain of 1708, and beyond (r.) in the SQUARE LOUVOIS (Pl. 14; 1), the attractive *Fontaine Louvois,* by the younger *Visconti* (1844).

The *Square* was laid out in 1839 on the site of a theatre built in 1792, which housed the Opéra from 1794 to 1820. On 13 Feb. 1820 the Abp. of Paris was called here to administer the last sacraments to the assassinated Duc de Berry, consenting to do so on such unholy ground on condition that the theatre was afterwards pulled down!—Donizetti lived at No. 5 Rue de Louvois in 1840.
Bossuet (1627-1704) died at No. 46 Rue Ste-Anne, the parallel street to the W.

On the E. side of the Square (and of the Rue de Richelieu) rises the W. façade of the **Bibliothèque Nationale.**

Admission. Most departments of the *Bibliothèque Nationale* are open daily from 9.00 or 10.00—17.00 or 18.00, except Sun., public holidays, and for a fortnight after Easter. Foreigners wishing to use the Library should apply to the Reception Desk with some form of identity, two identity photographs, a letter of recommendation (in the case of students, from their director of studies), etc. Information regarding the completion of requisition forms, photocopying services, etc., is freely available. Catalogues may be bought at No. 71 Rue de Richelieu, opposite. Frequent temporary exhibitions are also held in the building.

The Library is divided into the following departments: *Maps and Plans; Prints; Printed Books, Manuscripts; Oriental Manuscripts; Music* (at No. 2 Rue de Louvois); *Periodicals;* and *Medals* (see below). The *Bibliothèque de l'Arsenal,* a subsidiary collection, is at No. 1 Rue de Sully (see p. 137).

The *Bibliothèque Nationale* ranks with the British Museum as one of the two largest libraries in W. Europe. The extensive buildings were erected at various times on the site of the 17C *Hôtel Mazarin,* and include the *Hôtel Tubeuf,* whose brick and stone façade, set back in the Rue des Petits-Champs, was built by *Le Muet* in 1635.

Formerly known as the *Bibliothèque Royale* and the *Bibliothèque Impériale,* it originated in the private collections of the French kings. Largely dispersed at the end of the Hundred Years War, the Library was refounded by Louis XII, and moved to Blois. During the next two centuries it was removed to Fontainebleau, and then Paris, before finding its present home in the Rue de Richelieu in 1721. Guillaume Budé (c. 1468-1540) had earlier been appointed the first Royal Librarian. It was enriched by purchase or by gift of many famous private libraries and smaller collections (including that of Colbert), and at the Revolution its range was further increased with the confiscation of books from numerous convents and châteaux. In 1793 it was enacted that a copy of every book, newspaper, etc., printed in France, should be deposited by the publishers in the Bibliothèque Nationale.

The building is entered at No. 58 Rue de Richelieu; the main vestibule being on the r. of the *Cour d'Honneur*. The READING ROOM (seen through glass doors opposite), roofed by nine faience domes, seats 360 readers who have access to over 10,000 works of reference. The GALERIE MANSART, used for exhibitions, lying to the r. at the foot of the stairs, was formerly Mazarin's sculpture gallery; note his arms above the door, and the carved foliage and paintings by *Grimaldi*. The CABINET DES ESTAMPES, beyond, contains over 5 million prints.

The *Cabinet des Médailles et des Antiques, beyond the iron gates on the landing, is still under rearrangement and not normally on view to the general public, but may be visited by scholars. The collection, founded in the 16C, in addition to antiquities of outstanding quality, also contains c. 400,000 coins and medals. Among the more important objects displayed are: R1: a Parian marble torso of Aphrodite (Hellenistic period); French and foreign coins, engraved cameos, jewels, Renaissance medals, etc.; wall-cases contain Egyptian terracottas; bronzes; painted limestone statuettes.

R2: the central case—much of the furniture is by *Jacob*—displays an ivory chessman representing a Hindu king on an Elephant (reputed to have belonged to Charlemagne); a bust of Constantine the Great, once the head of the cantor's wand at the Sainte Chapelle; the 'Patère de Rennes', a Roman gold dish found in 1774; Merovingian chalice and oblong paten (6C), from Gourdon, in the Charollais; the *'Grand Camée' (also from the Sainte Chapelle), representing the Apotheosis of Germanicus, with Tiberius and Livia—it is the largest antique cameo known; agate nef from St-Denis; *Dish of Chosroes II, king of Persia (c. A.D. 600); *Cup of Ptolemy, in sardonyx; *Aquamarine intaglio of Julia, daughter of Titus, one of the best glyptic portraits extant; engraved Chaldaean stone (1100 B.C.) found near Baghdad.

In other cases: red-figured amphora, signed Amasis; cylix of Arcesilaus, king of Cyrene; vase of Berenice (239-227 B.C.) from Benghazi, and other ceramics; Roman curule chair of bronze, with arms and back added by Suger (12C), on which the kings of France were crowned, and known as the Throne of Dagobert; gold objects from the tomb of Childeric I, at Tournai; *Ivory consular diptychs, and Byzantine diptychs; gold bullae of Charles II of Anjou, king of Naples (1285-1309), of Baldwin I, Emperor of Constantinople in 1204-06, and of Edmund, Earl of Lancaster, titular king of Sicily, 1255-63; gold coins found at Chécy (Loiret); a Celtic bracelet (Aurillac, 5-6C); *Silver hoard from the temple of Mercurius Canetonensis (Berthouville, Eure), including silver figurines and vessels of the 2C B.C. and others of the best Greek period.

R3 contains Roman bronze statuettes, domestic utensils, ancient arms and armour, Greek and Etruscan vases, etc.—**R 5,** the Salon Louis XV, decorated by *Van Loo* and *Natoire,* and with dessus de portes by *Boucher,* retains its original coin cabinets.

Stairs ascend to the floor above, with (r.) the MANUSCRIPT ROOM (with more than 130,000 MSS., of which some 10,000 are illuminated); and l., the GALERIE MAZARINE, by *Mansart* (1645), with a ceiling by *Romanelli.* Beyond is the *Department of Maps and Plans.*

Immediately S. of the *Bibliothèque Nationale* we cross the Rue des Petits-Champs. No. 45 was the residence of Lulli until 1683, built by him with financial help from Molière; the garret of No. 57 was the home of Rousseau and Thérèse Levasseur c. 1754; Mme Récamier (1777-1849) died of cholera at No. 8.

Continuing S., at the corner of the Rue Molière (where at No. 37 lived Voltaire and Mme du Châtelet) is the *Fontaine Molière,* also by *Visconti* (1844; the dramatist by *Seurre,* and the figures of Comedy by *Pradier*). Molière (1622-73) died in a house on the site of No. 40 Rue de Richelieu; Denis Diderot (1713-84) died at No. 39; and Pierre Mignard (1610-95) at No. 23. No. 21, formerly the *Hôtel Dodun* by *Bullet* (1715), preserves some of its 18C grandeur; the composer Sacchini (1734-86) died at No. 14.

The street ends at the *Pl. du Palais-Royal.*

11   FROM THE PL. DU PALAIS-ROYAL TO THE PL. DE LA BASTILLE

MÉTROS: *Palais-Royal; Louvre; Les Halles; Étienne-Marcel; Châtelet; St-Paul; Sully-Morland; Bastille.*

Leaving the S. façade of the *Palais-Royal* on our l. (see p. 124; Pl. 14; 1), we follow the Rue St-Honoré. A short distance E. is the **Temple de l'Oratoire,** designed by *Clément Métezeau the younger* and *Jacques Lemercier,* and built in 1621-30 for Card. Bérulle, as the mother church in France for his Congregation of the Oratory. In 1811, Napoleon assigned it to the Calvinists. The portal was added in 1845.

Against the apse is a monument to Adm. Coligny (1519-72), the chief victim of the massacre of St Bartholomew, who was murdered in a house now replaced by No. 144 Rue de Rivoli. Here stood the *Hôtel de Ponthieu,* where the actress and singer Sophie Arnould (1764-1804) was born.

Further E. in the Rue St-Honoré, Molière was born on the site of No. 96 in 1622; opposite is the *Fontaine du Trahoir* (rebuilt by *Soufflot* in 1778, replacing an earlier fountain by *Goujon),* with its stalactites and shells. The chemist Lavoisier (1743-94) owned No. 47; and Riesener (1734-1806), the cabinet-maker, died at No. 2. Gallows stood at the point where the street is intersected by the Rue de l'Arbre-Sec, and nearby Card. de Retz was attacked during the Fronde (1648). Well-preserved 17C houses can be seen at Nos. 33-45.

A short distance past the *Oratoire,* at No. 11 Rue du Louvre leading N. to the small PL. DES DEUX-ÉCUS, are slight remains of Philippe Auguste's fortifications. Off the Rue J.-J. Rousseau (leading S.W. from this point) is the no longer fashionable *Véro-Dodat arcade* (1822), and beyond, the Rue du Pélican, which once lived up to its original name of 'Poilcon'.

To the E. of the Pl. des Deux-Écus stands the **Bourse du Commerce** (Pl. 14; 4), formerly the *Corn Exchange,* a circular 18C building remodelled in 1888, the westernmost and now the only remaining relic of the inadequate *Halles Centrales,* which until recently consisted of twelve huge pavilions.

Markets had stood here since the early 12C, but what Zola called "le ventre de Paris" has now been replaced by extensive modern markets at *Rungis-Halles,* a short distance N. of Orly airport (see p. 234). Work is still in progress with the complete restoration of the area; the plan for which will be a compromise between the designs for its redevelopment by *Bernard de la Tour d'Auvergne* and *Ricardo Bofill.*

A fluted Doric column abutting the *Bourse du Commerce* (S. side) is the only relic of the *Hôtel de la Reine* (later *Hôtel de Soissons,* in the garden of which stock-jobbing took place from 1720), built for Catherine de Médicis in 1572 on the site of the earlier *Hôtel d'Orléans* which had belonged to Blanche of Castile. The column may have been used as an astrologer's tower.

Further N. in the Rue du Louvre (r.) is the **Hôtel des Postes** (1880-84), the main *Post Office* of Paris: opposite, in the elegant *Hôtel d'Ollone* (built in 1639 and altered in 1730), the *Caisse d'Épargne* (or Savings Bank) is installed.

From the 13th to the 18C, the *University of Paris* was responsible for the postal service for private citizens, while from 1461 the royal mail was carried by relays of post riders. In 1719 the University lost its privilege and all mail was controlled by the royal service. In 1757 the postal headquarters was in the *Hôtel d'Hervart.*

On the E. façade of the *Hôtel des Postes,* facing the N. extension of the Rue J.-J. Rousseau (where, at No. 57, Rousseau lived with Thérèse Levasseur in 1776), is an inscription marking the site of the Hôtel which had been occupied by La Fontaine (1621-95) at the time of his death. Nos. 64 and 68 are worth noting.

Just N. of the *Bourse du Commerce,* the Rue Coquillière (with a remarkable shop selling kitchen utensils) leads E. to **St-Eustache* (Pl. 14; 2), in detail and decoration a Renaissance building, but in plan and in its general lay-out of medieval design.

Begun in 1532, perhaps by *Pierre Lemercier,* it was consecrated in 1637. The main W. doorway was rebuilt in 1754-88 in a completely inharmonious classical style. Both transepts have handsome round-headed doorways (c. 1638-40). The N. transept is approached by a passage from the Rue Montmartre. The open-work bell-tower ('Plomb de St-Eustache') above the crossing, has lost its spire. Above the Lady Chapel in the apse is a small tower built in 1640 and restored in 1875.

The church was the scene of the riotous Festival of Reason in 1793, and in 1795 it became the 'Temple of Agriculture'. Molière was baptized here in 1622, and Antoinette Poisson (Mme de Pompadour) in 1721; Lulli was married here in 1662. In 1791 the body of Mirabeau lay in state here before its removal to the Panthéon. Among those buried here are Colbert (1619-83), Adm. de Tourville (d. 1701), and Rameau (1683-1764). *St-Eustache* has always been noted for its music. Berlioz here conducted the first performance of his 'Te Deum' (1855), and Liszt his 'Messe Solenelle' (1866). Its organ recitals are worth attending.

The INTERIOR is unusual in its striking combination of classical forms with a Gothic plan. The double aisles and chapels of the nave are continued round a choir. The square piers are flanked by three storeys of columns in Renaissance variants of the classical orders. The chapels are decorated with paintings from the time of Louis XIII, but restored. The eleven lofty windows of the apse were executed by *Soulignac* (1631), possibly from cartoons of *Philippe de Champaigne*. The churchwardens' pew by *Pierre Le Pautre* dates from c. 1720. The stalls came from the convent of Picpus.

S. AISLE. The 2nd chapel commemorates Rameau; by the transept doorway is a 15C statue of St John the Evangelist; the 2nd choir chapel has a Pietà by *Luca Giordano* (?). In the Lady Chapel, on the altar, is a Virgin by *Pigalle;* the murals are by *Thos. Couture*.

N. AISLE. In the 1st choir chapel as we return is the tomb of Colbert, designed by *Le Brun*, with statues of Colbert and Fidelity by *Coysevox*, and of Abundance by *Tuby*. Above the W. door is the Martyrdom of St-Eustache, by *Simon Vouet*.

The Rue de Turbigo leads N.E. from *St-Eustache* to the *Pl. de la République*, soon reaching the Rue Étienne-Marcel, in which, to the l. (at No. 20), rises the *Tour de Jean-sans-Peur*, a graceful defensive tower of c. 1400 once incorporated in the *Hôtel de Bourgogne*. Part of this mansion (see No. 29) was used in the 16-18C as a theatre, where Corneille's 'Le Cid', and Racine's 'Andromaque' and 'Phèdre' were performed.

The next street to the E. is the old Rue St-Denis. At No. 135, in its N. section, an inscription shows the former position of the *Porte St-Denis* or *Porte aux Peintres*, a gateway in the *Walls* of Philippe Auguste. At the corner of the Rue Tiquetonne (then the Rue du Petit-Lion), stood the old shop bearing the sign of the 'Cat and Racket', celebrated in Balzac's story 'La Maison du Chat qui Pelote'. On No. 142 is the *Fontaine de la Reine* (1730).

Passing S. down the street, where at No. 133 are some old statues from the medieval *Hospital of St-Jacques* (on this site), we reach (l.) **St-Leu-St-Gilles**, built in 1235, and first rebuilt after 1319. The nave is of this date; the aisles were added in the 16C; the choir, still partly Gothic, in 1611, the last having been reconstructed in 1858-61 to make way for the adjacent boulevard. The façade and windows were remodelled in 1727, and a crypt excavated in 1780. The church contains three Nottingham alabaster reliefs (in the sacristy entrance) and a sculptured group of St Anne and the Virgin, perhaps from Écouen, by *Jean Bullant* (2nd S. chapel). The organ gallery is by *Nic. Raimbert* (1659).

Housed in the former presbytery (entered from No. 57 Blvd. de Sébastopol) is a *Musée d' Hygiène,* containing maps, plans, and models of sanitary installations, etc.

Marivaux (1688-1763) was born on the site of No. 106 Rue Rambuteau, two streets further S.

Continuing S. in the Rue St-Denis, we pass (r.) the small SQUARE DES INNOCENTS, on the edge of the Halles excavations, and on the site of the medieval *Cimetière des Innocents,* the main burial ground of Paris until 1785, when the remains were transferred to the *Catacombs* (see p. 64). Those of La Fontaine were probably among them. Traces of the arches of the cemetery galleries are still to be seen on Nos. 11 and 13 in the Rue des Innocents.

The charming Renaissance *****Fontaine des Innocents** (which may be re-sited when works are completed) stood in the centre of the Square. Erected in 1548 in the neighbouring Rue St-Denis by *Pierre Lescot*, with bas-reliefs by *Jean Goujon* (now in the Louvre), it was remodelled and set up here by *Payet* c. 1788, the S. side (for it had earlier abutted a building) being decorated by *Pajou*.

At the N.W. corner of the Square is the reconstructed doorway from the office of the *Marchandes Lingères* (1716).

To the S. is the Rue de la Ferronnerie, where, in front of No. 11, Henri IV was assassinated by Ravaillac in 1610.

No. 33 Rue St-Denis has an 18C sign, 'Au Mortier d'Argent'; the playwright Eugène Scribe (1791-1861) was born at No. 32.

Crossing the ugly BLVD. DE SÉBASTOPOL (l.) we may enter the narrow Rue Quincampoix (parallel to the E.), one of the oldest streets in Paris, although most of the houses date from the 17-18C. At No. 43 John Law (1671-1729), the celebrated Scottish financier, established in 1716 his Mississippi bank which, after frenzied speculation, obstructed by jealous rivals, ended in a bankruptcy (1720) even more catastrophic than the 'South Sea Bubble'. No. 54 (demolished) was the Cabaret de l'Épée de Bois, where the *Royal Academy of the Dance* had its origins in 1658. After the creation of Law's bank the wealthy 'Mississipiens' made it their club, when it was frequented by Louis Racine and Marivaux. Nos. 10, 12, and 14 (further S.) have rococo façades: No. 36 is also worth noting.

Further E., flanking the Rue St-Martin, on the so-called 'Plateau Beaubourg' is a large area under development, in which stands a curious 'modern' building (by *Piano, Rogers,* and *Franchini*) to house the new **Centre National d'Art Contemporain,** also known as the *Georges Pompidou Cultural Centre,* where it is planned to display most of the canvases from the *Palais d'Art Moderne* (see p. 168).

At No. 168 (then No. 96) in the Rue St-Martin Gérard de Nerval (1808-55) was born. To the S. in this street No. 89 has a 17C bas-relief of the Annunciation. Boccaccio (1313-75) was born at the junction of the Rue des Lombards and the Rue St-Martin. Adjacent is **St-Merri** (Pl. 15; 3), built in the Flamboyant Gothic style (1515-52) on the site of at least two older churches, which covered the grave of St Médéric of Autun (d. 700). In 1796-1801 it was called the 'Temple of Commerce'. The W. front is notable for its rich decoration, but the statues are mostly poor replacements of 1842. The N.W. turret contains the oldest bell in Paris (1331); the S.W. tower lost its top storey in a fire. The nave has a double aisle on the r.; a single, on the l. The pulpit was designed by *M.-A. Slodtz* (1753); who also altered the choir. The organ dates from 1567: Saint-Saëns was organist here. The remaining stained-glass windows, contemporary with the church, are of interest.

In the *r. aisle,* the 1st outer chapel has remains of the 13C church; further on is a large chapel by *Boffrand* (1743-44), with decorations by *P.-A. Slodtz.* In the *l. aisle,* the 1st chapel contains a 15C tabernacle; the 3rd a Pietà attr. to *Nic. Legendre* (c. 1670); the 4th, a painting by *Coypel* (1661). From the 5th, a staircase descends to the crypt (1515), which has grotesque corbels, and the tombstone of Guillaume le Sueur (d. 1530). In the N. TRANSEPT is St Merri delivering prisoners, by *Simon Vouet.* Among other paintings are a late-16C work of the Fontainebleau School (S. of the *Lady Chapel*) of St Geneviève guarding her flocks, with Paris in the background.

The old quarter round *St-Merri,* with its narrow and picturesque alleys, retains a number of interesting houses, which it is hoped will survive the present rage for demolition in the Halles-Beaubourg redevelopment scheme.

We reach the Rue de Rivoli just S. of *St-Merri,* this E. section of the street constructed by Napoleon III to allow a rapid access for troops to the *Hôtel de Ville* in case of emergency. In the centre of the SQUARE ST-JACQUES rises the only relic of the church of *St-Jacques-la-Boucherie* (demolished 1802), the Flamboyant Gothic **Tour St-Jacques,** dating from 1508-22, and now serving as a meteorological station. Among the 19C statues is one of Pascal, who in 1648 verified here (or on the tower of St-Jacques-du-Haut-Pas) the barometric experiments he had caused to be made on the Puy de Dôme. A tablet in the Square commemorates Gérard de Nerval, who was found hanged nearby (in the old Rue de la Vieille Lanterne) in 1855.

Adjoining, to the S.W., is the PL. DU CHÂTELET (Pl. 14; 4), bounded by the Seine, here crossed by the *Pont au Change* (see p. 43).

The Square is named after the vanished *Grand Châtelet,* a fortress gateway leading to the Cité, once the headquarters of the Provost of Paris and the Guild of Notaries. A plan of this fort may be seen on the front of the *Chambre des Notaires* on the N. side of the Square. On the E. side is the *Théâtre de la Ville;* on the W., the *Théâtre du Châtelet,* in which the Communards were court-martialled in 1871. The painter David (1748-1825) was born in a house which stood on the S. side of this site. In the centre of the Square is the *Fontaine du Châtelet* (or de la Victoire, or du Palmier) dating from 1806 and 1858. An inscription indicates the position of the 'Parloir aux Bourgeois', the seat of the municipality of Paris from the 13C until 1357 (see below).

From the N. side of the Square, the Av. Victoria (named in honour of Queen Victoria's visit to Paris in 1855) leads E. to the PL. DE L'HÔTEL-DE-VILLE (Pl. 15; 3), known until the Revolution of 1830 as the PL. DE GRÈVE, for here, since the 11C, ships had moored on the strand, or *grève.*

This Square was the usual site for public executions: among the more famous of which (many incredibly barbarous) were those of the Comte de St-Pol (1475), constable of France, on the orders of Louis XI; Briquemont and Cavagnes, the Huguenot leaders (1572; among many other Protestants); the Comte de Montgomery (1574), captured at the siege of Domfront and formerly captain in the Scottish Guard; François Ravaillac, the assassin of Henri IV (1610); Eléonore Galigaï (the favourite of Marie de Médicis), executed for sorcery in 1617; the Marquise de Brinvilliers (1676), poisoner; the highwayman Cartouche (1721); and Damiens (1757), for attempting to murder Louis XV. In 1789, Foullon (controller-general of finance) and his son-in-law Bertier were hanged here by the Revolutionary mob. In 1795 Fouquier-Tinville suffered the same fate as his countless victims. Louvel, who assassinated the Duc de Berry, was executed here in 1820.

It was often a rendezvous for the unemployed or dissatisfied workers, who were said to 'faire grève', which came to mean 'to go on strike'.

The present **Hôtel de Ville,** on the E. side of the Square, is of more interest for its history than its architecture. Its famous predecessor, begun c. 1532, was burnt down by the Communards in 1871, and this caricature replica, in the style of the French Renaissance, was erected (on a larger scale) in 1874-84 from the plans of *Ballu* and *Deperthes.*

Its over-decorated façades are embellished with statues of eminent Frenchmen; its interior is likewise lavishly adorned in the degraded official taste in architecture of the period, with sculpture, elaborate carvings, mural paintings, etc., including *Puvis de Chavannes'* The Seasons. Intending visitors (parties only, on Mondays at 10.30) should apply at the *Accueil de Paris* in the entrance vestibule, No. 29 Rue de Rivoli.

History. In 1264 St Louis created the first municipal authority in Paris by allowing the merchants to elect magistrates ('échevins'), led by the 'prévôt des marchands', who was also head of the 'Hanse des marchands de l'eau'. This merchant guild, which had the monopoly of the traffic on the Seine, Marne, Oise, and Yonne, took as their emblem a ship, a device which still graces the arms of the city. Their first meeting-place was known simply as the 'Parlouer aux Bourgeois'; later they met at the *Grand-Châtelet* itself; and finally, in 1357, the Provost Étienne Marcel bought the 'Maison aux Piliers' or 'Maison du Dauphin', a mansion in the *Pl. de Grève,* for their assemblies. In 1532 plans for an imposing new building were adopted, but work was stopped at the second floor, and the new designs approved by Henri II in 1549 were not completed until 1628.

In 1789, the 300 electors nominated by the districts of Paris met there. On 17 July, Louis XVI received the tricolour cockade from the hands of Bailly, the Mayor. On 10 Aug. 1792, the 172 commissaries elected by Paris gave the signal for a general insurrection. In 1794 Robespierre took refuge here, but was arrested on 27 July, and dragged hence, his jaw smashed by a bullet, to the guillotine. In 1805 it became the seat of the Préfet de la Seine and his council, and was the scene of numerous official celebrations (on Napoleon's marriage to Marie-Louise, etc.).

The Swiss Guards put up a stout defence of the building during the stormy days of 1830. In 1848 it became the seat of Louis Blanc's provisional government, and witnessed the arrest of the revolutionary agitators Barbès and Blanqui. Verlaine was employed here in the mid-1860s. The Third Republic was proclaimed here in 1870 (4 Sept.), and in the following March, the Commune. On 24 May 1871 the building was set alight by its defenders, many perishing in the flames.

In 1944 the *Hôtel de Ville* was the focus of opposition to the occupying forces by the Resistance movement, who by 19 Aug. had established themselves in the building, repelling German counter-attacks until relieved by the arrival of Gen. Leclerc's division five days later.

From behind the *Hôtel de Ville,* we may cross the Rue de Rivoli to visit the **Temple des Billettes,** at No. 22 Rue des Archives, which although properly in the *Marais* (see below, and Rte 12), is more conveniently approached from here. It was built in 1756 for the Carmelites, but since 1812 has been used as a Lutheran church. Its charming *cloister* (No. 24), the only medieval example in Paris, is a relic of an older convent (1427).

The Rue de Rivoli, and its E. extension, the Rue St-Antoine, split the ancient *Marais* district into two unequal sections; the smaller, to the S., is that part described in our route; for the area to the N., see Rte 12.

To the E. of the *Hôtel de Ville,* between two of its annexes, lies the PL. ST-GERVAIS, with its elm tree, a reminder of the famous elm of St-Gervais, beneath which justice used to be administered. The proverbial expression for waiting for Doomsday is ironically, 'Attendre sous l'orme' (the elm). This was one of the first inhabited areas on the Right Bank, and the Rue François-Miron follows the course of a Roman road which led from Lutetia to Senlis.

To the E. it is dominated by the church of *St-Gervais-St-Protais* (Pl. 15; 5), which, founded in the 6C, dates its present form from the rebuilding of 1494-1578 (choir and transepts) and 1600-57 (nave, chapels, and tower). The original plans are attributed to *Martin Chambiges,* whose work was continued by his son *Pierre.* The lower stages of the tower are an early-15C survival. The façade (1616-21), by *Clément Métezeau* and (probably) *Salomon de Brosse,* is the earliest example in France of the superimposition of the three classic orders— Doric, Ionic, and Corinthian. In 1795 the church was converted into a 'Temple of Youth'. Bossuet preached here; Mme de Sévigné was married here; and here are buried Philippe de Champaigne (1602-74), Scarron (1610-60), and Crébillon the elder (1674-1762).

The INTERIOR, impressive from its loftiness and unity of style, is remarkably rich in works of art. The high windows of both nave and choir contain much stained-glass of c. 1610-20 by *Robert Pinaigrier* and *Nic. Chaumet.* The nave was completed in Flamboyant Gothic at a time when Renaissance influence was strongest.

s. AISLE. The 2nd chapel has an altar commemorating victims of the bombardment of Good Friday, 1918, when a German shell struck the church. In the 3rd, seven low 17C painted panels of the Life of Christ; 5th and 6th, stained-glass of 1531. In the 8th chapel, the tomb of Michel Le Tellier (d. 1685), by *Mazeline* and *Hurtrelle;* the bearded heads supporting the Chancellor's sarcophagus are from the tomb of Jacques de Souvré (d. 1670), by *François Anguier,* the rest of which are in the Louvre. The *Lady Chapel,* an overdecorated example of Flamboyant Gothic (1517), has fine contemporary glass. The SACRISTY, in the N. choir aisle, retains a good iron grille of 1741. In the N. transept is a painting of the Passion (Flemish; mid-16C, at present under restoration). From the next chapel we may enter the well-restored *Chapelle Dorée* (1628); in the adjacent chapel are a 13C high relief of the Dormition of the Virgin (below the altar), and a portrait by *Pajou* (1782) of Mme Palerme de Savy.

In the CHOIR, the stalls are of the 17C (W. end) and mid-16C, the latter with curious misericords. Against the N. entry-pillar is a 14C Virgin, known as N.-D. de Bonne-Délivrance; and on either side of the altar, wooden statues of the patron saints, by *Michel Bourdin* (1625). The 18C bronze-gilt candelabra are by *Soufflot.*

François Couperin (1668-1733) and seven members of his family served as organist here from 1653 to 1830, and their organ, restored, still survives. Couperin 'le Grand' himself was born in a house on the site of No. 4 Rue François-Miron

The S. façade of the church can now be seen, since the area has been the subject of restoration: note also the façades of some houses in the Rue des Barres, behind the building.

The stepped Rue François-Miron, leading N.E. from *St-Gervais,* is one of the finest streets in the district, Nos. 2-14, built c. 1735, adorned with wrought-iron work displaying the famous elm (see above); Nos. 30, 36, and 42 all have good features.

No. 26 in the Rue Geoffroy-l'Asnier (r.) is the *Hôtel de Châlons-Luxembourg* (1608), with a magnificent doorway (1659) and an attractive Louis-XIII pavilion in the courtyard. No. 22 also retains a handsome 17C façade. No. 17 is a *Jewish Study Centre,* with a memorial.

Further E. in the Rue François-Miron (off which diverges the Rue de Jouy; see below) is the *Hôtel de Beauvais (No. 68; by *Le Pautre,* 1655), with a fine courtyard, an ornate circular vestibule, and a carved staircase by *Desjardins.* Anne of Austria and Card. Mazarin watched the entry of Louis XIV and Marie-Thérèse into Paris in 1660 from its balcony. Christina of Sweden was a later tenant, and here in 1763 Mozart (aged 7) was the guest of the Bavarian ambassador.

The balcony of the *Hôtel du Président Hénault* (No. 82) should be noted.

To the r. in the Rue de Jouy, No. 7, the *Hôtel d'Aumont,* by *Le Vau*

(1648) and *Fr. Mansart* (1656), retains some of its original decoration, including work by *Le Brun.*

Beyond, the Rue du Figuier diverges r. to the **Hôtel de Sens** (Pl. 15; 5), built c. 1474-1519 for the archbishops of Sens, at a time when the bishopric of Paris was suffragan to the metropolitan see of Sens (before 1623; see p. 233); it is older than the *Hôtel de Cluny* (see p. 58), the only other example of 15C domestic architecture in Paris. Unfortunately it has suffered a long period of neglect, and has been poorly restored. Marguerite de Valois (1553-1615), whose memoirs may well have assisted Brantôme in the composition of his 'Dames illustres', passed peccant years here with her younger lovers, one of whom, in 1605, she had executed for the jealous murder of another on her very doorstep.

Since 1962 it has housed the *Bibliothèque Forney,* a reference library devoted to the fine arts.

To the W. are the modern buildings of the *Cité Internationale des Arts,* providing accommodation and facilities for foreign art students, on the pattern of the *Cité Universitaire.*

To the E., the QUAI DES CÉLESTINS, commanding attractive views of the *Île Saint-Louis,* passes (l., at No. 32) the site of the *Tour Barbeau,* completing, on the river bank, the N. perimeter of Philippe Auguste's defensive *Wall,* a section of which may be seen from the Rue des Jardins-St-Paul, adjoining. Here also stood the tennis-court of the Croix-Noire, where Molière performed in 1645 until his arrest for debt. Rabelais (1494?-1553) died in the Rue des Jardins-St-Paul, and was buried in the vanished church of *St-Paul-des-Champs* (see below), as were the Mansarts (1666, and 1708), and the 'Man in the Iron Mask', who had died in the Bastille (1703). The neighbouring Rue St-Paul had acquired its name before 1350; at No. 32, part of the church belfry survives.—See below for the eastern end of the Quai des Célestins. Turning r. at the N. end of this street (restoration in progress on the r.), and then l. brings us to the Rue St-Antoine, an ancient thoroughfare retaining many elegant façades.

A few yards to the W. is the church of **St-Paul-St-Louis** (Pl. 15; 6), or the *Grands-Jésuites,* built for that Society by Louis XIII in 1627-41 to replace a chapel of 1582. St-Paul was added to the original name in 1796 to commemorate the demolished church of *St-Paul-des-Champs.*

Designed by *Père Fr. Derrand,* its florid style, founded on 16C Italian churches, is the earliest example of the Jesuit school of architecture in France. Richelieu said the first mass here. The handsome Baroque portal is by *Père Martellange.* The interior is over-decorated but imposing, and contains, in the l. transept, a Christ in the Garden by *Delacroix;* and in the r., Louis XIII offering a model of the church to St Louis, by *Simon Vouet.* By the high altar is a Mater Dolorosa of the School of Germain Pilon. Bp. Huet (d. 1721), the original editor of the Delphin classics, is buried here, and Louis Bourdaloue, who here made most of his famous orations: "he preached like an angel", commented Mme de Sévigné, herself a regular worshipper here.

Gérard de Nerval was educated at the adjacent *Lycée Charlemagne,* occupying a 17C Jesuit house.

Turning E. along the Rue St-Antoine, we shortly pass (l.; No. 62) the ***Hôtel de Sully** (or de Béthune-Sully), now occupied by offices of the *Monuments Historiques,* who can give information about any Guided Tours to the sites and monuments of Paris that may be joined, etc.; they also publish a review devoted to the restoration of architecturally important buildings: 'Les Monuments Historiques de la France'.

The mansion, by *Jean du Cerceau* (1624-30), was acquired by Sully, the minister of Henri IV, in 1634. The courtyard, a particularly fine example of the Louis-XIII style, the entrance pavilions, and the interior, retaining 17C ceilings and panelling, have been the subject of extensive restoration, and may be visited daily, except Tues., 10.00-12.00, 14.00-17.00 or 18.00. The *Hôtel de la Mouffle* had previously stood on this site, from 1407.

Further E., the Rue de Birague leads l. to the S. entrance of the *Pl. des Vosges* (see Rte 12); Nos. 12 and 14 have elegant features. Opposite this point, from the S. side of the Rue St-Antoine, we may follow the Rue Beautreillis. Beneath the carriage-entrance of No. 22, the *Grand Hôtel de Charny* (where Baudelaire lodged in 1858-59), are some wood-carvings in the purest Louis-XIII style. No. 16, the *Petit Hôtel de Charny,* was the birthplace of the dramatist Sardou (1831-1908).—To the r. in the Rue Charles V, is the imposing *Hôtel d'Aubray,* residence of the notorious Marquise de Brinvilliers (1630-76), the poisoner. No. 10, the *Hôtel de Maillé,* retains its Louis-XIII façade, and No. 15, opposite, dates from 1642.

No. 10 Rue Beautreillis was the *Hôtel des Princes de Monaco,* built c. 1650, but altered in the 18th and 19Cs; No. 7, with a wooden staircase and wrought-iron balcony, is one of the finest bourgeois houses of its period in Paris (late 16C).

On reaching the Rue des Lions, with a number of 17-18C mansions, including No. 10 (the passage in the modern façade leads to a courtyard of 1642) and No. 11, in which Mme de Sévigné lived in 1645-50, turn l. and then r. to regain the Quai des Célestins.

At No. 4 QUAI DES CÉLESTINS is the stately *Hôtel Fieubet,* with an interesting courtyard, built by *J. H.-Mansart* (1676-81) for Gaspard de Fieubet, chancellor to Anne of Austria; unfortunately it was badly disfigured in 1857, and now accommodates the *École Massillon.* The *Hôtel de Nicolaï,* No. 4, is also of the late 17C.

At No. 1 Rue de Sully, on the far side of the BLVD. HENRI-IV. in the Quartier de l'Arsenal (named after the arsenal established here by Henri IV), stands the **Bibliothèque de l'Arsenal** (Pl. 15; 6; open 10.00-17.00 daily; closed first fortnight in Sept. See *Bibliothèque Nationale,* p. 127, for rules regarding admission).

The library was founded in 1757 by Marc-René d'Argenson, Minister of War, and partly installed in the former residence of the Grand Master of Artillery, built in 1594 for Sully. The façade in the parallel BLVD. MORLAND (facing the *Préfecture de Paris*) is by *Boffrand* (c. 1723).

The library possesses some 15,000 MSS., one million printed volumes, and 120,000 engravings. It is known particularly for its incomparable series of illuminated MSS., and its almost complete collection of French dramatic works. The Gordon Craig collection was acquired in 1957. Among its archives are the papers of the Bastille; documents relative to the 'Man in the Iron Mask', and the 'Affair of the Diamond Necklace'; letters of Henri IV to the Marquise de Verneuil, etc.; also St Louis's Book of Hours, and Charles V's Bible, among others. Nodier, Hérédia, Mérimée, and Anatole France were librarians here.

Noteworthy among the rooms shown to the public (Thurs. 14.00-16.00) are the *Salon de Musique,* by *Boffrand,* with superb Louis-XV woodwork, and the *Apartment of the Duchesse de La Meilleraie,* with a ceiling by *Simon Vouet.*

Turning N.E. (r.) past the *Caserne des Célestins* (barracks of the Gendarmerie Mobile, built on part of the site of the famous Celestine monastery founded in 1362), we shortly diverge l. off the BLVD. HENRI-IV, to regain the Rue St-Antoine (viâ the Rue Castex). On the corner is the circular *Temple de Ste-Marie,* originally the chapel of the convent of the Visitation, and now a Protestant church. It was built by *Fr. Mansart* in 1632-34.

The unscrupulous Surintendant des finances Nicolas Fouquet (1615-80) and Henri de Sévigné (killed in a duel in 1651) were buried here. St Vincent de Paul was almoner of the convent for 28 years.

A few yards to the W., at No. 21, is the *Hôtel de Mayenne* (or d'Ormesson), retaining a turret and charming staircase. Now the *École des Francs-Bourgeois,* it was built by *Jean du Cerceau* in 1613-17.

Turning E. we pass (r.) the Rue de Lesdiguières, where at No. 9 was Balzac's first Paris lodging, in a garret at three sous a day. A tablet on No. 5 Rue St-Antoine marks the position of the court of the *Bastille* (see Rte 12), by which the Revolutionary mob gained access to the fortress. Near the junction of this street and the PL. DE LA BASTILLE was the site of the great barricade of 1848, and also the last stronghold of the Communards in 1871.

12   THE MARAIS

MÉTROS: *Bastille; St-Paul; Hôtel-de-Ville; Rambuteau; Temple; Arts-et-Métiers; Réamur-Sébastopol.*

The ****Marais,** one of the most interesting districts of old Paris, is bounded by the *Grands Boulevards* on the N. and E., by the *Blvd. de Sébastopol* to the W., and by the Seine to the S. It includes the greater part of the 3rd and 4th Arrondissements. In spite of past neglect, demolition, and some rebuilding, it remains substantially as developed in the 17C, and contains many scores of buildings of outstanding architectural interest, affording a fascinating and unique reminder of the elegance of this period.

Pioneers in the work of restoration were the *Association pour la sauvegarde et la mise en valeur du Paris historique,* with offices at Nos. 44-46 Rue François-Miron, who publish a detailed inventory map of the area.

The S. section of the *Marais* has already been described for convenience in Rte 11.

So called from the marshy land ('marais', marsh or morass), the *Marais* only became habitable with the arrival of the Knights Templar and other religious houses, who settled here in the 13C, and converted the marshes into arable land. Royal patronage began with Charles V, who, anxious to forget the associations of the *Palais de la Cité* with the rebellion of Étienne Marcel in 1358, built the *Hôtel Saint-Paul* here. In the 16C, the *Hôtel de Lamoignon* and *Hôtel Carnavalet* were built, but the seal of royal approval came with the building of the PL. ROYALE (1605; later known as the *Pl. des Vosges,* see below).

Courtiers unable to find room here began to build themselves houses as near to the Place as possible, and the Marais remained the most fashionable residential area of Paris until the creation of the Faubourg St-Germain in the early 18C. It was the Revolution which ended its long reign of splendour. The nobles had to flee; the State confiscated their property and sold it to the growing number of craftsmen, mechanics, and merchants who flooded into the area, who appeared to take a brutish pleasure in disfiguring as much as possible. Much of the Marais continues to be a commercial district, even if its architectural merits are more appreciated as the value of its properties has increased.

Immediately E. of the *Marais* lies the **Pl. de la Bastille** (Pl. 15; 6). The ground plan of the famous fortress prison is marked out by a line of paving-stones in the Place, beneath which some cellars are said to survive.

The main keep of the fortress (a model of which may be seen in the *Musée Carnavalet*) stood on the W. side, across the end of the Rue St-Antoine, and the main drawbridge was slightly N. of the junction of the *Blvd. Henri-IV* with the Place. The *July Column* (see below) stands approximately in the centre of what was the E. bastion. The *Canal St-Martin* now runs beneath the Place, appearing to the S. in the Gare d'eau de l'Arsenal, which shortly enters the Seine.

The **Bastille** (more correctly the *Bastille St-Antoine*) originated as a bastion-tower defending the E. entrance to Paris. It was developed under Charles V into a fortress with eight massive towers, immensely thick walls, and a wide moat. By the reign of Louis XIII, the Bastille had become almost exclusively a state prison for political offenders, among whom were the mysterious 'Man in the Iron Mask' (1698-1703) and Voltaire (twice). The arbitrary arrest by 'lettre de cachet' of persons obnoxious to the Court, and their protracted imprisonment without trial, made the Bastille a popular synonym for oppression. Bassompierre was imprisoned in 1629 for twelve years by Richelieu, "not that he had done wrong, but for fear he might be led into mischief". Vanbrugh enjoyed Louis XIV's hospitality (for obscure reasons) for most of 1692. Linguet's 'Memoires' (1783, published in London) describe his own experiences when incarcerated there in 1780-82. Another inmate was the notorious Marquis de Sade, who here wrote 'Justine' and other licentious works. Mirabeau the Younger was also imprisoned here, another victim of the practice of arrest by 'lettre de cachet', albeit at his father's instigation.

In 1789, the Revolutionary mob, aided by a few troops, attacked and overwhelmed its defenders, and murdered the governor, the Marquis de Launay, and freed a handful of prisoners. In the same year the building was razed to the ground, and its key, presented by La Fayette to Washington, is now at Mount Vernon. The anniversary of the fall of the Bastille (14 July) is celebrated by the French as a Fête Nationale.

The **July Column** (*Colonne de Juillet*) is in no way connected with the above event, but was erected by Louis-Philippe to commemorate the victims of the three days' street-fighting of July 1830, who are buried in vaults beneath the circular base of the column. The victims of the Revolution of February 1848 were subsequently interred there, and their names added to the inscription. The bronze-faced column, 169 ft high, is surmounted by a bronze-gilt figure of Liberty; its ascent is provisionally suspended.

Nos. 2-20 in the BLVD. BEAUMARCHAIS, leading N. from the *Pl. de la Bastille*, are built on the site of a luxurious mansion and garden belonging to the dramatist Caron de Beaumarchais (1732-99). The *Hôtel de Mansart-Sagonne* (see below) is well seen from Nos. 21-23 in the boulevard, which with its continuation, the BLVD. DES FILLES-DU-CALVAIRE (recalling the site of a former convent; 1633-1790) and BLVD. DU TEMPLE (see p. 154), leads to the *Pl. de la République*.

The Rue de la Bastille leads N.E. from the *Pl. de la Bastille* to the Rue des Tournelles, No. 28 in which is the *Hôtel de Mansart-Sagonne*, built for himself by *Jules Hardouin-Mansart* (1646-1708), and decorated by *Le Brun* and *Mignard*. No. 50 has a splendid façade. The cultured courtesan Ninon de L'Enclos (1620-1705) lived here from 1644, and died at No. 56. Before reaching these two houses, the Rue du Pas-de-la-Mule leads l. to the *Pl. des Vosges*.

The *****Place des Vosges** (Pl. 15; 6), the heart of the *Marais*, a large quadrangle surrounded by houses in red brick with stone facings, was built on a uniform plan with arcaded ground floors (1606-11), and is one of the most attractive squares in Paris. Trees were not planted in the central gardens until 1783, and although they provide welcome shade, they spoil the effect of harmonious symmetry. The main approach to the *Pl. des Vosges,* from the Rue St-Antoine, is by the Rue de Birague (see p. 137), passing through the *Pavillon du Roi* (see below). The whole Place is at present the subject of slow but thorough restoration.

The square occupies the site of the royal *Palais des Tournelles,* the residence of the Duke of Bedford, regent of France after the death of Henry V; in 1559 this was the scene of the fatal tournament when Henri II was accidentally killed by Montgomery, and it was in consequence abandoned by his widow, Catherine de Médicis. The square in its present form was laid out for Henri IV, probably by *Baptiste du Cerceau,* as the PLACE ROYALE, and opened in 1605; the king's pavilion was above the gateway in the centre of the S. side, while the queen's was the corresponding building on the N. (No. 28). In the earlier part of the reign of Louis XIV this was one of the most fashionable addresses in Paris, and the centre of the 'Nouvelles Précieuses' satirized by Molière. It only acquired its present name in 1799, the department of the Vosges having been the first to discharge its liabilities for the Revolutionary Wars.

At the corners of the square are fountains (1816), and in the centre a poor equestrian statue of Louis XIII (1825) set up to replace one destroyed in 1792. Mme de Sévigné (1626-96) was born in the *Hôtel de Coulanges* (No. 1bis; 1606), next to the *Pavillon du Roi;* No. 3 is the *Hôtel d'Estrades.* No. 6 (see below) was built in 1610 for the Maréchal de Lavardin (d. 1614). No. 7, the *Petit-Hôtel de Sully,* was built by *Jean Androuet du Cerceau.* Both Gautier and Daudet lived for a while in No. 8, the *Hôtel de Fourcy* (1605). No. 9, the *Hôtel de Chaulnes,* was the residence of Rachel (d. 1858), the tragedienne. No. 11 was occupied by Marion Delorme, the courtesan, in 1639-48. No. 21 was the mansion of Card. de Richelieu (1615), in front of which, on the very day after the cardinal's edict against duelling, took place the famous duel between François de Montmorency and Des Chapelles against Bussy and Beuvron (1627). No. 12 occupies part of the *Hôtel Dangeau,* the home of the Marquis de Dangeau (1638-1720), the historian.

No. 6 in the *Pl. des Vosges,* in which Hugo lived in 1832-48 (2nd floor), is now the **Musée Victor-Hugo** (adm. daily, except Mon. and Tues., 10.00-17.30), perhaps of more interest for the numerous pen and wash *Drawings (c. 350) by *Hugo* (1802-85) displayed there than for the family souvenirs. Note the bust of Hugo by *Rodin;* portrait of Juliette Drouet by *Bastien-Lepage;* The Première of Hernani, by *Besnard;* portrait of Adèle Foucher, the poet's wife, by *Louis Boulanger;* Hugo on his death-bed, by *Bonnat;* and works by *Célestin Nanteuil* and *Delacroix,* etc. Some furniture and woodwork, designed or carved by Hugo, is also of interest.

From the N.W. corner of the *Pl. des Vosges* we cross the Rue de Turenne (where l., in the court of No. 23, is the *Hôtel de Villacerf,* of c. 1660, with a fountain), and enter the Rue des Francs-Bourgeois, taking its name from the citizens who, being vassals to a feudal lord, were exempt from municipal taxes. For the N. section of the Rue de Turenne, see p. 146.

The *Musée Carnavalet, or *Musée Historique de la Ville de Paris* (Pl. 15; 4), at the corner of the Rue des Francs-Bourgeois and the Rue de Sévigné, is a highly important collection illustrating the history of Paris from the 16C to the middle of the 19C.

Musée Carnavalet

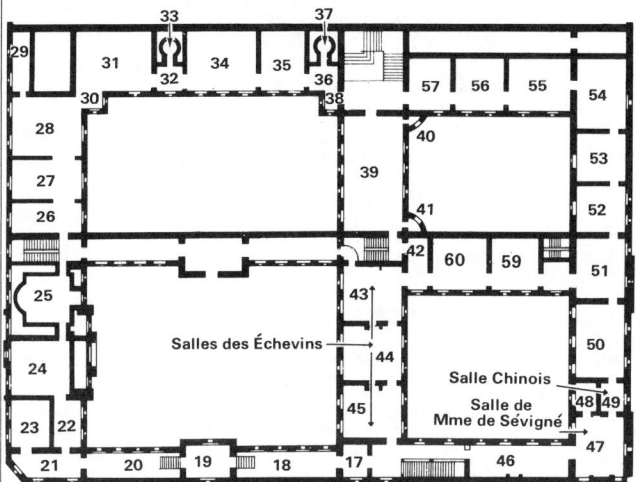

First Floor

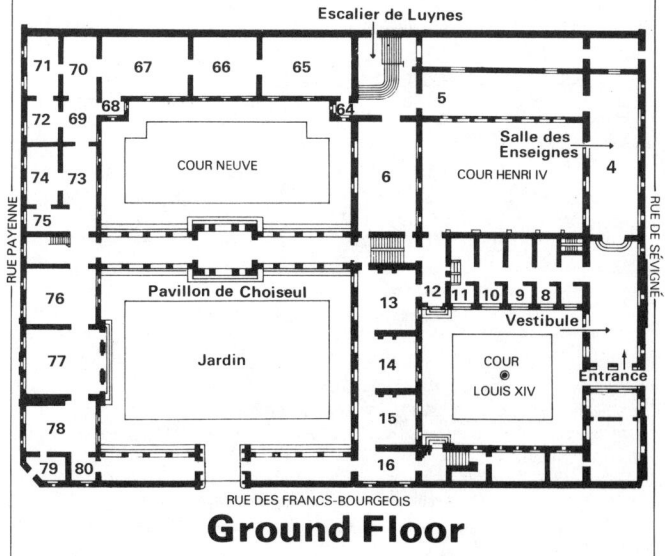

Ground Floor

MÉTRO: *St-Paul;* adm. 10.00-17.50 daily, except Tues.

The museum is housed in the *Hôtel Carnavalet,* a fine mansion begun in 1544 for Jacques de Ligneris, President of the Parlement, and adorned with sculptures by *Jean Goujon.* It was altered in 1660 by *Mansart,* who built the present façade, but retained the 16C gateway with its *Goujon* sculptures (on the keystone, a winged figure of Abundance standing on a globe which was later carved into a carnival mask, in punning allusion to Carnavalet). Further alterations and enlargements were made earlier this century.

The name Carnavalet was derived from the Breton family of Kernevenoy, the second owners of the building. Mme de Sévigné lived here from 1677 until her death in 1696; her apartments, which were shared by her daughter, Mme de Grignan, and her uncle, the Abbé de Coulanges, were in the S.E. corner of the First Floor.

The bronze statue of Louis XIV in the centre of the courtyard is by *Coysevox.* Of the sculptures in the courtyard, the best are those by *Jean Goujon* on the entrance arch and above the door on the l. The reliefs of the Seasons, on the side opposite the entrance, were probably done under his direction. On the r., the relief above the door is a 19C copy of the one opposite; those on the first storey are by *van Obstal* (1660).

Some rooms are in the process of rearrangement, but the following itinerary will take the visitor round the building in an approximate chronological progression, with one or two slight breaks in continuity.

From the entrance vestibule we enter the SALLE DES ENSEIGNES (R 4), with a wrought-iron grille, containing material relative to trades and guilds, including a collection of shop and tavern signs of the 15-19C. In the central cases are weights and measures, and models of glassworks and locksmiths' works, merchants' tokens, etc.—In R 5, continuing the display, is the front of an apothecary's shop of the First Empire.

R 6 (l.) conserves some magnificent gilt panelling from the *Hôtel d'Uzès,* Rue Montmartre, from designs by *Ledoux,* while the adjoining room, also by *Ledoux* (1752), was saved from the 'café Militaire' in the Rue Saint-Honoré. Behind the latter is a large 19C maquette of the *Palais-Royal.*

RR 12-16 contain a number of interesting maquettes of Paris from the Middle Ages to the time of Henri IV; in R 15 is a tapestry plan of 1540.— From R 16 (l.) ascend to the FIRST FLOOR.

RR 17-25 illustrate the topography of Paris from the 16C to the beginning of the 18C. Note also the *anon.* 16C Flemish painting of the Prodigal Son in the company of courtesans, and a portrait of Mary Stuart in a white mourning veil (1561) in R 19, and the views of Paris by *P.-D. Martin* in RR 20, 22, and 24 (the Inauguration of the church of Les Invalides). R 23 contains the richly painted and gilded woodwork (c. 1656) from the *Hôtel Colbert de Villacerf* at 23 Rue de Turenne; R 24 is the 'grand cabinet doré', by *Le Vau,* from 14 Pl. des Vosges; the ceiling painting is by *Le Brun,* as is that in R 25, of 1651, with decorations from the same hôtel.

Returning through these rooms, we may visit R 46, devoted to Mme de Sévigné, with a pastel of the marquise by *Nanteuil,* and of her daughter Mme de Grignan, by *Mignard,* and other souvenirs.—R 47 contains paintings of St-Germain and Vincennes, by *van de Meulen.*—

MUSÉE CARNAVALET *Plan p. 141* 143

RR 45-43, nearby, the SALLES DES ÉCHEVINS, contain portraits of aldermen by *Largillière, de Troy,* and *Duplessis,* and the Allegory of the Peace of Aix-la-Chapelle (1749) by *Dumont le Romain.* In **R 45** is a monumental chimneypiece of the Louis-XIII period.

Hence we may visit **R 39,** the first of a series of rooms (**RR 39-42, 60, 59, 58, 51-53**) accommodating the important collection of furniture donated by Mme Henriette Bouvier in 1965.—To the r. of **R 51,** in **R 50,** are interesting views of 18C Paris by *Nicolas Raguenet.* **R 49,** adjoining, also contains examples of 18C furniture, in the Chinese taste.

RR 54-57, well-panelled, concentrate on furniture of the period of Louis XV. **R 56** is devoted to the theatre; **R 57** to Rousseau and Voltaire, with a portrait of the latter, aged 24, *after Largillière;* while **R 54** contains an early painting by *Chardin* of a game of billiards.—Crossing the landing of the Escalier des Luynes (a reconstruction of a stairway from the *Hôtel de Luynes,* decorated with wall-paintings of the family, by *Brunetti,* of 1748), we reach **R 36,** with a portrait of B. Franklin, by *Duplessis,* and **R 37,** conserving the rotunda from the ground floor of the *Hôtel de Fersen.* The following suite of rooms is devoted to furniture from the Bouvier collection, of the Louis-XV-XVI period; **R 31,** painted by *Boucher* and *Fragonard* (1750-65), is from the house of the engraver Gilles Demarteau in the Rue de la Pelleterie.

R 26 contains views by *A.-J. Noël,* and *J.-B. Lallemand,* among others.

The adjoining stairs ascend to the LIBRARY, with an extensive reference section devoted to the history of Paris, etc.—By passing along the gallery opposite (**RR 61-63**), through **R 39,** and down the ESCALIER DE LUYNES, or alternatively by descending the first stairs and passing through the PAVILLON DE CHOISEUL below, and turning l., we reach **RR 64-75,** devoted largely to the Revolutionary and Empire periods.— **R 65,** the Pillage of the Invalides; **R 66,** with a model of the Bastille cut from one of its stones under the direction of *Palloy,* the demolition contractor; painting of the storming of the Bastille by *Singleton,* and its destruction, by *Hubert Robert;* 'Lettres de Cachet' signed by Louis XV, etc.—**R 67,** the Salle de la Convention, with busts, documents, and portraits (Marat, Danton, Robespierre, etc.) of the period; **R 70** (SALLE DU TEMPLE), with souvenirs of Louis XVI and his family during their imprisonment in the Temple; **R 74** is devoted to Napoleon, and in **R 75,** portraits of Napoleon by *Lefèvre,* of Mme Récamier by *Gérard,* of Talleyrand in 1809 by *Prud'hon,* and of Dr John Moore (1729-1802), the author of descriptions of Paris during this disturbed period, by *Vestier.* Personal souvenirs of Napoleon and his family are displayed in **R 74.**

RR 76-80, beyond the hallway, are devoted to various aspects of Paris (literary, theatrical, etc.) during the 19C. Returning to **R 76,** we may regain the entrance by turning r. along the central colonnade.

No. 29 Rue de Sévigné, formerly the *Hôtel Le Peletier de St-Fargeau* (by *Bullet;* 1687), is now the *Bibliothèque Historique de la Ville de Paris,* containing over 400,000 vols and 100,000 MSS. relative to the history of Paris and the Revolution. No. 48, opposite, the *Hôtel de Jonquières,* retains the relief (1810) from an old fountain; No. 52, built by *Pierre Delisle-Mansart* for himself, has been much altered.

In the Rue Payenne, immediately W. of the *Hôtel Carnavalet*, Nos. 11, the *Hôtel de Polastron-Polignac*, and 13, *Hôtel de Lude*, are good examples of early-18C mansions. There is a small lapidary collection in the SQUARE GEORGES-CAIN opposite.

S. of the *Hôtel Carnavalet*, on the corner of the Rue Pavée (No. 14), is the *Hôtel Lamoignon*, built in 1584 for Diane de France, the legitimized daughter of Henri II, but named after Lamoignon, President of the Parlement of Paris (1658), a later occupant, and enlarged in the 17C. Daudet set up house here on his marriage in 1867. Adjacent are traces of the notorious prison of *La Force* (demolished 1850), where many victims of the Revolution were massacred.

On the S. side of the Rue des Francs-Bourgeois (No. 31) is the *Hôtel d'Albret*, built c. 1640 by *Fr. Mansart*, with an 18C street façade. At the end of the courtyard of No. 33 is a fragment of the *Walls* of Philippe Auguste. The *Hôtel de Guillaume Barbès* (No. 35) was built in the second half of the 17C.

Ninon de L'Enclos lived in the neighbouring Rue Elzévir (No. 16) in 1642; No. 8 has a good façade.

No. 26, the *Hôtel de Sandreville* (late 16-18C); and No. 30, the *Hôtel d'Alméras*, a red-brick mansion of the Henri-IV period, are noteworthy. The Allée des Arbalétriers (No. 38) was one of the entrances to the *Hôtel Barbette* (see p. 146), and led to the field alongside the walls which used to be a practice ground for crossbowmen.

Beyond, the Rue Vieille-du-Temple (comp. below) diverges to the r. and l.

At No. 55, occupying part of the buildings (1685) of the adjacent church, are the head offices of the *Crédit Municipal*, formerly the *Mont-de-Piété* (or government pawnbroking establishment), founded by Louis XVI in 1777. The 18C doorway (opposite) of **N.-D. des Blancs-Manteaux** (deriving its name from the white habits of an earlier order of mendicant monks established here in 1285 by St Louis) comes from the church of *St-Barthélemy* in the Île de la Cité, demolished in 1863. The church contains a rococo pulpit in the Flemish style (1749).

Among other striking houses in the Rue des Francs-Bourgeois are Nos. 54, the *Hôtel de Camus;* 56, the *Hôtel de Fontenoy* (early 18C); 58, which belonged to Louis Le Tonnelier, baron de Breteuil, minister of Louis XVI; and 58bis, the *Hôtel d'Assy* (early 17C).

We now reach the imposing portal of the ***Hôtel de Soubise** (No. 60; Pl. 15; 3), the greater part of which was built by *Delamair* in 1706-12 on the site of the mansion of the Duc de Guise. The **Archives Nationales** have been housed here since 1808, the presence of which has ensured the survival of the interior decoration (1712-45) by *Natoire, Boucher, Van Loo, Restout, Lemoyne*, etc. The splendid *Cour d'Honneur*, with its colonnade, has copies of the Four Seasons by *Robert Le Lorrain* on the façade.

The earlier entrance, the turreted Gothic gateway of 1380 (at No. 58 Rue des Archives), was part of the *Hôtel de Clisson*, built in 1372-75 by the Constable Olivier de Clisson, a supporter of Charles V against the English. Bolingbroke (later Henry IV) gave a farewell banquet there in 1399 before setting out for England. During the English occupation of Paris (1420-35) Thomas, Duke of Clarence and later the Duke of Bedford lived here. With its purchase in 1553 by Anna d'Este, wife of François de Lorraine, Duc de Guise, it became the *Hôtel de Guise*, remaining in the family until 1696, when Anne de Soubise bought it. Another occupant during this period was Henri II de Lorraine, who killed the last of the Colignys in a duel in the *Pl. des Vosges* in 1643: his grandfather had instigated the murder of Adm. Coligny in the massacre of St Bartholomew. Here he entertained lavishly, and gave hospitality to Corneille.

The CHAPEL bears traces of the *Chapelle de Clisson* of 1375 transformed for the Guise by *Primaticcio*. The OVAL ROOM is a masterpiece of the style of transition from Louis XIV to Louis XV. Here and elsewhere are exhibited some of the outstanding documents arranged to show the development of French institutions, etc.

Among the earliest is a will of 627; others concern Clovis and Charlemagne. Letters from foreign potentates and statesmen include the Emperor Charles V, Christina of Sweden, Tamerlane, Franklin, and Washington, etc.; among treaties displayed are those of Brétigny, Westphalia, and the Pyrenees; the Edict of Nantes (with the signature of Henri IV) and its Revocation; the Oath of the Jeu de Paume; Marie-Antoinette's last letter, and Louis XVI's will; also his diary with 'rien' written against the date 14 July 1789, etc. The Orléans archives were donated to the Archives Nationales in 1969.

Opposite the W. side of the Hôtel de Soubise is the Rue de Braque. Nos. 4-6, the *Hôtel Le Lièvre de la Grange,* is a fine late-17C mansion; No. 7 belonged to Vergennes, foreign minister to Louis XVI and supporter of American Independence.

At the corner of the Rue des Archives and the Rue des Haudriettes is a pretty fountain, with a naiad by *Mignot* (1765). Diagonally opposite is the *Hôtel de Guénégaud* (No. 60 Rue des Archives) by *Fr. Mansart* (c. 1650), in which a **Musée de la Chasse** has been installed (1967), at the expense of the Sommer Foundation. It also houses an exclusive Hunting Club (with an annexe at Chambord).

The first room displays a portrait, in falconer's costume, of Philip the Fair (father of Charles V), and 'La Chasse de Diane' by *Brueghel le Velours* and *van Balen.* Stairs ascend to rooms containing hunting weapons, powder flasks, daggers, crossbows, etc., and to the second floor. Here are collections of stuffed big game, swords, porcelain decorated with hunting scenes, and paintings by *François Desportes* (1661-1743), *Chardin, Oudry,* and *Carle Vernet,* among others.

No. 62, adjacent, the *Hôtel de Montgelas* (1709), is also noteworthy.
On the corner (No. 54) survives the pretty turret (c. 1510; restored) of the *Hôtel Hérouët.* A short distance S. (l.) in the Rue Vieille-du-Temple is the **Hôtel des Ambassadeurs de Hollande** (No. 47), one of the most impressive mansions in the Marais, built by *Cottard* in 1657-60 on the site of the house of the Maréchal de Rieux, in front of which, returning from Isabeau de Bavière's house (see p. 146), the Duc d'Orléans was assassinated in 1407 by the hired bravos of John the Fearless, Duke of Burgundy.

The building was never in fact the property of the Dutch ambassadors, but in 1720-27 belonged to the chaplain of their Embassy, and its chapel was several times used for Protestant ceremonies. Mlle Necker (later Mme de Staël) was baptized there in 1766, and Franklin's daughter was married there. Beaumarchais also lived here, where he wrote his 'Mariage de Figaro'; in 1788 turning the house into a provident institution for poor nursing mothers.

Nos. 36, 24, and 15 (the *Hôtel de Vibraye*) further S., are noteworthy.
From this intersection, we may make a detour towards the N.E. section of the Marais, passing (No. 87 Rue Vieille-du-Temple) the **Hôtel de Rohan**, known also as the *Hôtel de Strasbourg,* begun in 1704 by *Delamair.*

It was successively occupied by four cardinals of the Rohan family, all of whom were bishops of Strasbourg; the most famous was the cardinal (Édouard) implicated in the 'affair of the diamond necklace' (1784-85). From 1808 to 1925 the mansion was occupied by the *Imprimerie Nationale* (see p. 86), after which it was thoroughly restored to accommodate certain departments of the *Archives Nationales* not accommodated in the neighbouring *Hôtel de Soubise* (see above). In the second courtyard is a fine relief of the Horses of Apollo by *Robert Le Lorrain;* the *'Cabinet des Singes' contains paintings by *Chr. Huet* (1745-50).

Slightly to the S.E., No. 17 in the Rue Barbette, recalling the name of the *Hôtel Barbette*, the favourite residence of Isabeau de Bavière, which stood on this site, retains a door with two medallions.

No. 22 Rue des Quatre-Fils (leading N.E.) was the home of the Marquise du Deffand (1697-1780). Her salon was frequented by Voltaire, Montesquieu, D'Alembert, Condorcet, Turgot, Hénault, and Horace Walpole. She later became blind, and Mlle de Lespinasse, her companion in 1754-64, set up a separate salon. No. 20, retaining a fine doorway, was the residence, after 1800, of de Sèze, Louis XVI's lawyer.

In the Rue Charlot, leading N.E. from the Rue des Quatre-Fils, is *St-Jean-St-François*, built as a Capuchin chapel on the site of a tennis-court, and completed in 1715. No. 7, opposite, the *Hôtel de Brévannes*, is partly 17C. Mlle de Scudéry (1607-1701) lived from 1670 and died in the Rue de Beauce, to the N.W. Turning r. into the Rue du Perche (off which, in the Rue de Saintonge, Nos. 2 to 24 form an attractive ensemble), we cross the Rue Vieille-du-Temple into the Rue des Coutures-St-Gervais, lined with many 17C houses, and (r.) the garden façade of the **Hôtel Salé**. The entrance of this impressive mansion, built in 1656 by *Jean Boullier de Bourges* for Aubert de Fontenay, the financier, is at No. 5 Rue Thorigny. Originally the *Hôtel de Juigné*, it became known as the *Hôtel Salé* on account of the profits its owner had made out of the salt tax. Its staircase is notable. When restored, it will house a museum devoted to the work of Picasso. It is likely that Marion Delorme died in a house on the site of No. 2 in 1650. Nos. 6, 8, and 10 were built together as the *Hôtel de Percey;* No. 8 belonged to Mme de Sévigné in 1669-72.

The Rue Ste-Anastase leads into the Rue de Turenne, where (r.) Nos. 52-54 form the 17C *Hôtel de Montrésor*. No. 56 was once the home of Scarron (1610-60; who died there) and his wife Françoise d'Aubigné (1635-1719; granddaughter of the poet Agrippa d'Aubigné), later Mme de Maintenon. No. 60 is the *Hôtel du Grand-Veneur*, with a boar's head on the façade, while No. 66 retains traces of the *Hôtel de Turenne*, built for the great marshal's father. On the site of the chapel of the convent later installed here, the church of *St-Denis-du-St-Sacrement* was built in 1835 in the Grecian style, by *Godde*. No. 80, a short distance N., belonged to the Marquis de Launay, the last governor of the Bastille.

The nearby Rue Debelleyme, leading N.W., crosses the Rue Vieille-du-Temple, at the junction of which (No. 110) is the *Hôtel d'Espinay* (which belonged to a favourite of Henri III), with a magnificent staircase. Nos. 106-100 (to the l.) all preserve features of the early 17C, when they were built. Just to the N., the Rue de Poitou leads back to the Rue Charlot (in which No. 28, a short distance to the r., is the *Hôtel de Béramcourt;* 1690), across which we continue N.E. by the Rue Pastourelle. To the l. in the Rue des Archives (the next main street), at No. 70, died Lamennais (1782-1854), the subversive religious writer. No. 78, to the r., was built by *Bullet* (c. 1660), with a beautiful staircase by *Le*

Muet, and was the residence of Marshal Tallard (1712). Further N. at No. 90 are traces of the *Hôpital des Enfants-Rouges*, founded by François I and his sister Marguerite in 1534, so-called because the children wore a red uniform. Just beyond is the SQUARE DU TEMPLE (Pl. 15; 2), the centre of the densely populated Quartier du Temple, laid out in 1857 on the site of the late-12C stronghold of the Knights Templar, and the headquarters of their order in Europe until 1313, when it was occupied by the Order of St John.

The area owned by the Templars lay mostly between this point and the *Pl. de la République*, to the N.E. (see p. 154). Before the Revolution it was occupied by wealthy noble families, artisans who did not belong to the corporations and therefore were free from many restrictions, and debtors who were protected here from action for debt.

The palace of the Grand Prior of the Knights of St John was renowned for luxurious living, but with the Revolution the Tour du Temple, of 1265, was transformed into a prison, and in Aug. 1792 Louis XVI and the royal family were incarcerated here. On 21 Jan. 1793, the king was taken hence to the guillotine; Marie-Antoinette was transferred to the *Conciergerie* on 2 Aug.; and on 9 May 1794, Mme Élisabeth was carried off to execution. The Dauphin (Louis XVII) is believed to have died here on 9 June 1795; and the sole survivor, Mme Royale, was released on 19 Dec. of the same year. The tower was demolished by Napoleon I, and its last vestiges were removed under Napoleon III.

A short distance to the N. (195 Rue du Temple) is the church of **Ste-Élisabeth**, founded in 1630 by Marie de Médicis. The façade is a copy of *Sta Maria Novella* at Florence. The main feature is the woodwork, including, in the ambulatory, 16C carvings of scriptural scenes from the abbey of *St-Vlaast* at Arras.

The Rue Réaumur leads W. from the *Pl. du Temple*, passing (l.) the Rue Volta, in which No. 3, of the 14C, is possibly the oldest surviving house in Paris. The Rue Réaumur crosses the Rue de Turbigo to meet the Rue St-Martin (the original Roman road from Lutetia to the N.) between the former Priory of *St-Martin-des-Champs* (r.) and (l.) *St-Nicolas-des-Champs*, see below.

We may regain the Rue du Temple by turning E. along the Rue des Gravilliers (just S. of *St-Nicolas-des-Champs*). Balzac lived at No. 122 Rue du Temple in 1814-19; at No. 13 Rue Chapon (the first turning r., going S.), with an interesting court, was the house of the archbishops of Reims. No. 115 marks the probable site of a residence of Jean Bart (1650-1702), a privateer created Admiral of the Fleet by Louis XIV. Nos. 101-103, the *Hôtel de Montmorency*, the residence of Fouquet in 1652, has its entrance at No. 5 Rue de Montmorency. No. 51 in this street, the *Maison du Grand-Pignon*, restored in 1900, was built in the early 15C.

The Rue Michel-Le-Comte, parallel to the S., retains a number of early 17C houses, including the *Hôtel Le Tellier* (No. 16), with a fine courtyard; No. 21, the home of Verniquet, architect to Louis XVI; and No. 28, the *Hôtel d'Hallwyll*, by *C. Ledoux* (18C), and probably the birthplace of Mme de Staël (1766).

The **Musée National des Techniques**, or *Conservatoire National des Arts et Métiers*, the Science Museum of Paris, with its entrance at No. 292 Rue St-Martin (Pl. 15; 1; adm. daily except Tues., 13.30-17.30; Sun. 10.00-17.00), occupies certain buildings of the ancient priory of *St-Martin-des-Champs*.

During the Revolution, these were taken over by the Société des Jeunes Français, an educational institution, and later were used as a small-arms factory.

In 1789 they were assigned to the Conservatoire des Arts et Métiers, which had been founded by a decree of the Convention in 1794, and here were assembled the collections of Vaucanson and other scientists. Two important buildings remain of the earlier priory, founded in 1060 by Henri I and presented to the Abbey of Cluny by Philippe I in 1079, which until the early 14C stood without the city walls.

To the r. of the entrance courtyard (its gateway is of 1850) is the ****Refectory**, a 13C masterpiece, built by *Pierre de Montreuil* (architect of the *Sainte Chapelle*). This remarkable hall (138 ft by 39 ft), its vaulting sustained by a central row of columns (recalling those of the *Église des Jacobins* at Toulouse), now accommodates the Library. Note the 13C reader's pulpit at the E. end. The external side of the S. doorway is a good example of decorated Gothic, and the sole relic of the original cloisters. Further S. one may see the restored 13C portal of the church (not entered from here, but see below). The turret is a recent addition.

As the main entrance is under restoration, we enter the museum at the N.E. corner of the courtyard. On the r., on the GROUND FLOOR, are models of locomotives and rolling-stock; rooms on the l., and in the wing beyond, display an extensive collection of astronomical and surveying instruments; clocks (by Berthoud, Lepaute, Bréguet, Janvier, and other famous 18C clockmakers); and a collection of elaborate automata, including Marie-Antoinette's 'Joueuse de Tympanon'.

From the provisional entrance vestibule, stairs ascend to the FIRST FLOOR, with rooms (l.) displaying examples of machinery employed in the processes of printing; apparatus used by Daguerre, Niepce, and Lumière, etc., in the pioneering days of photography and cinematography; and historical equipment illustrating the development of recording, television, radio-astronomy, etc.

To the r. on the First Floor, are rooms devoted to domestic lighting and heating; models of machines, including the 'Machine de Marly' (see p. 204). From the far end of this wing, steps descend to the former Abbey Church of **St-Martin-des-Champs**, now sheltering a curious congregation of cars and planes. Although 'restored' in 1854-80, the fabric of the Choir, with its 'chevet' of chapels, is perhaps the earliest Gothic vault in Paris (1130-40), while the aisleless nave dates from the 13C.

Among the prototypes of the motor-car are Cugnot's steam-carriage of 1770, and one by Serpollet (1888); petrol-driven vehicles include a Panhard (1896), Peugeots of 1893 and 1909, a Berliet phaeton (1898), a De Dion-Bouton (1899), a Renault of 1900, etc. Among the aeroplanes are those of Ader (1897), Esnault-Pelterie (1906), the plane in which Blériot made the first flight across the Channel (1909), a Bréguet of 1911, etc.

Most other sections of the museum are at present closed or are being reformed.

At the N.W. corner of the building is the *Fontaine du Vertbois* (1712), which, with the adjoining tower, has been restored.

The exterior of *St-Martin-des-Champs* is best seen from the Rue Réaumur, to the S.

Adjacent is **St-Nicolas-des-Champs**, with a square tower, built in 1420 but enlarged in 1541-87, when the choir was rebuilt and the outer nave aisles added. At the Revolution, it served as the 'Temple of Hymen'. The original W. doors have survived, and the fine S. portal (c. 1576), *after Philibert Delorme*, likewise retains its contemporary doors. There is good woodwork in the nave vestibule. Paintings include a Baptism of Christ by *Gaudenzio Ferrari*, a Madonna and Saints by *Amico Aspertini* (both c. 1500). The ambulatory chapels have 17C wall-paintings; also (1st S. chapel), Our Lady of Victories (c. 1610-20); and (6th chapel) a 14C Italian altarpiece. The Apostles at the tomb of the Virgin, with the Assumption (on the 17C high-altar), is by *Simon Vouet*.

Guillaume Budé (or Budaeus; 1468-1540), Théophile de Viau (1590-1626), Gassendi (1592-1655), the astronomer, and Mlle de Scudéry (1607-1701), are buried here.

Nos. 67-87, on the W. side of the Rue du Temple, provide a charming ensemble of 17C houses, of which Nos. 71, 73, and 75 form the *Hôtel de St-Aignan*, built by *Le Muet* in 1640-50; the courtyards and gate are particularly elegant. No. 79, dating from c. 1620, but altered after 1751, is the *Hôtel de Montmor*, also with a good gateway and attractive pediment in the courtyard.

No. 62 was the site of a house in which Anne de Montmorency, constable of France, died in 1567; No. 41, the *Auberge de l'Aigle d'Or* (17C), is the last remaining example in Paris of a coaching inn of the period. The square turret on No. 24 dates from 1610; and an inscription on No. 17 indicates the site of the house of Du Guesclin (1372-80). We regain the Rue de Rivoli at the *Hôtel de Ville* (see p. 133).

13   THE GRANDS BOULEVARDS: FROM THE MADELEINE TO THE PL. DE LA RÉPUBLIQUE

MÉTROS: *Concorde, Madeleine, Opéra, Richelieu-Drouot, Rue Montmartre, Bonne-Nouvelle, Strasbourg-St-Denis, République.*

The *Grands Boulevards*, a succession of wide thoroughfares extending in a curve from the Pl. de la Concorde to the Bastille, were laid out in 1670-85 on the site of the inner ramparts demolished in the reign of Louis XIV. These had comprised the E. part of the 'enceinte de Charles V', erected after 1370, and the new fortifications to the W. built by Louis XIII in 1633-37.

Although the Western Boulevards are no longer the centre of fashion they once were, they are still busy shopping and commercial areas.

The Rue Royale forms a convenient approach to the Boulevards from the PL. DE LA CONCORDE. As far as the Rue St-Honoré it is lined with uniform 18C houses, with shops below. No. 3, *Maxim's*, was a haunt of 'high society' in the 1890s; the *Café Weber,* celebrated earlier in the century as a literary forum, stood at No. 21. Mme de Staël lived briefly in 1816 at No. 6; No. 8 was the home of the architect Gabriel.

The street is dominated by the imposing church of *St Mary Magdalen,* better known as the *Madeleine (Pl. 7;8), built in the style of a Roman temple, and surrounded by a majestic Corinthian colonnade. Two earlier churches had been demolished unfinished in 1777 and 1789, before *P. Vignon* commenced work in 1806 on Napoleon's orders, who, before he had thought of the *Arc de Triomphe,* intended it as a 'Temple of Glory' for the 'Grande Armée'. It was finished by *Huvé* in 1842. In the pediment is a relief of the Last Judgement (restored), by *Lemaire;* the bronze doors are adorned with bas-reliefs from the Decalogue, by *Triqueti* (1838).

The interior consists of a domed cella, meretriciously decorated and inadequately lighted. In chapels on either side of the entrance are the Marriage of the Virgin, by *Pradier,* and the Baptism of Christ, by *Rude;* the affected group of the Ascension of the Magdalen, on the high-altar, is by *Marochetti.*

The church stands in the centre of the PL. DE LA MADELEINE, on the E. side of which is a small flower market. To the N. are Hediard and Fauchon, haunts of the gastronome. At No. 2 (now Thomas Cook's agency) stood the *Café Durand,* which played a dominant role in the 1848 Revolution, and where Zola wrote 'J'Accuse', an open letter denouncing the army, and in defence of Dreyfus, published in 'L'Aurore', 13 Jan. 1898.

Marcel Proust spent much of his youth at No. 9 in the BLVD. MALESHERBES, leading N.W. from the *Madeleine*, its S. section dominated by *St-Augustin*, an early and tasteless example of the use of iron in church-construction (1860-71), by *Baltard.*

The BLVD. DE LA MADELEINE, the westernmost of the Grands Boulevards, leads N.E. Marie Duplessis (1824-47), the prototype of the 'Dame aux Camélias', died at No. 15 (formerly 11); Nos 17-25 house the *Aux Trois Quartiers* department store; the *Crédit Foncier* occupies an 18C mansion in the neighbouring Rue des Capucines, leading S.E. towards the *Pl. Vendôme* (see p. 123).

The boulevard is continued by the BLVD. DES CAPUCINES, crossing the *Pl. de l'Opéra*. Offenbach (1819-80), who had lived in Paris since 1833, died at No. 8 Blvd. des Capucines.

Opposite the *Théâtre des Capucines*, the Rue Édouard-VII leads N. to a small Place containing an equestrian statue of Edward VII (by *Landowski*), who as Prince of Wales and King was a frequent visitor to Paris, and a promoter of the 'Entente Cordiale'.

At No. 14 in the boulevard a tablet records the first exhibition of a cinema film (in the 'Salon Indien' of the *Grand Café*) given by the brothers Louis and Auguste Lumière (28 Dec. 1895). The first demonstration of X-rays, a discovery of Dr Roentgen, took place in the same room a few days later.

The ***Musée Cognacq-Jay**, a small elegant collection of 18C furniture and works of art, occupies three floors at No. 25 Blvd. des Capucines, and was originated by the founder of the 'Magasins de la Samaritaine' (N. of the Pont Neuf).

Take the lift to the THIRD FLOOR, and turn r. into **R 7**, with 'Assemblée dans un parc' and other works by *Watteau*. In **R 8**, adjacent, are displayed in eight cases an impressive collection of enamelled and jewelled 18C boxes and other decorative objects. On the walls hang pastel portraits by *La Tour* (1704-88) of the Marquis de Bérenger and his wife, a Man in a blue waistcoat, and a self-portrait. On the landing, *Gérard*, portrait of Mme Bauguin du Boulay and her niece, and three scenes by *Louis Boilly* (1761-1845).

Descending the stairs, we pass some English pastels, the best of which are portraits of Princess Metternich, and Sarah Siddons, by *Lawrence*. On the landing below are two Venetian scenes by *Canaletto.*—**R 6** contains a good collection of marquetry furniture.—**R 5**, *Ruysdael*, the Old Oak, and an early *Rembrandt*, Balaam's ass (1626).—**R 4**, panelled, displays a well-preserved Louis XVI bed 'à la polonaise', a marquetry desk, and three colourful 'Kien-Lung' porcelain birds (18C). Among the portraits are *Gainsborough*, Charles Colmore; *Reynolds*, Lord Northington (once in an oval frame); and *Lawrence*, the Calmady children; also, *Drouais*, Alexandrine le Normant d'Etioles, daughter of Mme de Pompadour.

We pass, in descending to the FIRST FLOOR—and on the stair to the entrance vestibule—a series of charming scènes galantes, etc., by *Mallet, Lavreince, Baudouin,* and *Debucourt.* In **R 3** are a number of Meissen porcelain and French terracotta figures; while in **R 2**, adjoining, are terracotta busts by *J.-B. Lemoyne* of the Maréchal de Saxe and Maréchal de Lowendal; and chairs covered with Beauvais tapestry. Among the portraits are those of the Duchess of Beaufort by *Largillière; Boucher's* portrait of his daughter, Mme Baudouin; and Marie Leczinska, by *Nattier*. Also by *Boucher*, 'La Belle Cuisinière', and the

Music Lesson.—**R1**, with panelling from the château of Eu, in Normandy, displays *Vigée-Lebrun*, 'La Camargo'; *Morland*, the First Steps; a still life by *Chardin;* and among other works, two nudes by *Jollain*.

At No. 35 in the boulevard took place the exhibition of paintings (1874) by Renoir, Manet, Pissarro, and Monet, which included the latter's 'Impression—Soleil levant', which gave the group their name.

The PL. DE L'OPÉRA (Pl. 7; 6), a busy focus of traffic, is dominated to the N. by the opera-house, while to the N.W. is the *Café de la Paix*, once a fashionable meeting-place for visitors to Paris.

The grandiose **Opéra**, an appropriate monument to the most extravagant and brilliant period of the Second Empire, was built in 1861-75 from the designs of *Charles Garnier*, the successful entrant of 171 competitors. Although its superficial area is 3 acres, it contains only 2,158 seats as compared with the 3,000 of the Théâtre du Châtelet, and the 2,800 of La Scala at Milan.

The first opera-house in Paris was established in 1669 by Perrin, Cambert, and the Marquis de Sourdéac on the Left Bank, between the Rue de Seine and the Rue Mazarine, and the first director was Lulli, under whom it acquired its secondary title of *Académie Royale de Musique*.

The façade, flanked by a flight of steps, is lavishly decorated with coloured marbles and sculpture. On either side of the arcade opening into the vestibule are allegorical groups, including (r.) The Dance, by *Carpeaux* (a copy of the original, now in the *Louvre*). Above are medallions of composers; and bronze-gilt statues of other composers and librettists are seen between the monolithic columns of the loggia. Behind the low dome of the auditorium is a triangular pediment crowned by a statue of Apollo of the Golden Lyre.

The E. pavilion in the Rue Halévy is the subscribers' entrance; to the W., in the Rue Auber, is the 'Pavillon d'Honneur', and the entrance to the LIBRARY AND MUSEUM (with a complete collection of the scores of all operas and ballets performed here since its foundation).

This latter entrance, originally known as the 'Pavillon de l'Empereur', was designed so that his coach could be driven up to the level of the dress circle—a precaution welcomed since Orsini's attempt on the life of Napoleon III on his way to the old Opera-house in 1858, and a device which won Garnier the competition, so it was rumoured.
Passing through two vestibules, the second containing the box-office (open 11.00-18.30), we reach the GRAND STAIRCASE , with its white marble steps 33 ft wide, and with a balustrade of onyx and rosso and verde antico. On the first floor, where it divides, is the entrance to the stalls and the amphitheatre, flanked by caryatids, and on each floor are arcades of monolithic marble columns. The *Avant-Foyer* leads to the *Grand Foyer*; glass doors communicate with the Loggia overlooking the *Pl. de l'Opéra*, and by the middle door is a bust of Garnier by *Carpeaux*.
The AUDITORIUM, resplendent in red plush and gilt, and with five tiers of boxes, is—except during performances—not normally on view, but visitors may, on making application, be allowed to join an escorted group. The dome, resting on eight pillars of scagliola, was redecorated in 1964, many would say inappropriately, by *Chagall*. The huge stage is 118 ft high, 174 ft wide, and 85 ft deep, behind which is the *Foyer de la Dance* (the scene of many paintings by Degas), with a mirror measuring 23 by 33 ft.

The AV. DE L'OPÉRA leads S.E. to the *Pl. du Théâtre-Français* (see p. 124), its southern reaches now more oriental than occidental in character! It is crossed by the Rue Louis-le-Grand, in which Mme de

Montespan and the painter Hyacinthe Rigaud (1659-1743) had houses; while Napoleon and Joséphine Beauharnais were married in 1796 at No. 3 Rue d'Antin (the next cross-street), which was then the Mairie of the 2nd Arrondissement. The *Fontaine Gaillon* (1828), just to the E. in the Rue St-Augustin, is by *Visconti* and *Jacquot*.

Immediately behind the *Opéra*, facing the PL. DIAGHILEV, are the department stores of *Galeries Lafayette* and, to the W., *Du Printemps*, whose huge central halls should be seen to be believed.

Just E. of the *Galeries Lafayette* is the Rue de la Chaussée-d'Antin, leading N. to *La Trinité* (see p. 156). In its S. section, at No. 2, Rossini lived from 1857. No. 5 (rebuilt) sheltered Mozart after the death of his mother, and was the residence of Chopin in 1833-36. No. 7 (also demolished) was the home of the Neckers, who entertained Gibbon here; in 1798 it was bought by Jules Récamier, the banker, whose wife here presided over the most distinguished salon of the Directory, frequented also by Lord and Lady Holland, and many other English en passage.

The BLVD. DES ITALIENS (the continuation N.E. of the *Blvd. des Capucines*), whose many cafés have been largely replaced by cinemas and commercial buildings, derived its name from the *Théâtre des Italiens* (1783), where Donizetti's 'Don Pasquale' was first performed in 1843. Grétry lived at No. 7 from 1795 to 1813. In 1784-85, Jefferson had lodgings in the Impasse Taitbout (now Rue du Helder), leading l. No. 5 Rue Taitbout, further E., was the house of Sir Richard Wallace, where Lord Hertford accumulated the works of art now in the Wallace Collection, London (see also p. 176). Wagner lived at No. 25 in 1840-41.

At the corner of the next street, the Rue Laffitte, stood the house of Mme Tallien (1773-1835), daughter of the Spanish financier Cabarrus, and wife of the revolutionary, and later Princesse de Chimay. Part of the building (No. 20) became the *Café Hardy*, rival of the *Café Riche* at No. 16 ("Il faut être bien riche pour dîner chez Hardy, et bien hardi pour dîner chez Riche").

At the far end of Rue Laffitte (named after Jacques Laffitte, 1767-1844, the financier) is seen *N.-D.-de-Lorette* (p. 155), with *Sacré-Coeur* in the background. No. 17 was the residence of Queen Hortense of Holland, and here Napoleon III was born in 1808. From No. 27, then Laffitte's residence, was issued the manifesto of Thiers proposing the coronation of Louis-Philippe. At Nos. 39 and 41 stood Ambroise Vollard's art gallery, where so many paintings by Gauguin and Cézanne were first displayed. Vollard was also responsible for the first exhibitions in Paris of works by Picasso and Matisse (in 1901 and 1904, respectively).

It was in the parallel Rue Le Peletier (to the E.) that the 'Carbonaro' Orsini flung a bomb at the carriage conveying Napoleon III to the opera, killing and injuring many, but leaving the emperor unharmed (1858). No. 3 was the *Café du Divan*, frequented by Balzac, Gautier, de Nerval, and Baudelaire.

In the Rue de Marivaux (opposite) stands a building until recently the *Opéra-Comique*, but now housing an experimental *Opéra-Studio*.

The *Opéra-Comique* originated in a company which produced pieces during local fairs, and in 1715 purchased from the Opéra the right of playing vaudevilles interspersed with ariettas. Discord between the two theatres continued until in 1757 Charles Favart (1710-92) finally established the rights of the Opéra-Comique, which moved to the 'Salle Favart' on this somewhat confined site in 1783, since rebuilt.

At the junction of the boulevard with that of the BLVD. MONTMARTRE and BLVD. HAUSSMANN (the latter only extended to this point in 1927), the Rue Drouot leads N. past (No. 6) the *Mairie of the 9th Arrondissement* in a mansion of 1746-48, and No. 9 (l.), the *Hôtel des Ventes Mobilières*, or *Hôtel Drouot*, long the main auction-rooms of Paris, where important sales are held from Feb. to June, and which occupy the same place in Parisian life as Christies or Sothebys in London. It has been temporarily transferred to the Gare d'Orsay.

To the S., the Rue de Richelieu leads to the *Bibliothèque Nationale* (see p. 127). Thomas Paine wrote 'The Age of Reason' at No. 95 in this street (1793).

The short BLVD. MONTMARTRE, in spite of its name, is a long way from Montmartre. At No. 10 (l.) is the *Musée Grévin*, a waxwork collection equivalent to Mme Tussaud's. On the r. is the Rue Vivienne, leading to the *Bourse*; the *Passage des Panoramas* (named after an entertainment displaying views of cities, introduced to Paris by the American Robert Fulton, who had also tested his first steamboat on the Seine in 1803); and the *Théâtre des Variétés*, scene of several Offenbach successes.

The Rue Montmartre leads S.E. towards *St-Eustache* (p. 130), and was already so named in 1200. Émile Zola (1840-1902) was born at No. 10 Rue St-Joseph, a short distance S. on the l. The Rue du Faubourg-Montmartre, diverging N.W. towards the 'suburb' of Montmartre, recalls the time when the boulevard formed the city boundary. Lautréamont (1846-70) died at No. 7, where he had written 'Les Chants de Maldoror'. The Rue Geoffroy-Marie, a turning off to the r. (commemorating a saddler and his wife who in 1260 presented to the *Hôtel-Dieu* a little farm which sold for over 3 million francs in 1840), leads to the titillating cabaret known as the *Folies Bergère*, situated in a mainly Jewish enclave, and a centre of the diamond trade.

Continuing E. along the BLVD. POISSONNIÈRE (in which No. 27 was Chopin's first Paris home, in 1831-32), we pass (r.) the Rue du Sentier, where, opposite the end of the Rue du Croissant, Mozart and his mother lodged in 1778. In the same year she was buried in the vanished *Cimitière St-Joseph* nearby, the original burial-place of Molière also. M. and Mme Necker lived in 1766-89 at the junction of the adjacent Rue de Mulhouse and the Rue de Cléry (in a house replaced by No. 29).

To the N., at No. 2 Rue du Conservatoire (beyond the Rue Rougemont), is the *Conservatoire National d'Art Dramatique*, a small theatre of 1802, reputed for its excellent acoustics.

The boulevard is now crossed by the Rue Poissonnière (r.) and its N. extension, the Rue du Faubourg-Poissonnière, both named after the fishmongers who used to pass by on their way to the *Halles*. Beyond this junction, the line of boulevards is continued by the BLVD. DE BONNE-NOUVELLE, on the N. side of which is the façade (1887) of the *Théâtre du Gymnase*, where Rachel made her début in 1837. At the far end of the next street running N. is the church of *St-Vincent-de-Paul* (see p. 155). To the S. steps lead up to *N.-D. de Bonne-Nouvelle*, rebuilt in 1824. André Chénier (1762-94) lived in 1793 at 97 Rue de Cléry, close by; the same street was Corneille's home in 1665-81.

The short BLVD. ST-DENIS (Pl. 9; 7) lies between the *Porte St-Denis* and the *Porte St-Martin*, beyond which the *Blvd. St-Martin* continues as far as the *Pl. de la République*. The **Porte St-Denis**, a triumphal arch 72 ft high, designed by *Blondel*, was erected in 1672 to commemorate the victories of Louis XIV in Germany and Holland.

The bas-reliefs were designed by *Girardon* and executed by the brothers *Anguier*. It faces the Rue St-Denis, or 'Voie Royale', once the processional route of entry into Paris, and last so used on the occasion of Queen Victoria's visit in 1855.

On the far side of the BLVD. DE SÉBASTOPOL, which with its N. extension, the BLVD. DE STRASBOURG, stretches from the *Pl. du Châtelet* to the *Gare de l'Est*, we pass the **Porte St-Martin**, another supererogatory triumphal arch in honour of Louis XIV, 60 ft high, built in 1674 by *Bullet*, and decorated with bas-reliefs of contemporary campaigns by *Desjardins* and *Marsy* (S. side), and *Le Hongre* and the elder *Legros* (N.).

At No. 6 in the *Blvd. St-Denis* stood the 'Cinéma Saint-Denis', opened in 1896 by the brothers Lumière, which claimed to be the first cinema.

The Rue St-Martin (the original Roman road leading N. from Lutetia) leads S. to the *Conservatoire National des Arts et Métiers*, and *St-Nicolas-des-Champs* (see p. 148), off which the Rue N.-D. de Nazareth diverges l. The façades of Nos. 41-49 are of interest; Rudolf Diesel (1858-1913), the inventor of the engine which bears his name, was born at No. 38.

We pass two famous theatres in the BLVD. ST-MARTIN, just E. of the Arch, the *Théâtre de la Renaissance* and *Théâtre de la Porte-St-Martin*, both rebuilt after being burnt down during the Commune.

The 'Renaissance' was managed by Sarah Bernhardt in 1893-99. The 'Porte-St-Martin', in its original form a foundation of Marie-Antoinette (who had it built in seventy-five days in 1781 to house the opera), is remembered as being the theatre of Frédérick Lemaître (1800-76), and here Coquelin aîné (who created the name-part in Rostand's 'Cyrano de Bergerac') was seized by a mortal illness during a rehearsal of 'Chantecler' in 1909.
Paul de Kock (1794-1871) died at No. 8.

The **Pl. de la République** (Pl. 9; 8), on the site of the Porte du Temple, and the junction of seven important thoroughfares, was laid out in 1856-65 by Haussmann for strategic reasons, but it has maintained a political role as the scene of radical manifestations. The pedestal of the *Monument de la République* (82ft high), by the brothers *Morice* (1883), has bronze bas-reliefs by *Dalou*.

At the corner of the Rue Léon-Jouhaux (previously Rue de la Douane) leading N.E. from the Place, was Daguerre's workshop (1822-35). Gounod's 'Faust' was first performed in 1859 in the *Théâtre Lyrique*, one of many (including 'Des Funambules'; 1816-62) which stood on a section of the BLVD. DU TEMPLE demolished by Haussmann, known earlier in the 19C from the melodramas enacted here as the 'Boulevard du Crime', and immortalized by Carné in the film 'Les Enfants du Paradis'.

Beyond the *Pl. de la République* the boulevards are of little interest, and change their character. The BLVD. DU TEMPLE, with its continuations, leads S.E. to the *Pl. de la Bastille* (see Rte 12). Flaubert lived at No. 42 in this boulevard in 1856-69; and a little to the N. is the site of the house from which Fieschi discharged his 'infernal machine' at Louis-Philippe in 1835, killing Marshal Mortier and several others, but not the king. Just to the W., at No. 5 in the parallel street named after him, died Béranger (1780-1857).

14   GARE DE L'EST TO GARE ST-LAZARE (FAUBOURG ST-MARTIN AND FAUBOURG ST-DENIS)

MÉTROS: *République, Gare de l'Est, Gare du Nord, Poissonnière, N.-D.-de-Lorette, Trinité, St-Lazare, St-Augustin, Madeleine.*

The BLVD. DE MAGENTA leads N.W. from the *Pl. de la République* to meet the outer boulevards beyond the *Gare du Nord.* Just E. of its intersection with the BLVD. DE STRASBOURG is **St-Laurent**, one of the oldest foundations in Paris. Gregory of Tours mentions that a church existed here near the Roman road as early as 583. The present building, begun before 1429, retaining an older N. tower, was continued in the 16-17C, the nave having been vaulted in 1655-59, and the choir remodelled at the same time, with a high-altar by *Ant. Le Pautre.* The *Lady Chapel* dates from 1712. The 17C façade was demolished in 1862-65, when the flamboyant W. front was built and the spire erected. The roof has elegantly carved pendentives. Mme du Barry (Jeanne Bécu; 1746-93) was married here in 1764.

The courtyard of the **Gare de l'Est** (Pl. 9; 5; the terminus of the line to Strasbourg, etc.) just to the N., occupies the site of the medieval St Lawrence fair.

To the W. of the boulevard at this point stood the *Prison de St-Lazare* (since 1935 partly demolished and rebuilt as a hospital), from 1632 the headquarters of the Lazarists or Priests of the Mission, founded in 1625 by St Vincent de Paul (1576-1660). Among its inmates were André Chénier and Hubert Robert.

The boulevard next crosses the Rue La Fayette before passing (r.) the **Gare du Nord**, the terminus of the line from Calais, Boulogne, etc. (Pl. 9; 3).

There is little of interest in the thickly populated cosmopolitan Quartier de la Chapelle to the N., where adjacent to the ugly modern basilica stands the 13C *St-Denis-de-la-Chapelle,* much restored, where Joan of Arc received Communion in Nov. 1429 before besieging the walls of Paris.

Turning S.W. along the Rue La Fayette, we pass (r.) *St-Vincent-de-Paul* (1824-44), by *Lepère* and *Hittorf,* with two square towers dominating a pedimented portico of twelve Ionic columns, and approached by a monumental flight of steps.

At No. 58 Rue d'Hauteville, leading S., is the *Hôtel de Bourrienne* (1787), finely decorated in First Empire style by Napoleon's secretary.

This street is crossed by the Rue de Paradis, where at No. 30bis is the shop of the glass-maker Baccarat, with a *Museum* adjoining (adm. 9.00-17.30 weekdays). Corot (1796-1875) died at No. 56 in the Rue du Faubourg-Poissonnière, further W.; No. 9 Rue de Montholon (leading S.E. from the SQ. DE MONTHOLON) was the residence of Liszt in 1831.

We shortly diverge due W. along the Rue de Châteaudun, passing (r.) *N.-D.-de-Lorette,* another of the drearily magnificent basilican churches of the early 19C, built in 1823-36, with a portico of four Corinthian columns, by *Hippolyte Lebas.* Bizet (1838-75), born at No. 26 Rue de la Tour-d'Auvergne (leading off the Rue des Martyrs, ascending behind the church), was christened here. The Rue des Martyrs, the ancient approach to Montmartre, was already well known for its 'cabarets' in the 18C; Géricault (1791-1824) died at No. 49, later occupied by Béranger.

The Rue N.-D.-de-Lorette ascends N.W. from the church through a quarter whose name was synonymous with the *demi-mondaine* or *femmes entretenues* of the mid-19C who congregated here. These 'Lorettes', a favourite subject of the caricaturist Gavarni (1801-66), are represented on his monument in the small PL. ST-GEORGES, which the street crosses. Delacroix lived from 1844 to 1857 at No. 58 (then 54) in the Rue N.-D.-de-Lorette; Gauguin was born at No. 56 in 1848; while at No. 27 in the Place is the *Hôtel Thiers*.

This latter building, burned down by the Communards, was the residence of President Thiers (1797-1877), and reconstructed, it now contains the *Bibliothèque Thiers* (80,000 vols on the history of France since the Revolution; and the Napoleonic collection of Frédéric Masson, of 30,000 vols; drawings by *David*; bust of Joséphine by *Houdon*, etc.). Permission to visit must be requested of the Librarian, Institut de France, 23 Quai de Conti.

Mallarmé (1842-98) was born in the nearby Rue Laferrière (No. 12).

The Rue St-Georges runs downhill, and crosses the Rue de Châteaudun. The Goncourt brothers lived at No. 43 from 1849 to 1868; Auber (1782-1871) lived for thirty years and died at No. 22; Henry Murger (1822-61), author of 'Scènes de la Vie de Bohème', was born the son of a concierge at No. 19.

In the Rue Taitbout (parallel to the W.) lodged Rossini (at No. 28), when musical director of the *Théâtre des Italiens* (1824-25); and Mirabeau (1749-91) died at No. 42.

In 1842-47 Chopin and George Sand lived at Nos. 5 and 9 respectively in the SQUARE D'ORLÉANS, off the E. side of the N. end of this street. At No. 14 Rue de la Rochefoucauld, to the W. at this level, is the *Musée Gustave-Moreau* (adm. 10.00-13.00, 14.00-17.00 except Mon. and Tues.), containing an extensive collection of paintings and drawings left by Moreau (1826-98) to the State.

To the W. stands *La Trinité*, a conspicuously ugly church built in 1863-67 by *Ballu* in a hybrid style, with a tower 206 ft high.

From behind the church, the Rue Pigalle and Rue Blanche ascend N.E. and N. towards Montmartre. To the W. of the church the Rue Clichy (in which, at No. 21, Hugo lived in 1880) leads N. to the *Pl. de Clichy*. No. 16 is the *Casino de Paris*, a famous music-hall. To the S., the Rue de Mogador leads S. to the *Opéra*.

The Rue St-Lazare leads W. from the SQUARE DE LA TRINITÉ. Mme Vigée-Lebrun died at No. 29 in 1842. Just E. of the **Gare St-Lazare** (Pl. 7; 6), the Rue d'Amsterdam leads N., in which lived Manet (at No. 77; in 1879-83) and Alexandre Dumas (No. 97; from 1854).

The station itself is the terminus of the western region of the S.N.C.F. The *Hôtel Terminus* was the home of Georges Feydeau in 1909-19, who, intending to stay a week while his family moved house, remained a decade.

To the W. of the station, the Rue de Rome leads N.W., in which No. 89 was the home of Mallarmé (1842-98) from 1885, and here his friends would congregate on Tuesday evenings. At No. 14 Rue de Madrid, diverging W. off this street, is the **Conservatoire National Supérieur de Musique** (Pl. 7; 3), founded in 1765 as the *Académie Royale de Chant*, amalgamated with the École de Déclamation Dramatique in 1786, and refounded in 1795. It moved to these buildings, formerly a Jesuit college, in 1911.

The **Musée Instrumental** (adm. 14.00-16.30, Wed. and Sat.; closed Aug.) originated in the Clapisson collection. It includes the violins of Lulli, Kreutzer, and Sarasate; Beethoven's clavichord; Marie-Antoinette's harp; and many other instruments of historical or artistic interest. The *Library* possesses the most complete series in existence of musical scores, books on music, and MSS., including Mozart's 'Don Giovanni'. Jules Renard (1864-1910), author of 'Poil de Carotte', died at No. 44 Rue du Rocher, to the W., where he had lived since 1888.

The Rue du Havre leads S. from the *Gare St-Lazare*, where No. 8, the *Lycée Condorcet*, founded in 1804, occupies the former buildings (with a Doric cloister court) of a Capuchin convent; on the site of its chapel (in the parallel street to the E.) is *St-Louis d'Antin*, by *Brongniart* (1782). Proust was but one of the school's many famous pupils. The street is continued S. of the *Blvd. Haussmann* by the Rue Tronchet (in which Chopin lived, at No. 5, in 1839-42) to the *Madeleine* (see Rte 13).

The BLVD. HAUSSMANN, one of the main streets in the area, commemorates Baron Haussmann (1809-91) who, as Préfet de la Seine, initiated considerable urban development in central Paris. Work began here in 1857 as part of a scheme to construct an unbroken thoroughfare from the *Blvd. Montmartre* to the *Arc de Triomphe*, and was only completed in 1926.

A short distance to the W., on the S. side of the *Blvd. Haussmann*, is the SQUARE LOUIS XVI (Pl. 7; 6), formerly the *Cimetière de la Madeleine*, where rest the bodies of the victims of the panic of 1770 in the *Pl. de la Concorde* (see p. 87), the Swiss guards massacred on 10 Aug. 1792, and all those guillotined between 26 Aug. 1792 and 24 March 1794 (among them Charlotte Corday and Philippe-Égalité). The **Chapelle Expiatoire** (adm. 10.00-12.00, 14.00-17.00 or 18.00), erected in 1815-26 from the plans of *Percier* and *Fontaine*, stands in the S.W. corner of the Square. The chapel, in the style of a classical funeral temenos, was built by order of Louis XVIII and dedicated to the memory of Louis XVI and Marie-Antoinette, whose remains, interred in the graveyard on this site, were removed to St-Denis in 1815.

In the interior are two marble groups: Louis XVI and his confessor Abbé Henry Essex Edgeworth (1745-1807), by *Bosio* (below which is inscribed the king's will, dated 25 Dec. 1792); and Marie-Antoinette supported by Religion, by *Cortot*, the latter figure bearing the features of Mme Élisabeth. (Below is inscribed a letter said to have been written by the queen to her sister-in-law from the Conciergerie on 16 Oct. 1793.) The bas-relief by *Gérard* above the doorway represents the removal of the remains to St-Denis.

15   MONTMARTRE

Best approached from the MÉTRO stations of *Clichy, Lamarck-Caulaincourt,* or *Anvers.*

The PL. DE CLICHY (Pl. 7; 7) was the site of the 'Barrière de Clichy', which on 30 March 1814 was defended against the Russians by pupils from the École Polytechnique and the Garde Nationale under Moncey, an action commemorated by a bronze group 20ft high by *Doublemard* (1869). To the E. lies the wide BLVD. DE CLICHY, forming, with its continuation, the BLVD. DE ROCHECHOUART, the S. boundary of Montmartre proper.

The first turning r. off the Blvd. de Clichy, the Rue de Douai (where at No. 30, the house of Turgenev and Mme Viardot, the singer, Dickens met George Sand in

1856) shortly crosses the PL. ADOLPHE-MAX, in which Vuillard had a studio. Zola (1840-1902) died at No. 21bis Rue de Bruxelles, crossing this square; and Berlioz (1803-69) died at No. 4 Rue de Calais, leading S.E.

The *Blvds. de Clichy* and *de Rochechouart* are now the focus of the seedy night life of a sordid area, where *colour*-ful and motley crowds congregate in the cafés and around the so-called 'cabarets artistiques' of the PL. BLANCHE (on the N. side of which stood the *Moulin Rouge*), and PL. PIGALLE, etc.

A century has passed since *Montmartre* was rendered easier of access by the construction of new streets ascending through the N. slums, and poorer artists, migrating there because it was both picturesque and cheap, made it for about thirty years an artistic centre, vividly depicted by Toulouse-Lautrec (1864-1901), among others, whose studio was at No. 5 Av. Frochot, near the *Pl. Pigalle*. No. 16 in the adjacent Rue Frochot was the home of Mme Sabatier ('La Présidente'), often the rendezvous of de Musset, Flaubert, Sainte-Beuve, Gautier, and Baudelaire.

About 1881 the famous 'Le Chat Noir' (No. 84 Blvd. Rochechouart; closed in 1897) was opened, and the advertisement thus given to the attractions of the district invited a tide of pseudo-bohemians, tourists, and less desirable hangers-on, before which the serious artists retired, and have now all but vanished. There remain, however, a few old-fashioned streets and backwaters, made familiar in the paintings of Utrillo, among others, and an hour or two may be pleasantly spent wandering around the 'Butte' (see below), preferably during daylight.

Seurat and Signac had adjoining studios at No. 128bis BLVD. DE CLICHY in 1886; Seurat (1859-91) died at No. 39 Rue André-Antoine (leading N. from the Pl. Pigalle). Picasso lived at No. 130 in 1909; and Degas died at No. 6 in 1917.

The short Av. Rachel, the first turning on the l. off the *Blvd. de Clichy*, as we walk E., leads to the main entrance of the **Cimetière de Montmartre**, on the W. slope of the Butte.

Although less important than that of *Père-Lachaise*, it contains the graves of many famous 18-20C figures, among which may be listed Gautier, de Vigny, the Goncourt brothers, Alex. Dumas (fils), Stendhal, Heine, Murger, Maxime du Camp, Renan, and Giraudoux; among composers, Berlioz, Delibes, Offenbach, Halévy, Adam, and Ambroise Thomas; among artists, Fragonard, Greuze, Delaroche, Horace Vernet, and Degas; the actors Fr. Lemaître and Louis Jouvet; the dancers Vestris, Taglioni, and Nijinsky; Mme Récamier, Pauline Viardot, and Marie Duplessis ('Dame aux Camélias'); Ampère and Dr Charcot.

From the *Pl. de Clichy,* the Rue Caulaincourt is carried over the cemetery by a viaduct, the latter being the most convenient approach to Montmartre by car. Continuing along the BLVD DE CLICHY, we pass (l.) the famous *Moulin Rouge* (now a cinema), and turn l. up the steep Rue Lepic (at No. 54 lived van Gogh in 1886) towards the rebuilt *Moulin de la Galette*. Turning E. along the Rue Norvins, we shortly reach the central PL. DU TERTRE (Pl. 8; 2), with the former Mairie (No. 3), now surrounded by cafés, etc.

The **Butte Montmartre** rises 423ft above sea-level and 335ft above the level of the Seine, and the name has been variously derived from Mons Mercurii, Mons Martis, and Mons Martyrum. Of these, the two first presuppose the existence of a Roman temple on the hill; the last the probability that St Denis and his companions, SS Rusticus and Eleutherius, were beheaded at the foot of the hill, St Denis afterwards walking to the site of the Basilica of St-Denis (see p. 204), 'with his head in his hands'. The *Chapelle du Martyre* (in the convent at 9 Rue Yvonne-le-Tac, just E. of the Métro Abbesses) occupies the probable position of a chapel erected on the site of the martyrdom. It was in the crypt beneath this that St Ignatius de Loyola and his six companions, including St Francis Xavier, took the first Jesuit vows, in 1534, thus founding the Society of Jesus.

To the E. of the *Pl. du Tertre* stands the old church of **St-Pierre-de-Montmartre**, the successor of an earlier church erected to commemorate the martyrdom of St Denis, a relic of a Benedictine nunnery founded in 1134 by Adélaïde de Savoie (d. 1154). It was consecrated in the presence of her son Louis VII by Pope Eugenius III in 1147. In 1794 it served as the 'Temple of Reason'. The façade dates from the time of Louis XIV. Inside, against the W. wall, are two ancient columns with 7C capitals, the date also of two other capitals, one at the apse entrance and another in the N. aisle. The nave has 15C vaulting; the aisle vaulting was added in a restoration of 1900-05. The apse also has been almost entirely rebuilt, but the choir retains perhaps the earliest example of an ogee arch in Paris (1147). The foundress's tomb lies behind the altar.

In the JARDIN DU CALVAIRE, S. of the church, are stations of the Cross executed for Richelieu; to the N. of the building foundations of a Roman temple have been discovered, while in the derelict graveyard is the tomb of the navigator Bougainville (1729-1814).

The Rue Azais, to the S., leads past a reservoir to the terrace below the *Basilique du Sacré-Coeur*, with extensive views S. over the entire city with its changing denticulated horizon. Commanding Paris in this way, the history of the Butte Montmartre is one long series of sieges and battles. It was occupied by Henri of Navarre in 1589, and here in 1814 took place the final struggle between the French and the Allies. In 1871 it was held for two months by the Communards. In 1873 the National Assembly decreed the building of a church as an expiatory offering after the Franco-Prussian War of 1870-71. *Sacré-Coeur*, the resulting erection, only too visible from almost every part of Paris, is a conspicuous oriental-looking white stone edifice in a neo-Romanesque-Byzantine style derived from *St-Front* at Périgueux. Its ugliness does not seem to deter a constant press of pilgrims and visitors; see Pl. 8; 2.

Work was begun in 1876 from the plans of *Abadie* (who had restored *St-Front*), and although used for services in 1891, it was not consecrated as a basilica until 1919. 328 ft long, and 246 ft across the ambulatory, it is surmounted by a dome 197 ft high, and abutted by a square bell-tower of 308 ft (containing a bell weighing almost 17¾ tons). The undaunted tourist may survey its meretriciously decorated interior, and, for a fee, visit both the crypt and dome (for the panoramic view).

From the Sacré-Coeur, flights of steps descend the steep slope of the Butte to the SQ. WILLETTE (a funicular railway on its W. side will assist those making the ascent here), whence the Rue de Steinkerque leads downhill to the Pl. d'Anvers and Blvd. de Rochechouart.

Not much remains of 'Old Montmartre', with its cottages and little gardens, although in the Rue des Saules, leading N. from the Rue Norvins, one may see the last surviving vineyard of Paris. No. 4 in this street is 'Au Lapin Agile', made famous by its artistic clientele. Harriet Smithson (Mme Berlioz; d. 1854), Honegger (1892-1955), and Utrillo (1883-1956) are buried in the nearby *Cimetière St-Vincent*.

At No. 17 in the Rue St-Vincent, to the r. beyond the vineyard, steps climb to the *Musée de Vieux-Montmartre*, installed in a 17C house once belonging to Roze de Rosimond, a member of Molière's 'Illustre Théâtre'. It contains, apart from ephemera and material of very local interest, a small collection of Clignancourt (or Montmartre) porcelain, made in 1767-99 in a pottery at the junction of the Rues du Mont-Cenis and Marcadet. This house was occupied by Renoir in 1875, and later by Utrillo, and Dufy, among others.

At the corner of the Rue St-Vincent, at No. 24 Rue du Mont-Cenis (house rebuilt) lived Berlioz and Harriet Smithson in 1834-37.

Not far S. of the Rue Norvins, the PL. ÉMILE-GOUDEAU was a favourite 'artistic' residence c. 1910, where (at No. 13, the 'Bateau-Lavoir') lived Modigliani, Picasso, and Max Jacob, and where a banquet was given in honour of Douanier Rousseau.

16   FROM THE PL. DE LA CONCORDE TO THE ARC DE TRIOMPHE

A   Viâ the Champs-Élysées

MÉTROS: *Concorde, Champs-Élysées-Clemenceau, Franklin D. Roosevelt, George-V, Charles de Gaulle-Étoile.*

To the W. of the *Pl. de la Concorde* (see Rte 8) extend the *Champs-Élysées*, through which the wide *Av. des Champs-Élysées* gently ascends to the *Arc de Triomphe*. The lower-lying area, drained and planted in 1670 according to *Le Nôtre*'s designs, was rearranged in 1770 by the Marquis de Marigny (brother of Mme de Pompadour), who extended the avenue to the Pont de Neuilly in 1774. Cossacks encamped there in 1814, as did English troops in the following year. It must be admitted that however fashionable a promenade it may have been under the Second Empire, time has treated it harshly, and although still crowded, few of its attractions are of an aesthetic nature, however superb may be the vistas.

The **Champs-Élysées** consists of two parts; the first, forming a park, extends to the ROND-POINT DES CHAMPS-ÉLYSÉES; hence the increasingly commercialized avenue, largely flanked by the offices of airline companies, car showrooms, cinemas, banks, and a few expensive cafés, continues N.W. towards the commanding bulk of the *Arc de Triomphe*, a striking silhouette against the setting sun.

Skirting the N. side of the *Champs-Élysées* is the Av. Gabriel, with the *American Embassy* (1931-33) at the corner of the Rue Boissy-d'Anglas, built on the site of a mansion belonging to the gastronome Grimod de la Reynière. Further on (r.) are the gardens of the *British Embassy*, and next come the gardens of the *Palais de l'Élysée* (see p. 163).

From the PL. CLEMENCEAU, the Av. de Marigny leads N., off which (l.) is the *Théâtre Marigny*, and an open-air stamp market (Thurs. and Sun.); to the S. the Av. Winston Churchill, with a fine view of *Les Invalides* (see p. 81), leads between the *Petit-Palais* (l.) and *Grand Palais*, both built for the Exhibition of 1900, to the *Pont Alexandre-III* (1896-1900, a single steel arch, 350 ft long and 150 ft wide).

The **Petit-Palais**, or *Musée des Beaux-Arts de la Ville de Paris* (Pl. 7; 7), in itself a building of no great merit (1900, by *Girault*), contains various *Collections of paintings, etc., donated to the city by private collectors, which are often unjustifiably ignored by the visitor. Unfortunately the quality of display leaves something to be desired. It is often the site of temporary exhibitions.

MÉTROS: *Champs-Élysées-Clemenceau;* adm. 10.00-17.50 daily, exc. Tues. The entrance, with a domed vestibule, is in the Av. Winston-Churchill, on its W. side.

The collections may be roughly divided into four sections. First the 19-early 20C French paintings, including representative canvases by

Édouard Vuillard, Pierre Bonnard, and *Gustave Courbet,* with the latter's Portrait of M. Corbinaud, of his father, a Self-portrait with his dog, and Pierre-Joseph Proudhon and his children. Among other important works may be mentioned: *Cézanne,* Portrait of Ambroise Vollard, and wall-panels of the Seasons (signed 'Ingres' in derision); *Gauguin,* Old man with a stick; *Toulouse-Lautrec,* The Nice mail-coach, Portrait of André Rivoire; *Renoir,* Portrait of A. Vollard, Woman with a rose; *Mary Cassatt,* Head of a girl (pastel); Portraits of Lydia Cassatt and of 'M.D.'; Landscapes by *Sisley* and *Pissarro; Monet,* Sunset at Lavacourt; *Manet,* Portrait of M. Duret; *Marie Bashkirtseff,* Self-portrait; *Berthe Morisot,* A young girl, In the park; *Baudry,* Mme Singer; *Sargent,* Mme Allouard-Jouan; *Bonnat,* Mme Ehrler.

THE DUTCH SCHOOL: *W. van de Velde,* Marine views; *Hobbema,* Mills, Forest scene; *van Goyen,* Landscapes; *Guil. de Heusch,* Landscape; *Ter Borch,* The fiancée; *A. van Ostade,* The gazette,Woman with a letter, The analyst; *Pot,* Portrait of a man; *Metsu,* The toilet, Woman playing the virginal; *Rembrandt,* Self-portrait in oriental costume; *Neefs,* Church interior; *Palamedes,* Palace interior, 'Réunion galante'; *I. van Ostade,* Farmyard; *Teniers the Younger,* Tavern scenes; *Jan Steen,* Idiot begging alms; *W. K. Heda,* Still life; *Wouwerman,* Gypsies, The cavaliers' halt; *Jordaens,* Diana's repose; *Brakenburgh,* Tavern interior; *A. van de Velde,* Landscape; *van der Meulen,* Cavalry combat; *Both,* Landscape; *Berghem,* The watering-place; *Hackert* and *van de Velde,* Ash-trees; *Jouvet,* Portrait of Corneille.

The **Edward Tuck Collection:** Chinese porcelain of the Kang-Hi period (1662-1722) (famille noire); Battersea enamels; Meissen figures; 18C Beauvais tapestries, *after Boucher* and *Huet; Greuze,* Portrait of *Benjamin Franklin;* terracotta bust of Franklin by *Houdon;* and a representative collection of Louis-XV furniture.

The **Dutuit Collection:** among the paintings, *Cranach,* The burgomaster's daughter; *Brueghel ('de Velours'),* Wedding and *Cima de Conegliano,* Madonna and Child. Also an impressive collection of Grolier bindings, among others; Gubbio and Urbino ware; Limoges enamels; ivories; German and Burgundian wood carvings; Gallo-Roman bronzes; Egyptian statuettes; and an extensive collection of Greek ceramics, etc.

The **Grand Palais,** facing the *Petit,* with a classical façade, 260yds long, surmounted by a lofty portico, now accommodates various exhibitions; while its W. half contains a *Planetarium* and the *Palais de la Découverte* devoted to the popularization of scientific knowledge (adm. 10.00-18.00, except Monday; entrance in the Av. Franklin D. Roosevelt). Lectures on scientific subjects, film shows, etc. are also regularly held here.

Six avenues radiate from the ROND-POINT DES CHAMPS-ÉLYSÉES, with its six fountains.

To the r. in the Av. Matignon, Heinrich Heine (1799-1856) died, on the fifth storey of No. 3.

On the r., at the commencement of the built-up area of the Av. des Champs-Élysées, are the offices of the newspaper *Le Figaro.* Two streets beyond, at No. 107 Rue La Boétie, are showrooms of the *Institut Géographique National,* where a large range of French maps may be bought. At the corner of the Rue de Berri, further W., a plaque marks the site of a mansion in which Thomas Jefferson lived in 1785-89, as American minister.

At No. 25, on the S. side of the Avenue, lived Thérèse Lachman, later the Marquise de Païva, who held here the artistic and political salon (c. 1850-70) which advanced her career of adventuress and spy. Dickens lived at No. 49 in 1855-56.

At No. 127 (l.), beyond the Av. George-V, is the *Office de Tourisme de Paris*, whose long-suffering and helpful hostesses can often advise the tourist in distress or in need of information (see p. 31). Byron stayed in the street named after him, N. of and parallel to this section of the avenue.

Twelve avenues radiate starwise from the PL. CHARLES-DE-GAULLE (formerly *Pl. de l'Étoile*, and still commonly known as such; Pl. 6; 5). The uniform façades facing it between each avenue were designed by *Hittorf*. In the centre stands the **Arc de Triomphe,* the largest triumphal arch in the world (162 ft high, and 147 ft wide), beneath which is the *Tomb of the Unknown Soldier*, symbolic of the dead of both World Wars. Its constantly burning flame is revived every evening. At its foot is a bronze plaque representing the 'Shaef' shoulderflash, and dated 25 Aug. 1944, the day of the liberation of Paris after the German occupation.

Designed by *Chalgrin*, and begun in 1806, it was not completed until 1836. The main façades of the arch are adorned with colossal groups in high relief. Facing the *Champs-Élysées* are (r.) the Departure of the Army in 1792 (otherwise known as 'La Marseillaise') by *Rude*, and (l.) the Triumph of Napoleon in 1810, by *Cortot*; facing the Av. de la Grande-Armée are (r.) the Resistance of the French in 1814, and (l.) the Peace of 1815, both by *Étex*.

The four spandrels of the main archway contain figures of Fame by *Pradier*, and those of the smaller archways have sculptures by *Vallois* (S. side) and *Bra*. Above the groups are panels in relief of incidents in the campaigns of 1792-1805. On the row of shields in the attic storey are inscribed the names of 172 (victorious) battles of the Republic and the Empire; below the side arches are the names of generals who took part in these campaigns, those who fell in action being underlined.

On the summit is a platform (adm. 10.00-17.00 or 18.00 except Tues.; fee) commanding panoramic views of Paris.

Since 1840, when the route was followed by a cortège bearing Napoleon's ashes, watched, despite the intense cold, by 100,000 people, the Champs-Élysées has been used for state processions on a number of occasions, funereal, triumphal, and in celebration of liberation, etc.

Wagner lived in the Rue Newton, a short distance to the S., in 1859-60.

B   Viâ the Rue du Faubourg-St-Honoré

MÉTROS: *Concorde, Madeleine, St-Philippe-du-Roule, Pl.-des-Ternes, Villiers, Monceau, Charles de Gaulle-Étoile.*

The RUE DU FAUBOURG-ST-HONORÉ, the N.W. continuation of the Rue St-Honoré, extends from the *Rue Royale* (leading from the *Pl. de la Concorde* to the *Pl. de la Madeleine*; see p. 149) to the *Pl. des Ternes* (N.E. of the *Arc de Triomphe*), following the course of the medieval road from Paris to the village of Roule. It became fashionable at the end of Louis XIV's reign, and in the 18C its many splendid mansions made it a rival to the Faubourg St-Germain as an aristocratic quarter. Its pretensions are now sustained by a succession of luxurious and expensive boutiques, jewellers, etc., and houses devoted to the exploitation of female (and male) vanity, both cosmetic and sartorial, but, like Bond Street, its standards are sophisticated, and the tyranny of fashion is fragile.

At No. 8 Rue d'Anjou, leading N., died La Fayette in 1834; Benjamin Constant (1767-1830) died at No. 29.

We shortly pass (l.) the exclusive *Cercle Interallié* (No. 33; of 1714), and adjacent, the *Hôtel de Charost* (1723), now the **British Embassy** (Pl. 7; 7).

The mansion was bought in 1803 by Pauline Bonaparte, Princess Borghese (much of whose furniture remains), and was sold by her to Wellington in 1814 for £32,000. Sydney Smith preached an eloquent sermon in the dining-room (then serving as a chapel), and here were married Berlioz and Harriet Smithson (with Liszt as best man) in 1833; and Thackeray to Isabella Shawe in 1836. Somerset Maugham (1874-1965) was born here.
The *Embassy Church*, in the Rue d'Aguesseau, opposite, is at present closed.

No. 41 is the *Hôtel Pontalba*, built by *Visconti* and restored by E. de Rothschild; No. 45 was the residence of Thiers at the end of his term as President, in 1873. Nos. 55-57 are the **Palais de l'Élysée** (no adm.), at the corner of the Av. de Marigny. This heavily guarded mansion (since greatly altered and enlarged) was built as the *Hôtel d'Évreux* in 1718. It was occupied later by Mme de Pompadour, Murat, Napoleon I (who signed his abdication here in 1815), Wellington, and Napoleon III, who lived here as President from 1848 until he moved, as Emperor, to the Tuileries in 1852. It then reverted to its use as a residence for visiting heads of state (including Queen Victoria in 1855, and Elizabeth II in 1957), but since 1873 it has been the official residence of the President of the Republic.

To the r., the Rue des Saussaies leads to the PL. DES SAUSSAIES and the *Hôtel du Maréchal Suchet* (No. 16 Rue de la Ville-l'Évêque), built by *Boullée* c. 1750. Alexis de Tocqueville (1805-59), author of 'Democracy in America', was born at No. 12 in the same street.

Passing (r.) the *Ministère de l'Intérieur* (Home Office), built c. 1770, flanking the PL. BEAUVAU, we continue past No. 100 Rue du Faubourg-St-Honoré, Fanny Burney's residence in 1806-12. Beyond the Av. Matignon is the Rue de Penthièvre (r.), in which No. 26 may occupy the site of Benjamin Franklin's city office. Meyerbeer (1791-1864) died in the Rue Jean-Mermoz, to the l. Further on, to the r., stands *St-Philippe-du-Roule*, built in 1769-84 by *Chalgrin* on the site of the parish church of Roule and later enlarged.

At No. 45 Rue La Boétie (to the r.) is the *Salle Gaveau*, one of the more important concert-halls in Paris.

The Rue du Faubourg-St-Honoré soon meets the wide Av. de Friedland, which leads W. to the *Arc de Triomphe* (see p. 162), off which, to the l., at No. 12 Rue Balzac (then No. 22 Rue Fortunée, demolished), is the site of the house where Honoré Balzac (1799-1850) died.

Alfred de Vigny (1797-1863) died at No. 6 Rue d'Artois, parallel to and W. of the Rue du Faubourg-St-Honoré.

At No. 208 in the Rue du Faubourg-St-Honoré, beyond the Av. Friedland, are the buildings of the old *Hôpital Beaujon* (1784); opposite, at No. 11 Rue Berryer, in the former *Hôtel Salomon de Rothschild* (where President Doumer was assassinated in 1932), are the offices of the *Centre National d'Art contemporain*. Just beyond the intersection with the Av. Hoche is the *Salle Pleyel* (1927), the largest concert-hall in Paris. Mme de Caillavet held her salon at No. 12 Av. Hoche, which was frequented by Anatole France, Maupassant, and Proust. In the Rue Daru, parallel to the N., is the neo-Byzantine Russian Orthodox church of *St-Alexandre-Nevsky* (1859-61).

Gustave Flaubert (1821-80) lived from 1875 until his death at No. 240 Rue du Faubourg-St-Honoré; from 1869 to 1875 he had lived at No. 4 Rue Murillo, just S. of the Parc Monceau.

From behind the church of St-Philippe-du-Roule, the Rue de Courcelles crosses the *Blvd. Haussmann.* At No. 38 in the Rue de Courcelles (then No. 48) Dickens lodged in 1846; Proust lived at No. 45 in 1901-05 (before moving to No. 102 Blvd. Haussmann where he remained until 1919), containing his cork-lined 'sound-proof' room. Saint-Saëns occupied No. 83bis. There is a fine private collection of Chinese art at No. 48 (M. C. -T. Loo). Henri Barbusse (1873-1935) died at No. 105.

The **Musée Jacquemart-André* (Pl. 6; 6), at No. 158 BLVD. HAUSSMANN, contains an important collection of French art of the 18C (on the Ground Floor), and Renaissance and Italian art on the First Floor.

The house was built c. 1870 by Édouard André (d. 1894), who in 1881 married the painter Nélie Jacquemart, who survived her husband until 1912, bequeathing their collection to the Institut de France.
MÉTRO: *St-Philippe-du-Roule;* adm. 13.30-17.30 daily, except Mon. and Tues.

From the Vestibule, we turn l. into **R 2**, with four Gobelins tapestries, and a Savonnerie carpet (1663), and displaying *Nattier*, Portrait of the Marquis d'Antin; *Prud'hon*, Cadet de Gassicourt; and busts of Caumartin by *Houdon*, the architect Gabriel by *Coysevox*, the painter Nicholas Vleugels by *Slodtz*, and the Marquis de Marigny by *Le Moyne.*—**R 3**, with Beauvais tapestries of Russian games after *Le Prince.*—**R 4**: *Rubens*, Hercules strangling the lion, and (from his studio) Portrait of a Flemish couple; *van Dyck*, Count Henry of Peña; *Rembrandt*, Amalia von Solms, Pilgrims at Emmaus, Dr Arnold Tholinx; *Hals*, Portrait of a man; *Ph. de Champaigne*, Portrait of a man; *Ruysdael*, Landscape; *Jan de Bray*, Portrait; *School of Bruges*, Virgin and Child illuminating a book; and in a case, the *Boucicaut Book of Hours, which belonged to Diane de Poitiers.

R 5: *Canaletto*, St Mark's Square and The Rialto, Venice; *Chardin*, Still life, and drawings by *Lancret, Pater, Watteau,* and *Boucher.*—**R 6**: *Tocqué*, Portrait of a man; *Vigée-Lebrun*, Countess Skravonska; *Greuze*, Girl in confusion; *Perroneau*, Woman in a bonnet, Portrait of the painter Gillequin, and *Chinard*, A woman's head; in a case, bookbindings. We return to **R 7**, with *Mantegna*, Madonna and Child between two saints, and Mocking of Christ; *Quinten Massys*, Posthumous portrait of an old man; *Luini*, Virgin with SS Margaret and Augustine; a bronze plaquette of the Martyrdom of St Sebastian, by *Donatello;* a horse in gilt bronze, attr. to *Leonardo da Vinci;* ivories, and an enamelled plaque by *Jean Pénicaud I.*

From the Winter Garden (**R 8**) we turn l. into **R 9**, dominated by *Uccello*, *St George killing the dragon; *di Conti*, Head of a man; *Pontormo*, An old woman; book-bindings.—On the STAIRCASE, frescoes by *J. B. Tiepolo*, including Henri III welcomed by Fed. Contarini to the Villa de Mira. Passing through the gallery, we reach **R 10**, devoted to the arts of the Italian Renaissance, against the walls of which have been re-erected a number of 15C marble doorways, one with a frame sculptured by *Bened. da Rovezzano* (attr.). Among the terracottas from the della Robbia workshops, a Madonna and Child by *Luca della Robbia*; the Legend of St Emilian, a marble bas-relief in the form of a triptych (*Venetian School*); *Donatello*, two bronze winged torch-bearers, and bust of Lodovico Gonzaga, Marquis of Mantua; and *Ricciarelli*, posthumous bust of Michelangelo (bronze).

R 11, with Brussels tapestries, *after van Orley; Botticini*, The dead Christ with the Virgin, saints, and others; Portrait of a young man (*Venetian School*), and marquetry choir-stalls, c. 1505 (N. Italian). **R 12**, adjoining, with 25 ceiling panels in grisaille attr. to *Girol. Mocetto* (15C), is temporarily closed for restoration.

Descending to the Ground Floor, we turn l. into **R 13**, with a bust of Richelieu by *Warin*, and a fine collection of Sèvres, Meissen, Vincennes, and Vienna porcelain, and Chinese porcelain and stoneware.

A short distance E., the Rue de Téhéran leads N. across the Av. de Messine to meet the Rue de Monceau.

At No. 8 Théodore Herzl, proselyte of Zionism, lived in 1891-95; No. 28 belonged to Prince Murat; and No. 32 was the birthplace of Oscar I of Sweden (1799-1859), son of Bernadotte.

The **Musée Nissim de Camondo*, at 63 Rue de Monceau (Pl. 6; 4; MÉTRO: *Villiers*), housed in a tastefully furnished mansion, containing a large number of Savonnerie and Aubusson carpets, and now an annexe to the *Musée des Arts Décoratifs*, was bequeathed by Count Moise de Camondo as a memorial to his son Nissim, killed in 1917. A high proportion of the individual pieces of furniture are of outstanding quality.

Adm. 10.00-12.00; 14.00-17.10 daily, except Tues. and Wed.

From the entrance VESTIBULE, with a red marble fountain (1765) from the château de St-Prix, Montmorency, and a writing-desk by *Riesener*, stairs lead up past two lacquered Louis-XV corner cupboards in the Chinese style, and a pair of Regency armchairs upholstered in Savonnerie tapestry.

FIRST FLOOR. GRAND BUREAU: white marble chimneypiece of c. 1775, inlaid with bronze, etc.; a pair of low cabinets by *Leleu;* cylinder-top desk and secretaire by *Saunier*, the latter from the château de Tanly; desk-armchair of 1778; a white marble-topped table by *Carlin* from the château de Bellevue; pair of low chairs by *Séné;* eight chairs by *N.-Q. Foliot* covered in Aubusson tapestry (scenes from La Fontaine); Aubusson tapestries with six fables from La Fontaine after *Oudry*, and a Beauvais screen with the fable of the Cock on the Dunghill; bronze bust of Mme le Comte by *G. Coustou* (1716-77); *Vigée-Lebrun*, Bacchante.

GRAND SALON: White and gold panelling from No. 11 Rue Royale of c. 1775-80; marquetry cabinet and tables by *Riesener;* round table and bureau de dame (with Sèvres porcelain plaques) by *Carlin;* a pair of low tables by *Weisweiler;* oval table attr. to *Roentgen,* and one by *Lacroix;* suite of furniture (which belonged to Sir Richard Wallace), including two sofas and an armchair by *Georges Jacob;* four chairs by *Henri Jacob;* a six-leaved Savonnerie screen; 'L'Été' (Hubert Robert's daughter), a marble bust by *Houdon; Vigée-Lebrun,* Mme Le Coulteux du Molay; 'La Pécheuse', a Beauvais tapestry *after Boucher;* and among Savonnerie carpets, one ('L'Air') woven for the Grande Galerie of the Louvre (1678) and one made in 1660.—SALON HUET: Seven panels and three dessus de portes of 'Scènes pastorales' painted by *J.-B. Huet*, dated 1776; cylinder-top desk by *Oeben*; pairs of small cabinets by *Garnier* and *Carlin*, the latter once belonging to Adm. de Penthièvre; sofa, two bergères, and eight chairs by *Sené;* table with chased bronze given by Louis XVI to Vergennes; silver-gilt candlesticks by *F.-T. Germain* (1762) embossed with the arms of Mme de Pompadour.—SALLE À MANGER: console and a pair of ebony and chased bronze tables by *Weisweiler;* pair of small cabinets by *Leleu;* silver, including two tureens by *Auguste* and *Roettiers* (the latter's work was ordered by Catherine II of Russia for Orloff).—CABINET DES PORCELAINES (with a view of the *Parc Monceau*), with services of Sèvres, Chantilly, and Meissen porcelain; silver-gilt service by *Dehanne* and *Cardeilhac,* etc.—GALERIE: sofa and chairs by *Pierre Gillier;* Aubusson tapestries after *Boucher* ('La Danse Chinoise', etc.).—PETIT BUREAU: furniture by *Topino, Riesener,* and *Lacroix,* among others; snuffboxes, clocks, Chinese porcelain (Kien-Loung; 1736-95); terracotta medallions by *J. B. Nini;* marble bust of Mme Le Comte by *Coustou;* four views of Venice by *Guardi;* portrait of Necker by *Duplessis; Oudry,* eight sketches for Gobelins tapestries of 'Les Chasses de Louis XV'; three paintings by *Hubert Robert.*—On the STAIRS leading to the Second Floor, two Aubusson tapestries in the Chinese style, after *Boucher.*

SECOND FLOOR. GALERIE: sofa and chairs by *Nogaret;* a series of engravings after *Chardin;* 18C Chinese porcelain. Turning r. we enter the SALON BLEU: pair of tables attr. to *Riesener;* bookcase attr. to *Carlin;* red morocco casket embossed with the arms of Marie-Antoinette; views of Paris by *Bouhot* (1813), *Canella* (1830), *Demachy* (1774), and *Raguenet* (1754); a family portrait by *Gautier-Dagoty* (1740-86); watercolour of the Quai Malaquais by *Thomas S. Boys;* Chinese porcelain of the period 1662-1795.

BIBLIOTHÈQUE (oak-panelled): secretaire by *Leleu;* two bronze and Sèvres biscuit candelabras by *Blondeau* after Boucher; two paintings by *Hubert Robert;* Aubusson tapestry screen (1775).—CHAMBRE À COUCHER: furniture by *Cramer, Topino,* and *Jacob Frères;* six-leaved screen by *Falconet* (1743). Among paintings: *Danloux,* Rosalie Duthé; *Lavreince,* The singing lesson; *Lancret,* Les Rémois; *Houdon,* Sabine Houdin (?), a plaster bust; *Drouais,* Alexandre de Beauharnais as a child; Savonnerie carpet (1760) for the chapel at Versailles.—DEUXIÈME CHAMBRE: secretaire attr. to *Riesener;* screen by *Canabas;* 'Scènes de chasse' by *de Dreux, Shayer, Fontaine, H. Vernet,* etc.

At No. 7 Av. Vélasquez, a parallel street to the N. (MÉTROS: *Villiers* or *Monceau*), is the **Musée Cernuschi** (adm. 10.00-17.50 daily, except Mon., Tues., and holidays), bequeathed to the city in 1895, in many ways a pendant to the more comprehensive collections of Oriental art in the *Musée Guimet* (see p. 169). Of particular interest are the funerary figurines of the T'ang and Wei dynasties, neolithic terracottas, and bronze vases, etc., of the Chang dynasty (14-11C B.C.), while outstanding are the paintings on silk of horses and grooms of the T'ang period (8C). Note also the collections of clasps, mirrors, jade amulets, etc. On the *First Floor* is an extensive collection of bronze objects from

Louristan and Iran (8-7C B.C.), a bronze basin of 5-3C B.C., and porcelain of various periods.

The neighbouring ***Parc Monceau** (Pl. 6; 4; 217 acres) derives its name from a vanished village, and is a remnant of a private park laid out by *Carmontel* in 1778 for Philippe-Égalité d'Orléans, Duc de Chartres, and father of Louis-Philippe. It was then known as the 'Folie de Chartres', and certain 'picturesque' details remain. Near the N.E. corner is the *Naumachie*, with a Corinthian colonnade which may have come from either the château du Raincy or from the projected mausoleum at St-Denis for Henri II and Catherine de Médicis. To the E. of the lake is a Renaissance arcade from the *old Hôtel de Ville;* to the W., the round *Pavillon de Chartres*, a toll-house of the 18C city wall erected by the Farmers-General, is now used as a keeper's lodge.

There are a number of fine mansions in the streets to the N., including the Rue de Prony, leading N.W., off which the Rue Fortuny (where at No. 2 Edmond Rostand lived in 1891-97, and wrote 'Cyrano de Bergerac') turns N.E. to the PL. MALESHERBES. Slightly to the N. of the latter is the *Salle Cortot*, a concert-hall.

Further N.E., in the **Batignolles**, some quaint areas still survive the pressures of modernization, and deserve exploration. The Quartier gave its name to a school of impressionist painters under the leadership of Manet. In the *Cimitière des Batignolles* (best approached by the Av. de Clichy, and some distance N.W. of the Cimitière de Montmartre) lie Verlaine, André Breton, Léon Bakst, and Féodor Chaliapine.

The Av. de Villiers leads N.W. from the Pl. Malesherbes, in which No. 43 is the *Musée Henner*, devoted to the work of Jean-Jacques Henner (1829-1905). Some distance further W., near the *Porte de Champerret*, stands *Ste-Odile* (1938-46), with a flattened dome and rocket-like tower.

17   CHAILLOT, PASSY, AND AUTEUIL

MÉTROS: *Concorde, Alma-Marceau, Iéna, Trocadéro, Passy, Muette, Porte-d'Auteuil.*

From the *Pl. de la Concorde*, the COURS-LA-REINE (with its extension) leads W. to the *Pl. de l'Alma*. It was laid out in 1616, and followed the old road to the villages of Chaillot, St-Cloud, and Versailles, and the Roman canal which brought water from Chaillot.

The parallel PORT DE LA CONFÉRENCE, flanking the Seine, takes its name from the *Porte de la Conférence* (demolished in 1730), through which the Spanish ambassadors entered Paris in 1660 to discuss with Mazarin the projected marriage between Louis XIV and María Teresa.

The *Pont des Invalides*, beyond the *Pont Alexandre-III* (see p. 160), of 1827-29, was rebuilt in 1879-80 and enlarged in 1956. The new *Pont de l'Alma* (1970) retains the figure of a Zouave, which was long used as a gauge in estimating the height of the Seine in flood.

Several handsome streets radiate N. from the PL. DE L'ALMA (Pl. 11; 6), many of the mansions being the showrooms of 'haut-couturiers', who have replaced the once ubiquitous Parisian 'midinette' in the folklore of fashion. At No. 13 Av. Montaigne, leading N.E., is the *Théâtre des Champs-Élysées*, by *A.* and *G. Perret* (1911-13), with bas-reliefs by

Bourdelle. On the W. side of the Av. George-V, leading N., is the American church of the *Holy Trinity* (1885-88), built in a Gothic style by *G. S. Street.*

The Av. de New York, with its continuations, skirts the N. bank of the river for some distance before bearing W. to the *Porte de St-Cloud.* When parallel to the long narrow *Allée des Cygnes* (or 'Isle of Swans') lying in mid-stream S. of the *Pont de Bir-Hakeim,* the road passes (r.) the circular **Maison de la Radio** (or de l'O.R.T.F.), designed in 1960 by *H. Bernard,* impressive in size even if its tower is out of proportion to the rest of the building, the only one of note in the area (Pl. 10; 8). Regular guided visits are organized from 9.30 to 18.30. A museum devoted to Radio as a means of communication is in the process of being installed here.

On the S. extremity of the *Allée des Cygnes,* crossed here by the *Pont de Grenelle* (rebuilt 1875), and facing downstream, is a reduced bronze copy of *Bartholdi's* statue of Liberty, presented to France by the United States, where the original stands at the entrance to New York harbour.

The Av. du Président-Wilson leads W. from the PL. DE L'ALMA, from which the Av. Marceau immediately diverges r. uphill towards the *Arc de Triomphe,* passing (l.) *St-Pierre-de-Chaillot* (1937), built in a Byzantine Romanesque style by *Émile Bois,* and replacing the earlier parish church of 1750.

To the r. in the Av. du Président-Wilson is the main façade of the *Musée Galiéra* (1888), generally housing temporary exhibitions. Opposite stands the **Palais d'Art Moderne,** constructed for the Exhibition of 1937 (by *Aubert, Dondel, Viard,* and *Dastugue*) on the site of a military bakery, itself replacing the old *Savonnerie* (see p. 61). The wall of the terrace is decorated with bas-reliefs by *Janniot;* and here, with other statues by *Bourdelle,* is 'La France', in honour of French patriots who fell in the Second World War.

The building now houses three museums. The *Museum of Costume* is at present closed, and will probably be transferred to the Musée des Arts Décoratifs (see p. 94).

To the E. is the **Museum of Modern Art** *'de la Ville de Paris'* (adm. 10.00-17.45 daily, except Mon. and Tues.) as opposed to the **Musée National d'Art Moderne** in the W. wing (adm. 9.45-17.15 daily, except Tues.). It is planned to move the latter to the new *Centre Beaubourg* (see p. 132).

The former contains a somewhat miscellaneous collection of paintings by *Dufy, Utrillo, Suzanne Valadon, Matisse, Rouault, Vlaminck, van Dongen, Léger, Derain, Gris, Braque, Picasso,* and *Modigliani* (including the latter's **'Femme aux yeux bleus').

Of more interest is the *Musée National.* At present (1975) the rooms are arranged thus: **RR 1-2:** *Vuillard* and *Bonnard.*—**R 4:** *Matisse,* including 'L'Odalisque à la Culotte Rouge'.—**R 5:** *Dufy.*—**R 6:** *Sonia* and *Robert Delaunay,* and *Léger.*—**R 7:** *Derain,* including 'La tasse de thé'.—**R 8:** *Dunoyer de Segonzac.*—**R 9:** *Rouault.*—**R 10:** *van Dongen* and *Marquet.*—**R 11:** naïfs: *Utrillo* and *Suzanne Valadon.*—**R 12:** *Foujita, Soutine,* and *Modigliani.*—*****R 13:** *Picasso,* including 'Arlequin' (1923), portrait of Georges Coquiot (1901), 'La liseuse' (1920), and 'Nu assis' (1905).

RR 14-15: *Braque, Gris,* and *Picasso.*—**R 16:** the Donation *Braque,* including sculpture, and his 'Woman with a mandoline' (1903).—**R 17:** *Chagall,* including Double portrait with a glass of wine.—**R 18:**

Surrealism: *Dalí, Picabia, Tanguy, Miró, Arp,* and *Giacometti.*—**R 19:** *Kupka, Kandinsky,* and *Klee.*

Stairs lead down to a further series of rooms devoted to *Vasarely, Michaux, Dubuffet,* and *Jackson Pollock,* among others. Other galleries contain sculpture, including bequests by *Brancusi*(displayed in a reconstruction of his studio, once at No. 11 Impasse Ronsin), *Julio González, Zoltan Kemeny, Anton Pevsner,* and *Laurens.* Also to be seen are works by *Arp, Calder, Bernard Buffet, Ipousteguy, La Patellière* ('Le repos dans le cellier', 1926), and, returning to the entrance vestibule, works by *Sutherland* and *Bacon.*

To the W. is the PL. D'IÉNA (Pl. 11; 6), from which seven streets diverge. No. 2 Av. d'Iéna is the residence of the U. S. ambassador. To the N. of the Place stands the *Musée Guimet* (see below). At No. 24 Rue Boissière, to the N.W., the poet Henri de Régnier (1864-1936) died; at No. 44 Rue Hamelin (leading off the latter) died Marcel Proust (1871-1922). In the Rue Paul-Valéry (the continuation N.W. of the Rue Hamelin), No. 40 was the home of Paul Valéry (1871-1945) from 1902, and from 1883 had been the studio of his aunt by marriage, Berthe Morisot, and a favourite literary and artistic rendezvous.

The ****Musée Guimet**, installed at No. 6 Pl. d'Iéna, was founded at Lyon in 1879 by Émile Guimet, presented by him to the State, and transferred to Paris in 1888. In 1945 it officially became the *Département des Arts Asiatiques des Musées Nationaux,* the original collection having been considerably augmented, and now including those of the Asiatic department of the *Louvre,* illustrating the arts of India and the Far East. The building also houses a *Library* and photographic section.

MÉTROS: *Iéna* and *Trocadéro;* adm. 9.45-12.00, 13.30-17.15 daily, except Tues. Some sections are still undergoing rearrangement. The annexe, at No. 19 Av. d'Iéna, is devoted to *Oriental Religious Art.*

GROUND FLOOR. From the entrance vestibule we pass into **R 'N'**, which together with **RR 'L', 'O', and 'H'**, are devoted to Khmer sculpture from *Cambodia,* including a statue of Hari-Hara (pre-Angkorian style; late 6C), uniting in one person the two gods Siva and Vishnu; lintel of 7-12C; sculpture of 9-10C; Vishnu in the Kulen style; Brahma in the Koh Ker style; pediment from the temple of Banteai Srei (967); seated Buddha in the style of Angkor Wat (early 12C); carvings of a lion, an elephant, and of the magic serpent, Naga (12C). Also sculptures in the Bayon style (12-13C); each meditative statue wears the enigmatic 'Angkorian smile'; portrait of King Jayavarman VII; frieze of dancing *apsaras.*

R 'M': *Champa Art of Assam* (central Vietnam). Note the head of Buddha (9C), and a dancer with two young elephants (10C).

R 'K' (l.): *Java:* Heads of Buddha (8-9C); lintel decorated in the Prambanan style (9C); bronzes (7-9C), and statuettes of Avalokitesvara and Kubera, gods of riches—note the seven treasure-pots at his feet; leather marionettes for a shadow-theatre, and a painted fabric calendar from Bali.

(Centre): *Siam* (Thailand): stuccoes from P'ra Pathom (c. 8C); Buddhas of the Schools of Sukhodava and U-Thong (14-15C); head of Buddha (16C); on the walls, painted and worked leather hangings.— *Laos:* Buddha with a begging-bowl.—*Burma:* lacquered wooden Buddha, and illuminated MSS.

Tibetan Art (continued in **R 'J'**): Statue in gilded bronze of Dakini;

and statuettes decorated with coloured stones; religious objects, jewellery, silverwork, etc. On the walls, paintings illustrating the life of Buddha, gods and saints.—**R 'I'**: Nepal: Buddhist paintings and statues of wood and gilded bronze.

FIRST FLOOR. **RR 'K'** and **'J'**: *Indian Art*. Funerary furniture and stone sculpture from near Pondicherry; clay sarcophagus, pottery, and jewellery. Mathurâ and Amarâvatî sculpture (2-4C); serpent-king (sandstone); marble bas-reliefs; Buddhas. Among objects of the 'classical' period (4-8C), a Buddha in the Gupta style; steles of *Pâla Art* (8-12C); S. Indian stone sculpture; bronzes of Siva; *gouaches and watercolours of the Mogul, Rajput, and Pahâri period (16-18C), including one of Louis XIV when young.

RR 'M' and **'P'**: *Pakistan and Afghanistan*, including examples of Græco-Buddhist Gandara sculpture (1-c.5C); decorative bas-relief (schist); figurines from the Buddhist monastery of Hadda, including a Genie carrying a floral offering, and a demon in a fur; fragments of frescoes from the monastery of Kakrak (c.5C); and the Treasure of Begram (1-2C): Græco-Roman and Syrian objects, Indian ivories, and Chinese lacquer-work discovered together by the French archaeological mission to Afghanistan in 1937 and 1939-40.

RR 'N', 'F', 'G', and **'H'**: the *Arts of China*. Carved bone objects of the Chang Dynasty (16-11C B.C.), and important collections of archaic bronze implements, ritual vases, and arms, etc., from Ngan-Tang, capital city of the dynasty; ritual vase in the shape of an elephant; a 'p'an' bowl of the Chou Dynasty (11-5C B.C.); the Treasure of Li-Yu, a remarkable find from the 'Fighting Kingdoms' Dynasty (5-3C B.C.), notably a jade, turquoise, and gold-ornamented sword.—Jades: the earlier ones in the form of symbols (Pi, the sky; Tsong, the earth; Kwei, the mountain, etc.), and bronzes.—Han Dynasty tombstone (206 B.C.—A.D. 220); Buddha from Yun-Kang (5C); heads of Bodhisattva and Kasyapa, from Long-men (early 6C); Ananda and Kasyapa, disciples of Buddha (Suei Dynasty; 561-618); marble with traces of polychrome; Dvarapàla, guardian of the temple, and funerary statuettes of the T'ang Dynasty (618-906); gilded bronzes of the Wei, Suei, and T'ang dynasties (5-10C), including a small stele representing Sakyamuni and Pradhutaratna, dated 518; lacquer-work; polychrome bowls of the Han Dynasty and Sung Dynasty (960-1279); black lacquer cabinet decorated in gold (17C).

SECOND FLOOR. **R 'K'**: the *Arts of Japan*. Jômon and Yayoi pottery (2000-1000 B.C., and 1C B.C.-3C A.D. respectively); terracotta funerary figurines (Haniwa) of the era of the Great Tombs (5-6C); wooden Buddhas (8-9C); carved masks of the Nara Dynasty (8C); portraits of bonzes (14-15C); pottery for the Tea Ceremony ('Cha-no-yu'); Imari, Kakiemon, and Satsuma porcelain; sword-furniture (kozukas); screens, one illustrating the arrival of the Portuguese in Japan (16C).

R 'K': *Corea*. Gilded bronze crown, and silverware, from the kingdom of Silla (5-6C); and ceramics.

RR 'D', 'L', 'P', and **'I'** contain an important collection of *Chinese* porcelain, formed principally from the Calmann Collection—'three colour' ware (T'ang Dynasty), celadon, black, and white wares (Sung Dynasty)—and from the Grandidier Collection: Ming (1368-1643) and Ch'ing (1644-1912) dynasties.

R 'M': *Central Asia.* Buddhist paintings from Touen-houang; votive banners, one representing Kasyapa in old age, dated 729.

To the S.W. is the *Palais du Conseil Économique et Social*, by *A. Perret* (1937-38), originally designed for a Musée des Travaux Publics. The N. wing was added in 1960-62, to house the *Union Européenne Occidentale.* No. 34 in the Av. du Président-Wilson was the home of Laure Haymann, the model for Proust's Odette de Crécy.

The Av. du Président-Wilson ends at the PL. DU TROCADÉRO (Pl. 11; 5), almost circular in shape, from which six thoroughfares fan out. It is flanked to the S.E. by the *Palais de Chaillot* (see below). The Place is situated on the 'Colline du Trocadéro', named after a fort near Cádiz occupied by the French in 1823.

Catherine de Médicis built a country house on this eminence; later embellished by Anne of Austria, it was sold to Maréchal de Bassompierre, and in 1651 Henrietta Maria bought it from his heirs and established the *Convent of the Visitation of St Mary* here. This was destroyed during the Revolution, and Napoleon wanted to use the site for a palace for his son which would be more magnificent than the Kremlin, but the disasters of 1812 intervened.

To the W., steps ascend to the small *Cimitière de Passy*, where Debussy, Gabriel Fauré, Manet, Berthe Morisot, Marie Bashkirtseff, and Las Cases lie buried.

The **Palais de Chaillot** (MÉTRO: *Trocadéro*), flanking the S.E. side of the *Pl. du Trocadéro*, was erected for the Paris Exhibition of 1937, and replaced the earlier Palais du Trocadéro designed for the 1878 Exhibition. The new building (by *Carlu, Boileau,* and *Azéma*) encases in its two curved wings the two wings of the original structure. Between them is a square, its terrace affording a striking perspective towards the *Eiffel Tower* and across the *Champ-de-Mars* to the *École Militaire,* and the *Unesco* buildings beyond.

Below the square, adorned with gilded bronze statues, is an *Aquarium,* and the *Théâtre de Chaillot,* seating over 2,000, the home of the Théâtre National Populaire (decorated by *Bonnard, Dufy,* and *Vuillard,* among others). Here took place (in Sept.-Dec. 1948) the third General Assembly of the United Nations.

To the r. and l. of the Colline du Trocadéro, gardens flank fountains which include a battery of 20 jets shooting almost horizontally towards the Seine, crossed here by the *Pont d'Iéna* (1806-13, and since twice widened). The next bridge downstream is the *Pont de Bir-Hakeim* (formerly the *Pont de Passy;* 1903-06), a double bridge, the upper part being used by the Métro. It is named after a French exploit in N. Africa in 1942.

The *Palais de Chaillot* at present accommodates four museums: in the E. wing, the *Musée des Monuments Français* and *Musée du Cinéma;* in the W. wing, the *Musée de la Marine* and the *Musée de l'Homme.*

The **Musée des Monuments Français** (adm. 9.45-12.30; 14.00-17.15, daily, except Tues.) was founded by Viollet-le-Duc in 1879 as the *Musée de Sculpture Comparée,* and the unprejudiced must admit that although it only contains *copies* of masterpieces of French sculpture, mural paintings, and stained-glass, they are faithfully copied, and the collections are exhibited with much ingenuity and in perfect taste. It provides for the layman both an interesting introduction to the range of early French sculpture and architecture, displaying examples from all over France; and valuable reproductions of early wall-paintings, many of which have since deteriorated or are fast disappearing. The items shown are well lit and well labelled. The *Sculpture* is arranged in a series of rooms to the l. of the entrance.

The *Wall-paintings* occupy rooms to the r., and on the three floors above.

Among the latter, the following are outstanding. FIRST FLOOR: mural and ceiling paintings from St-Gilles (Montoire); Berzé-la-Ville (nr Cluny); St-Martin at Vicq (nr Nohant); St Michael from Le Puy cathedral; St-Aignan-sur-Cher; St-Chef (Isère); Rocamadour (Lot); St-Savin-sur-Gartemp. SECOND FLOOR: Asnières-sur-Vègre; St-Julien at Le Petit-Quevilly (nr Rouen); St-Jean at Vic-le-Comte (Puy-de-Dôme); dome of Cahors cathedral; Frétigny (Eure-et-Loire); Étigny (Yonne); La Clayette (Saône-et-Loire); Chapelle du Chalard, St-Geniès (Dordogne); the Tour Ferrande, Pernes (Vaucluse); Chartreuse at Villeneuve-lès-Avignon; crypt of Auxerre cathedral; walls of the château of Ravel (Puy-de-Dôme); Les Brignes (Alpes-Maritimes); Transfiguration from Le Puy cathedral. THIRD FLOOR: Kernascléden (Morbihan); Abondance (Haute-Savoie); La Chaise-Dieu; château de Dissay (Vienne); château du Pimpéan (nr Angers); Ennezat (nr Riom); château de Rochechouart (Haute-Vienne); and Albi cathedral.

The devotee of the art of the film will find much to interest him in the **Musée du Cinéma** located in the basement of this wing, and under the direction of M. Henri Langlois. Over 3,000 items are displayed in 60 sections, vividly presenting diverse aspects of the history of the film during its first 75 years. A small projection studio shows a range of old French films: see 'Le Monde' on Thursdays (under 'Spectacles') for the week's programme.

On the GROUND FLOOR of the W. wing of the *Palais de Chaillot* is installed 'the ***Musée de la Marine**, with a remarkable collection of material illustrating French naval history, including an outstanding series of ship models, and paintings of maritime subjects, among which are Vernet's *Ports of France*. Adm. 10.00-18.00, except Tues.

From the entrance, we turn r. into the main gallery, dominated by the richly carved poop of the 'Reale' (1690-1715), some of the sculpture of which is attributed to *Puget*. Note the paintings (nos. 61 and 62) of the Embarkation of Henry VIII for the Field of Cloth of Gold, by *Bouterwerke* (a copy of the original by *Vincent Volpi*) and a View of Amsterdam by *Bakhuysen* (1664). Four *anon.* views of Malta (Nos. 138-9) are also of interest; likewise two views of Port Mahon (nos. 147 and 416, the latter by *Joseph Chiesa*), and a number of marine paintings by *Jean-François Hue* (1751-1823).

In the centre of the gallery are displayed 13 (of the 15 completed of the original 24 commissioned) views of the *'Ports of France' by *Claude-Joseph Vernet* (1714-1789), depicting Dieppe, Antibes, tunny-fishing near Bandol, Rochefort, La Rochelle, Cette, two views of Toulon, two of Bordeaux, two of Bayonne, and Marseilles, and all painted between the years 1754 and 1765.

We pass the Emperor's Barge (1811) before entering a section devoted to early steamships. **R15**, at the far end of the wing, contains recent models and paintings, the fleet air arm, etc.

Returning along a parallel gallery, we pass further sections displaying marine instruments, diving and underwater exploration equipment, a model of a nuclear submarine, models of the careening of a ship, and of the raising and transportation of the obelisk of Luxor (now in the *Pl. de la Concorde*), of ship construction, etc., while among individual items are a sectional view of the transatlantic liner 'Normandie', and Dr Bombard's raft.

The **Musée de l'Homme** is housed on the First and Second Floors of this wing, and was formed by the amalgamation of the *Galerie d'Anthropologie* and the *Musée d'Ethnographie du Trocadéro.* A comprehensive Library, Photographic Library, Cinema, and various technical services are also accommodated in the building. Adm. 10.00-17.00 or 18.00 daily, except Tues.

In comparison with some more recently installed museums (such as the *Musée National des Arts et Traditions Populaires;* see p. 176), its quality of display leaves something to be desired, but the items exhibited are more or less self-explanatory.

The sections devoted to Anthropology, Paleoanthropology and Prehistory, Africa, the Near East, and Europe, are found on the FIRST FLOOR. On the SECOND are rooms displaying exhibits from the Arctic, Asia, Indonesia and Oceania, and America.

The Rue Franklin leads S.W. from the *Pl. du Trocadéro*, and is continued by the Rue Raynouard. At their junction, the Rue de Passy, high street of the old village of **Passy**, runs W. to the *Jardin du Ranelagh* (see below). No. 47 Rue Raynouard is **Balzac's House** (adm. daily except Mon. and Tues. 10.00-18.00), containing souvenirs of the novelist, who lived here in 1841-47. It is worthwhile entering the unexpected ivy-covered Rue Berton, behind the house, one of the most charming remaining in Passy.

Earlier inhabitants of the Rue Raynouard include the architect Robert de Cotte and the Abbé Prévost, and Benjamin Franklin (in 1777-85), who erected on his house (the *Hôtel de Valentinois*, which stood on the corner of the Rue Singer) the first lightning conductor seen in France.

In the Rue d'Ankara, between Rue Berton and the Seine, No. 17, now the *Turkish Embassy*, was once the residence of the Princesse de Lamballe, and later the private asylum of Dr Émile Blanche, where Maupassant died in 1893; Gérard de Nerval and Gounod had also sought treatment there.

Not far W. of Balzac's House (before reaching the *Maison de l'O.R.T.F.;* see p. 168), the Rue des Vignes leads N.W., where at No. 32 Gabriel Fauré (1845-1924) died; James Joyce lived at No. 34 during the latter period of his stay in Paris. Other distinguished residents of Passy include Fanny Burney (in 1802-06), Béranger (in 1833-35), Maeterlinck (in 1897-1910), and Rossini (1792-1868), who died there.

The Rue des Vignes also leads to the Chaussée de la Muette and the E. end of the **Jardin du Ranelagh** (Pl. 10; 7), part of the ancient royal park of *La Muette.* It was designed to emulate its fashionable namesake in London, and just before the Revolution was a favourite resort. The first balloon ascent in France was made nearby in 1783 by Pilâtre de Rozier and the Marquis d'Arlandes.

The royal *Château de la Muette*, originally a hunting-lodge, improved by the Regent Orléans, and restored by Louis XV for Mme de Pompadour, has completely disappeared. It is also associated with Marie-Antoinette, who was welcomed here by Louis XVI on her arrival in Paris on the eve of her wedding in 1770. Twelve years later she set forth hence for *Notre-Dame* and *Ste-Geneviève* on the occasion of the thanksgiving for the birth of the Dauphin. The Château was later occupied by Philippe-Égalité, who stood on the terrace watching the mob bringing Louis XVI from Versailles to the Tuileries in 1789. From 1820 to 1920 it belonged to the Erard family, piano manufacturers. The present mansion, just N. of the JARDIN DU RANELAGH and E. of the *Porte de la Muette*, was built by Baron

Henri de Rothschild, and is now the property of the *European Council for Economic Co-operation.*

At No. 2 Rue Louis-Boilly, leading off the W. side of the gardens, is the **Musée Marmottan** (MÉTRO: *La Muette;* adm. 10.00-18.00, daily, except Mon.). Regrettably (like so many buildings whose collections are under the aegis of the *Institut de France*) it is pervaded by a musty fin-de-siècle atmosphere; nevertheless, it contains, apart from the *Monet donation* (see below), a number of interesting paintings, among which are works attr. to *van der Weyden,* and *Schongauer.* Also displayed are portraits of Talma by *Riesener* and of Princess Metternich by *Lawrence;* and works by *L. de France* (1735-1805), *J.-B. Mallet* (1759-1835), *Carmontel* (1717-1806), *A.-I. Melling* (1763-1831), *Louis Boilly* (1761-1845), *A. Caizac,* and drawings by *Fragonard* and *Hubert Robert.* There are also some pleasant views of Schoenbrunn, etc., by *B.* and *C. Vernet,* and of Rowing at Fontainebleau by *J. Bidault* and *L. Boilly.*

In a gallery to the l. of the entrance are works by *Claude Monet* (1840-1926) and his friends, including *Berthe Morisot,* Young girl at a ball; *Carolus Duran,* Portrait of Monet; of Monet and his wife by *Renoir,* and by *Monet* himself, Argenteuil in the snow, Vertheuil in the mist, A train in the snow, and The beach at Trouville, together with sketches for his later canvases. Stairs descend to an underground gallery recently built to house the spectacular collection of *Monet's* colourful paintings of water-lilies, wisteria, and other flower-pieces, the majority of them donated to the museum in 1971 by the artist's son Michel Monet, and which form a complementary collection to those displayed in the *Orangerie* (see p. 90).

———

In the residential district of **Auteuil**, to the S., Henri Bergson lived at No. 47 Blvd. de Beauséjour, skirting the Jardin du Ranelagh, and the Goncourt brothers (Edmond, 1822-96; and Jules, 1830-70) lived and died at No. 67 Blvd. de Montmorency ('le Grenier'), its continuation S., where they entertained Huysmans, Zola, Daudet, and Maupassant. In parallel streets to the E. of the latter lived Dr Émile Blanche and his son, the painter J.-E. Blanche (at 19 Rue Docteur-Blanche), and André Gide, who lived in the Av. des Sycomores.

At the S. end of the Blvd. de Montmorency is the *Porte d'Auteuil,* the S.E. entrance to the *Bois de Boulogne,* and an approach to the A13 autoroute and Blvd. Périphérique; hence the BLVD. EXELMANS swings S.E. across the Seine by the *Pont du Garigliano* and the Rue d'Auteuil leads E. to *N.-D. d'Auteuil,* built in the Romanesque-Byzantine style (1877-88) on the site of the 12C parish church; in front is the tomb of the chancellor D'Aguesseau (d. 1751) and his wife. Sir Benjamin Thompson, Count von Rumford (1753-1814), lived at No. 59 Rue d'Auteuil from 1808 until his death. Proust (1871-1922) was born at a house on the site of No. 96 Rue La Fontaine, a short distance to the N.

18   THE BOIS DE BOULOGNE AND NEUILLY

MÉTROS: *Porte-d'Auteuil, Muette, Porte-Dauphine, Porte-Maillot, Les Sablons.*

The ***Bois de Boulogne** (Pl. 10;1-3), familiarly known as the 'Bois', lies immediately to the W. of the 16th Arrondissement of Paris (*Chaillot, Passy,* and *Auteuil:* see Rte 17), and was originally bounded on the E. by part of the peripheral fortifications of the city. Now the BLVD. PÉRIPHÉRIQUE tunnels below the E. and S. edges of the Bois, which is bounded on the N. by *Neuilly;* the suburb of *Boulogne-Billancourt* to the S.; and by the Seine to the W., on the far side of which rise the hills of Mont Valérien, St-Cloud, Bellevue, and Meudon.

Although the châteaux of La Muette, Madrid, and Bagatelle, and the abbey of Longchamp were erected on its borders, until the middle of the last century the Bois was utterly neglected. Much timber was cut down for firewood during the Revolution, and part of the Allied army of occupation bivouacked there after Waterloo. It was often the scene of suicides and duels. In 1852 it was handed over by the State to the City, was transformed into an extensive park (2,155 acres), and became a favourite promenade of the Parisians. The model was Hyde Park, which had so impressed Napoleon III.

There are four main entrances to the 'Bois' from Paris, namely the *Porte Maillot* (at its N.E. corner); the *Porte Dauphine* (at the W. end of the Av. Foch); the *Porte de la Muette* (at the S. end of the Av. Victor-Hugo); and the *Porte d'Auteuil* (at its S.E. corner). Between the last two is the subsidiary *Porte de Passy.*

The usual approach to the Bois is by the imposingly wide, garden-flanked AV. FOCH (opened in 1855 as the Av. de l'Impératrice), leading W. from the *Étoile* to the *Porte Dauphine.* Note one of the original art-nouveau entrances to the *Métro* on the N. side of the avenue here.

Not far from the *Étoile* is a monument to Adolphe Alphand (1817-91), who laid out the Bois and many other parks in Paris in their present form.

At No. 59 Av. Foch, on the l., is the **Musée d'Ennery** (adm. Sun. only; 13.00-17.00 or 18.00), with a collection of oriental art formed by the dramatist d'Ennery (1811-99); the building also houses a small museum of Armenian art.—Anatole France (1844-1924) died at No. 5 Villa Said, leading N.W. off the avenue, while No. 80 Av. Foch was the home of Claude Debussy (1862-1918), who died at No. 24 Square de l'Av. Foch (off the Rue Le Sueur). The Av. Foch is crossed diagonally by the Av. de Malakoff, No. 122 in which is the *Palais Rose,* built by *Sanson* for Boni de Castellane.

There is a curious *Museum of Forgeries* (Musée de la Contrefaçon) at No. 16 Rue de la Faisanderie, leading S. near the Porte Dauphine. S.W. of the park entrance is a huge building (1955-59) constructed for N.A.T.O., but now accommodating *Paris Université IX.* Claudel (1868-1955) died at No. 11 Blvd. Lannes, skirting the Bois to the S.; Supervielle lived from 1918 to 1943 at No. 47.

The direct approach to the *Porte de la Muette* from the *Étoile* may be made by following the Av. Victor-Hugo, in which Victor Hugo (1802-85) died in a house on the site of No. 124. The poet Lamartine (1790-1869) died near the square named after him off the S. section of this avenue (house demolished).

The '**Bois**' is divided diagonally by the long ALLÉE DE LONGCHAMP, leading S.W. from the *Porte Maillot* towards the CARREFOUR DE LONGCHAMP, and a popular equestrian rendezvous. It is intersected by the ROUTE DE LA REINE MARGUERITE (from the CARREFOUR DE LA PORTE DE MADRID to the PORTE DE BOULOGNE, on the S. side of the Bois). The equestrian scenes which were such a favourite subject of Constantine Guys often had the 'Bois' in the background.

Of particular interest in this N. section of the Bois is the *****Musée**

National des Arts et des Traditions Populaires (Pl. 10; 2), approached with ease from either *Porte Maillot* or *Porte Dauphine,* or, more directly, from the MÉTRO: *Les Sablons.* The Museum (adm. 10.00-12.30; 14.00-17.00 daily, except Tues.) is housed in a not unattractive functional building by *Jean Dubuisson,* completed in 1966, standing just W. of the CARREFOUR DES SABLONS. It contains an auditorium, library, laboratories, etc., forming a centre for the study of French ethnography. Those sections of this fascinating museum at present open are exceptionally well displayed in a series of nine parallel passages or 'rues', while adjacent are audio-visual cabins. By the entrance is a bell-forge.

Rue 1. Farming equipment: yokes, harnesses, traps, etc.—2. Harrows, hoes, rakes, flails, scythes and sickles, and vinicultural implements.—3. Cowbells, branding-irons, protective collars, crooks; bee-keeping equipment; sheepshearing, and dairy implements.—4. Spinning, carding, rope-making, and basket-weaving; brick and tile manufacture; surveying equipment and carpenter's tools.—5. Lamps and candlesticks; and irons, jacks, and bedwarmers; kitchen utensils—jars, waffle-irons, butter-moulds, etc.; furniture and lacework.—6. Ritual costumes; rural medicine; cradles and early toys; regional and traditional costumes: capes and *sabots,* etc.—7. Games and pastimes: archery, tennis, skittles and *boules,* marbles and croquet. Musical instruments: rattles, hurdy-gurdies, flutes, and whistles; bagpipes, etc.—8. Fairs and circuses: puppets, marionettes, and silhouettes.—9. Graphic arts: metal and wood blocks; engraving and lithographic equipment: stencils, etc.

N.W. of the museum is the *Jardin d'Acclimatation,* with a small-scale zoo and children's playground. To the W., near the *Porte de Madrid,* stood the *Château de Madrid,* built in 1528 by François I (who is said to have named it in memory of his captivity in Spain, after Pavia). It was gradually demolished between 1793 and 1847.

Further W., skirted by the ROUTE DE SÈVRES À NEUILLY, are the walls of the park of **Bagatelle** (59½ acres), famous for its rose-garden, at its best in mid-June. This elegant little domed *Palace* was built for a wager within 64 days by *Bélanger* for the Comte d'Artois, later Charles X, in 1779.

Henry Swinburne observed that during the Revolution it had been turned into a tavern. It was later the residence of Sir Richard Wallace (1818-90), supposed natural son of the Marchioness of Hertford. Wallace had a town house at No. 25 Rue Taitbout, where he accumulated art treasures in addition to those he had inherited from the eccentric 4th Marquis of Hertford, which are now in the *Wallace Collection* in London. He was also a great benefactor of Paris, which he provided with drinking fountains, and helped to equip ambulances during the 1870-71 war. He founded the *Hertford British Hospital* in Paris, and built the Anglican church of St George (1887-88; Rue Auguste-Vacquerie, off the Av. d'Iéna).
The attractive **Bagatelle Gardens* are open to the public until dusk (fee); the restaurant is expensive.

To the W. are various sports grounds (including polo); to the S.W. is the *Hippodrome de Longchamp,* opened in 1857, seen at its gayest on the day of the 'Grand Prix' in June. On the N. side is a windmill (restored), practically the only relic of the *Abbey of Longchamp,* founded in 1256 by St Isabel of France, sister of St Louis.

From the CARREFOUR DE LONGCHAMP (just E. of the windmill), a road leads due E. past the *Grande Cascade* (an artificial waterfall) to skirt the enclosure of the *Pré-Catelan* (named after the troubadour Arnaud Catelan, murdered here c. 1300), with a huge copper beech, and 'Jardin Shakespeare' (containing all the plants and trees mentioned in his plays).

Further E. are buildings of the *Racing Club de France,* flanking the W. bank of the *Lac Inférieur,* with two linked islands. Boats may be hired on the E. bank. Further S. is the *Lac Supérieur,* beyond the CARREFOUR DES CASCADES; in the S.E. corner of the Bois is the *Hippodrome d'Auteuil* (steeplechasing).

Just S. of the Bois is the *Jardin Fleuriste* (municipal nursery gardens), with occasional flower-shows. *N.-D.-des-Menus,* in the Av. J.-B. Clément, leading S.W. from the *Porte de Boulogne,* although frequently restored (by Viollet-le-Duc among others), preserves a 14C nave. Beyond (r.) are the *Jardins Albert Kahn* (including one laid out in the Japanese style), open daily Apr.-Nov.

From the *Arc de Triomphe* (see p. 162), the Av. de la Grande Armée slopes gently N.W. (passing at No. 65 the offices of the *Touring-Club de France*) to the **Porte Maillot** (Pl. 11; 1), the site of extensive works in recent years, and commanded on the N. side by a complex of buildings comprising the *Palais des Congrès,* a hotel, shopping-centre, and one of the *Aérogares* (or air terminals) of Paris.

A short distance to the N.W., near the PL. DE LA PORTE DES TERNES, stands *N.-D. de la Compassion,* a mausoleum in the Byzantine style (1843) moved here from its original neighbouring site, where stood an inn at which Ferdinand, Duc d'Orléans, son of Louis-Philippe, died as the result of a carriage accident. As a travesty of taste it equals the other Orléans mausoleum at *Dreux,* see p. 257.

Beyond the *Porte Maillot,* we continue to approach, viâ the Av. Charles-de-Gaulle, the concrete jungle known as **La Défense** (named after a monument commemorating the defence of Paris in 1871), an aggressive example of high-rise building housing miscellaneous international companies (among others), against which there appears to be no defence. Few will appreciate its attractions, and those who may wish to do so at close hand will have to cross the *Pont de Neuilly* (or take the R.E.R. from *Étoile*). The stone bridge, by *Perronet* (1768-72, almost entirely rebuilt in 1935-39), replaced an earlier bridge erected in 1606 after Henri IV and Marie de Médicis were almost drowned here. On the l. beyond the bridge is the *Tour Nobel,* built on the site of the house in which Bellini died in 1835, while to the N.W. of this area is a triangular-shaped domed edifice covering 18 acres, built to accommodate exhibitions, etc., and known as the C.N.I.T. building.

To the N. of the *Île de Puteaux,* crossed by the *Pont de Neuilly,* is the *Île de la Grande Jatte,* painted by Seurat in 1884.

Neuilly itself, once the most fashionable suburb of Paris, was partially laid out in what was formerly the park of Louis-Philippe's château (built in 1740 and burnt down in 1848), and later developed as a colony of elegant villas, but the construction of blocks of flats has overwhelmed the distinctive character of the neighbourhood. In its S. half, which has the attraction of being adjacent to the *Bois de Boulogne,* at a house on the site of No. 33 Rue de Longchamp (leading S. from near the bridge), Théophile Gautier died in 1872. Further to the E., in the old cemetery, lie Anatole France and André Maurois.

19   THE EASTERN DISTRICTS: FROM THE BUTTES-CHAUMONT TO THE FAUBOURG ST-ANTOINE

MÉTROS: *République, Buttes-Chaumont, Jourdain, Télégraphe, Philippe-Auguste, Nation, Bastille, Faidherbe-Chaligny, Gare-de-Lyon.*

The first main turning r. off the BLVD. DE MAGENTA, leading N. from the *Pl. de la République,* the Rue de Lancry, shortly crosses the *Canal St-Martin,* beyond which the Rue Bichat leads r. to the entrance of the **Hôpital St-Louis* (Pl. 9; 6; for skin diseases), founded by Henri IV and built by *Claude Vellefaux* in 1607-12. It is an excellent and now rare example of the Louis-XIII style, and its Courtyards and *Chapel* may be visited on application at the porter's lodge; the latter is not normally open except on Sundays.

Turning r. on making our exit, we follow the Rue de la Grange-aux-Belles, where to the N. of the next crossroad stood a small Protestant cemetery, now built over, where in 1792 Paul Jones was buried (and subsequently exhumed; and now at Annapolis). Nearby stood the *Gibet de Montfaucon,* the 'Tyburn' of Paris, set up in the 13C and finally removed in 1790.

It proved fatal to three 'surintendants des finances': Enguerrand de Marigny, who erected it; Jean de Montaigu, who repaired it; nor did Semblançay, who tried to avoid it, fare better. Olivier le Daim, confidential barber to Louis XI (1484; comp. 'Quentin Durward'), was hanged here, and Coligny's body exposed after the massacre of St Bartholomew.

Further up the hill is the PL. DU COLONEL-FABIEN, to the N. of which the BLVD. DE LA VILLETTE bears l. over the canal at the PL. DE STALINGRAD, with a *Rotonde,* which was a toll-house (built by *Ledoux* in 1789), and now a repository for archaeological finds in the Paris area.

Further N.E., at the junction of the *Canal de l'Ourcq* and the *Canal St-Denis,* are the *Abattoirs de la Villette,* built by *Baltard,* and adjacent markets, beyond which circles the Blvd. Périphérique.

Hence we may follow the Av. Mathurin-Moreau to the W. entrance of the **Parc des Buttes-Chaumont,** one of the more picturesque, and least known, of Parisian parks (almost 60 acres) lying in the midst of the district of *Belleville* (which belies its name).

It was laid out under Haussmann's régime in 1866-67 by *Alphand* and *Barillet* on the bare hills ('*monts chauves*') which had long been used as a general rubbish-dump and slaughterhouse for horses, etc., its extensive gypsum ('plaster of Paris') quarries being ingeniously transformed into rock-scenery. These heights had been the scene of the 'Battle of Paris' in 1814, and in 1871 were held by the Communards until dislodged by bombardment from Montmartre to the W.

From near the S. end of the park, the Rue Fessart leads E., crossing the Rue de la Villette, where at No. 51 the painter Rouault (1871-1958) was born, to the Gothic-revival church of *St-Jean-Baptiste* (by *Lassus,* 1854-59). From the S. side of the church, the Rue de Belleville continues E., passing a developing area to the N., to the *Cimetière de Belleville,* the highest point in Paris (419 ft). An inscription to the r. of the entrance in the Rue du Télégraphe records that Claude Chappe here experimented with the aerial telegraph that was to announce the victories of the French Revolutionary Wars. In the Rue Haxo, parallel to the E., at No. 79 (r.), is the *Chapelle des Otages,* built in 1936-39 on the site of the Villa des Otages, behind which (at the end of the passage just N. of the chapel) 52 hostages held by the Communards were shot on 26 May 1871.

The return to the centre may be made from the *Métro Télégraphe*, viâ *République*.

———————

From the PL. DE LA RÉPUBLIQUE, the Av. de la République leads E.S.E. across the BLVD. RICHARD-LENOIR, built over the *Canal St-Martin* in 1860 by Haussmann, to the N.W. corner of *Père-Lachaise*, the main entrance of which is in the BLVD. DE MÉNILMONTANT.

The quarter of *Ménilmontant*, N. of the cemetery, was the home of the philosophical fraternity of the Saint-Simoniens in the 1830s.

The *Cimitière de l'Est*, better known as ***Père-Lachaise,** is the largest (116 acres) and long the most 'fashionable' cemetery in Paris, and its tombs display the work of many 19C French sculptors, funerary and otherwise.

Père François de La Chaise (1624-1709) was the confessor of Louis XIV, and lived in the Jesuit house rebuilt in 1682 on the site of a chapel. The property, situated on the side of a hill from which the king, during the Fronde, watched skirmishing between Condé and Turenne, was bought by the city in 1804 and laid out by *Brongniart*, and since extended.

The first interments were those of La Fontaine and Molière, whose remains were transferred there in 1804. The monument to Abélard and Héloïse, set up in 1779 at the abbey of the Paraclete, was moved here in 1817, its canopy composed of fragments collected by Lenoir from the abbey of Nogent-sur-Seine. In the E. corner of the cemetery is the *Mur des Fédérés*, against which the last of the Communards were shot in 1871 (28 May); and here also is a monument to the many thousand Frenchmen who died either in German concentration camps or during the Resistance of 1941-44.

Some thousands still converge on the cemetery on 1 and 2 Nov. ('Jour de la Toussaint'—All Saints' Day—and 'Jour des Morts'). A guide-plan may be obtained for a nominal sum from the keeper's lodge at the main entrance, which will indicate the position of the tombs of the illustrious dead interred here, which indeed make an impressive list.

Among other writers: Beaumarchais, Hugo, Béranger, Proust, Balzac, Constant, Mme de Genlis, Gérard de Nerval, de Musset, Daudet, Rémy de Gourmont, Daniel Stern, Apollinaire, de Régnier, Barbusse, Bernardin de Saint-Pierre, Villiers de L'Isle-Adam, Colette, Éluard, and Gertrude Stein.

Among *musicians*: Méhul, Gossec, Grétry, Boïeldieu, Hérold, Pleyel, Lesueur, Rossini (removed to Florence in 1887), Cherubini, Bellini, Bizet, Hahn, Chausson, Chopin, Lalo, Gustave Charpentier, Auber, Poulenc, Dukas, and Enesco, and the librettist Scribe.

Among *artists:* David, Corot, Doré, Ingres, Gros, Daumier, Daubigny, Delacroix, Géricault, Seurat, and Modigliani.

Among *Maréchaux de l'Empire:* Davout, Kellerman, Lefebvre, Masséna, Murat, Ney, Victor, Macdonald, Suchet, Gouvion-Saint-Cyr, and Augereau; and generals Foy, Junot, and Marbot.

Other famous names in their respective 'fields' are: Mlle Mars, and Mlle George; Rachel, Talma, and Sarah Bernhardt; Isadora Duncan, Adelina Patti, Yvette Guilbert, Edith Piaf; Brillat-Savarin; Champollion, the egyptologist; Baron Taylor, Baron Haussmann; the philosophers Saint-Simon and Comte; Lammennais, Michelet, Arago, Cuvier, Monge, Barras, and Thiers.

Among Englishmen interred here are Oscar Wilde (1856-1900; with a monument by *Epstein*); Sir William Keppel (1702-54), second Earl of Albemarle; Adm. Sir Sidney Smith (1764-1840), who had been imprisoned previously for two years in the Temple, from which he escaped in 1798; and Sir Richard Hertford-Wallace (1818-90), the connoisseur and benefactor of Paris (see p. 176).

N. of the Rue de la Roquette, opposite the main entrance to the cemetery, stood the *Prison de la Grande-Roquette,* itself on the site of the convent of the

Hospitalières de la Roquette, founded in 1639, replaced in 1899 by the *Petite-Roquette* (for women). From 1853 to 1899 condemned prisoners were held at La Roquette while awaiting execution. Some Commune hostages were also shot there.

To the S.E. of the cemetery, approached by the BLVD. DE CHARONNE and Rue de Bagnolet, stands *St-Germain-de-Charonne,* a rustic church of the 13-15C, restored in the 19C, retaining its village cemetery (the only other in Paris being *St-Pierre-de-Montmartre*). To the S.E. is *St-Jean-Bosco* (1937), of concrete, and with a lofty tower.

The Faubourg St-Antoine

The BLVD. DE MÉNILMONTANT, with its continuation S., the Av. Philippe-Auguste, leads S.E. to the *Pl. de la Nation,* also approached direct from the *Pl. de la Bastille* by Métro. The RUE DU FAUBOURG-ST-ANTOINE leads E.S.E. from the Bastille to the *Pl. de la Nation,* through an area memorable in the history of the Revolutions of 1789 and 1848. It was also the scene of skirmishing during the Fronde (1652), when Turenne defeated Condé.

Since the late 13C it has been a centre of cabinet-making, and many courtyards and passages are still the site of busy workshops behind 18C façades.

At No. 1 Rue du Faubourg-St-Antoine, Fieschi hatched the plot against Louis-Philippe. At No. 61 (l.), at the corner of the Rue de Charonne, is the *Fontaine Trogneux* (1710). Further on (r.), the SQUARE TROUSSEAU occupies the site of the *Hospice des Enfants-Trouvés,* in the graveyard of which the Princesse de Lamballe was buried after her corpse had been paraded through the streets. In front of No. 151, Baudin, representative of the people for the department of the Ain, was killed on a barricade while inciting the Parisians to protest against the coup d'état of Napoleon III (1851).—To the l., the Rue St-Bernard leads to the church of *Ste-Marguerite,* built in 1634 but many times altered since. Behind the high-altar is a Pietà by *Girardon.* It is believed that the 10-year-old Louis XVII, who in all probability died at the *Temple,* was buried in the graveyard here, with other victims of the Revolution.

S. of the Rue du Faubourg-St-Antoine at this point lies the *Hôpital St-Antoine,* rebuilt in 1905 but retaining part of *Lenoir's* 18C building for the former *Abbaye de St-Antoine-des-Champs.*

A number of thoroughfares converge on the spacious **Pl. de la Nation,** at the hub of which is a colossal bronze group representing the 'Triumph of the Republic', by *Dalou* (1899). It was known formerly as the *Pl. du Trône* (named after the throne erected for Louis XIV's triumphal entry in 1660 with María Teresa); in 1794 no less than 1,300 victims of the Terror were guillotined here. To the E. of the 'circus' are two pavilions, built as toll-houses by *Ledoux* in 1788, each surmounted by a Doric column 100 ft high; one with a statue of Philippe Auguste (by *Dumont*), the other, of St Louis, by *Étex.*

The COURS DE VINCENNES (the scene in Easter Week of the Foire aux Pains d'épice, a festival dating back to the 10C, when bread made with honey and aniseed was distributed by the monks of the Abbey of St-Antoine) leads directly E. from the *Pl. de la Nation* to the *Porte de Vincennes,* and beyond to the *château de Vincennes* (see Rte 20), also reached direct by the Métro.

The Rue Fabre-d'Églantine leads S. to the Rue de Picpus, where, at the end of the garden at No. 35, a convent of Augustinian nuns, is the little ***Cimitière de Picpus** (open 14.00-16.00 or 18.00, except Mon.), a private burial-ground for 'émigrés' and descendants of victims of the Revolution.

Among individuals interred there are André Chénier, and Gen. La Fayette; among famous families, those of Chateaubriand, Crillon, Gontaut-Biron, Tascher de la Pagerie, Choiseul, La Rochefoucauld, Du Plessis, Montmorency, Talleyrand-Périgord, Rohan-Rochefort, Noailles, Quélen, Salignac-Fénelon, etc., as well as sixteen Carmelites of Compiègne martyred in 1794. In a second section are buried members of the house of Salm-Kyrbourg, and those guillotined in the PL. DU TRÔNE-*renversé* (as the *Pl. de la Nation* was known from 1793 to 1880), including Chénier.

A short distance S.E. of the PL. DE LA BASTILLE, in the Rue de Charenton, is the *Hospice des Quinze-Vingts,* an asylum for 300 blind persons founded by St Louis in 1260. The building was before 1775 the *Caserne des Mousquetaires-Noirs.* Note also Nos. 20-25 in this street; Nos. 40-60 occupy the site of the *Couvent des Filles-Anglaises de la Conception,* which from 1635 to 1655 accepted only daughters of English parents.

The Rue de Lyon leads S. from the *Pl. de la Bastille* to the **Gare de Lyon** (Pl. 19; 4), the terminus of the railways to Geneva, Lyon, Marseilles, etc., on the S. side of which the Rue de Bercy leads S.E. to the extensive *Entrepôt des Vins,* with bonded warehouses and cellars.

The BLVD. DIDEROT leads W. from the *Gare de Lyon* to the *Pont d'Austerlitz* (also approached direct from the *Pl. de la Bastille* by the BLVD. DE LA BASTILLE), built in 1802-07, rebuilt in stone in 1855, and widened in 1884-86.

To the N.W., the QUAI HENRI-IV occupies what was until c. 1840 the *Île Louviers,* now joined to the Right Bank. To the S.E., at No. 12 QUAI DE LA RAPÉE, is the *Institut Médico-Légal* (no adm.), which took the place of the old Morgue, which stood at the S. end of the *Île de la Cité.* Just beyond it the Métro crosses the Seine on a single span of 450 ft. Other bridges seen in this direction are the *Pont de Bercy* (1864), *Pont de Tolbiac* (1879-84), *Pont National* (1852, enlarged in 1939-42), and the new bridge carrying the Périphérique. The *Porte de Bercy,* on the N. Bank here, is the commencement of the A4 autoroute to the E.

The *Pont d'Austerlitz* crosses the Seine to *Gare d'Austerlitz,* see p. 60.

20 VINCENNES: THE CHÂTEAU AND PARK

Approx. 2 km. E. of the *Porte de Vincennes,* and reached directly from the centre by the MÉTRO (*Château de Vincennes*), stands the impressive bulk of the historic ***Château de Vincennes,** rectangular in plan, and flanked by nine square towers. With the exception of the entrance tower, the finest and largest, which lost only its statues, the others were reduced to the level of the walls in the 19C. Michelet called it 'the Windsor of the Valois'.

Visitors are conducted in small groups to the Keep and Chapel. Adm. 10.00-12.00; 14.00-17.00 or 18.00, daily, except Tues.

History. The present castle, succeeding an earlier royal hunting-lodge fortified by St Louis, was begun by Philippe VI in 1337, and its fortification was completed by his grandson Charles V (1364-73), who also commenced work on the Chapel, which was not finished until 1552. Some idea of how it once looked may be gained from the illustration of December in the 'Très Riches Heures of the Duc de Berri', or *Fouquet*'s panel of Étienne Chevalier. The foundations of the *Pavillons du Roi* and *de la Reine* (to the S.) were laid in the 16C, but these buildings were not completed for nearly a century, when the château, then in Mazarin's possession, was altered and decorated by *Le Vau*.

With the completion of the palace at Versailles (c. 1680), Vincennes was deserted by the court, and the château was occupied in turn by a porcelain factory (1745; transferred to Sèvres in 1756), a cadet school, and in 1757, a small-arms factory. Offered for sale in 1788, it found no purchaser, and in 1791 La Fayette rescued it from destruction by the Revolutionary mob. In 1808 Napoleon converted it into an arsenal, when the surviving 13C buildings were demolished. In 1840 it was made into a fortress, and much of Le Vau's decoration was destroyed or masked by casements. During the Second World War, German occupying forces had a supply depot here, and the *Pavillon de la Reine* was partially destroyed by an explosion in 1944 during their evacuation of the building. Restoration continues to be undertaken sporadically, but much work is still to be done.

The historical associations of Vincennes are endless. It witnessed the deaths of Jeanne de Navarre in 1305, Louis X in 1316, Charles IV in 1328, Charles IX in 1574, and of Mazarin in 1661; and Charles V was born here in 1337. In 1326 the 'Auld Alliance' or treaty between France and Scotland was signed here. Henry V of England died here in 1422, seven weeks before the death of Charles VI, whom he was to succeed as king of France. During the reign of Louis XIII, the keep was used as a state prison; and among its inmates were the Grand Condé, Card. de Retz, Fouquet, Diderot (visited there by Rousseau in 1749), and Mirabeau (who here wrote his 'Essai sur les lettres de cachet' in 1784). Prince Charles Edward Stuart was imprisoned here briefly after Culloden. A later prisoner was J.-H. Latude (1725-1805), who, for a fraudulent attempt to extract money from Mme de Pompadour, was incarcerated here (and elsewhere), untried, for thirty-five years.

In 1804 the Duc d'Enghien, son of the Prince de Condé, arrested five days before on Napoleon's orders, was tried by court-martial and shot here the same night. Gen. Daumesnil was governor of the château from 1809 to 1814, during the Hundred Days, and from 1830 until his death in 1832. When summoned to surrender to the Allies in 1814, his answer was "First give me back my leg" (which he had lost at Wagram). In 1830, when the mob broke into the building in search of some former ministers of Charles X, he dispersed them by threatening to blow up the powder-magazine. In 1944, three days before evacuating it, the Germans shot some thirty hostages against the interior of the ramparts.

Crossing the moat, we enter the fortress beneath the imposing *Tour du Village,* 155 ft high, and pass between a range of tawdry buildings in military occupation to reach the central courtyard. The *Keep, 170 ft in height, a square tower flanked with round turrets, is enclosed in a separate turreted enceinte, and is the finest of its type in France (since the *Château de Courcy* was blown up by the Germans in 1917), and as such deserves further restoration. The two doors on the ground floor facing the postern came from the prison of Louis XVI in the Temple. A wide spiral stair ascends to the first and second floors (third floor closed), supported by vaults springing from a central column; the corbels at each corner of the room symbolize the four Evangelists. Note the oak beams between the ribs. The SECOND FLOOR was a favourite residence of Charles V, and contains a fine chimneypiece, and an oratory in the N.W. turret. Henry V (of England) and Charles IX died on this floor. 17C prisoners of state were lodged above. The energetic may climb to the roof, commanding a wide view of the area, with the main landmarks of central Paris easily discerned to the W. The kitchen, with its internal well, is shown on the ground floor as we make our exit.

The **Chapel** opposite was founded by Charles V in 1379, and, retaining the Gothic style, was only completed in 1552. The Flamboyant *Façade has a magnificent rose-window surmounted by an ornamental gable filled with tracery. The interior, bare of furniture, contains graceful vaulting, and at the E. end, seven *stained-glass windows by *Beaurain* (16C), restored after an explosion in 1870. A monument to the

Duc d'Enghien (see above; by *Deseine*, 1816) may be seen in the oratory.

To the S., approached through a portico, lies the immense COUR D'HONNEUR, and beyond, the monumental *Tour du Bois*. To the r. stands the *Pavillon du Roi* (now containing military archives), and opposite, the *Pavillon de la Reine*, where Mazarin died in 1661. Both were completed by *Le Vau* in 1654-60. The latter houses the *Musée de la Guerre de 1914-1918*.

The **Bois de Vincennes,** first enclosed in the 12C, was replanted in 1731 by Louis XV and converted into a park for the citizens of Paris. It was further enlarged in 1860. To the S.E. of the château are extensive *Floral Gardens,* and beyond are various stadiums and sports grounds. Further E. is the *Lac des Minimes,* a *Jardin Tropical,* and an *Indo-Chinese pagoda.* S.W. of the château, beyond University buildings, and bordering the Av. Daumesnil, is the *Parc Zoölogique de Vincennes* (open 9.00-17.30 or 18.00), the main zoo of Paris, containing an impressive collection of birds and mammals.

At the W. end of the Bois is the *Lac Daumesnil,* and beyond a partially subterranean section of the Blvd. Périphérique, the **Musée National des Arts Africains et Océaniens,* recently reformed, and housed in a building erected in 1931 for a Colonial Exhibition, with a sculpted façade. It also accommodates an important *Aquarium.*

As its name implies, it concentrates on the *arts* of the ci-devant French colonies rather than their ethnography, for which see *Musée de l'Homme,* p. 173. Adm. 9.45-12.00; 13.30-17.00 daily, except Tues. and holidays.

GROUND FLOOR: l., the Oceanian Collection: masks, wooden drums, and statues from the New Hebrides: to the r., naïf bark paintings from Australia.

FIRST FLOOR: l., arts of the W. African coast, including gold figurines, etc., from Akan; brass and gold powder figures from Ghana and the Ivory Coast; note also the carved wood woman and child from Kran (Liberia). To the r., work from the Niger and Congo basins, Yoruba (Nigeria), and the Cameroons; Benin bronzes; nail-studded magic statues from the Congo; Bembe figurines, masks, jewellery, and pottery.

SECOND FLOOR: l., Moroccan jewellery, including a fine necklace from Fez (16-17C); arms; and a section devoted to fabrics, brocades, embroidery, caftans, etc. To the r., the arts of Tunisia and Algeria, including bonnets, pendants, fibulas, etc.

IV THE ENVIRONS OF PARIS

21 PARIS TO VERSAILLES

BY ROAD. Versailles is best approached by taking the A13 motorway and turning 1. at the first exit after passing through the tunnel at St-Cloud. Hence a road leads S.W. towards the palace of Versailles (parking in the *Pl. d'Armes*).

BY RAIL. From the *Gare Montparnasse* to *Versailles-Chantiers;* from the *Gare St-Lazare* to *Versailles-Rive Droit;* and from the *Gare des Invalides* to *Versailles-Rive Gauche* (the station nearest the palace).

Those wishing to visit Sèvres and Meudon should follow the N10 W. from the *Porte de St-Cloud.* The famous *Porcelain Factory* at **Sèvres** lies immediately to the N. on crossing the Seine. Founded in 1738, it was moved here in 1756 from Vincennes, at the instance of Mme de Pompadour. Since 1760 it has been State-controlled. Among designers of Sèvres ware *E.-M. Falconet* (1716-91) and *J.-B. Pigalle* (1714-85) may be mentioned.

There are guided tours of the workshops (no children) on the first and third Thurs. of each month, from 14.00 to 15.30: the sale-room is open Mon.-Fri., 9.00-12.00, 13.30-18.00. A fine historical collection of the ware produced here may be seen in the *Musée Céramique* (adm. 9.45-12.00, 13.30-17.15, except Tues.), which also displays china and porcelain other than that of Sèvres.

The road continues S.W. to Versailles.

Immediately S. of Sèvres lies **Meudon,** once the home of Rodin (whose villa, 'des Brillants', is now a museum; adm. 13.30-18.00, Sat., Sun., and Mon.), and, in 1841, Wagner, who composed 'The Flying Dutchman' here, at No. 27 Av. du Château. Rabelais held the benefice of Meudon in 1551-52.

The *Musée de l'Air* at Meudon, with a notable collection of early aircraft, is in the process of moving to *Le Bourget.* Nearby is the *Observatoire d'Astronomie Physique.* The building, formerly the *Château Neuf,* was built for the Grand Dauphin ('Monseigneur', the son of Louis XIV), by *Mansart,* but a fire in 1870 reduced it to the single-storeyed building which it is today. The Terrasse commands an extensive view.

2 km. N. of Sèvres lies the suburb of **St-Cloud.** The royal castle, in which Henri III was assassinated in 1589, and where Napoleon's second marriage was celebrated in 1810, was burned down during the German occupation in 1870; but the park (1,000 acres), with its cascades and fountains, is open to the public. The views to the N.E., towards Paris, are not without interest. Some 4 km. to the N. is the fort of *Mont Valérien,* where 4,500 Frenchmen were murdered during the German occupation of 1941-44. At *Montretout,* the upper part of St-Cloud, are the headquarters of Interpol.

Some 3 km. to the W. is the park of *Villeneuve-l'Étang,* with a memorial to American airmen of the First World War. Pasteur died in the château, which is now a medical research institution.—At *Ville d'Avray,* to the S., and 2 km. W. of Sèvres, is the *Villa des Jardies* (nr the station), the country retreat of Balzac, where he was visited by Hugo and

Gautier. Later the house belonged to Léon Gambetta (1838-82), who died there. The 18C church, in the Rue de Sèvres, contains frescoes by *Corot,* who often painted the two Étangs to the S.W. in the *Bois de Fausses Reposes.* The palace of Versailles lies 5.5 km. S.W. of Ville d'Avray.

VERSAILLES (93,500 inhab.; *Hotels*), 23 km. S.W. of Paris, and the main town of the department of Yvelines, lies in a low sandy plain between two lines of wooded hills, in danger of becoming further spoilt by encroaching suburban developments. With its regular streets and its imposing avenues converging on the palace, it still seeks to retain its royal cachet, although the palace quite overshadows it in interest (see p. 187).

History. Versailles emerged from obscurity in 1624, when Louis XIII built a hunting lodge here, which subsequently developed into a small château. But the real creator of Versailles was Louis XIV, who in 1661 conceived the idea of building a lasting monument to his reign—a trophy of self-glorification. *Louis Le Vau* was entrusted with the renovation and embellishment of the old building round the Cour de Marbre, while *Le Nôtre* laid out the park. After Le Vau's death in 1670 the work was continued by his pupil *François d'Orbay,* while the interior decoration was superintended by *Charles Le Brun.* In 1682 Louis XIV transferred here from St-Germain, the court and seat of government. *Jules Hardouin-Mansart,* appointed chief architect in 1676, remodelled the main body of the palace and built the two great N. and S. wings, giving the immense façade (with its 375 windows) a total length of 634 yds. The chapel, begun by him, was finished by his brother-in-law *Robert de Cotte* in 1710.

More than 30,000 workmen were employed at one time on the building of the palace and in laying out and draining the grounds; the cost, impoverishing France, amounting to over 60 million livres. In 1687 *Mansart* built the *Grand Trianon.* Under Louis XV a series of royal apartments, decorated in the current style, were incorporated; and one of the colonnaded pavilions in the entrance court, the interior of the opera-house, and the *Petit Trianon* were built by *J.-A. Gabriel.* Louis XVI redecorated a suite of apartments for Marie-Antoinette and built the 'rustic village' or *Hameau.*

Not all visitors from England were impressed by Versailles. The poet Gray, in 1739, wrote of it as "a huge heap of littleness"; Dr Johnson was more interested by the menagerie than the palace; Smollett described it as a "most fantastic composition of magnificence and littleness, taste and foppery".

The independence of the United States was formally recognized by England, France, and Spain, at the Treaty of Versailles, signed in 1783. The meeting of the Assembly of the States-General was held in Versailles in 1789, where on 20 June the deputies of the Third Estate constituted themselves into the National Assembly. On 6 Oct. the Paris mob, led by the women of the Halles, marched to Versailles, massacred the bodyguard, and conveyed the king and the royal family to the Tuileries. In 1792, when Richard Twiss visited Versailles, he found it almost bare: glasses, tapestries, and pictures removed. It had been uninhabited for over two years, and the Grand Canal was quite dry. In 1814 the palace was occupied by Tsar Alexander I and Frederick William III of Prussia. Under the Restoration, the second colonnaded pavilion was completed by *Dufour,* but the building later fell into disrepair. Louis-Philippe did irreparable damage to the palace in housing a pretentious museum there, containing few canvases of any importance, and reflecting his prodigious lack of taste.

In the Franco-Prussian War Versailles became the H.Q. of the German armies operating against Paris, the palace being used as a hospital, and Moltke occupying No. 38 Blvd. de la Reine. On 18 Jan. 1871, William I of Prussia was crowned German Emperor in the *Galerie des Glaces;* and on 26 Jan. the peace preliminaries were signed at Bismarck's quarters at 20 Rue de Provence. In 1871-75 the National Assembly sat in the opera-house, and here the Republic was proclaimed on 25 Feb. 1875.

During the First World War Versailles was the seat of the Allied War Council, and the Peace Treaty with Germany was signed in the *Galerie des Glaces* on 28 June 1919. Extensive restorations were made in 1928-32, and have continued since the Second World War. During that war, the Allied G.H.Q. was at Versailles from

Sept. 1944 until the following May, and many buildings were requisitioned by the military.

Versailles was the birthplace of Louis XV (1710-74), Houdon (1741-1828), the sculptor, Marshal Berthier (1753-1815), Louis XVI (1754-93), Louis XVIII (1755-1824), Charles X (1757-1836), Kreutzer (1766-1831), the violinist, Gen. Hoche (1768-97), and de Lesseps (1805-94; at 18 Rue des Réservoirs). Mme de Pompadour died in the palace in 1764; the painter Georges Rouault (1871-1958) is buried in the St-Louis cemetery. Ambroise Vollard (1865-1939) also died at Versailles.

The **Town** of Versailles contains a certain number of buildings of interest, among them, in the Rue des Réservoirs (to the N. of the palace), No. 7, the *Hôtel des Réservoirs,* built by *Lassurance* for Mme de Pompadour (but since much altered), still bearing the marquise's arms. The *Théâtre Montansier* (No. 13), founded by the actress Mlle Montansier, was built by *Heurtier* and *Boulet* in 1777, and since restored. La Bruyère (1645-96) lived and died at No. 22, the *Hôtel du Prince de Condé.*—A few minutes walk to the N.E., at 54 Blvd. de la Reine, is the **Musée Houdon,** occupying the 18C *Hôtel Lambinet,* containing sculptures by *Houdon,* paintings by *Dunoyer de Segonzac,* and religious art of the 14-18C (adm. Tues., Thurs., Sat., and Sun., 14.00-18.00). Nearby, to the S., stands *Notre-Dame,* built by *J. H-. Mansart* in 1684 as the parish church of the palace, with a pulpit of the period, and interesting registers.

Immediately to the S. of the Palace, in the Rue de l'Indépendance-Americaine, is the *Grand-Commun* (now a hospital), built by *Mansart* in 1684 to house a swarm of minor court functionaries, with fine bas-reliefs and courtyard. At No. 3 is the former *Hôtel de la Guerre* (1759), and (No. 5) the old *Hôtel de la Marine et des Affaires Étrangères* (1761), now the municipal library, with a small museum and Louis-XV decorations (open weekdays, 14.00-18.00). The Marquis de Louvois (1641-91), Louis XIV's great War minister, died at No. 6, once the *Hôtel de la Surintendance.*

Hence the Rue du Vieux-Versailles (l.) brings us shortly to the **Jeu de Paume,** the royal-tennis court, built in 1686, but of little interest in itself (adm. on application to the Conservateur, Château de Versailles).

In 1789, the deputies of the Tiers-État, finding themselves locked out of the States-General, adjourned here, and with the astronomer Bailly as their president, swore not to separate until they had given France a proper constitution. It was later used as a studio by Gros and Horace Vernet.

In the Rue du Maréchal-Joffre, to the S., stands a rare but somewhat frigid example of a Louis-XV church, the **Cathedral of St-Louis** (1743-54), by *Jacques Mansart de Sagonne.* To the W. is the former royal kitchen-garden, now a horticultural college (entrance No. 4 Rue du Potager). To the S.E. is the PL. DU MARCHÉ-ST-LOUIS, with quaint 18C houses. Further on, at No. 4 Rue St-Médéric, was the *Parc-aux-Cerfs,* purchased in 1755 by Louis XV—when in rut—for the indulgence of his amours.

In the Av. de Paris, leading directly E. from the palace, No. 3 occupies the *Hôtel de Mme du Barry* (1751; adm. on application), preserving contemporary woodwork. Robert de Montesquiou lived at No. 53, where he entertained many writers and dillettantes. Further on, at Nos. 57-61, are the *Laiterie de Madame* and *Pavillon de Musique,* built by *Chalgrin* in 1780 in emulation of the 'hameau' at the Petit Trianon, for Mme Élisabeth, Comtesse de Provence, wife of the future Louis XVIII.

**The Palace of Versailles

Admission. In order to accommodate the press of visitors, particularly noticeable between Easter and late Sept., the palace is open every day during this period from 9.30 to 18.00; at other times of the year it is likely to open later and close earlier. The visit of groups is sensibly restricted between 12.30 and 14.30. However, as individuals are not normally able to visit certain suites of rooms unescorted, it is strongly recommended that the traveller wishing to see, even if cursorily, the *Petits-Appartements,* among a number of other galleries, should endeavour to arrange to make up a group (minimum 10), which will be escorted round these rooms by an English-speaking guide. If possible, an appointment should be made in advance through the *Service éducatif* (Tel. 950 5832), but there should be little difficulty in joining a small group on making enquiry at the entrance vestibule, and the visit will be undertaken without the delays and inconvenience attendant on those attempting to cover the ground unaided. There is a snack-bar in the *Galerie Napoléon,* near the main entrance.

It is virtually impossible to visit all the galleries, the park, and the Trianons in one day, although many endeavour to do so.

To the E. of the palace lies the PL. D'ARMES, where the wide Avenues de St-Cloud, de Paris, and de Sceaux, converge, bounded on the E. by the **Grandes-Écuries** and the **Petites-Écuries,** the royal stables, which once accommodated 2,000 carriages and 2,500 horses. Built by *Mansart* in 1679–85, they are now barracks.

Flanking the gateway to the palace, with *Mansart*'s original grille, are groups of sculpture: (r.) France victorious over the Empire, by *Marsy,* and over Spain, by *Girardon;* and l., Peace, by *Tuby,* and Abundance, by *Coysevox.* The *Avant-Cour* or *Cour des Ministres* is flanked by detached wings once assigned to secretaries of state. Beyond the equestrian statue of Louis XIV (1837) is the COUR ROYALE, between two colonnaded pavilions dating from 1772 (r.) and 1829.

In the time of Louis XIV, only those who possessed the honours of the Louvres—those called 'cousin' by the king, and who had the right to bring their coach or chair or liveried servants into the great Courtyard of the Louvre—could enter this court in a similar fashion.

The visitors' entrance to the palace is in the r.-hand pavilion. Before entering, walk over to the COUR DE MARBRE, a deep, marble-paved recess at the end of the *Cour Royale;* this was the courtyard of Louis XIII's château and the nucleus of the whole palace, before being transformed by *Le Vau* and *Mansart.*

The ticket-office, cloakroom (obligatory for umbrellas, parcels, etc.), and bookstalls are accommodated in the VESTIBULE GABRIEL (**R 23**).

Beyond this is the VESTIBULE DE LA CHAPELLE, which has handsome carved and gilded doors and contains a bas-relief by *Nicolas* and *Guillaume Coustou* of Louis XIV crossing the Rhine. To the r. we get a view of the **Chapel** (adm. only for mass on Sun. at 11.30), with its colonnade of Corinthian columns, begun by *Mansart* in 1699 and completed in 1710 by *Robert de Cotte.* The high-altar is of marble and bronze, with sculptures by *van Cleve* and *G. Coustou,* above which is the organ. François Couperin was but one of the great organists who played here. The central ceiling-painting is by *Antoine Coypel,* and above the royal pew is a Descent of the Holy Ghost, by *Jouvenot.*

From the vestibule we may enter the 17C GALLERY (*Salles du Dix-septième Siècle*), with an impressive collection of portraits displayed in eleven rooms. **R 2:** *Rubens,* Marie de Médicis and her parents. **R 3:** Richelieu, by *Ph. de Champaigne.* **R 4** is devoted to the Jansenists of

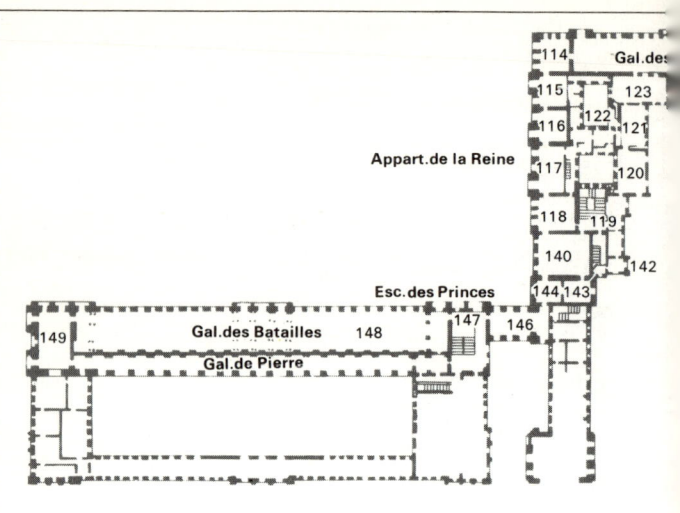

Gal.des

114

115 123

116 122 121

117 120

Appart.de la Reine

118 119

140

144 143 142

Esc. des Princes

147 146

149 Gal.des Batailles 148

Gal.de Pierre

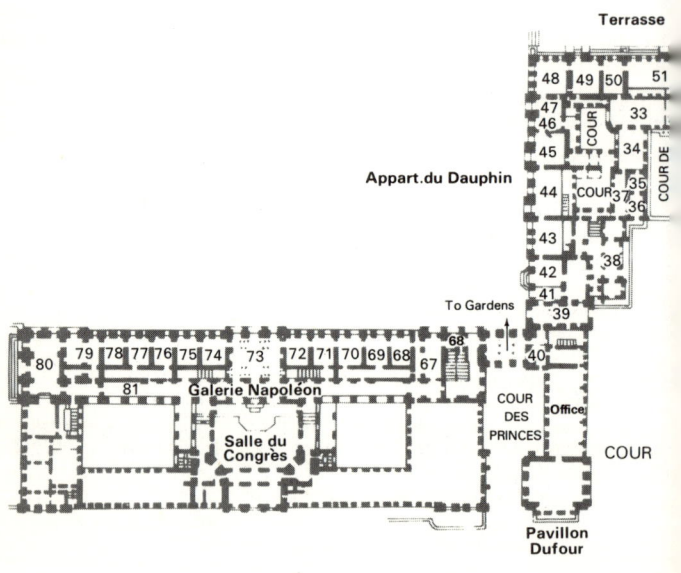

Terrasse

48 49 50 51

47 33

46 COUR

45 34

Appart.du Dauphin

44 COUR 35

37 36

43

42 38

41

39

To Gardens

80 79 78 77 76 75 74 73 72 71 70 69 68 67 68 40

81 Galerie Napoléon

Salle du Congrès

COUR DES PRINCES

Office

COUR

Pavillon Dufour

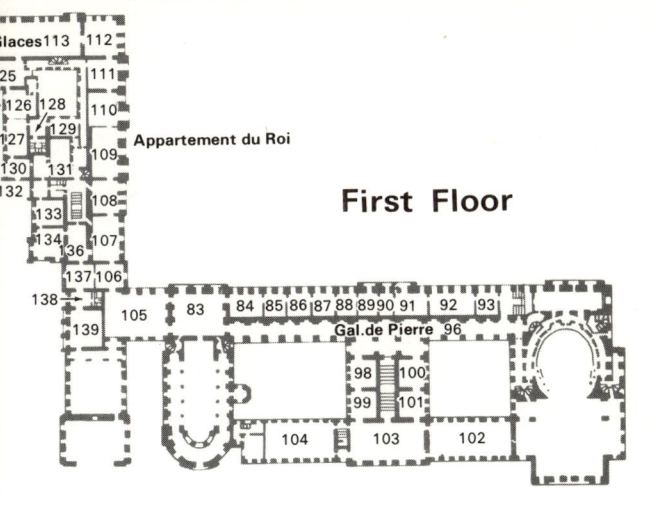

First Floor

Appartement du Roi

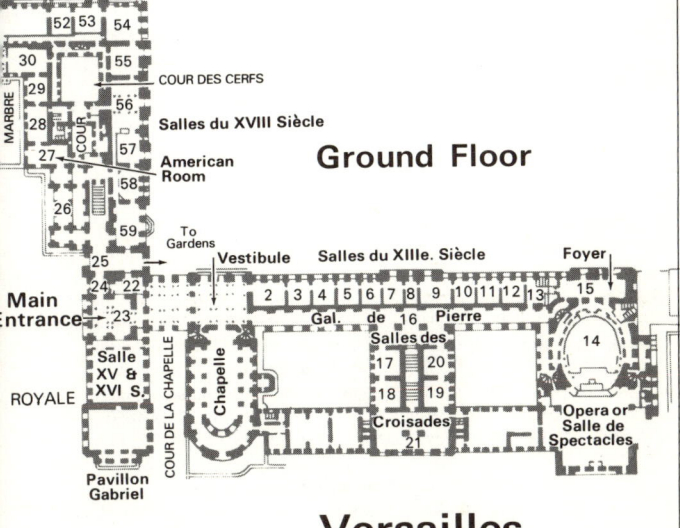

COUR DES CERFS

Salles du XVIII Siècle

American Room

Ground Floor

To Gardens

Vestibule   Salles du XIIIe. Siècle   Foyer

Gal.   de   Pierre

Salles des

Croisades

Main Entrance

Salle XV & XVI S.

ROYALE

Pavillon Gabriel

Opera or Salle de Spectacles

Versailles
The Palace

Port-Royal, with perspectives and portraits, including *Ph. de Champaigne,* Angélique Arnauld, and the architect Lemercier. **R 8:** portraits of Racine, Molière, La Fontaine, etc. **R 9:** views of Versailles by *P.-D. Martin,* and others; and of sieges, by *van der Meulen,* and a portrait of Mansart by *De Troy.* **R 11:** portraits by *Beaubrun* of the royal family.

At the far end of this gallery is the FOYER DE L'OPÉRA, retaining its 18C decoration by *Pajou.* Off the parallel GALERIE DE PIERRE, to the r., are the SALLES DES CROISADES, etc. **(RR17-21)**, of very slight interest.—The **Opéra,** or *Salle de Spectacles,* was built for Louis XV by *Gabriel* in 1753-70, and first used on the occasion of the marriage of the Dauphin (Louis XVI) and Marie-Antoinette.

It was later repainted in the poor taste of the period of Louis-Philippe, and in 1855 was the scene of a banquet given in honour of Queen Victoria.

Modelled on the King of Sardinia's theatre in Turin, it is a perfect example of Louis-XV decoration, having been skilfully restored (1955-57) by *Japy,* even the upholstery being copied from the original specifications. Seating 700 spectators and with a stage second in size only to the Paris Opéra, it is now reserved for rare gala performances.

Stairs ascend to **RR 93-84,** continuing the series of 17C portraits and busts, etc. **R 92:** four battle scenes by *van der Meulen,* and equestrian portrait of Louis XIV by *Houasse.* **R 91:** views of palaces: St-Germain and Vincennes by *J.-B. Martin,* Marly and Trianon by *P.-D. Martin,* and St-Cloud by *Allegrain.* **R 88:** Mme de Maintenon by *Mignard,* and Fénelon by *Vivien.* **R 87:** *Rigaud,* Marquis de Dangeau. **R 86:** Princesses, including the Duchesse de Bourgogne in a red dress, by *Gobert.* **R 85:** *Benoist,* wax portrait of Louis XIV aged 68, with his own (?) wig. **R 84:** *Rigaud,* the Duchesse d'Orléans.

From the UPPER VESTIBULE **(R 83)**, with figures of the Virtues by various sculptors, a striking view may be had of the *Chapel* and *Royal Gallery,* the door of which has a chased lock by *Desjardins.*

We now enter the SALON D'HERCULE **(R 105)**, fitted up by Louis XV in the Louis-XIV style. The elaborate decorations were sculptured by *Vassé* (1729-34). On the ceiling is the Apotheosis of Hercules by *Fr. Lemoyne,* who, after three years' work (1733-36), committed suicide on its completion. Swiss Guards used to be posted here to prevent the intrusion into the State Apartments of 'those freshly marked with smallpox, the shabbily dressed, petitioners, begging friars, and dogs'.

The SALON DE L'ABONDANCE **(R 106)** is the first of the *King's State Apartments,* which, although they have lost their original furniture, have preserved their decorations of marble inlay, sculptured and gilded bronzes, carved doors, and painted ceilings, executed under the supervision of *Charles Le Brun.* The ceiling-painting here—used as a refreshment room at royal receptions—is by *Houasse* (freely restored).

The SALON DE VÉNUS **(R 107)**, named after its ceiling-painting (also by *Houasse*), is noteworthy for its marble decorations in the early Louis-XIV style. The carved doors are by *Caffieri;* above are bronze bas-reliefs. The mural decorations of this salon (and the succeeding one) are original. In the central alcove is a statue of Louis XIV in Roman costume *and* wig, by *Warin;* and on either side of the room are trompe-l'oeil paintings by *Jacques Rousseau.*

The SALON DE DIANE **(R 108)**, the former billiard room, has a ceiling by *Blanchard,* and contains a bust of Louis XIV by *Bernini* (1665).

The SALON DE MARS (**R 109**), once the *Salle des Gardes*, later a gaming-room and subsequently a ballroom and concert-room, has a ceiling by *Audran, Jouvenet*, and *Houasse*. The dessus de portes are by *Simon Vouet*, and the portrait of Marie-Antoinette and her children by *Mme Vigée-Lebrun* (1787). The tapestries are the first of a series by *Le Brun*, illustrating 'The Life of the King', and are among the earliest works from the Gobelins manufactory (1668-72).

The SALON DE MERCURE (**R 110**), a card-room under Louis XIV, where that monarch lay in state for eight days, has a ceiling by *J.-B. de Champaigne*. The Savonnerie carpet and the clock (by *Morand*) should be noticed.

The SALON D'APOLLON (**R 111**), the former throne-room, is the last of the King's State Apartments. On the ceiling, by *Lafosse*, is Louis XIV (the 'Roi Soleil') as Apollo in a chariot escorted by the Seasons.

The three following rooms—the *Galerie des Glaces*, with its antechambers, the *Salons de la Guerre* and *de la Paix*—together form a grandiose decorative ensemble. The SALON DE LA GUERRE (**R 112**), completed in 1678, has preserved its original decoration of coloured marble and bronze, and contains six busts of Roman emperors, bequeathed by Mazarin. Over the mantlepiece is a stucco relief of Louis XIV on horseback, by *Coysevox*.

The ceiling-painting, the first of a series designed by *Charles Le Brun*, represents France victorious, with a thunderbolt in one hand and a laurel-wreathed portrait of Louis XIV in the other; in the semicircles appear Bellona in anger, and figures of defeated Germany, Holland, and Spain.

The **Galerie des Glaces* (or *Grande Galerie;* **R 113**), 235 ft long, 30 ft wide, and 43 ft high, is a masterpiece of the Louis-Quatorze style. It was begun by *Mansart* in 1678, and its decoration, designed by *Le Brun*, was completed in 1686. Among the artists employed were *Caffieri, Coysevox, Le Comte*, and *Tuby*, for the sculptures; *Cucci*, for the mirror frames; and *Ladoiseau*, for the trophies on the walls.

The gallery is lighted by seventeen windows looking on to the park, and facing these are as many bevelled mirrors of equal size. The red marble pilasters have bronze capitals decorated with cocks' heads, fleurs-de-lys, and suns. The cornice of gilded stucco is adorned with crowns and the collars of the Orders of the Saint-Esprit and St Michael. The marble statues of Venus, Paris, Mercury, and Minerva in the niches are copies from the antique.

The central ceiling-painting represents Louis XIV omnipotent, while the numerous other paintings depict the subjection of Holland, Germany, and Spain, the Peace imposed by Louis on his enemies, his embassies abroad, the Protection of the Arts, and of the People, and the great Foundations established during his reign.

Opposite the windows are two doors adorned with mirrors. For the *Salon de la Paix*, see below.

We pass through the first door into the CABINET DU CONSEIL (**R 125**), which dates in its present form from 1753. The carved woodwork is by *Antoine Rousseau*. Off this room open the *Petits Appartements du Roi* or *Cabinets du Roi* (**RR 126-130**), constructed by Louis XV in 1738 to provide a retreat from the tedious etiquette of his court.

The CHAMBRE DE LOUIS XV (**R 126**) has carved woodwork by *Verberckt*. Here the king died of smallpox in 1774.

The CABINET DE LA PENDULE (**R 127**) derives its name from *Passemant*'s clock (1749), executed by *Dauthiau*, with chased designs by

Caffieri, surmounted by a crystal globe marking the phases of the sun, moon, and planets. Five tables (1730-57) illustrate the evolution of Rococo furniture.

The CABINET DES CHIENS (**R 128**), with a frieze of hunting-scenes, and decorated with flower paintings, was occupied by the lackeys and the king's favourite hounds. On the staircase descending hence, Damiens attempted to assassinate Louis XV in 1757.

The SALLE À MANGER (**R 129**) overlooks the Cour des Cerfs (much altered). We return to **R 127** to enter the CABINET DE TRAVAIL (**R 130**); the woodwork (1753) is by *Verberckt.* The ornate desk, the Bureau du Roi, ordered by the king in 1760 for this room, was designed by *Oeben* and *Riesener* (1769), with bronzes by *Duplessis, Winant,* and *Hervieux.*

Adjoining is the CABINET DE MME ADÉLAÏDE (**R 132**), with woodwork by *Verberckt,* where, in 1763, Mozart played before Mme Adélaïde (1732-1800), 4th daughter of Louis XV.—The Bibliothèque de Louis XVI (with Louis-XV furniture) (**R 133**) is decorated by *Antoine Rousseau,* with a chimneypiece by *Boizot* and *Gouthière,* and a candelabrum attr. to *Thomire.*

The SALON DES PORCELAINES (**R 134**), with a desk by *Leleu,* was so called because of the annual sale of Sèvres ware arranged for the Court, which occupied also the two following rooms. These, the SALLE DE BILLARD and SALLE DES JEUX (**RR 136-137**), where Louis XIV's collections of paintings and gems were housed, later became part of Mme Adélaïde's suite.

The adjoining staircase ascends to the **Apartments of Mme du Barry** on the second floor. The beautiful woodwork here has been restored and repainted in its original colours.—The attic floor contains the diminutive **Apartments of Mme de Pompadour.**

The CHAMBRE DU ROI (**R 124**), Louis XIV's bedchamber (in which he died in 1715), opens on the r. of the CABINET DU CONSEIL and overlooks the *Cour de Marbre.* Here took place the ceremonious 'lever' and 'coucher' of the king, who used to lunch daily at a little table placed before the middle window. It was from the balcony of this room that Marie-Antoinette and Louis XVI, at La Fayette's suggestion, showed themselves to the mob on 6 Oct. 1789. The decorations of carved wood and the balustrade separating the bed from the rest of the room are original. The sculpture of gilded stucco above is by *N. Coustou.* The chimneypieces date from 1761, with bronzes by *Caffieri;* on one is a bust of Louis XIV, on the other, the Duchesse de Bourgogne, mother of Louis XV, both by *Coysevox.*

The *Chambre du Roi* is followed by the OEIL-DE-BOEUF (**R 123**), named after a small 'bull's eye' window. Here, scandalmongering courtiers used to wait for admission to the king's 'lever'. The decorations are original, including the stucco frieze showing children's games on a gold background, by *van Cleve, Hurtrelle,* and *Flamen.* A curious picture by *Nocret* represents the royal family in mythological costume.

We now return to the *Galerie des Glaces,* and at its l. end enter the SALON DE LA PAIX (**R 114**), the queen's card-room. The ceiling completes *Le Brun's* scheme (see above), depicting France as bringing the benefits of peace to Europe, etc. Over the chimneypiece (left unfinished by *Le Brun*) is a painting by *Lemoyne* (1729), showing Louis XV following his great-grandfather's example as the bringer of peace.

The CHAMBRE DE LA REINE (**R 115**), the first of the *Queen's State Apartments,* has been restored to its pre-Revolution appearance, the chimneypiece having been brought back from the Trianon and the silk hangings copied (at Lyon) from pieces of the original material. Here died Marie-Thérèse (1683) and Marie Leczinska (1768), and here took place the confinements of the queens of France. The jewel cabinet of Marie-Antoinettte (by *Evalde;* 1770) was brought from the Château of St-Cloud. Above the doors are allegorical paintings of the children of Louis XV by *Natoire* and *De Troy.* The grisaille panels of the ceiling are by *Boucher,* and the portrait of Marie-Antoinette is by *Mme Vigée-Lebrun;* the unfinished pastel of the queen is by *Kucharski* (1792).

From the *Chambre de la Reine* we may visit the *Petits Appartements de la Reine (**R 122**), the small and cramped private suite of Marie-Antoinette, preserving its superb decoration. The BOUDOIR or *Petite Méridienne,* with its gilded woodwork and mirror-frames, and the LIBRARY, with imitation bookshelves, were designed by *Mique* (c. 1781). In the SMALL LIBRARY, used by the ladies-in-waiting, is a marriage-chest of Marie-Antoinette. In the SALON DE LA REINE, with elaborate decoration by the brothers *Rousseau,* she received her intimate friends, and her musicians, Gluck and Grétry, and sat to Mme Vigée-Lebrun for her portraits. The last two rooms are the BATH ROOM, and the CHAMBRE DE REPOS or *Salon Jaune.*

R 116, the SALON DES NOBLES (or *Salon de la Reine*), was the queen's presence chamber. The ceiling is by *Michel Corneille* (d. 1708); the busts are of Louis XVI by *Pajou,* and Marie-Antoinette by *Le Comte.*

In the ANTICHAMBRE (**R 117**), where the queen dined in public, are Gobelins tapestries, and busts of Louis XIV by *Coysevox* (1681), Louis XV by *Gois,* and Louis XVI by *Houdon.*

The SALLE DES GARDES DE LA REINE (**R 118**), with marble decoration of the period of Louis XIV, retains its ceiling by *Noël Coypel, the Elder.* It was here, on 6 Oct. 1789, that the revolutionary mob burst in, and three of the Swiss Guards died in the queen's defence.

To the l. is the landing of the ESCALIER DE MARBRE or *de la Reine,* built by *Le Vau* and *Mansart,* with an interesting perspective painting in the Italian style. Across the landing is a LOGGIA (**R 119**) overlooking the *Cour de Marbre,* in which a door on the r. admits to the *Apartments of Mme de Maintenon* (see below), while on the l. open the SALLE DES GARDES DU ROI (**R 120**) and the ANTICHAMBRE DU ROI (**R 121**), where Louis XIV dined in private on the rare occasions when he did so.

Hence it is convenient to visit **R 140,** the SALLE DU SACRE (previously the *Grande Salle des Gardes*), recently restored since its mutilation by Louis-Philippe. The ceiling-painting is by *Callet;* the dessus de portes by *Gérard;* and the walls are adorned by huge paintings depicting Napoleon presenting eagles in the Champ-de-Mars (1804), and his coronation at Notre-Dame, both by *David;* and *Gros,* Murat at the battle of Aboukir (1799).

In the adjoining GRAND CABINET (**R 143**), Racine's 'Esther' was played before the king, and in 1702 his 'Athalie' was presented by the princes and princesses.—**R 144** leads to the SALLE DE 1792 (**R 146**), now containing military portraits, and originally the 'Salon des Marchands', to which vendors of goods were admitted for the convenience of the inmates of the palace.—The ESCALIER DES PRINCES (**R 147**), by *Mansart,* gave access to the S. wing, once reserved for the princes of the blood.

The series of rooms beyond this point are of little interest. The GALERIE DES BATAILLES, nearly 400 ft long, constructed under Louis-Philippe by throwing into one most of the rooms on the first floor, displays a sad selection of huge canvases representing French military achievements—perhaps the only one of note being The Battle of Taillebourg, by *Delacroix*—indeed Thackeray considered them among "the worst pictures that eye ever looked on".

Returning to **R 119,** we may visit (r.) the **Apartments of Mme de Maintenon (RR 141-142;** shown on request), furnished by Louis XIV in 1682 for Mme de Maintenon, who became his second wife probably the following year. The ANTICHAMBRE, and BEDCHAMBER (where most of the business of State was transacted), now accommodate a fine collection of 16C portraits by *Corneille de Lyon* and other artists of the School of Clouet.

The adjoining ESCALIER DE STUC (built under Louis-Philippe) ascends to the SECOND FLOOR. Here, in the **Attique de Chimay** (r.) and **Attique du Midi,** are displayed an outstanding *Collection of Historical Paintings illustrating the early Napoleonic period. Unfortunately, the galleries are not always open, and it is as well to check beforehand.

We first enter **R 174,** with battle scenes by *Bacler d'Albe*, Arcole, and Lodi, by *Lejeune;* and other views by war-artists of the period including *Lecomte, Morel, Taunay, Mulard, Berthon,* and *Boguet.* Note also *Gros,* Napoleon at Arcole, and the impressive collection of scenes by *Bagetti* (in display cases). In the small room to the r. are sketches by *Vernet* and others.—To the l. is **R 176,** dominated by *Lejeune*, Battle of the Pyramides (among other scenes of the Egyptian Campaign).— **R 177:** *Lejeune*, Battle of Marengo; *Mongin*, Passage of the army through the defile of Albaredo; and *David*, Napoleon crossing the Alps.

R 178: *Hue*, Napoleon visiting the camp at Boulogne.—**R 179:** *Desoria*, Portrait of Letourneur, member of the Directoire; *Gérard*, Joachim Murat; and miniatures by *Gauffier*.—**R 180:** *Gilbert*, Combat between 'La Canonnière' and 'The Tremendous' (1806); *Hoppner*, copied by *Healy*, Lord Nelson, and Lord St Vincent; *Lawrence*, copied by *Healy*, William Pitt.—**R 181,** the first of a series devoted to *Small portraits by *François Gérard*.

We cross to **R 171,** dominated by *Gérard*, Napoleon as Emperor of the French, and 'Madame Mère'; *Lethière*, Joséphine; *Vigée-Lebrun*, Marie-Annunciade-Caroline Bonaparte, among other members of the Imperial family.—**R 170:** *Kinson*, Bernadotte; *Meynier*, Ney; and *Lejeune*, Napoleon visiting the bivouacs before Austerlitz.—**R 169:** *Lefèvre*, Napoleon I, and Augereau.

R 168 (Life in Paris): *Lefèvre*, Baron Denon; *Girodet*, Chateaubriand; *David*, Pope Pius VII.—**R 167:** *Roehn*, Napoleon at Wagram (night scene).—**R 166:** *van Bree*, Launching of 'Le Friedland'; *Franque*, Marie-Louise and the King of Rome.

R 165 (Peninsular War): *Lejeune*, Passing the Somosierra; Assault on the monastery of S. Engracia, Zaragoza; and The Battle of Chiclana (Barrosa); *Taunay*, Crossing the Guadarrama; *Heim*, Defence of the castle at Burgos. The second half of this gallery is devoted to the Russian Campaign.

Returning to **R 119,** we descend to the GROUND FLOOR, and visit the **Salles du Dix-huitième Siècle.** These, looking out on the gardens, were occupied at various times by the Regent Orléans, and the sons and daughters of Louis XV, and are also known as the Appartements du Dauphin et de la Dauphine, et de Mesdames. They have been repeatedly altered, and most of the original decorations were swept away by Louis-Philippe. They contain an admirable collection of 18C portraits, but some rooms may be closed for restoration.

R 42: *Rigaud*, Louis XV; *Santerre*, The Regent Orléans.—**R 43:** *J.-B. Van Loo* and *Parrocel*, Louis XV on horseback.—Note the organ in **R 44.**—**R 45:** Louis XVI, Louis XVIII, and Charles X were born in this room, which was also the bedroom of Marie-Antoinette on her arrival in France; *Nattier*, Mme de Pompadour; the Marquis de Marigny, her brother, by *De Troy;* and Lenormant de Tourneheim (her mother's protector, and Marigny's predecessor as director of the royal buildings), by *Tocqué.*—**R 46:** *Nattier*, Marie-Josèphe de Saxe (mother of Louis XVI).—**R 47** has retained some of its Louis-XV decoration.—**R 48** (GRAND CABINET DU DAUPHIN): *Nattier*, Portraits of the daughters of Louis XV; the balcony of wrought and gilded iron commands a splendid view of the gardens.

R 49 was the Regent's study, where he died in 1723, and was later the bedroom of the Dauphin Louis, son of Louis XV. It preserves decorative details, including woodwork by *Verberckt*, and a red marble chimneypiece with figures by *Caffieri;* also *Nattier*, Infanta Luisa Isabel (1759), and *N. Coustou*, bust of Marie Leczinska.—**R 50** retains traces of Louis-XIV decorations.

The GALERIE BASSE (**R 51**), below the *Galerie des Glaces*, has been completely altered since the reign of Louis XIV, when Molière gave several of his plays in it, including the first performance of 'Tartuffe' (1664). It contains a series of paintings, by *Martin* and *Lenfant*, of battles; *Van Loo*, Louis XV; *Nattier*, Mme Anne-Henriette, 2nd daughter of Louis XV, playing the viola da gamba.

R 52, once part of a suite of bathrooms, and later occupied by Mme de Montespan, Mme de Pompadour, and the daughters of Louis XV, contains *Nattier*, Mme Adélaïde as Diana, and Mme Henriette as Flora; and gouache drawings by *van Blarenberghe* of the campaigns of 1744-48 in Flanders.—**R 53:** *Nattier*, the Duc de Bourgogne as an infant, Marie Leczinska (1748), and Isabel, daughter of the Infanta Luisa Isabel (Louise-Élisabeth, eldest daughter of Louis XV).—**R 54:** *Roslin*, The Dauphin, son of Louis XV.—**R 55:** *L.-M. Van Loo*, Choiseul; *Rigaud*, Chancellor Maupeou, Comte d'Argenson; *Carle Van Loo*, Soufflot; *Drouais*, Louis XV.—In **RR 56-59** a portrait of Louis XVI standing, by *Duplessis*, and two views of Versailles by *Hubert Robert*, are noteworthy. The 'perspective' decoration of **R 59** has been restored; note also the clock.

We turn r., through **R 26,** into **R 27,** that of 'American Independence', with portraits of Washington, *after C. W. Peale;* van Blarenberghe, Capture and siege of Yorktown; *G. P. A. Healy*, Portraits of Americans painted for Louis-Philippe.—**R 28:** *Vigée-Lebrun*, Marie-Antoinette; *Duplessis*, Louis XVI.—**R 29:** *Vigée-Lebrun*, The Dauphin Louis-Joseph and Madame Royale as children.—**R 30:** *Duplessis*, Portraits of M. and Mme Necker; *Houdon*, bust of La Fayette.—We pass through **R 32** into **R 33,** with scenes from the Revolution, including *David*, Death of Marat; two cartoons; and a bust of the Dauphin (Louis XVII) as a child, by *Deseine* (1790).—**RR 34-35** are devoted to the Convention and the Directory.

The rooms on the ground floor of the S. wing (**RR 67-80**) are of only slight interest. They contain some paintings by *Gros,* and *H.* and *C. Vernet,* among others, and furnishings, made in the 1950s, reproducing original Napoleonic designs.

The **Gardens of Versailles* are best approached by a passage just W. of the main visitors' entrance.

André Le Nôtre (1613-1708), the celebrated landscape-gardener (to whom London owes Greenwich Park, and Rome the Quirinal and Vatican gardens), designed the gardens for Louis XIV, although the fountains and hydraulic machinery were the work of *J. H.-Mansart* and the engineer *François Francini,* while the sculptural decoration was executed under the supervision of *Le Brun* and *Mignard.*

The gardens were first laid out in 1661-68. The preliminary work of levelling and draining the site was prodigious, and thousands of trees were brought here from all parts. Inspired by Italian originals which were interpreted with an amplitude and harmony hitherto unknown, Versailles is the masterpiece of French gardening. In their general lines and their sculptural decoration, with the characteristic stressing of the 'classical' note, the gardens remain as they were laid out, but it was not until the 18C that the planting of trees was developed to its present extent, so that what we now see is basically the gardens of Louis XV and Louis XVI.

They are essentially formal, with their carefully planned vistas and straight tree-lined walks, their artificial lakes and ponds, arranged with geometrical precision, their groves and clumps of trees, lawns, and terraces, all interspersed with innumerable statues and vases of marble and bronze, and embellished with fountains of infinite variety.

Admission. The gardens and park are normally open free all day to pedestrians (no picnics); cars are admitted to the park on payment.

The *Fountains* play on the first and third Sun. of the months May-Sept. inclusive, at 16.30; the *Fêtes de Nuit,* at the Bassin de Neptune, take place at dates varying annually, which should be checked in advance; *Son et Lumière* also takes place on 27 July and 7 Sept.

The most direct approach to the **Grand Trianon** for the pedestrian is to follow the *Allée d'Eau* (see below), leading N. from the terrace behind the central block of the palace to the *Grille de Neptune,* thence bearing N.W. along the Av. de Trianon, approx. 20 mins. brisk walk. But by taking this route, one sees little of the Gardens of Versailles, which themselves merit exploration.

The central axis of the main TERRACE commands splendid *Views, and the terrace itself is adorned with bronze statues after the antique, and with marble vases of War, by *Coysevox,* and Peace, by *Tuby.* Beyond the PARTERRES D'EAU, two large ornamental pools decorated with bronzes (1690), are the *Marches de Latone,* monumental flights of steps, from which one may obtain an impressive view of the palace, and, in the opposite direction, a famous vista of the gardens. Flanking these steps are the *Fontaines de Diane* (r.) and *du Point-du-Jour* (Dawn). By the former are statues of Air, by *Le Hongre,* and Diana the Huntress, by *Desjardins.*

On the r. of the Terrace extend the PARTERRES DU NORD, where the original design of Le Nôtre has been largely respected. Just beyond is the *Fontaine de la Pyramide* (in lead), by *Girardon,* and among the sculptures in the cross-walk (l.) is Winter, also by *Girardon.*—The ALLÉE D'EAU, designed by *Perrault* and *Le Brun* (1676-88), with its groups of children, leads directly to the BASSIN DE NEPTUNE (1740), the largest fountain-basin in the gardens, whence we may return by the ALLÉE DES

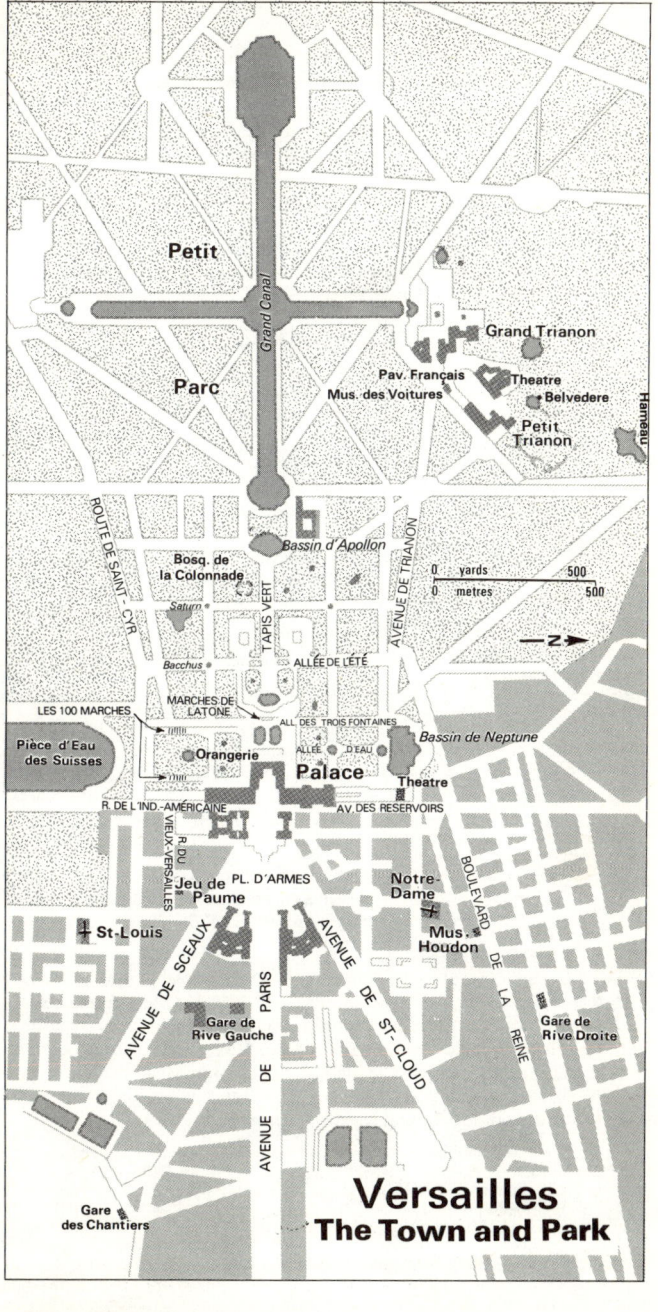

Petit

Grand Canal

Parc

Grand Trianon

Pav. Français
Mus. des Voitures

Theatre

Belvedere

Petit
Trianon

Hameau

ROUTE DE SAINT-CYR

Bosq. de
la Colonnade

Bassin d'Apollon

Saturn

TAPIS VERT

Bacchus

ALLÉE DE L'ÉTÉ

AVENUE DE TRIANON

0   yards   500
0   metres   500

→N→

LES 100 MARCHES

MARCHES DE
LATONE

ALL. DES TROIS FONTAINES

Pièce d'Eau
des Suisses

Orangerie

ALLÉE   D'EAU

Bassin de Neptune

Palace

R. DE L'IND.-AMÉRICAINE

Theatre

AV. DES RESERVOIRS

R. DU
VIEUX-VERSAILLES

Jeu de
Paume

PL. D'ARMES

Notre-
Dame

BOULEVARD
DE
LA
REINE

St-Louis

Mus. s
Houdon

AVENUE DE SCEAUX

AVENUE
DE
PARIS

AVENUE
DE
ST-CLOUD

Gare de
Rive Gauche

Gare de
Rive Droite

AVENUE
DE

Gare
des Chantiers

Versailles
The Town and Park

TROIS FONTAINES (parallel to the ALLÉE D'EAU), to reach the BAINS D'APOLLON (r.), a grove laid out by *Hubert Robert* under Louis XVI, in a 'romantic' spirit very different from the formal symmetry of Le Nôtre.

To the W., the ALLÉE DE L'ÉTÉ leads to the so-called TAPIS VERT (or *Allée Royale*), a lawn 360 yds long and 40 wide, lined with marble vases and statues, many of them copies from the antique. Note (on the l.) Venus, by *Le Gros,* and Achilles at Scyros, by *Vigier*. Towards its far end (r.) is the entrance to the BOSQUET DES DÔMES, with several statues, including Acis and Galatea, by *Tuby*.—Almost opposite, on the far side of the *Tapis Vert,* in the BOSQUET DE LA COLONNADE, is a *Circle* of marble arches by *Mansart* (1685-88), in the centre of which is the Rape of Proserpine, by *Girardon*.

At the end of the *Tapis Vert* lies the BASSIN D'APOLLON, in the centre of which is the impressive group of Apollo's Chariot, by *Tuby*. To the r. is the *Petite Venise,* where Louis XIV's Venetian gondoliers were housed. Beyond the *Bassin d'Apollon,* and separated from the gardens by railings, is the PETIT PARC, divided by the GRAND CANAL, just over one mile long, and 60 yds wide, the scene of Louis XIV's boating parties. Almost at its centre point it is crossed by a transverse arm (c. 1,200 yds), extending from the *Grand Trianon,* to the N., to the few remaining buildings of the former royal *Menagerie*.

To regain the palace, we may traverse the 'SALLE DES MARRONNIERS' (so-called), a chestnut grove behind the *Colonnade,* and passing the BASSIN DE SATURNE and BASSIN DE BACCHUS, with sculptures by *Girardon* and *Marsy,* reach the BOSQUET DE LA REINE.

This glade was notorious as the scene of the court scandal known as the 'Affair of the Necklace' (1784-85), in which the Card. de Rohan (seeking the favour of Marie-Antoinette by means of a costly gift) was duped by the Comtesse de la Motte.

The PARTERRES DU MIDI lead hence to the palace. To the r., two flights of steps, known as the *Cent Marches,* descend alongside the *Orangerie,* by *Mansart*.—To the S., beyond the St-Cyr road, is the PIÈCE D'EAU DES SUISSES (800 yds long, by 150 wide), excavated in 1678-82 by the Swiss Guards, many of whom are said to have died of malaria during the operation.

The **Trianons** are normally open daily (except Tues.), visitors being conducted round in small groups, but at present (1976) the *Petit Trianon* is closed for extensive renovation. The *Musée des Voitures* is open, however (see below).

The ***Grand Trianon,** a miniature palace designed by *J. H.-Mansart* and *Robert de Cotte,* was built for Louis XIV in 1687 as a retreat from the formality of court life, yet retaining sumptuous marble decorations comparable with those of Versailles itself. It replaced a flimsy earlier building or Summer-house for picnics, tiled within with blue and white Delftware, and known as the 'Porcelain Trianon', which had been erected on the site of the village of *Trianon*.

The palace was occupied for a time by Mme de Maintenon. It was redecorated for Napoleon, who frequently stayed there, and the Empire furniture which he installed still remains. In 1818 the Duke of Wellington dined here with Louis XVIII. Louis-Philippe did his best to spoil the interior decoration in 1837. A restoration of both *Trianons* was carried out in 1925-27, and of the *Grand Trianon* (again) in 1963-66.

While a special note of admiration must be recorded for the accurate work of reproduction of fabrics of the period, undertaken during the 1960s, it must be admitted that the sheets of plastic protecting them detract from the splendid effect intended. Somehow it is all too new, and however historically irreproachable the decoration may be, a little 'faded glory' would perhaps have been more becoming.

On reaching the courtyard, with the open colonnade or Péristyle ahead, we turn l. to the visitors' entrance. From the entrance Vestibules (**RR 1-2**) we reach **R 3,** with views of Versailles and Chambord by *Allegrain* and *P.-D. Martin* respectively, and a console table by *Jacob-Desmalter.*—A corridor leads to a small BOUDOIR (**R 8**), containing a gondola-shaped sofa, to the r. of which we enter the splendidly mirrored SALON DES GLACES (**R 7**), furnished with a handsome set of white and gilt chairs covered with Beauvais tapestry.—**R 6,** the SALON DES COLONNES, with Napoleon's bed (1809) from the Tuileries, later broadened and mutilated by Louis-Philippe. Passing through **RR 5** and **4,** we cross the open Péristyle of Languedoc marble pillars to the *Right Wing,* first entering the circular DRAWING-ROOM (**R 9**), with paintings of American flowers and fruit, by *Desportes.*—**R 10** (SALON DE MUSIQUE): note the bronze table with Vosges granite top, two consoles by *Jacob-Desmalter,* and the Beauvais tapestry-covered set of chairs.—We are next conducted through the GRAND SALON and MALACHITE ROOM (**R 12**), the latter with a malachite bowl given to Alexander I of Russia after the Treaty of Tilsit, in 1807.—From the adjoining SALON FRAIS, with a painting of the view E. from Versailles by *J.-B. Martin,* we turn l. into the GRANDE GALERIE, decorated by *Mansart,* with good views S. over the terrace. It contains 24 allegorical views, almost all similarly framed, of the Gardens of Versailles and Trianon, twenty-one by *Jean Cotelle* (1645-1708), two by *Allegrain,* and one by *J.-B. Martin.* The suite of rooms beyond, known as the *Trianon-sous-Bois,* is not open to the public.

Returning through the *Salon Frais,* we reach the SALON DES SOURCES, with views of Versailles by *P.-D. Martin* (1663-1742) and *Charles Chastelain* (1672-1740) and turn r. through a further series of tastefully furnished rooms, the APARTMENTS OF MME DE MAINTENON, subsequently occupied by Stanislas Leczinski, former king of Poland (1741), Mme de Pompadour, and Napoleon and Marie-Louise.—The remaining rooms (**RR 23-24**) were installed on the site of a theatre which stood here until 1703, and from 1845 they formed a suite of rooms for Louis-Philippe's daughter, Louise-Marie, and her husband, Leopold I of Belgium.

The gardens were laid out by *Mansart* and *Le Nôtre.* To the W. is the *Buffet* (the main fountain), also designed by *Mansart,* with bas-reliefs and figures of Neptune and Amphitrite. A bridge leads from the JARDIN DU ROI, behind the palace, to the gardens of the *Petit Trianon.*

Between the *Grand* and *Petit Trianons* is the **Musée des Voitures,** containing among others the carriage used at the marriage of Napoleon and Marie-Louise (1810), the state coach used at the coronation of Charles X (1824), and the marriage of Napoleon III with the Empress Eugénie (1853); also *berlins* and *calèches* of the 18C.

To the E. is the ***Petit Trianon** (1751-68) on two floors, unlike the Grand Trianon, built by *Gabriel* for Louis XV as a country retreat for himself and Mme de Pompadour, who did not survive its completion. Mme du Barry then occupied it; and it was a favourite residence of Marie-Antoinette. The palace was subsequently occupied by Pauline Borghese, Napoleon's sister.

To the l. of the courtyard is a derelict *Chapel* (not shown). The interior of the palace, at present undergoing extensive restoration, contains an elegant suite of rooms on the first floor, many of them retaining their original decoration, including chimneypieces by *Guibert* in the DINING ROOM and GRAND SALON, etc. In the former, traces of the trap-door, through which, in Louis XV's reign, the tables used to appear ready-laid, are still visible in the floor.

The GARDENS of the *Petit Trianon* were originally a menagerie and botanical garden laid out by *Jussieu* for Louis XV, but were altered for Marie-Antoinette in the English style (1774-86). Here, so Thicknesse was told, the king "had a little garden . . . where he often picks his own salad, makes his own soup, and enjoys the conversation of a few select friends, without the plague, impertinence, and above all, the parade that generally attends royalty".

To the W. of the main building is the *Pavillon Français*, built in 1751 by *Gabriel*, with a good view hence of the façade of the palace. To the N. is the *Theatre* (1780), where Marie-Antoinette made her début in court theatricals, beyond which is the octagonal *Belvedere* (by *Mique*), with charming interior decoration, overlooking a small lake. In a grotto here, the queen was resting when, on 5 Oct. 1789, she was told the news that a revolting mob had broken into Versailles.

Some few minutes walk to the N.E., on the far side of a larger lake, is the **Hameau,** a sort of theatrical village built by Marie-Antoinette to gratify her taste for 'nature', as popularized by Rousseau, although, apart from churning butter, the queen left the work of the farm to real, not royal, peasants. It comprises a mill, the *Maison de la Reine* (with a dining-room, billiard-room, and card-room, etc., with a kitchen or 'Réchauffoir' behind), and the 'Boudoir' on the r.; a *Colombier*, with pigeon-cote and chicken-run; the *Dairy;* the 'Tour de Marlborough'; and farm-buildings.

Hence we may return past the *Temple d'Amour*, with its Corinthian colonnade and Mouchy's copy (1780) of *Bouchardon*'s statue of Love, to the courtyard of the *Petit Trianon*, and make our exit.

22   PARIS TO MALMAISON AND ST-GERMAIN-EN-LAYE

Malmaison may be approached either by road (N13; 7.5 km.) from the *Pont de Neuilly*, or on the R.E.R. from *Auber* viâ *Étoile* to *La Défense*, there taking the 158 bus to within a few minutes walk of the château.

The **Château of Malmaison,* built in 1622 on the site of a leper colony dependent on the Abbey of Saint-Denis, was the home of Joséphine Bonaparte after 1798, and was enlarged in 1800. It now contains collections of considerable historical interest, as does its annexe, the *Musée du Château de Bois-Préau* (see below; adm. every day except Tuesday, 10.00-12.00, and 13.30-17.00).

At the height of her power, the empress held a literary and artistic salon at Malmaison, and after her divorce in 1809 she retired here and devoted herself to gardening, dying only five years later of a chill caught while doing the honours of the grounds to the allied sovereigns. Napoleon spent five days here in 1815, between Waterloo and his departure for St Helena. Malmaison was later bought by María Cristina of Spain, and by Napoleon III in 1861. Despoiled of most of its contents, it was sold in 1896 to the philanthropist Daniel Osiris, who refurnished it and in 1906 presented the château to the State as a Napoleonic Museum. Further appropriate acquisitions have been made since, and the rooms redecorated.

GROUND FLOOR. From the entrance vestibule in Antique style, displaying busts of the Imperial family, we turn r. into the BILLIARD ROOM, containing Napoleon's throne from Fontainebleau, his portrait in Gobelins tapestry, and a Savonnerie carpet with his insignia. The SALON DORÉ, with a chimneypiece given to Napoleon by Pope Pius VII (its decoration torn off by the Germans occupying Malmaison in 1871), contains *Girodet's* painting of Ossian welcoming the dead to Valhalla, a portrait of Joséphine by *Gérard,* and her embroidery frame, etc. The adjacent MUSIC ROOM, restored in 1975 to its original appearance, displays instruments which may have belonged to Joséphine, and her marble bust by *Chinard.*

Returning through these rooms, we enter the DINING ROOM, with its original frescoes of Pompeian dancers by *Lafitte,* restored, and the silver-gilt 'surtout' of table decorations presented by the city of Paris to the emperor on the occasion of his coronation. The COUNCIL CHAMBER, shaped like a tent, contains a yew-wood desk (gift of the city of Bordeaux), and a clock from the Tuileries. The adjoining LIBRARY, retaining its original decoration by *Percier* and *Fontaine,* accommodates a number of books from Napoleon's personal collection, which, previously widely dispersed, have been purchased and reassembled on their original shelves. Here also are Napoleon's bureau and armchair, and a clock made in 1791 for Louis XVI by *Janvier,* and purchased by Napoleon.

Stairs ascend to the FIRST FLOOR, with, on the landing, a Gobelins tapestry, after *Gérard,* of Joséphine at Malmaison.—SALON DE L'EMPEREUR, a reconstruction of Napoleon's bedroom at the Tuileries, with the original furniture and hangings, and a drawing by *Isabey* of Napoleon as First Consul at Malmaison. The three following rooms contain sumptuous services of Sèvres ware; the 'Table d'Austerlitz' decorated with portraits of Napoleon and his marshals; the silver-gilt ewer and basin used at his coronation, etc.—JOSÉPHINE'S APARTMENTS: Antechamber, with water-colours of Malmaison by *Garnerey,* of topographical interest; portraits of the empress, and personal souvenirs. In her BEDROOM is the bed, designed by *Jacob-Desmalter,* in which she died; other contemporary furniture, and a fine Sèvres clock. The silk-lined SALLE DES ATOURS contains a work-table (from *St-Cloud*), etc.; the BOUDOIR is likewise hung with silk; and in the BATHROOM are Joséphine's dressing-table and dressing-case by *Rémond.*

On the SECOND FLOOR is the SALLE DE STE-HÉLÈNE, hung with the brocade that covered the catafalque in which the emperor's remains were transported to his tomb. It contains the camp bed on which Napoleon died in 1821, his death-mask moulded by Antommarchi (his Corsican doctor), clothing, MSS., and paintings. Other rooms are devoted to souvenirs of Queen Hortense (mother of Napoleon III) and Eugène de Beauharnais, Joséphine's children by her first marriage, etc.

The PARK, of which but 15 acres remain of 500, contains a rose garden planted with the varieties of rose that were grown by Joséphine. The *Coach House,* to the r. of the entrance lodge, contains the 'Opal', the state carriage in which Joséphine drove to Malmaison after her divorce, a gala coach (temp. Louis XIV) used by Napoleon; his 'dormeuse' used at Waterloo, and Blücher's landau en berline. Behind is the *Pavillon Osiris,* with collections of caricatures, medallions, and snuffboxes propagating the Napoleonic legend, and a portrait of Tsar Alexander I, by *Gérard.* Beyond the other side of the entrance drive is a *Summer-House* used as a study by Napoleon when First Consul.

A few minutes' walk to the E. will take one to the **Musée du Château de Bois-Préau,** in the Av. de l'Impératrice Joséphine, admirably displayed in a building bought by Joséphine in 1810, and in 1926 bequeathed to the State by Edward Tuck, its American owner (see also Petit-Palais, p. 161).

To the r. of the entrance is a room containing portraits by *Gérard* of 'Madame Mère'; Joséphine in her coronation robes; Joseph Bonaparte as King of Spain, and his wife; and Napoleon's sister, Elisa.—To the l. of the entrance we pass through a series of rooms containing such souvenirs as a 'surtout' or epergne given to the emperor by Carlos IV of Spain; a portrait of the King of Rome by *Georges Rouget;* the King of Rome's cradle by *Jacob-Desmalter,* and other mementoes; and Marie-Louise, by *Gérard.*—On ascending the stairs, turn r. past a collection of sabres, Napoleon's grey coat and hat, flask, and nécessaire, his mantle (note bees), and Hortense's court dress. Other rooms display Murat's splendidly ornate bed, and sabre-legged tabourets or stools, and *Gérard*'s portrait of Murat; Napoleon's hat and coat (and chairs) from St Helena; *Marchand*'s sketch of the dead emperor; and a book given to Napoleon by Lord Holland.

In the church of *Rueil,* nearby, is the tomb of the Empress Joséphine, erected in 1825 by her children, Eugène and Hortense de Beauharnais. The tomb of Queen Hortense, in the chapel opposite, was erected by her son, Napoleon III, in 1858, who also donated the 15C Florentine organ-case, by *Baccio d'Agnolo.*

The N13 skirts the S. bank of the Seine, passing at *Bougival,* the house where Bizet died (1875), to *St-Germain-en-Laye.*

St-Germain-en-Laye (37,400 inhab.; *Hotels*) may be reached with ease from central Paris by the R.E.R. from Auber or Étoile. By road, it may be approached from the *Pont de Neuilly* by the N13 (taking in en route the *Château of Malmaison,* see above), or by the N190 branching r. off the latter, which passes through the garden suburb of *Le Vésinet* (18,000 inhab.). The TERRASSE, to the N.E. of the Castle, commands a splendid *View of Paris (and particularly of *La Défense*): *Notre-Dame* itself is approx. 21 km. to the E. James II once compared the view to that from the Terrace at Richmond.

Claude Debussy (1862-1918) was born at St-Germain, where his statue, by *Maillol,* may be seen in the PL. M.-BERTEAUX, just S. of the castle. Thicknesse rented a house here in 1766; Henry Swinburne lived 5 km. N. at *Les Mesnils* in 1786, and again in 1796.

Its strategically placed royal château, overlooking a bend of the Seine, was built first in the 12C by Louis VI, and in 1539-48 completely rebuilt by François I, except for the keep. The so-called *Château-Neuf,* below the original castle, constructed for Henri II and Henri IV, was demolished in 1776, except for the *Pavillon Henri-IV* and the *Pavillon Sully,* at the foot of the steep slope E. of the town, in the suburb of *Le Pecq.*

It was in this 'new' castle that Louis XIV was born in 1638, five years before the death of his father in the same building; and it remained one of the principal seats of the French Court until the completion of Versailles in 1682. Meanwhile, the older château afforded refuge to the widowed Queen Henrietta Maria of England; after 1688 it was also the residence—and Court—of James II in exile, who died there in 1701, as did his wife, Mary of Modena, in 1718. His tomb, erected by George IV in the church opposite the castle, contains only his heart.

In 1962, a century after the setting-up of an earlier museum in the château, the **Musée des Antiquités Nationales** was installed here, and has more recently been tastefully reorganized to display its impressive collections in chronological order, which are well labelled and described. Crossing the courtyard, we ascend stairs and turn r. to reach **R 1,** devoted to *Neolithic* finds.—**R 2:** *Bronze Age,* including (*Case 3*) swords and sword moulds, and (*Case 13*) torques, bracelets, and other gold objects.—**R 3:** *Hallstatt* period (1st Iron Age; 800-450 B.C.).—**R 4** (across landing): *La Tène* culture (450-52 B.C.), with a good collection of bronze vessels and vases—note that in *Case 18*—and jewellery.—**R 6:** reconstituted chariot-burial from La Gorge-Meillet.—**R 9,** with a model of the important fortified site of Alesia.

The series of rooms on the floor above concentrate on *Roman and Merovingian Gaul.* **R 10** contains Celtic divinities; **R 11,** divinities of the Graeco-Roman world, including some fine figures of Mercury, ex-votos and their moulds; note the Venus in *Case 5.* Here is also an exemplary display of silver utensils, etc., also glassware, bronze lamps, scales, handles, keys, etc., and sigillate pottery.—Across the landing are rooms displaying small sculptured objects—birds, boars, horses, and human figures: note the charming couple in bed, with a dog at their feet, from Bordeaux (*Case 6*); a collection of jewellery, buckles, and fibulas; games, etc.—**R 16** contains a large mosaic pavement (3C A.D.) from St-Romain-en-Gal (Rhône), showing a rustic calendar of the seasons, while various agricultural implements, etc., are also shown here.—Articles of jewellery, plaques, glassware, and buckles, etc., of the *Merovingian* period are displayed in the adjoining room. Another section has been opened recently, devoted to the *Paleolithic* period.

———————

The adjacent *Chapel* of 1230-38, just predating the *Sainte Chapelle* in Paris, also by *Pierre de Montreuil,* has been sadly disfigured over the years, but nevertheless is of considerable architectural interest. It contains copies of tombs from the Aliscamp at Arles. Here were baptized François I, Claude de France (1499-1524), daughter of Louis XII and first wife of François I, and Louis XIV.

To the N. of the castle is the PARTERRE, originally a park laid out by *Le Nôtre,* beyond which is a JARDIN ANGLAIS. At its S.E. corner is the Pavillon Henri-IV (see above), since 1836 a much-frequented hotel: Dumas wrote 'The Three Musketeers' and 'Monte Cristo' here; and Thiers died here in 1877.

To the N.E. extends the TERRACE OF ST-GERMAIN (see above). At the far end is the *Grille Royale,* the entrance to the *Fôret de St-Germain,* the former royal hunting preserve, once over 9,000 acres in extent, and still retaining a number of pleasant drives and walks.

Some 4 km. further N. is **Maisons-Laffitte** (23,500 inhab.), birthplace of Jean Cocteau (1889-1963). Its celebrated *Château, the masterpiece of *François Mansart* (1642-51), is notable for its interior decoration and collection of 17-19C furniture (adm. Wed. and Sat. at 15.30; Sun., 15.00 and 16.30: Oct.-May, Sun. only at 15.30. Guided tour).

The Château was bought in 1818 and the park cut up into building-lots by Jacques Laffitte, a speculator and banker who had already profited in the Napoleonic Wars. Voltaire's bed caught fire when he was staying there; later visitors were La Fayette and Benjamin Constant, among others.

Maisons-Laffitte also possesses important training-stables and a racecourse.

At *Chambourcy*, 4 km. W. of *St-Germain,* are the tombs of the Chevalier d'Orsay and his wife, Marguerite Power, Countess of Blessington (1789-1849). The white cheese of Chambourcy has been famous since the 17C.

Some 4 km. S. of *St-Germain,* to the W. of the N148A, stood the royal château of *Marly* (its name preserved in the town of **Marly-le-Roi**), built in 1679-86 by *J. Hardouin-Mansart* for Louis XIV, and a favourite retreat from Versailles: indeed, regular visits to Marly were essential, to allow Versailles to be aired and cleaned.

The château was destroyed at the Revolution, and although vestiges of the park remain, with an impressive fountain, the famous hydraulic *Machine de Marly,* originally constructed to raise water from the Seine to the Marly aqueduct, which in turn carried it to Versailles, was dismantled in 1967. New machinery had been installed in 1855-59, taking its water from underground sources, recently replaced by electric pumps.—The church of *Marly-le-Roi* was also built by *J. H.-Mansart* (1689), and contains some works originally in Versailles.

23   PARIS TO ST-DENIS

St-Denis (96,000 inhab.) is best approached by car, by turning off the A1 autoroute c. 3 km. N. of the *Porte de la Chapelle;* or alternatively, by taking the MÉTRO recently extended to its terminus at *St-Denis-Basilique.*

The **Basilica of St-Denis** stands in the centre of one of the most unattractive and derelict of the northern suburbs of Paris, beyond the site of the celebrated 'Foire du Lendit' which was held here from Dagobert's time until 1552. It was founded on the probable site of *Catolacus,* where the missionary apostle of Lutetia was almost certainly buried.

The basilica itself is a fine example of Gothic architecture, but is overshadowed in interest by the *Tombs it contains. Unfortunately, these may not be studied in detail in the normal course of the rapid conducted visit (commencing every ½ hour), for chains obstruct their closer inspection, and the tedious monologue of the attendant guide is equally disconcerting. Application should be made in advance to the *Administration des Beaux-Arts,* 3 Rue de Valois, for permission to view the monuments at leisure.

History. The abbey of St-Denis was founded c. 475, perhaps at the instance of St Geneviève, and rebuilt in 630-38 by Dagobert, who also founded a monastery for Benedictines. The first substantial church on the site was built by Abbot Fulrad in 750-75, and here in 754 Pope Stephen III consecrated Pepin le Bref and his wife and sons, thus establishing them securely on the throne. This church was itself replaced by another built by Abbot Suger, of which the narthex (W. porch) and apse (c. 1136-44) survive, ranking among the most important examples of the earliest Gothic architecture. Recent excavations in the crypt, also of this period, and retaining the Romanesque arch, have brought to light Gallo-Roman Christian tombs, and remains of the earlier churches. The rest of the building dates from 1231-81, following the designs of *Pierre de Montreuil* (d. 1267), while c. 1375 the chapels on the N. side of the nave were added.

Most of the effigies of earlier kings were made during the reign of Louis XI (St Louis; d. 1270), when St-Denis became recognized as a royal mausoleum; others were brought here during the Revolution. With the exception of Philippe I, Louis XI, Louis-Philippe, and Charles X, all the French kings since Hugues Capet are buried here. In 1422 the body of Henry V lay in state here on its way from Vincennes to Westminster, and seven years later Joan of Arc dedicated her armour here. In 1567 Condé's Huguenots captured the place, but he prevented them from despoiling the basilica: later in the year he was defeated in the plain to the S. by Anne de Montmorency, who was himself mortally wounded. Henri IV abjured Protestantism here in 1593.

After injudicious alterations in the 18C, the abbey was suppressed at the Revolution, the church unroofed, its tombs rifled and their contents dispersed, but the best of the monuments were saved from destruction by Alexandre Lenoir, who preserved them in his *Musée des Petits-Augustins* (École des Beaux-Arts), whence they were later returned, and drastically restored. Restoration of the fabric of the basilica was taken in hand in 1813, but it was so incompetently carried out that the stability of the N. tower was endangered, and in 1847 it had to be taken down. A subsequent 'restoration' by Viollet-le-Duc and Darcy went some way to repair the harm; but the explosion of a nearby bomb-dump in 1915 caused further damage. It is at present undergoing cleaning.

EXTERIOR. The W. front, although disfigured at the Revolution, retains one good 12C tower with a low modern steeple. The transeptal portals, each with a rose-window, are of mid-13C work.

Interior. Only the more important tombs are listed. The conducted visit begins in the S. AISLE, with, among others, the tomb of *Louis d'Orléans* (d. 1407; see p. 145) and *Valentine de Milan* (d. 1408), a fine Italian work of 1502-15, commissioned by their grandson, Louis XII. Opposite, against the S.W. pillar of the crossing, is the heart-tomb of *François II* (d. 1560), by *Germain Pilon* and *Ponce Jacquiau*. Also in the S. AISLE, the Urn (1549-55) by *Bontemps*, containing the heart of *François I*. In the S. TRANSEPT: the *Tomb of *François I* (d. 1547) and *Claude de France* (d. 1524), a masterpiece by *Philibert Delorme, Pierre Bontemps, Primaticcio*, and others, begun in 1548. The royal pair appear both recumbent and (above) kneeling with their children: reliefs depict the king's military exploits. On the E. side of this transept are the tombs of *Charles V* (d. 1380) by *André Beauneveu* and *Charles VI* (d. 1422) with their queens; and of *Bertrand Du Guesclin* (d. 1380), one of the few commoners buried here (his heart is at Dinan; his entrails at Le Puy).

CHOIR AND AMBULATORY. At the W. end of the CHOIR are the tombs of *Philippe III*, le Hardi (d. 1285), by *Pierre de Chelles* and *Jean d'Arras*, remarkable as being one of the earliest known French portrait-statues. The effigy of his queen, *Isabel of Aragón* (d. 1271), is particularly fine. Also *Philippe IV*, le Bel (d. 1314). Following the AMBULATORY, we pass (to the l. of the steps) the tomb of *Dagobert* (d. 638), showing reliefs of the torment and redemption of the king's soul, and with a beautiful *Statue (13C) of *Queen Nanthilde*: the figures of Dagobert and his son are 19C restorations. We next pass the tomb of *Léon de Lusignan* (d. 1393). Note the 12-13C glass in the LADY CHAPEL, and adjacent chapels, including a Tree of Jesse. Turning W. along the N. side of the Ambulatory we pass (l.) *Blanche* and *Jean* (both d. 1243), children of St Louis (from Royaumont), with fine enamelled plaques; *Frédégonde* (d.

597), queen of Chilperic I, a remarkable slab in cloisonné mosaic (11C, from St-Germain-des-Prés); and also from St-Germain, *Childebert I* (d. 558), a 12C statue. In the chapel at the top of the steps, draped statues of *Henri II* (d. 1559) and *Catherine de Médicis* (d. 1589) by *Germain Pilon* (1583). In the SANCTUARY is the *Altar of the Relics* (by *Viollet-le-Duc*), on which are placed the reliquaries, given by Louis XVIII, of St Denis and his fellow-martyrs.

In the N. TRANSEPT is the splendid tomb of *Henri II* and *Catherine de Médicis,* designed by *Primaticcio* in 1560-73, with recumbent and kneeling effigies of the king and queen, and supporters and reliefs by *Germain Pilon* and other contemporary sculptors. The king and queen were kneeling at a bronze prie-dieu melted down at the Revolution. Here also are the tombs of *Philippe V* (d. 1322), *Charles IV* (d. 1328), *Philippe VI* (d. 1350), and *Jean II* (d. 1364, prisoner at the Savoy, London), the last two by *André Beauneveu.* Opposite (l., in the choir) are tombs of *Louis X* (d. 1316) and his son *Jean I* (d. 1316).

In the N. AISLE, the *Tomb of *Louis XII* (d. 1515) and *Anne of Brittany* (d. 1514), made by *Jean Juste* (Giov. di Giusto) in 1516-32. The royal pair are depicted naked and recumbent on the tombstone, and kneeling on the canopy above (the conventional design for Renaissance tombs); bas-reliefs illustrate episodes in the king's career. Lastly, among other 13-14C tombs, that of *Louis de France* (d. 1260), the eldest son of St Louis, with Henry III of England as one of the bearers.—Note, before entering the Crypt, the *High Stalls* of the Ritual Choir (1501-07) from the chapel of the château de Gaillon; the *Low Stalls* are 15C work from St-Lucien, near Beauvais.

The CRYPT, entered on either side of the Choir, was constructed by Suger round the original Carolingian 'martyrium', the site of the grave of St Denis and his companions, and retains some 12C capitals. Here are seen the sarcophagi of Louis XVI, Marie-Antoinette, Louis XVIII, among other 18-19C royal personages. The ossuary on the N. side contains the bones that were thrown into a pit when the tombs were rifled in 1793. In a side chapel is a charming 12C Virgin, originally at the abbey of Longchamp.

———————

To the S. of the basilica, the monastic buildings, rebuilt in the 18C by *Robert de Cotte* and *Jacques Gabriel* (under restoration), have been occupied since 1809 by a *Maison d'Éducation de la Légion d'Honneur.*

The *Museum* opposite contains the reconstituted pharmacy of the *Hôtel-Dieu,* on whose site it stands, and drawings by Cézanne, Léger, Dufy, etc., and the study of the poet Paul Éluard (Eugène Grindel; 1895-1952), born in St-Denis.

24   PARIS TO ÉCOUEN, CHANTILLY, AND CLERMONT (FOR AMIENS)

N16 for 20 km.   *Écouen.*—41 km.   *Chantilly.*—64 km.   *Clermont.* For the alternative road direct to *Chantilly* viâ the N17 and N324A, see Rte 25.

From the *Porte de la Chapelle,* the N16 drives N. towards *St-Denis* (see Rte 23), which it is preferable to bypass, rejoining the old road to the N. At 15 km. we fork r. past (l.) *Sarcelles,* with a much-altered church (12C choir and belfry, 15C Gothic nave, and Renaissance façade), and r., *Villiers-le-Bel,* with a 13-16C church, to reach (20 km., l.) *Écouen.*

Écouen (4,500 inhab.) is commanded by a magnificent Renaissance *Château begun c. 1535 for the Constable Anne de Montmorency; among the artists employed in its construction were *Jean Goujon* and *Jean Bullant,* to the former of whom are ascribed the façade and Right Wing, and the chimneypiece of the great hall. The vaulting of the main staircase and of the chapel is noteworthy. For some years work has been in progress thoroughly to restore the building and install therein a **Museum of the Renaissance.** Certain pavilions will be open to the public by the spring of 1976 (early 16C Brussels tapestries of David and Bathsheba in the GAL. DE PSYCHÉ, etc.), and other sections will be opened progressively.

The choir (1544) of the church (*St-Acceul*) contains fine contemporary *Stained-glass, attr. to *Jean Cousin.*

N. of *Écouen* we pass (l.) *Le Mesnil-Aubry,* with a charming Renaissance church of 1531-82, and (27 km., l.) the fine 18C château of *Champlâtreux,* built by *Chevotet* for the Molé family.

At 29 km. bear l. for **Luzarches** (2,500 inhab.; *Hotels*), once famous for the relics of the saintly physicians Cosmas and Damian, martyred in 303. The interesting *Church* dedicated to them bears, within its porch, sculptured medallions relating to their lives. The building, although preserving important 12C remains, dates principally from the mid-16C, and, like *Le Mesnil,* is the work of *Nicolas de St-Michel.* Robert de Luzarches, architect of Amiens cathedral, was born here. The gateway to the castle, to the W. of the town, leads to the ruins of the collegiate church of *St-Côme,* largely destroyed at the Revolution.

About 3 km. E. lies the château d'*Hérivaux,* ruins of an abbey founded in 1160, also demolished at the Revolution, and once the property of Benjamin Constant, who entertained Mme de Staël there. He sold it in 1802 and moved to a smaller house, 'Les Herbages', at *St-Martin-du-Tertre,* nearer Luzarches.

Chantilly (see below) lies 11 km. N. of Luzarches.

———————

A detour may be made to *Royaumont,* by driving W. from *Luzarches* to (4 km.) *Viarmes,* with a church preserving a 12-13C nave.—*Asniers,* 1 km. beyond, has a 12-13C church.—2.5 km. N. of *Viarmes,* to the r. of the D909, lies **Royaumont,** retaining the considerable remains of the great Cistercian abbey founded in 1228 by St Louis, who in 1234 was married in the church. With the exception of a tall stair-turret, the huge church was dismantled in 1791. The beautiful *REFECTORY (used as a cotton-mill in the 19C; and which would be better stripped of its furnishing), has vaulting sustained by five monolithic columns, and retains the tomb of Henri of Lorraine, by *Coysevox;* the KITCHEN, and CLOISTER, with its simple clustered columns, may be visited.

Adm. 10.00-12.00; 14.00-17.00 or 18.00; closed Tues.; time is wasted waiting for a group to accumulate. During the 1914-18 War it accommodated a Scottish Women's Hospital for French soldiers run entirely by women; it now houses an international cultural foundation (Gouin-Lang).—The nearby château, by *Le Masson,* dates from 1785-89.

At 2 km. N. we turn r. for (6.5 km.) *Chantilly.*

Boran-sur-Oise, a riverside resort 2.5 km. S.W. of this junction, has a 13-15C church with a Gothic belfry.

40 km. **Chantilly** (10,700 inhab.; *Hotels*), the 'Newmarket' of France, where important race-meetings have been held since 1836, is also famous for its château, containing outstanding works of art.

From the N16 we approach the château by turning r. along the Rue du Connétable in the centre of the town, which passes (r.) the church of *Notre-Dame* (1686-92), built by the son of the Grand Condé, and the *Grandes-Écuries* (open Sat. and Sun. afternoons in summer), built by *Jean Aubert* in 1719-35, with room for 240 horses. Passing through the *Porte St-Denis,* we see the château on our l. A more direct approach from the Paris road may be made by turning r. after the railway bridge, and driving through the park along the Route de l'Aigle, passing behind the grandstands and the chapel of *Sainte-Croix* (one of seven erected by Madeleine of Savoy, wife of the Great Constable) to the CARREFOUR DES LIONS.

An alternative route from Paris is the N17 to (34.5 km.) *La Chapelle-en-Serval;* there branching l. onto the N324A through the forest to the Carrefour des Lions.

The *Château de Chantilly,* standing in a lake stocked with carp, consists of two connected buildings, the *Petit Château* or Capitainerie, on the S.W., and the *Grand Château* to the N.

History. Chantilly came into the possession of the Montmorency family in 1484, and after the execution of Henri II Montmorency passed to the Grand Condé (whose mother was a Montmorency) in 1632. The present *Petit Château* was erected about 1560 (probably by *Jean Bullant*) for the Constable Anne de Montmorency. The *Grand Château,* rebuilt by *Mansart* for the Grand Condé on the site of a mansion built by *Chambiges* for Constable Anne in 1528-31, was described, by Lord Herbert of Cherbury as "an incomparably fine residence, admired by the greatest princes of Europe". Molière's 'Les Précieuses ridicules' was given for the first time at Chantilly in 1659. During the visit of Louis XIV in 1671, François Vatel, his maître d'hôtel, committed suicide because he thought the fish would be late (as described by Mme de Sévigné). In 1777 Philip Thicknesse saw the Prince de Condé at supper with some friends—8 people waited on by 25 servants!
    The *Grand Château* was destroyed at the Revolution, but after some repairs had been carried out by the last of the Condés (d. 1830), it was entirely rebuilt in 1875-81 by his heir, the Duc d'Aumale (1822-97), fourth son of Louis-Philippe, from the designs of *Daumet.* Unfortunately, he also inherited his father's 'taste' in many respects. After the confiscation of the property of the Orléans family in 1853, the Château was bought by the English banking firm of Coutts, but the property was returned to its rightful owner by a decree of the National Assembly in 1872. In spite of his banishment from France, the Duc d'Aumale bequeathed the whole domain, together with his art collections, to the *Institut de France.* Chantilly marks the farthest advance in this direction of German troops in Sept. 1914; it was later the headquarters of Marshal Joffre.
    Admission. Every day except Tues., 10.30-17.00.

After passing the iron Grille d'Honneur, we leave on our r. the *Château d'Enghien* (1770), built by *Leroy* for the unfortunate Duc d'Enghien (comp. Vincennes), and now the curator's residence. We cross the *Terrasse du Connétable,* with a statue of the Constable Anne de Montmorency (1492-1567) by *P. Dubois,* pass between two bronze groups of hounds by *Cain,* cross the moat, and enter the *Cour d'Honneur* through a colonnade.

The **Musée Condé,** one of the most interesting collections (although a number of paintings reflect a certain lack of discrimination on the part of the Duc d'Aumale) within easy reach of Paris, is installed on the ground floor of the *Grand Château* and part of the first floor of the *Petit Château.* Containing a unique concentration of French paintings and illuminations of the 15-16C, it offers also a comprehensive range of

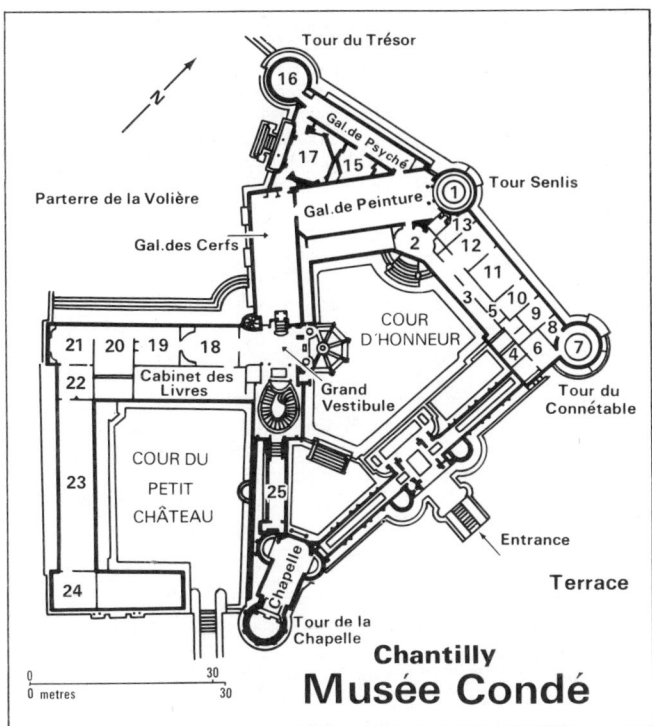

Chantilly
Musée Condé

Chantilly ware from the factory founded by the Duc de Bourbon in 1730, an important Library, and other works of art.

GRAND VESTIBULE. On the l. is the *Grand Staircase,* but we ascend steps to the r. to enter the GAL. DES CERFS, on the ceiling of which are the arms of the successive owners of Chantilly. The walls are hung with 17C Gobelins tapestries of hunting scenes. Above the chimneypiece, the Vision of St Hubert; dessus de portes of Venus and Cupid, and Diana, all by *Baudry.*—Among the more important paintings displayed in the GAL. DE PEINTURE (r.), many of which have two catalogue numbers, are: 528 *Fromentin,* Hawking; 383 *Lancret,* 'Déjeuner au jambon'; 94/309 *Ph. de Champaigne,* Mazarin, and 95/308 Richelieu; 150 *Lampi,* the Tsarina Marie Féodorowna; 148-149 Views of Chantilly by *De Cort;* and 124/343 *Nanteuil,* portrait of Colbert.—From the end of the gallery we enter the ROTUNDA (**Pl. 1**) in the *Tour Senlis,* with a mosaic pavement from Herculaneum: 7/48 *Clouet,* Odet de Châtillon; 75/278 *anon.,* Gabrielle d'Estrées in her bath; 134/306 *after Poussin,* Landscape; and portraits by (41) *Andrea del Sarto,* (61) *Annibale Carracci,* and (13) *Piero de Cosimo,* Simonetta Vespucci.

The GAL. DE LOGIS (**Pl. 3**) contains a magnificent collection of *French portrait drawings of the 16-17C, including 43/558 Anne de Montmorency; 9/561 Charles IX; 48/555 Henri II; 41/579 *Marc Duval*, Gaspard de Coligny; 3/570 *after Fouquet*, Charles VII; 47/573 *anon.*, Double portrait; 6/576 *after Jean Perréal*, Charles VIII; 21/590 *after Clouet*, François de Scepeaux; 25/589 Marguerite de Navarre; 13/571 François II; 38/567 *after Decourt*, Henri III; 42/568 attr. *Le Mannier*, Charles IX aged three playing with a cat; 46/583 *Corneille de Lyon*, Old man; 57/596 Anne, Duc de Joyeuse; 51/563 Antoine de Bourbon; 59/564 and 60/586 Unknown woman; 71/581 Duc de Nemours; 73/583 Mary Tudor; 74/592 Laure de Noves; 76/595 Gabrielle d'Estrées; and 153/587 Marguerite-Charlotte de Montmorency. Opposite is 158/346 *anon.*, Fagon (?).

In the adjoining room are: 148/287 Sully; 136/288 attr. *Quesnel*, Martin Ruzé; opposite: 99/598 *after Dumoustier*, Rogier de Saint-Lary; 150/604 James I of England; 134 *Wouwerman*, Cavalry combat.—**Pl. 6:** 439 *Perrault* (after Horace Vernet), Louis-Philippe and his sons leaving Versailles, and 553 *Bonnat*, the Duc d'Aumale.

ROTONDE DE LA MINERVE **(Pl. 7)**, in the *Constable's Tower:* Minerva, a Greek statuette of the best period; vase from Nola; Pourtalès Amphora, a red-figured vase of the time of Pheidias; Tanagra figures; bronze ewers from Herculaneum, etc.; 119/315 *after Mignard*, Henriette d'Angleterre, Duchesse d'Orléans.

CABINET DES ANTIQUES **(Pl. 8)**. On the l.: *Lawrence*, Francis I of Austria; Wall-cases: vases and bronze utensils, and coins minted within ten years of the eruption of Vesuvius in A.D. 79, found at Pompeii.

CABINET DU GIOTTO **(Pl. 9)**: 1/111 *Enguerrand Quarton*, Virgin; 14 *Iacopo del Sellaio*, Madonna; 1 *School of Giotto*, Death of the Virgin; 42 *Andrea del Sarto*, Young Man; 18 *Ghirlandaio*, Louis de la Trémoille; 122bis *Frans Francken* (?), Ecce homo.

SALLE ISABELLE **(Pl. 10)**: 506 *Rousseau*, Landscape; 140 *W. van de Velde the Younger*, Calm sea; *J. van Ruisdael*, Coast at Scheveningen.

SALLE D'ORLÉANS **(Pl. 11)**: 552 *Bonnat*, Duc d'Aumale (1880); 521 *Jalabert*, Queen Marie-Amélie (1865); a collection of *Chantilly Porcelain*, and portfolios of drawings (not exhibited through lack of space) by *Primaticcio* (decorations for Fontainebleau), *Watteau*, the *Clouets*, and *Carmontelle* (18C portraits in water-colour), among others.

SALLE CAROLINE **(Pl. 12)**: *Greuze*, 393 Affection, 391 Girl, a study for the 'Village Marriage Contract' in the Louvre, 394 'La Surprise'; 386 *Duplessis*, Duchesse de Chartres watching her husband's departure for Ushant (1778); 372 *Watteau*, 'L'Amante Inquiète'; 319 *Mignard*, Comtesse de la Suze; 376 *Nattier*, Duchesse d'Orléans as Hebe; 419 *Carle Vernet*, Duc d'Orléans and Duc de Chartres (1788); 334 *Largillière*, Portrait; 371 *Watteau*, 'La Sérénade'; *Nattier*, Duchesse de Nantes, daughter of Mme de Montespan; 92/325 attr. *Seb. Bourdon*, Portrait; 138/338 attr. *Rigaud*, Portrait; 156/339 Princesse des Ursins.

Pl. 13: 8 attr. *Clouet*, Jeanne d'Albret; and *after Clouet* or from his studio: 10 and 16 Charles IX; 11 Elisabeth of Austria; 12 Odet de Châtillon; 20 Catherine de Médicis; 23 Marguerite de Valois as a child; 26 Henri II as a child; attr. to *Corneille de Lyon* or his studio: 27 Gabrielle de Rochechouart (?); 33 the Dauphin François, son of

François I; 36 *Jean Decourt,* Henri III (?); 37 Albert de Gondi; 40 *Marc Duval,* Jacques de Savoie; 49 *anon.,* Marguerite d'Angoulême; 50 *anon.,* Henri d'Albret, King of Navarre; 55 *anon.,* Michel de l'Hôpital; 77 *anon.,* François I; 78 *anon.,* Ferdinand of Austria; 81 *anon.,* Claude de France (?); 86 *anon.,* Montaigne.

Returning through Pl. 5, we pass portraits by *Mierevelt* of Grotius, and of Elizabeth of Bohemia, to regain the *Gal. de Peinture,* crossing which, we enter the GAL. DE PSYCHÉ. 42 of the original 44 sepia *Stained-glass windows representing the Loves of Cupid and Psyche (as related by Apuleius in 'The Golden Ass') were made about 1541 for the Constable de Montmorency's château at *Écouen,* and were probably designed by *Michiel Coxie.* At the end is a wax portrait bust of Henri IV (1610) by *Guillaume Dubois.*

On the wall are important *Portrait drawings, many ascribed to the *Clouets,* and others to *Jean Perréal.* They include: 1 Diane de Poitiers, 5 Marshal Strozzi, 9 Hercule-François d'Alençon, 13 Marguerite d'Angoulême, Queen of Navarre, sister of François I, 15 Jeanne d'Albret, mother of Henri IV, 20 Henri II, 21 Henri, Duc de Guise, 22 François, Duc de Guise, 23 Jeanne, Queen of Navarre, 24 François II, 25 Marguerite de Valois (La Reine Margot), first wife of Henri IV, 26 Charles IX as a child, 27 Anne de Montmorency, 30 Admiral Coligny, 35 Henri II as a boy, 41 Marshal Brissac.

The SANTUARIO (Pl. 15), off the centre of the room, contains the main treasures of the collection, including *Raphael,* 39 Madonna of the House of Orléans (painted about 1505), 38 the Three Graces (or the Three Ages of Woman), an earlier panel. Between these, 19 Esther and Ahasuerus, a long panel painted in tempera, which, although catalogued as by Filippino Lippi, is probably by an unknown pupil of Botticelli (*'Amico di Sandro'*). It is likely (by 1976) that reproductions only will be on view of **200-240, forty (of 47) miniatures executed in 1453-60 for the Book of Hours ordered by Étienne Chevalier (1410-74), Treasurer of France. They were acquired by the Duc d'Aumale in 1891, and while plausibly ascribed to *Jean Fouquet* (1415-81), they have not yet been proved to be the work of that master. Nos 201 and 202 (r. wall) represent Étienne Chevalier and his patron saint adoring the Virgin and Child.

Re-entering the *Gal. de Psyché,* we turn l. to reach the CABINET DES GEMMES (Pl. 16) in the *Tour du Trésor* (views). In the table-case near the centre window are an enamel of Apollo guiding the Chariot of the Sun, attr. to *Cellini,* and the rose diamond known as the 'Grand Condé'. In the wall-cases: a Cross from the treasury of Basle (15C); snuff boxes, with views and plans of Chantilly (by *Roussel,* 1775); a collection of fans, miniatures, and enamels, etc.

We return to the *Gal. de Psyché,* turn r., and pass through a small room in which is a bas-relief of the Departure of Phaethon, by *Jean Goujon,* to enter the TRIBUNE (Pl. 17), a large octagonal room in the middle of which is a vase by *Clodion.* On the panels above the cornice are represented eight houses and châteaux connected with the Duc d'Aumale: Collège Henri-IV, Aumale, Palais-Royal, Palermo, Écouen, Guise, Villers-Cotterets, and Twickenham.

On the walls hang: 146 *Reynolds,* Countess Waldegrave and her daughter (1761); 445 *A. Scheffer,* Prince Talleyrand; 370 *Watteau,* 'Plaisir pastoral'; 125 *van Dyck,* Gaston, Duc d'Orléans; 107, 108

Memling (?), Diptych of the Virgin appearing to Jeanne de Bourbon, daughter of Charles VII, and Christ on the Cross; 15 *Perugino*, Madonna with SS Jerome and Peter; 16 *Botticelli* (?), Autumn (once attr. to Mantegna); 48 *Fr. Clouet*, Card. Odet de Châtillon; 105 *Flemish School*, Anthony, the 'Grand Bastard' of Burgundy; 10 *Sassetta*, Mystic Marriage of St Francis (1444); 11 *Pesellino*, Madonna with SS Peter and Anthony; 313 *Mignard*, Molière; *Ingres*, 431 Mme Devauçay, painted in Rome in 1807, and 430, Self-portrait; 93 *Ph. de Champaigne*, Angélique Arnauld; 114 *Mignard*, Card. Mazarin; 125 *H.-G. Pot*, portrait of Andres Hooftman; 141 *after Rigaud*, Armand-Jean le Bouthillier de Rancé, Abbé de la Trappe; 155 *anon.*, Marquise de Montespan; 137 *Rigaud*, Louis XIV; 165 and 166 *anon.*, the Duc du Maine, and Duc d'Anjou (later Philip V of Spain); and three portraits by *Mme Vigée-Lebrun*.—In the small room beyond is the Fall of Phaethon, by *Goujon*, a pendant to the bas-relief in the other vestibule.

We now return through the *Gal. des Cerfs* to the *Grand Vestibule* and turn r. to visit the apartments in the **Petit Château,** decorated in honour of the Grand Condé, from 1686, by *J. H.-Mansart,* and furnished with Beauvais tapestry and contemporary clocks, ornaments, and woodwork.—ANTECHAMBER **(Pl. 18)**: dessus de portes of dogs by *Oudry* and *Desportes;* enamel of Henri IV by *Claudius Popelin;* and Sèvres, Chinese, and Rouen porcelain.—SALLE DES GARDES **(Pl. 19)**: 126 and 127 *van Dyck*, Comte Henri de Bergues and the Princesse Marie de Brabançon; four enamel portraits by *Léonard Limousin;* 132 *Justus van Egmont*, the Grand Condé (1658); 125 *after Nanteuil*, the Grand Condé in 1662; 157 *anon.*, Abraham de Fabert, Maréchal de France; and 168 *anon.*, François II de Montmorency, Duc de Luxembourg. The mosaic above the chimneypiece is from Herculaneum.

The richly decorated BEDROOM **(Pl. 20)**, with white and gilt wood, and painted panels by *J.-B. Huet,* contains a commode by *Riesener,* chairs by *J.-B. Sené,* and a fine chandelier.—CABINET **(Pl. 21)**: Equestrian statue of the Grand Condé by *Frémiet.*—*THE SALON DES SINGES **(Pl. 22)** is named from the highly decorative chinoiserie panel-paintings of "Singeries ou différentes actions de la vie humaine" by *Christophe Huet.*

*GAL. DES ACTIONS de M. Le Prince **(Pl. 23)**. The panels of this long room were painted in 1686-96 by *Sauveur Lecomte* with scenes from the battles fought by the Grand Condé, whose despatch-case lies on the bureau of the Duc de Choiseul. Over the fireplace is a *Trophy formed of his swords and pistols; above is his portrait when twenty-two years of age, at Rocroi, by *J. Stella;* below, a medallion by *Coysevox* of 1686, the year of the Prince's death. The bust of the Grand Condé in bisquit de Sèvres on the mantlepiece is by *Roland* (1785); those in marble of Turenne, and of the Grand Condé, are by *Derbais* (1695).—The next CABINET **(Pl. 24)** contains a portrait of the Duc d'Enghien by *Vallain*, and miniatures; and 90 *Triophime Bigot*, the Supper at Emmaus.

Retracing our steps to the *Antichambre,* we turn r. to enter the CABINET DES LIVRES, containing some 13,000 volumes of the 13-18C, many of great rarity. The superb bindings are worthy of study. Perhaps the greatest treasure here is the **'*Très Riches Heures du Duc de Berri*'** (acquired in 1855), with magnificently illuminated pages of the Months, executed about 1415 by *Pol de Limbourg* and his brothers, direct from nature and not treated conventionally as had previously been the universal practice. Only reproductions of the delicate originals are now on view.

We return to the *Grand Vestibule*. On the r. is the GRAND ESCALIER (no adm.), with its superb balustrade of steel and copper, designed by *Daumet* and executed by the brothers *Moreau*, with caryatids by *Chapu*, and Gobelins tapestry after *Boucher* and *De Troy*.—Passing the staircase, we enter the GAL. DE LA CHAPELLE (**Pl. 25**), with drawings by *Dürer*, Annunciation (1526); *Domenichino*, Flight into Egypt; *Seb. del Piombo*, Head of Christ; and *Raphael*, Madonna.

The CHAPEL, founded early in the 14C, but many times rebuilt, was virtually destroyed during the Revolution. It was restored in 1882 by *Daumet*. Behind the altar is the mausoleum of Henri II de Condé (d. 1662), with bronze sculptures by *J. Sarazin*. The Altar itself, by *Jean Bullant* and *Jean Goujon*, the woodwork of 1548, and the stained-glass (1544; portraits of the Great Constable's children), were all brought here from Écouen. The flag, taken at Rocroi, 19 May 1643, is claimed to be the oldest captured colour in France.

The *PARK, with impressive parterres, was laid out for the most part by *Le Nôtre* for the Grand Condé, and is adorned with sculptures and ornamental water. Among the buildings which may be visited are the *Maison de Sylvie*, to the S.E. behind the Château d'Enghien, to reach which we pass the *Chapelle de St-Sébastien* (1552) and the *Cabotière* (Louis-XIII period). 'Sylvie' was the name given to Marie Félice Orsini, Duchesse de Montmorency, by the poet Théophile de Viau, who, when he was condemned to death in 1623 for his licentious verses, was hidden by the duchess in this building. Rebuilt by the Grand Condé in 1684, the Maison de Sylvie was in 1724 the scene of the romantic affair of Mlle de Clermont, sister of the Duc de Bourbon, and M. de Melun, who was killed in a hunting accident. It now contains Chinese curios, wood-carvings, tapestry, etc.

To the N.E. stand a group of cottages, the 'Hameau', built in 1776 by the penultimate Condé, and once the scene of many 'fêtes champêtres' of the period. To the W., near the stables, is the *Jeu de Paume,* of 1757, containing carriages, two leaden dogs from Twickenham, Abd-el-Kader's tent, etc.

The ***Forest of Chantilly**, of 5,190 acres, composed of oaks, limes, birches, and clumps of Scots pines, is intersected by numerous roads or sandy tracks (in the interest of the training-stables), the latter being closed to cars.

The N324 leads 10km. E. to *Senlis* (see p. 215) viâ *Courteuil*, where the Abbé Prévost (1697-1763) died.

FROM CHANTILLY TO BEAUVAIS (47 km.). **St-Leu-d'Esserent**, 5.5km. N.W. of *Chantilly* by the D44, has a particularly fine 12C *Church, with later additions, and recent restorations. To the N., the cloisters of the priory may be visited. The local quarries supplied stone for the cathedrals of Chartres, Sens, and later, the Palace of Versailles; in 1944 it was used for the assembly of VI and V2 rockets.— From *St-Leu* we turn N.W. through *Cramoisy*, with a 12-13C church, to (15km.) *Mello*, with an 11-13C church altered in the 16C, and an ancient château largely rebuilt in 1770.—20km. *Bury* has an interesting 11-13C priory-church containing a carved wood altarpiece of the Passion (16C).—23km. *Mouy*, with a 12-13th, and 16C, church, 6km. W. of which is the restored Renaissance château of *Mouchy-le-Châtel*, with a 12C tower.—27km. At *Fillerval* (2km. N.E.) is a château built by the geographer Cassini (see below), with a remarkable pediment displaying astronomical instruments.—34km. *Villers-St-Sépulcre*, named from a sculptured Entombment, and incorporating a slab from the Holy Sepulchre in Jerusalem.— 47km. *Beauvais*, see p. 267.

The N16 leads N. from Chantilly to (48km.) **Creil** (75,000 inhab.), an industrial town and important railway junction, which made it a military target in both World Wars. It retains a small museum (18-19C furniture, and a collection of Creil pottery and stoneware for which this expanding town is famous) housed in the remains of the royal castle. The church of *St-Médard* (13-16C) may also be visited.—*Montataire,* immediately to the W. of *Creil,* has a 12-15C church and a château of the 14-16C.—*Nogent-sur-Oise,* N. of *Creil,* has a 12-13C church, as has *Villers-St-Paul* (to the E. of *Nogent*), the latter with a geometrically decorated porch.

57 km. **Liancourt** (2 km. E.) retains a 15-17C church with curious bell-turrets, and a marble monument with good effigies of Charles du Plessis and his wife, but the site of the 17C château of the Dukes of la Rochefoucauld-Liancourt has been built over.

It was Duc Frédéric-Alexandre (1747-1837) who made the celebrated retort when Louis XVI remarked (on the evening of 14 July 1789) on hearing of the disturbance in Paris, "Mais c'est une révolte!": "Non, Sire, c'est une révolution!"
Cambronne-lès-Clermont, 4 km. to the E. of the N16, has a good 12-13C church with a Romanesque belfry, capitals, and remains of murals.

64 km. **Clermont** (8,700 inhab.), built on a hillside above the Brèche, in the Middle Ages seat of powerful countship, retains its *Hôtel de Ville* of 1328 (restored), preserving a portrait of Berwick, Duc de Fitz-James (natural son of James II), by *Van Loo.* Berwick acquired the village of *Fitz-James* (formerly *Warty*), N.E. of *Clermont,* in 1704. A statue in the *Hôtel de Ville* of *Clermont* commemorates C.-F. Cassini de Thury (1714-84), the geographer, who first employed the method of triangulation in making maps of France, and one of the celebrated local family (of Italian origin) of astronomers and cartographers. The church of *St-Samson,* later substantially altered after a fire, contains some good 16C stained-glass. To the l. of the church are the ruins of a 13C *Gateway.* Crowning the hill are the walls and keep of the *Castle* (views), which was twice captured by the English, in 1359 and 1434, and was the birthplace of Charles IV, le Bel, in 1294.

The N31 leads W. to (26 km.) *Beauvais,* see p. 267, passing near (2 km., l.) *Agnetz,* with a 13-16C church, and through part of the FORÊT DE HEZ. —Also 31 km. E. to *Compiègne,* see p. 217. The N16 leads N.W. to (66 km.) *Amiens.*

25   PARIS TO SENLIS AND COMPIÈGNE (FOR NOYON)

N17 to (44 km.) *Senlis* and N32 to (75 km.) *Compiègne.*
While the A1 motorway is the most rapid approach to *Senlis,* the N17 is the route described, leaving Paris by the *Porte de la Villette.*

At 16 km., just beyond the airport of **Le Bourget** (where the *Air Museum* at Meudon is to be transferred), passing extensive tulip fields (at their best in April-May), *Gonesse* lies to the l., the birthplace of Philippe Auguste, with a 12-13C church, behind which is the *Hôtel-Dieu,* built on the site of one founded in 1208.—*Goussainville* (4 km. N.) has a Renaissance church built by *Jean Bullant,* and 4 km. beyond, to the N.W., at *Fontenay-en-Parisis,* is an interesting 12-13C church.

23.5 km., l. (after passing, r., the W. end of the **Charles de Gaulle Airport**) is *Louvres,* where *St-Justin* preserves an 11C W. portal; the rest of the church is 13-16C. The tower of the church of *St-Rieul* has a pointed vault said to date from c. 1110, and claimed to be the oldest existing example of the kind.—2.5 km. N.E., towards *Villeron,* is an impressive 13C tithe-barn.

31 km. *Survilliers,* with an interesting 16C church.—6.5 km. E. lies *Mortefontaine,* with an old château, once the property of Joseph Bonaparte, where a commercial treaty between the First Consul and the United States (represented by Franklin) was concluded in 1803. In the nearby *Parc de la Vallière* is a pretentious château built in the Renaissance style in 1897 by the Duc de Grammont.—Hence the N17 may be regained by following the D607 viâ *Thiers* to *Pontarmé.*

At 34.5 km. the N324A diverges l. through the forest to the *Château of Chantilly* (8 km. beyond; see p. 208).

At 37.5 km. *Pontarmé,* we enter the FORÊT DE CHANTILLY.

44 km. **SENLIS** (14,400 inhab.; *Hotels*), while not quite the peaceful old town it once was, still retains many attractive alleys, particularly those within the Gallo-Roman ramparts of the Silvanectes.

The gâteau senlisien, game, and venison pâtés, and cèpes from the adjacent forests should be sampled.

Senlis was a royal residence from the time of Clovis to Henri IV; Hugues Capet was elected 'Duc des Francs' here in 987; in 1358 it was the scene of a massacre of nobles by the Jacquerie. The bishopric founded in the 3C lapsed in 1790. The town was briefly in German hands in Sept. 1914, who set fire to some streets and plundered the town.

From the S., the Rue de la République crosses the S.E. section of the town, the site of its outer medieval ramparts forming a concentric ring of tree-lined boulevards, except to the S.E., where some fortifications are preserved, including the *Porte de Paris.* In this quarter, reached by the Rue de Meaux, leading E. off the Rue de la République, lies the ancient *Abbaye St-Vincent* (adm. 8.30-12.00; 14.00-19.00), founded in 1062, and retaining a 12C belfry and cloister of 1680. It was rebuilt in the 17C, and is now a theological college. Also in the Rue de Meaux is the former hospital-chapel of *La Charité* (1704).

In the Rue Ste-Geneviève, on the W. side of the Rue de la République, is the *Logis du Haubergier* (16C), with a hexagonal turret-stair, housing a good regional *Museum* (10.00-12.00; 14.00-17.00 or 18.00, except Tues., and Wed. morning). A few yards W. is the *Hôtel de Ville,* rebuilt in 1495. Beyond, in the Rue de Beauvais, is the former church of St-Aignan (now a theatre), and several 14-15C houses. The Rue du Châtel leads N. from the Hôtel de Ville into the Gallo-Roman enceinte, with 16 towers remaining, and among the most complete in existence, but most of them are hidden by abutting houses. We pass (No. 20) the old *Hôtel-Dieu.* At the far end of the street is the *Hôtel des Trois-Pots,* first mentioned in 1292, and now with a 16C façade. Here is the entrance to the ruins of the royal castle (4th, 11th, and 16C), the *Priory of St-Maurice* (14C), and *Musée de la Vénerie* (Hunting), with canvases by *Oudry, Desportes,* and *Snyders,* etc. (adm. 10.00-12.00; 14.00-17.00 or 18.00, except Tues., and Wed. morning). To the N. of the cathedral is the *Hôtel de Vermandois* (13-16C).

The ***Cathedral** was built in 1155-84 (almost coeval with St-Denis and Notre-Dame). Its S. Tower is surmounted by a fine 13C spire 256 ft high. The central door of the W. façade is embellished with statues and reliefs relative to the Life of the Virgin; the eight statue-columns were badly restored in the 19C. The transepts were rebuilt by *Pierre Chambiges* in 1530-56 after a fire, in a rich Gothic style, but displaying Renaissance tendencies. From the same period date the side portals and the five shallow E. chapels, of which that in the centre was remodelled in 1840.

The INTERIOR is notable for the beauty of its triforium gallery. The E. chapel of the S. transept has a remarkable 16C vault. From the S.W. chapel in the nave a staircase leads to the beautiful *Chapter-house* (late 14C), with a central pillar (apply to the sacristan). The *Sacristy*, octagonal in plan, in part a relic of the original early 11C church, should also be visited.

To the E. of the cathedral is the *Palais de Justice* (previously the Bishop's), to the S. of which is the disused church of *St-Frambourg* (1177-85), now a workshop. Behind the Bishop's Palace is the former church of **St-Pierre** (now a market), a handsome building with a façade in the Flamboyant style (1516); one of the towers has a dome and is of Renaissance date; while the other, partly Romanesque, has a spire of 1432. The building is open Tues. and Fri.; at other times enquire for the concierge.

A short distance S.E., at No. 12 Rue Bellon, is the *Hôtel Saint-Simon* (18C), belonging to the family of the industrious author of the famous 'Mémoires', who was himself a governor of the town.

A few minutes walk S.W. of the PL. DE CREIL (at the far end of the Rue de Beauvais) are the remains of a Gallo-Roman *Amphitheatre* (138 ft by 105 ft), discovered in 1863, and probably earlier than that of Nîmes.

The N324 leads 10 km. W. to *Chantilly*, see p. 208.

2.5 km. S.E. of Senlis lie the picturesque ruins of the *Abbaye de la Victoire*, founded by Philippe Auguste to commemorate the Battle of Bouvines (1214), rebuilt in the 15-16C, and suppressed at the Revolution. Adm. 9.00-12.00; 13.00-19.00.

5 km. E. of Senlis, to the r. of the N324 leading to (21 km.) *Crépy-en-Valois* (see p. 221), are the ruins of the château of *Montépilloy* (12C), partly rebuilt c. 1400, and dismantled at the end of the 16C.—3 km. N.E., at *Rully*, is a 12-13C church with a fine belfry.—Hence the N32 (from Senlis to Compiègne) may be gained by driving N. through *Raray*, with a 17C château built on the site of an earlier one, with a remarkable decorated *Courtyard, which served as the location for Cocteau's film 'La Belle et le Bête'; the church is 15-16C.

10 km. N. of Senlis, on the N17, lies **Pont-Ste-Maxence,** taking its name from a bridge over the Oise built here by *Perronnet* in 1774-85, and damaged in 1914; its replacement has been rebuilt since its destruction in 1940. A good view may be obtained from the *Moulin de Calipet* (1694) to the S.E. The church of *Ste-Maxence* dates from the 15-16C. Of more interest is the *Abbaye de Moncel, E. of the town (off the D123), partly 14C, and with the exception of the church, almost entirely preserved (adm. 10.00-16.00 or 18.00, Sun. and holidays; otherwise by appointment). Hence the N32 for Compiègne may be gained 10 km. to the E., passing *Pontpoint*, where the 12C church preserves its Romanesque belfry, and (7 km.) *Rhuis*, with an interesting 11C church.

Shortly after leaving Senlis by the N32, we pass (r.) the 12-15C church of *Chamant.*—55.5 km. *Villeneuve-sur-Verberie*, with an 11-12C church, with a nave altered in 1510.—*Raray* (see above) lies 2 km. S.E.

61 km. **Verberie** (2,500 inhab.), an ancient town once residence of Merovingian and Carolingian kings, has a 13-15C church. *St-Vlaast-de-*

Longmont, 1 km. S.E., has a 12C church preserving good Romanesque decoration and a square tower surmounted by a stone spire, also 12C.

A number of early churches may be seen in the *Vallée de L'Automne,* through which the D123 leads to Villers-Cotterets, among them those at *Saintines, Béthisy-St-Pierre, Béthisy-St-Martin,* and (9.5 km. from Verberie) *Orrouy. Morienval* (see p. 221) lies c. 5 km. further E.

2 km. N. of Orrouy, on the ancient track (the 'Chaussée Brunehaut') from Senlis to Soissons, lies **Champlieu,** an important centre for Gallo-Roman remains (2-3C), which may be visited 10.00-12.00; 14.00-18.00; or 14.00-16.00 only from Nov. to Mar. The ruins, on the supposed site of Rotomagnus or Ratumacos, a city of the Sylvanectes, comprise a theatre, baths, and temple. Adjacent are remains of a little Romanesque church on earlier foundations, a cemetery, and early Christian catacombs.—Continuing N. from this point we shortly meet the N332 some 10 km. S.E. of Compiègne.

Beyond Verberie we skirt the W. side of the FORÊT DE COMPIÈGNE, and at 75 km., after passing *Royallieu,* the sad site of a concentration camp for deportees during the years 1941-44, enter *Compiègne* itself.

COMPIÈGNE (40,700 inhab.; *Hotels*), the *Compendium* of Latin chronicles, so called from its position on the 'short cut' between Beauvais and Soissons, was later a country seat of the Frankish kings, and the site of the Benedictine monastery of St-Corneille.

Joan of Arc, leading a sortie from Compiègne in 1430, was captured by the Burgundians, who sold her to the English. The Treaty of Compiègne (in 1624, between Richelieu and the Dutch), and other treaties, were signed in the château, which was a favourite residence of royalty, perhaps because of the facilities for hunting in the adjacent forest. Many of the hunting-paths and avenues therein were cut by Louis XIV and Louis XV. Here Marie-Antoinette was received by Louis XVI in 1770, and Marie-Louise by Napoleon in 1809. It was also frequently visited by Napoleon III in preference to his other palaces, and the fatuities of court junketings here reached their zenith. It was occupied by the Germans 1-12 Sept. 1914, and was bombarded by them in June 1918. On 11 Nov. the Armistice was signed 6 km. N.E. of *Compiègne* (see p. 219). A large section of the town was destroyed by German bombs in June 1940. The town is famous for its chocolates.

Convenient parking-sites may be found adjacent to the château (or palace).

The **Palace of Compiègne,** nearly 5 acres in extent, designed by *Gabriel* under Louis XV and restored by Napoleon I, is an example of French neo-classic decadence, imposing in its mass-effect, but unattractive in its extreme bareness and sobriety. The façade facing the PL. DU PALAIS is relieved, however, by a graceful portico and columns of the main courtyard; the façade giving upon the terrace and park is 114 yds in length. The interior contains a number of handsomely decorated apartments, many retaining the Empire furniture installed here by Napoleon.

The entrance lies to the r. of the courtyard, whence groups are escorted round the building. Adm. 10.00-12.00; 13.30-17.30, except Tues.

On ascending the ESCALIER D'HONNEUR to the SALLE DES GARDES, impressive in size and decorated with trophies in grisaille by *Crosnier,* we enter the SALON DU ROI DE ROME, with furniture by *Jacob-Desmalter,* and chairs covered with Beauvais tapestries of the fables of La Fontaine after designs by *Oudry.* Note also the Gobelins tapestry after *Coypel.* To the r. is the QUEEN'S SALON DES JEUX, with silk hangings made at Lyon after original patterns, and two commodes by *Stockel.* Retracing our steps, we pass through the SALON À MANGER, with tromp-l'oeil dessus de porte by *Sauvage,* and furniture by *Jacob-Desmalter.*—The adjoining SALON DES CARTES contains three huge wall-maps, two by *Pierre-Denis Martin* (1738-39) of Compiègne and the forest. The chairs are covered with Beauvais tapestries after cartoons by *Casanova.*—Note the chairs made by *Jeanselme* in 1859 in the Louis-XV style in the adjacent SALON DE FAMILLE, commanding a good view of the gardens and forest beyond.—The CABINET DU CONSEIL, next visited, contains an impressive silk hanging of the Crossing of the Rhine by *François Bonnemer* (1682-84) after *van der Meulen.* The woodwork in this room and the next has been restored after a fire in 1919.—The LIBRARY and its furniture were designed by *Jacob-Desmalter.* The emperor's bureau has been returned from Malmaison. Note the biscuit figures of Molière and Corneille by the mirror.—The adjacent MUSIC ROOM is hung with two Beauvais tapestries (c. 1685) in the Chinese taste, and two from the Gobelins factory, after *Amédée Van Loo,* from the 1780s.

Passing through the CHAMBRE, and BOUDOIR, of the empress, we enter the SALON DES FLEURS, with panels painted by *Dubois* after Redouté.— Leaving the main wing, we are escorted through the EMPRESS'S DINING-ROOM, with mahogany furniture by *Jacob-Desmalter,* to Louis XV's GAL. DES CHASSES, with Gobelins tapestries of hunting scenes *after Oudry.*—Paintings of dogs by *Oudry* and *Desportes* are seen in the adjoining GAL. DES CERFS.

We now enter the heavily gilt GAL. DE BAL, lit by fifteen chandeliers, and resplendent in its ugliness.—In the GAL. NATOIRE (r.) *Coypel*'s 'Histoire de Don Quixotte' (at present under restoration) may be placed.—The VESTIBULE TO THE CHAPEL (l.) displays Gobelins tapestries *after Raphael;* the CHAPEL itself is particularly tasteless.—Hence we may pass through a series of rooms designated **Musée du Second Empire,** with contemporary furniture and decoration, including a Gobelins copy of *Winterhalter*'s painting of the Empress Eugénie and Napoleon III, and descending stairs at the far end of the wing, make our exit.

Also accommodated in the palace is the **Musée National de la Voiture et du Tourisme** (opened here in 1927 under the auspices of the Touring-Club de France), with an interesting collection of coaches and carriages, and chaises, etc. Other sections are devoted to sledges, early bicycles, and cars, including examples by Amédée Bollée fils (1895), a Renault of 1900, a Panhard-Levassor phaeton of 1891, a de Dion limousine of 1907, etc.

The long S.E. façade lies on the perimeter of the old defensive walls of Compiègne, the best preserved section of which leads from the palace to the river. Another segment of the semicircle is hidden by abutting houses just S. of the Rue F.-Sarlovèze; the Rue Martel approximately marking the site of their position to the W.

From the N.W. corner of the PL. DU PALAIS, the Rue des Minimes (whose ancient church serves as a gymnasium) leads shortly to the PL. DE L'HÔTEL DE VILLE. The Flamboyant **Hôtel de Ville** (1502-10) is decorated with late 19C statues; the tall belfry contains a bell cast in 1303 and a 16C clock, which sets in motion every ¼-hour three wooden figures known as 'Picantines'. The building also accommodates sections of the *Musée Vivenel* (see below), and another devoted to the art of 'Figurines historiques', a collection of c. 100,000 items, the majority being lead soldiers. Among the various dioramas displayed is one of the Battle of Waterloo.

Off the Rue St-Corneille, and leading W. from the opposite side of the square, is (l.) the 14C *Cloister of St-Corneille* (damaged in 1940), sole relic of the ancient abbey. To the r., the Rue Jeanne d'Arc descends to the old *Hôtel-Dieu,* founded by St Louis, with a 13C façade, and preserving good woodwork. To the W. is the cylindrical *Tour Beauregard* (or *Tour Jeanne d'Arc;* 12C), beyond which is the **Musée Vivenel,** housed in the *Hôtel de Songeons* (late 18C), built on the ruins of a church of the Jacobins, fragments of which are visible in the adjoining park.

The collections of Antoine Vivenel (1799-1868) form the basis of this interesting museum, those of *Greek Vases taking second place only to the Louvre collection. Apart from Antiquities, representative examples of 12-13C ivories, Mennecy and Chantilly porcelain, etc., are displayed, besides paintings and drawings. Adm. 9.00-12.00; 14.00-18.00, except Tues.

A short distance to the S.E. stands *St-Antoine,* a plain Gothic building (13-16C) with a florid portal, raised choir, and good gargoyles. The Rue St-Antoine is continued E. by the Rue des Lombards, No. 10 in which is a gabled house of the 16C. Beyond is the 13-15C church of *St-Jacques,* with a lofty bell-tower with a Renaissance lantern. Continuing E., we shortly regain the *Pl. du Palais.*

To the W. of the château, the Rue d'Ulm leads to the *Porte Chapelle,* built in 1552 by *Philibert Delorme.*

Hence the N31 leads 28 km. W. to *Clermont,* see p. 214.—*Noyon* lies 24 km. N.E. on the N32; *Amiens* 71 km. N.W. on the N35.

A circuit of the **Forêt de Compiègne,** with an area of 55 sq. miles, may be made to include a visit to the '*Clairière de l'Armistice*', *Pierrefonds,* and *St-Jean-aux-Bois.*

The former is approached by following the D66 driving E. from the *Porte Chapelle,* and is reached after 6 km. German plenipotentiaries had presented themselves at the railway siding at *Rethondes,* 3 km. to the E., on 8 Nov., to sue for an armistice, which was signed at 5.00 on the morning of 11 Nov. 1918 in this clearing in the forest, and hostilities were ordered to cease on the whole front at 11.00.

Marshal Foch's railway-coach, in which the armistice was signed, was later preserved in a building erected for the purpose adjacent to the site. In June 1940 Hitler vindictively forced the French to sign an armistice in the same carriage. This was later destroyed by the Germans and replaced by an identical one, which may be entered on payment of a fee: thus is the memory of such solemn occasions hallowed and turned to profit.

On regaining the D66, at a point just N. of LES BEAUX MONTS (views), we turn r. onto the D547, passing through *Vieux-Moulin,* and skirting the ÉTANGS DE ST-PIERRE (to the S. of which is MONT ST-PIERRE, with a Roman camp), soon entering (c. 20 km.) *Pierrefonds,* a village on the S.E. border of the forest. Its restored 11-14C church has a crypt of 1060, and tower of 1552.

The huge and commanding bulk of the **Castle of Pierrefonds** was long considered one of the outstanding examples of medieval military architecture; but a critical reaction to Viollet-le-Duc's criteria of restoration has since taken effect. Adm. 10.00–12.00; 13.30–16.00 or 14.00–18.30.

Built in 1392–1407 by Louis I d'Orléans, the ambitious brother of Charles VI, it passed to Charles d'Orléans, the poet. In 1422 it was occupied by the English; in 1617 it was dismantled, and remained in a state of picturesque ruin until the mid-19C. In 1813 Napoleon I had acquired the pile, which in 1857 was entrusted by Napoleon III to *Viollet-le-Duc*, whose scholarly excesses were regarded by some as his crowning achievement. Be that as it may, the powerfully constructed building impresses in spite of his questionable 'restorations'.

Built in the form of an irregular quadrilateral enclosing a central court, the castle is strengthened by massive towers at the angles and in the middle of each side, while two rampart walks, one above the other, are carried round the walls. To the l. of the entrance is the *Salle des Gardes*, with the *Salles des Preuses* above it; to the r. the *Keep*, and beyond, the Gothic *Chapel*, among other parts of the castle which may be visited.

The D85 leads W. to *St-Jean-aux-Bois*, with a 13C church, and remains of a Benedictine abbey founded in 1152, shortly beyond which we bear N.W. to regain *Compiègne*.

26   PARIS TO VILLIERS-COTTERÊTS AND SOISSONS (FOR LAON)

N2 to (38km.) *Dammartin-en-Goële*, (77km.) *Villers-Cotterêts*, and (102km.) *Soissons*. The distance will be slightly less on the completion of a section of the motorway S. of the *Aéroport Charles-de-Gaulle*.

The N2, leaving Paris from the *Porte de la Villette* (and skirting *Le Bourget* airport; see Rte 25), may also be approached by either the A1 motorway driving N. from the *Porte de la Chapelle*, or by a branch (B3) of the A3 driving N.E. from the *Porte de Bagnolet;* these converge S.W. of *Roissy-en-France* and continue almost due N. to *Senlis*. We bear N.E. again towards *Dammartin-en-Goële*, passing (30 km. r.) *Le Mesnil-Amelot*, preserving a 15-16C Gothic church, with a robust belfry and Flamboyant façade.

38 km. **Dammartin-en-Goële** (3,500 inhab.), a picturesque hilltop town (views) once defended by a castle, demolished in the 17C. The rebuilt church of *St-Jean* preserves a porch (1482) and other features of the original 13C building; *Notre-Dame*, dating from 1480, contains the *Tomb of the founder, Antoine de Chabannes (d. 1488), a companion of Joan of Arc.

A detour can be made hence to Ermenonville. The D13 leads N. viâ (2 km.) *Othis*, with a 16C church (Renaissance façade), shortly passing near *Ève*, to the E., with a 12-16C church surmounted by a 14C spire.

9 km. *Ermenonville* (600 inhab.; *Hotels*), bounded to the N. and N.W. by the extensive FORÊT D'ERMENONVILLE, parts of it now spoilt by over-exploitation, is famous for its association with Jean-Jacques Rousseau (1712-78), who died in a pavilion (no longer existing) of the elegant 18C château of M. de Girardon; and was buried on the *Île des Peupliers*, near the S. end of the lake in the PARC D'ERMENONVILLE (adm. 9.00-17.00 or 19.00; entrance opposite the château).

Rousseau's remains were removed from his tomb in 1794 and placed in the *Panthéon,* Paris. The sandy nature of the soil in the vicinity has earned it the soubriquet 'Desert'.

Some 2.5km. N., to the r., stands the domain of **Chaalis,** once a famous and wealthy Cistercian abbey, founded in 1136, suppressed in 1785, and sold at the Revolution. Tasso paid a visit here in 1570. In 1912 it was bequeathed by its last proprietor (Mme Jacquemart-André; see p. 164) to the *Institut de France.* Of the ruined 13C church, the only relic is the N. transept. To the E. is the Prior's chapel (late 13C; restored in the 19C).

Visitors are taken on a guided tour, but few individual items merit attention among the miscellaneous collections of medieval, Egyptian, and Italian furniture, and antiquities. The first room entered contains a work ascribed to *van Orley,* and two by *Giotto,* but the majority of other paintings in the building are of doubtful attribution and little interest, with the exception perhaps of four battle-pieces by *J.-B. Martin* (in the billiard room) and, at the foot of the stairs, a portrait of Henrietta of England; and a view of the Tour de Nesle, Paris. Other rooms contain a watercolour of Rousseau's tomb by *G.-F. Meyer,* and a portrait of the Duc de Bourgogne, by *Nattier.*

4km. E. of Ermenonville lies *Montagny-Ste-Félicité,* its church remarkable for its slender belfry. *Baron,* 5km. N. of Montagny, has a 12-13C church with a 15C spire, and woodwork by the brothers *Slodtz.*—We may regain the N2 at *Nanteuil-le-Haudoin,* 6km. E. of Montagny.

Another detour may be made from (52km.) *Nanteuil-le-Haudoin,* its church retaining a fortified portal, to *Crépy-en-Valois,* 12km. N.E. by the D136.

Crépy-en-Valois (10,900 inhab.), retaining picturesque corners, was in medieval times the capital of Valois, an appanage of a branch of the royal family. Parts of the old walls survive on the valley side. Crépy suffered severely during the Hundred Years War; in 1431 it was sacked by the English; in 1814 it withstood a Prussian attack; it was also occupied briefly by the Germans in 1914, and damaged by them in 1940.

Towards the centre, approaching from the S., is the *Porte de Paris* (18C). *St-Thomas,* to the E., begun in 1180 and dedicated to Thomas Becket, retains only a 13C façade, and a tower with a 15C spire. To the N. in the old town stands *St-Denis,* with a Romanesque nave, and graceful 15C choir (and 19C steeple). By the scanty remains of its castle an *Archery Museum* has been installed. Note the *Hôtel de la Rose* (1537) in the PL. DE LA HAUTE.

9km. N.E., on the N335, lies **Morienval,** its *Church,* with three Romanesque towers, preserving fine Gothic vaulting of the early 12C.— *Pierrefonds* (see p. 220) lies 9km. further N.

We may gain the N2 some 7km. E. of Crépy.

62km. *Betz,* 5km. S.E., has a church with a Romanesque portal.

69km. *Vez,* 3km. N., is dominated by a 13-14C castle (restored by Viollet-le-Duc), with a fine pentagonal keep. Its chapel contains various antiquities, some from *Champlieu* (see p. 217). The church is of the 12-13C, with a nave covered by 16C timbers.—2km. W. lie the imposing ruins of the 12C abbey of *Lieu-Restauré,* restored in 1540, with a Flamboyant rose-window on one façade.—At *Largny-sur-Automne,* between Vez and Villers-Cotterêts, is a 12C church.—70km. Both *Vauciennes* and adjacent *Coyolles* retain 13C churches, the former unaltered.

At 77km., bypassed to the N., lies **Villers-Cotterêts** (9,000 inhab.; *Hotels*), almost surrounded by the extensive FORÊT DE RETZ. The town suffered severely in June 1918, but on 18 July it saw the opening action of the great Allied offensive under *Mangin* (when 20,000 German prisoners and 400 guns were captured) which lasted until the Armistice.

Alexandre Dumas (père; 1802-70) is its most famous native, who was born at No. 50 in the street which bears his name. He is buried in the cemetery here. A small Museum devoted to the family is in the Rue Demoustiers. Dumas commended the local andouillettes.

The **Château** was built in 1522-45 by *Philibert Delorme* and *Jacques* and *Guillaume Le Breton* for François I, to replace an earlier castle burnt down by the English in 1429. The park was laid out by *Le Nôtre*. Although the building is now used as an old people's home, parts of the interior may be visited (8.30-10.30; 14.00-17.00).

A detour may be made by following the D80 E. to (9 km.) *Corcy,* there turning N. to **Longpont,* with the impressive ruins of a Cistercian abbey founded in 1131, parts of which have been converted into a château. The church (13C), of which some walls and buttresses remain, was as large as the cathedral at Soissons.—By turning W. along the D2, we regain the N2 after 4.5 km.

At *Montgobert,* 3 km. on the far side of the main road, is the château of Pauline Bonaparte and the tomb of her first husband, Gen. Leclerc (1772-1802).

102 km. **SOISSONS** (32,100 inhab.; *Hotels*), although one of the oldest towns in France, has few relics of its past remaining. Its oval-shaped cheese 'de clovis' should be tried; also its pralines.

History. Soissons is believed to have been the *Noviodunum* of Caesar, known later as *Augusta Suessionum* or *Suessiona,* the second capital of Gallia Belgica. Here the Roman army was defeated by Clovis in 486, and in 511 Soissons became the capital of the kingdom of Neustria. Pepin le Bref was proclaimed king in the abbey of St-Médard in 752. Charles le Simple was defeated outside its walls in 923, and the town was captured in 948 by Hugues le Grand. Its medieval history is one list of sieges, frequent during the Hundred Years War. In 1814 and 1815 the fortress failed to prevent the passage of the Aisne by the Allies. In 1870 it fell after three days' bombardment. It was twice entered by the Germans in the 1914-18 War, and, on their final retirement in Aug. 1918, their gunners revenged themselves on its smoking ruins. It was spared such barbarities in the Second World War.

The two most important monuments remaining are the ruins of **St-Jean-des-Vignes* and the cathedral. The former, part of an important abbey founded in 1076, in which Becket once resided, was suppressed at the Revolution, and dismantled in 1804, with the exception of the **Façade,* which bears a striking resemblance to Reims cathedral. The imposing towers, completed in 1506, and differing from each other in style, scarcely harmonize with the rest of the façade. The large 13C cloister and cellar, and 14C refectory, among other buildings, may be visited.

Some distance to the N. stands the **Cathedral,** which although very considerably restored, still retains important sections of the original 12C Romanesque and 13C Gothic edifice. The N. side was mutilated, and the nave shattered, leaving the W. façade standing detached, and except for damage to the 14C tower, comparatively intact. The choir, completed in 1212, and the transepts, escaped without vital injury in 1918.

The **S. Transept* is the oldest (1177) and most beautiful part of the building, with an apsidal ending, and above its graceful arcades are two triforium galleries beneath the loftily placed clerestory. The N. Transept has a straight façade of the 14C, and on its E. side, a portal of the same date, with pointed and decorated gables. Its 13C stained-glass in the apse and an Adoration *after Rubens* had been removed to safety before the bombardment.

To the N. of the apse, the PL. DU CLOÎTRE (note No. 10) leads to the Rue du Collège, where, to the l., is a fine 17-18C gateway to the college.

To the E. of the cathedral is the central PL. F.-MARQUIGNY, on the far side of which are the 12C façade and two bays of the secularized church of *St-Pierre-au-Parvis*. Not far S. the Rue des Feuillants (l. off the main Rue St-Martin) leads to the *Pavillon des Arquebusiers* (1626) with an Ionic entrance-gate of 1638.

The Rue du Commerce leads N. from the main square to the rebuilt 18C *Hôtel de Ville*, on the site of the earlier castle of the Counts of Soissons. Just beyond is the church of *St-Léger*, relic of an abbey founded in 1152, retaining 13C transepts and choir, and an 11C crypt approached from the 13C cloister, and now housing an interesting provincial Museum.

Some distance to the E., on the far bank of the Aisne, are the remains of the Abbey of **St-Médard** (entrance in the Rue de Bouvines), with a 13C chapter-house and 9C *Crypt, containing the tombs of Clotaire (d. 561) and Sigebert (d. 575), son and grandson respectively, of Clovis.

From *Soissons* the N31 leads E. to (57 km.) *Reims;* the N2 leads N.E. to (30 km.) *Laon;* and N37 N. to (61 km.) *St-Quentin.*
The N31 leads due W. to (38 km.) *Compiègne*, see p. 217.

27   PARIS TO MEAUX AND CHÂTEAU-THIERRY (FOR REIMS)

N3 to (45 km.) *Meaux*, (65 km.) *La Ferté-sous-Jouarre*, and (91 km.) *Château-Thierry.*
From the *Porte de Bagnollet* we may follow the A5 for 7 km. before turning r. onto the N3; or alternatively follow the N3 direct from the *Porte de Pantin*, running parallel to the Canal de l'Ourcq, to the N. of which is *Bobigny*, the new departmental capital of Seine-St-Denis.

At 19 km. (r.) stood the FORÊT DE BONDY, once the haunt of highwaymen.—At 31 km., the D404 leads N. to (7 km.) *Nantouillet*, with the interesting remains of a 16C château built by Card. Duprat, chancellor under François I, and a 13C church with a fine Renaissance portal.—7 km. beyond lies *Dammartin-en-Goële*, see p. 220. Just N. of Nantouillet is the *Collège de Juilly*, founded by the Oratorians in 1638, which numbers among its eminent pupils Marshal Villars, Montesquieu, the Duke of Berwick, D'Artagnan, Adm. Dupetit-Thouars, Berryer, etc.

At 40 km. (r.) we pass a Monument to Gen. Gallieni (1849-1916), military governor of Paris in 1914.—Some 4 km. to the N. is a Memorial to some of the first victims of that war, among them the Catholic poet Charles Péguy (1873-1914).

46 km. **MEAUX** (42,000 inhab.; *Hotels*), whose main attraction is now the old quarter near the cathedral, was originally a stronghold of the Meldi, a Gallic tribe, commanding the abrupt river bend. Meaux was later the capital of the Haute-Brie. During the revolt of the Jacquerie (1358) nine thousand peasants were massacred here and the town was sacked. It was twice besieged by the English in the 15C. Although its

bridges were blown up by the retreating British army on 3 Sept. 1914, von Kluck's patrols entered Meaux two days later only to retire the same afternoon in the face of Gen. Manoury's advancing forces.

One of four types of Brie cheese comes from Meaux. Other varieties are those of Melun, Montereau, and Nangis. This form of cheese is recorded as early as 1217. Its andouillettes, and a confection known as 'croquettes d'or', have a local reputation. Meaux has long been famous for its mustard, which is now in fact made at Lagny-sur-Marne.

An early Bp. of Meaux was the poet and musical theorist Philippe de Vitry; more famous was Jacques-Bénigne Bossuet (1627-1704), bishop from 1681.

The *Cathedral of St-Étienne is a beautiful but weather-worn structure of the 12-16C built over an earlier sanctuary. The Flamboyant W. front, although it lacks a S. tower (merely a slated stump), is imposing. The statues of its triple portal have been destroyed, but it retains some bas-reliefs in the tympana over the doors, and some quaint gargoyles. The N. portal (13C) has a 12C statue of St Stephen and bas-reliefs illustrating his life. The S. portal (also 13C) resembles the S. portal of Notre-Dame, Paris. The *Porte Maugarni*, in the choir, dates from the 15C.

In spite of the short nave, the INTERIOR is elegant and airy. Bossuet is buried in the *Choir*, although his Monument (by *Dubois*, 1907) is in the N. nave aisle. Some panels of his pulpit have been incorporated into a reconstructed version. The organ (1627) rests on a 15C arcade.

To the N. of the cathedral is the **Bishop's Palace,** comprising various buildings of the 15-17C, and a 12C chapel. It now contains a *Museum*, which although largely devoted to Bossuet, contains paintings by *Largillière, Bouchardon, Millet*, and *Courbet*, etc. (Adm. 14.00-15.00 or 16.00 on Sun. and holidays; occasionally at other times; the gardens are open daily 10.00-12.00; 14.00-18.00 or 19.00). In the GARDEN is the Pavilion known as the '*Cabinet de Bossuet*', where many of his famous sermons were composed.

To the E. of the palace is the **Old Chapter-House** (restored), a valuable example of 13C domestic architecture, with a covered exterior staircase (15C woodwork). Passing through an archway and turning l., we shortly reach a tree-lined boulevard, flanked by a section of the defensive *Town Wall* (with the episcopal gardens above), incorporating Roman work.

Ronsard lived during 1552-54 at *Mareuil-lès-Meaux,* 5 km. S.W.

FROM MEAUX TO VILLERS-COTTERETS (41 km.). The D405 shortly passes (r.) an American Monument—one of many in this area—to the Soldiers of the Marne, beyond which (7 km.) *Vareddes* experienced a sanguinary three-day battle centred on *Côte 139,* a good viewpoint to the W.—*Germigny-l'Évêque,* 2 km. S.E., retains slight remains of Bossuet's country retreat.—12 km. *Lizy-sur-Ourcq,* 3 km. to the r., has a 15C church conserving some old glass, and a 17C market; *Ocquerre,* on the far bank of the river, preserves a Renaissance building with monumental chimneys.—16 km. *May-en-Multien* has a curious church, partly 12C.—Hence a lane descends to (5 km.) *Crouy-sur-Ourcq,* with a ruined 14C château with an imposing keep, and a church retaining a Romanesque tower and Renaissance porch.—At *Acy-en-Multien* (7 km. N.W. of May) is another 12C church altered in the 15-16C, with a 19C spire.—30 km. *Marolles* has a church with a good 12C belfry and curious Romanesque portal.

32 km. **La Ferté-Milon** (1,900 inhab.) was the birthplace of Jean Racine (1639-99). The two churches retain good stained-glass (15-16C), while above the once-fortified town are the impressive ruins of the castle (1382-1407), with a regular keep, to which the name Ferté (fermeté) refers. Note the monumental portal.—For *Villers-Cotterets,* 9 km. N. in the centre of the FORÊT DE RETZ, see p. 221.

At 54 km. (8 km. E. of Meaux), a turning (r.) leads 2 km. to the imposing ruins of the château of *Montceau* (1547-60), built by *Philibert Delorme* for Catherine de Médicis, and altered by Henri IV for Gabrielle d'Estrées; it was dismantled in 1798.

66 km. **La Ferté-sous-Jouarre** (6,900 inhab.) derives its name from a 10C fortress, later held by the Bourbons, on a now vanished island. Louis XVI and Marie-Antoinette, after the arrest of their flight at Varennes in June 1791, were brought here on their way back to Paris. The millstones in the vicinity are of great repute. A pontoon bridge thrown across the river here by the British on 9 Sept. 1914 to replace the bridge destroyed by von Kluck, allowed the advance to be made which diverted the Germans from Paris.

Jouarre (2,700 inhab.) 3 km. S., with the 13C tower remaining of its once-famous Benedictine abbey, also preserves (behind its 15C church) the important remains of a *Merovingian* *Crypt (634), with porphyry and jasper columns, surmounted by white marble capitals, and the *Sarcophagi of sundry saints (one hypothetically an Irish princess). Note also the decoration of the walls, etc. Adm. 9.00-11.30; 14.00-18.30, except Tues.; 10.30-12.00; 14.00-18.30 on Sun.; enquire at the abbey, 9 Rue Montmorin.

FROM LA FERTÉ TO MONTMIRAIL (33 km.). A pleasant detour may be made up the valley of the Petit Morin, S.E. of La Ferté, by the D204 and D31 (viâ *St-Ouen-sur-Morin*, with a 17C château by *de Brosse*) to (17.5 km.) *Sablonnières* (on the British front during the Battle of the Marne), with a church of the 12th and 16C, regaining the D407 at *Viels-Maisons* (11 km. N.E.), 21 km. E. of La Ferté.—6 km. S.W. of Sablonnières lies *Rebais*, see p. 228.

33 km. *Montmirail* (3,400 inhab.), the birthplace of Card. de Retz (1614-79), with a 14-16C church, and château commenced in 1553 by *Jean de Lilly* and finished by *Louvois*. On 11 Feb. 1814 Montmirail was the scene of Napoleon's victory over the combined forces of Russia and Prussia.—*Sézanne*, see p. 228, lies 24 km. S.E.; and *Épernay* lies 40 km. N.E.

Although the direct road (N3) between *La Ferté* and *Château-Thierry* (26 km. N.E.) is the most rapid, it is of little interest.

At 69 km. *Chamigny* (r.) has a partly 13C church, as does (75 km.) *Montreuil-aux-Lions*.—At 89 km. the D9 leads 7 km. N.W. to BOIS BELLEAU, with a large American military cemetery (1918); to the r. at this junction a lane leads 1.5 km. S. to *Côte 204*, with another American Monument (commanding a good view of—92 km.—*Château-Thierry*, see below).

The alternative road (D402) leads N.E. from La Ferté, crossing the Marne, and threads its way through a number of riverside villages. At 17 km. the church of *Nogent-l'Artaud* (on the S. bank) has a 12C choir and nave, altered in the 16C.—*Chézy-sur-Marne* (4.5 km. N.E.) has a 15C church with a fine tower, and to the N.W. the ruins of a Benedictine abbey founded in the 9C.—Regaining the N. bank, we pass (6 km. N.) *Essômes*, with a 13-14C church (restored), before turning E. into *Château-Thierry*.

Château-Thierry (13,900 inhab.), with the old town sheltering below the castle-crowned hill, and guarding the river-crossing, was the birthplace of Jean de la Fontaine (1621-95).

History. Said to be named from a castle built by Charles Martel for the Frankish king Thierry IV (d. 737), Château-Thierry was later held by the counts of Champagne. It was captured in turn by the English (in 1421), by Charles V (1544), and by the Leaguers in 1591; pillaged in 1652 during the War of the Fronde; and bombarded in 1814, when Napoleon defeated the Russians and Prussians in the neighbourhood. It was held briefly by the Germans in 1914, and was re-entered by them on 31 May 1918; and until their withdrawal on 21 July, was the centre of bitter fighting both in containment and counter-attack. The town also suffered by bombardment in the invasion of 1940.

From the bridge, the Rue Gén.-de-Gaulle leads N., passing (r.) a 16C belfry, to the central PLACE, with the *Hôtel de Ville* ahead. Steps to the W. of the latter ascend to a footpath, which, followed to the r., leads to the *Porte St-Jean*, the entrance to the castle enceinte (views). Beyond is the *Porte St-Pierre*, a gateway in the town walls. This may also be approached by the Rue du Château, climbing N.E. from the S. side of the PLACE, passing the modern hospital (r.) preserving a late-17C chapel, and (at No. 32), the old *Hôtel de Marnay d'Hangest*.

By turning l. at the top of the steps behind the Hôtel de Ville, we shortly reach the Rue de la Fontaine, where at No. 12, dating from 1559, is the birthplace of the fabulist, the most eminent of the Castelthéodoriciens, and now a Museum. Lower down the hill, by turning r. across the Av. de Soissons, we reach *St-Crépin* (15-16C, restored), with a heavy square tower.

Montmirail (see p. 225) lies 24 km. S.E.; *Épernay* lies 48 km. E. on the N3, and *Reims*, 62 km. N.E., may be reached by following the N3 and N380.

FROM CHÂTEAU-THIERRY TO SOISSONS, VIÂ OULCHY-LE-CHÂTEAU (41 km. on the N37). At 14 km. *Coincy* (3 km. E.) is an interesting 12-15C church (restored) with a 12C crypt; at *Brécy*, 2 km. S., is another church of the 11-14C.—17 km. *Armentières-sur-Ourcq*, to the E., retains picturesque ruins of a 14C castle.— 21 km. *Oulchy-le-Château*, one of many villages in the vicinity damaged in the fighting of July 1918, retains a Romanesque church within the enceinte of a castle of the counts of Champagne. There is a small British cemetery behind the church. Beyond, to the E., rises the *Butte de Chalmont*, with a Monument by *Landowski* to the Second Battle of the Marne.—2 km. N.W. of the N37 lies *Oulchy-la-Ville*, and *Rozet-St-Albin* (further S.W.), both with 12C churches.

33 km. (r.) at *Buzancy* is a Monument inscribed "Ici fleurira toujours le glorieux Chardon d'Écosse parmi les Roses de France" after the Scots entry into the victorious attack of 22 July 1918.—35.5 km. *Berzy-le-Sec* and *Courmelles*, to the l. of the road, contain interesting 12C churches, the latter with a remarkable apse.—41 km. *Soissons*, see p. 222.

FROM CHÂTEAU-THIERRY TO SOISSONS, VIÂ FÈRE-EN-TARDENOIS (48 km. on the N367 and D6). The N367 climbs N.E. from Château-Thierry, at 17 km. passing near *Villeneuve-sur-Fère* (2 km. N.W.), birthplace of Paul Claudel (1868-1955), and at 22 km. entering *Fère-en-Tardenois* (3,100 inhab.; *Hotels*), British G.H.Q. during the First Battle of the Aisne (Sept.-Oct. 1914), and the scene of fierce fighting in May-Aug. 1918. The 15-16C church has interesting painted woodwork and other carving. The robustly pillared market-hall (of 1552) has been reroofed.—3 km. N.E. lie the ruins of the 13C *Castle of Fère*, approached by a Renaissance galleried viaduct of five arches, 66 ft high, built by *Jean Bullant*.— Continuing N. on the D6, we soon bear N.W. to (48 km.) *Soissons*, see p. 222.

28   PARIS TO SÉZANNE (FOR ST-DIZIER)

A   Viâ Champs and Coulommiers

N34 (21.5 km. *Champs*).—61 km. *Coulommiers*.—111 km. *Sézanne*.

From the *Porte de Vincennes*, after passing (r.) the *Château de Vincennes* (see Rte 20), we bear l. through the N.E. corner of the Bois. Beyond the park, the N34 climbs N.E. through the suburb of **Nogent-sur-Marne**. The château in which Charles V died in 1380 was given by Charles VII to his mistress Agnès Sorel, and was afterwards occupied by Diane de Poitiers; it was demolished in the 18C. Watteau died at Nogent in 1721. Louis Daguerre (1787-1851), who gave his name to the daguerreotype, died at *Bry-sur-Marne,* further to the E.

At 18.5 km., the D104 turns r. through *Gournay-sur-Marne,* to the E. of which (after 3 km.) is the *Château de Champs. (Adm. 11.00-16.30 or 19.00 depending on the season; closed Tues. and when in official occupation. Visitors are accompanied.)

The château was built in 1703-07 by *J.-B. Bullet* on the site of an earlier building. It was later the residence of the Princesse de Conti (daughter of Louis XIV and Louise de la Vallière), and in 1757 of Mme de Pompadour. Pillaged during the Revolution, it was restored in the 1890s and since 1934 has been used by visiting heads of state.

From the entrance vestibule we ascend to the FIRST FLOOR and turn into the MUSIC ROOM, with a frieze of instruments and dessus de portes by *Monnoyer,* and commanding an impressive view of the *Gardens,* laid out by *Claude Desgots,* a nephew of Le Nôtre. To the l., the GUEST ROOM, with dessus de portes by *Boucher;* to the r., MME DE POMPADOUR'S BEDROOM, with good painted woodwork, and dessus de portes by *Carle Van Loo.* The following room contains a portrait of Mme de Pompadour as 'La belle jardinière' by *Drouais;* the scenes of sheep and goats are by *Desportes.*

We descend to the GROUND FLOOR and to the GRAND SALON, with a Coromandel screen, and furniture covered with Aubusson tapestry. To the l. is the DINING ROOM, with pink marble fountains and serving tables. *Desportes* and *Oudry* were responsible for the dessus de portes. A large canvas depicts a hunting-scene at Champs, by *J.-B. Martin* (?). To the r. is the sober SMOKING-ROOM, with good panelling, 18C Beauvais tapestries, a *Boulle* bookcase, and a portrait of Louis XV by *Van Loo,* given by the king to Mme de Pompadour. We next enter the *SALON CHINOIS, decorated c. 1740 by *Christophe Huet.* Note the fine chandelier, Tabriz carpet, furniture covered with Beauvais tapestry depicting La Fontaine's fables, and console table in onyx. The next room displays *Mignard*'s portrait of Louis XIV in his minority. The penultimate room which may be visited is the BLUE BOUDOIR, also attractively decorated by *Huet.*

Hence we continue E. on the D217 bis—skirting the New Town of *Marne-la-Vallée* under construction—at 7.5 km. passing (r.) the château of *Guermantes* (17C), a name made familiar by Proust (adm. 14.00-17.45 on Sat., Sun., and holidays, from 15 Mar. to 15 Nov.).

Some 3.5 km. S., at the next crossroad, stands the château of *Ferrières,* rebuilt in the Renaissance style for the Rothschild family by *Joseph Paxton* in 1857. *Lagny* (see below) lies 2 km. N. of this junction.

The detour may be continued viâ (12.5 km.) *Jossigny,* with a château of 1743 (adm. weekends and Mon.). Continuing E., we regain the N34 at *Villiers-sur-Marne.*—There is a fine 13C church at *Villeneuve-le-Comte,* a planned village of 1203, 7 km. S.E. of Jossigny, on the edge of the FORÊT DE CRÉCY. where in Sept. 1914 the British army rested after its retreat from Mons, and before advancing on the Marne.

20.5 km. *Chelles,* where stood a Merovingian palace in the 6C, where Chilperic I was murdered at the instigation of his wife Fredegonde. Nothing remains of the famous abbey founded here in 660. The *Alfred-Bonno Museum* contains local prehistoric and medieval collections.— Passing (r.) the château of *Pomponne* (1682; restored in the 19C), we enter (29 km.) **Lagny** (16,300 inhab.), the ancient *Latiniacum.* The church of *St-Pierre* (or *N.-D. des Ardents*), the choir of an unfinished abbey-church of the 13-14C, contains several fine tombs. Of the abbey (founded in 643 by a Scottish monk, St Furcy, and destroyed by the Normans), only a large 17C building remains, now used as the Hôtel de Ville. Other objects of interest are a 13C fountain, a 14C archway, and the ruined 15C church of *St-Furcy.*—The Romanesque church of *St-Thibault-des-Vignes* (12C), 3 km. S.W., retains some fine capitals.

32 km. (r.) *Montévrain* has a 12-13C church, with curious capitals.—36.5 km. Louis Braille (1809-52) was born at *Coupvray,* to the l. To the N. and E. of this point took place the Battle of the Ourcq (Sept. 1914). We cross the Grand-Morin at (42 km.) *Couilly,* with a Romanesque tower to its church.—*Meaux* (see p. 223) lies 10 km. to the N.

Just to the S.E. of Couilly is *Pont-aux-Dames,* named after the Bernardine nunnery to which Mme du Barry retired after the death of Louis XV, and destroyed at the Revolution.

47 km. **Crécy-en-Brie,** retaining a number of mills, and remains of ancient fortifications.—*La Chapelle-sur-Crécy* (2 km., E.) has a fine 13-14C church, with a beautiful triforium, and a series of curious masks in the choir. The road climbs up above the valley, descending again to (61 km.) *Coulommiers.*

Coulommiers (11,400 inhab.), the birthplace of the painter Jean de Boullogne (1591-1634), and a busy but dull market town, was the ancient *Columbariae.* The château built by *De Brosse* for the Duchesse de Longueville in the 17C, and described in Mme de La Fayette's 'La Princesse de Clèves', was demolished (with the exception of two pavilions) by the Duc de Chevreuse in 1737. Adjacent to the site is the church of the Capuchins (17C) with a small museum. Of more interest, situated on the hill to the N.E. of the town, is the chapel (13C) and buildings (15-16C) of a *Commandery of the Templars,* now part of the Hospital farm.

Mauperthuis (6 km. S.W.) is described in Gautier's 'Mademoiselle de Maupin'.
Rebais (12 km. N.E. on the D222) retains a 12C Romanesque church, part of an abbey founded c. 615 by St Ouen, with a good 13C tomb.
Jouarre (see p. 225) lies 14 km. N. of Coulommiers.

The N34 ascends the plateau at (65.5 km.) *Chailly-en-Brie,* and continues due E. to (79 km.) *La Ferté-Gaucher.* This is also approached by the more picturesque road following the river valley, viâ (18 km.) *Jouy-sur-Morin,* with a 13-16C church.—*La Ferté-Gaucher* also has a church of the same period.

98 km. *Esternay,* just beyond which (l.) lies its 16-17C château.—111 km. **Sézanne** (3,500 inhab.; *Hotels*), lying amidst vineyards, retains an interesting 15-16C church with a Renaissance S. portal and upper windows, and a good stone reredos. Its andouillettes are worth tasting.

To the N. and N.E. of the chalk plateau of Sézanne is a 'pocket' of clay forming the MARSHES OF ST-GOND, in the neighbourhood of which was the scene of Foch's victory over von Bülow in the Battle of the Marne (9 Sept. 1914).
St-Dizier lies 92 km. further E. on the N4, off which the D5 leads N.E. to *Châlons-sur-Marne,* 55 km. from Sézanne.

B   Viâ Rozay-en-Brie

This faster but duller road (N4) drives E. from the *Porte de Picpus,* passing at (13.5 km.) *Champigny* a 13-14C church of some interest. At 17 km. (r.) it also passes near the château of *Ormesson* (see p. 229).—32.5 km. *Presles* (r.) has an imposing 16C church-tower.—The road bypasses (34.5 km.) *Tournan-en-Brie,* with a restored 13C church and 15C town gate used as the Hôtel de Ville.

At 37.5 km. (r.) lies the château *des Boulayes* (1785).—At 44 km. we bypass *Fontenay-Trésigny.*—5 km. N., at *La Houssaye,* is the château where Marshal Augereau received Napoleon in 1807, and died in 1816; his tomb is in the 13-14C church.

51 km. (r.) **Rozay-en-Brie** (1,800 inhab.), an attractive village with traces of fortifications, and a 13C church restored in the 16C, with a 12C belfry.—2 km. S. stands the Château of *La Grange-Bléneau* (16-17C), which belonged to La Fayette from 1799 until his death in 1834, and retains his library. He received Pitt here in 1802.

From the crossroads at 62 km., the D231 leads 21 km. S.E. to *Provins* (see p. 230), passing, at 2.5 km., *Jouy-le-Châtel,* with remains of a 13C keep and other fortifications, a restored château, and a 12C church with 15-16C alterations.

74 km. *Beton-Bazoches* retains ·a 12C church, as does (89 km.) *Montceaux-lès-Provins,* the latter with 17C additions.—98 km. *Esternay,* and (111 km.) *Sézanne,* see p. 228.

C. The A4 motorway, driving E. from the *Porte de Bercy,* will in due course facilitate the exit from Paris in this direction. It will meet the N34 S. of *Couilly,* before bearing N.E. between *Meaux* and *La Ferté-sous-Jouarre* towards *Château-Thierry* (see Rte 27).

29   PARIS TO PROVINS (FOR TROYES)

N19 to (29.5 km.) *Brie-Comte-Robert.*—63.5 km. *Nangis.*—84 km. *Provins.*

From the *Porte Picpus,* we follow the N19 S.E.

At 12 km. the N186 leads l. past the church of *St-Christophe* (13C, with a remarkable tower-porch of the 12C), and across the Marne to *St-Maur des-Fossés,* once famous for its Benedictine abbey, where the entrails of Henry V were buried. The magnificent château, a disfigured entrance of which may be seen at No. 36 Rue du Four, bought by Catherine de Médicis in 1563; visited by Budé, Ronsard, Rabelais, Desportes, etc.; and where Mme de La Fayette wrote her 'Princesse de Clèves', was destroyed during the Revolution.

At 15 km. the D60 (continued by the D185) leads 5.5 km. E. (and S. of the *Porte de Bonneuil*) to the château of *Ormesson* (16-17C; for authorization to visit, apply to the owner), passing to the S., *Sucy-en-Brie,* with the châteaux of *Sucy* (under restoration), built by *Lambert de Thorigny* in 1640, and of *Montaleau* (now the Mairie), where Mme de Sévigné, when a girl, frequently visited her uncle.

21.5 km. To the l. lies the château of *Gros-Bois,* built by the Duc d'Angoulême at the beginning of the 17C, and sumptuously furnished during the First Empire by Marshal Berthier. The interior may be visited by appointment.—The churches at adjacent *Villecresnes* (with a Romanesque tower and 12C nave), at *Marolles-en-Brie* (2 km. E.), and at (26.5 km.) *Servon* (13C), are of interest.

29.5 km. **Brie-Comte-Robert** (8,700 inhab.), founded by Robert, Comte de Dreux in the 10C, is situated on the rich Plateau de la Brie, long famous for its cheese. The ruins of the castle (c. 1170), opposite No. 35 Rue du Gén.-Leclerc, and six 13C arches, the remains of the chapel of the old Hospital (1207) in the Rue des Halles, are of interest. *St-Étienne,* 13C but altered in the 15-16C, contains 15C wood-carving, 16C glass, and a fine 13C rose-window in the apse.

34.5 km. *Suisnes,* 1 km. S., retains a château once owned by Adm. de Bougainville, who initiated, with his gardener Cochet, the rose-culture

of the area.—36.5 km. *Coubert,* with a château built in the 18C by
Samuel Bernard, the financier.—*Soignolles* (1.5 km. S.) has interesting
stalls with misericords (1530-40) in its church.

41 km. *Ozouer-Courquetaine* (1 km. E.) has a late 16C church with a
copper font-cover by *Robbe* (1731), and picturesque remains of a
château.—6 km. beyond, at *Chaumes-en-Brie,* the 13-14C church
contains a Christ by *Ph. de Champaigne.* The father and grandfather of
Couperin 'le Grand' were organists here.—The ruined château of *Vivier,*
3 km. N., was once the rendezvous of royal hunts.

52.5 km. *Mormant,* 5 km. N. of which, at *Courtomer,* is a 13C
church.—Beyond Mormant, we pass the extensive petrol refineries of
Grandpuits, and at 63.5 km. enter *Nangis,* an old town with a 13-15C
church with elegant flying buttresses, and remains of a 14-16C castle
now partly occupied by the Hôtel de Ville.

68 km. The *Church at **Rampillon,** 1 km. S., with a remarkable
sculptured portal, and flanked by a tower attributed to the Templars,
whose quarters here were burnt by the English in 1432, is of considerable
interest; of equal importance is the *Church of **St-Loup-de-Naud,** 4 km.
S.E. at 79.5 km., one of the earliest in the Île de France. Partly of the
11C, its sculptured portal is among the best-preserved examples of 12C
work, but the interior of the church deserves a restoring hand.

84 km. **PROVINS** (12,300 inhab.; *Hotels*), one of the most attractive
towns within easy reach of Paris, is finely situated at the junction of the
Voulzie and Durteint. Once the capital of the Brie, with an important
fair, and with a prosperous population of 80,000 (?), it was ruined by
plague (1373), the English wars, and the Wars of Religion. Among its
natives were the trouvères Guyot de Provins (12C) and Thibaut IV,
Comte de Champagne (1201-53).

Provins has long been celebrated for its crimson roses (wrongly called Provence
roses), which are said to have been originally brought by the Crusaders from the
Holy Land. They were introduced into the coat-of-arms of Edmund of Lancaster
(1245-96) when he married the widow of Henri le Gros, Comte de Champagne.

Provins consists of an upper and lower town, the former still partially
surrounded by well-preserved *Ramparts,** seen to advantage on
approaching the town from the W. It is advisable to turn l. off the N19
and follow the tree-lined lane parallel to the walls, passing first the *Porte
St-Jean,* and the so-called 'Brèche des Anglais' (through which the
English forced their way into the town in 1432), entering the Old Town
by the *Porte de Jouy.* A short distance W. of the central PL. DU CHÂTEL is
the *Grange-aux-Dîmes* (13C), the tithe-barn of the canons of St-
Quiriace, consisting of two vaulted storeys resting on piers, in the
pointed style. It now contains a small 'Musée lapidaire'.

To the S.E. rises the impressive *Tour de César** or *Grosse Tour,* a
massive 12C keep on a motte now surrounded by a rampart ('Pâté-aux-
Anglais'), added by Thomas Guerard, an Englishman, during their
occupation of Provins. The tower (adm. 9.30 or 10.00-12.30; 14.00-16.00
or 18.00) is curiously constructed, and worth visiting.

Further downhill stands the conspicuous church of *St-Quiriace,**
begun in 1160, and remarkable for its plain massive architecture. The
large choir is early 12C; the unfinished nave, with a fine triforium, is
13C. The cupola over the crossing dates from 1665. The crypt may be

just seen. St Quiriace was a converted Jew (of which there were once many in Provins), who assisted the Empress Helena in her search for the True Cross.

A museum is projected in the Rue du Palais, just to the N.

The Upper Town also commands a good view N. towards the **Hôpital Général** on the far side of the valley, beyond the umbrageous BLVD. D'ALIGRE, built on the site of a monastery of the Cordeliers founded by Thibaut IV in 1237. Two sides of a beautiful 14-15C *Cloister,* and a chapter-house, survive; the heart of Thibaut V is enshrined in the chapel.

The Rue St-Thibault descends into the Lower Town, passing (r.) the *Hôtel-Dieu,* with a 13C portal. Further along this street (Rue des Capucines) are the *Hôtel de Vauluisant* and *Hôtel de la Croix d'Or,* both dating from the 13C.

To the N. of the PL. DU GÉN.-LECLERC stands *Ste-Croix,* with a nave and aisles of the 13C, and a choir of the 16C. Further E. is *St-Ayoul* (11-16C), with a 12C portal, and a reredos and other wood-carvings by *P. Blasset* (1612-63), buried in the church. Abelard sought refuge in the priory of which this church was a dependency, in 1122, the year before he founded the *Abbaye du Paraclet* (c. 25 km. S.E., beyond *Nogent-sur-Seine).*

A few yards N. of St-Ayoul stands the 16C *Tour Notre-Dame-du-Val,* surviving from an earlier cloistered church. Some defensive walls of the Lower Town may be seen along the BLVD. CARNOT, and its extensions, skirting the river to the S. and E.

The church at *Voulton* (12-13C), 7 km. N.E., on the D71, is of interest for its elegant vaulting.

From PROVINS TO SENS, see p. 234. *Troyes* lies 65 km. E. on the N60.

30   PARIS TO MELUN AND SENS (FOR AUXERRE)

N5 to (46 km.) *Melun.*—76 km. *Montereau.*—112 km. *Sens.*

From the *Pl. de la Bastille,* we follow the Av. Daumesnil to the *Porte de Picpus,* and shortly bear S. through an industrial area to (18 km.) *Villeneuve-St-Georges.* At adjacent *Crosne* (to the S.E.) was Boileau's country house, 'Les Préaux', from which he took his name.

Further along the valley at *Yerres,* in the Pl. du Taillis near the church, is the entrance to a manor owned by Guillaume Budé.—*Brunoy,* 2 km. S., with a curiously decorated church, gave its name to a marquisate conferred on Wellington after Waterloo by Louis XVIII.—The picturesque *Moulin de Jarcy* lies some 4 km. S.E. We may regain the N5 from either Brunoy or Jarcy.

At 21 km. we enter the FORÊT DE SÉNART, once sacred to Druids, beyond which the New Town of *Melun-Sénart* is under construction.

46 km. **Melun** (37,000 inhab.; *Hotels*), one of the capitals of the Brie, and now of the department of Seine-et-Marne, is of Gallo-Roman foundation. The oldest part of the town lies on an island in the Seine, connected to either bank by bridges rebuilt since blown up during the heavy fighting here in 1944. Abélard founded a school of philosophy at Melun in 1101, when he was only twenty-two. Jacques Amyot (1513-93), the humanist, was born here. Its eel-pies are a local delicacy.

St-Aspais (15-16C), on the N. bank, was also damaged. *Notre-Dame,* on the island, was founded by King Robert, who died at Melun in 1031. It was much altered in the 15C.

6 km. N.E., off the D215, stands the château of **Vaux-le-Vicomte, built by *Le Vau* in 1656-61 for Fouquet, Louis XIV's superintendent of finance, and adorned with paintings by Mignard and decorated by Le Brun. The formal **Gardens were one of *Le Nôtre*'s first commissions.

Molière's 'Les Fâcheux' was performed here on the occasion of the extravagant fête given on 17 Aug. 1661 in honour of the young king, which also caused Fouquet's downfall. La Fontaine described this splendid entertainment, and after Fouquet's arrest (only nineteen days later), wrote his 'Élégie aux nymphes de Vaux'. The tapestries were woven for the château in a manufactory specially set up locally, which was then transferred to the Gobelins at Paris. The building, which survived the Revolution, was bought in 1873 by an industrialist, Alfred Sommier (whose family still live there), and thoroughly restored.

The sumptuously furnished rooms on the Ground Floor, including the impressive domed *Grand Salon*, may be visited from April to Oct., 10.00-12.00; 14.00-18.00; 10.00-18.00 on Sun. and holidays. The fountains play on the 2nd and last Sat. of each month between 15.00 and 18.00.

At *Champeaux,* 7 km. further E., birthplace of the scholastic philosopher Guillaume de Champeaux (d. 1121), is a large 12-14C church, with quaint stalls and misericords by *Richard Falaise* (1522), 14C monuments, and good glass by *Nicolas Masson* and *Alain Courjon.*—At *Blandy* (3 km. S.W.) is a ruined castle of the 12-14C.

3 km. S.W. of *Melun* (by the N372), in the park of the château, are the ruins of a Cistercian nunnery, the *Abbaye du Lys,* built in 1244 by Blanche of Castile.

The N5 drives S. from Melun through the forest, by-passing the resort of *Bois-le-Roi,* to (18 km.) *Fontainebleau,* see Rte 31.

5.5 km. S.E. of *Melun,* at *Chartrettes,* is a château built by Henri IV for Gabrielle d'Estrées.

The N5bis leads S.E. from Melun. At 64 km. *Machault* (3 km. to the W.) was the home of Guillaume de Machault (c. 1300-77), an important figure in medieval music.

76 km. **Montereau-faut-Yonne** (21,600 inhab.), at the confluence of the Yonne and Seine, derives its name (*Monasteriolum*) from a monastery founded in the 6C. In the church hangs the sword of Jean sans Peur, Duke of Burgundy, assassinated on the bridge here in 1419 by partisans of the Dauphin, afterwards Charles VII. A statue of Napoleon (between the restored 18C bridges) commemorates his defeat of the Germans here in Feb. 1814.

Some 15 km. N.E., off the D18, lie the impressive ruins of the Cistercian abbey of *Preuilly,* founded in 1118 by St Stephen Harding, Abbot of Cîteaux (a native of Sherborne in Dorset).—3 km. beyond, at *Donnemarie,* are remains of ancient fortifications and a 12-13C *Church, the figures in its portal decapitated at the Revolution, and with two galleries of a 16C cloister.

3 km. S. of Montereau, we turn l. onto the N5, which ascends the valley of the Yonne past (100 km.) *Pont-sur-Yonne,* with an interesting 12-15C church.—The château of *Fleurigny* (13 km. E. on the D25), of c. 1526, retains a window by *Jean Cousin* in its chapel, and a fine carved chimneypiece in the Salle des Gardes.

112 km. **SENS** (27,900 inhab.; *Hotels*), lying for the most part on the E. bank of the river, and on the borders of Burgundy, was described by Thicknesse as 'a large ragged ancient city, but adorned with a most noble cathedral well worthy of the notice of strangers'. It has been praised for its gastronomy, particularly its andouillettes.

History. Known in antiquity as *Agedincum* or *Agendincum,* Sens was the chief town of the Senones, a powerful Gallic tribe to which Brennus, who (according to tradition) captured Rome in 390 B.C., belonged. Christianized in the 3C, it became the seat of a widely-spread archbishopric, to which even Paris was suffragan until 1627. In 1140, the council at which St Bernard secured the condemnation of the doctrines of Abélard met here; in 1234 Louis IX was married to Margaret of Provence in the cathedral. During the Wars of Religion, its citizens were enthusiastic supporters of the League.

Thomas Becket spent part of his exile (from 1166) in the Abbaye de Ste-Colombe (see below); the architect William of Sens was born here, as was the poet Rutebeuf (d. 1285); Marivaux (1688-1763) lived some years in the town; as did Mallarmé in 1857-60.

We pass, to the r. on approaching Sens on the N5, the *Abbaye de Ste-Colombe,* founded in the 6C, rebuilt in the 13C, and restored since its destruction in 1793.

The old centre of *Sens* (pronounced *Sánss*) is surrounded by a pleasant oval of wide tree-lined boulevards, some sections of which are abutted by medieval walls, of which an isolated tower and a postern of 1260 survive.

From the PL. J.-JAURÈS (in the centre of the N. perimeter) this oval is bisected by the Rue de la République, in turn bisected at right-angles by the narrow Grande-Rue, leading W. to the river, and the church of *St-Maurice* (12-16C). To the N.E. of this intersection stands the earliest Gothic cathedral in France, coeval with the choir of Suger's basilica at St-Denis.

The *Cathedral of St-Étienne was begun c. 1130 by Abp. Sanglier, and after alterations in the 13-14C, was completed in 1490-1520. Several of its features were reproduced at Canterbury by William of Sens, to whom the rebuilding of the E. end of the English cathedral was entrusted in 1175.

The W. front, with three richly-sculptured portals, was ruthlessly mutilated in 1793; only the figure of St Stephen on the main pillar of the central portal escaped, being protected from the general destruction by the words 'La Loi' engraved on the book in his hand! The sculptures here are of the 12C, except the tympanum (Legend of St Stephen), which is 14C. The statues above the windows over the door are modern.

The N. portal has two 12C reliefs, and the legend of St John the Baptist in the tympanum; the S. portal (14C) contains statuettes of prophets, and is devoted to the Death, Assumption, and Coronation of the Virgin.

The S. Tower (240 ft) or 'Tour de Pierre' is mainly 14C (completed 1535); the N. Tower is known as the 'Tour de Plomb' from its former lead covering, destroyed in 1845. The richly-decorated transeptal portals, by *Martin Cambiges,* date from 1490-1513.

INTERIOR. The *Stained-glass throughout the cathedral is worthy of note. The nave is supported by piers alternating with coupled columns. The altarpiece on the l. side dates from a tomb of 1515. The four marble columns of the 18C high-altar once formed part of the original monument of Louis XIV in the Pl. des Victoires, Paris.

The transepts contain early 16C glass. On the N. side of the Ambulatory are the oldest *Windows. In the CHAP. STE-COLOMBE (1st on l. of Choir) is the tomb of Dauphin Louis (1729-65), father of Louis XVI, by *G. Coustou.* Here are also reliefs from the destroyed tomb of Card. Duprat, Abp. of Sens (1525-35), and the fine kneeling statues of two other archbishops (1636). In the CHAP. DE ST-THOMAS-DE-CANTORBÉRY is a 12C statue; the saint's vestments and mitre may be seen in the

Treasury, containing a 10C carved ivory coffin, among other objects.

Immediately to the S. of the cathedral is the *Palais Synodal*(13C), but restored in 1860 by Viollet-le-Duc, who was impelled (it is said) by admiration of its six fine windows. The Provincial Estates of Central France were assembled here by Charles V in 1367.

Further E., beyond a vaulted passage with a Renaissance doorway, stands the *Archbishops' Palace* (1510-65). The old *Seminary* nearby contains good 18C wood-carvings.

Opposite the cathedral, to the N. of the decrepit Market-Place, is the *Hôtel de la Pointe,* erected by the Card. de Bourbon in 1567.

To the S. of the cathedral, at the corner of the Rue de la République and Rue Jean-Cousin, is the *Maison d'Abraham,* with quaintly carved beams (but in urgent need of repair) and the *Maison du Pillier.* At No. 8 (16C) in the latter street is the *Musée Jean-Cousin,* devoted to the artist (1501-89), born at *Soucy,* 7 km. N.E. of Sens.

Beyond is *St-Pierre-le-Rond* (13-16C; under restoration); while in the adjacent *Hôtel Vésou* is the local *Museum* and *Library,* containing Gallo-Roman sculpture, etc., and early MSS.

To the E. of the main boulevard, in the grounds of a hospital, is *St-Jean* (13-17C), with a fine 13C apsidal chapel, a rare type of Burgundian Gothic.—Further E. is the ill-restored church of *St-Savinien* or *St-Pierre-le-Vief,* with an 11-13C belfry, and crypt of 1001.

From SENS TO (47 km. N.) PROVINS, follow the D412, turning r. off the N5 at (12 km. N.) *Pont-sur-Yonne.* The D81, continued by the D225, leads W. to (46 km.) *Nemours,* see p. 242.

Troyes lies 65 km. E. on the N60; *Auxerre,* 51 km. S.E. on the N6; and *Montargis,* 51 km. S.W. on the N60.

31 PARIS TO FONTAINEBLEAU, NEMOURS, AND CHÂTEAU-LANDON (FOR GIEN AND BOURGES)

A6 for 49 km.; N7 to (64 km.) *Fontainebleau;* N7 to (79 km.) *Nemours.*—94 km. *Château-Landon.*

Although Fontainebleau may also be approached viâ *Melun* (see Rte 30), the most direct (and recommended) road is the A6 motorway, leaving Paris by the *Porte de Gentilly* or *Porte d'Italie.* Just after leaving the Blvd. Périphérique we pass a new hospital, replacing the *Hospice de Bicêtre,* a famous lunatic asylum founded by Richelieu in 1634 on the site of a 13C castle built by John, Bp. of Winchester (whose name Bicêtre is thought to be a corruption).

At 11 km. the l.-hand bifurcation leads past *Rungis-Halles,* the main market complex of Paris, built to replace the congested Halles Centrales (see p. 130).—16 km. **Orly Airport** (*Hotels*). The old village of *Orly,* N.E. of the airport, clusters round its church.

Shortly beyond this intersection the A10 (for *Orléans*), off which diverges the A11 (for *Chartres;* see Rte 33C), bears S.W.

The A6 bypasses (29 km., l.) the New Town of *Évry;* and at 32 km. (l.) *Corbeil-Essonnes.* Near the church of *St-Spire* (close to the Seine at *Corbeil*), with a 12C nave and earlier transept (the Romanesque part of the choir has been detached from its 15C addition), is the 14C gatehouse of a former abbey.

At 49 km. we bear S.E. of the A6 which continues across country towards Nemours, Auxerre, etc.

51 km. The N372 leads S.W. to (9.5 km.) *Milly-la-Forêt,* passing (5.5 km.) *Courances,* with a château in the Louis-XIII style, and gardens designed by *Le Nôtre.* It was briefly Gen. Montgomery's residence during the Liberation. The *Moulin de Grena* (1370) may be seen at adjacent *Moigny.* **Milly-la-Forêt** (3,500 inhab.; *Hotels*), on the W. outskirts of the FORÊT DE FONTAINEBLEAU, has an 11-12C church, a ruined 12C castle, and market-hall of 1479. The 12C *Chapelle St-Blaise* was restored and decorated by *Jean Cocteau*(1889-1963), who died at Milly, and is buried there. The *Botanical Garden* of medicinal plants is of interest. *Fontainebleau* lies 17 km. due E.

At 52 km. (r.) *Fleury-en-Bière,* is an imposing *château built by *Pierre Lescot* and enlarged by Richelieu, containing fine woodwork, furniture, and paintings (by *Natoire, Oudry,* and *Rigaud,* etc.).

55 km. Millet and Th. Rousseau are both buried at *Chailly-en-Bière,* 1 km. N.; Bazille, Monet, Renoir, Sisley, and Seurat also painted there.—1 km. S. at this junction lies the village of **Barbizon** (1,200 inhab.; *Hotels;* the tenines de gibier should be sampled), which although more sophisticated than it was in its early days, is still the resort of artists. It gave its name to the Barbizon School of painters in the last century, who made it their headquarters; among them Millet, Corot, Th. Rousseau, Diaz, and Daubigny (as described in the Goncourts' novel 'Manette Salomon', 1867).

On meeting the N7, we enter the FORÊT DE FONTAINEBLEAU, and at 64 km. reach the CARREFOUR DE LA LIBÉRATION, on the perimeter of the town itself.

FONTAINEBLEAU (16,600 inhab.; *Hotels*), from *Fons Blandi* or *Fontaine de Bland,* with its palace, and finely situated in the middle of its forest, is one of the pleasantest resorts in the neighbourhood of Paris.

The station (regular service from the *Gare de Lyon*) is c. 2 km. N.E. of the palace; bus service between the two. S.I., 38 Rue Grande (for information regarding autocar circuits of the forest, etc.).

History. Fontainebleau is first mentioned as a royal hunting-seat in 1137, and was later fortified. In 1169 Thomas Becket, then in exile, consecrated the chapel of *St-Saturnin.* In 1259 St Louis founded, nearby, a monastery for the Trinitarians, who had a hospital here. Philippe IV was born at Fontainebleau, and died here; but its real creator was François I, who here assembled a group of Italian artists, including Serlio, Rosso, Primaticcio, Vignola, and Nicolo dell'Abate. The keeper of the Library was the poet Mellin de Saint-Gelais (1487-1558). François found the palace almost derelict, for Charles VII and his successors had deserted it for the Loire. His grandsons François II and Henri III were also born here. Henri IV spent vast sums on the building, where in 1601 his son Louis XIII was born. Queen Christina of Sweden retired here in 1657. In 1685 Louis XIV signed the revocation of the Edict of Nantes at Fontainebleau; and Louis XV received many distinguished visitors here, including (during his minority) Peter the Great (1717), and in 1768, Christian VII of Denmark.

Napoleon I spent 12 million francs on the restoration of the palace, where in 1804 he received Pope Pius VII, who in 1811 was kept prisoner here, before renouncing temporal power the following year. Here in 1814 Napoleon signed the act of abdication, and said farewell to his Old Guard; and on his return from Elba, he reviewed his grenadiers here before leading them to the Tuileries. The palace was again restored by Louis-Philippe, at enormous cost, but in his usual questionable taste. From 1941 it was the headquarters of Gen. von Brauchitsch, until liberated by Gen. Patton in Aug. 1944, and for some years after was the military H.Q. of the Allied powers in Europe. Dancourt (1661-1725), author of 'Chevalier à la mode', was born, and died, in Fontainebleau.

From the CARREFOUR DE LA LIBÉRATION, the BLVD. A. MAGINOT and the

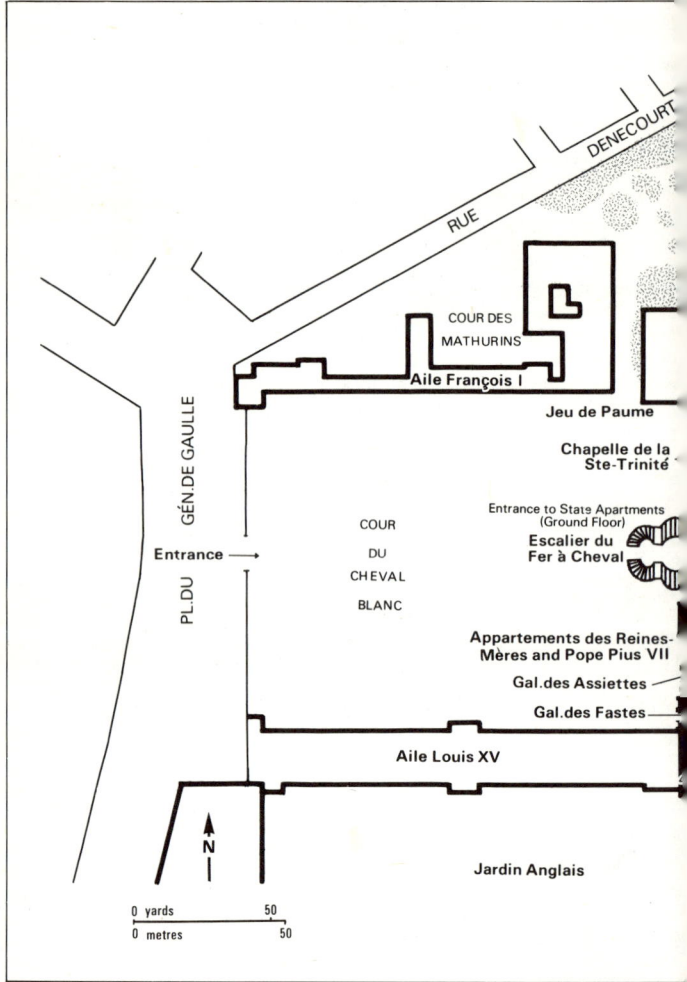

RUE

DENECOURT

COUR DES
MATHURINS

Aile François I

Jeu de Paume

Chapelle de la
Ste-Trinité

Entrance to State Apartments
(Ground Floor)
Escalier du
Fer à Cheval

PL. DU   GÉN.DE GAULLE

Entrance →

COUR
DU
CHEVAL
BLANC

Appartements des Reines-
Mères and Pope Pius VII

Gal.des Assiettes —

Gal.des Fastes—

Aile Louis XV

N

Jardin Anglais

0 yards   50
0 metres   50

Rue Royale approach the PL. DU GÉN.-DE-GAULLE opposite the W. façade
of the palace. Facing it is the *Hôtel du Card. de Ferrare,* its doorway the
only authentic work of *Serlio* surviving. Relics of other old mansions
remain in the BLVD. MAGENTA, to the S., and in the Rue Royale, where, at
No. 15, is a small museum of military costume.

The ****Palace** is composed of many distinct buildings erected over the
years, and for the most part two-storeyed. Because some of the stone
used was unsuitable for sculpture, the exterior is comparatively plain
when compared with the sumptuous interior decoration.

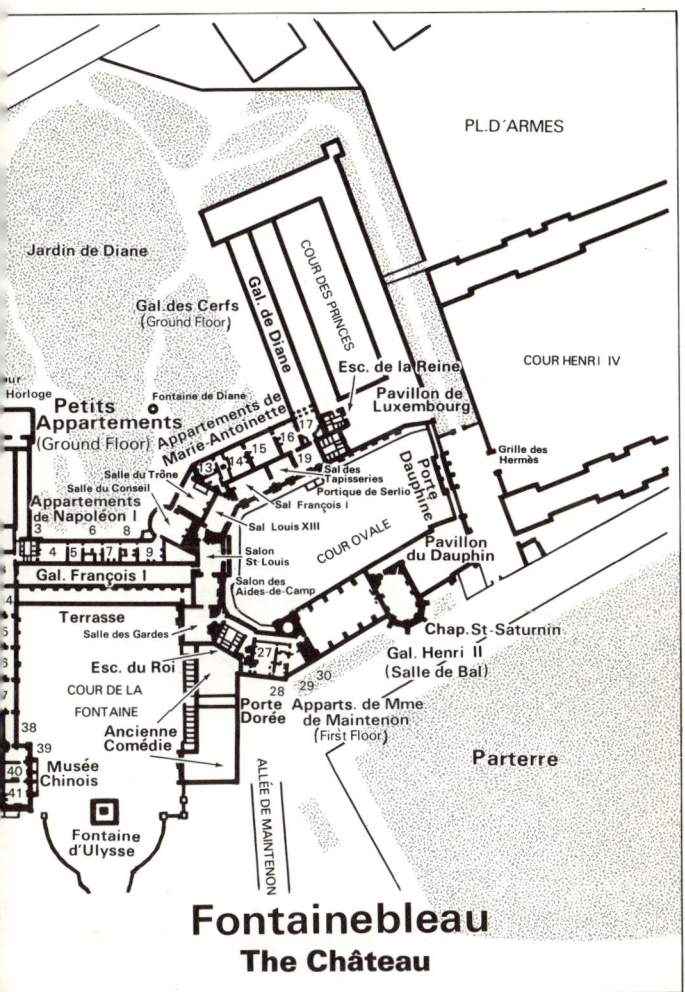

PL. D'ARMES

Jardin de Diane

Gal. des Cerfs
(Ground Floor)

COUR DES PRINCES

Gal. de Diane

Esc. de la Reine

COUR HENRI IV

ur
Horloge

Petits
Appartements
(Ground Floor)

Fontaine de Diane

Appartements de
Marie-Antoinette

Pavillon de
Luxembourg

Grille des
Hermès

Salle du Trône

17
16

Salle du Conseil

13 14 15 19

Appartements
de Napoléon I

Sal des
Tapisseries

Porte
Dauphine

3   6   8

Portique de Serlio

Sal François I

Sal Louis XIII

4 5 7 9

Salon
St-Louis

COUR OVALE

Pavillon
du Dauphin

Gal. François I

Salon des
Aides-de-Camp

Terrasse

Salle des Gardes

Chap. St-Saturnin

27

Esc. du Roi

Gal. Henri II
(Salle de Bal)

COUR DE LA
FONTAINE

30

28   29

38

Ancienne
Comédie

Porte
Dorée

Apparts. de Mme
de Maintenon
(First Floor)

39

Musée
Chinois

Parterre

40
41

Fontaine
d'Ulysse

ALLÉE DE MAINTENON

Fontainebleau
The Château

Adm. daily, except Tues., 10.00-12.30; 14.00-17.00 or 18.00. The main courtyards and gardens are open all day. Some apartments are closed at present for restoration.

The COUR DU CHEVAL-BLANC (500 ft by 370 ft), which we first enter, is named after a vanished cast of the horse of an equestrian statue of Marcus Aurelius in Rome; it is also known as the *Cour des Adieux*, after Napoleon's farewell to his Guards (see History).

In front of the central pavilion is the *Escalier en Fer-à-Cheval*, a horseshoe-shaped staircase by *Jean du Cerceau* (1634) ascending to the

FIRST FLOOR. To the l. of the VESTIBULE D'HONNEUR (**Pl. 33**), with six massive oak doors, two of them original (Louis XIII period), is the gallery (**Pl. 2**) of the CHAPELLE DE LA SAINTE-TRINITÉ, built by *Philibert Delorme* for Henri II and decorated during the reign of Henri IV. The chapel was the scene of the marriage of Louis XV and Marie Leczinska in 1725 and of the baptism of Napoleon III. In the centre of the ceiling are five religious paintings by *Fréminet* (1608-14), while the woodwork and elaborate reredos (by *Bordoni*) are of the time of Louis XIII.

To the r. of the entrance vestibule are the **Apartments of the Queens-Mother** and of *Pius VII* (**Pl. 34-43**), at present only visited in guided groups. They were occupied by Catherine de Médicis, Anne of Austria, and Marie-Thérèse, and by the Pope as both guest and prisoner. From the ANTECHAMBER, we enter the SALON DES OFFICIERS (**Pl. 35**), with a splendid marquetry commode by *Riesener*, and the adjacent GRAND SALON DE RÉCEPTION, with a ceiling designed by *Philibert Delorme*, and over the doors, portraits of Charles IX and Catherine de Médicis. The QUEEN-MOTHER'S BEDROOM (**Pl. 37**) has a fine old Gobelins tapestry (*after Raphael*) and a *Ceiling decorated with paintings by *Cotelle de Meaux;* above the doors are portraits of Anne of Austria and Marie-Thérèse, by *Desève;* the furniture is upholstered in Beauvais tapestry, with subjects taken from La Fontaine's fables. The clock, with ten dials, was made for Napoleon.—The adjoining POPE'S STUDY contains a replica of *David*'s portrait of Pius VII; also his calotte.

In the CABINET DE TOILETTE (**Pl. 39**) are tapestry portraits of Henri IV and Louis XIII. The POPE'S BEDROOM contains a Louis-XVI bedstead, and another fine commode, by *Beneman*, and two cabinets de nuit. Note the furniture by *Jacob*, combining Joséphine's rose and Napoleon's bees. The Pope used to say mass during his captivity in the SALON D'ANGLE.—In a room beyond (**Pl. 43**) are displayed two Venetian scenes, and a painting of Napoleon's meeting with the Pope, by *J.-L. Demarne*. The SALLE D'ATTENTE has an 18C 'Chinese' lacquered commode.

The GALERIE DES FASTES (under restoration), which we next enter, has superb carved foliage (Louis-XV period) and three fine tapestries of the Victories of Louis XIV (*after Le Brun*). The GALERIE DES ASSIETTES is decorated with Sèvres plates (1837) painted with views of French royal palaces, etc. On the ceiling are frescoes by *Ambroise Dubois*.

Opposite the main entrance is the *Galerie François-Premier, 210 ft long, built in 1528-44 in the Renaissance style; the initial and salamander device of the king are conspicuous. The paintings and stucco reliefs, by *Rosso*, were completed after his death by *Primaticcio*. The frescoes represent allegorical and mythological scenes, with references to the life of François I. It is one of the few extant rooms of the original palace of François, and here the Italian influence is seen at its strongest.

At the far end we turn r. into the SALON DES AIDES-DE-CAMP (or *Salle du Buffet*), containing two fine ebony cabinets of the Louis-XIII period, and three paintings removed from the Salon Louis-XIII (see below), and other works by *Dubois*.

The adjacent SALLE DES GARDES (r,), completed in 1564 by Charles IX, was redecorated in 1834. The ceiling and frieze, however, date from François I and Henri II. The magnificent marquetry floor reproduces the design of the ceiling. The chimneypiece, with figures of Strength and

Peace, by *Jacquet,* was made up, under Louis-Philippe, of sections of the great chimneypiece of Henri IV removed from the next room (not visited), when it was turned into a theatre by Louis XV.

The ESCALIER DU ROI was built by *Gabriel* in 1749, the upper part having been the *Bedchamber of the Duchesse d'Étampes in François I's time. The sculptures are ascribed to *Primaticcio:* the nude figures ('the nymphs of Fontainebleau') were veiled at the request of Marie Leczinska! The frescoes, in which François I is depicted as Alexander the Great in eight episodes from the life of the Macedonian hero, were painted by *Nicolo dell' Abate* from Primaticcio's designs, and restored by Pujol. The stucco figures are of the period of Jean Goujon.—Passing through a vestibule containing a statue of Mercury by *Francavilla,* we traverse a narrow corridor.

The *Salle de Bal or *Galerie Henri-II,* 100ft long, the most splendid room in the palace, was built by François I and decorated under Henri II, *Philibert Delorme* being the designer. The windows command the best view of the COUR OVALE. The elaborate ceiling is of walnut, and the design of the parquet floor (made under Louis-Philippe) corresponds with it. Everywhere are seen the interlaced monograms of Henri II and Diane de Poitiers and the emblems of Diana (bows and arrows, and crescents). The mythological paintings were designed by *Primaticcio,* executed by *Nicolo dell' Abate*(1552), and restored under Henri IV, and again in 1834. The satyrs flanking the fireplace are copies of the originals melted down at the Revolution.

Returning, we visit the APARTMENTS OF MME DE MAINTENON, with *Boulle* furniture, and a fine clock. It is said that the Revocation of the Edict of Nantes (1685) was signed in her salon. Originally the royal suite of François I, they were converted by Louis XIV into salles de réception.

Passing through the Salle des Gardes, we enter the first of the Appartements Royaux, overlooking the Cour Ovale. The SALON DE ST-LOUIS, in the original keep of the castle, was the king's bedchamber until the 17C; it was redecorated by Louis-Philippe with paintings of episodes in the life of Henri IV. On the chimneypiece is an equestrian statue of the king by *Jacquet* (1599) from the 'great chimneypiece' (see above).

The *SALON LOUIS-TREIZE, known also as the *Grand Cabinet du Roi* or *Chambre Ovale,* one of the most interesting rooms in the palace, was decorated by *Paul Bril* under Henri IV, and restored in 1837. Marie de Médicis gave birth to Louis XIII here in 1601. *Ambroise Dubois* painted thirteen pictures (the Loves of Theagenes and Chariclea) for this room, but three were removed (see above) during the reign of Louis XV, when the doors were widened to admit the voluminous dresses of the period. The little Venetian mirror was one of the first to be seen in France.

The SALON FRANÇOIS-PREMIER, adjoining, a dining-room under Napoleon, has an original chimneypiece with a medallion of Venus and Adonis by *Primaticcio,* and several Gobelins tapestries depicting hunting scenes.—The *Salon des Tapisseries,* once the anteroom of the queen, contains 17C Gobelins tapestries of the Story of Constantine. Three Gobelins tapestries of the Seasons are displayed in the adjoining Antechamber.

We now reach the vestibule of the GALERIE DE DIANE (**Pl. 17**), over 260ft long, built by Henri IV and remodelled under the Restoration, and with ceiling-paintings of that period. Since 1859 it has served as a Library, and includes several early printed books (15-16C; no adm.).

The APPARTEMENTS DE LA REINE (or *de Marie-Antoinette*, who chose the decorations) were built between 1545 and 1565. The first two rooms contain Louis-XIV woodwork, and Louis-XVI furniture by *Stockel* and *Beneman*. The MUSIC ROOM (**Pl. 15**) was Marie-Antoinette's card-room. The bust of the queen, in Sèvres biscuit-ware, is by *Pajou*. Note also the grisaille dessus de porte, and table of Sèvres ware (1806). The BEDROOM (**Pl. 14**), with its fine ceiling, was occupied successively by Marie de Médicis, Marie-Thérèse, Marie Leczinska, Marie-Antoinette, Joséphine, Marie-Louise, Marie-Amélie, and the Empress Eugénie, and is sometimes known as the 'Chamber of the six Maries'. The silk hangings of the bed, and on the walls, were given to Marie-Antoinette by the city of Lyon.—The adjoining BOUDOIR, beautifully proportioned, has a ceiling-painting of Aurora by *Barthélemy*, and stucco dessus de portes by *Beauvais*.

The SALLE DU TRÔNE was first used as a throne-room by Napoleon; it served previously as the king's bedroom. The magnificent ceiling dates from the time of Louis XIII. The fine portrait of Louis XIII is after an original by *Philippe de Champaigne*, which was burned in 1793. The lustre-candelabrum is of rock-crystal; the carpet is from the Savonnerie. The woodwork is of the period of Louis XIV.—A small adjacent cabinet was the 'Brûle-Tout', where state papers were burned after council-meetings.

The magnificent ***Salle du Conseil** (so used by Charles IX) is decorated by *Boucher, C. Van Loo*, and *J.-B. Pierre*, c. 1753; the bay, with a ceiling by *Lagrenée*, was added in 1773.

The APARTMENTS OF NAPOLEON I, in a wing built by Louis XVI abutting the Galerie François-Premier, are furnished partly in the Empire style, and contain a number of Napoleonic relics. In the BEDROOM (**Pl. 9**), with Louis-XVI decoration, is the emperor's bed; in the adjacent *Study*, his camp-bed, and a desk by *Jacob-Desmalter*.—The CABINET DE L'ABDICATION or *Salon Rouge* (**Pl. 7**) contains the little table on which Napoleon signed his abdication in 1814 (although probably not in this room), and a facsimile of the document.—In the ANTICHAMBRE DES HUISSIERS (**Pl. 4**), with the emperor's hat, worn on the return from Elba, and relics, the painting of the Duchesse de Bourgogne is a copy of the original, by *Godert*.

On the GROUND FLOOR are the **Petits Appartements de Napoléon et de Joséphine,** preserving their Louis-XV and Louis-XVI decoration, and Empire furniture and Napoleonic relics. Beyond, below the Galerie de Diane, is the GALERIE DES CERFS (so called because of the stag-heads which form part of the decoration), where Christina of Sweden had Monaldeschi, her favourite, murdered (1657).

Also opened on request are the **Chinese Museum** (entered from the Cour de la Fontaine), displaying in three rooms, once part of the suite of the 'grand maréchal', a small collection of oriental art. The APPARTEMENTS DES CHASSES (entered from the Escalier de la Reine), containing paintings by *Oudry, Desportes,* and others, illustrating the hunting achievements of Louis XV, are still under rearrangement.

The Conservateur, on receiving written application, may authorize a visit to the *Chapelle St-Saturnin*, in the S.E. wing, rebuilt for François I, the *Theatre,* and the *Musée de l'Histoire du Château* (on the Second Floor).

Exterior. A pleasant walk may be taken round the outside of the château, starting at the N.E. corner of the COUR DU CHEVAL-BLANC, passing the *Jeu de Paume* (Tennis Court; r.), and entering the JARDIN DE DIANE, with a bronze fountain-figure of Diana (1684). Passing (r.) the *Galerie des Cerfs*, we bear round the N. wing, following the line of the old moat, to reach the *Grille des Hermès* (l.) adorned with heads of Hermes (Mercury) by *Gilles Guérin* (1640) facing the COUR HENRI-IV (1609), the main entrance of which faces the PL. D'ARMES; and r., the *Porte du Dauphin,* by *Primaticcio,* one of the entrances to the COUR OVALE.

Beyond the *Pavillon du Dauphin,* we reach the PARTERRE, a formal garden with ornamental ponds, laid out by Henri IV and again by *Le Vau* for Louis XIV. To the r. is the apse of the *Chapelle St-Saturnin* (poorly restored), beyond which a passage admits to the COUR DE LA FONTAINE, to the S. and S.E. of which are the ÉTANG DES CARPES and the JARDIN ANGLAIS, laid out for Napoleon. Somewhere in these gardens Thomas Coryate, passing through Fontainebleau in May 1608, was amazed to see ostriches running wild.

The PARK (212 acres) extends to the E. of the Parterre. On the S. side, beyond the canal dug by order of Henri IV, are the buildings of the former School of Artillery, now barracks.

Beyond the walls lies the suburb of **Avon** (15,400 inhab.), with a 13-16C church entered below a curiously gabled porch. It contains the tombs of Monaldeschi, the painter Ambroise Dubois, and the naturalist Daubenton. In the cemetery lies Katherine Mansfield (1888-1923), who died at the *Prieuré des Basses-Loges,* while under the influence of Gurdjieff, the mystic. Avon had a thriving pottery in the early 17C. There are notable vineyards at *Thomery,* further to the E.

The *Forest of Fontainebleau,* surrounding the town, is approx. 42,000 acres in extent, and although traversed by a number of good roads, is best explored on foot. Its thick glades and picturesque groups of ancient oaks, which with beech, hornbeam, birch, and Scots pine, are the commonest trees; its sandy clearings, and wildernesses of rocks, make it a pleasant centre for excursions. The legend of the 'Grand Veneur' tells how Henri IV, shortly before his assassination, hearing the sound of a rapidly approaching hunt, was suddenly confronted by a Black Huntsman of huge and hideous appearance, who on uttering a warning cry, as abruptly vanished.

The best general view of the forest is commanded by the *Tour Denecourt* (4.5 km. N.E. of the palace), erected in 1851 by C.-F. Denecourt (1788-1875), nicknamed 'Le Sylvain', who devoted his life and fortune to the study of the forest. Among the more picturesque sites are the *Gorges de Franchard* (4 km. W. of the CARREFOUR DE LA LIBÉRATION), a rocky wilderness lying not far S. of the D409; and the *Gorges d'Apremont* (6 km. N.W., S. of the N7). Although skirted by roads, the exploration of these areas must be undertaken on foot.

At *Valvins,* 1.5 km. N.E. of Fontainebleau station. lived Mallarmé (1842-98) from 1884 until his death; he is buried in the cemetery.

FROM FONTAINEBLEAU TO SENS (53 km.). From the CARREFOUR DE L'OBÉLISQUE, immediately S.E. of the palace, we follow the N5, after 6.5 km. turning l. for **Moret-sur-Loing** (3,100 inhab.; *Hotels*), an ancient town retaining two of its 14C *Gates,* besides a tower and part of its walls. *Notre-Dame,* consecrated to Thomas Becket, has a fine portal (15C), and contains some remarkable wood-carvings. In an old timbered house to the r. of the church, is sold the famous barley-sugar of the nuns of Moret. Behind the church, at No. 9 Rue du Château, Sisley (1840-99) spent the last four years of his life. Pissarro painted here in 1901-02. Just beyond is the castle-keep (1128), in which Fouquet was imprisoned for some months in 1664. Good view from the bridge. Its quails are famous, prepared in the style of *St-Mammès,* an adjoining village.

Regaining the N5, at 18 km. we may bear l. to *Montereau-faut-Yonne,* see p. 232.

For the road hence to *Sens,* 33 km. further S.E., see p. 232.

FROM FONTAINEBLEAU TO PITHIVIERS (44 km.). We follow the N51 S.W.

through the forest, at 10 km. crossing the A6.—At 13 km. **Larchant** (3.5 km. S.) is a fine 12C church, with a richly decorated apsidal chapel of the 13C.—25 km. **Malesherbes** (3,900 inhab.). In the 12-13C church is a bust of Guillaume de Lamoignon de Malesherbes (1721-94), Louis XVI's minister and defender, who owned the château to the S. of the town, rebuilt in the 15C, with a huge barn, and pigeon-house. To the N. of the town lies the château *de Rouville* (late 15C, but over-restored in the 19C).—At *Champmotteux,* 10 km. N.E. on the N449, the church contains the reconstructed tomb of Chancellor Michel de l'Hôpital (d. 1573), which was smashed in 1793.—44 km. *Pithiviers,* see p. 245.

Following the N7 S. from *Fontainebleau,* we bypass (72 km. l.) *Grez-sur-Loing,* with an interesting 12-16C church, containing Romanesque capitals. Louise de Savoie (1476-1531), mother of François I, died in the castle, now ruined. R. L. Stevenson moored his canoe here after his 'Inland Voyage', and the composer Frederick Delius lived here from 1900 until his death in 1934.

79 km. **Nemours** (11,200 inhab.; *Hotels*) stood originally on an island in the Loing, and was once the capital of the Gâtinais. It now covers the adjacent island, and the E. bank of the river. *Nemoracum* was fortified at an early date, and between 1420 and 1437 was in English hands.

A local confection, known as coquelicots, is worth sampling, as are its hams and pâtés.

Eleuthère-Irénée, one of the family of Du Pont of Nemours, founded in the State of Delaware a factory which formed the basis of the chemical 'empire' which bears his name.

The fortified château (15C, but parts of it dating from the 12C) defending the river crossing, is under restoration. An interesting view of the outer walls and keep may also be obtained from the river side. preserving some old mills. The *Grand Pont* commands a view of the apse of *St-Jean Baptiste* (16C; built to house relics of the saint), with a fan-vaulted nave, with pendant bosses, in the vicinity of which a few quaint old houses survive.

The D40 follows the W. bank of the river to (94 km.) **Château-Landon** (3,000 inhab.), on a bluff above the Fusain valley, and birthplace of ancestors of the Plantagenets. The church of *Notre-Dame* (11-14C), with a 13C tower, is remarkable, and the view from the terrace adjoining the main square of the ancient fortifications, and the ruined Romanesque tower of St-Tugal, is impressive. The ruins of the abbey of *St-Séverin,* founded by Childebert in 545, at the E. end of the village, may be visited (enquire at the S.I.).

The churches of *Arville* and *Puiseaux* (12 and 19 km. N.W. of Château-Landon respectively), *Boësse* (7 km. S.W. of Puiseaux), and *Mondreville* (7 km. W. of Château-Landon) are of interest.

At *Ferrières,* 8 km. S.E., is an abbey church (11-15C) remarkable for a rotunda formed of eight columns at the crossing, and for its 16C stained-glass; also a pilgrimage chapel of 1620.

FROM CHÂTEAU-LANDON TO SENS (46 km.). The D43 crosses the N7 at *Dordives,* beyond which the road skirts the impressive ruins of the 13C castle of *Mez-le-Maréchal.*—15 km. **Égreville,** with a 13-15C church and 15C beamed market-hall. The Duchesse d'Étampes, mistress of François I, lived in the 16C château, where Jules Massenet (1842-1912) passed his last years; he is buried in the cemetery.—There are remains of 13C ramparts and a fortified church at *Lorrez-le-Bocage,* 7 km. N.—Veering S.E., we regain the so-called 'Chemin de César', a Roman road leading due E. to (46 km.) *Sens,* see Rte 30.

Montargis lies 1.8 km. S. of Château-Landon on the D40; *Gien* is 39 km. further S. (N7 and N140); and *Bourges* lies 74 km. S.E. of Gien.

32   PARIS TO SCEAUX AND ÉTAMPES
(FOR ORLÉANS OR TOURS)

N20 to (51 km.) *Étampes.*

We drive S. from the *Porte d'Orléans* parallel to the A6; the roads converge some 15 km. S. of Paris.

At 7 km. (l.; 2 km. S. of the Blvd. Périphérique) we pass the double *Aqueduct* crossing the valley of the Bièvre, the lower part of which was built in 1613-24 by Marie de Médicis to supply the Luxembourg fountains; it was preceded by a Roman one, built in the 4C to bring water to the Palais des Thermes (see p. 58).

11.5 km. (r.) *Sceaux.* The suburb may also be approached by rail from Luxembourg (or Denfert-Rochereau) to Sceaux or Bourg-la-Reine.

A broad avenue (the Allée d'Honneur) ascends W. from the N20 to the entrance of the *château* of **Sceaux,** a 19C building replacing the sumptuous 17C château built by *Claude Perrault* for Colbert, which, during the first half of the 18C, was the scene of the brilliant literary and artistic court of the Duchesse du Maine. Here Voltaire wrote three of his tragedies, and works by Racine, Molière, and Lulli were performed in the adjacent **Orangerie** (l.), constructed by *J. Hardouin-Mansart* (1684; restored).—To the r. is the *Pavillon de l'Aurore,* also by *Perrault.*

Since 1937 the **Musée de l'Île de France** has been installed in the château, illustrating the history and topography of the area now covered by the departments of Hauts-de-Seine, Seine-St-Denis, Val-de-Marne, Essonne, Yvelines, and Val-d'Oise. It is well worth visiting, not only for its site, but for the wealth of interesting material depicting the appearance of, and life in, the environs of the capital in past centuries. The building also contains a Reference Library, etc. Adm. Mon. and Thur., 14.00-17.00; Wed. and Fri., 10.00-12.00; 14.00-17.00; open until 19.00 at weekends.

The majority of the rooms are devoted to specific regions. **R 2** contains a model of the château, and **R 3** portraits of Colbert attr. to *Lefebvre,* and of the Duchesse du Maine by *De Troy.*—**R 4** (note the view): Sceaux ceramics (1754-95).—**R 5**: Sèvres and St-Cloud ware.— **R 7**: Views of St-Cloud by *Dunouy, Fleury,* etc.—**R 8** is devoted to Meudon. Stairs ascend to the SECOND FLOOR, where a series of rooms display views of the Machine de Marly, of St-Germain by *James Basire* (1730-1802); of Mousseau, by *J.-M. Morel;* drawings, watercolours, and engravings by *Dunoyer de Segonzac* (1874-1946); two of Etry occupied by Cossacks in 1814, by *J. Randon,* and a number of attractive views by *Paul Huet* (1803-69), among others of great topographical value, including also the Tower of Vincennes, by *Bonington.*

The extensive **Park,** laid out by *Le Nôtre,* forms one of the most attractive open spaces near Paris, and contains, S. of the château, a series of cascades leading to the OCTAGON, to the W. of which is the GRAND CANAL. Hence we have a view of the *Pavillon de Hanovre,* removed here in 1832 from the Blvd. des Capucines, 9e. It was built in 1760 with money extorted from the Hanoverians in the Seven Years War.

A short distance N.W. of the château, approached across the park, is the old churchyard of *Sceaux,* where the fabulist Florian (1755-94) lies buried. The simple tombs of Pierre and Marie Curie, the discoverers of radium, may be found in the local cemetery.

At 24 km. we pass (2 km., l.) **Longpont-sur-Orge,** with a *Church of considerable archaeological interest, begun c. 1060 and formerly attached to a Cluniac priory. The choir, transepts, and spire were unhappily demolished in 1822 to save the cost of upkeep, but the two former were rebuilt in 1878. The W. front is original, with a 13C portal surmounted by a 15C rose-window. In the doorway are headless statues (13C); that of the Virgin has been restored (badly). In the archivolts are 13C statues of the Wise and Foolish Virgins. The nave, remodelled in the 12C, has fine Romanesque arches and foliate capitals, with a blind triforium above. Behind the high-altar is the statue of N.-D. de Bonne-Garde, with ex-votos. Among the tombs are those of the foundress, the Comtesse de Montlhéry, and Louis of France, grandson of St Louis (d. 1318).—S. of the church is the château of *Lormoy* (rebuilt 1837), with a fine chestnut avenue.

25 km. **Montlhéry** (3,700 inhab.). Near the church is the *Hôtel-Dieu,* founded by Louis VII in 1146, with a mutilated 13C carving on the door. Spanning the Grande Rue is the massive *Porte Baudry,* with an inscription recording its history. The town is dominated by the * *Tour de Montlhéry,* a cylindrical keep 105 ft high, a relic of a famous medieval fortress and dating from the 13-15C. By the entrance are some tombstones from a Gallo-Roman cemetery. The tower may be ascended (for the view) 9.30 or 10.00-12.00; 14.00-16.00 or 18.00.

There is an interesting 15-16C church at *Marcoussis,* 3 km. to the W. Also noteworthy is the *Collégial St-Merry* at *Linas,* just S. of Montlhéry, altered in the 16C, but retaining a 13C choir and belfry.

At 26 km. (r.) is the 'Autodrome' of Montlhéry, a popular motor-racing track.

30 km. **Arpajon** (8,100 inhab.), called *Châtres* until 1720, takes its name from a marquisate in Auvergne. The church dates from the 13C, and there is a 17C market-house.

FROM ARPAJON TO ABLIS (34 km.). The D19 leads S.W. viâ (2 km.) *Égly,* with 15-17C paintings in its church, to (11 km.) *St-Chéron,* just N. of which is the château of *Baville.* 3.5 km. N.W. of St-Chéron stands the château *du Marais,* c. 1770, by *Barré,* in an extensive park. The château of *Villeconin* (8 km. S. of St-Chéron) retains a gatehouse of the 13C.—20 km. **Dourdan** (7,400 inhab.; *Hotels*), the Gallo-Roman *Dordincum,* and later capital of the Hurepoix, has a curious church of 12C foundation, but provided with two steeples and an elaborate vault in the 15C. The comic dramatist Jean-François Regnard (1655-1709), who owned a property nearby, is buried here. The royal * **Castle,** preserving its square turreted rampart and its keep (under restoration), was rebuilt by Philippe Auguste in 1220 on the site of an earlier fortress, where Hugues Capet was born c. 941, and where his father Hugues le Grand died in 956. It was besieged and taken many times: by Salisbury in 1428; by Montgomery in 1567; and by Biron in 1591, in the name of Henri IV.—The village of *St-Cyr-sous-Dourdan,* 5 km. N., retains a 16C church and fortified priory.—*Ablis* (see p. 246) lies 14 km. W. of Dourdan.

FROM ARPAJON TO MILLY-LA-FORÊT (31 km.). The N499 leads S.E. to (16 km.) *La Ferté-Alais* (the fortress of Adélaïde, wife of Guy Trousseau, lord of Montlhéry in the 11C), whose castle no longer exists; boulevards have replaced the former ramparts. The church dates from the 11-12C.—The S105 leads S. along the E. bank of the Essonne before bearing S.E. to *Milly* (see p. 235).

At 38 km., a lane leads 2.5 km. r. to *St-Sulpice-de-Favières,* with an unexpected elegant *Church, built in 1260-1320 to accommodate pilgrims to the shrine of St Sulpicius. It has an exceptionally fine tower and choir, and contains two good contemporary stained-glass windows, and a 17C altarpiece in painted wood. The chapel with the saint's relics, adjoining the N. aisle, is a survival from an earlier 12C church.

The N10 ascends the once notorious hill known as the 'Côte de Torfou', just to the E. of which is *Chamarande,* with a 17C château built by *Fr. Mansart* on the site of a 9C castle.—The road now passes (r.) *Étréchy,* with a graceful Gothic church, at 45 km. passing (l.) the château of *Jeurre,* in the park of which are many 18C follies, including some taken from *Méréville* (see p. 246).

47 km. *Morigny* (1 km. E.) has a church occupying the 13-15C choir of a late 11C Benedictine abbey. The château (adm. on application) contains an interesting prehistoric collection, and three Gallo-Roman mosaics.

49 km. **Étampes** (19,000 inhab.), with a bypass, is an ancient town (known as *Stampae* in the 6C) strung out along the old Orléans road, and dominated by the *Tour Guinette,* a huge 12C keep where Philippe Auguste confined his queen, Ingeborg of Denmark, for 12 years (1201-13). Geoffroy St-Hilaire (1772-1844), the naturalist, was a native of Étampes. Its pâtés d'alouettes are famous.

Near the town centre stands *St-Basile* (15-16C), retaining an elaborate Romanesque W. door and a 12C tower, and within, ten 16C reliefs of the Passion, three of them mutilated. The Rue de la République leads S.E. to *N.-D. du Fort,* an interesting church preserving much 11C work in its nave; the steeple (204 ft) is a fine 12C composition. The W. and S. doorways are somewhat later, while the transepts and choir (with 16C glass) are of the 14C. In the N.E. chapel are some 12C figures, and beneath is a crypt, possibly Merovingian.

A short distance S. in the Rue de la Tannerie, is the early 16C *Hôtel St-Yon.* Further S., seen from the *Pont Doré,* spanning a branch of the Juine, is the *Tour de Jean-le-Bâtard,* a relic of the ancient ramparts. Turning N. along the Rue Ste-Croix, we pass (l.) the *Hôtel de Ville,* with two turrets of 1614, and the Renaissance *Hôtel d'Anne de Pisseleu.*— The *Palais de Justice,* to the S.W., contains a curious 14C mural painting. Further N., behind St-Basile, is the so-called *Maison de Diane de Poitiers* (1544), with a good courtyard.

Some distance S.W. along the main street lies *St-Gilles,* a 16C church (badly damaged in 1940), with a 12C doorway and grotesque carvings in the N. aisle. 1 km. beyond is *St-Martin* (12-13C), with a beautiful apse, and a dangerously leaning tower displaying Renaissance decoration.

From this end of the town, the D21 leads W. to (8 km.) *Châlo-St-Mars,* with a 12C church, 6 km. S.W. of which, in the valley of the Chalouette, at *Chalou-Moulineux,* are two late-12C churches, one (ruined) dedicated to Becket.

The most rapid road from ÉTAMPES TO CHARTRES is the N191 to (30 km. W.) *Ablis,* there turning l. onto the N10 to (58 km.) *Chartres,* see p. 247.

FROM ÉTAMPES TO FONTAINEBLEAU (44 km.). The N191 leads E. passing at 10 km. (l.) the château of **Farcheville,** with well-preserved fortifications built in 1291.—25 km. *Milly-la-Forêt* (see p. 235).—44 km. *Fontainebleau,* see Rte 31.

FROM ÉTAMPES TO PITHIVIERS (32 km.). The direct road (N721) runs S. across the plateau viâ *Sermaises,* with an interesting church, to **Pithiviers** (8,000 inhab.), noted for its almond cakes, a rather dull old town (whose original site was probably at *Pithiviers-le-Vieil,* 2 km. W.), which sprang up after 874 around the shrine of the sainted king Salomon II of Brittany, whose body was brought here to save it from desecration at the hands of the Normans.

In the medieval centre, surrounded by tree-lined boulevards on the site of earlier ramparts, stands the church, dedicated to St Salomon and St Gregory (a 10C hermit of Armenia, who died near the town), dating mainly from the 16-17C, but the mid-12C crossing of an older church (now at the E. end of the S. aisle) supports a tower of 1180, with a spire of 1855. The 17-18C furniture is handsome.

The *Hôtel de Ville* adjoins the 13C tower of the former church of *St-Georges,* while a *Museum* occupies the chapel and other rooms of the former *Hôtel-Dieu* (18C). Among the paintings are works by *Coypel, Carle Van Loo, Natoire, Leprince, David, Fragonard, J.-B. Huet,* and *Corot,* among others; and some of the Italian Schools. A *Transport Museum* may also be visited in Pithiviers.

The village of **Yèvre-le-Châtel** (6km. E. on the D123) lies adjacent to the ruins of a *Castle* built c. 1236 by Amaury de Montfort. Only a gate remains of the outer ward, but the square inner ward, with four drum towers and immense supporting arches, is still to be seen. The 11-13C chapel serves as a parish church.

For the route from PITHIVIERS TO CHARTRES, see p. 251; to *Fontainebleau,* Rte 31.

The D26, continued by the D7, leads 38 km. E. to *Château-Landon,* see p. 242.

The N20 continues S.W. from *Étampes* across the monotonous but fertile Beauce plateau. At 62 km. *Méréville* (5 km. S.E.), with a 16C market-house, is a château on which, from 1784, the banker Laborde spent a fortune. The park was designed by the painter Hubert Robert in the 'English' style (comp. *Jeurre; p.* 245).

67 km. *Angerville,* bypassed, has a 15C church with a 12C tower.— 82 km. *Toury* retains a 13C church with a curious porch. A monument on the Orléans road commemorates Blériot's first monoplane flight (31 Oct. 1908) to *Artenay,* some 12 km. S.

Orléans lies 34 km. S. of Toury.

33   PARIS TO CHARTRES (FOR TOURS OR LE MANS)

A   Viâ the N10 (Rambouillet and Ablis)

The A12 and N186 converge a short distance S.W. of Versailles (approx. 18 km. from the *Porte d'Auteuil*), where we diverge onto the N10.

At 32 km. we pass near (r.) *Élancourt,* where the church retains a 12C choir and Romanesque tower.—To the l. the New Town of *St-Quentin-en-Yvelines* is under construction.

48.5 km. *Rambouillet* (see p. 253). The N10 circles round the E. side of the town before continuing S. to (60 km.) *Ablis,* whose church has a Romanesque nave, and a late Gothic choir, with 16C stained-glass.— 7.5 km. S.W., at *Auneau,* is a fine 11-14C castle, 4.5 km. S.E. of which, at *Aunoy-sous-Auneau,* is a notable Gothic church (13-15C).

At *Ablis,* the N10 turns abruptly W. across the Beauce plateau, parallel to the A11.—65.5 km. *St-Symphorien,* to the N., where stands the first of the 'Bornes de la Liberté' (1946), stones set up to mark the advance of the army of liberation through France in 1944.—1 km. N.E. is the imposing but over-restored 16C château of *Esclimont.*

69 km. *Gallardon* (4 km. N.W.) retains a ruined cylindrical keep (11C), the 'Épaule de Gallardon', below which is a notable 12-13C church, with a large choir; also a number of 16C houses.

The N10 drives directly towards the spires of Chartres cathedral, which are seen from some distance away, Crossing the A11, we enter the town through an unattractive industrial zone, and ascend the Blvd. de la Courtille towards (83 km.) the centre.

CHARTRES (71,500 inhab.; *Hotels*), the old capital of the province of Beauce, and now of the department of Eure-et-Loir, is chiefly famous for its magnificent cathedral, one of the noblest creations of medieval architecture, its tall but unequal spires still dominating the town, itself retaining an attractive quarter of ancient houses. The town has a reputation for its gastronomy, its pâtés being famous for centuries; also its pain d'épices.

History. Chartres, the chief place of the Carnutes, called by the Romans *Antricum,* was one of the main strongholds of Gallic Druidism. Edward III's siege of Chartres in 1360 was his last military operation before the Treaty of Brétigny (see p. 251); and in 1417-32 the town was held by allies of the English until retaken by Dunois. It was besieged again in 1568 by the Huguenots, and in 1591 by Henri IV, who, after his renunciation of Protestantism, returned here to be anointed in 1594. During the Franco-Prussian War, Chartres was for almost five months the centre of German operations against the second army of the Loire. It suffered some damage in 1944, before being liberated by the Americans on 16 Aug.

John of Salisbury (1120-80) was Bp. of Chartres from 1176 until his death. Philippe Desportes (1546-1606) and Mathurin Régnier (1573-1613) the poets, the Marquis de Dangeau (d. 1720), author of the famous 'Journal', Jean-Pierre Brissot (1754-92), the Girondist, and François Marceau (1769-96), a soldier at 16 and a general at 23, were natives of Chartres; Jean Moulin (1899-1944), founder of the Conseil National de la Résistance, who was deported and murdered by the Germans, was prefect of the department. J.-K. Huysmans's 'La Cathédrale' (1898) is largely concerned with Chartres. 'Mont-St-Michel and Chartres', by Henry Adams, is also of interest.

The PL. DES ÉPARS, the modern centre of the city, where the Hôtel Grand Monarque has an 18C façade, lies on the perimeter of the old ramparts, to the N. of which, flanked by the P.O. (l.), is the BLVD. DE LA RÉSISTANCE, with a monument to Jean Moulin. The line of boulevards continues downhill (BLVD. CHARLES PÉGUY), with a view of the N.E. ramparts, to the PL. DROUAISE and the river.

From the Pl. des Épars, the Rue Colin-d'Harleville leads directly N.E. to the cathedral, passing (r.) the *Chapelle Ste-Foy* (16C, with an 11C portal), and l., the *Préfecture,* with the 16C *Hôtel de Champrond* opposite.

An alternative route is that viâ the Rue Noël-Ballay, in which No. 8 is the 16C *Maison de Claude-Huvé,* the Rue Serpente, and Rue des Changes, in which the last house on the r. is 13C.

The ****Cathédrale de Notre-Dame,** is, as it stands, almost entirely a work of the 13C, only the W. front, with its twin towers, and the crypt, having survived from its predecessors, while later additions have been relatively unimportant. Among its most striking features, apart from its sheer size, are the rich lateral portals, the wealth of its stained-glass, scarcely equalled in France, and the three rose-windows.

A cathedral, with St Aventinus as the first bishop, was founded here in the 4C, on the site of a Druidic sanctuary and a temple of the Dea Mater; and this, the earliest church in France dedicated to the Virgin Mary, became an important goal of pilgrimage. This building and its successors were repeatedly destroyed or burned, and the first great church erected on the site was begun by St Fulbert (960-1028), bishop, after 1020. The oldest parts of the existing building, above ground, are the W. tower and the lower part of the façade of this Romanesque cathedral, which survived the fire of 1194.

It was rebuilt in the first quarter of the 13C, and was consecrated in its present form in 1260, although additions were made in the 14-16C. Almost miraculously, it escaped the ravages of the Religious Wars, the Revolution, and the Second World War; but a fire in 1836 destroyed the ancient wooden roof, which was replaced in metal.

The cathedral is open 7.00-19.00; the towers may be ascended 9.30-12.00; 14.00-

18.00, or 10.00-12.00; 14.00-17.00; the treasury is open 10.00-12.00; 14.00-18.00 or
15.00-17.00; the crypt (guided visit) at regular intervals throughout the day.

Exterior. The splendid *W. façade is pierced by the triple *Portail
Royal* (1150-75), decorated with statues and statuettes, mainly
illustrating the Life of Christ. The doorways are flanked by statues of
biblical kings and queens, attenuated figures with formal pleated
drapery, characteristic of 12C sculpture. In the central tympanum is
Christ Blessing, with the symbols of the Evangelists, and the Apostles
below; the side arches represent the Ascension (N.) and Nativity (S.).
The western rose-window, and the gallery with 16 statues of the kings of
Judah, were added in the 13C.

The greater part of both *Towers* dates from 1134-44. The elegant
crocketed N. spire (371 ft), and the 'Clocher Neuf', were raised in 1507-
13, partly at the expense of Louis XII, by *Jean Texier* (Jehan de Beauce).
The S. tower (339 ft without the cross), or 'Clocher Vieux', is the tallest
Romanesque steeple in existence. At the corner a 12C angel bears a
sundial of 1528. The Renaissance clock beside the N. tower was made in
1520 by *Jehan de Beauce.*

The two portals on the N. and S. sides are triple projecting Gothic
porticoes resting on piers or clustered pillars with side openings between
them. The stately sculptures are of a later date (1225 et seq.) than those
of the W. front, but equally impressive. The N. portal alone is
embellished with more than 700 figures symbolic of the Coming of
Christ; the S. portal is dedicated to the Glorification of the Saints, and
the Last Judgment. Above each portal is a fine rose-window. The tall
windows of the nave and choir are separated by huge flying buttresses
unique of their kind, particularly impressive at the E. end.

Interior. The cathedral is 422 ft in length, and its height to the spring of
the vaulting is 106 ft. The nave is the widest in France (52 ft between the
piers). The style throughout the nave and choir is the most vigorous
early Gothic, and the grandeur of proportion is enhanced by an extreme
sobriety of sculpture. It too often remains unlit in dull weather.

More than 160 windows are filled with superb **Stained-glass, dating
for the most part from the 13C, although that of the three fine W.
lancets, one of which contains a Tree of Jesse, survived the fire of 1194.
The rose-windows of the nave and transepts are remarkable for their size
(30-40 ft in diameter) and their graceful tracery. The windows in general
illustrate legends of saints; the representations of various trades in the
lower compartments of many indicate that they were presented by the
trade guilds or corporations.

The St Fulbert window (E. side of S. Transept) was donated in 1954 by the Inst.
of American Architects.

In the middle of the NAVE (too often covered with chairs) a circular
maze or labyrinth, called 'La Lieue' from its supposed length, is marked
on the pavement in coloured stone; to follow its windings on one's knees,
saying prayers at various points, was probably at one time a penitential
exercise. The CHAP. DE VENDÔME, off the S. side-aisle, was added by
Louis, Comte de Vendôme, in 1417.

The **Choir** is enclosed by a magnificent stone *Screen, begun in 1514
from designs of *Jehan de Beauce,* and completed under Louis XIV, and
of interest as being one of the last examples of Gothic art. Its 40
remarkable sculptures of events in the Life of Christ and of the Virgin

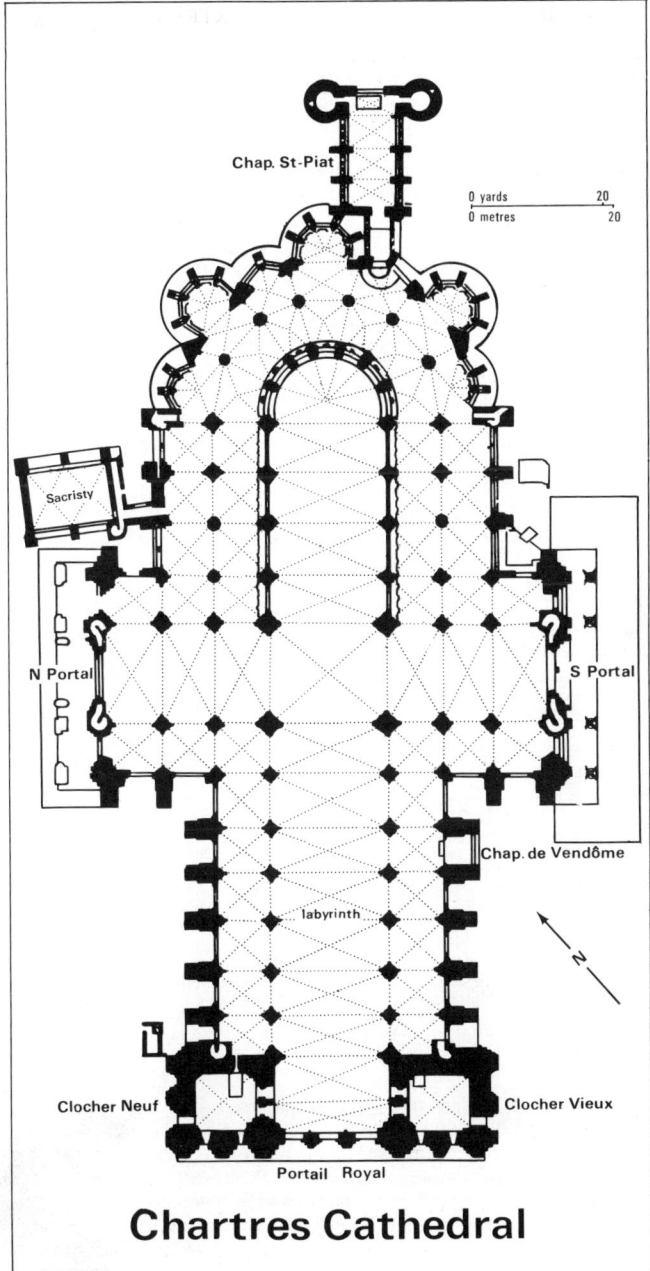

Chap. St-Piat

0 yards 20
0 metres 20

Sacristy

N Portal

S Portal

Chap. de Vendôme

labyrinth

N

Clocher Neuf

Clocher Vieux

Portail Royal

Chartres Cathedral

Mary (by *Jehan de Beauce, François Marchand, Jean Soulas,* and others) are surrounded by elaborate tracery and tabernacle-work. The inappropriate marble retable of the Assumption is the work of *C.-A. Bridan* (1767-73), who also carved the marble bas-reliefs around the sanctuary (1788). In the N.W. chapel of the ambulatory is the 'Vierge du Pilier', an early 16C image that was crowned with the Cap of Liberty at the Revolution. The window of the S.W. chapel enshrines 'N.-D. de la Belle Verrière', a 12C survival in a setting of 13C glass.

The *Treasury,* behind the altar, contains the reliquary of the 'Sancta Camisia', said to be a garment of the Virgin sent to Charlemagne by the Empress Irene, and presented to Chartres by Charles le Chauve (c. 876).

From the apse a staircase and corridor lead to the CHAP. ST-PIAT (1349), flanked on the outside by round towers; its lower storey (1323-35), originally the chapter house, is now the bishop's funerary chapel.

The **Crypt,** dating partly from the 11C, is the largest in France, and is dedicated to 'N.-D. sous Terre', the earliest of the Christian Virgins, venerated on the supposed site of the Druidic sanctuary. We descend into the S. gallery, on the l. of which is a Gallo-Roman bas-relief. In the CHAP. ST-MARTIN are fragments of the 13C rood-loft of the cathedral and the cenotaph of St Calétric, Bp. of Chartres (557). Near the CHAP. ST-NICOLAS is a piscina surmounted by a 13C fresco, and further on, a 12C font. Returning past the entrance, we pass the seven apsidal chapels, four of them added in the 13C; a 9C inner crypt (no adm.), opposite the CHAP. STE-VÉRONIQUE, is dedicated to St Lubin or Leobinus, a shepherd, afterwards Bp. of Chartres (6C). Passing the well in which the earliest martyrs of Chartres are believed to have been drowned, we reach the sanctuary of N.-D. SOUS TERRE, with a 19C image, in the N. gallery; to the r. of it is the CHAP. DES SAINTS-FORTS, containing a 13C triptych.

The *Maison Henri-III,* opposite the N. portal, retains six windows of the 13C. To the r., installed in the former *Bishop's Palace* (17-18C), the **Musée des Beaux-Arts** is not without interest.

Among paintings displayed in its fine rooms are *Hubert Robert,* L'Aqueduc de Maintenon; *Rigaud,* portrait of the Duc de Saint-Simon, and Molière, by *Mignard;* Fontenelle, by *Largillière;* Turenne, by *Ph. de Champaigne;* a pastel of Molière by *Nanteuil;* and St Lucy, by *Zurbarán.* In the **Chapel** (1764-74), decorated by *Bridan,* are *Twelve enamels (16½ by 11 inches) of the apostles, executed in 1545-47 by *Léonard Limousin* for the castle chapel of Diane de Poitiers at Anet, moved here from the church of *St-Pierre* (see below). Also from the same church is the statue of St Paul, by *François Marchand* (d. 1553).

Other paintings of merit include *Bol,* La kermesse d'Hoboken; *Teniers the elder,* Les joueurs de boules; *Teniers the younger,* Tabagie des singes, and Le Concert; two works by *Verdussen;* Catherine of Russia on horseback, by *Erichsen.* Note also the anon. 15C Flemish pietà, and a collection of alabasters. On the upper floor is a small collection of armour, and a section devoted to the architectural history of the cathedral.

The terraced gardens below form an approach to the lower town.

By turning r. on making our exit from the Museum and then l. we reach the **Cellier de Loens,** the 13C storehouse of the chapter, a fine vaulted crypt, to be reopened shortly as a *Museum of Stained-Glass,* with a section describing the techniques of its manufacture.

Further S., in the Rue du Cheval-Blanc, are the *Maison de l'Homme-Sauvage,* and other old houses.—Turning N. we shortly enter the Rue Chantault, with, at No. 29, a 12C house. Just beyond, passing (r.) the gabled *Cloître St-André,* is the Rue de la Brèche, with (r.) the disused and mutilated church of *St-André,* a 12C building with a Romanesque façade and nave, and a 15C N. chapel with the grave of Jehan de Beauce. Thence we may return to the *Musée des Beaux-Arts* by stairs ascending from the PL. ST-ANDRÉ; or turning l., cross the Eure beside the chapel of *N.-D. de la Brèche,* erected in thanksgiving for the successful outcome of the siege of 1568, when the Protestants abandoned the breach made in the walls here (note the stone cannon-balls). From the bridge we follow the quaint Rue du Massacre, Rue de la Tannerie, and Rue de la Foulerie to the *Pont St-Hilaire.* The ramparts on the W. side of this island are best seen from the BLVD. MARÉCHAL-FOCH, on the far bank (where the *Porte Guillaume,* a 14C town gate, survived until its deliberate destruction by the Germans in 1944). Recrossing the stream, we reach **St-Pierre,* once the church of the powerful Benedictine abbey of St-Père-en-Vallée. It preserves a massive low tower of c. 1150, a 13C nave, and a 14C choir with a 12C apse. The flying buttresses and the stained-glass (late-13th and 14C) are notable.

The Rue St-Pierre (No. 16 in which is the Renaissance *Maison des Trois-Pigeons*) passes below the church of *St-Aignan,* a 16-17C building with a wooden roof of 1625, and is continued by the Rue des Écuyers, where at No. 35, a turret encloses the 16C *Escalier de la Reine-Berthe,* a spiral staircase of carved oak. The Rue St-Eman leads W. to the PL. DE LA POISSONNERIE, in which are the 15C wooden houses called the *Maison du Saumon* and *Maison de la Truite-qui-File.* Hence the Rue de la Petite-Cordonnerie and narrow Rue aux Herbes lead back to the S. front of the Cathedral.

Many ancient houses in this old quarter S.E. of the Cathedral are undergoing restoration; others of interest may be seen in the Rue des Grenets (No. 12), the continuation of the Rue des Changes (leading S. from the Cathedral), and beyond St-Aignan, at Nos. 8 and 10 PL. DE L'ÉTAPE-AU-VIN. Not far W. of this point is the *Hôtel Montescot* (1614), restored since the Hôtel de Ville was destroyed, with its valuable library, in 1944. A new town hall flanks the PL. DES HALLES, from the N.W. corner of which we may regain the *Pl. des Épars.*

A short distance to the S., approached by the Rue St-Brice, stands *St-Martin-au-Val* (now a hospital chapel: admission may be granted on request), a 12C abbey church on the l. of which, although much restored, are preserved some remains of a basilica dating from before the 10C. The vaulted crypt has Gallo-Roman capitals and contains sarcophagi of early bishops.

For the route from CHARTRES TO DREUX, see p. 258; *Verneuil* lies 56 km. N.W. on the D393; *Le Mans* (119 km. S.W.; N23); *Tours* (129 km. S.W.; N10); *Blois* (92 km. S.); and *Orléans* (72 km. S.E.; N154 and N20).

A short excursion may be made to **Illiers,** 25 km. S.W. of Chartres on the N821, a little town on the Loir (which here divides the Beauce from the Perche-Gouët) famous as the 'Combray' of Marcel Proust's 'À la recherche du temps perdu'. The 14C church has a fine roof. Proust spent his childhood holidays with his uncle and aunt, M. et Mme Amiot (tante Léonie), whose house, No. 4 Rue du Docteur-Proust, is preserved as a literary shrine (and 'centre de documentation proustienne'); for details of the many associations, refer to *George D. Painter*'s 'Marcel Proust; a Biography', vol. 1 (1959).

FROM CHARTRES TO ÉTAMPES, see p. 245.

FROM CHARTRES TO PITHIVIERS (73 km.). We follow the N154 S.E. across the monotonous Beauce plateau. Shortly after passing beneath the motorway, a turning (l.) leads to the hamlet of *Brétigny* where the famous treaty was signed in 1360, in accordance with which Jean II, le Bon, paying a ransom of 3 million crowns to regain his liberty lost at the battle of Poitiers, surrendered the whole of S.W. France to Edward III, who, in return, renounced all claim to the French crown. At 21 km. a crossroads leads 10 km. N.E. to *Santeuil*, with an important Romanesque church, once fortified, with a 13C apse.—*Voves*, 7 km. S.W. of the crossroad, has a 12-15C church.

38 km. *Allaines-Mervilliers*, 2 km. to the S. of which, a disused church preserves a remarkable 12C sculptured tympanum, said to represent St-Fiacre refusing the Scottish crown. We bear l. onto the N827, crossing the A10, past (41 km.) *Le Puiset*, with a beautiful 12C church and the ruins of a castle, which defied Philippe I but was destroyed by Louis VI. Most famous of its robber-barons was Hugh du Puiset (d. 1195), nephew of King Stephen, and Bp. of Durham.—47 km. *Toury*, see p. 246.—73 km. *Pithiviers*, p. 245.

Le Mans lies 119 km. S.W. of Chartres on the N23; *Tours* is 138 km. S.W. on the N10 (viâ *Châteaudun* and *Vendôme*).

B   Viâ the Valley of the Chevreuse, Port-Royal, Rambouillet, and Maintenon

N306 to (40 km.) *St-Rémy-lès-Chevreuse*; (*Port-Royal-des-Champs*); (*Dampierre*).—61 km. *Rambouillet*.—81 km. *Maintenon*.—102 km. *Chartres*.

The N306 and the road bearing S. off the N10 at *Sèvres* towards the A10 converge at *Porte Clamart* (8 km. S.W. of the *Porte de Châtillon*, and 13 km. from the centre of Paris).

At 16.5 km. we cross the valley of the Bièvre, where, 4 km. to the W., at *Jouy-en-Josas*, with a 13-16C church, Oberkampf founded the famous manufacture of printed calico, called 'toiles de Jouy', c. 1780.—At **Bièvres** itself (4,100 inhab.), just N. of this junction, an interesting *Musée de la Photographie* has been installed in the Mairie.

3 km. E. of the next main junction at (31 km.) *Saclay*, lies *Vauhallan*, where the church, originally 6C, was rebuilt in the 13C, and altered in the 18C.—We diverge r. onto the N306, passing, W. of Saclay, the research laboratories of the Centre d'Études Nucléaires, and climb down into the VALLÉE DE CHEVREUSE.

40 km. *St-Rémy-lès-Chevreuse*, 2.5 km. N. of which are slight remains of a 12C castle at *Châteaufort*.

At 41 km. a detour may be made to **Port-Royal-des-Champs**, 6 km. N.W. by the D46 (r.), passing at 5 km. the church at *St-Lambert*, where in the cemetery a granite pyramid marks the common fosse where the remains of the nuns of Port-Royal were reinterred.—On reaching the D91, a footpath leads N. to the entrance of the enclosure (adm. 10.00-12.00; 14.00-18.00 from 15 Apr. to 15 Oct.; rest of the year 14.00-17.00 only, except Sun. and holidays; shut every Tues., and Wed. morning).

The celebrated abbey of *Port-Royal-des-Champs*, founded in 1204, played an important part in the religious history of France, being the headquarters of the Jansenists. Mère Angélique, abbess 1605-61, removed the community from Paris in 1625 (see p. 63). In 1638 the abbey-buildings were taken possession of by the 'solitaires', among whom were Mère Angélique's nephews, and later, her father. Their 'Petites Écoles' (1648-55) attracted much attention by their 'natural' methods of education; James Duke of Monmouth is said to have finished his education at one of them. The nuns, who returned in 1645, devoted themselves to the education of girls. Racine spent three years (1655-58) at the abbey, as a pupil of Pierre Nicole. Pascal, whose sister Jacqueline was a nun there, championed the Jansenists in their protracted quarrel with the Jesuits (comp. 'Lettres Provinciales', 1656-57).

In 1709, as a result of these religious wranglings, a Papal bull authorized the immediate demolition of the abbey and dispersal of its inmates. On the night of 28 Oct. the abbey was quietly surrounded by detachments of French and Swiss guards, and next morning, after being given a quarter of an hour to pack, the old nuns were led to waiting coaches, and driven to distant destinations. Most of the extensive buildings were then razed to the ground, the materials sold, and the site ploughed over: such was the inexorable and predatory power of the Jesuits.

Little remains to be seen: merely the foundations of the 13C church, the cloister wall, a dovecote, one of the towers built to defend the abbey during the Fronde, Mère Angélique's fountain, and the 'Solitude' (reconstructed). The tombstones of thirty members of the community are now in the church of *Magny-les-Hameaux,* an attractive village 4.5 km. to the E.

Regaining the road (D91), we may drive N. to the top of the hill to visit (l., along an avenue) the *Musée National des Granges de Port-Royal (adm. 10-11.30; 14.00-17.00 or 17.30, except Mon., Tues., and holidays) installed in a building of 1651-52, and devoted to the history of the Jansenists and, more particularly, of *Port-Royal,* and including some portraits by *Ph. de Champaigne.*

5.5 km. S. of Port-Royal-des-Champs lies *Dampierre,* see below.

———————

42 km. **Chevreuse** (4,200 inhab.), with a church dating from the 12th to the 17C, is dominated by the imposing ruins of the château *de la Madeleine* (12th and 15C), once the home of the intriguing Duchesse de Chevreuse, the enemy of Richelieu.

The D58 diverges r. to (4 km.) **Dampierre,** with a splendid * *Château* rebuilt for the Duc de Luynes by *Jules Hardouin-Mansart* in 1675-83, and restored in 1840 (adm. suspended). The park was laid out by *Le Nôtre.*

5 km. N.W. along the D58 is the church of *N.-D. de la Roche,* containing (after those in Poitiers cathedral) the oldest choirstalls in France, c. 1275.—A short distance beyond, at *Le Mesnil-St-Denis,* is an attractive 16-18C château.

From Dampierre, the D91 leads S., passing (l.) the château of *Cour-Senlisse* (15-16C) to regain the N306 just beyond *Cernay-la-Ville.*

2.5 km. W. of this junction (by the D24) are the ruins of the abbey of **Les Vaux-de-Cernay,** founded by the Cistercians in 1128, and suppressed at the Revolution. These comprise the church (c. 1170), the monks' parlour and dormitory adjoining the N. transept, a superb example of the Romanesque style, a chapel, and a well. The prior's lodging is now a modern residence (for adm. apply to the Régisseur, Abbaye des Vaux-de-Cernay, par Auffargis).

At 44.5 km. (2.5 km. S.W. of *Chevreuse* on the N306) the château of *Breteuil* (17-19C), now somewhat commercialized, lies to the l.—49 km. *Cernay-la-Ville,* see above.—53 km. The château of *La Celle-les-Bordes* (1610) lies 4 km. to the S.E.

61 km. **Rambouillet** (18,700 inhab.), where since 1897 the Château has been the official country residence of the President of the French Republic.

In 1547 François I died in the château, which then belonged to Jacques d'Angennes, one of his officers. Charles IX and Catherine de Médicis took refuge there during the Religious Wars; and here Charles X signed his abdication in 1830. The Marquise de Rambouillet (1588-1665), who held her famous salon in the *Hôtel de Rambouillet* in Paris in the early 17C, was a member of the Angennes family, who owned the castle from the 14C until 1700. After that date the Comte de Toulouse, son of Louis XIV and Mme de Montespan, greatly enlarged the building: his son, the charitable Duc de Penthièvre, was left undisturbed by the Revolution. Florian lived here in 1768-83. Louis XVI was a frequent visitor, but Marie-Antoinette found the place unbearably dull. After 1830 the estate was used as a pleasure-resort, until restored by Napoleon III.

The **Château** may be visited when the President is not in residence (adm. 10.00-12.00; 14.00-16.00 or 18.00; closed Tues.). Only one machicolated tower of the original 14C castle survives; the remainder is a sombre pile of red brick, with five flanking towers of stone. It contains some good oak panelling, Gobelins tapestries, etc.

The *GARDENS (open daily until dusk) are mainly due to Penthièvre. Beyond the Parterre is the JARDIN D'EAU, a lake with formally designed islands; the central 'Grand Canal' being extended by a Tapis Vert. To the E. is an avenue of Louisiana cypresses, while to the W. is the 'Jardin Anglais', with a shell grotto. To the N.W. is the *Laiterie de la Reine* (adm. at the same hours as the château), built to amuse Marie-Antoinette, and decorated with sculptures and grisailles. Beyond is the national sheep-farm, endowed by Louis XVI.

The FORÊT DE RAMBOUILLET, a presidential chase of some 30,000 acres, extends to the S.E. and to the N.W., but is perhaps best explored from *Montfort-l'Amaury* (see p. 255), 18 km. to the N. viâ the N836. Near *Poigny-la-Forêt*, 4.5 km. N. and to the W. of this road, are the ruins of a 12C priory church on the bank of the picturesque ÉTANG D'ANGENNES.

74 km. *Épernon* (4,200 inhab.), an old town on a hillside, with a 13C vaulted cellar ('the winepress of Épernon'), and a large late Gothic church. Its game-pies should be sampled.

81 km. **Maintenon** (3,300 inhab.). The *Château* (adm. daily except Tues.; 14.00-17.30 or 18.30) was given by Louis XIV in 1674 to Françoise d'Aubigné (1635-1719), later Marquise de Maintenon who in 1683 became his second wife, and remains the property of her heirs, the Noailles family. Damaged in 1940, and since restored, it preserves a 13C keep and two 14C towers, but is mainly a 16C building, with additions due to Mme de Maintenon, personal souvenirs of whom may be seen, together with family portraits, etc.

We turn S. onto the D6, shortly passing the ruins of an *Aqueduct* designed by Louis XIV to bring water from the Eure to Versailles, but the project was never completed.—86 km. *St-Piat* preserves an ancient (5C) sculptured sarcophagus of the patron saint in its church.—At (91 km.) *Jouy*, the church has a charming 13C W. front.—Beyond *St-Prest*, with a 11-13C church, and before joining the main road, we pass the buildings of the *Hospice d'Aligre*, incorporating parts of the Benedictine abbey of Josaphet (founded 1117), including the tomb of John of Salisbury (see p. 247); also tombs of the Aligre family, and a 16C cloister brought from Coulombs (see p. 258).—102 km. *Chartres*, see Rte 33A.

C   Viâ the A10 and A11

This is the most rapid but least interesting road. Making our exit from Paris by either the *Porte d'Italie* or the *Porte de Gentilly*, after approx. 12 km. (6 km. from the Portes), we veer S.W., at 18 km. turning W. again near *Palaiseau* (with a 12-15C church), taking its name from the Merovingian palace which once stood there.

23 km. (l.) *Orsay*, with the late-18C château of Gen. Moreau, victor of Hohenlinden, built on the site of a castle taken by the English in 1424, and later the home of the Chevalier d'Orsay, the famous 19C dandy. The grounds now accommodate an annexe of the Faculté des Sciences, with spacious laboratories, etc.
    Hence the N188 leads S.W. to (11 km.) *Limours* (4,200 inhab.), with a church built by François I in the Flamboyant style, containing 16C stained-glass (restored).—5.5 km. S.E., at *Briis-sous-Forges*, is a square tower, which is supposed to be a remnant of a convent where Anne Boleyn was educated.—The N188 continues S.W. to (21 km.) **Rochefort-en-Yvelines,** on the S. limit of the FORÊT DE RAMBOUILLET, retaining a number of 15-16C houses, the mairie

occupying a 17C bailliage, and with a partly Romanesque church dominated by a ruined castle. Hence we may rejoin the A10.—*St-Arnault,* 4 km. W., has a church showing a strange mingling of Romanesque and late Gothic work. No. 9 Rue de Paris has a façade of 1523, restored in 1770.

48 km. *Rochefort-en-Yvelines* (see above) lies 2 km. N.—At 53.5 km. the A10 diverges S. towards *Orléans.*

60 km. (l.) *Ablis* (see p. 246).—At 83 km. we diverge r. to (88 km.) *Chartres,* the A11 bypassing the town to rejoin the N10 to the S. Work is in progress with its extension to *Le Mans.*

34   PARIS TO HOUDAN AND DREUX (FOR ALENÇON)

N12. (46 km.; *Montfort-l'Amaury*).—63 km. *Houdan.*—84 km. *Dreux.*

The A12 and N186 converge a short distance S.W. of Versailles (approx. 18 km. from the *Porte d'Auteuil*), where we diverge onto the N12.

2 km. N.E. of this intersection stood the famous Military Academy of **St-Cyr,** founded by Napoleon in 1808, but destroyed in 1944; the academy has since been transferred to *Coëtquidan* in Brittany. It occupied the buildings of the school of St-Louis, established in 1680 for the daughters of poor but noble families by Mme de Maintenon, who was buried there in 1719. Racine's 'Esther' (1689) and 'Athalie' (1691) were written specially for, and played by, the schoolgirls.
34 km. The D30 leads N. c. 10 km. to the château of *Wideville (off the N307), built in 1630 for Claude de Bullion (1580-1640), able minister and friend of Richelieu, containing interesting paintings, and a fine fresco by *Simon Vouet.*

39 km. **Pontchartrain,** with a château built by *Fr. Mansart* for the Phelypeaux family, the last member of which, better known as the Comte de Maurepas (1701-81), was a minister under both Louis XV and XVI.—Just to the S., at *Jouars,* is a church with a 13C choir and 18C nave.

At 41 km. the N191 leads N. to (13 km.) *Maule,* with a late 11-12C church with a Renaissance tower. There is a curious *Musée du Velocipède* 1 km. N., with c. 200 examples dating from the 17C to 1925.

At 42 km. the N191 leads 3.5 km. S. to crossroads.—At *Bazoches-sur-Guyonne* (1 km. E.) the church has a Romanesque portal and 12C tower.—There is a 17C château at *La Tremblaye-sur-Mauldre,* just beyond.—S. of these crossroads lies *Les Mesnuls,* with a fine château built in 1530 and altered by Marshal Villars (adm. by appointment).— 3 km. N.W. (and also approached direct from the N12 at 46 km.) lies **Montfort-l'Amaury** (2,300 inhab.; *Hotels*), the ancient seat of the medieval counts of Montfort, notable among whom were Simon IV (d. 1218), leader of the Albigensian Crusade, and Simon V (?1208-65), Earl of Leicester.

The church of **St-Pierre,** with an attractive S. doorway, and containing some remarkable 16C *Stained-glass, and elaborate roof-bosses, was rebuilt by Anne of Brittany (Countess of Montfort) at the end of the 15C, but was not completed until the 17C. A fragment of its Romanesque predecessor survives on the N. side of the nave.

A short distance N.W. is the *Old Cemetery,* preserving a 15C gateway and three galleries (16-17C). The Rue St-Laurent leads uphill to the *Porte Bardoul,* the most conspicuous section of the town walls, overlooked by ruins of the castle (10th and 15C). Nearby, in the Rue Maurice-Ravel, is the *Villa de Belvédère* (museum), home of Ravel

(1875-1937) from 1921. There are a number of attractive old houses in the lower town.

From Montfort-l'Amaury, the D138 leads through part of the FORÊT DE RAMBOUILLET to (17 km.) *Rambouillet*, see p. 253, viâ (7 km.) *St-Léger-en-Yvelines*, with a 12C church, passing (l., after 5 km.) the ÉTANGS DE HOLLANDE, a series of artificial lakes created by order of Louis XIV.

63 km. **Houdan** (2,900 inhab.) preserves a 12C keep flanked by four turrets, all that remains of the castle of the Montforts, a handsome 15-16C church with an impressive apse, and a number of old houses in the Rue Ernest-Chapelier. Houdan is also known for its breed of poultry and its pâtés.—*Dreux,* see below, lies 21 km. W.

At *Richebourg,* 5 km. N.E., is a 15C church retaining 16C glass; 8.5 km. beyond lies *Montchauvet,* an attractively situated fortified village.

An interesting DEVIATION VIÂ ANET AND IVRY may be made by driving N.W. on the N833.—17 km. **Anet** (1,800 inhab.), famous for its **Château* (adm. 10.00-11.30; 14.00-17.00 or 14.30-17.30) built by Henri II for his mistress Diane de Poitiers in 1548-55. *Philibert Delorme* was the architect, and the decoration was entrusted to *Jean Goujon, Germain Pilon,* and *Benvenuto Cellini.* The building later passed to the Duchesse du Maine, visited there by Mme du Deffand, Mme du Châtelet, Fontenelle, and Voltaire, but was sold at the Revolution, and the greater part was demolished in 1804-11. The entrance gate, W. wing, and chapel survive. The original central façade has been re-erected in the courtyard of the École des Beaux-Arts in Paris, see p. 74. The first performance of Lulli's last work, 'Acis et Galatée' (1686), took place here.

The main entrance, in the form of a triumphal arch, is adorned with a copy of *Cellini*'s Nymph of Fontainebleau, above which is a clock surmounted by a sculptured stag-hunt. Beyond it is what is left of the château, with a vestibule and staircase added by the Duc de Vendôme in the 17C, and panelled rooms containing tapestries, portraits, old furniture, and mementoes of Diane.

The *Chapel,* on the plan of a Greek cross, with a central cupola, contains sculptured reliefs by *Goujon.* The tomb of Diane was rifled in 1795, but her body was rescued and buried outside the E. end of the parish church (which dates from the 13th and 16C).

The hare and venison pâtés of Anet have a local reputation.

Just E. of the château, a lane skirts the river Eure, which we shortly cross to **Ivry-la-Bataille** (1,500 inhab.; *Hotels*), where a 12C doorway is the sole remnant of an abbey of which the architect Philibert Delorme (1515-70) was titular abbot. A doorway of the 14-16C parish church is ascribed to him. Ivry owes its name to the decisive victory which Henri IV won over the forces of the Ligue in 1590.

Hence the N836 leads N. to (17 km.) *Pacy-sur-Eure,* see p. 258.

The direct road FROM IVRY TO DREUX (N828) is reached by recrossing the river to *Ézy-sur-Eure,* thence driving S. through the FORÊT DE DREUX. An alternative route is that running parallel to the river through (11 km. from *Anet*) *Marcilly-sur-Eure,* shortly beyond which, in the grounds of a château near the river, stands the nave of the abbey church of *Le Breuil-Benoît* (1137).—16 km. *St-Georges-Motel,* where the 12C church contains fragments of a Tree of Jesse in 16C stained-glass.—

Passing (l.) *Montreuil,* with an 11-15C church, we shortly enter (18.5 km.) *Dreux.*

DREUX (34,000 inhab.), once an attractive old town, now retains few vestiges of its historic past. Its pâtés are worth tasting.

History. Capital of the Gallic tribe of the Durocasses, it was in the Middle Ages the headquarters of a powerful line of counts, and although the county passed to Charles V in 1378, it was not formally united to the French crown until 1556. Henry V occupied the town in 1421. The 'Journée de Dreux' (1562), one of the bloodiest battles in the Religious Wars, was fought in the plain between the Blaise and the Eure, when Montmorency and Guise defeated the Huguenots under Louis de Condé. The fortifications were dismantled by Henri IV in 1593, after a stubborn siege. The place passed by marriage in the 18C into the hands of the Orléans branch of the Bourbons, who built there their mausoleum.
Among natives of Dreux ('Drouais') are the Métezeau family of architects: Clément (1479-1555), Thibault (1533-1600), Louis (1559-1615), and Clément (1581-1652); Antoine Godeau (1605-72), précieux, Bp. of Vence, and one of the original members of the Académie Française; Jean Rotrou (1609-50), the poet; and Danican Philidor (1726-95), the composer and chess-player.

On the N. side of the PL. MÉTEZEAU, in the centre of old Dreux, in a loop of the river Blaise, stands **St-Pierre** (13-17C), much of which is the work of the Métezeau family. It was considerably damaged in the Revolution. The earliest part of the church is the N. transept, with the piers in the choir and in the aisles of the nave. The fine but mutilated W. doorway (1524) is flanked by two 16C towers, that on the r. remaining unfinished. The 15C nave contains contemporary glass in the first window on the l., and a carved Romanesque capital serving as a bénitier by the first pier (r.). There is noteworthy glass in the LADY CHAPEL (15C) and in several of the aisle-chapels (16C). The fine organ-case (1614) in the 17C S. transept was carved by *Toussaint Fortier* of Dreux.

There is a small *Museum* of local antiquities housed in a chapel a short distance S. of the main square.

On the W. side of the square, facing down the Grande Rue, stands the sturdy Renaissance **Beffroi* (1512-37), with two elegant turrets and windows with stone mullions (adm. 10.00-11.30; 14.00-17.00 or 18.00).

Beyond the far end of the Grande Rue rises a hill surmounted by the Orléans mausoleum. This may be approached by car by circling to the W. of the hill, and immediately climbing to the r.; on foot, it may be reached by turning r. into the Rue Parisis (towards the far end of the Grande Rue) and taking the first lane on the l. A steep flight of steps ascends to the summit (views).

The **Chapelle Royale St-Louis** (adm. all day except between 11.45 and 13.30; also to the park, with remains of a keep and other fortifications) was begun in 1816 by the Dowager Duchess of Orléans and enlarged and completed by her son, Louis-Philippe, in his usual decadent taste. It is a pseudo-Gothic domed apsidal building, and is lavishly adorned with sculptures and stained-glass (those in the nave, dome, and lower crypt being executed at Sèvres after designs by *Larivière*). Those depicting saints, round the choir, are from cartoons by *Ingres,* and include portraits of Louis-Philippe as St Louis, Queen Marie-Amélie as St Amelia, and the Duc d'Orléans as St Ferdinand, etc.

In the UPPER CRYPT are the tomb of Louis-Philippe (1773-1850) and his wife, whose remains were transferred here in 1876 from Weybridge, their home in exile in England.

Beyond the adjacent tomb of Ferdinand d'Orléans is that of his wife, Hélène of Mecklenburg-Schwerin (1814-58), placed in a separate chapel, because she was a Protestant. Among the funerary sculpture on the ostentatious tombs of this illustrious family are examples of the work of *Chapu, Walhain, Pradier* (of Mlle de Montpensier), and Princess *Marie d'Orléans* (d. 1839).

Argentan lies 112 km. W. of Dreux viâ the N12 and N24bis; *Alençon* 100 km. S.W. on the N12; and *Nogent-le-Rotrou* (for *Le Mans*) 56 km. S.W. on the D928.

FROM DREUX TO ÉVREUX (42 km.). We follow the N12 W. towards (13 km.) *Nonancourt* (bypassed), where we diverge r. onto the N154, after passing (10 km., l.) *St-Rémy-sur-Avre*, with a 12th and 16C church. The road beyond crosses a flat plain before descending into the valley of the Iton at *Évreux*, see p. 258.

Nonancourt (1,900 inhab.) grew up around a castle built in 1113 by Henry I of England, where in 1189 was signed a treaty between Philippe Auguste and Richard Coeur-de-Lion determining their share in the Third Crusade. Henri IV slept at Nonancourt the night before the Battle of Ivry (see p. 256). Here, in Nov. 1715, the local postmistress saved the life of James Francis Edward, the 'Old Pretender', who would otherwise have been assassinated by hirelings of the Earl of Mar, as described by Saint-Simon (whose home at *La Ferté-Vidame* lay 31 km. S.W.).

The church (1511) contains some good stained-glass, and an organ-loft, both of the 16C, and a 14C stone Virgin.

The direct road (N154) leads 32 km. S. from DREUX TO CHARTRES, see p. 251; a more attractive road (N829) follows the valley of the Eure viâ (11.5 km.) *Villemeux-sur-Eure*, with a Romanesque church altered in the 16C, with a rose-window.—17 km. **Nogent-le-Roi**, an old fortified town retaining some 16C houses, with a Gothic and Renaissance church, with an elegant apse. On the opposite bank of the river are remains of the 12C abbey of *Coulombs*.—At 25 km. we enter *Maintenon*, see p. 254, and follow the road thence to Chartres.

35   PARIS TO ÉVREUX (FOR LISIEUX AND CAEN)

A13 to (56 km.) *Mantes;* at 71 km. bear l. onto N13.—80 km. *Pacy-sur-Eure.*—96 km. *Évreux.*

For the road to Mantes, see Rte 36A, 15 km. beyond which we leave the A13, and drive due W. to (80 km.) *Pacy-sur-Eure,* with an interesting church dating from the 12C.

Hence the N836 leads N.W. along the charming valley of the Eure, through (6.5 km.) *Cocherel,* scene of Du Guesclin's victory over the troops of England and Navarre in 1364, when Jean de Grailly, the 'Captal de Buch', was taken prisoner.—13 km. *Autheuil-Authouillet.* The church in the latter village contains remarkable 18C woodwork, including an elaborately carved priest's chair.—3 km. beyond, at *La Croix-St-Leufroy,* the moated castle of 1620 is the abbot's lodge of a former abbey, some sculptures and paintings from which are preserved in the church.

96 km. **ÉVREUX** (50,400 inhab.; *Hotels*), capital of the department of the Eure (one of the five departments of Normandy), stands on three branches of the Iton, the well-rebuilt town centre preserving a cathedral of considerable interest. It is reputed also for its rillettes, quenelles, poultry, and cider, etc.

History. Gallo-Roman *Mediolanum* seems to have occupied a site on the plateau some 5 km. S.E., but a town existed on the present site in the time of Augustus. A bishopric was founded by St Taurinus in the 4C, and the town walls were built 100 years later. Évreux was burned in 1119 by Henry I, who received permission to do so from the bishop on condition that he rebuilt the cathedral. In 1193 the principal citizens were treacherously massacred by Prince John of England, and in 1365 the town was burned by the Norman governor before its surrender to the king's troops. It was finally united to France in 1404, but in 1418-27 was again in English occupation, having been captured by Thomas, Duke of Exeter. Meanwhile (1427) Charles VII had bestowed the countship of Évreux on Sir Charles Stuart of Darnley, sieur d'Aubigny (d. 1429), commander of his Scottish bodyguard.

Évreux experienced another devastating fire in June 1940, on being bombed by the Germans, which caused extensive damage; Allied air attacks in June 1944 were confined to an area near the station.

The *Cathedral of Notre-Dame, many times ruined, rebuilt, and restored between the 12th and 17C (and again since 1940), atones for its lack of unity by presenting in juxtaposition successive phases of medieval and Renaissance architecture. The main façade is Renaissance (1575-91), with a large portal flanked by towers (one of which was crowned by a cupola and stone lantern until 1940). The rose-window is an unusually late example, dating from c. 1591. The N. façade exhibits the richest style of Flamboyant Gothic. The central tower, dating from 1467, had its elegant spire destroyed in 1940.

In the NAVE, the Romanesque main arcades date from the rebuilding of Henry I, while the upper part is due to a later reconstruction following a fire in 1194. The E. parts of the church are noticeably sumptuous in contrast. The aisles were added in the 14C, but the window-tracery was altered in the 15th and 16C. Some of the aisle chapels preserve fragments of 13C glass. The pulpit (1675), by *Guillaume de la Tremblaye,* was brought from the abbey of Bec.

In the TRANSEPTS are an open triforium with Flamboyant arches, and good 16C rose-windows. The choir screen is iron-work of the 18C; the stalls date from the 14C, as do the *Stained-glass windows (well restored), which are among the finest of their period in France. Delicate wooden Renaissance screens separate the transepts from the Ambulatory, where most of the chapels have screens of the same period. The 15C glass in the LADY CHAPEL is remarkable for its fine execution and perfect preservation, and much of the other glass in the ambulatory chapels is equally noteworthy. In the apse is a fine 15C Virgin and Child. The restored Gothic *Cloister* is entered from the S. transept.

To the S. of the cathedral is the former *Bishop's Palace,* a Flamboyant building of 1481 (considerably restored), and now containing the **Museum.**

The collections include prehistoric and Gallo-Roman antiquities, including a bronze statue of Jupiter Stator, and a 4C glass goblet, from *Mediolanum;* two tombstones, one (1317) from the abbey of *Bonport,* and another (1290) from *Chanteloup;* Rouen faience, etc.; the mitre of Jean de Marigny, Abp. of Rouen (1317-57), 13C Limoges enamel crosses, and 14-15C English alabasters. The paintings include portraits by *Ph. de Champaigne* of Angélique Arnauld (Abbess of Port-Royal), and more modern works.

Parts of the old town *Moat* can be seen from the Public Gardens behind the cathedral, from the N.W. of which one may follow a pleasant riverside walk, skirted by *Ramparts,* to the graceful Flamboyant **Tour de l'Horloge,** containing a bell of 1406.

The Rue de Verdun leads E. from the cathedral, passing (l.) the *Palais de Justice,* to meet the Rue Joséphine. A short distance further W., to the r., stands **St-Taurin,** the church of a vanished abbey founded in 1026 on the site of the saint's grave. The W. front dates from the mid-18C. Built over a crypt, the interior preserves some Romanesque arches and capitals (N. side), but the general effect is that of a 14C building, although parts of the triforium (S. side) are Renaissance work. The beautiful 14C CHOIR contains 16C glass. To the N. of the choir is preserved the magnificent 13C *Shrine of St-Taurinus.*

The château (1676-89) of the Duc de Bouillon, built on the site of a castle of Charles the Bad of Navarre, which stood c. 2 km. to the W., was demolished in 1834.

Les Andelys (see p. 262) lies 36 km. N.E. on the N154 and N316 viâ *Gaillon*, see p. 261.

For the route from ÉVREUX TO DREUX, see p. 258. The N154 leads N. to (51 km.) *Rouen*, and the N13 to (72 km.) *Lisieux*, 49 km. further W. of which lies *Caen*.

36   PARIS TO LES ANDELYS (FOR ROUEN)

A   Viâ Mantes and Vernon

A13 to (56 km.) *Mantes.*—80 km. *Vernon.*—106 km. *Les Andelys.*

From the *Porte d'Auteuil* the A13 drives W., shortly spanning the Seine, and entering the tunnel below St-Cloud.—At 18 km. the N10 bears l. for *Chartres* and *Dreux,* see Rtes 33 and 34A respectively.

56 km. **Mantes** (42,400 inhab.), an industrial town, which hardly deserves its sobriquet 'la Jolie'.

It was burned in 1087 by William the Conqueror, whose horse is said to have trodden on a cinder, causing the fall from which the corpulent king died at Rouen. Philippe Auguste died here in 1223, and his heart is buried in the church. Sacked by Edward III in 1346, recaptured by Du Guesclin in 1364, but soon after retaken by the English, Mantes finally passed to France in 1440. Gabrielle d'Estrées, who had a house here (destroyed), was frequently visited by Henri IV. The R.A.F. destroyed the main bridge over the Seine here in 1944, but it says much for the accuracy of the bombing that the beautiful collegiate church was left untouched.

Notre-Dame, dating mainly from the 12-13C, resembles Notre-Dame in Paris in style. The 12C façade, with a rose-window, has three fine doorways, that on the S. having an elaborate 14C gable: in the lintel of the N. door is a charmingly naïve Resurrection. The upper part of the N. tower and the gallery between the towers is an addition of 1844, while the apse-chapels and the *Chap. de Navarre* (S.) are of the 14C. The interior is notable for its lightness, for the absence of a transept, and for the remarkable *CHAP. DE NAVARRE (restored), vaulted from a central pier, and containing four 14C statuettes of queens.

A short distance to the W. is the *Tour St-Maclou* (14-15C), relic of an earlier church.

E. of Notre-Dame, opposite the ancient bridge (see *Limay,* p. 262), survives the 14C *Porte aux Prêtres,* part of the old fortifications.

Some 1.5 km. N.W. of the central Pl. A.-Briand, lies the interesting church of *Gassicourt* (restored after damage in 1944), with a late 12C nave and 13C choir and transepts.

We now follow the N13, skirting the Seine, to (62 km.) **Rosny-sur-Seine,** with the château built by Maximilien de Béthune, Duc de Sully (1559-1641), Henri IV's favourite minister, who was born at Rosny. Henri IV retired here after the Battle of Ivry (see p. 256), in which Sully was wounded. A later owner was the Duchesse de Berry, who made additions in 1818-26.

We shortly climb the Corniche de Rolleboise, before descending through *Bonnières-sur-Seine,* where a Neolithic multiple grave has been exposed, near the church.

Évreux (see Rte 35) lies 32 km. W., on the N13, off which we bear r. onto the N13bis for (80 km.) **Vernon** (23,600 inhab.; *Hotels*), an old town visited by both Bonington and Turner, but much damaged in 1940. It was the first meeting-place of the Estates of Normandy, in 1452. In Aug. 1944 the Allies threw bridges across the Seine here.

The church of *Notre-Dame,* mainly of the 14-15C, has an elaborate W. front with a good doorway, and a striking rose-window between low balustrades; at the E. end of the lofty nave is an unfinished 13C tower. Within are 16C stained-glass; some Flemish tapestries; a fine 17C tomb; and a 16C sculptured organ-loft. The Choir preserves a Romanesque arcade.

Adjacent is a half-timbered 15C house; others may be seen in the Rue Potard and Rue Carnot. Beyond the Rue d'Albuféra, leading from the rebuilt bridge, is the bold *Tour des Archives* (1123), attr. to Henry I.

At *Bizy,* on the W. outskirts of the town, is a château (rebuilt), where the Duc de Penthièvre died in 1793.—Some 4 km. beyond, *Brécourt* gives its name to a skirmish between the Girondins and Sanscoulottes (July 1793), known also as the 'Battle without tears', because there were no casualties.

The N13bis continues N.W. to (94 km.) **Gaillon** (4,300 inhab.), where Card. Georges d'Amboise, the art-loving Bp. of Rouen, erected a sumptuous château (1500-10), in the building and embellishment of which many Renaissance masters took part. This was destroyed in 1798, except for the entrance gateway and the lower part of the N. wall. Near the church, with 16-17C statues, is a fine 16C half-timbered house.

Évreux lies 24 km. S.W.; *Les Andelys* (see p. 262), 12 km. N.E.; and *Rouen* 42 km. N.W.

B   Viâ Poissy, Meulan, La Roche-Guyon, and Château-Gaillard

N190 to (28 km.) *Poissy.*—42 km. *Meulan.*—56 km. *Limay (Mantes).*—71 km. *La Roche-Guyon.*—84 km. *Vernonnet.*—106 km. *Les Andelys.*

From the *Porte Maillot,* we follow the N190 W. to (20.5 km.) *St-Germain-en-Laye,* see Rte 22.

Hence the N184 leads N. through the FORÊT DE ST-GERMAIN to (10.5 km.) **Conflans-Ste-Honorine** (30,600 inhab.) dominated by the ruins of a Romanesque keep, at the confluence of the Oise and the Seine, and a river-port since the 9C. The pseudo-Renaissance château houses a *Museum of the Inland Waterways,* with models of lighters, barges, etc. The church of *St-Maclou* is of the 12-16C.— *Pontoise* (see p. 264) lies 8.5 km. to the N.—The church of *Andrésy* (2.5 km. S.W.) contains good 16C glass.

The N190 leads N.W. from St-Germain to (28 km.) **Poissy** (37,100 inhab.), a favourite residence of St Louis and once the scene of an important cattle market. The modern bridge spanning the river replaces one of the 13C almost destroyed during the last war. A few arches remain of the *Dominican Abbey,* in the refectory of which, in 1561, took place the fruitless conference of Poissy between Protestants and Catholics, their respective protagonists being Théodore de Bèze and Card. Lorraine. The church of *Notre-Dame* (1130-40, with later additions) retains two fine Romanesque towers, and three ambulatory chapels, two of which take the place of transepts. The Font of St Louis is somewhat worn, owing to the popular belief that its scrapings swallowed in a glass of water would cure a fever.

34 km. *Triel-sur-Seine* has a 13-15C church, the choir of which is built above a street, containing good Renaissance glass.

There is a 12C church at *Vernouillet,* on the opposite bank of the Seine, with a Romanesque belfry; 2.5 km. S. of which, at *Médan,* was Zola's country house from 1877 until his death in 1902.

42 km. **Meulan** (8,500 inhab.), an ancient town, with slight remains of a castle, and the church of *St-Nicolas,* with a 12C choir.—4 km. N.W., at *Gaillon,* is a 12-13C church with an octagonal stone spire.

Hence we follow the N. bank of the Seine through (47 km.) *Juziers,* with a fine late-12C apsed church, to (56 km.) **Limay,** also with an interesting 12-13C church with a graceful steeple, and rich in works of art. The composer Chausson (1855-99) was killed here in a bicycle accident, near his country villa.

Mantes, see p. 260, lies on the opposite bank of the Seine. The ancient bridge crossing to the ÎLE AUX DAMES was partly destroyed by the French in 1940.

From *Limay,* the D147 leads N.W. to (62 km.) *St-Martin-la-Garenne,* with an interesting church with a 12C choir, a rebuilt tower, and fine Renaissance façade.—**Vetheuil,** 3 km. beyond, was Monet's home in 1878-81. The church (12-16C) has a remarkable early Gothic choir, and an attractive Renaissance façade.—We pass troglodyte dwellings at *Haute-Isle.*

71 km. **La Roche-Guyon** (600 inhab.), with the château of the La Rochefoucauld family, and where the author of the 'Maximes' (1665 and later editions) wrote a large part of his work. The keep, a remarkable example of military architecture, was built in the 10C by a baron named Guy. It was Rommel's H.Q. during part of the Battle of Normandy (1944). In the church is the tomb of François de Sillery, Duc de La Roche-Guyon (d. 1627).

Beyond La Roche-Guyon, the N313 climbs steeply, off which (r.) runs the 'Route des Crêtes', with extensive views.—We descend to (74 km.) *Gasny.*—6.5 km. N.E. lies *Bray-et-Lû,* see p. 263.—6 km. S.W. lies **Giverny,** the residence, from 1883, of Claude Monet (1840-1926), who died there, and is buried near the Romanesque apse of the church. It is also well-known for its filet de boeuf en brioche.

We follow the N313 W. to (84 km.) *Vernonnet,* the N. suburb of *Vernon* (see p. 260), with the château *des Tourelles,* a 12C keep, and fragments of an ancient bridge.

11.5 km. N., off the N181, are the villages of *Tourny,* and beyond, *Fontenay,* the former with an interesting 13th and 16C church. The lane joining them passes near the famous avenue of the château of *Beauregard.*

The N313 continues to skirt the Seine, with the FORÊTS DE VERNON, and DES ANDELYS, to the r., to (106 km.) **Le Petit-Andely.**

The lesser of the twin towns of **Les Andelys** (7,300 inhab.; *Hotels*) came into existence as a bridgehead below the fortress of Château-Gaillard. *St-Sauveur* dates from 1197, while the domed *Hospice St-Jacques* was rebuilt by the Duc de Penthièvre in 1785.

Évreux (see p. 258) lies 36 km. S.W., beyond *Gaillon,* and reached by the N316.

Le Grand-Andely was partially destroyed in the air attacks of 1940, but some half-timbered houses survive to the W. of the central PL. POUSSIN, near the *Tour de la Madeleine.* To the N.E. stands the 13C church of *Notre-Dame* (restored), with additions of the 15-16C. Within are good stained-glass (16C), an Entombment (16C), and a carved

Renaissance organ; also, in the Renaissance N. transept, several paintings by *Quentin Varin,* Poussin's first master. Thomas Corneille (1625-1709), younger brother of Pierre, died here. Nicolas Poussin (1594-1665) was born in the hamlet of *Villers-sur-Andelys,* 1.5 km. S.

Opposite the church, a lane leads S. Turning l. across the bridge, we climb steeply, bearing r. at the next crossroad, and shortly reach a viewpoint overlooking the impressive ruins of *Château-Gaillard,* and the Seine beyond.

This fortress was built on the chalk cliffs above the river by Richard Coeur-de-Lion in 1196, when the loss of Gisors left the frontier of Normandy undefended. Only eight years later this 'saucy' castle was starved into surrender by Philippe Auguste, after a six-month siege. In 1314 Marguerite of Burgundy and her sister Blanche, the frail wives of Louis X and Charles IV, were immured here, where the former was strangled on her husband's orders. In 1334 the castle afforded asylum to David II of Scotland, who had fled before Edward III. In 1603 it was dismantled by order of Henri IV.

The ruins of this remarkable and picturesque example of military architecture (adm. mid-Mar. to mid-Oct.; 10.00-12.00; 14.00-17.30, except Tues., and Wed. morning) include two main enceintes, of which the outer has almost disappeared, the keep, and a southern outwork or châtelet.—The lane descends steeply to *Le Petit-Andely.*

C   Viâ Magny-en-Vexin

For the route to (33 km.) *Pontoise,* see p. 264.—59 km. *Magny-en-Vexin.*— 89 km. *Le Grand-Andely.*

At Pontoise we bear l., continuing on the N14 to (46 km., l.) *Vigny,* with a Renaissance château built by Card. Georges d'Amboise, retaining pepper-pot towers.

52 km. *Guiry-en-Vexin* (1.5 km., l.) has a 17C château attr. to *François Mansart;* a church containing good 14-16C sculpture; and a small archaeological museum devoted to the Vexin.—54.5 km. *Cléry-en-Vexin* has an early 13C church altered in the 16C, with a Flamboyant Gothic portal and nave.

59 km. **Magny-en-Vexin** (4,100 inhab.). We pass on entering the town two 18C pillars on the site of medieval gates. To the N. of the town centre, preserving a number of old houses, is the church of *St-Martin,* rebuilt in the 16C (under restoration), containing notable monuments, a 14C stone Virgin, and a curious Font of 1534.

There is an interesting late-13C church with a double portal (16C) at *Genainville,* 4 km. S.—6 km. S.W., at *Villarceaux,* are two châteaux: one of 1737; the other, 15C, where Ninon de L'Enclos lived with Louis de Mornay (adm. Fri.-Sun. afternoons).

Amberville, with a 16-18C château, and *Bray-et-Lû,* with the ruined château of *Beaudemont,* lie 7 km. and 10 km. W. of Magny, respectively.—At *Ecos* (4 km. N.W. of Bray) there is a fine group in high-relief of c. 1400 in the church.—Hence the N14 may be regained viâ *Aveny* (4 km. E.), with a 15C bridge, *Berthenonville,* with a charmingly situated old church, and *Château-sur-Epte,* with remains of a keep of c. 1087.

2 km. N.W. of *Magny,* to the r. of the N14, the church of *St-Gervais* is of the 12-13C, with a Renaissance façade of 1550, 1.5 km. N. of which is the château of *Alincourt,* a cluster of buildings dating from the 14th to

the 17C. *Parnes,* beyond, retains a Romanesque church altered in the 15C.

At 69 km. *St-Clair-sur-Epte* a treaty in 912 between Rollo and Charles le Simple established the river as the boundary of the Duchy of Normandy.—70.5 km. (r.) *Guerny* retains good sculpture in its church.

7 km. beyond St-Clair, after passing through *Les Thilliers-en-Vexin,* we turn off the N14 onto the D125, at 89 km. entering *Le Grand-Andely,* see p. 262.

Rouen lies 44 km. N.W. on the N14.—To the r. of N14, 3 km. beyond the junction with D125, is *Hacqueville,* birthplace of Marc Isambard Brunel (1769-1849), the engineer.

37   PARIS TO PONTOISE AND GISORS

N14 to (33 km.) *Pontoise;* D915 to (79 km.) *Gisors.*

Both the N14 (from the *Porte de Clignancourt*) and the N309 (from the *Porte d'Asnières*) converge c. 16 km. N.W. of central Paris. An alternative route, at least until the main exit of the N14 is constructed, is the N192, leading N.W. from *La Défense,* which meets the N14 some 5.5 km. further N.W.

A short distance E. of the former junction lies *Enghien-les-Bains* (10,700 inhab.) on the bank of a small lake, which as the nearest watering-place (sulphur-baths) to Paris, enjoyed a certain vogue in the 19th and early 20C.—5 km. N.E. of the second intersection, at *Taverny,* is a noteworthy 13-14C church, restored by Viollet-le-Duc, with a fine Renaissance stone altarpiece.

Between the N309 and N192, on the N. bank of the Seine, lies *Argenteuil* (102,400 inhab.), often painted by the Impressionists, and where Braque was born in 1882.—*Cormeilles-en-Parisis,* adjoining to the N.W., was the birthplace of Louis Daguerre (1787-1851). The church here has a Romanesque nave and Gothic and Renaissance choir. Adjacent *La Frette,* and *Herblay,* to the W., have early churches, the latter with good 16C glass.

33 km. **Pontoise** (24,100 inhab.; *Hotels*), also bypassed, and now part of the conurbation of *Cergy-Pontoise,* was the ancient capital of the VEXIN FRANÇAIS, and birthplace of Philippe le Hardi, Duke of Burgundy. Of its fortifications, which guarded the river-crossing, nothing remains but the shell of a castle, dismantled in 1742. In the snowy winter of 1437 these were stormed by Talbot's English troops which, clad in white, approached the walls unnoticed.

Pontoise was the birthplace of Pierre Lemercier (d. 1570), and his grandson Jacques Lemercier (c. 1585-1645), and Fontaine (1762-1853), all architects; Camille Pissarro spent the years 1872-84 at Pontoise, moving hence to *Eragny,* on the opposite bank of the river, where he lived until 1903; but see also *Eragny-sur-Epte,* below.

The church of *St-Maclou,* with a 15-16C façade, has a single tower (1547), and three portals, two late Gothic, that on the S., of the Renaissance. The choir and transepts date from 1140-65; the nave is of the 16C, with two 15C W. bays. The N. arcade and N. aisle (1525), with three windows of contemporary glass, have interesting capitals. In the N.W. corner is the chapel of the Passion, containing a fine Holy Sepulchre (c. 1550) and two stained-glass windows of 1545. The Renaissance work in the church is due to *Pierre Lemercier* and his son *Nicolas* (1541-1637).

A short distance to the E. is the *Hôtel de Ville,* accommodated in what was part of a Franciscan convent, altered in the 19C. A local Museum is housed in a nearby mansion of 1477-83.

S.W. of St-Maclou, in the lower town, is the late-16C church of *Notre-Dame,* with an early 13C Virgin, and the tomb of St Gautier, founder of the 11C abbey of St-Martin-de-Pontoise.

The church of *St-Ouen,* on the E. bank, is partly Romanesque, N. of which are the ruins of the Cistercian abbey of **Maubuisson** (cons. 1244), founded by Blanche of Castile, who died there in 1251, with the remains of a 13C chapter-house, refectory, and tithe-barn.

The abbey was notorious for the amorous exploits of Marguerite of Burgundy and her sister Blanche, and later for those of Angélique d'Estrées (sister of Gabrielle), who was appointed abbess by Henri IV, but whose conduct was such that she had to be forcibly removed by Louis XIII; her successor, Angélique Arnauld (1618-25), introduced the austere morals of Port-Royal.

Cergy itself (7,400 inhab.), described as 'a pleasant village' in a previous edition of this *Guide,* but no longer so, retains a 13C church with a Renaissance doorway opening on to the site of its vanished nave.—*Jouy-le-Moutier,* further S.W., has an interesting church; that at *Ennery,* 3.5 km. N. of Pontoise, of the 12-13C, has additions by the *Lemerciers.*

42.5 km. *Cormeilles-en-Vexin* has a curious church with a Romanesque nave and Gothic and Renaissance choir.—47 km. *Marines* is an old town with a château that belonged to Sillery, chancellor of Henri IV, and an elegant Renaissance church porch.

51 km. *Chars* has a church with a Romanesque nave, 12C rose-window, a striking late-12C choir, and Renaissance tower.—*Santeuil* (4.5 km. S.) has a Romanesque church with a 13C nave.

54.5 km. The church at *Lavilletertre* (3 km. N.E.) preserves interesting Romanesque capitals. — At *Nucourt* (5 km. S.W.) the church (12C; altered in the 16C), with a fine stone altarpiece, stands a short distance N.W. of the village; key at the mairie. Nucourt was a site for the assembly of V1 rockets in 1944.—*Magny-en-Vexin,* see p. 263, lies 5.5 km. further W.—*Serans* (4 km. N. of Nucourt) has a Gothic church with a Flamboyant façade and Romanesque tower.

62 km. *Montjavoult,* 3.5 km. W., has a Renaissance church with a portal similar in style to St-Gervais at Gisors.

69 km. Gisors (8,300 inhab.; *Hotels*), the former capital of the VEXIN NORMAND, a territory long contested by English and French, suffered severely during the German invasion of 1940 (and again in 1944), when the Hôtel de Ville and museum were burnt out, and many of its timbered houses destroyed. The Duc de la Rochefoucauld, cousin of the Duc de Liancourt, was brutally murdered at Gisors in 1792. The quality of its food has the flavour of Normandy, particularly the pâtés de lapins truffés.

The imposing church of **St-Gervais-St-Protais* (13-16C) presents a succession of styles. The 16C S.W. tower remains incomplete. The sculptured W. porch (1537-62) and its carved doorways were badly burnt. The Renaissance work is by *Robert* (fl. 1518-48) and *Jean Grappin* (fl. 1537-98). The side portals are Gothic; the N. doorway, the more elaborate, was also the worst damaged. The nave, seriously injured by fire, has been restored; the mural painting of the Bearing of the Cross (1561) in the N. aisle, and the large Tree of Jesse (16C) in the S. aisle, have been saved. In the ambulatory of the Gothic choir (1240) are a series of 16C painted panels depicting the legend of SS Gervase and Protase, and the Life of Christ; also two stained-glass windows of the 17C.

Slightly to the N., the PASSAGE DU MONARQUE is prolonged to the postern gate of the *Castle, the extensive ruins of which dominate the town. This famous fortress, begun in 1097 by William Rufus, being an outpost of Normandy towards the Île de France, was for a hundred years an object of strife between the two countries, until by the Treaty of Louviers (1196) Richard Coeur-de-Lion ceded it to Philippe Auguste. Richard then hastened to compensate his loss by erecting Château-Gaillard, see p. 263.

The 12C keep, with an octagonal staircase-turret added in the 15C, rises from a mound in the centre of the enceinte, which retains 12 towers overlooking the double fosse, and enclosing a public garden. The *Keep* and the cylindrical *Tour du Prisonnier* (95 ft high), built by Philippe Auguste, with three vaulted storeys and a dungeon, may be visited.

The N181 leads S.W. from Gisors towards (31 km.) *Les Andelys* (see p. 262) passing (3 km., r.) *Neaufles-St-Martin,* with ruins of a keep built by Henry II (1182), (8 km.) *Dangu,* with good sculpture in its church, and (12 km.) *Vesly,* with 14th and 16C statues in its church, a feature of the district.

3 km. N. of Gisors, at *Bazincourt,* adjoining *Eragny-sur-Epte,* lived Camille Pissarro and his son Lucien; the latter village giving its name to the Eragny Press (London, 1894-1914).—The N15 continues N. to (25 km.) *Gournay-en-Bray.*

The N181 leads N.E. to (32 km.) *Beauvais,* see Rte 38, passing (4 km.) *Trie-Château,* its church with a restored Romanesque façade and early-13C choir. A round tower remains of the medieval castle (11C) on which site the 17C château was built. Here in 1767 Rousseau, when a guest of the Prince de Conti, finished writing his 'Confessions'. The tiny *Hôtel de Ville* preserves two Romanesque windows.—Just beyond, the N323 leads 4 km. S.E. to *Chaumont-en-Vexin,* with slight remains of the castle which once commanded the town, and with a Gothic church (1417-16C), with a fine Renaissance tower and N. doorway, by *Robert Grappin,* combining Gothic and Renaissance motives, and a charming choir.

38   PARIS TO BEAUVAIS (FOR AMIENS OR ABBEVILLE)

N1. (35.5 km. *Beaumont-sur-Oise* lies 3 km. N.E.).—76 km. *Beauvais.*

We follow the N1 N. from the *Porte de la Chapelle.*

At 17 km., shortly before the N16 to Chantilly forks r. (see Rte 24), the D125 leads W. to (2.5 km.) **Montmorency,** now a hilltop outer suburb of Paris (20,800 inhab.) and retaining few relics of its fashionable past, with its elegant villas, its 'cherries, pears, and its donkey-rides'. We pass (l.) remains of the *Ermitage,* where in 1756 Rousseau began his 'Nouvelle Héloïse'; the composer Grétry died in the Ermitage in 1813. After his rupture with Mme d'Épinay, Rousseau moved to *Montluis* (a short distance S.W., approached viâ the Rue de Grétry and its continuation), where he wrote the 'Lettre à D'Alembert', 'Émile', and 'Du Contrat Social' (1762). A small museum here is devoted to Rousseau who, fearing arrest, took refuge in Switzerland in 1762. Further S.W. stands the 16C church of *St-Martin,* situated on a terrace (views). The stained-glass, representing members of the Montmorency and Coligny-Châtillon families, most famous of whom was Anne de Montmorency (1493-1567), for whom the dukedom was created, has been drastically restored. Note also the memorials to Polish refugees, who congregated in Montmorency in the 19C. The painter Le Brun had a château near here, demolished in 1814.—At *Deuil,* further S., at the foot of the hill, is an 11-12C church with an elegant choir, almost completely restored after war damage.

20.5 km. (l.) *Domont,* adjacent to the extensive FORÊT DE MONT-MORENCY, stretching to the N.W., has an interesting church preserving a fine 12C apse.

25.5 km. At *Belloy-en-France* (6 km. N.E. off the D909) is a 14-16C church with an impressive Renaissance portal, and elegant vaulting. The road continues N. to (11 km.) *Royaumont,* see p. 207.

27.5 km. (l.) *Maffliers* has a church with a choir rebuilt in 1643 by *Philibert Delorme.*

At 32 km. we reach a crossroad.

6 km. S.W. (off the D9) are the ruins of the Cistercian *Abbaye du Val,* founded in 1136, but largely demolished after 1845.—The D64 leads 4.5 km. W. through the FORÊT DE L'ISLE-ADAM to **L'Isle-Adam** (9,900 inhab.), where the Renaissance church of *St-Martin,* with a façade attr. to *Jean Bullant* (damaged in 1940), contains a carved wood pulpit (German; 1560), stalls with quaint misericords (late-15C), and a fine 15C carved altar-screen.—4.5 km. S., on the far side of the Oise, lies **Auvers** (with a 12-16C church), a riverside village (now 5,800 inhab.) much painted by Corot, Daumier, Daubigny (who died there in 1878), Pissarro, Cézanne, etc. Dr Gachet (see p. 90) lived here, and his most famous patient, Van Gogh, who died in the Café Ravoux (1890; now called 'Chez Van Gogh'), is buried in the cemetery.

At *Méry,* on the opposite bank of the river, is a fine *Château* (16-18C), built on the site of an earlier monastery, containing interesting works of art (visits are authorized).

Nesles-la-Vallée, 4 km. N.W. of L'Isle-Adam, has a 12C church with a Romanesque belfry, curious vaulting, and three Virgins (13C and later).—*Champagne-sur-Oise* (3 km. N. on the W. bank of the river) retains a fine 13C church (restored by Viollet-le-Duc).

2 km. N. of the junction at 32 km. (on the N1) lies *Presles,* where the church preserves some curious misericords.—3 km. beyond, passing (r.) *Nointel,* whose château's gardens were once famous, lies **Beaumont-sur-Oise** (7,700 inhab.). Its ancient castle, guarding the river-crossing, was dismantled in 1422. The view from the ramparts is now largely of factories, and, further W., of a nuclear power station. The late-Transitional church of *St-Laurent,* with good capitals and a Renaissance tower, is of interest.—The N1 may be regained 6 km. N.W., beyond *Chambly,* with a fine 13-14C church containing 16C paintings and a Flemish altarpiece.

Immediately N. of Chambly, the N323 leads N.W. to (11 km.) *Méru,* with a 12-16C church; another interesting example of the 12-13C may be visited at *St-Crépin-Ibouvillers,* 5 km. beyond.

At 36 km. the N1 crosses the Oise.

53 km. *Noailles,* formerly *Longvilliers,* which assumed the name of the ducal family of Noailles in the 17C.—The villages of *Tillard* and *Silly,* not far W., preserve curious churches.—64 km. (l.) *Allonne* has an interesting 13-16C church.

68 km. **BEAUVAIS** (56,800 inhab.; *Hotels*), capital of the department of the Oise, is very largely a new town, the centre having been almost totally burnt out by German incendiary bombardment in June 1940, which also destroyed the buildings of the famous tapestry factory; miraculously, the cathedral was virtually untouched. The town is also known for its

patisserie, quiches, fruits confits, saucissons chauds, and 'côte de veau bellovaque'.

History. The *Bratuspantium* mentioned by Caesar occupied a site in this neighbourhood, and after its destruction or abandonment, Beauvais became the capital of the Bellovaci, from whom it took its name. In the 9C it became a countship (Beauvaisis), and was later controlled by its worldly bishops, peers of France, who were frequently at odds with the townspeople. In 1358 it was a centre of the 'Jacquerie' or peasants' revolt. In 1472 Beauvais withstood a siege by Charles the Bold, Jeanne Laisné ('Jeanne Hachette') leading the womenfolk in its defence. In 1664 Colbert founded the Tapestry Factory. The town was bombed in 1918, the damage being slight compared with the holocaust of 1940, when 2,000 houses disappeared, 75 of which, mostly of the 15-16C, were classified as Historic Monuments. Pierre Cauchon (d. 1442), Joan of Arc's accuser and judge, was Bp. of Beauvais.

Dominating the centre of the town by its great height, somewhat like a stranded whale, rises the ****Cathedral of St-Pierre,** which, had it been completed on the original scale, would have been the largest Gothic cathedral in the world; its choir and transepts alone form one of the most ambitious masterpieces of medieval architecture, although reflecting more the hauteur than the humility of the church.

The foundations were laid in 1227, and work continued until 1578. The inordinate boldness of the ground plan, with infrequent pillars and weak buttresses, made the building peculiarly vulnerable, and twice the roof caved in (1247 and 1284), and the tower erected above the crossing in 1550 by *Jean Vast,* together with its spire (502ft high), collapsed in 1573. *Martin Cambiges* (1500-48) and then *Michel Lalye* (after 1532) worked on the transepts; the former built the N. portal at the expense of François I (whose salamander emblem and unfinished genealogical tree may be seen in the interior), while to the latter is due the S. portal.

Exterior. The transepts end in superb Gothic façades; the S., framed by two highly decorative turrets, is approached by a flight of fourteen steps. Its portal, denuded of statues, is surmounted by a double open gallery, a rose-window, and pediment; the Renaissance doors of carved oak (mutilated) are by *Jean le Pot.* Those of the N. portal, in perfect preservation, are also by *Le Pot.* The W. end is somewhat abruptly and inelegantly finished by a covering of slate.

Interior. The unfinished cathedral is 238ft long and 153ft high. The CHOIR itself is 120ft in length, its vaulting supported by twelve double flying buttresses. Above the seven ambulatory chapels and the rectangular choir chapels are a blind triforium and a series of windows. The main triforium is glazed. The glass in the galleries of the S. transept is ascribed to *Nicolas Le Prince.* The rose-window dates from 1551. Note also the window depicting St Peter and St Paul in the CHAP. DES MORTS, and one devoted to St Hubert.

The gallery windows in the N. transept represent the sibyls, by *Jean Le Prince.* In the rose-window are figures of the sun and of a flame-coloured seraphim. In the CHAP. DU SACRÉ-COEUR (l.) are windows by *Eugrand Le Prince* (1522). To the r. of the N. portal is the famous *Astronomical Clock,* constructed in 1865-68 by a local horologist, with 52 dials, etc. Various figures perform evolutions at each hour; that of the Last Judgment working only at noon.

AMBULATORY. The 4th, 6th, and 8th chapels retain some 13C glass (restored). The *Organ* (1530) is under restoration, and will be moved from its present position.

From the W. end of the cathedral (or HAUTE-OEUVRE) we may enter the so-called BASSE-OEUVRE, in the place of the nave, and dating from 997

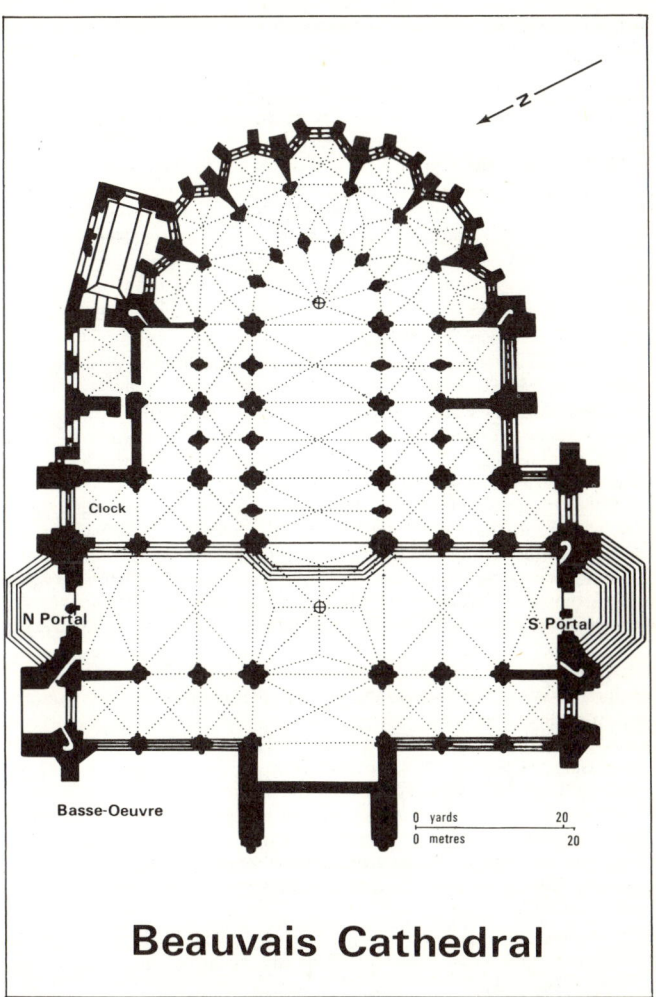

Beauvais Cathedral

(one of the very few churches extant in France prior to the 11C), which served as the cathedral until the 13C. Here also is the restored *Cloister.*

The magnificent series of ***Beauvais Tapestries** are being placed in a new building immediately to the E., abutting the remains of the Gallo-Roman walls, where it is hoped they will be more secure than in the cathedral choir, from which five were mysteriously removed in 1974.

The finely woven *Beauvais Tapestry,* made of wool and silk, and often designed as panels or furniture coverings representing landscapes, flowers, or pastoral scenes, is made on a horizontal or 'low' warp (unlike *Gobelins,* which is made on a vertical or 'high' warp), and is woven from the reverse side. The looms from the manufactory, which stood S.E. of *St-Étienne,* were sensibly evacuated to *Aubusson* in 1939, and are now at the *Gobelins* in Paris.

Immediately to the W. of the cathedral are the two pepper-pot towers (14C) of the entrance to the courtyard of the *Palais de Justice* (previously the Bishop's Palace; mostly 14th and early-16C), at the far end of which is the entrance (in a stair-turret) to the ***Museum** (adm. 10.00-12.00; 14.00-17.00 or 18.00; closed Tues.), an interesting collection saved from its previous site, destroyed in 1940. Outstanding among the sculpture is a St Barbara by *Jean le Pot,* a Decapitation of St Paul (16C); also, among the paintings, a portrait of Card. de Gesvres, by *Pompeo Batoni.* In an adjoining building are the prehistoric and Gallo-Roman collections, further examples of Gothic sculpture, Merovingian arms, etc.

On the W. side of the *Palais de Justice* is a restored Romanesque tower on a Gallo-Roman base.

A few minutes walk S.E. from the cathedral will bring one to the modern PL. DE JEANNE-HACHETTE, flanked to the S. by the new *Hôtel de Ville,* behind which the Rue du Dr-Gérard leads W. to the Rue de la Banque, in which a few old houses remain.

S. of the town hall stands ***St-Étienne,** an interesting building (12-16C) in two distinct styles, with a large W. tower of 1598. The nave and transepts illustrate externally the developments of later Romanesque, and internally, those of early Gothic architecture. The N. transept has a rose-window representing the Wheel of Fortune, and a reticulated gable. The contrast between the restored Romanesque nave and the late Gothic choir (1506) is striking. The stained-glass (1518-54) in the ambulatory chapels includes a remarkable window of the *Tree of Jesse. The animal painter J.-B. Oudry (1686-1755), also a director of the Tapestry Factory, is buried here.

1.5 km. E., off the Clermont road (N31), is the interesting church of *Marissal,* painted by *Corot* in 1866, with a tower and apse of the 12C, choir of the 13C, and nave, portal, and spire of the 16C.

Also of interest in the immediate vicinity of Beauvais are the church at *Guignecourt,* 6.5 km. N.E., off the N181; *N.-D.-du-Thil,* 1 km. N.W., with the remains of the ancient *Abbaye de St-Lucien;* and the leper-house of *St-Lazare* and adjacent buildings in the suburb of *Voisinlieu,* 1.5 km. S.E.

The N181 leads S.W. to (32 km.) *Gisors,* see Rte 37, off which, after 13 km., the D3 bears S. to (6.5 km.) *Jouy-sous-Thelle,* with an interesting late Renaissance church.

The N31 leads 26 km. E. to *Clermont,* see Rte 24.

Amiens lies 60 km. N. on the N181 and N16; *Abbeville,* 86 km. N. on the N1; *Dieppe,* 104 km. N.W. on the N31 and D915; and *Rouen,* 80 km. W. on the N31 and N30.

INDEX

Topographical names in Paris are printed in Roman type; those in the Environs in **Bold**. The names of eminent persons are in *italics*; those listed as buried in the larger cemeteries are not included unless they are also referred to in the text. Places named after saints are printed alphabetically under St- (e.g., St-Denis), but saints themselves are listed as Denis, St.

Avenues, Boulevards, Gares, Hôpitaux, Hôtels (mansions), Musées, Places, Ponts, Portes, Quais, Rues, Squares, *in Paris* are indexed alphabetically in sub-groups in Roman type under these headings.

Note that streets, etc., named after persons are known by and indexed under the full name: i.e., Rue Antoine-Bourdelle, not Rue Bourdelle (which can be confusing when the visitor is not aware of the Christian name in question).

Subject entries are printed in CAPITALS.

Set by Cold Composition Ltd, Tonbridge, Kent

Printed in Great Britain by Fletcher & Son Ltd, Norwich

BLUE GUIDE
TO
PARIS
AND ENVIRONS

Atlas Contents

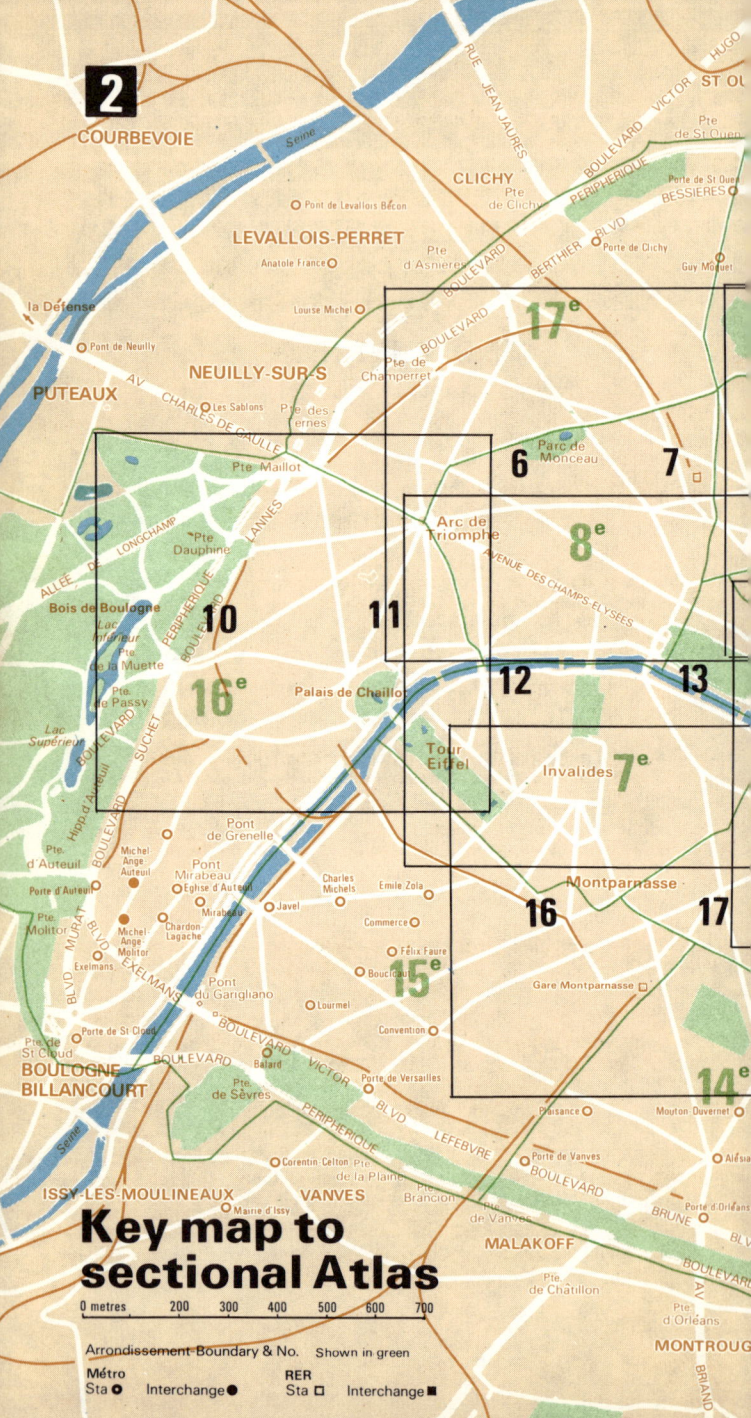

Key map to sectional Atlas

0 metres   200   300   400   500   600   700

Arrondissement Boundary & No. Shown in green

Métro — Sta ● Interchange ●
RER — Sta □ Interchange ■

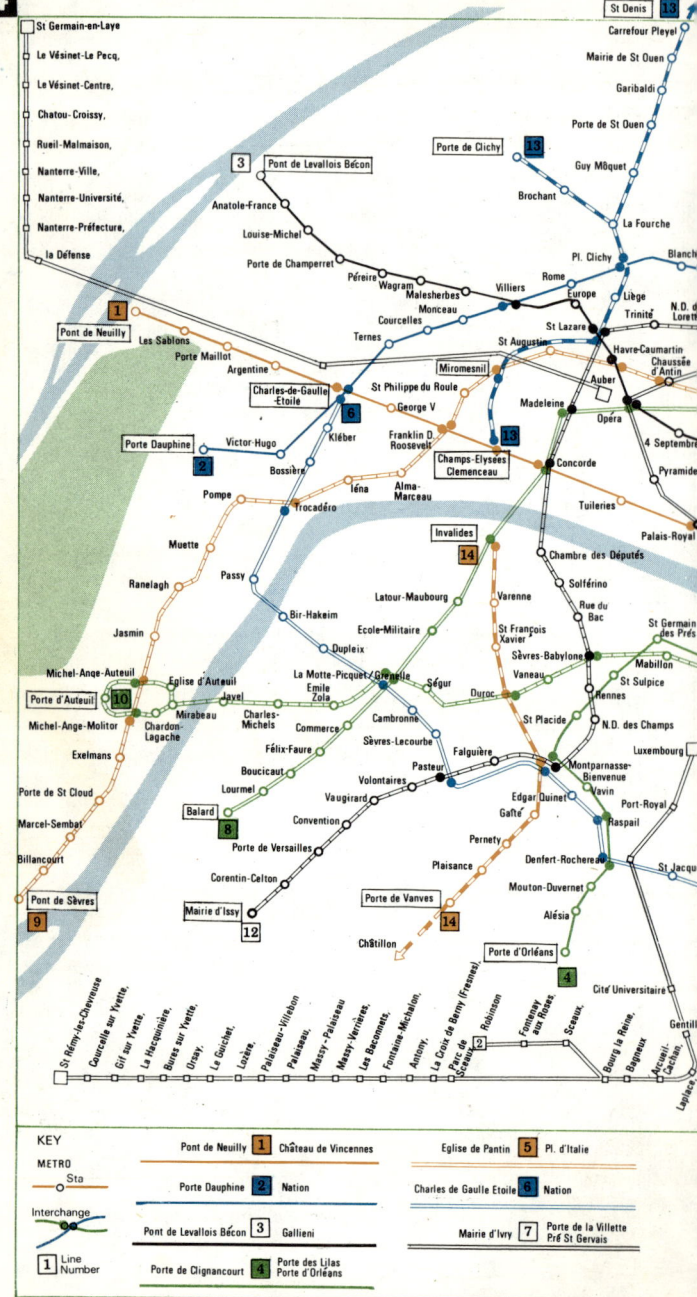

4

St Germain-en-Laye
Le Vésinet-Le Pecq,
Le Vésinet-Centre,
Chatou-Croissy,
Rueil-Malmaison,
Nanterre-Ville,
Nanterre-Université,
Nanterre-Préfecture,
la Défense

St Denis **13**
Carrefour Pleyel
Mairie de St Ouen
Garibaldi
Porte de St Ouen
Guy Môquet
Brochant
La Fourche
Blanch
Pl. Clichy
Porte de Clichy **13**

3 Pont de Levallois Bécon
Anatole-France
Louise-Michel
Porte de Champerret
Péreire Wagram Malesherbes
Courcelles
Ternes
Monceau
Villiers Rome Europe Liège
N.D. d
Loreti
St Augustin
St Lazare
Havre-Caumartin
Chaussée d'Antin
Auber
1 Pont de Neuilly Les Sablons
Porte Maillot
Argentine
Charles-de-Gaulle Étoile **6**
St Philippe du Roule Miromesnil
George V
Kléber
Franklin D. Roosevelt
Madeleine
Opéra
4 Septembre
Pyramide
Porte Dauphine **2**
Victor-Hugo
Boissière Iéna
Champs-Elysées Clemenceau **13**
Concorde
Tuileries
Palais-Royal
Pompe Trocadéro
Alma-Marceau
Muette
Chambre des Députés
Ranelagh
Passy
Latour-Maubourg
Varenne
Solférino
Rue du Bac
St Germain des Prés
Jasmin
Bir-Hakeim
Ecole-Militaire
St François Xavier
Sèvres-Babylone
Mabillon
Duplex
Invalides **14**
St Sulpice
Michel-Ange-Auteuil
Eglise d'Auteuil
La Motte-Picquet / Grenelle
Ségur
Vaneau
Rennes
Porte d'Auteuil **10**
Javel Emile Zola
Cambronne
Duroc
St Placide
N.D. des Champs
Michel-Ange-Molitor
Chardon-Lagache
Mirabeau
Charles-Michels
Commerce
Sèvres-Lecourbe
Falguière
Luxembourg
Exelmans
Félix-Faure
Pasteur
Montparnasse-Bienvenue
Porte de St Cloud
Boucicaut
Volontaires
Vavin
Port-Royal
Marcel-Sembat
Lourmel
Vaugirard
Edgar Quinet
Gaîté
Raspail
Billancourt
Balard **8**
Convention
Pernety
Denfert-Rochereau
St Jacque
Pont de Sèvres **9**
Porte de Versailles
Plaisance
Mouton-Duvernet
Corentin-Celton
Porte de Vanves **14**
Alésia
Mairie d'Issy **12**
Châtillon
Porte d'Orléans **4**
Cité Universitaire
Gentilly

St Rémy-les-Chevreuse
Courcelle sur Yvette,
Gif sur Yvette,
La Hacquinière,
Bures sur Yvette,
Orsay,
Le Guichet,
Lozère,
Palaiseau-Villebon,
Palaiseau,
Massy-Palaiseau,
Massy-Verrières,
Les Baconnets,
Fontaine-Michalon,
Antony,
La Croix de Berny (Fresnes),
Parc de Sceaux,
Robinson
Fontenay aux Roses,
Sceaux,
Bourg la Reine,
Bagneux,
Arcueil-Cachan,
Laplace
2

KEY

METRO
○ Sta

Interchange

1 Line Number

Pont de Neuilly **1** Château de Vincennes

Porte Dauphine **2** Nation

Pont de Levallois Bécon **3** Gallieni

Porte de Clignancourt **4** Porte des Lilas Porte d'Orléans

Eglise de Pantin **5** Pl. d'Italie

Charles de Gaulle Etoile **6** Nation

Mairie d'Ivry **7** Porte de la Villette Préf St Gervais

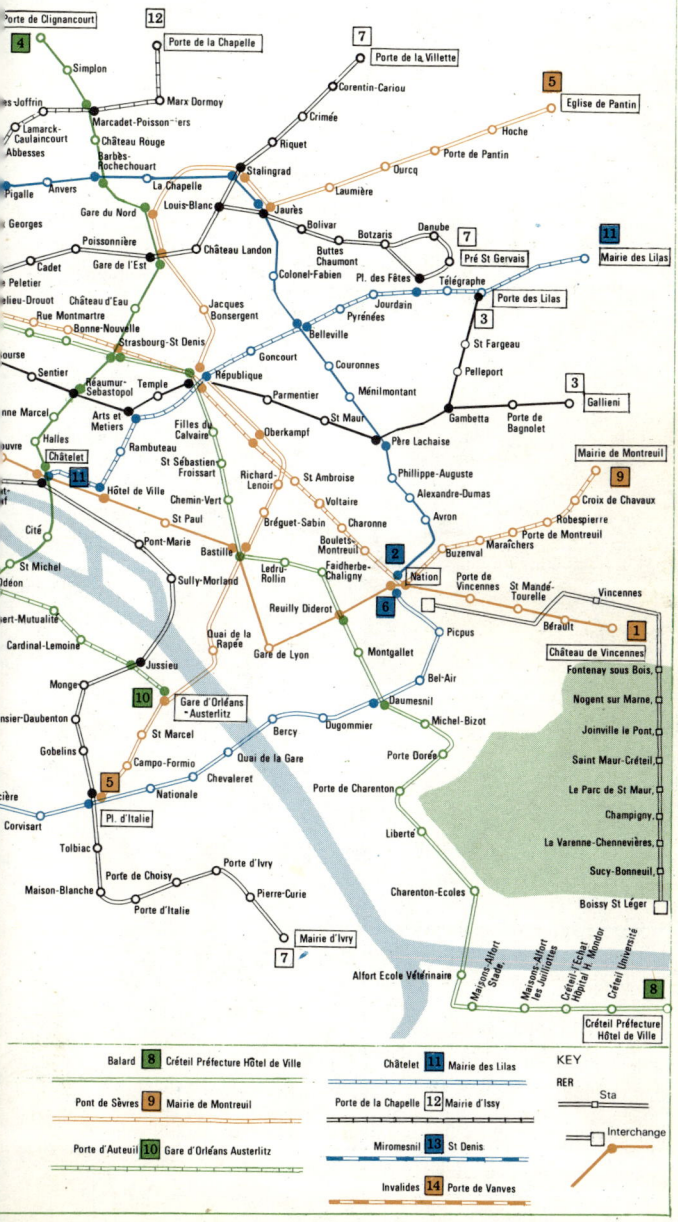

Métro

Porte de Clignancourt
12
Porte de la Chapelle
7
Porte de la Villette
5
Eglise de Pantin
es Joffrin
Simplon
Corentin-Cariou
Marx Dormoy
Lamarck-
Caulaincourt
Abbesses
Marcadet-Poisson·ers
Château Rouge
Crimée
Hoche
Riquet
Porte de Pantin
Barbès-
Rochechouart
Stalingrad
Ourcq
Pigalle
Anvers
La Chapelle
Laumière
Georges
Gare du Nord
Louis-Blanc
Jaurès
Bolivar
Danube
11
Mairie des Lilas
Poissonnière
Château Landon
Botzaris
7
Cadet
Gare de l'Est
Buttes
Chaumont
Pré St Gervais
Peletier
Château d'Eau
Colonel-Fabien
Pl. des Fêtes
Télégraphe
Porte des Lilas
lieu-Drouot
Rue Montmartre
Jacques
Bonsergent
Pyrénées
Jourdain
3
Bonne-Nouvelle
Strasbourg-St Denis
St Fargeau
Gallieni
3
ourse
Sentier
Goncourt
Belleville
Réaumur-
Sébastopol
Temple
République
Couronnes
Pelleport
ne Marcel
Arts et
Métiers
Parmentier
Ménilmontant
Mairie de Montreuil
9
Filles du
Calvaire
St Maur
Gambetta
Porte de
Bagnolet
uvre
Halles
Rambuteau
Oberkampf
Père Lachaise
Croix de Chavaux
Châtelet
11
St Sébastien
Froissart
Richard-
Lenoir
St Ambroise
Phillippe-Auguste
Robespierre
Hôtel de Ville
Chemin-Vert
Voltaire
Alexandre-Dumas
Porte de Montreuil
Cité
St Paul
Bréguet-Sabin
Charonne
Avron
Maraîchers
St Michel
Pont-Marie
Boulets-
Montreuil
Buzenval
1
Château de Vincennes
déon
Bastille
Ledru
Rollin
Faidherbe-
Chaligny
2
Nation
Porte de
Vincennes
St Mandé-
Tourelle
Vincennes
ert-Mutualité
Sully-Morland
Reuilly Diderot
6
Bérault
Cardinal-Lemoine
Quai de la
Rapée
Picpus
Château de Vincennes
Fontenay sous Bois
Jussieu
Gare de Lyon
Montgallet
Nogent sur Marne
Monge
10
Gare d'Orléans
- Austerlitz
Bel-Air
Joinville le Pont
ensier-Daubenton
Bercy
Daumesnil
Michel-Bizot
Saint Maur-Créteil
Gobelins
St Marcel
Dugommier
Le Parc de St Maur
Campo-Formio
Quai de la Gare
Porte Dorée
Champigny
cière
5
Chevaleret
Nationale
Porte de Charenton
La Varenne-Chennevières
Corvisart
Pl. d'Italie
Liberté
Sucy-Bonneuil
Tolbiac
Porte de Choisy
Porte d'Ivry
Boissy St Léger
Maison-Blanche
Pierre-Curie
Charenton-Ecoles
8
Créteil Préfecture
Hôtel de Ville
Porte d'Italie
7
Mairie d'Ivry
Alfort Ecole Vétérinaire

KEY

Balard	8	Créteil Préfecture Hôtel de Ville		Châtelet	11	Mairie des Lilas
Pont de Sèvres	9	Mairie de Montreuil		Porte de la Chapelle	12	Mairie d'Issy
Porte d'Auteuil	10	Gare d'Orléans Austerlitz		Miromesnil	13	St Denis
				Invalides	14	Porte de Vanves

RER   Sta
Interchange

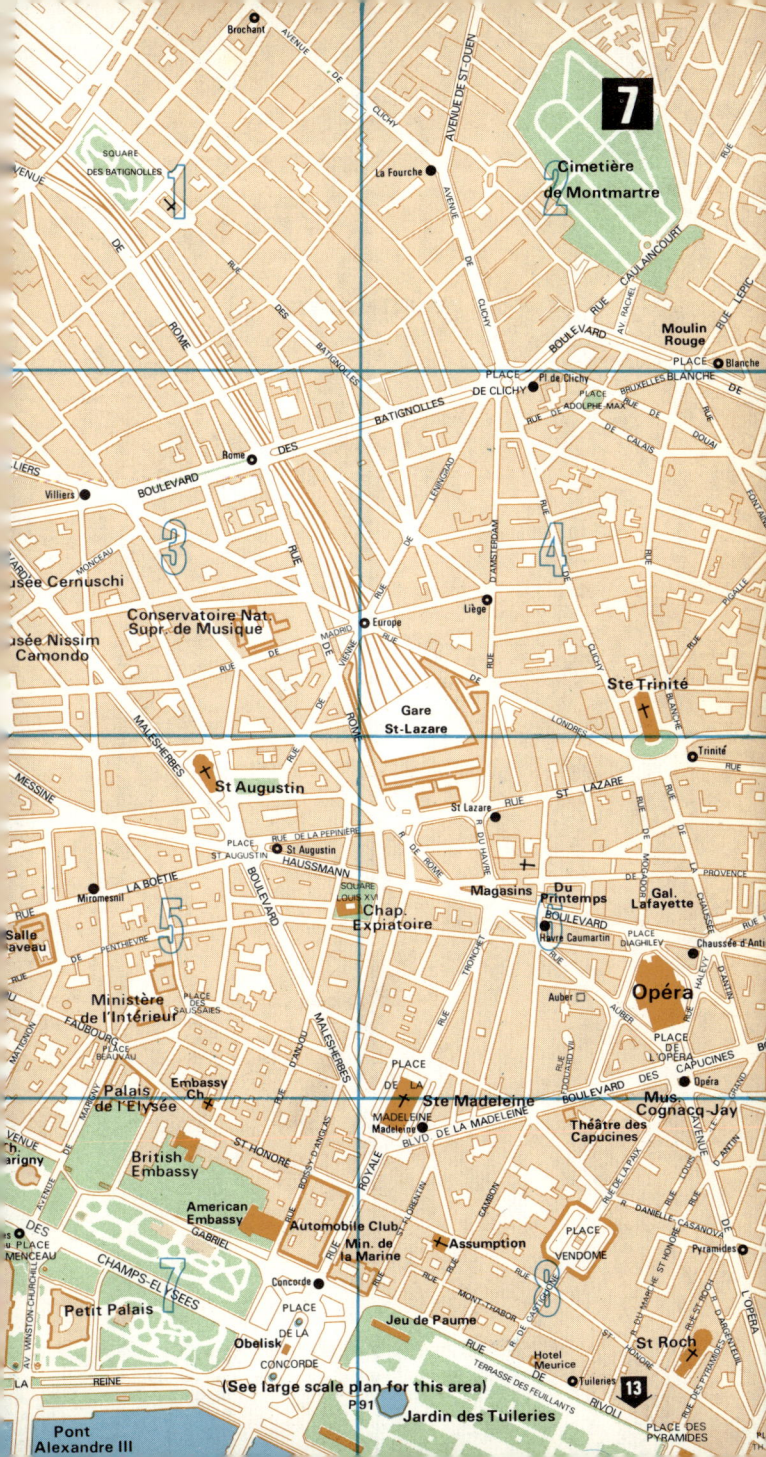

7

Brochant

AVENUE DE ST-OUEN

AVENUE DE CLICHY

SQUARE
DES BATIGNOLLES

1

AVENUE

La Fourche

AVENUE DE CLICHY

RUE

DE

ROME

RUE

DES

BATIGNOLLES

Cimetière
de Montmartre

2

RUE CAULAINCOURT

AV. RACHEL

RUE

LEPIC

BOULEVARD

AV. DE CLICHY

Moulin
Rouge
PLACE
Blanche

PLACE
DE CLICHY

Pl de Clichy

BLANCHE

RUE DE ADOLPHE MAX

PLACE
DE CLICHY

BRUXELLES

RUE DE CALAIS

DOUA

BATIGNOLLES

BOULEVARD

Rome

RUE

DES

RUE DE L'ENERGIE

RUE

D'AMSTERDAM

RUE

FONTAINE

VILLIERS

Villiers

BOULEVARD

3

MONCEAU

RUE

RUE

DE

ROME

DE

VIENNE

MADRID

Europe

Liège

PLACE

Ste Trinité

Trinité

BLANCHE

4

RUE DE CLICHY

RUE

RUE DE ROCHE

usée Cernuschi

Conservatoire Nat.
Supr. de Musique

RUE DE

Gare
St-Lazare

RUE DE LONDRES

ée Nissim
Camondo

RUE

MALESHERBES

St Augustin

St Lazare

RUE

ST LAZARE

RUE DE ROME

RUE DU HAVRE

MESSINE

PLACE
ST. AUGUSTIN

RUE DE LA PEPINIERE

HAUSSMANN

BOULEVARD

RUE DE MOSCOU

RUE

DE

PROVENCE

Magasins

Du
Printemps

Gal.
Lafayette

5

LA BOETIE

Miromesnil

RUE

DE

PENTHIEVRE

RUE DE

SQUARE
LOUIS XVI

Chap.
Expiatoire

BOULEVARD

Havre Caumartin

BOULEVARD

PLACE
DIAGHILEV

Chaussée-d'Anti

Salle
aveau

Ministère
de l'Intérieur

PLACE
DES
SAUSSAIES

RUE

TRONCHET

RUE

Auber

Auber

Opéra

PLACE DE
L'OPÉRA

HALEVY

Opéra

RUE

MALESHERBES

RUE

DANIOU

FAUBOURG

RUE
BEAUVAU

Palais
de l'Elysée

Embassy
Ch.

PLACE
DE LA

Ste Madeleine

MADELEINE

Madeleine

BOULEVARD DES
CAPUCINES

Mus.
Cognacq-Jay

VENUE
h.
arigny

ST HONORE

RUE ROYALE

BLVD DE LA MADELEINE

Théâtre des
Capucines

British
Embassy

RUE BOISSY D'ANGLAS

American
Embassy

GABRIEL

Automobile Club.

Min. de
la Marine

Assumption

RUE CAMBON

PLACE
VENDOME

R. DANIELE CASANOVA

Pyramides

St Roch

7

CHAMPS-ELYSEES

DES
u. PLACE
MENCEAU

AVENUE WINSTON CHURCHILL

Petit Palais

Concorde

PLACE
DE LA
CONCORDE

Obelisk

Jeu de Paume

RUE

MONT-THABOR

Hotel
Meurice

Tuileries

RIVOLI

RUE ST HONORE

RUE DE L'ORATOIRE

REINE

(See large scale plan for this area)
P 91

TERRASSE DES FEUILLANTS

Jardin des Tuileries

13

PLACE DES
PYRAMIDES

Pont
Alexandre III

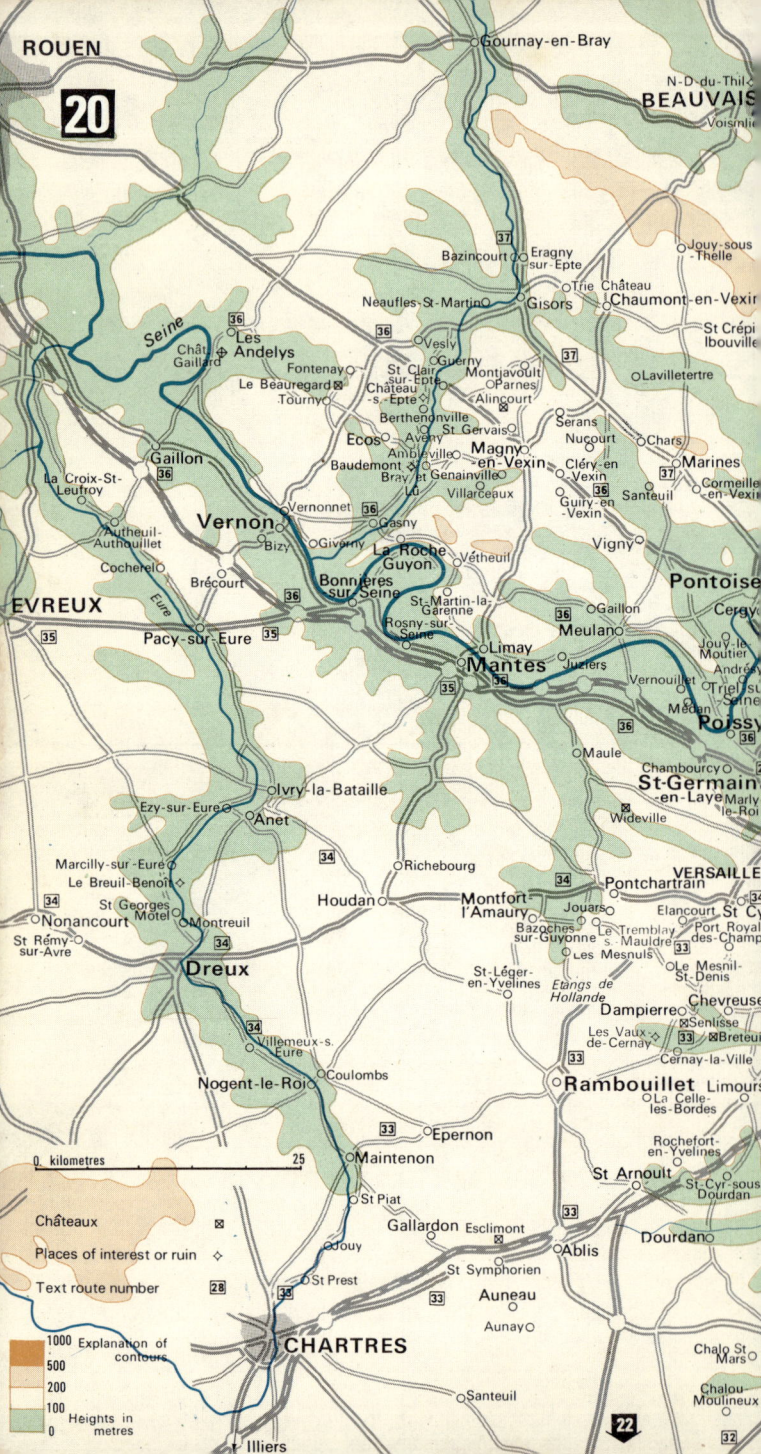

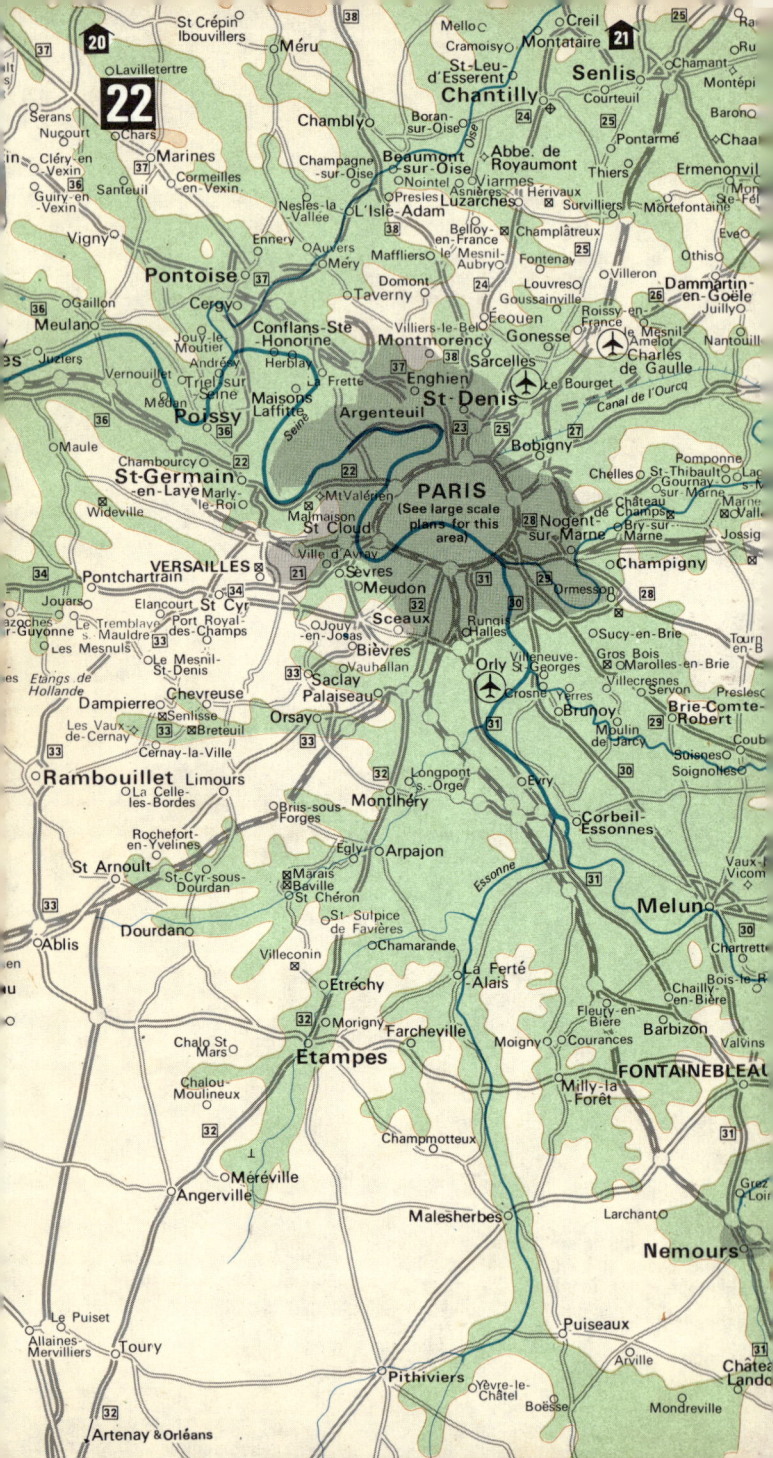

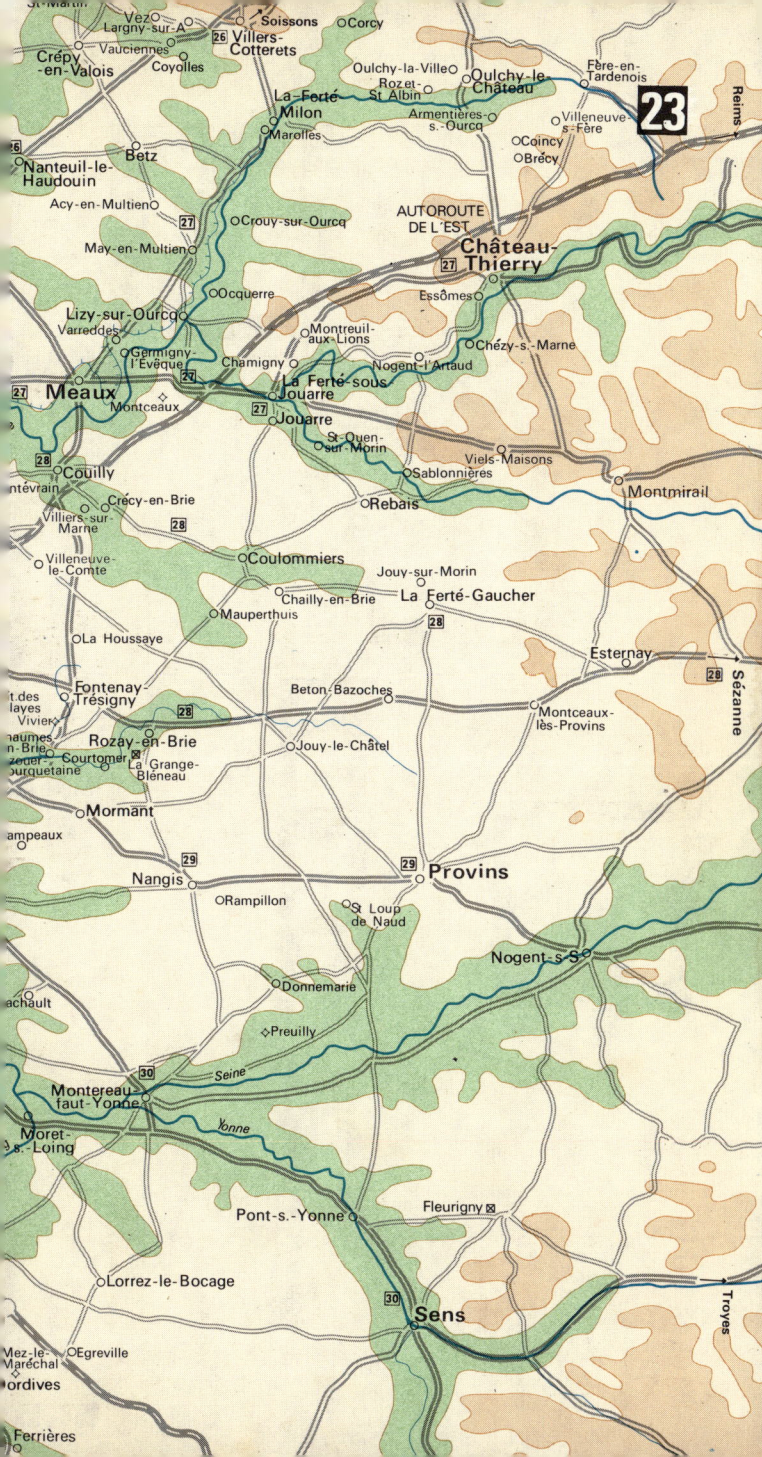

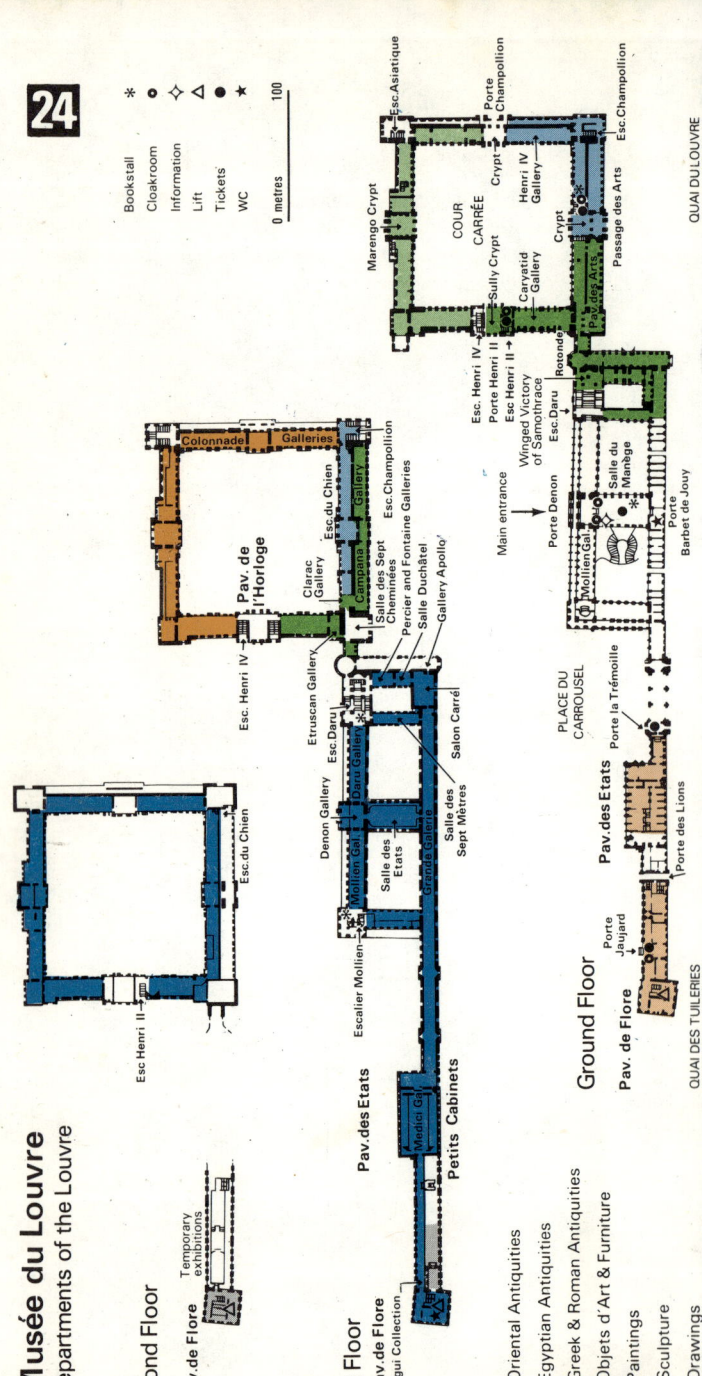

Musée du Louvre
Departments of the Louvre

Second Floor

Pav. de Flore

Temporary exhibitions

Esc Henri II

First Floor

Pav. de Flore

Beistegui Collection

Pav. des Etats

Petits Cabinets

Medici Gal.

Escalier Mollien

Mollien Gal.

Salle des Etats

Grande Galerie

Salle des Sept Mètres

Denon Gallery

Daru Gallery

Esc. Daru

Etruscan Gallery

Salon Carré

Salle des Sept Cheminées

Percier and Fontaine Galleries

Salle Duchâtel

Gallery Apollo

Clarac Gallery

Campana Gallery

Gallery

Esc. du Chien

Esc. Champollion

Pav. de l'Horloge

Esc. Henri IV

Colonnade

Galleries

Esc. du Chien

Ground Floor

Pav. de Flore

Porte Jaujard

QUAI DES TUILERIES

Pav. des Etats

Porte des Lions

Porte la Trémoille

PLACE DU CARROUSEL

Main entrance

Porte Denon

Winged Victory of Samothrace

Mollien Gal.

Salle du Manège

Porte Barbet de Jouy

Esc. Daru

Rotonde

Esc. Henri II →

Porte Henri II

Esc. Henri IV →

COUR CARRÉE

Marengo Crypt

Sully Crypt

Caryatid Gallery

Crypt

Henri IV Gallery

Crypt

Porte des Arts

Passage des Arts

Esc. Champollion

Esc. Asiatique

Porte Champollion

Esc. Champollion

QUAI DU LOUVRE

Pav. des Arts

24

* Bookstall
○ Cloakroom
◇ Information
△ Lift
● Tickets
★ WC

0 metres   100

Oriental Antiquities
Egyptian Antiquities
Greek & Roman Antiquities
Objets d'Art & Furniture
Paintings
Sculpture
Drawings